P9-DBQ-415

Issues in Business and Society

Consulting Editor

BARRY RICHMAN
University of California

Los Angeles

Issues in Business and Society

SECOND EDITION

GEORGE A. STEINER
University of California Los Angeles

JOHN F. STEINER
California State University Los Angeles

Random House New York

Second Edition
987654

All inquiries should be addressed to Random House, Inc., 201 East 50th Street, New York, N.Y. 10022. Published in the United States by Random House, Inc., and simultaneously in Canada by Random House of Canada Limited, Toronto.

Library of Congress Cataloging in Publication Data

Steiner, George Albert, 1912– comp.
Issues in business and society.

1. Industry—Social aspects—United States—Addresses, essays, lectures. 2. Industry and state—United States —Addresses, essays, lectures. I. Steiner, John F. II. Title.
HD60.5.U5S83 1977 658.4'08 76–30754
ISBN–0–394–31289–9

Manufactured in the United States of America

Design: Vladimir Yevtikhiev

PREFACE

The relationships of the business institution to society are broad and many-sided, and the issues have not just one, two, or several sides, but often are multifaceted. For this reason, it is necessary that students at both the undergraduate and graduate levels supplement their understanding of the basic elements in the business-environment relationship, as presented in textbooks, with the living controversy of the contemporary literature.

This volume, like the first edition, provides such an exposure to the major arguments of the day in this field of study. Most of this second edition is composed of entirely new readings that raise new issues or treat old issues in a current context. Only a few fundamental articles that have not lost importance with time have been retained from the first edition.

In selecting articles, we have emphasized current and potentially important future issues. Also, whenever possible and appropriate, we have chosen articles on different sides of an issue. A number of articles have been included because they integrate or summarize a multiplicity of views on issues. To vary the pace of the intellectual demands on the reader, we have included long and short articles; some are easy to read and a few are rather rigorous, some are tendentious and some are scholarly, but all, we think, are authoritative. Most of the pieces have been written by distinguished and well-known authors. We have also included a number of boxed short items that present provocative thoughts to complement the readings.

To facilitate classroom discussion, we have prepared questions about the content of all the readings. Sometimes questions are better raised after reading several articles. So if questions do not appear at the end of a reading, they will be found after succeeding selections. Some of the questions may be answered by a simple review of an article, but others are mind-stretching and demand creative thought for adequate response. Some are designed to teach the student that a high degree of tolerance for ambiguity is needed in dealing with the subject matter of the interface between business and society.

We have eliminated footnotes in the readings. Those who wish to pursue a subject in greater depth can, of course, return to the original article for references.

This volume has been compiled in such a way as to be informative to undergraduates and stimulating enough for more advanced graduate students. We hope that in addition to classroom use it will appeal to business executives and general readers who want to be informed about the social, moral, and political environment of business. It is our judgment that the subject matter of this book should be part of the intellectual equipment of managers who think of themselves as enlightened and socially conscious.

We acknowledge the help of many in the preparation of this edition. We wish to thank a number of faculty members across the country who took the time to respond to our queries about the first edition and this revision. These include David Author, Oregon State University; Jeffrey A. Barach, Tulane

University; Daniel Kasper, University of Southern California; Steven E. Goodman, St. John's University; Robert D. Henderson, University of Tampa; Robert J. Holloway, University of Minnesota; O. J. Krasner, Pepperdine University; D. MacKintosh, University of New Orleans; Philip H. Mounts, University of Wisconsin-Oshkosh; Harold Oaklander, Pace University-New York; James E. Post, Boston University; Thomas Rotondi, Marquette University; Dan Stage, Loyola Marymount University; Edward N. Strader, University of Wyoming; Joseph W. Towle, Washington University; and L. M. Wooton, Southern Methodist University. We are also grateful to those who returned anonymous questionnaires. We thank the many authors represented in this book and their publishers for permission to use their writings.

We wish to thank, finally, Mrs. Betty Delbridge for her help in the preparation and duplication of this manuscript.

Los Angeles
April 1976

GEORGE A. STEINER
JOHN F. STEINER

CONTENTS

1. Past Critics of the Business System 3

Protest Movements and Their Effects on American Business, THEODORE SALOUTOS 4

2. Current Criticisms of Corporations and Capitalism 21

The Corporate Impact, RALPH NADER, MARK GREEN, and JOEL SELIGMAN 22

Capitalism Has Created Great Social Ills, JOHN G. GURLEY 36

Capitalism, Militarism, Poverty, and the Environment, NEIL H. JACOBY 45

The Economics of Dissent, CAMPBELL R. McCONNELL 55

On the Legitimacy of Business, DANIEL YANKELOVICH 76

The Parable of the Dam, GEORGE W. BALL 80

3. Perspectives on Business Power 81

Is There a Ruling Class in America? G. WILLIAM DOMHOFF 82

Social Responses to Corporate Power: A Condition Without a Remedy? SUMNER MARCUS 90

Corporate Bigness—For Better or For Worse? ARTHUR A. THOMPSON 102

The Businessman's Shrinking Prerogatives, PAUL A. SAMUELSON 126

4. Changing Social Values and the Business Role 131

Business and the Changing Society, GEORGE CABOT LODGE 132

The Quality of Working Life, JAMES C. TAYLOR 153

5. Business Social Responsibilities 167

The Social Responsibility of Business Is to Increase Its Profits, MILTON FRIEDMAN 168

A Case for Social Responsibility, DOUGLAS A. HAYES 175

Five Propositions for Social Responsibility, KEITH DAVIS 181

Institutionalizing Corporate Social Decisions, GEORGE A. STEINER 189

The Social Audit, JOHN J. CORSON and GEORGE A. STEINER 198

Corporate Social Responsibility Precisely Defined at Shell 209

6. What Is the Proper Role of Public Directors? 215

Public Directors Merit a Try, CHRISTOPHER D. STONE 216

7. Business Ethics and Moralities: Universal Aspects 229

Is the Golden Rule a Useful Guide to Business Decision Making? CRAIG C. LUNDBERG 230

Is Business Bluffing Ethical? ALBERT Z. CARR 236

The Business of Ethics, NORMAN C. GILLESPIE 248

Major Forces Upgrading and Downgrading Business Ethical Behavior, JOHN F. STEINER 255

8. Business Ethics and Moralities: Foreign "Payoffs" and Recommended Solutions for Unethical Behavior 259

Reform of Bribery Abroad Involves U.S. Policy, MILTON S. GWIRTZMAN and ALAN R. NOVAK 260

Results of a Survey of Payoffs, JAMES R. BASCHE, JR. 267

The Basics of Bribery, EDITORS OF *The Wall Street Journal* 268

What to Do About Corporate Corruption, RALPH NADER and MARK GREEN 270

The Failings of Business and Journalism, LOUIS BANKS 275

Standards for Business Conduct, BUSINESS ETHICS ADVISORY COUNCIL 279

The Prospect of Ethical Advisors for Business Corporations, JOHN F. STEINER 284

9. Multinational Corporations: Good or Bad for Host Countries? 291

There's No Love Lost Between Multinational Companies and the Third World, LOUIS TURNER 292

In Defense of the Multinational Corporation, EMILIO G. COLLADO 302

Do Multinational Corporations Stand Guilty as Charged? RICHARD EELLS 312

10. Business, Environment, and Energy 321

The Environmental Crisis, NEIL H. JACOBY 322

Trade-Offs in Assessing Environmental Impacts, STAHRL EDMUNDS 340

Don't Confuse Us with Facts, *Forbes* 351

The Energy Problem: What Should Be the Government's Policy Toward Business? JOHN C. SAWHILL 360

11. Business and Consumers 369

Consumer Discontent: A Social Perspective, ZARREL V. LAMBERT and FRED W. KNIFFIN 370

Consumerism and Marketing, MAX E. BRUNK 383

12. Business and Minorities 393

What Does "Equal Employment Opportunity" Really Mean? WILLIAM H. BROWN, III 394

Exploding Some Myths About Women Managers, WILLIAM E. REIF, JOHN W. NEWSTROM, and ROBERT M. MONCZKA 405

No Easy Victories on the Voyage to Equality, JACQUELINE PINCKNEY 417

13. Renovating Governmental Regulatory Machinery 431

The Consensus on the Major Issues About the Business-Government Relationship, NEIL H. JACOBY 432

The Limits of Legal Compulsion, JOHN T. DUNLOP 443

The Case for Economizing on Government Controls, MURRAY L. WEIDENBAUM 452

Changing Modes of Government Regulation of Business, JOHN R. MEYER 464

Historical Accident, JOHN P. CARTER 470

14. Should We Slow Down Economic Growth? 475

Growth vs. No Growth: An Evaluation, ROLAND N. McKEAN 476

The Future of Mankind, HERMAN KAHN 495

15. Should We Have National Aggregate Economic Planning? 505

The Humphrey-Javits Bill, HUBERT H. HUMPHREY and JACOB K. JAVITS 506

Laissez Faire, Planning, and Reality, ARTHUR SCHLESINGER, JR. 511

In Opposition to the Humphrey-Javits Bill, T. A. MURPHY 515

Proposal for a National Policy Assessment and Action Program, GEORGE A. STEINER 518

16. Diverse Views on the Future of the Corporation and Capitalism 529

The Emerging Public Corporation, JOHN KENNETH GALBRAITH 530

What Is the Future of the Corporation? REGINALD H. JONES 534

The Crisis of Capitalism: A Marxist View, JOHN G. GURLEY 544

The Corporation and Liberal Democracy, IRVING KRISTOL 548

Will U.S. Capitalism Survive? OTTO ECKSTEIN 551

A System Worth Improving, LEON H. KEYSERLING 555

Issues in Business and Society

1 PAST CRITICS OF THE BUSINESS SYSTEM

PROTEST MOVEMENTS AND THEIR EFFECTS ON AMERICAN BUSINESS

THEODORE SALOUTOS

It is a premise of this book that there are significant and fundamental changes taking place in the business-society relationship that are not mere extensions of past relationships. They are deep and are bringing basic changes in the role of business in society. If this view is accepted, and it is difficult to reject it, it still is worthwhile to look at past business-society relationships to gain a valuable perspective in viewing today's changes and tomorrow's potential variations in this nexus. Theodore Saloutos, professor of history, University of California at Los Angeles, in this first reading skillfully traces historical protest movements in the United States from the Civil War to the present time.

Businessmen who today find themselves harassed by consumerists, environmentalists, politicians and reformers for polluting the atmosphere, producing inferior goods, failing to honor warranties, providing unhealthy working conditions, seeking federal loans, tax breaks, and excessive profits, may find some comfort in knowing that businessmen, large and small but mostly large, have been the targets of social critics for many years. Contrary to what the chairman of one of the nation's largest corporations said not too long ago—that the "unjustified harassment" to which the businessmen of today are subjected was "unknown to businessmen in other times"—the evidence is much to the contrary. There is hardly a decade in the history of this country since the Civil War in which corporations or large businesses, justifiably or unjustifiably, have not been subjected to attack by critics and reformers. These attacks assumed a variety of forms; and they came from labor unions, agrarians, preachers of the social gospel, politicians, reformers such as Henry George, Edward Bellamy, Henry Demarest Lloyd, scholars such as Thorstein Veblen, the Socialists, the muckrakers and the Progressives on up through the New Dealers and the Fair Dealers, and the consumerists and environmentalists of today. Some years ago Miriam Beard observed in her *History of the Businessman* (New York, 1938) that, "Such antagonisms have been endemic in all societies whether headed by a king, the nobility, the landed gentry, a dictator, by warriors or by priests."

Perhaps three things should be made clear at the outset. One is that I have chosen to confine myself to the more significant developments since the Civil War. The reasons for this are perfectly obvious to the historian who has some familiarity with the wide variety of reform movements that mush-

Theodore Saloutos, "Protest Movements and Their Effects on American Business," *Contemporary Challenges in the Business-Society Relationship,"* George A. Steiner (ed.), Los Angeles, California: Graduate School of Management, UCLA, 1972. Reprinted by permission.

roomed during these years. To attempt anything more would be to invite confusion, if not disaster; for as stated, there have been many such movements, and they have come in cycles, in periods of prosperity as well as of depression; and those that came to an urban-industrial society are perhaps more understandable than those of the antebellum period. A second point is to remind you that my observations are designed to focus on the major protest movements since the Civil War, and where possible indicate their effects on business, and not to spotlight the contributions of American business as a means of answering the critics. One must concede at the outset that taking a survey of the protest movements of the past is a far easier undertaking for the historian than assessing their effects on business. For how can one make such an assessment? Often there is a wide discrepancy between the rhetoric of the businessman and his deeds. A good deal of research remains to be done in a neglected area. The records of the businesses concerned are not open to scholars to study, hence the kind of evidence needed is not readily in hand. Much more than public-relations handouts are required. About all one can do is to observe the movements, the nature of their demands, and where possible determine the reactions or responses of businessmen to them. And a third point is that my observations have to do primarily with big business, corporate leadership, the "top brass" in the business community and not the small.

The business community normally has been one of the first to feel much, if not most, of the impact of the protest movement. Business has been a ready, often vulnerable, target because of its visibility and the deep-seated belief, ingrained through years of agitation, that business's greedy, grasping ways have been responsible for many of the ills of society. Whether this is true or not is beside the point, because this is precisely the way much of the public has felt and continues to feel. Often what one believes to be true is more important than the truth itself.

Business historians like to think that the drive for wealth had been "tempered by a strong sense of moral obligation" at least until the middle of the nineteenth century, and that this so-called "peace between profit and piety" more or less broke down during and after the Civil War, when many behaved as though the future belonged to the fittest. This post-Civil War period, it should be emphasized, has been the era that critics of American business usually have singled out as being representative of business at its worst. This was the era of the so-called "robber barons," "the boodlers," and the trusts who brazenly carried on their piratical forays in one of the ugliest, slimiest and sleaziest periods in history. This was the time when Daniel Drew fed his cattle salt to make them thirsty and forced them to drink a lot of water before they were taken to market; when Cornelius Vanderbilt bragged of how he busted "the hull damn legislature"; when John D. Rockefeller eliminated his competition as though they were clay pigeons; and when Jay Gould cornered the nation's gold supply and systematically robbed the Erie Railroad. Andrew Carnegie's efforts to control his appetite in accumulating wealth by appealing to the ideals of "social stewardship" were ignored for the most part even in his own corporation.

Some of the most vigorous protests against such practices, though by no means the only ones, were voiced by the farmers, who then constituted the bulk of the population of the nation, through the Granges and the Alliances they organized. The farmers had a general distrust of the emerging large corporations, the railroads in particular, and their allies. The farmers believed they were getting less than a fair return on their products, and they blamed this on the railroads and middlemen whom they charged with exacting more than their fair share for inadequate service, warehouse charges and commissions.

And the reactions of the farmers to such practices, real or imagined, were double-edged; and they affected the business community in one fashion or another. In response the farmers sought to build their own marketing agencies, such as cooperative marketing grain and livestock associations; establish consumer stores, factories to manufacture their machinery and equipment; and even mutual insurance companies. For a time they even talked earnestly about building a farmer-owned railroad system that would be owned and managed by the farmers, that would free them from the clutches of the railroad monopolists. The fact that most of these farmer enterprises encountered reverses of one sort or another traceable to poor management, the lack of capital, and competition from the more efficient traditional business agencies, did not minimize the new competitive threat that the farmers' actions posed, and it served as a warning to business of what could be in store in the future.

A second and better known kind of reaction assumed the form of regulatory legislation aimed to control the "soulless" corporations. Such actions, the hope was, would bring the railroads, the largest corporations of the day, under public control, protect the helpless masses, preserve and perhaps expand competition, protect the farmer and the small businessman, and thus enable the small man to survive.

The difficulties of the farmers cooperatives during the 1870s, 1880s, and 1890s did not mean the end of them; far from it. Although weak and ineffective in the earlier formative years, they blossomed forth after many self-inflicted wounds and much opposition into the large-scale cooperative associations of the 1920s that became the cornerstone of the farm policy of Herbert Hoover. The cooperatives in both their cruder and more sophisticated forms represented an attack on the traditional ways of doing business. They were in large measures protests against the commodity exchanges, the so-called "gamblers" in farm products, the grain brokers, the cotton merchants, the meat-packing interests and their allies the bankers, the railroads, the insurance companies and the profiteers, who were blamed for many, if not most, of the ills of society.

As indicated, this agitation against the traditional marketing agencies continued for many years before the legislators came to the aid of the farmers. Eventually most of the state legislatures and Congress enacted laws to protect farmers who banded together into cooperatives and received patronage dividends. The opposition of many companies to the cooperatives was fierce and prolonged, as hearings before investigating committees of the House and Senate, and the literature distributed by those businesses most affected by the cooperatives, attest. Companies that competed with the cooperatives were disturbed by the patronage-dividend feature, which they labeled a rebate, as well as by some of the tax exemption features in laws that placed established institutions at a competitive disadvantage. This has been part of the price that some businesses have had to pay for the distrust that had accumulated against them in the past.

During the early 1890s a fresh wave of anti-business sentiment burst forth that assumed the name of Populism; it was political in orientation and designed to free the small people from the financial and corporate interests. The ensuing attacks on the bankers, the deficient money and credit supply of the nation that made it difficult for the small businessman and farmer to survive, the protective tariff system viewed as profitable to the few and expensive to the many, land monopolists, tax dodgers, conscienceless profiteers and those associated with the financial establishment, were in effect a major assault on business.

Ironically, the monetary views of the Populists, which businessmen and prominent economists of the day branded as the harebrained schemes of the crackpots of their generation, today have become part of the thinking of the establishment and even have become enshrined in some of our important citadels of higher learning. The Populists, as you may recall, believed that the basic economic ills of society could be eliminated if only more money were pumped into the economy by the federal government, and this same government assumed the initiative in liberalizing the credit facilities of the nation.

The Populist argument has even haunted the post-World War II generation. In fact, the monetary views of Milton Friedman, professor of Economics at the University of Chicago and one of the leading classical economists and theoreticians, whose name was linked with Senator Barry Goldwater in the presidential campaign of 1964, sound very similar to those of the Populists. Friedman, if I understand him correctly, argues that "the key to capitalistic economic stability is monetary policy—the factors that govern the rate of growth or decline in the money supply."

What has happened in effect is this. One of the foremost conservative economists of the 1960s and 1970s has been advocating that the money supply of the country be increased at a rate of 3 to 5 percent annually, which not only goes to the heart of the Populist argument, but exceeds it. The Populist proposal, by comparison, was modest—increase the money supply of the country until it reached $50 per capita. Even more startling is that the once heretical views of the Populists have acquired respectability in the very same institution in which it was roundly denounced by one of the foremost economic critics of the 1890s.

Americans, who have grown accustomed to reading about or viewing on their TV screens stories of marches on Washington and the presentation of demands to Congress and the President, may be sobered by the fact that this is not a new phenomenon. During the first half of the 1890s a number of industrial armies of unemployed people marched on Washington to protest the adverse state of the economy and demand appropriate legislation to help remedy matters. All this is linked with Jacob Coxey of Coxey's Army fame and his son "Legal Tender Coxey," and his army of unemployed who wanted Congress to finance a road-building program that would provide jobs for the unemployed.

Business was partly blamed for this by none other than the conservative editor of the *Nation,* E. L. Godkin, an indefatigable foe of the protective tariff who complained that the tendency for everybody who was "down on his luck [was] to go to Washington for relief." "It never showed itself before the period of high tariffs," wrote Godkin, and "the protectionist gospel has worked its natural and legitimate results. . . ." Godkin added that, ". . . as long as there is a large party, containing 'our best people' in this country, preaching the doctrine that American industry cannot flourish without government aid, that the withdrawal of that aid means ruin and misery, and that every man in business who finds that his market is poor go to Congress for relief, we shall every year find ourselves face to face with the rising tide of Coxeyism. . . ."

Although a broad overall public impression of the businessman during the nineteenth century, at first glance, would be that of a self-centered irresponsible person propelled exclusively by the profit motive, documented evidence of the philanthropic activities of some of the early business leaders indicates a breadth of interest on their part that should caution one against accepting such oversimplifications. Businessmen, whether they liked it or not, could hardly avoid the fact that their economic interests and conditions in the communities were closely interwoven, especially in the hundreds of company towns that sprang into existence in the isolated river valleys and mining areas of nineteenth-century America.

The efforts of businessmen to concern themselves with the welfare of their employees spread throughout the Middle States, gradually to the South and West, was not confined strictly to the Boston area, and eventually assumed the form of the company town which came to have so many sinister connotations. These company towns, often the creation of a single man or enterprise, were compelled to win and hold workers; and to do so, they had to provide supplemental facilities and services. They provided company housing and stores, libraries, schools, and similar institutions to attract a stable and contented labor force. The motives that inspired such undertakings were mixed, and so were their results. All too often exploitation and bitterness resulted instead of harmony. Meanwhile, "The hierarchical structures of business, and particularly of the single-company town, encouraged employers to assume that the wealth and power at their command made them the best judges of the entire community's welfare needs."

After the single-company town was superseded by urban centers of greater complexity, it became more difficult to assign to any given employer responsibility for conditions affecting residents. This, combined with the growing impersonality of the urban community, discouraged business philanthropy; hence from here on it was the individual rather than the company contributions that provided the chief support of urban charities.

Andrew Carnegie did as much as any single individual to popularize the idea that the successful business leader should consider himself a trustee of the interests of the community at large. His ideas and actions regarding the distribution of his fortune for social ends anticipated in many ways the later development of corporate philanthropic and community relations programs. Judge James Hall's advice that the successful business leader "be a patron of the arts, a promoter of education, a friend to literature and science, an active agent in all public improvement . . ." won only a limited, and primarily an individual, response in the nineteenth century. Of course this kind of giving and these kinds of concessions did not go to the heart of the complaints made by the protesting groups.

By the end of the nineteenth century company contributions to the local and national welfare causes had become an accepted, if not a common, practice. The YMCA and the Red Cross had established a claim in business interest and support, and businessmen were demonstrating a growing sense of involvement with the conditions of other social groups, such as workers, immigrants and the urban masses. "What the nineteenth century lacked, and what the twentieth was to supply, was a rationale—a concept of the relationship of business to the community—in which social responsibility was clearly seen as a charge not merely upon individual conscience and concern, but upon corporate resources as well."

It would be misleading to assume that the criticisms of business stemmed exclusively from the kind of protest movements that I have been describing, because they also emanated from other, in some instances more powerful, quarters, as well. Three other particular fields contributed, and these were (a) fiction, (b) history writing, and (c) the ministers of the social gospel. The influence of these groups was enormous and for the most part went unchallenged until more recent years.

The preachers of the social gospel, largely Protestants, complained that the churches had become too engrossed in theological disputes and too little concerned with the problems of the little man in a growing urban-industrial society. These churches, furthermore, were dominated by men who either belonged to or were in sympathy with the capitalist classes, and were equally indifferent to the need of applying the principles of Christianity to industrial matters. One preacher found that members of the working classes did not attend church because they were unable to dress as well as the average member of the congregation. Said one workingman, "When the capitalist prays for us one day in the week, and preys on us the other six, it can't be expected that we will have much respect for his Christianity."

The solution of all these problems, according to the exponents of the social gospel, was to remove the temptation of sin by doing away with starvation, poverty, disease, overwork, and the bad conditions that depressed workers and turned virtue into vice. God had to become a matter of transforming life on earth into the harmony of heaven, rather than of getting individuals into heaven. The greatest kind of evil was that which used up the wealth, happiness, and virtue of a community in gratifying one's self; and the greatest kind of goodness was that which put freely at the service of the community all that a man could offer. Christian principles had to be applied to the solution of social problems. And finally the attack had to be on the causes or conditions that produced these evils instead of on the effects.

Most of the larger Protestant denominations became convinced of the responsibility of the Church in the amelioration of social problems, and this brought about the formation of the Federal Council of the Churches of Christ in America in 1908. The program of the Federal Council of Churches called for the elimination of poverty, the shorter workday, a living wage, the abolition of child labor, better housing, protection for the worker in the factories and the like, which in effect constituted an attack on the functioning of capitalism and the businessman who was at its very foundation. And you will note the program of the churches came to a fruition at the height of the Progressive era in politics.

The attacks on business during the Progressive period that were joined by the muckrakers, the Socialists, the preachers of the social gospel and other social critics resulted in the enactment of regulatory curbs on business and legislation designed to broaden the base of our social and political economy. Among the significant pieces of legislation passed by Congress before the outbreak of World War I in 1914, in response to such protests, were those that provided for the direct election of United States Senators, the federal income tax, lower tariffs, the Federal Reserve Act, which aimed to bring about a better distribution of the banking and credit facilities of the nation, the Federal Trade Commission Act, the Clayton Anti-Trust Act, workmen's compensation, and greater protection of women and children in factories.

The picture portrayed of the businessman through the years in fiction has been rather ugly, and for the most part it has stuck. Themes in these novels ranged from the practice of cannibalism by businessmen in Washington to tycoons that sold cracked steel to the government, soldiers who were corrupted in youth by a business society, to the masculine tycoon father who produces a son who combines military skill with homosexual urges. Other themes have dwelled on the interminable hypocrisies and frauds of the advertising industry, the jungle in which big businessmen and manufacturers roamed, the rich father's children who make a cult of failure just to get even with the old man, and the traveling salesman who seduced an avant-garde girl novelist on a transcontinental train. Certain novels of the 1920s and 1930s stress the war of class against class. Some of the authors were Socialists by conviction who were trying to anatomize the abuses of capitalism and what capitalism did to one's personality.

The response of businessmen to such evaluations has been that business has not exactly been free of unethical practices, but that writers have an obligation to place their themes and subjects in better perspective, which is an involved way of saying that all businessmen do not fall into this unsavory category. Industrialists kept insisting they were open to suggestions and that changes had taken place for the better.

Many also became concerned with what they believed were the great injustices being done the businessman by the historians. Among the few early historians who wrote in an unflattering and even a scornful fashion about the vulgar, crass and dull businessmen were William H. Prescott, Henry Adams, Charles Francis Adams and Charles Beard. This list, incomplete as it is, gives one some idea of the high pinnacles such attitudes had reached in the profession. And the antagonism of some historians increased as the power and influence of the businessman grew.

What a few historians had been able to say about business and businessmen, in due time a group of able journalists, whom Theodore Roosevelt labeled as muckrakers, were able to proclaim to the world at large. The muckrakers, it should be kept in mind, were not historians; but one of them, Ida Tarbell and her *History of the Standard Oil Company,* played an important part in molding the attitude of a generation of readers toward the company and industrial combinations in general.

> For ten years, between 1902 and 1912, there was incessant hammering at business in the nation's most widely read magazines. Their combined circulation totaled several million at a time when the magazine did not have to compete with radio, television, and the motion picture for the public interest. When the mold of opinion toward business was still plastic and warm, the muckraker by sheer reiteration drove the stereotype of the businessman—as motivated by greed and lust for profit, as utterly ruthless toward his competitors, as socially irresponsible—deep into the public consciences. And to a considerable extent it has remained there, because the muckraker indictment of business was one of the streams that fed the progressive movement of the early twentieth century, the New Deal, and the Fair Deal.

The findings of the muckraker, which for the most part were accurate, revealed much that was bad about business, and they had great appeal. But this was a one-sided indictment that failed to give business credit for its creative accomplishments. This phase of business achievement needed telling along with the more sordid phases to bring about a better-balanced picture of business and to rub off some of the anti-business bias that prevailed.

Curiously enough the indictment against business was left unanswered for the most part. With few exceptions, most businessmen ignored the criticisms, concentrated on their business endeavors and tried to justify their conduct as best as they could. The "Gospel of Wealth" gave way to the "Gospel of Production," or the turning out of "more for less and less," and this in due time was followed by the "Gospels of Distribution and Service." During the post-World War II years the concept of business as an institution was aimed at "achieving a just and working balance between the conflicting interests of labor, capital, and the general consumer."

Attitudes toward the businessman shifted with the trend of events, the state of the economy, the tide of public opinion, and the needs of the hour. During the 1920s public sentiment turned more favorable to the businessman than it had been for many years, and this friendliness was best reflected in the administrations of Warren G. Harding, Calvin Coolidge, and Herbert Hoover. Although academicians such as Charles and Mary Beard, and Vernon Parrington, continued to point to the defects in American society, popular writers issued a series of laudatory biographies in book and article form with the intention of molding public opinion. Such works, despite their limitations and the unwillingness of scholars to accept them at face value, cannot be ignored because they represent a popular approach to a significant topic at a particular period in our history. Meanwhile, many of the financial and industrial magnates had become oracles of the day on almost everything under the sun. "When the whole country went into a frenzy of speculation in 1928 and 1929, these high counsellors, with few honorable exceptions, were all on the side of more frenzy. . . ."

Then the pendulum began to shift in the opposite direction. As the economic crisis of the 1930s worsened, the attacks on big business were intensified. The American people had become disenchanted with the business community and its gilt-edged promises of yesteryear that ended in disaster. Double discredit fell upon business leadership which not only had failed to lead but had given false counsel. Frustration turned into despair. Many Americans, disillusioned with the state of our economy, came to distrust business in general.

When the depression struck the nation, the business corporations which had long emphasized private philanthropy and "character-building" services were unprepared to deal with mass unemployment. Hoover and those of his political persuasion insisted on local and voluntary responsibility for the relief of the needy; these elements continued to insist on self-help and limited government, and opposed federal relief expenditures. Business had to give more to charitable agencies or reconcile itself to added taxes for relief until jobs appeared.

For a brief period it appeared that some of the more enlightened employers of the 1920s might offer the kind of business leadership the nation needed so badly. Gerard Swope, whose unemployment benefit plan for General Electric workers attracted particular attention, was viewed as an industrial statesman of the first order. Swope's much discussed plan for national economic stabilization through private economic planning was hailed in some quarters as a step forward by American business leadership, but in others it was criticized for vesting too much power in private hands. For the most part the best of these plans turned out to be mere straws in the wind.

While business representatives were seeking to counteract the depression and build more effective relations with the general community, a series of vigorous and very threatening movements shaped up that were decidedly anti-business in tone. Besides the Socialists and the Communists, who were in disagreement with each other, there were: the farm strikers of the early 1930s who were anti-New Deal as well as anti-business; Huey Long and his "Share-the-Wealth" and "Every Man a King" program that appealed to the downtrodden; Dr. Francis Townsend and his $200-a-month pension for the aged; the Farmer-Labor Party of Minnesota which was to the left of the New Deal and anxious to expand nationally; the Reverend Charles Coughlin,[with] his assaults on the bankers and the international financiers, the New Deal, and his formation of the Union Party in 1936, which ran "Liberty Bell" Bill Lemke of North Dakota for President; and the Technocrats who, if granted their way, would have liquidated our money economy and substituted in its place a system of continental totalitarianism based on energy units.

Although with the coming of the New Deal in 1933 the federal government began to administer relief on a broad scale, businessmen, private agencies and even the federal government were anxious that the entire program not be relinquished to Washington. Appeals in 1933, 1934 and 1935 laid stress on individual responsibility, private philanthropy and local agencies. Managers of large corporations were beginning to view corporate philanthropy as a possible counterweight to the expanding role of the government. Corporate, rather than individual, contributions seemed the likeliest source of increased giving. The sad state of our economy was beginning to drive home the meaning of the interdependence of business and the community. Although Roosevelt had demonstrated misgivings about tax deductions for corporate contributions in 1935, he emphasized the obligations of industry to support private social welfare services, so did other New Dealers. But in the meantime the role of the government kept expanding.

The New Deal left little doubt that it posed a challenge "to the primacy of business leadership and initiative." Businessmen who viewed the expansion of government with feelings ranging from "hesitant acceptance to apoplectic antagonism" could hardly argue convincingly that they had proved themselves equal to the task of serving the general welfare. Throughout the 1930s business faced a resentful, if not a hostile, public. Every group that business had designated itself as trustee of during the 1920s seemed to turn against it. Many business leaders considered the Wagner Act, the Social Security Act, the Public Utilities Holding Company Act and other pieces of New Deal legislation as hostile to business. Roosevelt, in the opinion of many, was steering clear of business.

Roosevelt's insistence on major tax reforms opened the door slightly to the amendment for which the community chests and their backers had been contending for so long. The Revenue Act of 1935 included a graduated corporate income tax and a tax on intercorporate dividends that was aimed at the holding companies, an act business viewed as unfriendly to its interests. Provisions originally made for an undistributed profits and an inheritance tax were dropped and replaced by an excess profits tax. New Dealers defended the tax package as an effort to build justice and equality in the national tax structure, while businessmen attacked this as another "soak-the-rich tax."

Meanwhile, community chest officials, anxious to obtain a tax exemption, visited Treasury department officials, lobbied in Congress, and testified before the House Ways and Means Committee, but their requested exemption of 15 percent was reduced to 5 percent of the taxable income. They placed stress on the growing dependence of private philanthropy upon corporate support. After a great deal of pressure, lobbying and debating, the measure passed Congress despite the disapproval of the President.

The 5 percent amendment did not inundate philanthropic coffers. The corporate givings of between $30 and $33 million annually reflected the shifting economic conditions more than anything else. Not until 1940 and the return of favorable business conditions did significant increases in corporate donations occur. The tax exemption for corporate contributions directed some of these funds into private philanthropic channels, just as the Revenue Act and the Social Security Act of 1935 tapped corporate surpluses for the general welfare.

Business's response to changing conditions had been questioned before the Great Depression. Dean Wallace B. Donham of Harvard University argued that a better understanding of social relationships and corporate philanthropy were only surface manifestations of the problems at hand. Something more fundamental was needed. "No amount of support of hospitals and charities, of fine arts and universities, will serve to remove the stigma of materialism from our civilization. The idealism of our business leaders must be focused on business itself, on the great task of adjusting business progress to community happiness." Regulation from the outside would not enforce the kind of social responsibility the times required. Only direct and intimate knowledge on the part of the businessmen of the relationship of business to social conditions could adopt economic institutions to social needs. "We build great industrial corporations which introduce amazing novelties into life," continued Donham. "Their executives behave first, last, and nearly all times as if their companies had no function except to manufacture and sell. They have a fine understanding of their own business, too little grasp of their industries as a whole, almost none of the relations between their particular interests and our general social and economic structure, and far too little grip on the social consequences of their activities." Corporate philanthropy, it should be added, failed to impress many. Roosevelt was of the belief that it was aimed at influencing public opinion more than in meeting fundamental needs.

Businessmen tended to stress shortcomings in the public's understanding of the economic forces at work, rather than in the performance of the economy. But this was a difficult argument to maintain in the depth of the depression, even for the most ardent defenders of business themselves. Still these elements hoped that as conditions took a turn for the better, the failures of the past would be forgotten and obscured by the perplexities and prospects of the future, and in the meantime they could argue that the chief failure of business came from the lack of good public relations.

In all fairness there were individual businessmen who recognized the emergence of new economic and political relationships during the 1930s, a decade of unprecedented change and experimentation. Such attitudes were best reflected by Ralph E. Flanders, Alfred P. Sloan, Jr., of General Motors, and Paul W. Litchfield of Goodyear Tire and Rubber Company. The election of 1936 had a sobering and chastening effect on some of those who believed that the public favor could be regained simply by insisting on the need for it. Flanders pointed out that business had done much to provide economic opportunities for Americans, although it had failed to raise wage levels adequately and promote economic stability. Now management had better accept "the social ideals which they had indicated are the evident purposes of the American people" and cooperate with the government and organized labor. The one big lesson the depression and the New Deal taught business leadership was to be more sensitive to public opinion.

When all is said and done little progress was made beyond the levels of the 1920s. The chief interest of business leadership still was to stress "fundamental principles essential to the maintenance of a free and competitive economy." Most businessmen failed to consider seriously the relationship of social responsibility to key issues of the 1930s such as social security and industrial relations. Only with the community chest and comparable welfare agencies were they able to find outlets for specific notions of responsibility.

As international problems superseded domestic issues and the depression slowly came to an end, the pace of change was influenced by the new circumstances. Ideas and policies that developed slowly under peace-time conditions and found business and community closer together were speedily forged into strong ties. Corporate giving through the established channels, such as the community chest, the Salvation Army, hospitals, etc., had increased. The approach of war loosened the purse strings of the corporations and quickened their consciences; and the war itself accelerated the process.

Despite the growth of tax-induced philanthropy, corporate giving barely kept pace with the overall rate of economic expansion. Corporate giving reached 1 percent of the company profits in 1945, even though a 5 percent exemption had been provided by law since 1936. Furthermore, the smaller corporations gave more generously in relation to their resources.

World War II did much for ideas concerning the role of business in society. The doubt and defensiveness of the 1930s rapidly faded into the background. Business emerged from the war in a triumphant mood with renewed confidence and leadership. The climate of opinion encouraged an exploration of the social dimensions of corporate enterprise. Business publications of the 1950s were filled with discussions of social problems and the responsibilities of management in dealing with them. They elaborated on the trusteeship concept enunciated during the 1920s and also injected the idea of social responsibility. Business gradually was drawn into the participation of a range of social interests extending well beyond what hitherto had been considered appropriate: education, the fine arts, religion, recreation, and even politics. This continued until the 1960s, when the tide of public opinion began to shift once more.

For me to recite the list of charges that have been leveled against business within recent years would be to belabor the obvious charges of corporate irresponsibility ranging from a disregard of the working conditions of its employees to seeking favorable tax breaks, producing inferior and even unsafe products, deceptive advertising, crimes at the executive level, fraud and the sale of adulterated products, investing money in under-developed countries, the exertion of too much influence over universities and colleges through boards of trustees or regents, and comparable grievances have been voiced repeatedly.

The reactions to these complaints have varied. Some corporations, it appears, have profited from past experiences, and others have not. Some executives argue that the profit motive has to be defended at all costs and have behaved accordingly; others have been dazed by the barrage of attacks that have been hurled against them. There are those, such as members of the American Bankers Association, who are relying on better public relations and who hope to improve their image and the image of the bankers in general by preparing a series of glossy films of the industry. Some companies are making genuine attempts to resolve the problems the consumers are complaining about. Some, of course, maintain that businessmen who accept the argument of "social responsibility" are the "unwilling puppets of the intellectual forces that have been undermining the basis of a free society." Company executives who decide in the general social interest to hire hard-core unemployed instead of better-qualified workmen or install more pollution control equipment than required to improve the environment, according to this line of reasoning, do so at the expense of their shareholders, higher prices to the customers of the company's product or lower wages to the employees.

Consumerism has reached the point where it can no longer be ignored as it has been for the most part in the past. The Office for Consumer Affairs in the White House says that it receives about 2,500 complaints a month, and the Federal Trade Commission says that it averages about 20,000 complaints a year.

Although consumerism is gaining some recognition, there is little evidence that the business community has been caving in to the militants. However, these are some of the things that have been happening. During the past year and a half more than a dozen major companies have appointed top-level officers to new positions dealing with consumer affairs; those of Chrysler, Pan-Am and RCA are at the vice-president's level; and others such as that of Swift and Company have imposing titles like "director of public responsibility." Some companies have installed toll-free telephone lines for use by consumers who want to bypass dealers and other intermediaries to lodge complaints directly at headquarters; and still other companies have advised consumers through advertising to forward their complaints to headquarters in writing. Ford Motor Company, we are told, recently put its service division on a par with its sales division. Some companies have been liberalizing their guarantees and warranties.

Consumerism of today differs from the consumerism of the early 1900s and the 1930s, when social critics led campaigns against fraud, deceit, price-fixing and unsafe or unwholesome products. Such complaints are still being heard today. But the consumer movement of today, which began in the late 1950s, "is more concerned with the quality of products and services and increasingly complex and technical products." The consumers want: "safe, reliable products and services that perform as advertised and that are repaired or remedied promptly when they fail. In addition, the activists say, consumers want more detailed information about goods and services to enable intelligent comparison before a purchase is made."

The response of the corporations has a long way to go before the consumer advocates will be entirely satisfied with the results, even though some headway is being made. The actions of some of the major companies have been viewed with caution in other quarters. As someone said: "Frankly the more money and ingenuity these companies spend telling us how much they care about us, the more skeptical I am that they're actually doing anything that will result in better treatment of customers."

This, then, is a thumbnail sketch of protest movements and what they mean and did not mean to business in the past. This, I should repeat, is a focus that has not been given to business too much by historians. Business, until perhaps very recent times, did not begin to respond to critics as forthrightly and directly as it could have all along. Contributions to charity, community chest drives, the YMCA, the Salvation Army, the Red Cross, hospitals and similar institutions represented a partial response to the needs of the community and society, as well as an evasive way of responding to legitimate complaints. Larger doses of realism and forthrightness would have helped.

Businessmen will have to learn to reconcile themselves to criticisms, justified or unjustified. Complaints will be lodged against them as long as business exists, people continue to buy its products, and society is faced with problems. The nature of the grievances and the names of the products attacked and of the men and women doing the complaining will change, but the complaints will continue. Business will always remain a convenient target as long as the nation is faced with urban problems, a racial issue, unemployment, . . . and inflation—a mean set of problems by any standard; and the belief [will] persist that business had something to do with creating these conditions. Politicians unresponsive to the needs of the day tend to aggravate matters. Popular means of communication and the ability to link business with a war-oriented foreign policy will continue to feed the fires of protest. To me, at least, the writing of some good business history in the long run will help remove some of the misunderstanding and stigma that is attached to business, but I am afraid it will not offer any instant relief. At least this is how I, as a historian, see it.

CHAPTER ONE QUESTIONS

1. Saloutos argues that antagonisms between businessmen and the broader public interest have been present throughout American history. What are some underlying causes of this antagonism?
2. Are the stresses and tensions of the business–public interest controversy healthy or unhealthy for society? Is either (or both) side guilty of excess?
3. What will be the nature of the business–public interest dialectic in the future? Can you speculate which of today's potential problems in business practice will arouse the wrath of reformers ten or twenty years from now?
4. Do you think Saloutos has been fair and objective in his treatment of past and present viewpoints? For example, does he overemphasize the reluctance of business leaders to respond to and initiate reform?

CURRENT CRITICISMS OF CORPORATIONS AND CAPITALISM

THE CORPORATE IMPACT

RALPH NADER, MARK GREEN, AND JOEL SELIGMAN

Ralph Nader, a well-known consumer advocate, and two of his top staff present in the following analysis a broad range of criticisms of the modern corporation.

> *The corporation is a creature of the state. It is presumed to be incorporated for the benefit of the public. It receives certain special privileges and franchises, and hold them subject to proper government supervision. . . .*
>
> —United States Supreme Court in *Hale v. Henkle,* 201 U.S. 74 (1906).

If the Constitutional Convention were convened in 1976 instead of 1787, can we imagine that this time the Founding Fathers would fail to mention the corporation?

Two centuries ago Americans were keenly aware of the tyrannical potential of unlimited governmental power. In rejecting the arbitrary abuses of King George III, the colonists embraced the philosophical premises of Locke and Montesquieu in their constitution: power would be dispersed among countervailing institutions; political officials would be electorally, and hence personally, accountable for their actions; delegations of power would be limited to those specified in written law. What began as a daring experiment in political self-governance has endured the erosion of time, becoming a model for constitutional democracy.

With a glaring exception: the Constitution of the United States does not mention the business corporation. It neither explicitly defines the relation of the individual to the business corporation nor the relation of the business corporation to the federal government. The small scale of business enterprise two hundred years ago led such prominent thinkers as Adam Smith and Benjamin Franklin into such poor prophesies. Smith thought that the corporate form, where a few people manage other people's money, would lack the entrepreneurial incentive and spirit to survive; and Franklin, like most of his illustrious colleagues, was far more worried about political oligarchy than corporate oligarchy.

So today, while the United States Constitution governs every federal, state, county and local authority, no matter how small, it is silent about the giant corporations which govern our economy. The fact of their impact is not difficult to trace. In 1974 the 100 largest corporations held one-half of the assets of the other 1.8 million corporations—which was the same percentage of industrial assets that the top *200* corporations held just 20 years before. Of *Fortune*'s top 1000 corporations, the largest 10 corporations had 16 percent of the workforce, 20 percent of the profits and 23 percent of the assets. Exxon had greater sales in 1974 than each of the GNPs of Austria, Denmark and South Africa. General Motors employs more people—734,000—than the states of California, New York, Pennsylvania and Michigan combined. ITT has operations in all 50 states, and has employees in 70 countries as well.

Mere brobdingnagian size, however, only begins an analysis of corporate power. Herbivorous dinosaurs were also huge—but weak, dumb and helpless before predators. Our giant firms, on the other hand, have both size *and* power. A couple of hundred corporate managers, who could fit comfortably into a small auditorium, can make decisions controlling most of our industrial economy. How many hundreds of billions of dollars will be paid out in dividends and wages; how many billions will be invested in capital investment or research and development? It is an exercise in power when an electronics firm important to an eastern city shifts production to a newly built Mexican plant; when U.S. Steel decides to raise its price substantially in the face of slackening demand, thereby accelerating inflation; when B. F. Goodrich in the 1960s decides to sell an aircraft brake which its technicians know will fail under normal stress; when the American auto industry in the 1950s commits itself to bulky chariots rather than smaller, fuel-efficient vehicles; or when General Motors in 1929 refuses to install shatterproof glass on its cars. In all these instances, consumers, workers, shareholders and citizens can be very dramatically affected by Corporate America.

Theory, however, has lagged behind reality. Classical economists still appear to assume that if the government would only mind its own business we could have a self-correcting, perfectly allocating market and that the Gross National Product could be the proper barometer of societal wealth. Many businessmen—of the sort who inveigh against "Big Government" at annual meetings—treat the *Fortune 500* as if they were competing Ma & Pa groceries—just like small firms, except larger. But a giant corporation is not merely an inflated version of a small business firm—any more than a man is just an oversized infant or an elephant simply a large mouse since both are mammals. For corporations, as well, a vast increase in quantity involves a shift in the quality and nature of the enterprise as well.

Thus, prominent analysts like A. A. Berle, Walton Hamilton, Robert Dahl, Earl Latham, Richard Eells, Arthur S. Miller and John Kenneth Galbraith have correctly perceived the giant corporations to be more like a private government. "The corporate organizations of business," wrote Professor Wolfgang Friedman, "have long ceased to be private phenomena. That they have a direct and decisive impact on the social, economic and political life of the nation is no longer a matter of argument." Worse, these private governments also produce costly side-effects, or what economists call "externalities." As K. William Kapp argued in his prescient 1950 book, *The Social Costs of Economic Enterprise,* GNP and production data usually "leave out important social costs of production borne by third parties and future generations. . . . [T]he institutionalized system of decision-making in a system of business enterprise has a built-in tendency to disregard those negative effects on the environment that are 'external' to the decision-making unit."

For those who simply assume that big business is what has made America great and that there is no need for a major redesign of our large corporations, it would be useful to catalogue some of the social costs of corporate impacts. In brief fashion, to be discussed subsequently, they sketch the invisible taxes our private governments levy on all Americans.

INDUSTRIAL POLLUTION

Until the recent environmental movement caught much of business short, industrial pollution was considered a free form of waste disposal. Free, that is, for the company. But society generally pays the bill in impaired health, damaged property and aesthetic despoilation. In the early 1970s, as companies such as Reserve Mining Company dumped 67,000 tons of waste rock and asbestos fibers a day into Lake Superior, as American Cyanamid poured 6 million gallons of waste water into the Savannah River daily, and as U.S. Steel released 225 tons of pollutants into the air each day at its Clairton coke plant near Pittsburgh, the link between industrial production and environmental pollution became clear. "A factory dumps its wastes into an adjoining river," observes economist Anita Summers, "and consequently fishermen no longer fish, sailors no longer sail, and nature lovers search for another retreat. Urban centers swarm with autos, the pollution index soars, eyes burn, shirts get dirtier, and the view from the city's highest point is no longer a source of delight."

Between 1946 and 1971, levels of pollution in many industries rose from 200 percent to 2000 percent, though production grew only 126 percent in the same period. Industrial pollution accounts for one-third of all solid waste, one-half of all air pollution and more than one-half of total water pollution. According to a 1970 Public Health Service (PHS) study, 36 percent of 2600 tap water samples contained bacteria or chemicals in excess of PHS standards. The National Cancer Institute has estimated that, contrary to previous assumptions, 80–90 percent of all human cancers are caused by environmental factors, including industrial pollution. For example, its computer analysis of death certificates from 1950–1969 found an extremely high incidence of bladder cancer in heavily industrialized areas around Newark, Chicago, St. Louis and New Orleans.

TOXIC SUBSTANCES

Business not only often pollutes its surrounding environment but its internal environment as well. The chemicalization of the workplace threatens the well-being of millions of American workers. The 1972 *President's Report on Occupational Safety and Health* said that perhaps 100,000 deaths annually are caused by occupational disease. For example, in January 1974 the B. F. Goodrich company reported to the National Institute of Occupational Safety and Health (NIOSH) that several employees had died of a rare form of liver cancer, angiosarcoma. The workers had been exposed to vinyl chloride, a colorless gas used in the production of the common plastic polyvinyl chloride. At the Johns-Manville plant in Manville, New Jersey, writes reporter Phil Greer, "people are dying of diseases virtually unknown elsewhere; they are dying, medical experts agree, because they work in the biggest asbestos processing plant in the world." A 1970 PHS survey showed that over 30,000 workers are routinely exposed to beryllium, which can produce severe inflammation of the lungs, nose and throat, chest pains, pulmonary dysfunction, congestive heart failure, enlargement of liver and spleen, and discoloration of skin from oxygen deficiency.

Still, in the view of a lawyer in a silicosis compensation case in 1970, "with a maximum liability of only $12,500 plus medical and funeral expenses, it has been so inexpensive to disable and kill a man . . . that it has not been worthwhile to clean up."

DISCRIMINATION

Although many large corporations appear today to be in a race to place on their boards of directors women and blacks (or better yet, black women), the record behind the window-dressing is unimpressive. In 1973 alone, the Equal Employment Opportunity Commission moved against nine of the largest 25 firms in the nation for alleged discrimination against black and/or female employees. A survey of the top five officers of 44 American based multinational companies found not one woman among them; a study of the 1008 directors of the 67 largest California corporations found no blacks and six women (three being the wives of the company's chairman or president).

It should not be surprising, then, that black male workers earned 69 percent of the salary of their white counterparts in 1972 and that full-time female workers had a median income only 60 percent of their male counterparts in 1973.

WHITE-COLLAR BLUES

Most students of the business world are familiar with the phenomenon of "blue-collar blues"—where worker powerlessness and alienation lead to job dissatisfaction and hostility to management. But a comparable despair has begun to afflict businessmen as well. Based on a survey of 2800 corporate executives, the American Management Association observes that job alienation "has not merely spread to, but may even thrive in, the managerial suites of American business." Though businessmen may maintain an image of rugged individualistic enterprise—a cross between *Cash McCall* and *Major Barbara*'s Mr. Undershaft—William H. Whyte Jr.'s *The Organization Man* appears the more apt characterization.

Consider John DeLorean who, with a $550,000 salary and a shot at the presidency of General Motors at age 48, suddenly quit. He complained that one simply couldn't be an innovator, a planner on the 14th floor of the G.M. building in Detroit. "You were too harassed and oppressed by committee meetings and paperwork. . . . GM has gotten to be a total insulation from the realities of the world." At a May 1972 conference in Wilmington, Delaware, on business management structures in major countries, Charles Wilson, a historian at Cambridge University, thought that the drive for more security through mergers and diversification was blotting out individuality and self-determination. *Washington Post* reporter William Jones, summarizing the conference's findings, wrote that "Many large business enterprises around the world are being turned into bland, unimaginative [institutions]. . . . And the men who run the large corporations follow similar patterns in their management direction, seeking to avoid controversy or competition and striving for perpetual security."

Sometimes the corporate culture is worse than just bland. *Business Week* prints a symposium on executive stress; the *Wall Street Journal* runs a series on executive dropouts; two former Ford Motor Co. executives in separate actions sue their former employer on the grounds that its demands and pressures forced them to become alcoholics. Their lawsuits may be bizarre, but their condition is not. A recent study by the National Institute on Alcohol Abuse and Alcoholism found that some 20 percent of America's top business executives are "irresponsible alcohol users."

POLITICAL POWER

In the political marketplace there is the danger that powerful corporations by the weight of their wealth can overwhelm the voices of individuals. This link between corporate power and political power existed long before Dita Beard held center stage for two months in 1972, but ITT's self-inflicted anguish over its antitrust problems spotlighted the problem for all to see: too often when a major company has much at stake, it possesses the resources and contacts to lobby the government into acquiescence.

The techniques of converting economic strength into political strength are reasonably clear. First, campaign contributions can help put sympathetic legislators into office. As Senator Boies Penrose candidly explained to a group of his business patrons at the turn of the century, "You send us to Congress; we pass laws under which you make money; . . . and out of your profits you further contribute to our campaign funds to send us back again to pass more laws to enable you to make more money." The 1925 Campaign Finance Act notwithstanding, Penrose's ethic prevailed and was the source of so much of the Watergate Special Prosecutor's business; and since the Federal Election Commission has decided to allow corporations to raise money in political action committees, the vaunted 1974 campaign finance act will actually encourage more corporate money in politics. Second, there is the benefit of having friends in high places. President Gerald Ford regularly golfs with U.S. Steel lobbyist William Whyte, not John Gardner. When Elmer Bobst, chairman of Warner-Lambert and godfather to Tricia Nixon, had an antitrust problem, he felt free to bypass the Justice Department. "I never opened my mouth to the President about the case," protested Bobst, adding however that "I did talk to other people in the White House about it though."

Third, prominent businessmen enter and exit prominent government positions with rapid-fire regularity. Large contingents of oil men at the Federal Energy Administration; generals in defense firms; businessmen like Roy Ash, William Simon, Peter Flanagan and Bryce Harlow in cabinet level posts—the examples are many. Fourth, large companies can employ fleets of lobbyists to push for favorable policies—some 80 percent of the largest 1000 corporations have lobbying offices in Washington—and can call upon affiliated interests to reinforce their positions; thus, GM in early 1975 sent a letter to 1.3 million shareholders, 13,000 dealers and 19,000 suppliers asking them to press their congressmen to postpone safety and emissions standards for five years. Finally, big business can possess the kind of technical data that the federal government does not have, or does not want to have—natural gas reserve data, for example.

Together the above methods create an unhealthy dependence by government on business, or what a July 4, 1972 *New York Times* editorial called "The Corporate State." The editorial concluded that "The overriding issue is how to prevent powerful special interests from frustrating the democratic process."

PRIVACY INVASIONS

Confronted by employee theft or disloyalty, overzealous companies have at times fulfilled Orwell's worst fears. During the labor violence in the 1930s—three decades before Vince Gillen began investigating Ralph Nader—General Motors' "spy system was one of the most vicious in the country" according to William Manchester in *The Glory and the Dream*. Hearings before Senator Edward Long's Subcommittee on Administrative Practices and Procedures in 1965 documented a pattern of "eavesdropping techniques":

corporations testified to monitoring telephone conversations, placing hidden microphones in washrooms and lounge areas, deploying company spies, installing false ceilings with peepholes, and bribing the employees of rival companies. In 1975, ATT admitted that, in order to catch "phone freaks" dodging tolls, it had randomly monitored as many as 33 million calls in six U.S. cities between 1964 and 1970, taping part or all of 1.5 million of these calls. Such privacy invasions can involve millions of unsuspecting citizens and workers; but workers hostage to their need for employment can do little about such intrusions.

LOCAL SWAY

Perhaps the most obvious hostages of corporate power are those communities who depend on large companies for their existence, even as these companies tax these communities in numerous ways.

Local plants can provide employment—and pollution, as Gary, Indiana, understands about U.S. Steel. Subsidiaries of giant firms can exploit and damage local services: when a Union Camp manager was asked whether his company's heavy industrial pumping might dry up Savannah, Georgia's underground water supplies, he replied, "I don't know. I won't be here." Large companies possess and often exploit their leverage to bargain down the amounts of local tax they must pay. The Mayor's office in Gary, Indiana, estimated that U.S. Steel properties there had been under-assessed by about $140 million in 1971, enabling the firm to avoid paying $16–23 million in taxes. "Avoidance of state tax liabilities by America's largest corporations," concludes Byron Dorgan, North Dakota's tax commissioner, "has reached scandalous proportions."

Especially in company towns, like a St. Marys, Georgia, or Pullman, Illinois, the dominant corporation can control public opinion and political activities—a syndrome which can apply as well to "company states" like Delaware. In January 1974, four editors at Wilmington's *The Morning News* and *The Evening Journal,* both run by DuPont interests, either resigned or were fired; the editors said that their boards of directors opposed news stories that embarrassed or reflected adversely on the DuPont family. While locally dominant corporations can be oppressive, absentee corporations with national interests can be indifferent to community needs. For many plant managers at local subsidiaries, their town is a temporary station on the way to success in New York City or Los Angeles. "IBM is famous for never allowing anyone to take up roots . . . they're constantly moving people around the country," complains Congressman Hamilton Fish (R.–N.Y.), who has IBM facilities in his district. Sociological, economic and congressional studies have documented this lack of civic involvement, and its erosive effects on community well-being.

To take one example, Professor C. Wright Mills in 1946 compared three pairs of cities: in each pair was a "big-business city," where a few, large absentee-owned firms provided most of the industrial employment, and a "small-business city," where many smaller, locally owned firms comprised the community's economic life. Using such variables as unemployment rates, suburban sprawl, income distribution, the frequency of home ownership, death rates, the number of libraries and museums and per capita expenditures for schools, Mills concluded that "big business tends to depress while small business tends to raise the level of civic welfare."

DECEPTIVE INFORMATION

Large corporations also possess, in Richard Neustadt's description of American presidents, "the power to persuade." The average American adult sees 40,000 commercials *a year* on television. The top 100 national advertisers spent $3.6 billion in 1974 in the effort to favorably shape their corporate image and consumer purchasing decisions, an effort which to a large extent succeeds: one study concluded that if advertising expenditures were limited to 3 percent of the sales revenues for 14 specific industries that exceeded that level, their aggregate sales would have declined by 16.7 percent.

Ideally, informational advertising can educate consumers about best buys and, hence, encourage the intelligent allocation of economic resources. All too often, however, corporate advertising is the inane, misleading or deceptive fare we digest daily on television. Instead of advertising about price and quality, leading companies strive to associate their products with alluring superstars or beckoning moods—Catherine DeNeuve and Chanel, or the Marlboro Country. In the food industry, ads as informational as "Mmm, Mmm good" and "Anyone can be a Frito bandito" prevail, as the least nutritious foods tend to be the most heavily advertised. Potlatch Forests illustrated its environmental concern by a nationwide advertisement showing a picture of a spanking clean Clearwater River in Idaho, where it has a pulp mill, which carried the caption, "It cost us a bundle, but the Clearwater still runs clear"; sadly, the photograph had been taken many miles *upstream* from its polluting pulp mill. When a public interest law firm affiliated with Georgetown University studied advertising submissions by television manufacturers to the Federal Trade Commission, it found that nearly 60 percent of the ads were inadequately substantiated.

PRODUCT SAFETY

Perhaps it is a lingering belief in *caveat emptor,* or the knowledge that judicial hurdles make successful suits unlikely, but American business has a poor record on product safety. Too often its products add to the GNP in two ways: in manufacturing output and in increased health expenditures for those injured, maimed or killed.

There are several gauges to measure this consumer cost. The 1966 Traffic Safety Act has led to the recall of 35 million cars between 1967 and 1974. Recent data indicate that overprescription promoted by drug companies leads to 60,000 to 140,000 deaths and 5 to 10 million serious cases each year. Cosmetics injure 60,000 people annually, mostly women who suffer skin eruptions, loss of hair, severe allergic reactions and burns. Then there was the engineering director at General Dynamics who sent the following memorandum to his superior a few years ago: "It seems to me inevitable that, in the 20 years ahead of us, DC 10 cargo doors will come open and cargo compartments will experience decompression for other reasons and I expect this to usually result in loss of the airplane"; he added that floor changes would be costly, but "may well be less expensive than the cost of damages resulting from the loss of one plane-load of people." This advice was ignored, and two years later a Turkish Airlines DC-10 crashed after its cargo door blew open, killing all 346 passengers.

In 1968, the National Commission on Product Safety reported that each year 20 million Americans were injured severely enough in product related accidents to require medical treatment; 585,000 were hospitalized, another 110,000 permanently injured and 30,000 died—at a cost to the economy of $5.5 billion. This grim roll-call led to the creation of the Consumer Product Safety Commission in 1973.

THE PRICE OF TECHNOLOGY

Luddites notwithstanding, advancing technology can of course greatly enhance the quality of life. Which is why the Greek word *"techne,"* from which technology is derived, meant "art." From penicillin to transistorization, the benefits of research and development can be seen all around us. "Modern technology is creating a society of such complex diversity and richness," observes Buckminster Fuller, "that most people have a greater range of personal choice [and] wider experience than ever before."

On the other hand, technology is also quite capable of exacting a catastrophic price from society. This is especially true given the complexity and interconnection of modern life—e.g., a power failure at a single switching station in Canada throws the east coast of the United States into darkness. It was one thing when an individual consumer bought and drank some noxious snake oil potion from a traveling salesman a century ago; but when thousands of pregnant women abroad consume Thalidomide, leading to horribly deformed babies, it is quite another.

The Janus-like quality of technology takes numerous forms. In Japan it has been necessary to hand pollinate apple blossoms because pesticides have killed so many bees. Or consider the terribly mundane aerosol spray can. Aside from keeping wetness away, many scientists and a 14 member interagency task force have concluded that the gases released by hundreds of millions of such cans are slowly depleting the ozone layer in the atmosphere. As the ozone layer thins, more of the sun's ultraviolet wavelengths will reach the earth, causing increased eye damage, cancer, blindness, earlier skin aging and destructive changes in plant and animal life.

When problems involving nuclear power or pesticides or aerosol cans become public, those industries with financial interests in these technologies often simply assert that they are the experts and that their technology is safe. But when the health and safety of hundreds of millions of citizens are at stake, the assertions of business are not enough—especially given how wrong self-serving experts can be. The *Titanic* was supposedly unsinkable; it sank. The Maginot Line was a supposedly impregnable barrier; it was flanked in three days.

CORPORATE CONCENTRATION

Our economy, and certainly college economics courses, assume the existence of and benefits of a competitive enterprise system. Judge Learned Hand most practically appreciated the virtue of competition and evil of monopoly when he wrote, in 1946, "Many people believe that possession of unchallenged economic power deadens initiative, discourages thrift and depresses energy; that immunity from competition is a narcotic, and rivalry a stimulant, to industrial progress; that the spur of constant stress is necessary to counteract an inevitable disposition to let well enough alone." Yet by 1976, in John Kenneth Galbraith's useful dichotomy, the American economy could be functionally divided into two economies: the market system and the planning system. In the former, small businessmen and service firms compete among themselves according to the model of the marketplace. But the planning system, by and large the manufacturing and mining sectors, is dominated by our giant corporations—Alcoa, Kaiser and Reynolds in aluminum; U.S. Steel and Bethlehem Steel in steel products; IBM in computers. Beyond specific markets, huge conglomerate firms such as Textron and Gulf & Western have acquired holdings in numerous industries. In 1955 it was estimated that 44.5 percent of those working in manufacturing worked for the top 500 companies; in 1970 it was 72 percent. Between 1948 and 1968, the largest 200 U.S. industrial firms increased their share of all industrial assets by 25 percent. Today, these 200 control two-thirds of all industrial production.

This corporate concentration traces back to the three giant merger waves in the past three-quarters of a century and the historic ineffectuality of antitrust law. The resulting combinations practice not competition but market power, i.e., the ability to administer price and restrict output. Thus, in much of American industry, a few giant firms jointly act as would a monopolist or cartel. There are higher prices: the Federal Trade Commission has estimated that car and camera consumers overpay, respectively, 7 and 11 percent for their products due to the concentrated structure of their industries. There are higher profits, as studies by Joe Bain and Leonard Weiss have documented. There is the frustration of federal monetary and fiscal policy, since our large corporations will maintain their high prices even if demand falls during periods of tight money. There is waste: without the "stimulus" of competition, economist Frederic Scherer estimates monopoly waste and inefficiency at 10 percent of costs.

Like many consumer problems, the high cost of monopoly is invisible to the naked eye. If it could be transmuted into black children riding school buses into white neighborhoods, or a comatose consumer kept alive by lifesaving devices as an overreaching businessman threatens to pull the plug, perhaps the subject would work its way into the headlines. But Professor Walter Adams understands the problem even without these dramatics. "It poses the No. 1 domestic problem of our time—the prevalence of private socialism in what we like to think of as a free enterprise economy."

MULTINATIONAL CORPORATIONS

As the world GNP increases at about 5 percent annually and the world's multinational community grows by some 10 percent annually, one can understand why the U.S. Chamber of Commerce predicts that by the year 2000 a few hundred multinational corporations would own $4 trillion in assets, or 54 percent of the projected world wealth. To the managers of American-based worldcrops—and 13 of the largest 20 in the world are American—this is an encouraging development toward world peace and prosperity.

But there are vigorous dissenters. To the American labor movement, these companies are the modern version of the runaway shop: they flee to non-unionized, low-paying outposts like Singapore (Gulf) or Spain (Ford), thereby exporting jobs (the AFL-CIO has estimated that multinationals cost 900,000 American workers their jobs between 1966 and 1971). Labor is also anxious that they can lose their ability to strike—and hence their collective bargaining leverage—if multinationals can move abroad when American labor increases its demands or if these firms can simply increase production in their foreign facilities when they are struck in the United States. When Ford's English workers at Dagenham began organizing, an irritated Henry Ford said after a meeting on the subject, "Behave yourselves or we will go elsewhere."

These worldcorps cite the multiple benefits they bestow on underdeveloped countries, though often the benefits flow in the opposite direction. They often merely buy out existing local firms rather than build new facilities, use local capital rather than importing U.S. capital, and, between 1960 and 1968 according to a U.N.-sponsored study, were able to take 79 percent of their profits out of Latin America. Between 1950 and 1965, the profit inflow to the United States from third world investments was 264 percent of its capital outflow. These companies, with subsidiaries in many countries, can manipulate its charges for services and transactions via intra-firm transfer payments to disguise earnings and minimize tax payments to their host countries. (For example, the United Kingdom Monopolies Commission recently discovered that while the Hoffman La Roche drug firm had earned 25 million pounds between 1966–1972, it declared only 3 million pounds—passing on the difference from high-tax Britain to low-tax Switzerland.)

Multinationals may use underdeveloped countries as dumping grounds for products they have trouble marketing elsewhere due to strict regulatory laws. Hazardous drugs are marketed abroad that are either prohibited in the United States or that require warning labels regarding their use. Finally, however benevolent their intentions, multinational corporations often fail to adapt their technology to the needs of their underdeveloped host nations. They may insist on capital-intensive production to the labor-intensive facilities needed in densely populated areas. Or they may unwittingly promote a cultural imperialism which perverts local custom for "western progress." Richard Barnet and Ronald Müller, in their *Global Reach,* write that "It is not uncommon in Mexico, doctors who work in villages report, for a family to sell the few eggs and chickens it raises to buy coke for the father while the children waste away for lack of protein."

CONCENTRATION OF WEALTH AND INCOME

Business managers proclaim a "People's Capitalism" in which 25 million Americans are shareholders, while labor leaders—whose unions represent under 25 percent of all workers—understandably extol their influence on maintaining decent wages. The large companies, to be sure, are our major disbursers of income in the form of dividends, interest and wages. But a concentration of ownership and income misdistributes these benefits toward an elite who are already wealthy and away from most Americans who are not.

A study conducted by Senator Lee Metcalf (D.–Mont.) found that the largest 30 shareholders of Ford Motor Company stock—largely institutional holders disguised under street names—held 35 percent of the total common stock. The comparable figures for General Electric were 21 percent, for Chrysler 40 percent and for Mobil 28 percent. According to a 1962 Federal Reserve System study, 1 percent of all shareholders held 72 percent of all corporate stock. Based on Census data, the top 5 percent of Americans hold 53 percent of net private wealth, while the bottom 60 percent holds only 7.5 percent. While the poorest fifth of the United States earned 3.7 percent of the nation's income, the top fifth earned 47.9 percent; the top 1 percent earned 10.5 percent of all income, or 51 percent per capita earned by the poorest fifth.

BUSINESS CRIME

"If the word 'subversive' refers to efforts to make fundamental changes in a social system," sociologist Edwin Sutherland wrote more than two decades ago, "business leaders are the most subversive influence in the United States." In the past that notion would either rankle or amuse most corporate managers, but today, in the midst of what can only be called a corporate crime wave, they cannot dismiss its relevance.

The Special Prosecutor's office has successfully prosecuted 22 individuals and 18 companies—Phillips Petroleum, 3M, American Airlines, Goodyear Tire, among others—for violations of the campaign finance laws. The Securities and Exchange Commission has sued nine firms for their failure to disclose, as required under the securities laws, the existence of political slush funds at home and bribes abroad. Admitted foreign law violations include a $4 million payoff by Gulf Oil to South Korea, a $1.25 million bribe by United Brands to reduce export taxes in Honduras, and a $450,000 bribe by the Northrop Corporation to two Saudi Arabian generals to obtain lucrative arms contracts. There have been numerous and confirmed reports of payoffs to foreign political parties by major American companies, especially oil firms. According to a Library of Congress study, between January and November of 1975, two dozen major American corporations admitted to making more than $300 million in illegal bribes in recent years in this country and overseas.

Further, Gulf Oil has admitted to the SEC how it disbursed $4.1 million in illegal campaign contributions to numerous politicians between 1960 and 1972. The money, in cash, was delivered by Gulf lobbyists in blank envelopes to politicians or their aides in their offices, hotel rooms and airports. The Internal Revenue Service obtained an indictment of 3M for tax fraud relating to its slush fund, and is currently investigating 111 other companies for similar violations. The Civil Aeronautics Board has uncovered how Braniff Airways failed to record the sale of 3626 ticket sales in order to finance its illegal campaign giving. And press reports have disclosed how aerospace firms seeking Pentagon contracts have lavished valuable benefits on procurement officials; Northrop had Defense Department personnel to its duck hunting lodge 144 times between 1971 and 1973—activities that appear to violate Executive Order 11222, which prohibits procurement officials from accepting anything of monetary value from companies seeking contracts.

It is difficult to believe that these cases are mere aberrations. Some of the most important and established corporations in the country are involved, firms apparently no more or less prone than other firms to prevailing political and commercial pressure. These companies involve such diverse industries as aerospace, food processing, oil, sewing machines, airlines, banking, and office supplies. Indeed the prevalent rationales for these crimes—it's the way business is done abroad; if we don't do it, our competitors will—lead to the conclusion that this pattern of illegality is customary and pervasive.

This conclusion is corroborated by the general empirical data which exist on business crime and morality: in the 18 months ending in December 1974, the FBI announced that white-collar convictions were up 30 percent; Public Citizens' 1974 Staff Report on White Collar Crime reports that frauds and embezzlements have increased 313 percent since 1969; in a study by the Corporate Accountability Research Group of the presidents of *Fortune*'s top 1000 firms, 60 percent of the 110 respondents agreed that "many price-fix"; in a recent poll by University of Georgia professor Archie Carroll, three-fifths of corporate executives say that young managers in business would commit unethical acts to exhibit their loyalty to superiors. "At Carthage," said Greek historian Polybius, in words still echoing two millennia later, "nothing which results in profits is regarded as disgraceful."

Large business firms, to be sure, have been creators of wealth and jobs, a major reason why our real per capita income has tripled in the past forty years. Corporate philanthropy totals some $1 billion annually—or 6 percent of all philanthropy in the country. Still, invocations of corporate responsibility notwithstanding, the social balance sheet of big business contains enormous debits. In the last decade alone, an avalanche of congressional, academic and journalistic reports on business bilks can lead only true believers or Dr. Pangloss to remain upbeat about corporate power in America.

Which leads naturally to the question: where is the law? When confronted with social or economic wrongdoing, presumably the law—that reflection of democratic will—can provide a remedy. Has it historically done so?

QUESTIONS

1. The authors argue that the corporation is like a private government. What kind of case do they make to back up this argument?
2. How would traditional proponents of business defend themselves against the charges made by the authors? Are some of the areas of condemnation more damning than others? Which ones?
3. What other criticisms of business and the business institution might be added to those in this article?
4. On net balance, is the flow of business executives in and out of government positions a good or bad thing for the country? Explain.
5. It is, of course, important to catalogue and correct major social costs of industrialization. What benefits have we in the United States received from industrialization that should be identified on the other side of the scales?
6. With your background of economic history and a little library research, how would you appraise the cost-benefit equation of industrialization in the 1830s? The 1890s? The 1920s? The 1940s? The 1950s?

CAPITALISM HAS CREATED GREAT SOCIAL ILLS

JOHN G. GURLEY

John G. Gurley, professor of economics, Stanford University, argues in the following article that the great social ills of the United States are products of our capitalistic system, and he presents a challenge to the belief that the best hope for improving life in this country lies in continued support for its current economic system.

I shall first describe, in thirty-three words, what I consider the problem to be. I'll then try to analyze its basic causes. Finally, I'll turn to some possible solutions. In between, I'll hedge.

THE PROBLEM

What is the problem? It is that many of our economic resources are apparently being used for wasteful and destructive purposes when, all around us, there is so much poverty, oppression, and maltreatment of people and nature. Yet, economists have traditionally viewed economic activity in ways that question the very existence of such a problem. That is, the U.S. economy has been described in terms of a competitive model. In this model, consumers demand various goods and services, either directly in marketplaces or indirectly through their government representatives, in accordance with their preferences and their incomes, while private businessmen, seeking profits, produce the goods demanded, and produce them efficiently at low costs and prices. Hence, the things that are wanted get produced, and those that are not wanted are not produced. Under these conditions, there is no point at all in trying to convert anything!

While most economists recognize flaws in this picture, and would therefore want to modify the conclusion just drawn, it is still true that the influence of the competitive model has been so strong and so pervasive that it has all but eliminated economists as critics of the society in which they live. It is this model, applied domestically and internationally, that explains to a large degree why many economists have had to be told by their students and others what the actual situation is. This is an embarrassing fact, but it is a fact nevertheless.

CAUSES

What are the causes of the poverty, the environmental and urban decay, and the bloated military expenditures that concern us all? Surely, some of the

John G. Gurley, "Economic Conversion and Beyond," *Industrial Management Review,* Vol. 11, No. 3 (Spring 1970), pp. 17–25. Reprinted by permission.

environmental and urban decay is caused by the very processes of industrialization itself, whether they occur in the Soviet Union or in the United States. And some of this decay has roots in large and growing numbers of people crowding into already densely populated areas. Some of our military expenditures are certainly necessary in view of the nuclear weapons now aimed at us. Poverty is relative—a reflection of the fact that in no society does everyone move up together at exactly the same pace. Much of what we observe and do not like can be seen most anywhere in the world.

But that is not the whole story. Much of the rest has to do with capitalism itself. One of the main roots of the problem is that there is a private capital-owning class, whose interests are largely supported by the State, and which benefits from private profit-making within the context of a U.S. dominated international capitalist system. The system itself is under severe attack from anti-capitalist forces, both at home and abroad. These threats to global capitalism and the system's own driving forces and values largely determine how the surplus economic resources will be used.

MILITARY EXPENDITURES

These statements require some explanation. Let's start with military expenditures. Why have these expenditures risen so rapidly in the postwar period? Certainly it is not because consumers have expressed, through any sort of marketplace or voting mechanism, growing demands for: invasions by our military forces of one country after another, proliferation of nuclear, chemical and biological weapons, military aid to dictators, or counterinsurgency in dozens of poverty-stricken countries. These expenditures are not meant to maximize consumer utility by giving them what they request.

Instead, most of these expenditures are intended to support the interests of a small class of people who control much of the business wealth in this country and who have business interests and ideological commitments to capitalism throughout a large part of the world. These expenditures are intended to defend and, if possible, extend the area of the "Free World."

I don't think that anyone can really come to grips with this problem unless he realizes two things: first, that the "Free World" has relatively little to do with freedom and democracy and everything to do with free enterprise, foreign investment, and capitalism; and second, that the defense of the "Free World" is a very serious business, with not only the preservation of capitalist ideology at stake but also billions upon billions of dollars riding on every turn of the revolutionary wheel.

The "Free World" *does* exist. It is an international capitalist system with hierarchical structures, composed of countries favorably disposed to private enterprise. The United States, at the top of this structure, dominates most of the countries just below it, which include the advanced capitalist countries of western Europe, Canada, Japan, Australia, New Zealand, and perhaps Israel and South Africa. The United States, and many of these countries, in turn, heavily influence the economic and political destinies of quite a few low-income countries—in Latin America, Africa, and Asia—which are hospitable to free enterprise and especially to U.S. private investment, and which are at the bottom of the capitalist structure. Many of these satellite countries are ruled by the rich and the powerful—by dictators, sultans, monarchs, feudal landowners, oligarchs of one sort or another. In most of them, the people are not free. The "Free World," as I have said, is not necessarily receptive to freedom, but it is always receptive to capitalism.

In this international capitalist system, individuals and corporations in the wealthy countries own large amounts of land, natural resources, and capital goods in the satellite countries, while the latter are often heavily in debt to the former. The wealthy countries have the industrial power that is fed by the oil, minerals, and raw materials of the satellites, and the latter in return receive industrial goods and basic food items. Mostly by design, rather than by accident, there is much more trade between the wealthy and the poor countries than among the poor countries themselves. Finally, the international capitalist system is not really an alliance of "countries" or of "people." It is an alliance of the ruling classes in the underdeveloped countries with the capital-owning classes and their supporters in the industrialized nations.

So there *is* a "Free World"—and, what is most important for our purposes here, it is under attack. It is threatened from almost every direction by anti-capitalist forces. Some of the danger has been exaggerated, and some has been misrepresented. But most of it has been real enough to justify, in the name of the "Free World," not only billions of dollars of economic and military aid to the trouble spots, but also an extensive network of military bases, tens of thousands of troops in strategic locations, large-scale counterinsurgency operations, and numerous instances of military intervention.

It is true that some of our military expenditures can be explained, not in terms of the defense of the entire "Free World," but on the ground that nuclear weapons are in fact aimed right at us. As John Kenneth Galbraith has emphasized, some military spending has served the needs of a Technostructure that has generated increasing demands for weapons systems quite independent of real dangers and threats. But most of this activity does not float on a cloud of Cold War Myth, as Galbraith supposes. It is instead firmly based on something very real, the defense of the international capitalist system in the interests of a capital-owning class.

Vietnam, the forty-first military intervention by the United States since the turn of the century, was no blunder. Every piece of the "Free World" is potentially of great importance for the viability of the whole system. Each part plays its role—economically, politically, and psychologically. A victory for Communism in Vietnam would increase the danger to capitalism everywhere. It would weaken the economic structure of capitalist countries and satellites in Southeast Asia; it would shake public confidence in leaders who have been propped up by a United States that may no longer be willing to meet its commitments; it would strengthen anti-capitalist forces, directly by economic and military aid from a Communist Vietnam to neighboring countries and friendly groups, and indirectly by example to national liberation movements everywhere.

This view has recently been presented by a group of industrialists, bankers, militarists, and others, who call themselves the Citizens Committee for Peace with Freedom in Vietnam. As the *New York Times* reported:

"[Their] statement said that an abrupt withdrawal of United States forces would 'represent an American sellout and encourage the victors to try for one, two or three more Vietnams . . . America's word and leadership would be sharply devalued throughout the world. Every treaty that we have made, every agreement and commitment that we have entered into would be looked upon with suspicion by those countries who have counted on them. . . . The development of freedom and democracy would be reversed in Southeast Asia, and slowed in Africa and even in Latin America. Peaceful methods of social and economic change would be downgraded and violent methods encouraged. A huge part of the world would be increasingly vulnerable to Communist subversion and control . . . And the lesson of the success of violent guerrilla tactics to bring about change would not be lost on those who seek to use violence to effect social change here at home.' "

If, in this statement, "freedom and democracy" are understood to mean "free enterprise," then the statement, in my judgment, reflects a fairly realistic picture of the dangers now confronting global capitalism. So long as the dangers persist and we insist on defending the international capitalist world, it will be terribly hard to hold back the growth of military spending—especially if we also permit the military and their industrial contractors to play games with our scarce economic and natural resources.

POVERTY AND ENVIRONMENTAL DECAY

I previously suggested that the causes of environmental and urban decay and poverty are complex enough that no single determinant is likely to explain at all fully these social ills. Nevertheless, there is very little doubt that capitalism itself, through its private profit-making drives and its values, must be held accountable for some of the inequities and deterioration that we observe and smell every day of our lives.

It seems clear that if substantial private profits could be made in cleaning up our rivers and lakes; in restoring fresh, clean air to us once again, in eliminating hunger, malnutrition, substandard housing, and poor education, in doing something about congested and ugly urban areas and subhuman ghetto living, then, by God, they would be done faster than you could get a man to the moon.

In fact, however, not only is there very little private profit to be made in cleaning up the mess left in the wake of industrial capitalism, but, worse yet, it is the *creation* of much of the mess, not its elimination, that inflates the profits. Businesses make profits by keeping their costs as low as possible, and by charging higher prices for the products they produce. The costs involved here are private costs, the costs incurred by the firms themselves in production. The social costs, those costs imposed on the rest of us by the firms' operations—river and air pollution, traffic congestion, blighted landscapes, for example—do not have to be paid by the businesses and hence are no financial burden on them. In fact, the dumping of wastes into a river may be the cheapest way for firms to dispose of them. If so, the drive for minimum costs and high profits would dictate that this be done. Industrialists, of course, are very reluctant to spend money to meet the social costs of their operations—simply because such costs lie beyond their private profit calculations.

This, indeed, is the way industrialists *should* be expected to behave, according to the rules of capitalism. Milton Friedman, as usual, has given the clearest statement of what capitalism expects of its capitalists.

"The view has been gaining widespread acceptance that corporate officials . . . have a 'social responsibility' that goes beyond serving the interest of their stockholders . . . This view shows a fundamental misconception of the character and nature of a free economy. In such an economy, there is one and only one social responsibility of business—to use its resources and engage in activities designed to increase its profits so long as it stays within the rules of the game, which is to say, engages in open and free competition, without deception or fraud."

This doctrine of "open and free competition" has recently been invoked by Harrison Dunning, Chairman of the Board of Scott Paper Company, when he argued, in effect, that so long as there is open and free competition among many firms in polluting a river, no one firm significantly lowers the quality of the water, and hence no one firm should be held responsible for its actions. This may seem a strange use of "open and free competition," but it is a reasonable one within capitalist rules.

At a recent conference in Washington, called by the Department of the Interior's Water Pollution Control Administration and attended by 700 business executives, industry spokesmen made it clear that "they were all for the abatement of water pollution but that it should not be carried to the point of trying to make waterways too clean too soon or causing too great an impact on company profits." Brooks McCormick, President of the International Harvester Company, was reported to have said: "Any management today that does not understand its responsibility to society for degradation of the environment is derelict in its duty. But an even greater dereliction would be its failure to perceive and adopt a strategy of action that will provide the income for maintaining the profitability of the enterprise." Edgar B. Speer, President of the United States Steel Corporation, in discussing water pollution, said that "we oppose treatment for treatment's sake." There is something in that, but it does reflect less than complete enthusiasm for getting the job done.

And a few weeks ago, the *New York Times,* in an editorial on the construction of a giant pipeline for carrying oil across Alaska, rebuked the oil companies on Alaska's North Slope for "the greedy haste with which they are prepared to endanger a vast territory—the land, its people and its wildlife—for the sake of a quick and enormously profitable return on their investment."

But what do you expect? These are not evil men, and they are not necessarily cheating or engaging in fraud or deceit. The point is that private profit-making *demands* that they ignore the social costs of their operations. They should not be so castigated for doing what is required of them.

In saying this, I do not mean to deny the fact that some industrialists have made serious efforts and have spent large sums of money to clean up the mess they and others have made. But what they are doing is something that runs against the grain of capitalism, which is exactly why most of them acted only after heavy pressure by social-action groups of one type or another. The private profit-making drive is so strong and so much a part of our society that industrial capitalists must make heroic efforts to act in ways contrary to it.

The values of profit-making run even deeper, however. Private profit-making requires efficiency. To be efficient, a business firm builds on the best. This means that it does not hire the worst-trained workers, the disadvantaged, the poorly educated. Further, it locates where the most profits can be made, next to other factories that can give it low-cost access to supplies, or near markets where it can sell its products, even though a great social good might be served by locating in a depressed, poverty-ridden area. For the same reason, a banker extends loans to those who are already successful, or to those with the best prospects.

Such values not only permeate the business world, but also society as a whole. For example, primary and secondary education systems tend to devote their best teachers and best efforts to the superior students; universities offer admission to the ablest students, those who are best prepared; cultural centers are located in urban areas near the most cultured people; and even anti-poverty programs concentrate on those who have the best chance for success.

All of this ensures efficiency; it ensures the greatest returns for the cost, the best chance for making the operation profitable, whether it is business, education, or culture. However, when such a high value is placed on efficiency, as it is throughout our society, the economic and social development that results is almost bound to be inequitable. An economic development that builds on the best bestows riches on some people while leaving many others in society's stagnant backwaters. An economic development that stresses efficiency creates both wealth and poverty, fancy suburbs and miserable ghettos.

Capitalism is highly efficient, marvelously innovative, technologically progressive. Being all of these things, it has created great material prosperity for many people. But, at the same time, it has created the opposite—poverty and maltreatment of many of its people and much of its natural environment. Consequently, these social ills aren't just *problems* of capitalism; they are to some extent *creations* of capitalism. The wealthy industrialist and the poor tenant farmer are both products of the same system.

SOLUTIONS

What can be done to convert wasteful and destructive economic pursuits to ones more worthy of mankind?

If it is true that militarism, poverty, environmental decay, and other social ills are to a substantial extent products of U.S. capitalism, then there would appear to be only narrow limits within which economic conversion can be carried out, these limits being imposed by the existence of capitalism itself. Blueprints for economic conversion will turn out to be utopian, and rather useless, unless they reflect these limitations. And if they do reflect them, then they won't amount to much. These are the grounds for pessimism.

The prospects are not that bleak, however. For capitalism is not a static, unchanging creature, just daring someone to try to give it a once-and-for-all face-lifting. It is in fact a dynamic system, continually in the process of economic conversion. The question, therefore, is not whether to have economic conversion, or even how to achieve it, but rather how to respond to, reshape, and take advantage of, the broad developments that are now taking place in our own and the world's economy.

Professor Kindleberger has recently pointed out that, three-quarters of a century ago, private corporations in this country broke out of local markets and developed into national corporations. In the past several decades, many corporations have burst their national bonds to acquire overseas operations. Out of these activities has come the proliferation of multinational corporations—those firms with allegiances to two or more countries—and the initial development of true international corporations—those with no strong loyalties to any one nation.

International business expansion has radiated from the United States to other advanced capitalist countries, raising and tending to equalize technological capabilities throughout the advanced capitalist sector, and thereby stimulating reciprocal movements of business expansion. At the same time, U.S. capitalism has expanded, almost explosively, into many Third World countries, drawing them more tightly into the exploitative capitalist structure. Capitalism has been and is a system in expansion.

So is Communism. In the past half century, Russian, Chinese, and other Communisms have grown to cover a third of the world's population and almost that percentage of the world's land surface. This has greatly reduced the area and increased the dangers for capitalist expansion; the United States has already collided with these Communist countries on several occasions, and the two Communist giants themselves are in territorial and ideological disputes.

These global economic trends both strengthen and weaken the international capitalist system. It is being strengthened at the top by the growing economic cooperation and integration of the advanced capitalist countries. There are even indications that this affluent group will eventually draw eastern Europe and the Soviet Union into its economic orbit, and so further strengthen itself.

As U.S. capitalism has spread to the Third World, it has simultaneously encountered increasing resistance which has come basically from expanding socialist forces and from growing nationalist movements. Both of these forces have tended to weaken global capitalism at the bottom of the structure, and have in fact defeated it on several occasions, Vietnam being potentially the most damaging defeat of all.

So capitalism is gaining some strength at the top, losing some at the bottom. The strength at the top helps to hold the system together at the bottom; it pits a strong combination of industrial countries (including, at times, the U.S.S.R.), supported by the IMF and the World Bank, against weak, developing countries. But the decay at the bottom tends to spread to the top. There are now vigorous movements within the advanced capitalist countries, and especially within the United States, against capitalism. Capitalism in the advanced countries may be gaining technologically, but it is surely losing ideologically, as its blacks, its youth, it minorities, and its poor turn against its values, and more and more associate themselves with anti-capitalist forces abroad.

I started out by suggesting that, if consumers always got what they wanted, as in the competitive model so dearly loved by academic economists, the correct position of this Conference would be: There is nothing that we should do, for the system is working just fine.

I also noted that, if most of our economic and social ills are, in fact, created by an unchanging capitalism, the correct position would be: There is much that we should do, but nothing short of revolution that we can do.

If, on the other hand, our economic and social ills are unrelated to capitalism and so are correctable within the capitalist system—as many young people with environmental concerns seem to think, and as Galbraith apparently views the military scene—then the Conference should adopt the position: There is much that we should and can do.

I have taken still another position: that many of our difficulties come directly from capitalism itself—from a capitalism that is in constant change, a capitalism that is still very strong but is presently on the defensive. Within this context, there is certainly room for some progress by way of economic conversion.

But economic conversion, if pursued within the context of the existing capitalist system, is not likely to change by very much the basic drives of capitalism itself. By this route of economic conversion, there is room for correcting some of the worst effects of capitalism, but little room for any fundamental changes.

If this is so, there is a question as to whether we should devote our best efforts to trying to get a few more dollars eliminated from a huge military budget, a few more dollars devoted to alleviating hunger, a few more businessmen interested in the mess they create, and a few more city fathers concerned about ghettos—all the while trying to work within the present system. Or whether we should direct our energies forcefully to exposing the system itself. It can be argued that the former will achieve the latter. It may, if in the process of trying to improve things we increase our own awareness and the awareness of many others of the limits on our actions imposed by the system.

CAPITALISM, MILITARISM, POVERTY, AND THE ENVIRONMENT

NEIL H. JACOBY

Neil H. Jacoby, professor emeritus of business economics and policy, Graduate School of Management, University of California at Los Angeles, responds in the following article to the assertions and arguments of Professor Gurley presented in the previous article. Jacoby takes the position that the common welfare is best served by progressive reforms of the American economic and political systems and not, as Gurley suggests, by radical changes.

In his article, "Capitalism Has Created Great Social Ills," Professor John G. Gurley argues, in substance, that the American "capitalist" system (*i.e.,* competitive private enterprise) is mainly responsible for extravagantly high military expenditures and for poverty and environmental decay in the United States. Conceding that these problems may be caused in part by the very process of industrialization, by a large and increasing population, and by necessity, he nevertheless concludes that these evils are inescapable creations of capitalism. Because a fundamental reform of the system is in his view improbable, he suggests that capitalism should be replaced by a different system.

Had these propositions been advanced by Suslov in the columns of *Pravda,* the reader would not be surprised. Coming from the pen of a respected American economist, they provoke astonishment. Notwithstanding his commendable motive to improve our society, Professor Gurley gravely errs both in the premises and in the conclusions of his argument. Because these errors are common in the contemporary literature of social criticism, it is desirable to expose them. In the process of doing so, we shall show that American capitalism *is* achieving social goals, that its adaptation to new public priorities has indeed already begun, and that the common welfare will be served best by progressive reforms of the American economic and political system, not by radical change.

CAPITALISM AND MILITARISM

In his article, Professor Gurley notes the rapid rise since World War II of military expenditures for such things as aid to dictators and nuclear, chemical, and biological warfare. He contends that the high level of the U.S. military budget does not reflect the demands of the American people. "Instead,

Neil H. Jacoby, "Capitalism and Contemporary Social Problems," *Sloan Management Review,* Vol. 12, No. 2, Winter 1971, pp. 33–43. Reprinted by permission.

most of these expenditures are intended to support the interests of a small class of people who control much of the business wealth in this country and who have business interests and ideological commitments to capitalism throughout a large part of the world. These expenditures are intended to defend and, if possible, extend, the area of the 'Free World.' " They defend "the international capitalist system in the interests of a capital-owning class."

The familiar argument of the New Left that a "military-industrial complex" is able to boost military expenditures to levels higher than are in the public interest has been broadened. It is suggested that not only the Pentagon and the military hardware producers but also the entire American enterprise system is behind the conspiracy. The implication is that U.S. defense spending would drop substantially if only the nation could rid itself of the baneful influence of selfish corporate owners and managers.

These fanciful notions do not withstand objective analysis. The plain fact is that the level of U.S. military expenditures primarily reflects Congress' perception of the magnitude of world threats to national security. During the past decade, the Soviet Union and Communist China have devoted a rising fraction of their GNP's to military purposes. It is these countries, not the United States, which have taken the initiative in expanding nuclear armaments.

The level of military expenditures needed to assure national security is set in accordance with the public interest rather than business interests. "The Federal executive has repeatedly cancelled large military procurement programs that caused severe distress to defense firms and the communities in which they operated. Examples include the precipitous drops in military procurement after World War II and the Korean War, the cancellation of the B-70 manned bomber program in 1959, the termination of the Nike-Zeus ABM project in 1962, and recent drastic cutbacks in military and civilian aerospace programs. If the 'military-industrial complex' really dominated defense spending decisions, surely it would have been able to prevent the painful industrial adjustments it has endured." The truth is that the openness of the annual debate on the defense budget, the wide divergences of opinion among the generals, the Executive, and the Congress, and the great inequalities in the economic benefits accruing to various regions from defense spending, all combine to guard against the undue influence of business interests.

Moreover, the American business system benefits more from peace than from war or the preparation for war. There is abundant evidence that procurement contracts for weapons carry vast risks, produce relatively narrow profit margins, and provide highly unstable markets for business firms. That is why every large aerospace corporation has sought desperately to diversify into civilian products. That is why those companies which have not succeeded in their diversification efforts—Lockheed and General Dynamics, for example—are beset by financial troubles. If war and armament-making were good for American business, why does the stock market consistently collapse at every suggestion of armed international conflict and soar at every improvement in the prospects for peace?

The contention that the United States needs a huge defense budget to prop up its capitalist economy has become so discredited that even Communist propagandists have abandoned it. There is now universal recognition that a large drop in defense spending is needed to enable this country to fulfill its housing goals, to rebuild its cities, to restore the environment, and to underwrite the welfare of its people. Professor Gurley appears unaware of the fact that a massive reduction in defense expenditures *has already begun* and that, with the expected withdrawal of U.S. forces from Vietnam, further large reductions are scheduled. President Nixon noted that in 1971, defense spending would claim a *smaller* percentage of Federal expenditures than in any year since 1950, and that expenditures for pollution control, crime reduction, transportation, and housing would rise substantially in the years ahead.

Another fallacy in the Gurley theory is that U.S. military expenditures protect American business investments abroad rather than the security of the American people. If this were true, one should be able to cite many instances of U.S. military intervention to protect the property of U.S. corporations abroad or to recover damages suffered from expropriation by foreign governments. One should be able to demonstrate that U.S. foreign policy is dominated by the narrow economic interests of American multinational corporations rather than by political and social concepts of human freedom and dignity, national self-determination, and world comity and order.

When an American corporation goes abroad today, it cannot expect the U.S. government to protect its property. The era of "gunboat diplomacy" has passed. The political risks of investment in the less developed countries have risen since World War II as a result of strongly nationalistic feelings and of changed world attitudes toward intervention by one nation in the internal affairs of another. Recent expropriations of American corporate property in Bolivia, Peru, and Algeria, and the nationalization of Anaconda Copper Company's properties by Chile in 1969, did not lead to official interventions, despite the fact that the prompt, adequate, and effective compensation required by international law was not paid. Indeed, the U.S. government did not even apply the Hickenlooper Amendment—shutting off economic aid—to Peru when that country seized International Petroleum Corporation's properties without compensation. These instances demonstrate the "depoliticization" of private foreign investment since World War II.

Even more telling evidence that business corporations do not dominate U.S. foreign policy is found in the Middle East. One of the largest concentrations of American foreign investment is found in the petroleum industries of the Arab countries of the Persian Gulf and North Africa. Yet the United States provides military and economic support to Israel, whose importance to American business is negligible, thereby provoking bitter hostility among the Arab states and recurrent threats of expropriation of American oil properties.

CAPITALISM AND POVERTY

A second basic proposition advanced by Professor Gurley is that capitalism has created "poverty and maltreatment of many of its people and much of its natural environment. Consequently, these social ills aren't just *problems* of capitalism; they are to some extent *creations* of capitalism. The wealthy industrialist and the poor tenant farmer are both products of the same system." These evil results are said to be inherent in a system that responds to profit incentives and seeks to minimize business costs.

Taken literally, the assertion that capitalism "created" poverty is manifestly false. Poverty has been the lot of mankind since the beginning of recorded history. Before the Industrial Revolution and the emergence of the competitive market economy, almost every human being lived in "poverty" by contemporary standards, whatever the nature of the social system. The capitalistic economy that developed in Europe after the Middle Ages progressively *reduced* the endemic poverty that long antedated it.

Let us assume, however, that Professor Gurley intended his statement to mean that poverty can coexist with capitalism, and that capitalism does not necessarily abolish poverty. Because this is true, the salient issue is to define the role of the capitalist economy with respect to poverty. American society is composed of *two* related systems. The *economic system* is composed of private enterprises competing in the markets to acquire factors of production and to sell products. This system, called "capitalism," allocates resources in response to opportunities for profits. There is also the *political system,* composed of governmental and public institutions, which responds to the votes of citizens and representatives in legislatures. The political system allocates public resources and establishes the legal framework for the economic system. Each of these systems has unique capabilities and limitations; both must function properly if our society is to reach its goals. Failure to solve a social problem may be due to a malfunctioning of the economic system, the political system, or both. One system should not be blamed for failures of the other.

Over a long period of time and especially since World War II, both the economic and the political systems of the United States have operated to reduce poverty dramatically. The capitalist economic system, by offering strong incentives to individual creativity and effort, has recorded astonishing gains in productivity and in real output per person. Real income per person, measured in 1958 dollars, more than doubled during the periods 1950–1968, from $1,501 to $3,409. Because the distribution of money income among families at different income levels remained nearly constant, rising affluence was proportionately shared. The percentage of American families with annual incomes under $3,000 (in 1958 prices) fell from 26 percent in 1947 to 10.3 percent in 1968.

The American political system has also contributed to this remarkable reduction of poverty. It has transferred income and wealth from the rich to the poor via progressive income and estate taxation. It has supported massive public expenditures for assistance, medical and health services, and other benefits to children, the aged, the handicapped, and the poor. Most important, however, has been the massive public financing of education and manpower training and relocation. These public expenditures have expanded the opportunities and the productivities of millions of workers, enabling them to rise out of poverty. Collectively, expenditures on "human resources" now exceed military outlays.

Social critics often confuse poverty with inequality of individual incomes, although the two concepts are completely different. A capitalist economy (as well as other kinds of economies) pays individuals for their productive services in proportion to their marginal productivities. Productivities differ widely because of differences in energy, skills, education, mental ability, and other factors. Some persons have so low a level of productivity, owing to physical or mental handicaps or to lack of education and skill, that the incomes they can earn in a competitive labor market fall below the poverty line fixed by our society. It is the responsibility of the *political system* to try to raise the productivity of such persons, and to supplement their earned incomes by public assistance, so that they have a decent level of living. The primary goal of our society is affluence (*i.e.,* non-poverty) for all, and not equality of incomes. Indeed, a degree of income inequality helps to achieve generalized affluence by offering strong incentives for productive effort, efficient use of resources, and innovation.

CAPITALISM AND THE ENVIRONMENT

Although he concedes that the causes of environmental decay are complex, Professor Gurley asserts that "there is very little doubt that capitalism itself, through its private profit-making drives and its values, must be held accountable for some of the inequities and deterioration that we observe and smell every day of our lives." As he correctly points out, businessmen make profits by minimizing the costs of production, and hence are motivated to impose part of these costs on society in the form of air, water, and noise pollution. He sees no solution to the problem of environmental decay within the capitalistic system.

As in his discussion of poverty, Professor Gurley ignores the existence of the political system as the guide and monitor of the economic system in American society. The environmental problem of the United States was generated primarily by the tardy response of the *political system* to the higher value placed on environmental amenities by the people, and is only secondarily due to faults in the capitalistic economic system.

Environmental degradation occurs when there are significant external (or social) costs associated with producing or consuming commodities. When paper mills emit chemical wastes into lakes and streams, or motor vehicles cause air and noise pollution, external costs are being thrust on society in the form of reduced environmental amenities. The keystone of environmental improvement must be the internalization of these external costs, so that the prices of all goods and services reflect their full costs. While there are several alternatives open, the most efficient instrument in most cases is governmental regulation of the emissions of pollutants. If the government orders polluters to reduce their emissions to a prescribed legal standard, polluters then incur (or internalize) costs in order to conform to the standards. They thereby relieve the public of even greater costs of maintaining personal health and property damaged by pollution. Society has gained in its aggregate well-being.

Governmental action is essential in solving the problem of pollution because a competitive market economy is incapable, by itself, of internalizing external costs. This was demonstrated recently by a well-advertised effort of General Motors Corporation to sell a $26 pollution-reducing kit to motorists in the Phoenix region. During the first month, only a few hundred kits were sold in a market with several hundred thousand motor vehicles. The selling effort was then terminated. Few motorists would spend this small sum to install the device, because other persons would also reap the benefits. No auto manufacturer will voluntarily install costly pollution-reducing equipment on his own initiative; it would add to his costs and put him at a disadvantage in competing with auto manufacturers who did not do so. Society cannot reasonably expect *individual* producers or consumers to shoulder external costs in the name of "social responsibility" when the competitive market puts strong pressure on each to minimize costs in order to survive. A political decision by government is needed to put *all* producers and consumers on the same footing. It is the responsibility of the people, acting through their government, to create a market for pollution-reducing devices. Once government has acted, the competitive enterprise system will respond to produce them—and the pollution problem will be solved.

Although the political process has been sluggish in responding to the rising demands of the public for environmental amenities, reallocation of public and private resources has already begun. Heeding advice from many sources, including the Task Force on Economic Growth, President Nixon outlined a strategy in his budget message to the Congress early in 1970 which called for a shift in public priorities. Top priority was assigned to protecting the physical environment through substantial increases in Federal appropriations for clear air, clean water, and open space for recreation. The Council on Environmental Quality was created to review and coordinate all Federal programs affecting the environment. High Federal standards for water and air quality were established, and enforcement of anti-pollution laws was strengthened. Legislation has been enacted by Congress to require the production of nearly pollution-free motor vehicles no later than 1975.

One can posit a model of the dynamic relationships between changes in social values, governmental actions, and corporate behavior (see Figure 1). The *primary* sequential flow of influence (indicated by the solid line) runs from changed social values, via the political process, to changes in governmental regulations and public resource allocations. The market process then leads to corporate reallocations of private resources. However, changes in social values respond to certain *secondary* influences (indicated by the broken line), including political leadership and the advertising and selling efforts of corporations. Governmental actions are also influenced by corporate lobbying and other political activities of businesses.

This model enables us to identify the salient ways to improve the working of the social system. They are (1) to reform the political process so that

Figure 1

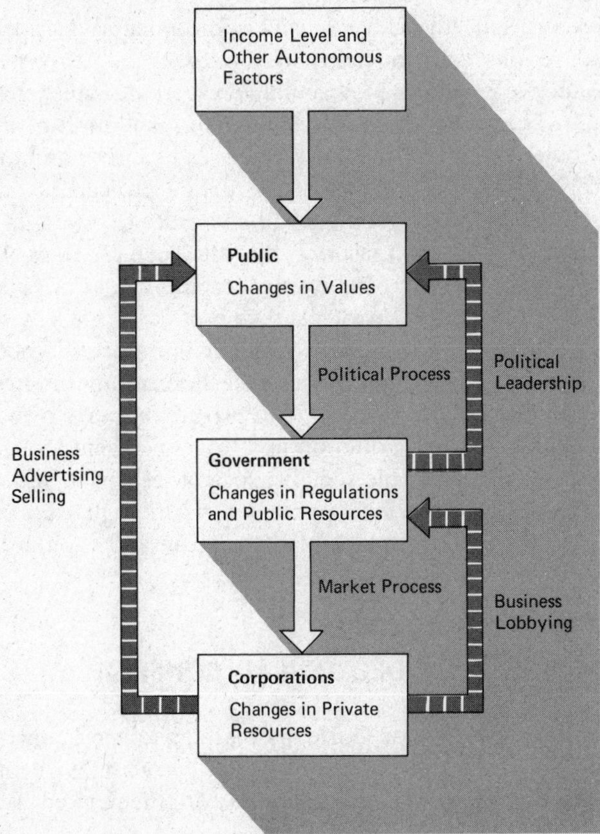

governmental actions will more rapidly and accurately reflect shifts in social values, (2) to reform the market process so that corporate behavior will respond more rapidly to changes in social values and governmental regulations, and (3) to reform political and business behavior so that their secondary influences will facilitate rather than obstruct the changes in resource usage that the public demands. With respect to the final point, it can be said that American business corporations have, until very recently, displayed a disturbing insensitivity to rising public demands for a better environment. They have been reluctant, if not obstructive, reactors to new social values instead of innovative leaders in devising means to satisfy them. Their lobbying and advertising activities have defended the *status quo* rather than helped to shape the future.

Although the creation of a satisfactory American environment will require the investment of tens of billions of dollars a year for many years to come, a strong start has been made, and we know that the problem is soluble under capitalism. Meanwhile, it would be an egregious error to suppose that pollution is indigenous to capitalist and absent from socialist economies. The primary causes of environmental pollution are the same: population growth and urban concentration, rising per capita production and consumption, and enormous increases in the utilization of energy and materials. Scientific investigation reveals that "the U.S.S.R. has environmental disruption that is as extensive and serious as ours [and] in some ways state ownership of the country's productive resources may actually exacerbate rather than ameliorate the situation." There are abundant evidences of pollution of the rivers and lakes of the Soviet Union, of chronic smog over its cities, and of soil erosion from ill-conceived timber cutting and construction projects.

A solution to the pollution problem will be harder to attain under socialism than under capitalism. One reason is that the socialist reward system puts strong emphasis upon growth of output and achievement of production quotas. It offers little incentive to officials who seek to preserve the environment, because that does not appear to be a "productive" activity. Even more important, the absence of private ownership of land and capital means that, unlike the United States, there are no private property owners to protest the loss of amenities through pollution and to act as agents for reform of the economic system. A monolithic socialist society lacks a separate mechanism for political control of economic processes. Although environmental improvement is clearly *possible* under both socialism and capitalism, it is more likely to occur in competitive market economies.

CAPITALISM AND THE IDEOLOGICAL CONFLICT

A final contention of Professor Gurley is that capitalism is on the defensive, both at home and abroad. "There are now vigorous movements within the advanced capitalist countries, and especially in the United States, against capitalism. Capitalism . . . is surely losing ideologically, as its blacks, its youth, its minorities, and its poor turn against its values, and more and more associate themselves with anti-capitalist forces abroad."

It appears that Professor Gurley mistakes recent noisy criticisms of "the establishment" by small minorities of students and other alienated persons for a vigorous and rising anti-capitalist movement. In fact, this fringe of political activists is bent on an unthinking destruction of the allegedly "repressive" American society, and any criticism of capitalism has been quite incidental to this purpose. Indeed, members of the New Left have been singularly barren of cogent ideas for reforming capitalism so that it may serve society better in the future. Basically, they are anarchistic rather than anti-capitalistic. Capitalism has always had and will always have critics. Professor Gurley presents no evidence that their number or influence is greater today than in the past, either at home or abroad.

More valid tests of the course of the ideological conflict between capitalism and socialism are (1) the *comparative performance* of the two systems in recent years, and (2) the *directions of reform* of each system. When these tests are applied, the weight of the evidence supports the proposition that *the "command economy" of centrally planned socialism is on the defensive throughout the world and is losing ideological support outside as well as within socialist countries.* During the past decade, the growth rates of the advanced market economies of Japan, West Germany, Italy, and France have exceeded those in the Soviet Union and most socialist countries; and the growth of small less developed nations like Korea, Taiwan, Thailand, Malaysia, Iran, Brazil, Zambia, Uganda, and Cyprus have been proportionately high. Although a sustained growth of production has not characterized all nations with capitalist institutions, neither has it occurred in all socialist countries. Capitalism has demonstrated an ability to bring broad-based welfare to underdeveloped as well as more advanced societies wherever political conditions have been conducive to its operation.

Even more impressive evidence of ideological gains by capitalism is that socialist countries are in the midst of a massive reform of their economic systems to incorporate more of the concepts and institutions of capitalism. The primary changes are decentralization of economic decision-making to the enterprise level, wider substitution of market prices for bureaucratically determined prices, wider usage of incentive compensation systems, and charging costs of capital into production costs in rejection of Marxist dogma that capital is functionless and costless. These changes, found in varying degrees in all Eastern European nations, are openly recognized and amply documented in the economic literature of both East and West. As the socialist nations have become more affluent and complex, they have found that mandatory central planning breaks down as a method of resource allocation, and that price and quality competition between enterprises in free markets is a more efficient guide. It appears likely that, in the end, public ownership of enterprises will remain as the only major distinction between socialist and capitalist economies. Should the present strong trend in the advanced capitalist countries toward dispersion of the ownership of shares in private business corporations among ever more people continue, even this distinction will become blurred. The conclusion is clear: socialism is converging toward capitalism, and socialism rather than capitalism is on the ideological defensive.

QUESTIONS

1. Strongly opposing views are expressed in these two articles. On the one hand, Gurley alleges and argues that capitalism itself is responsible in major degree for rising military expenditures, poverty, and environmental decay. Furthermore, he says, capitalist ideology is on the defense around the world. Present Gurley's arguments for each of these issues, and compare them with the arguments of Jacoby.
2. Do you think that Gurley has presented a uniformly fair assessment of the causes of social inequality and environmental degradation in American society? Why or why not?
3. In your judgment, does Jacoby overlook some of the faults of the present system?
4. Which of the two cases rests on more solid factual evidence? Explain.
5. Gurley argues that the cost-benefit tradeoff between economic efficiency and the public interest has gone awry. Which of his arguments effectively demonstrates this imbalance?
6. Has Gurley left room in his analysis for improving our present economic system through incremental change? Given Gurley's arguments, what concrete measures could business and government leaders take to improve the workings of the system?
7. Is Gurley's case something like that of throwing the baby out with the dirty bathwater? Explain your position.
8. Extreme positions are sometimes taken on each side of an issue in order to emphasize a point. In matters of important socioeconomic policy, do you think extreme positions help or hinder informed and rational debate?

THE ECONOMICS OF DISSENT

CAMPBELL R. McCONNELL

Campbell R. McConnell is professor of economics at the University of Nebraska. In the following article, he presents the major criticisms of capitalism made by radical economists and the responses of orthodox economists.

In the 1960s and early 1970s there has emerged a group of economists, variously labeled "New Left," neo-Marxist, or radical economists. Although radical economics encompasses an important intellectual tradition which traces back to Karl Marx, its recent growth is rooted in (1) the radicalization of university campuses in the late 1960s which occurred primarily in response to the Vietnam war and racial injustice and (2) the apparent inability of capitalistic society to resolve a number of deeply rooted problems such as the unequal distribution of income, wealth, and power both domestically and internationally; the wasteful use of resources; deterioration of the environment; discrimination; the urban malaise; and the inability to achieve full employment and price level stability simultaneously. More generally, radical economists flatly reject the orthodox or mainstream portrayal of mixed capitalism; they regard orthodox economics as essentially an apology for, or a legitimization of, the existing system. Furthermore, the radicals are decidedly pessimistic about the prospects for reform of the capitalistic system from within. They argue, on the one hand, that the laws of capitalistic development lead in a deterministic fashion to certain unpalatable characteristics and consequences and, on the other, that those who benefit most from the status quo dominate and control the political system.

The primary purpose of this article is to present some of the basic ideas and contentions which constitute radical economics. This is not a simple task. In the first place, just as there are many different postures or schools of thought within orthodox economics, for example, monetarists versus Keynesians, so there are many divergent views within the radical position. Hence, there is little doubt that some radicals would disagree, not only with the emphasis given to various points in the following presentation, but also with the very content of the model outlined herein. Second, the literature of radical economics is vast, diverse, and multidisciplinary; hence, any summary statement such as that offered here is necessarily abrupt and incomplete.

Campbell R. McConnell, "The Economics of Dissent," pp. 27–40, *MSU Business Topics,* Autumn 1975. Reprinted by permission of the publisher, Division of Research, Graduate School of Business Administration, Michigan State University.

ORTHODOX AND RADICAL ECONOMICS: BASIC DIFFERENCES

The ensuing discussion is in three parts. First, certain fundamental differences between orthodox and radical economics in methodology and problem perception are examined. Second, a radical model of modern capitalism is outlined. Finally, the orthodox rebuttal to the radical position is summarized.

In the radical or New Left view, the methodological shortcomings of orthodox economics render it incapable of understanding, and dealing effectively with, the "big problems" of capitalistic society. Radicals envision two related methodological deficiencies: First, orthodox economists have a naive and incorrect conception of the realities—the institutions and operations—of the capitalistic system; second, orthodox economics is too narrow a discipline to permit a clear understanding of real-world problems. Let us consider these two criticisms in the order stated.

HARMONY OR CONFLICT?

A leading Marxist commented as follows:

> Orthodox economics takes the existing social system for granted, much as though it were a part of the natural order of things. Within this framework it searches for harmonies of interest among individuals, groups, classes, and nations; it investigates tendencies toward equilibrium; and it assumes that change is gradual and nondisruptive.

But it is contended that capitalist reality is not so placid:

> The world we live in is not one of harmonies of interest, tendencies to equilibrium, and gradual change. . . . Conflicts of interest, disruptive forces, abrupt and often violent change—these are clearly the *dominant* characteristics of capitalism on a world-wide scale today.

Orthodox economists, in other words, envision a basic harmony in capitalism which allows the system to realize a satisfactory and workable reconciliation of divergent interests. Where product and resource markets are reasonably competitive, the market system promotes a rough identity of private and social interests through Adam Smith's "invisible hand." In other cases, countervailing power prevails; monopoly is countered with monopoly—big business faces big labor—so that market outcomes usually are socially tolerable. Where the market fails—for example, in the case of unbridled monopoly, spillover costs, and income inequality—orthodox economics holds that a benevolent government will intervene so as to protect and promote the general welfare. Modern capitalism is a pluralistic system wherein power is rather widely dispersed among business, labor, consumers, and government so that a consensus consistent with the general welfare can be reached. Hence, argue mainstream economists, the system's problems and shortcomings can be ameliorated or resolved within its present institutional and ideological framework. Indeed, the system is not only viable, but in most respects works quite well.

But the radical economists see in modern capitalism the deep class conflicts envisioned by Marx. In particular, in capitalist reality, power lies with the giant, monopolistic corporation—with the capitalist class—which dominates the productive system of industrialized capitalism. Furthermore, rather than functioning as a catalyst in the resolution of conflicts of interest, the public sector is dominated by, and is an instrument of, the large corporations. Instead of promoting socioeconomic harmony and furthering the general welfare, the public sector is essentially a tool by which the capitalists preserve and promote their own selfish interests—both domestically and internationally—to the detriment of the rest of society. Following Marx, the radicals conclude that the system is laden with contradictions and irrationalities and therefore is beyond redemption. The "solution" to capitalism problems lies in a radical change in the institutions upon which it is based; in particular, the private ownership of capital goods and reliance upon the market system as a decision-making mechanism must be eliminated in favor of some new form—presumably socialistic—of socioeconomic organization.

DISCIPLINARY NARROWNESS

A related criticism centers upon the disciplinary narrowness of economics. The radicals charge that orthodoxy concentrates upon the purely economic aspects of society and turns it back upon the critical interactions among economic, political, sociological, and technological facets of modern society. Establishment economists, the radicals argue, devote their energies to the technical treatment of highly specialized and esoteric matters which are remote from the real problems of the day. A primary example of this shortcoming is the failure of orthodox economics to recognize the political character of the modern corporation:

> When the modern corporation acquires power over markets, power in the community, power over the state, power over belief, it is a political instrument, different in form and degree but not in kind from the state itself.

The net result is that fundamental questions surrounding the distribution and use of *power* in capitalistic society are largely ignored by orthodox economists. This neglect allegedly results in a failure to understand the root causes of most of the problems which plague modern capitalism.

THE RADICAL CONCEPTION OF CAPITALISM

Modern radical economists have constructed a model of American capitalism which is essentially an updating and extension of Marxian thought. Let us outline the main features of the radical conception.

CORPORATE OR MONOPOLY CAPITALISM

The radical view holds that capitalism has reached an advanced stage in the United States wherein huge monopolistic corporations dominate the economy. Small corporations have succumbed through merger or bankruptcy or survive as a "competitive fringe" of an otherwise oligopolistic industry and exist largely at the discretion of the industry's dominant firms. Proprietorships and partnerships flourish only on the relatively unimportant fringes of the economy. Even agriculture is increasingly dominated by corporate farming. The dynamics of capitalist expansion have resulted in gigantic multiproduct enterprises, frequently of a multinational character. All major industries are now characterized by a high degree of concentration of economic activity among a small number of giant corporations. Hence, the two hundred or so largest industrial, financial, and commercial corporations shape and define the character of our economy and society.

> The reality is we now have an integrated industrial economy dominated by corporate collectives with resources greater than those of most States and many nations. These control technological innovation, administer prices, generate unending consumer wants while expanding to an international scale. . . . Highly accomplished profit gatherers, they are able to shift risk and social costs to the consumer, the taxpayer and the less powerful.

DOMINATION OF THE STATE

The evolution of corporate giants might not be such an ominous development if appropriate public surveillance through antitrust laws or regulation were to yield socially satisfactory (near-competitive) results. The radical view, however, is that the corporate giants have come to dominate the political state; hence, rather than control corporate power in socially desirable ways, the public sector has become the handmaiden of the corporate giants. Or, at a minimum, a situation of mutual interdependence—a symbiotic relationship—has developed between the corporate giants and government. The success of political parties in realizing and maintaining power depends upon the financial support of wealthy corporations; in turn, government follows policies which are responsive to the needs of the large corporations. The radicals contend that there is substantial evidence of this mutual dependence of big business and government. Consider some of the ways by which government allegedly has catered to the corporate giants.

Failure of Social Control

The regulatory commissions which are designed to control natural monopolies in the public interest are ineffective for the simple reason that they are controlled by the very corporate monopolies they are supposed to regulate! Witness, for example, the assessment of government regulation recently offered by the chairman of the Federal Trade Commission:

> Though most government regulation was enacted under the guise of protecting the consumer from abuse, much of today's regulatory machinery does little more than shelter producers from normal competitive consequences of lassitude and inefficiency. In some cases, the world has changed reducing the original threat of abuse. In other cases, the regulatory machinery has simply become perverted. In still other cases, the machinery was a mistake from the start. In any case, the consumer, for whatever presumed abuse he is being spared, is paying plenty in the form of government-sanctioned price fixing.
>
> The fact of the matter is that most regulated industries have become federal protectorates, living in the cozy world of cost-plus, safely protected from the ugly specters of competition, efficiency and innovation.

Similarly, antitrust legislation is applied half-heartedly, if at all, to large corporations; at best, the flagrant violations of antitrust by giant enterprises result in harmless admonitions or token penalties.

Public Subsidies

Radical economists also argue that the public sector uses tax revenues derived from a basically proportional tax system to subsidize the corporate giants in a variety of ways. For example, the tax-supported educational system provides corporate enterprise with the technical, scientific, and administrative manpower which it needs to operate profitably. Similarly, government finances most of the new scientific and technological developments upon which corporate enterprise depends. Governmentally sponsored construction of streets and highways has amounted to a tremendous subsidy to the automobile industry and all the related industries which feed inputs to it. The radicals emphasize that, in striking contrast, underprivileged minorities are powerless to obtain quality education, decent health care, and, frequently, adequate housing and food from the public treasury.

Provision of Markets

Government has also played a primary role, both directly and indirectly, in providing markets for the output of the corporate giants. High levels of military spending—at times in excess of $80 billion per year—have created major markets for many of the large corporations. Similarly, monetary and fiscal policies have tended to eliminate or mitigate recessions, the major sources of financial losses and insecurity for corporate monopolies. Finally, the government has assisted corporations in establishing and expanding their overseas markets through various "imperialistic" measures. To illustrate: In the radical view, foreign aid is basically a means of propping up governments which are receptive to American political and economic domination, typically at the expense of the economic and cultural welfare of the populations of these Third-World nations.

DYNAMICS OF CAPITALIST EXPANSION

Despite their friendly affiliation with the state, capitalist expansion does involve dynamics that pose a serious problem for the corporate capitalists. This problem, the radicals argue, spawns a variety of evils and irrationalities within the capitalistic system. The problem is this: As Marx saw it, the accumulation of real capital by the corporate giants increases their productive capacity; therefore, their continued prosperity depends upon ever-expanding markets.

> The pressure created by the necessity to find markets for expanding production constitutes one of the most fundamental characteristics of capitalism. . . . competition induces capitalists to expand sales and production of goods in order to realize profits. Greater output leads to expanded profits and capital accumulation. . . . but in order to realize profits on the newly accumulated capital even greater sales of output are required.

According to the radicals, the consequences of corporate capitalism and capitalist expansion are manifold and uniformly bad. The domination of society—including the political state—by huge, powerful, profit-seeking corporations creates a variety of "big" problems and inhibits the resolution of others. The problems allegedly spawned or aggravated by corporate capitalism run the gamut from worker exploitation, income inequality, and alienation to militarism and imperialism.

EXPLOITATION

Orthodox economics explains the distribution of income largely in terms of marginal productivity. That is, under competitive conditions any resource, say some particular kind of labor, will be employed up to the point at which its wage rate equals the value of its marginal product. Putting the matter very simply, this implies that any specific kind of labor is paid in accordance with its contribution to the national output at the margin. The theory also can be applied to land or capital so that all resources are rewarded in accordance with what they have contributed to the national output. Furthermore, it is a situation wherein one class of resources cannot possibly exploit or take advantage of another. Note: Neither radical economists nor most mainstream economists believe the resulting distribution of income is equitable or just. For example, even under pure competition, differences in natural abilities and the random (unequal) distribution of misfortune can result in a highly unequal distribution of wage incomes.

Radical economists stress three basic defects in the marginal productivity theory of income distribution. They point out, first, that this theory rests upon the assumption of competitive markets, while in fact monopoly has replaced competition in both labor and product markets. Corporate capitalists thus have the power to exploit workers in both labor and product markets. Monopsonistic employers—the large corporations—find it profitable to pay workers an amount *less* than the value of their marginal product. Similarly, the markets for most products are dominated by a few large corporations which use their market power to "rig" the market against workers as consumers.

A second point is less obvious. Even if all markets are competitive and labor resources are paid in accordance with the value of their marginal product, the ability of workers to generate output—to be productive—may be constrained arbitrarily by exploitative or discriminatory factors. That is, if the opportunity of individuals to develop their natural abilities through education and training is arbitrarily and unequally distributed *or* if society discriminates among workers on the basis of race or sex, then those workers are exploited in that the "actual" value of their marginal product and hence their wage payments will be arbitrarily held below the "potential" value of their marginal product.

Third, radical economists challenge the legitimacy of income payments to the owners of real capital. Their reasoning goes thus: To be sure, physical capital is productive; when combined with labor, machinery and equipment obviously enhance total output. *But* the productivity of real capital—created by the past efforts of labor—must be distinguished from the capitalist owner's ability to command profit income from the productive contribution of real capital.

> Radicals admit that a machine may increase production, that workers need them, and that they increase the worker's productivity. . . . But it is the physical capital that is productive (jointly with the worker), not the capitalist. The capitalist owns the capital, but he is not himself the machine. The machine does the work (with the worker), the capitalist gets the profit.

Stated somewhat differently, the mere owning of capital is *not* a productive activity and the income derived from capital ownership is therefore unearned and unjustified.

INEQUALITY

The factual characteristics of income inequality in the United States are well known. The top fifth of all families receive about 42 percent of total income and the bottom fifth receive about 5 percent, a relative distribution which has not changed significantly since World War II. Over time the incomes of rich and poor have been growing at about the same rate. The result is that the absolute dollar gap between the median incomes of the top and bottom fifth of all income receivers has widened substantially; this gap which was $10,565 in 1947 grew to $19,071 (in constant 1969 dollars) by 1969. The point stressed by radicals is that capitalistic institutions create most of this inequality and cause it to persist. The following comments on inequality tie in with the discussion of exploitation.

First, by providing unearned incomes to capitalist owners, the institution of private property is a basic source of income inequality. Wealth is even more highly concentrated than is income. One authoritative study, for example, concluded that 1.6 percent of the adult population owns 27.6 percent of the nation's total personal wealth, while at the other extreme one-half the adult population owns only 8.3 percent. Radicals hold that weak and easily avoided inheritance taxes allow the economic inequality arising from private property to be perpetuated through time.

In the second place, inequality is created and fostered by the exercise of economic power by one group against other groups. As the comments on exploitation indicate, in corporate capitalism giant firms can use their market power in both labor and product markets to the detriment of noncapitalists as workers and consumers. As a result, monopoly profits accrue and income inequality is reinforced.

Third, political power has sustained economic inequality. Given the domination of the state by the monopoly capitalists, it is no surprise that big business has benefited from a variety of tax loopholes and subsidies, from protection against foreign competition, and from lucrative government contracts. The progressivity of the federal tax system has been eroded over time and when coupled with regressive state and local tax systems, the overall tax structure turns out at best to be proportional. Therefore, the tax system has failed to function as a "great equalizer" of incomes. Furthermore, the so-called welfare system has been underfinanced and of little benefit to those groups most deeply mired in poverty. Indeed, American capitalism has displayed no propensity to alter significantly the distribution of income which the market provides.

These factors which cause and sustain income inequality, argue the radicals, are cumulative and self-reinforcing. The high concentration of wealth fattens the bank accounts of those at the top of the income distribution. And it is only these high-income receivers who are able to save in substantial amounts. What do they do with their savings? They invest it in more income-providing assets from which they receive still more income, which they reinvest in still more property resources, and so on. Much the same holds true with respect to economic opportunity. Education—particularly higher education—is traditionally viewed as an income equalizer; college is the ladder by which the children of the poor presumably gain the human capital—the skills and training—to climb out of poverty and into higher income brackets. Not so, say the radicals. The rich have not only more real capital, but also greater access to human capital. Those who go to college are increasingly the youth from higher income groups. The poor and middle-income groups find it increasingly difficult to afford college training, not merely because of the rising out-of-pocket costs associated with higher education, but because the opportunity cost—the income foregone by not entering the labor market—is relatively high. Crudely stated, poor families attach greater relative importance to the income which a son or daughter could earn by *not* attending college. Thus, the educational system has become a mechanism for the intergenerational perpetuation of economic inequality. And, finally, the college graduate from the rich family is likely to get a better job than the graduate from the poor family because of his or her "connections."

In the past several years the foregoing explanation of capitalist inequality has been supplemented by the concept of dual or segmented labor markets. In abbreviated form, the radical view is that labor markets are increasingly of two distinct types. The primary labor market is characterized by relatively high and rising wage rates, employment stability, good and well-defined opportunities for advancement, and the presence of advanced production techniques and efficient management. The secondary labor market embraces the opposite characteristics: wages are low and stagnant; employment is casual and unstable; available jobs are "dead ends"; relevant technology is archaic; and management is inefficient and exploitative.

The historical reasons for the evolution of these two distinct labor markets are diverse and largely complementary. One view is that dual labor markets are essentially a reflection of the alleged duality found in product markets. That is, the giant corporations which dominate major industries—John Kenneth Galbraith's "planning system"—give rise to primary labor markets, while the competitive fringes of the economy—Galbraith's "market system"—are conducive to secondary labor markets. Another position is of a more conspiratorial nature: labor market segmentation is the result of an historical effort by capitalists to retard the evolution of a homogeneous and unified labor force which might threaten and overthrow capitalist dominance of the economy.

A third interpretation is that the characteristics of both primary and secondary labor markets are self-reinforcing and over time cause the two markets to diverge. The features of the primary labor market lead to a benign cycle of progress; those of the secondary labor market spawn a vicious cycle of perpetual stagnation and poverty. That is, the high wages of the primary labor markets put firms under constant pressure to innovate and use technologically advanced capital goods. But such progress calls for more skills, and management invests in the training of its work force. Improved real capital and investment in labor's human capital both increase labor's productivity and lead to further wage increases which cause the cycle to repeat itself. Similarly, the fact that employers have invested in the training of their work force gives them a vested interest in greater employment stability; a firm must keep labor turnover low to realize a return on its investment in human capital. Hence, a self-reinforcing cycle of events occurs which allows those workers fortunate enough to be in the primary labor market to be relatively well off and to share in the gains of general economic advance. Substantially the opposite occurs in the secondary labor market. At poverty wage rates there is no reason for a firm to be labor-saving or technologically innovative; technology and capitalization languish. Indeed, secondary labor markets are typically highly competitive and, motivation aside, firms are financially unable to invest in real or human capital. Workers therefore tend to be unskilled and relatively unproductive. And high worker turnover is acceptable to the firm; indeed, it may be helpful in discouraging unionization. In fact, a kind of symbiotic relationship evolves wherein worker behavior mirrors the characteristics of the secondary labor market. Employment is unstable, so workers become "unreliable." Because production is technologically backward, workers have no motivation to upgrade their education and skills. The important point is that, while workers in the primary labor market achieve some economic progress, those in the secondary labor market are confined to a vicious cycle of stagnation and poverty. Furthermore, as the two labor markets diverge it is increasingly difficult for workers to achieve mobility between the markets.

The growing skill gap between the two markets, reinforced by discrimination based on race and sex and the geographic segregation of secondary labor markets in urban ghettos, makes upward occupational mobility less and less likely for secondary labor market workers. In the radical view this scenario is meaningful in explaining the persistence of income inequality through time.

ALIENATION

Radical economists argue that the institutions and operation of capitalism are a major source of alienation. That is, under corporate capitalism, individuals have less and less control over their lives and activities; the masses of people are increasingly remote from the decision-making processes which determine the character and quality of their lives.

> In general people in capitalist society do not participate in making the basic decisions that affect their lives; instead, these decisions are made through capitalist institutions over which most individuals have little or no control. The actual decisions are likely, if not inevitably, independent of the interests of the persons involved, and the consequences of these decisions will be contrary to their needs.

The causes of alienation are manifold. First, corporate dominance has largely eliminated the possibility of achieving independence and autonomy by going into business for oneself. Second, the sheer size of corporations and their bureaucratic structure put most workers—both blue- and white-collar—

in positions where they have little or no decision-making power. Blue-collar workers face repetitious, monotonous jobs which stifle creativity and any sense of craftsmanship. While spared the dehumanization of the production line, most white-collar jobs involve work which is as segmented and authoritarian as work in factories. Keypunch operators and typing-pool clerks bear a certain kinship to automobile assembly-line workers. Even middle-managers feel that they have no influence upon the organizational decisions which they are obligated to implement. In general, the sheer size of corporations is conducive to jobs which are constrained by inflexible work rules and procedures. In the corporations' drive for profits, they ride roughshod over the individual's needs and his or her desire for self-fulfillment. If profit maximizing calls for a mass-production technology, boring and stultifying jobs, and constraining work rules, then so be it.

THE IRRATIONAL SOCIETY: PRODUCTION FOR WASTE

Orthodox economists generally argue that one of the great virtues of capitalism is the capacity of the market (price) system to allocate resources with considerable efficiency. Radical economists, however, cite what they feel is overwhelming evidence that resources are used most irrationally under capitalism. Furthermore, this wasteful production is rooted in the institutions of capitalism and, ironically, in the price system itself.

The radical position is that simple evidence of the eye makes clear that capitalism uses its resources irrationally. The economy produces incredible quantities of automobiles, television sets, cosmetics, and alcoholic beverages, while at the same time many families are without adequate housing, medical care, or diet. The fact that some $25 billion is squandered each year on advertising is ample evidence that the production of many consumer goods fails to fulfill the true needs of consumers. At a time when the nation spends $70 or $80 billion per year on military hardware, the maintenance of overseas military bases, and "space circuses," such areas as urban decay, mass transit, and social services are woefully ignored. Furthermore, environmental pollution has been an inevitable by-product of capitalist production.

Why do these apparent irrationalities—this gross misuse of scarce resources—occur under capitalism? The answer, according to the radical position, lies basically in the dynamics of capitalist expansion abetted by the system's emphasis upon market signals, individual profit incentives, and its highly unequal distribution of income and wealth.

The essence of capitalistic expansion is that the pursuit of profits induces the giant corporations to expand their productive capacities. But this enhanced capacity necessitates ever-expanding markets if this additional productive capacity is to be profitably utilized:

> The pursuit of profits and the desire to accumulate lead to more and more production for the sake of production.

The consequences are quite obvious. In the first place, the great emphasis upon industrial growth and materialism in capitalism exacerbates the problem of environmental deterioration. Resources are devoured and waste products are dumped into the environment at an accelerating rate. The monopoly capitalist's concern is solely with private benefits and costs; spillover or external costs are uniformly ignored. Second, an ever-expanding demand is required if the expanding productive capacity of the monopoly capitalists is to be profitably utilized. Capitalists attempt to assure themselves of an adequate demand for their products both directly and indirectly. Direct efforts center upon want-creating, consumer-manipulating activities. Given the highly unequal distribution of income under capitalism, the poor cannot afford to partake of an expanding output. The rich, in contrast, are already glutted with most goods. Hence, the heavy hand of advertising and the technique of "planned obsolescence" are mustered to induce the consumption of essentially unneeded output. The demand for capitalistic production is supported indirectly by the public sector. Starkly put, government engages in wasteful and unnecessary military spending to absorb the output of the capitalistic system. Furthermore, government engages in imperialistic activities on a global basis to create and sustain overseas markets and to secure cheap sources of inputs. The basic point is that under capitalism, production priorities are determined not on the basis of the real needs of the people, but rather in accordance with what is profitable to the capitalist class. The outcome is the irrational use of resources, on the one hand, and the creation of a "commodity fetish culture" with undue emphasis upon rank materialism, on the other. Capitalism, so to speak, is producing more and enjoying it less.

IMPERIALISM

Given the dynamics of capitalism, it is inevitable that monopoly capitalism will transcend national boundaries to dominate and exploit the less-developed areas of the world. This "internationalization of capitalism" is, of course, imperialism.

Radicals envision orthodox explanations of underdevelopment as canards. In particular, they argue that it is patently incorrect to explain underdevelopment in terms of overpopulation or natural resource deficiencies.

High population density and economic growth do not correlate significantly and, in fact, the Third World is a major source of natural resources. Similarly, the familiar "vicious circle of poverty"—the argument that in poor countries, incomes are so low that there is no economic surplus to invest in capital goods with which to increase productivity and per capita incomes—is rejected by radical economists.

> In the radical view . . . the main obstacles to development are *not* natural or biological factors inherent in the underdeveloped countries, and *not* sexual desires and procreation, laziness, low intelligence or lack of natural

> resources. The obstacles are in the present social relationships of man to man: the fact that all the peasants' and workers' surplus over immediate need is extracted from them by the landlords, moneylenders, tax collectors, and foreign corporations.

Furthermore, orthodox economics' theories of underdevelopment provide

> the perfect defense against the suspicion of these peoples that their problems are due to antiquated social systems, rapacious ruling classes and—above all—foreign domination and exploitation.

More specifically, radicals contend that imperialism is the basic obstacle to Third-World development. In the first place, capitalist aid supports reactionary ruling classes (landlords, moneylenders, and the government itself) who in turn expropriate the economic surplus of workers and peasant farmers. For what purposes? For luxury consumption, for show-case (nonproductive) construction projects, for investment in advanced nations, and for military goods to repress domestic "liberation" movements. Second, contrary to the Marxian view that imperialism entails a flow of investment from mature capitalist countries to the underdeveloped areas of the world, modern radicals hold that the Third World has in fact made very substantial contributions to the capital accumulation of the United States and other imperialistic countries. That is, over time the imperialistic countries derive profit incomes from their overseas investments which far exceed the value of these investments, thereby contributing to a growing income gap between the have and have-not nations. Finally, trade between the advanced capitalist nations and the Third-World countries occurs on terms which are highly favorable to the former; in addition, the pattern of that trade tends to inhibit growth in the underdeveloped countries. That is, the underdeveloped countries are essentially exporters of raw materials and importers of finished goods, a trade pattern which fosters economic dependence rather than industrialization and growth.

It is perhaps in connection with imperialism or neocolonialism that the domination of the state by monopoly capitalists is most apparent.

> On the international front, U.S. trade and especially foreign investments grew enormously throughout the capitalist world during the postwar period and became increasingly important as sources of profits for U.S. corporations. Successive national administrations protected these expanding profitable international activities by the general policy of keeping as much of the world as possible open for trade, investment, and raw materials acquisition by giant corporations. This aim was pursued by economic aid to "friendly" governments (that is, those receptive to U.S. direct investment and trade or those in strategic positions to further the global aims of the U.S.), partly to strengthen them economically, partly to provide supporting overhead capital for U.S. private enterprise, and partly to increase export

markets for U.S. corporations. Postwar administrations have also extended military aid to "friendly" governments, for the purposes of fostering the weapons and aircraft output of U.S. corporations and of protecting these client governments from the militant opposition of some of their own people. The U.S. has, moreover, conducted counterinsurgency operations throughout the underdeveloped capitalist world, and when all has failed, it has used military force in pursuit of its basic aim—the maximization of the area of the world that is open for profitable corporate activities.

SOCIALIST VISIONS

What kind of new society do the radicals envision or advocate? The heterogeneity of radical thought becomes most apparent at this point.

> Every radical in the United States has his own view of exactly what socialism should be like. All agree that there should be no private profit, that it should be decent and human, that it should be based on a genuinely democratic process. But beyond that, there is disagreement on every particular.

A few radical economists are attracted to the Soviet model, but most are repulsed by its repressive features. Others recommend market socialism, that is, public ownership and the preservation of the price system. A few are content to advocate anarchism; others espouse some new form of economic organization based upon producer cooperatives. Some kind of socioeconomic organization along the lines of China's communes appeals to many radicals. Still others advocate "participatory socialism."

> Most fundamentally, socialism means democratic, decentralized and *participatory* control for the individual: it means having a say in the decisions that affect one's life. Such a participatory form of socialism certainly requires equal access for all to material and cultural resources, which in turn requires the abolition of private ownership of capital and the redistribution of wealth. But it also calls for socialist men and women to eliminate alienating, destructive forms of production, consumption, education and social relations. Participatory socialism requires the elimination of bureaucracies and all hierarchical forms and their replacement, not by new state or party bureaucracies, but by a self-governing and self-managing people with directly chosen representatives subject to recall and replacement. Participatory socialism entails a sense of egalitarian cooperation, of solidarity of people with one another, but at the same time it respects individual and group differences, and guarantees individual rights. It affords to all individuals the freedom to exercise human rights and civil liberties that are not mere abstractions but have concrete day-to-day meaning.

THE ORTHODOX REBUTTAL

The radical critique of capitalism is not merely an enumeration of this or that sin but rather a unified and systematic frontal attack on the whole system. That is, the entire spectrum of socioeconomic problems—exploitation, inequality, alienation, pollution, militarism, imperialism, and so forth—has a common cause. That cause, of course, is the ideology of capitalism; the private ownership of property resources and the functioning of the price system have spawned monopolistic corporations and their ultimate domination of the state and society. Let us briefly consider the response of orthodox economists to the economics of dissent.

> Capitalism relies for its operation on selfish motives. Its prized efficiency depends on the greed of the owners and managers of firms, on their desire for increasing profits. Further, the success of capitalism depends on careful calculation, on a nice balancing of costs and benefits. The reliance on selfishness is defended as a realistic evaluation of human motivations. But neither selfishness nor calculation are goals for which men are willing to make deep commitments. It is a fear of many conservative thinkers, the late Joseph Schumpeter being perhaps the best known and most thoroughgoing and Irving Kristol being the latest, that the ideological commitment to capitalism is too weak to resist the idealistic appeal of socialism or similar doctrines, which promise a daily contribution to the common good.
>
> Kenneth J. Arrow, "Capitalism, For Better or Worse," in Leonard Silk, ed., *Capitalism: The Moving Target,* Quadrangle/The New York Times Book Co., © 1974, pp. 107–108. Reprinted by permission.

INVALID PERCEPTIONS

We have seen that radical economics rejects the orthodox perception of modern capitalism as a pluralistic system characterized by a socially-responsive public sector. Similarly, orthodox economists reject the radical model of capitalism as a grossly distorted caricature; the radical view, they argue, is inconsistent with common-sense observation and therefore not realistic and believable.

Consider, for example, the following points. If worker exploitation depends directly upon the degree of monopsony power possessed by a firm, why is it that the large corporations generally pay the highest wages? How can radical economics square the upward drift of labor's share of national income and the virtual constancy of the corporate profit share with their contention that monopoly capitalists are exploiting labor? Where do such phenomena as the social security and welfare systems, Medicare, and minimum-wage legislation fit into the conception of government as handmaiden of the monopoly capitalists? Similarly, how does the long-term decline in protective tariffs square with government as a protector and promoter of capitalist profits? Is the radical notion that militarism is necessary to sustain aggregate demand credible in view of the fact that inflation, not overproduction and unemployment, has been the primary problem of capitalist countries since World War II? How is prosperous, capitalist Japan, with its minimum military establishment, to be reconciled with the radical notion of militarism as an economic prop? As for imperialism:

> it seems to be a mistake to believe that the business society generally considers foreign-policy confrontations advantageous to the business community. This is certainly suggested by the declines in stock exchange prices that usually accompany international political crisis and the rises that usually follow rumors of peace.

Is the radical notion of imperialism consistent with the fact that

> the great bulk of . . . (our) exports and of our foreign investments involve the developed areas of Europe and Canada, rather than areas where we are fighting wars or supporting dictators and supplying arms.

At a more philosophical level, orthodox economists detect an unexplained inconsistency in the radical conceptions of the historical development of capitalistic and socialistic societies. The basic issue involved is the old one of determinism versus free-will. Orthodox economists accuse the radicals of saying that capitalistic systems are burdened by determinism and therefore cannot effectively alter the character or consequences of the system. In contrast a socialistic system presumably would enjoy the advantages of free-will in that conscious policy choices can adjust the system to resolve problems and restructure outcomes to more closely meet the needs of the people. More specifically, radicals assert that the problems and contradictions of modern capitalism are the *inevitable* consequences of the laws of capitalist production. The underlying mode of production necessarily results in a highly unequal distribution of income, wealth, and power; in worker alienation; in wasteful production; and in imperialism and militarism. Orthodox economists are unwilling to accept this deterministic interpretation of capitalism. Furthermore, even if technology, production relationships, and social forces *do* impose significant constraints upon the capacity of any society to change and reform, would not such constraints transcend ideology and institutional arrangements and therefore also apply to socialist systems?

> Is there any logical or philosophical basis for this complete shift of philosophy (from determinism to free will) regarding the driving forces of historical development, simply because there has been a transfer of ownership of the means of production from one group of people to another?

Assar Lindbeck suggests that, in fact, there may be more-or-less inevitable consequences of socialistic systems, for example, that the seizure of power by force (socialist revolution) may be conducive to the selection of an "authoritarian and cruel" leadership, and that viable socialistic systems are necessarily highly centralized and bureaucratic.

NONOBJECTIVITY

Orthodox economists have grave reservations concerning the methodology of radical economics; radicals, they contend, are strongly inclined to substitute rhetoric for reasoning. The claim is that radical economics is doctrinaire, dogmatic, and deficient in scientific objectivity. Put uncharitably, radicals are alleged to employ a "cowboys and Indians mentality" in their interpretation of capitalism. Any and all actions by capitalists or government are envisaged within a conspiratorial framework for they are the "bad guys." The "good guys"—those who ultimately suffer from the actions of monopoly capitalists and government—are, of course, "the people." The radical method, argue orthodox economists, is to interpret current problems and policies to fit their preconceived conception of capitalist society, rather than to modify or retreat from their conception when the problems and policies in fact do *not* fit. Radicals, it is alleged, display a cavalier disregard for facts—both statistical and anecdotal—and for alternative explanations which are at odds with the neoMarxist paradigm. In interpreting problems to dovetail the radical model great reliance is placed upon simple two-variable analysis to explain issues and situations which are decidedly more complex. For example, to the radical economist the pollution problem is simply the consequence of profit-hungry corporations shifting costs to society, an indirect form of exploitation. Alternative explanations, for example, those centering upon population growth and its geographic concentration, are conveniently ignored. Similarly, we have seen that the radical conceives of the relationships between rich and poor countries entirely within an imperialistic framework, stressing the flow of benefits (capital) from the Third World to the advanced capitalistic nations. The concept of comparative advantage and the consequent possibility that international intercourse could be *mutually* advantageous are carefully excluded from their thinking.

At a more sophisticated level, orthodox economists contend that the multidisciplinary character of radical economics precludes it from being an objective, scientific endeavor. For example, when the concept of political power is introduced as a critical explanatory variable, the possibilities of empirical testing diminish dramatically. This may be an important reconsideration in explaining Bach's observation that radical literature

> seems . . . strangely barren of concrete, scientifically testable propositions on the relations between classes, "the power structure," and income distribution—or even of concrete suggestions as to how such a testable theory might be developed.

IMPORTANCE OF IDEOLOGY

Orthodox economists are highly skeptical of the radical assertion that each and every problem present in American capitalism is traceable to the ideological-institutional bases of the system. Other world economies with very different ideological bases seem to suffer from the same kinds of problems. Consider, for example, the question of income inequality. What is there to guarantee that the socialization of any economy will result in greater income equality? Socialization might simply redistribute income from private to public sectors and not from rich to poor. Furthermore, empirical studies show that a substantial portion of income inequality in the United States results from differences in the distribution of *human,* rather than property or real, capital. Hence, the nationalization of real capital would lessen, but not nearly resolve, the inequality issue. We note, incidentally, that wage income is unequally distributed in the Soviet Union, perhaps as much so as in the United States.

Consider imperialism. Can one seriously argue that imperialism correlates highly with the private ownership of resources and monopoly capitalism?

> Preindustrial and precapitalist societies certainly have been characterized by militarism, aggressive foreign policy, and imperialism—and present day noncapitalist societies are hardly free of a military-industrial complex and an aggressive nationalist foreign policy!

Soviet policy toward Estonia, Latvia, and Lithuania, among other countries (and more recently, toward Hungary and Czechoslovakia), makes it abundantly clear that monopoly capitalism does not have a monopoly on imperialism.

What about the critical problem of the distribution of *power?* One might concede the existence of casual evidence suggesting that the distribution of power has become increasingly concentrated in the United States. But by what means is the nationalization of property resources going to alleviate the problem?

> We would expect the problem to be accentuated, for then the bulk of economic power over physical assets would be concentrated in the one hand which also happens to exert political and military power: that is, the hand of centrally placed politicians and administrators.

Similarly, there is ample evidence of environmental pollution, alienation, discrimination, not to mention repression, in other systems with widely varying ideological bases and institutions. The point is this: Radical economics offers no convincing evidence that the ideological-institutional changes which it prescribes will provide the will, the resources, and the social technology to remedy the problems and contradictions it envisions in capitalism. Is the ideological-institutional structure of a society really the crucial determinant of its character and the source of its shortcomings? Or are such problems as inequality, imperialism, alienation, pollution, and so on, indigenous to any complex social system?

VIABLE OPTIONS

It is relatively easy to criticize the existing system; it is much more difficult to set forth a viable system which will effectively overcome the fancied and real deficiencies of modern capitalism. The essence of rational choice calls for the objective comparison of realistic and attainable alternatives. The radical economists are therefore obliged to state clearly and in detail the nature of the alternative system which they advocate. This they have not done.

> What the New Left lacks . . . is a practical, comprehensive solution. . . . The radicals know what must come down, but not what should be left standing or what should go up. . . . revolutionaries call for destruction first and experimentation afterward. One may be reluctant to sign up for such an uncertain future.

Orthodox economists argue that the radical position is bankrupt insofar as viable alternatives are concerned. Specifically, most radicals reject *both* the market system *and* the bureaucracy of government as means of providing a satisfactory solution to the economic problem. Since the price system and the public bureaucracy are the only two basic alternatives for economic decision making, the rejection of both leaves an operational vacuum. The orthodox economist says, in effect, "reread the earlier statement on the character of participatory socialism and attempt to discern how that system would actually operate." How would the system respond to the everyday questions which are at the core of *any* economy's functioning? How, specifically, would it decide what to produce? How would production be organized? What productive techniques would be selected? How would output be distributed? How would the "What, How, and For Whom" decisions be coordinated? Would resources be fully employed? How would resources be reallocated over time from uses of declining importance to those of increasing importance? And what incentives would exist for citizens to undertake all the required tasks and decisions? To paraphrase Assar Lindbeck, radical conceptions of idyllic communal societies (wherein the distinction between director and worker is obliterated and "self-fulfillment" is given priority over materialistic objectives) are superficially attractive, but they fail to respond to the hard question: "How do you plan to run the steel industry?"

Looked at more narrowly, the basic point of contention may be reformulated in terms of an inequality-incentives tradeoff. Radical economists may have a telling point when they cite income inequality as the Achilles Heel of modern capitalism. But it must also be recognized that their proposed solution may merely substitute the equally perplexing problem of achieving adequate economic incentives. The hard fact may be that private property and substantial income inequality are prerequisite to strong economic incentives. Hence, there may exist a critical tradeoff: other things being equal, the choice may be between a larger output distributed unequally under capitalism *or* a smaller output allocated more equally under some form of socialism. One may personally favor less income inequality in the United States and still argue that it is not necessarily true that the latter choice is inherently preferable to the former.

Radical response: We are not irresponsible, scatterbrained critics. Our movement is relatively new and our energies have been absorbed in uncovering and articulating the shortcomings of the existing system and in developing a critique of orthodox economic analysis. Radicals are just now getting seriously into the formidable task of framing meaningful, workable alternatives which will avoid the evils of both the market system and the bureaucracy. It is not a simple matter to create a viable system based upon equality and egalitarianism, cooperation, and self-realization as opposed to inequality, competition, and alienation. But give us time!

The evidence is quite clear that radical economics has established itself as an alternative, competing explanation of socioeconomic phenomena. And whether one greets the economics of dissent with delight or dismay, there is no doubt that a nodding acquaintance with the radical view contributes a new, skeptical dimension to one's interpretation of the economic, political, and social milieu. Furthermore, whether one finds their answers relevant or reasonable, the radical economists perform a useful service in underscoring some of the perennial problems associated with advanced capitalism. Finally, radical economics is useful in reminding us that economics, narrowly defined, provides only a limited perspective on the real world and that this perspective is not always the most relevant for understanding.

QUESTIONS

1. What, according to the author, are the most important differences between radical economics and traditional theories? How great a gap exists between the two?
2. Do radical economic theories present an adequate platform from which to advocate major changes? Do their ideas point to practical options or impractical ones?
3. Putting yourself in the position of a radical economist, respond to the defense of present economic arrangements set forth by Jacoby in this chapter.
4. Choose a significant objection of the radicals to the present system. Draw up a scenario for change in which you consider the practical aspects of public policy necessary to deal with the problem and the sources of resistance to change.

5. In the box presented in this chapter, Kenneth J. Arrow, a Nobel laureate for his economic contributions, comments on the selfish motives that capitalism depends upon to advance the public interest. How do you view his comments? Is there a paradox here that is responsible for much criticism of business? Do abuses of self-interest cause a greater adverse public criticism of business than warranted?

ON THE LEGITIMACY OF BUSINESS

DANIEL YANKELOVICH

Daniel Yankelovich, head of a leading polling company, points out in the following statement that people in this society overwhelmingly accept the basic attributes of the free enterprise system, and that in appraising popular attitudes toward business, one should keep in mind three types of legitimacy. This excerpt from "A Conversation on the Future of the Mixed Economy," also includes pertinent questions by Albert T. Sommers, Senior Vice President and Chief Economist of The Conference Board.

. . .

MR. DANIEL YANKELOVICH: The poll data over the past four or five years, showing a precipitous decline in respect for all institutions across the board, have disturbed everyone. But there are some ambiguities in those data that have to be clarified. Otherwise, I think one could be rather seriously misled.

In polls and surveys we usually use the concept of "confidence" in institutions. But confidence means many different things. It's more illuminating to use the more theoretical but precise concept of "institutional legitimacy." The idea here is that a society achieves a certain amount of political stability from the balance achieved between power and authority. The authority derives from the free acceptance by the people of institutions as meeting their purposes and values.

In a democracy, the balance should tip in favor of authority and away from naked power. The concept of institutional legitimacy has a number of different meanings historically. We have found in our research that three very different meanings attach to the concept of institutional legitimacy and the way people respond to institutions. It's rather important to keep them separate. The three are: (1) the *ideological legitimacy* of institutions; (2) their *functional performance capability,* that is, how well they do their job; and (3) the *moral aspect of legitimacy*.

Today, the relationship of the American public to its institutions is rather different from what it used to be on each of the three facets of legitimacy. Let me comment briefly on each one and offer some supporting data.

First, on the ideological side. Among the public, there is very strong, unified support for the concept of the welfare state and the idea of private property and the free enterprise system. At the level of abstract ideas, the notions of a market economy and free enterprise system are very widely supported. I'll give you some numbers in a minute. There is the very widely held view that the government should not run things, but should serve in the role of regulator-referee —protector of the public interest. The dispersion of the benefits of the system should be used to meet certain group rights, entitlements and the like. In sum, the welfare state. Here now are some statistics:

From Albert T. Sommers, ed., *The Free Society and Planning: A Conversation on the Future of The Mixed Economy,* New York: The Conference Board, 1975, pp. 3–6. Reprinted by permission.

A rather overwhelming 91 percent of the public feels that the government should not own or run big business as business is run in socialist European countries. There is, however, a desire for greater regulation of business. Seventy-four percent now want increased regulation.

Over seven out of ten people hold the traditional view that "private property is sacred." And more than three-quarters of Americans believe that "the Federal Government should not run the life of the country but should regulate major companies, industries and institutions, to be sure they don't take advantage of the public." That is the referee-regulator function I mentioned earlier.

About six out of ten people say that they're ready to sacrifice, if need be, to preserve the free enterprise system. This is one of the places where there is a split between people who consider themselves conservative or liberal. Conservatives hold this view to a much greater extent than moderates and liberals.

A majority of the people feel that the Federal Government has an obligation to see to it that the poor are taken care of, that no one goes hungry.

We see, therefore, that there is no withdrawal, in any fundamental ideological sense, from the system we've been living with and evolving toward. In fact, there is a very strong endorsement of the "rules of the game." When people say they lack confidence in our institutions, they clearly do not mean that they want fundamental ideological change.

On *functional* legitimacy, things are a little more complicated. Most institutions are assumed to be working fairly well. There are a lot of complaints about local and state government, but they're not regarded as being any worse than they were at any earlier period. Confidence has declined in the courts, in the press, in the professions, in the unions—but not usually on the grounds of their inability to do the job. There's a split here, between the general public and elite or leadership groups, who do feel that there has been a decline in the capability of the courts and other institutions to function properly.

The public's complaint about business is not that it's unable to do its job of making and delivering goods. The public feels that, if anything, big business is all too effective.

As far as the Federal Government is concerned, there has been a real change and a real decline in confidence. A majority today believes that the Federal Government is less effective than it was in the past: 61 percent of the public faults the government for its inability to solve the nation's problems. Here we have a very interesting contrast, because only about half that number among the political leadership hold this view. Here is a case where the people who are accused of not doing the job don't agree with the public's assessment.

There is a tremendous ambivalence in the country toward the idea of the "imperial presidency." On the one hand, there is the response to Watergate and the abuses of the past few years, leading to support for the idea that the presidency should be limited and weakened; but, on the other hand, people reach out automatically toward the presidency whenever there is any kind of trouble. If I had to make a judgment about which is the stronger of those two impulses, I would say it was the latter—reaching out toward a stronger presidency to meet more fundamental needs.

The third aspect of legitimacy, *moral legitimacy,* is where the decline is more clear-cut, and most sharp. Irving Kristol makes the distinction between profiteering and profit making. Profit making is when everyone benefits; but profiteering is where you benefit at my expense.

It was profiteering, of course, that was behind the populism of the 1890's. And that same cry about profiteering was raised against what was regarded as the oil companies' exploitation of the oil crisis. First, there was disbelief that the crisis *was* real—a feeling that the oil companies were making it up. Second, as it became clear that there was a real problem, the feeling grew that the oil companies and other big businesses were using the situation to line their own pockets and to take advantage of the problem in order to reap a profit rather than serve the public. This is *the* fundamental issue about confidence.

It also has to do with the government. The Nixon presidency was seen as power aggrandizement, as an institution serving its own interests—not in a financial sense but in the sense of power. Mr. Agnew was a symbol of old-fashioned corruption, serving himself, lining his own pockets at the expense of the country.

We now see a general carry-over of mistrust to all the other institutions in the society, with government and big business leading the way. The past tendency of the American public to blame itself for its own problems, by and large, has given way to blaming the major institutions of society. The institutions it blames most are big business and the Federal Government. It depends on the nature of the problem as to which of these two "villains" it selects. The percentage of people expressing loss of faith in government, according to the University of Michigan statistics, went from 12 percent in 1958 to 20 percent in 1964, and to 27 percent in 1968. Then it really picked up steam; from 1968 to 1973, which is the last figure we have, it rose to 51 percent. It must be beyond that now.

MR. ALBERT T. SOMMERS: What you're saying is that the reason for that rise is not disagreement with the rules of the game, but a sense that the rules are being violated. Is that the distinction?

MR. YANKELOVICH: Yes it is. The rules of the game are what I call *ideological legitimacy,* and that has not eroded. Now, playing within these rules of the game, you can play well or poorly. Most of the players are not regarded as playing any more poorly than in the past, except the Federal Government. The third aspect is this matter of *moral legitimacy;* you may be effective, you may make the trains run on time but use the benefits for your own selfish purposes. This viewpoint lies behind the startling decline in the percentage of people who have confidence in business, which went from 70 percent in the late 1960's to 19 percent in 1974. Business is seen as having too much power. There is a general feeling throughout the society that *all* the institutions have too much power, except the public—which doesn't have enough power. There has been a very sharp increase in the level of mistrust of those in power.

MR. SOMMERS: This moral disappointment can lead back into the ideological structure, in the sense that there is latent criticism here of a structure that permits this kind of misbehavior.

MR. YANKELOVICH: There are signs of that. A lot of things are happening now that may cause the ideological support to begin to erode. But, as of the moment, the clearest picture is of people still accepting the rules of the game within the generalized welfare-state concept, but holding the view of moral decline—of institutions serving their own self-interests by profiteering. Greed, I think, is the key word in people's minds.

. . .

QUESTIONS

1. What can business executives do to improve their public image in light of the concepts of legitimacy set forth by Yankelovich? Are there concrete actions that might be taken to restore eroded foundations of public trust?
2. What implications for reform do the legitimacy shortcomings of big business hold? How can these shortcomings be remedied? What kinds of reforms would the general public be most receptive to?
3. Do schools of business or management have any responsibility to help business improve its public image? If your response is affirmative, do you think this should take the form of helping to explain the business role in society? Should it take only the form of pointing out how business should reform in order to meet public approval? Should schools be doing anything else?

THE PARABLE OF THE DAM

GEORGE W. BALL

George W. Ball in the following parable cautions those who would "tear down the establishment" to pause and reconsider.

Since the beginning of time, so my story went, the villages in a mountain canyon had been periodically ravaged by floods. Finally, the leaders convened a great meeting and decided to invest their efforts and resources in building a large, strong dam. Thereafter, for a quarter of a century, the dam sheltered the villages from disaster, prosperity prevailed, and life was tranquil—until, at last, a new generation began to grow up, free from the apprehensions of the past and filled with exciting ideas about a world of song and beauty.

Inevitably the new leaders turned their attention to the dam. It was, they announced, huge and ugly and an affront to the environment. Besides it blocked out the sunset and had to be repaired every year. One leader wrote a folk song proclaiming it a symbol of imperialist megalomania, and people spoke excitedly of little else, until someone brought forth an argument that seemed quite unanswerable. After all, it was pointed out, no one ever talked about flood damage except the old fogies over 30 who were not to be trusted anyway. Who among the new leaders could recall any floods in his lifetime? It was perfectly clear that floods were completely outmoded, a matter of the past—perhaps just a fiction manufactured to frighten the people. Since there had not been one for 25 years, clearly there would not be another.

So, after a season of demonstrations, more speeches, a pageant and several rock festivals, they blew up the dam and used the fragments for a people's playground. And let me tell you straight, man, when the waters came down it was really the Age of Aquarius!

3

PERSPECTIVES ON BUSINESS POWER

IS THERE A RULING CLASS IN AMERICA?

G. WILLIAM DOMHOFF

G. William Domhoff is assistant professor of psychology and fellow of Cowell College, University of California at Santa Cruz. In the following excerpt he lays out the proposition that there is a ruling class in America and describes how he will go about proving it. The question of whether or not he is correct arises, of course.

. . .

Our starting point . . . must be the demonstration of an observable, differentiated, interacting social group with more or less definite boundaries. In other words, does an identifiable social upper class exist in the United States? This question is closely related to a second empirical question which interests us in the light of Mills's objection that "class" is an economic term: Does this social upper class overlap in membership with any particular economic "class"? The answer to both of these questions . . . is "Yes," thus making Mills's point primarily a semantic one. It will be shown that there is a national upper class made up of rich businessmen and their families, an "American business aristocracy," as Baltzell calls it. Although this national upper class has its ethnic, religious, and new-rich–old-rich antagonisms, it is nonetheless closely knit by such institutions as stock ownership, trust funds, intermarriages, private schools, exclusive city clubs, exclusive summer resorts, debutante parties, fox hunts, charity drives, and, last but not least, corporation boards. This information, when fully elaborated, can be considered a direct answer to sociologist William Kornhauser, who claims that one of the main weaknesses of Mills's work was that he did not sufficiently demonstrate the interaction of the various cliques making up his "power elite." If such a weakness existed, it was in Mills's presentation and not in a lack of such interaction.

In addition to demonstrating the reality of a national upper class, we will emphasize that this social group, whether its members are aware of it or not, has well-established ways of "training" and "preparing" new members. This point must be stressed because it is certainly the case that people are moving into (not to mention out of) this group all the time. "Social mobility" is a distinct reality, and this study will document its occurrence at the highest levels of society as well as at the middle levels where it is usually studied. Social mobility can be looked at from many points of view and in terms of many different questions, but the important thing to keep in mind in understanding this phenomenon in a sociological study of the upper class is the process of "co-optation." For our purposes, we will mean by co-optation the processes whereby individuals are assimilated and committed to the institutions and values of the dominant socioeconomic group. In studying co-optation we want to know which institutions select and prepare those who are assimilated, as well as the ideas and values that make a person acceptable. To anticipate somewhat, the co-optation of bright young men into the American upper class occurs through education at private schools, elite universities, and elite law schools; through success as a corporation executive; through membership in exclusive gentlemen's clubs; and through participation in exclusive charities.

Is this social upper class, with its several institutional focal points and its several means of assimilating new members, also a "governing class"? It is with this question that new ground must be broken, for systematic data are lacking. To begin with, "governing class" must be defined. Our definition is as follows:

> A "governing class" is a social upper class which owns a disproportionate amount of a country's wealth, receives a disproportionate amount of a country's yearly income, and contributes a disproportionate number of its members to the controlling institutions and key decision-making groups of the country.

Disproportionate wealth and income are important in this definition because they imply that the upper class has interests that are at least somewhat different from those of other socioeconomic groups. As we will see, members of the upper class have different sources of income as well as more income than persons of other income levels. By the same token, a disproportionate number of leaders is important because it implies control of these institutions and decision-making groups. . . . these criteria, while not infallible, are at least as good as those used in other approaches to this difficult question. And if, as Dahl says of the decision-making methodology, a group is more or less a ruling elite depending upon how many decisions it controls, we can say that a social upper class is more or less a governing class depending upon the percentage of wealth it possesses, the income it receives, and the leaders it contributes. Finally, we would stress that our minimum definition is valuable because it can be related to empirical data.

Although our definition may not be acceptable to everyone, it does meet Dahl's stricture that the hypothesis contained in such a definition must be capable of disproof as well as support. In fact, the methods we will use in testing the hypothesis are similar to those used by Dahl in his study of New Haven, Connecticut. Since Dahl and one of his former students, Nelson Polsby, have been the most articulate critics of previous studies of the American power structure, we have followed their criticisms and comments with some care. We do not wish to have it pointed out to us, as Dahl did to Mills and Polsby did to Baltzell, that we did not test our hypothesis. Dahl relied primarily on three methods to determine who governed in New Haven. He described them as follows:

1. To study changes in the socioeconomic characteristics of incumbents in city offices in order to determine whether any rather large historical changes may have occurred in the sources of leadership.
2. To isolate a particular socioeconomic category and then determine the nature and extent of participation in local affairs by persons in this category.
3. To examine a set of "decisions" in different "issue-areas" in order to determine what kinds of persons were the most influential according to one operational measure of relative influence, and to determine patterns of influence.

Dahl's first two methods are aspects of what we will call the "sociology-of-leadership" methodology. The essence of this methodology is the study of the sociological composition of leadership groups in order to determine whether or not the leaders come from any given socioeconomic class, ethnic group, or religious group. Dahl used this method in the first six chapters of *Who Governs?* With it he showed quite conclusively that members of the middle class had taken over the decision-making roles he studied in New Haven. Dahl's third method focuses on the decision-making process. With it he showed that different members of the middle class in New Haven were influential in different issue-areas. There was no one "ruling elite" that made decisions on a wide variety of issues.

Unfortunately, the decision-making method is difficult to apply because the "operational measure" of influence is the frequency with which a person "successfully initiates an important policy over the opposition of others, or vetoes policies initiated by others, or initiates a policy where no opposition appears." Inferences about who initiates and who vetoes must be made after "reconstructing" the decision "by means of interviews with participants, the presence of an observer, records, documents, and newspapers." However, we believe with Baltzell and Raymond Bauer, an expert in the study of policy formation, that even when the information with which to reconstruct a specific decision seems to be available, it is a very risky and tricky business. Many aspects of the situation may remain secret, the participants themselves may not be able to correctly assess the roles of the various members, the "real" interests of the participants are complex and often impossible for even them to determine, and the larger context within which the issue arises may be as important in understanding the eventual decision as the decision-making process itself. Thus, we have relied on Dahl's third method somewhat less than on his first two. At the same time we have tried to remain faithful to Dahl's concern with specific issue-areas by studying the sociological backgrounds of members of decision-making groups and by studying institutions and associations which are known to have a great amount of influence in specific issue-areas. Polsby seems to be recommending our approach when he says:

> If there exist high degrees of overlap among issue-areas in decision-making personnel, or of institutionalization in the bases of power in specified issue-

> areas, or of regularity in the procedures of decision making, then the empirical conclusion is justified that some sort of "power structure" exists.

However, since studying decision-making groups and institutional personnel is not the same thing as studying the decision-making process itself, it is very important in using this method to state explicitly the scope and limits of the powers of the given institution, association, or decision-making group. (One of the main criticisms of Mills's thesis was that he did not spell out the powers of his power elite.) The kind and limits of the powers of the groups and institutions which concern us will be noted as each one is studied. . . .

. . . the less than 1 per cent of the population comprising the American upper class, if it is a governing class, does not rule alone. Thus, it will be necessary to demonstrate that most of the non-upper-class leaders are selected and trained by members of the upper class (co-opted), or, to say the same thing differently, that the advancement of these non-upper-class leaders is dependent upon their attaining goals that are shared by members of the upper class. This leads to a discussion of our concept of the "power elite," a term borrowed from Mills but defined in a slightly different manner. We agree with Mills in defining the power elite as those who have a superior amount of power due to the institutional hierarchies they command, but we deviate from Mills by restricting the term to persons who are in command positions in institutional hierarchies controlled by members of the American upper class, or, in the case of members of the federal government, to persons who come to the government from the upper class or from high positions in institutions controlled by members of the upper class. By this definition, any particular member of the power elite may or may not be a member of the upper class. It not only allows for co-optation and for control through hired employees, but it agrees that some members of the upper class—what Baltzell calls the functionless genteel—may not be members of the power elite. This definition of the power elite is very similar to Baltzell's concept of an "establishment":

> The upper class, in other words, will be a ruling class or, as I should prefer to say, its leaders will form an *establishment*. . . . In a free society, while an establishment will always be dominated by upper-class members, it also must be constantly rejuvenated by new members of the elite who are in the process of acquiring upper-class status.

While our definition of the power elite is somewhat different from that given by Mills, the final result of our research will show that our power elite is very similar to his. This difference lies in the fact that (1) we have not assumed *a priori* that any group is part of the power elite as Mills did in so designating the corporate leaders, military leaders, and political leaders; and (2) we have grounded the power elite in the upper class. Putting it another way, we will attempt to show that Mills's power elite has its roots in Baltzell's

"American business aristocracy" and serves its interests. In the case of each institution hypothesized to be a basis of the power elite, control by members of the upper class must be demonstrated empirically. Thus, when we arrive at the crucial institution in this study—the federal government—we will be in a position to show just which parts of it can be considered aspects of a power elite that is the operating arm of the American upper (governing) class. We will not assume, as Mills did, that the Executive branch of the federal government is part of a power elite, but will instead show that its leaders are either members of the upper class or former employees of institutions controlled by members of the upper class. Perhaps several examples from recent Democratic administrations will make this final point clear. Franklin D. Roosevelt, John F. Kennedy, Adlai Stevenson, Dean Acheson, Averell Harriman, Douglas Dillon, McGeorge Bundy, and Nicholas Katzenbach were hereditary members of the upper class, while Robert McNamara was president of the Ford Motor Company, Dean Rusk was president of the Rockefeller Foundation, and John Gardner was president of the Carnegie Corporation. We consider all of these men to be members of the power elite, for they are either old-line members of the American business aristocracy or former high-level employees of institutions controlled by members of that social group. We are quite aware of the humble origins of McNamara and Rusk, whose children may or may not become members of the upper class depending upon the stock accumulations of their fathers, the schools they attend, and the persons they marry. However, we think that the nature of McNamara's and Rusk's previous employment, and the consequent status and income this afforded them, is what is important in understanding their appointment to government.

We believe that the relationship between the concepts of "governing class" and "power elite" is quite straightforward, but it is also true that there can be confusion unless the two are compared and contrasted. To repeat, "governing class" refers to a social upper class which owns a disproportionate amount of the country's wealth, receives a disproportionate amount of the country's yearly income, and contributes a disproportionate number of its members to positions of leadership. However, some of the members of this social group may not be involved in anything more relevant than raising horses, riding to the hounds, or hobnobbing with the international "jet set." The "power elite," on the other hand, encompasses all those who are in command positions in institutions controlled by members of the upper (governing) class. Any given member of the power elite may or may not be a member of the upper class. The important thing is whether or not the institution he serves is controlled by members of the upper class. Thus, if we can show that members of the upper class control the corporations through stock ownership and corporate directorships, the military through the Department of Defense, and the corporate law profession through large corporate law firms and major law schools, we will have gone a long way toward demonstrating that the aims of the American power elite, as defined by either Mills or [us], are necessarily those of members of the upper class.

Perhaps the relationship between "governing class" and "power elite" can be made even clearer by outlining the steps that we will follow in attempting to answer the question: Is the American upper class a governing class?

First, we will show the existence of a national upper class that meets generally accepted definitions of social class.

Second, we will show that this upper class owns a disproportionate amount of the country's wealth and receives a disproportionate amount of its yearly income, and that members of the American upper class control the major banks and corporations, which in turn are known to dominate the American economy.

Third, we will show that members of the American upper class and their high-level corporation executives control the foundations, the elite universities, the largest of the mass media, and such important opinion-molding associations as the Council on Foreign Relations, the Foreign Policy Association, the Committee for Economic Development, the Business Advisory Council, and the National Advertising Council.

Fourth, we will show that the power elite (members of the American upper class and their high-level employees in the above institutions) control the Executive branch of the federal government.

Fifth, we will show that the power elite controls regulatory agencies, the federal judiciary, the military, the CIA, and the FBI through its control of the Executive branch of the federal government. It will be shown also that this control by the Executive branch is supplemented by other lines of control in the case of each of these branches or agencies of the government.

After it has been shown that the power elite does not control but merely influences (1) the Legislative branch of the federal government, (2) most state governments, and (3) most city governments, it will be argued that its control of corporations, foundations, elite universities, the Presidency, the federal judiciary, the military, and the CIA qualifies the American upper class as a "governing class," especially in the light of the wealth owned and the income received by members of that exclusive social group.

It should be added that by "control," we mean to imply dominance, the exercise of "power" (ability to act) from a position of "authority" (the right to exercise power by virtue of some office or legal mandate). Synonyms for control would be rule, govern, guide, and direct. "Influence," for us, is a weaker term, implying that a person can sometimes sway, persuade, or otherwise have an effect upon those who control from a position of authority. Since these vague terms can be the subject of much debate, let us once again make clear that we will try to show that members of the upper class dominate major corporations, foundations, universities, and the Executive branch of the federal government, while they merely have influence in Congress, most state governments, and most local governments. This does not mean that they are never influenced in areas where they have control, nor does it mean that they never get their way where they merely exert influence. However, the interesting thing about "control" and "influence" in a country where the concept of a governing class calls forth notions of sinister men lurking behind the throne, is that members of the American governing class in fact serve their interests from positions of authority. Authority-based control, rather than covert influence, is their dominant mode.

A NEW CLASS OF BUSINESS CRITICS

In earlier times, criticism was largely confined to the radical left and the spokesmen for labor. Neither had much of a voice or influence. But today there is a new class hostile to business in general, and especially to large corporations. As a group, you find them mainly in the very large and growing public sector and in the media. This new class consists of well educated and intelligent professionals who work in all levels of government: public officials, civil servants, bureaucrats; doctors, lawyers, and engineers in some form of public service; teachers and school administrators; psychologists, sociologists, and environmentalists; members of the media; foundation managers (who are not in the public sector, but think that way) and more. No one knows how large this group is, but it could amount to as much as 15 percent of our population. These people are smart and articulate. They share a disinterest in personal wealth, a dislike for the free market economy, and a conviction that society may best be improved through greater governmental participation in the country's economic life. As a result of technological, economic, and social developments, this group has become terribly influential. They *are* the media. They *are* the educational system. Their dislike for the free market economy originates in their inability to exercise much influence over it so as to produce change. In its place they would prefer a system in which there is a very large political component. This is because the new class has a great deal of influence in politics. Thus, through politics, they can exercise a direct and immediate influence on the shape of our society and the direction of national affairs.

Irving Kristol in *Exxon USA,* quarterly publication of Exxon Company, U.S.A., Third Quarter 1975, p. 9. Reprinted by permission.

QUESTIONS

1. Do you agree with Domhoff's claim that the American social upper class is also the "governing class in the country"?
2. If the assertion of the author is indeed true, that is, that less than 1 percent of

the American population comprises the upper class and the governing class, how do you suppose we can claim that this is a "political democracy"?

3. Read Domhoff's book, and report on whether or not, in your opinion, he makes his case.
4. Where does Kristol's new class of business critics fit in "a governance class in the country?" (See box.) Assess the actual and potential power of this new class.

SOCIAL RESPONSES TO CORPORATE POWER: A CONDITION WITHOUT A REMEDY?

SUMNER MARCUS

Sumner Marcus, professor of business, government, and society, University of Washington, focuses on five major means that have been tried or proposed in the United States for dealing with what is considered excessive or undesirable corporate power. He concludes that, as things now stand, these responses do not cope effectively with the problem of corporate power. Excessive corporate power, he says, is a condition without a remedy.

This paper seeks to identify, clarify, and evaluate actual and potential responses of society to excessive corporate power. It is not concerned with the many debates regarding what constitutes excessive corporate power or about whether corporate power is or is not desirable under different sets of circumstances. The focus of the paper rather is on the efficacy of various means which have been tried or proposed in the United States for dealing with corporate power considered excessive or undesirable.

The responses to excessive corporate power may be classified into five fundamental categories. These are: (1) reliance on competitive processes to prevent the accumulation and persistence of corporate power; (2) the shoring up through special legal mechanisms of competitive processes when these processes have not effectively dissipated corporate power; (3) governmental participation in basic corporate decisions, such as entry into business, the setting of prices and wages, and product design; (4) governmental action helping other societal institutions and less powerful businesses in their efforts to cope with excessive corporate power; and (5) exhortations by public and private institutions to corporations to employ their power wisely in the "public interest," however that may be defined.

The current "energy crisis" is only the latest development to create apprehension concerning the acquisition by large corporations of substantial economic and political power. There gradually seeped into the public consciousness during the past year a more precise awareness of the many ways that decisions by powerful corporations—in this case mainly in the oil industry—could affect substantially the economic fabric of not only the United States but the whole of the non-communist world, developed and developing countries alike. Those previously concerned about the growth of corporate power—the consumerists, the populists, the Naderites, the environmentalists—could now find among the general public many more supporters for their various

From A Presentation to the Division of Social Issues in Management, Academy of Management, 1974 Annual Meeting, Seattle, Washington, August 18–21.

prescriptions for countering corporate power than they could before the gasoline tank became the national preoccupation.

At the same time, the very existence of the crisis and the apparent ability of the oil industry to affect substantially its intensity could not help but raise again questions concerning the efficacy of past responses to corporate power. After all, the oil industry had not been among the least targets of the almost century old antitrust laws. On the contrary, one of the first major prosecutions under the Sherman Act had resulted in the well-publicized break up of the Standard Oil monopoly at the turn of the century. And oil companies have not been strangers to antitrust proceedings in the intervening years. Furthermore, a frequent subject of specific governmental regulation at both the federal and state levels has been the oil industry. When the "environmental crisis," the "crisis" which preceded the "energy crisis," became sufficiently significant to justify additional participation by government in corporate decision making, the petroleum industry was again not among the least of the industries affected. In addition to the imposition of legal sanctions on the industry, governmental and non-governmental institutions alike exhorted the oil companies on many occasions to act responsibly; and the oil companies spent and continue to spend substantial amounts on advertising and public relations to demonstrate how socially responsible they have been and are. Yet despite all the past societal responses to corporate power in the oil industry, there remains the impression that oil companies, both individually and in the aggregate, possess enormous power in that they are able to influence the availability and distribution of oil not only in the United States but throughout the world.

Is this impression valid? The structure of the industry suggests strongly that it is. The major oil companies are among the largest in the United States. Seven of them are among the top 20 of *Fortune*'s list of the 500 largest industrial corporations. The oil industry in the United States is relatively concentrated at all levels—crude oil production, refining, and marketing; and there is a substantial coincidence among the top four, eight, and 20 companies in all three categories. Admittedly, there is some disagreement among economists whether and to what extent various levels and types of concentration measure the economic power of firms and the effectiveness of competition in an industry. But the conclusion that the major oil companies possess substantial economic power may be deduced also from their cooperative activities in relation to the exploitation of new oil fields, the transportation of crude oil, exchanges of gasoline, and the like. These circumstances make the oil industry a particularly suitable focus for a study of social responses to corporate power.

In any event, since the emergence of the energy crisis, Congress, the various executive agencies, the public interest groups, and the public at large have increasingly turned their attention to the phenomenon of corporate power generally, and in the oil industry in particular, . . . to consider ways to reduce this power and to make it better serve the "public interest." What is the likelihood that these efforts will be more successful now than in the past?

INACTION AS A RESPONSE TO CORPORATE POWER: RELIANCE ON COMPETITION

Before proceeding further with our analysis, let us consider briefly the likelihood that, if nothing positive were done to change existing power relationships, corporate power would vanish, dissipated by the forces of competition. There are few students of the economy who believe this could happen. Even those who believe strongly that the competitive process will in the long run diminish the power of corporations relative to that of other institutions assert the need for more positive societal responses to achieve this desired state, such as the enlarging of markets by government, the lowering of barriers to entry, and changes in the composition of corporate boards of directors. It is these and the other possible societal responses to corporate power which provide the main focus of this study.

THE ANTITRUST RESPONSE TO CORPORATE POWER

A well-known student of business-society relationships wrote recently that "There is nothing wrong with the energy industry that a stiff dose of free enterprise and strict enforcement of antitrust policies can't remedy." This conclusion seems less inevitable when the history of antitrust is examined and the antitrust process is analyzed. As indicated previously, the oil industry is dominated by a relatively few powerful firms which collaborate rather extensively in significant areas despite the industry's seemingly perpetual exposure to the attentions of antitrust officials over the years. Is this because antitrust enforcement was not "strict" in the past? Has antitrust been "strict" in relation to industries other than the oil industry?

The extensive literature dealing with antitrust and its shortcomings is replete with assorted explanations of why the theoretically ideal process of antitrust has not dealt successfully with corporate power in a wide spectrum of industries.

One explanation is that antitrust has not been strictly enforced. But here we are confronted immediately with a profusion of further "explanations." Not enough money has been appropriated by the Congress for enforcement. Too many top antitrust officials have lacked the personalities which would have made antitrust enforcement congenial to them. They have not been sufficiently sold on the efficacy of antitrust, or they lacked the requisite administrative abilities to create an effective enforcement agency, or they have been too timid to resist effectively the political pressures constantly swirling about the antitrust enforcement agencies, or they have just not understood antitrust and its potentialities, or they have been corrupt. The "explanations" for the lack of strict enforcement over a period of 80 years or more are so numerous and varied that a visitor from Mars would be forced to conclude that antitrust is inherently incapable of being enforced "strictly."

Although not entirely unrelated to the matter of "strict enforcement," there are a number of other explanations that are advanced for the shortcomings of antitrust. The Antitrust Division of the Department of Justice and the Federal Trade Commission, the principal enforcement agencies, have consistently expended their meager enforcement resource on the wrong targets; they have not made optimal use of their resources. Another explanation is that the prescribed sanctions are inadequate for effective enforcement; the criminal penalties are too mild; the dominant enforcement technique of the consent decree too often amounts only to a slap on the wrist and an exhortation not to violate the laws again; even those decrees which require corporations to divest themselves of parts of their businesses often don't hurt the companies at all, or enough to dissuade them from their existing policies. Assuming that a sanction such as divestiture might be effective to prevent or reduce corporate power in some cases, the affected company can delay interminably the imposition of the sanction by litigating its propriety to the bitter end, as IBM now seems to be doing, as Alcoa did in the 1940's, as the completely vertically integrated major oil companies doubtless will litigate in the 1970's and into the 1980's the suit which could involve divestiture of their refining, transportation and marketing facilities. The FTC instituted this suit in 1973 after years of discussion of such a remedy for dealing with the power of industry.

The most vigorous proponents of antitrust acknowledge the unfeasibility of current antitrust laws when, in addition to offering one or more of the numerous explanations for failure outlined above, they also urge the adoption of a relatively new legislative approach such as that being considered by Senator Hart and his Antitrust and Monopoly Subcommittee. This would provide for the comprehensive review by a new set of administrative and judicial mechanisms of competitive conditions in certain specified leading industries of the United States, including oil, with the contemplation that the leading companies in these industries would be broken up unless they could establish that the public interest required their maintenance in their present state. The likelihood of the enactment of such a law at this time is not perceived as substantial even by its proponents. But even if the emotions generated by the current crisis were to lead to more serious consideration of such a radical remedy, one might reasonably ask why the "strict enforcement" of such a plan for divestiture would not be subject to many of the same disabilities as the prevailing antitrust laws. Furthermore, as we shall see below, there is a serious question concerning the ability of government regulation in general to cope.

Before we leave antitrust, a brief recapitulation is in order. Antitrust has failed to deal effectively with corporate power. This is conceded even by its strongest adherents, although they may not be willing to put it so baldly. And there is nothing to suggest that tinkering with it further along the lines discussed above will, in any important way, enhance its effectiveness in reducing the power of powerful corporations.

PARTICIPATION BY GOVERNMENT IN THE SUBSTANCE AND PROCEDURE OF CORPORATE DECISION MAKING

Can corporate power be checked significantly by the participation of government in the basic decisions of powerful corporations? There can be no question that some types of governmental intervention could and do affect corporate power. But how greatly? Only a summary treatment of such a vast subject is possible here. For the purposes of this paper, it will be sufficient to suggest some reasons why government will usually fail when it seeks to curb corporate power by intervening in corporate decisions.

One reason is that the government rarely, if ever, intervenes at only one point in an industry's decisions. On the contrary, the government's influence or participation is more usually reflected at many points in corporate decision making. And what is most important in this regard is the fact that this government influence and participation is the work not of one or a few governmental agencies but frequently of many, situated in different parts of the legislative and executive branches, and in many different courts, speaking in different and often conflicting voices.

There is perhaps no better example of the diversity in governmental objectives and procedures than in efforts to regulate and influence the oil industry. The energy crisis has only made more evident in this regard what has always been there to see. During most of the period that one agency alone, the FTC, was conducting over 300 formal investigations of antitrust violations in the oil industry and both the FTC and the Antitrust Division were prosecuting oil companies both criminally and civilly for a variety of antitrust violations, including price-fixing, price discrimination, and the unjustified use of tying and exclusive dealing contracts, the very same Antitrust Division was granting antitrust immunity, sometimes at the urging of the State and Defense Departments, to collaborative efforts of the major oil companies in their negotiations with oil producing countries. At the same time, the five states accounting for the bulk of the oil production in the United States (Texas, Louisiana, Oklahoma, New Mexico, and Kansas) have restricted the production of oil for conservation purposes in a way that has maintained supply at a level which would permit the producers to obtain optimal prices for their products. When foreign supplies from the mideast and production from other states became increasingly important in the 1950's, the federal government, acting through yet another set of agencies, imposed stringent import quotas on oil to protect the price of domestic oil. At the very same time, the Congress provided through special tax treatment of the oil companies subsidies for oil exploration which not only enhanced the profits of these companies but also, and what is important for our present discussion, encouraged the companies to vertically integrate in order to take the best advantage of these subsidies. This in turn encouraged the very growth of corporate power which the antitrust laws are designed in theory to minimize. Conflicting threads of public policy thus stem not only from the fragmentation of the agencies which develop and implement the policy but even more from the lack of consensus in the government concerning what a policy should be. The fragmentation of public policy among many agencies with diverse or conflicting objectives is more the result than the cause of differences concerning the content of policy.

Moreover, there is far less optimism in 1974 than in, say, 1934, among students of the regulatory process about the likelihood that even an agency possessing more or less complete responsibility for the operations of an industry will operate as an effective counterpoise for the power of the industry in resolving questions significantly affecting the public interest. In recent years, the tendency for regulatory agencies to become "captives" of the industry being regulated has been often noted. There are various possible reasons for this, ranging from the susceptibility of administrators to the lures of industry lobbyists to the difficulty of the agency's maintaining an objective view about an issue where only one side of an issue is effectively presented to it.

Events in recent years may have increased an agency's ability to maintain its independence and objectivity with respect to its regulatory target. The emergence of public interest advocates and an increased sensitivity among administrators as a result of "Watergate" to the dangers of responding to pressures from the industry being regulated will doubtless help. But even when the agency can maintain its objectivity with respect to an industry, there is still no guarantee that the regulation will be effective to cope with the power of the industry being regulated. This is in part because regulators, whether they be legislators or administrators (but particularly the latter), tend to issue regulations without adequate concern about whether they will achieve their announced objectives. When one regulation has proved ineffective, the answer usually is to add more regulations. It is significant and somewhat perplexing that Ralph Nader's group, which has made one of the most comprehensive analyses of the failures of regulation in the United States, nevertheless prescribes *more* regulation as a remedy for the regulatory ills which they have discovered.

This attitude reminds one of a contemporary comment about the report of a governmental commission, which made an extensive investigation of the prohibition laws in 1931, concluded that the laws were unenforceable, but nevertheless recommended that the laws not be repealed:

> Prohibition is an awful flop.
> We like it.
> It can't stop what it's meant to stop.
> We like it.
> It left a trail of graft and slime,
> It don't prohibit worth a dime,
> It's filled our land with vice and crime,
> Nevertheless, we're for it.

Any analysis of governmental participation in corporate decision making as a possible method of coping with corporate power must, of course, deal not only with the more traditional regulatory agency established to approve or ratify corporate decisions about entry, product, price, and the like, but must also take into account the proposals being advocated with renewed vigor for the incorporation of governmental representatives into the actual decision making framework of the corporation. The idea that corporations might exercise their power more in the "public interest" if they were required to include in their board of directors members representing the public has intrigued reformers for some time. In recent years, the Project on Corporate Responsibility, attempted, through stockholder action, to place on the board of directors of General Motors representatives of the public. There have also been proposals for governmental requirements that "public directors," elected perhaps by the stockholders, perhaps by the electorate, perhaps by a federal agency, be included on boards of directors. If such a proposal were adopted, probably it could be carried out only by transferring the responsibility for chartering or licensing corporations from the states with their diverse laws regarding the organization and operation of corporations to the federal government which could then impose the requirement for public directors.

There are at least two significant considerations which would militate against the effectiveness of public directors in curbing undesirable exercises of corporate power, even assuming that the Congress were to become sufficiently exercised about corporate power to take the radical step of depriving the states in whole or in part of the power to create corporations, which they have possessed from the beginning of the Republic. One is that the public directors and any governmental agency responsible for placing them and supervising their activities on corporate boards would be subject to the same pressures and constraints in the performance of their duties as any other regulatory agencies to adopt a corporate rather than a "public" point of view. The other is that, by their very nature, boards of directors which not infrequently comprise so-called "outside" directors, appointed by management to represent points of view outside the corporation, have not generally functioned as the real policy making body in the corporation, no matter what the law may have contemplated in this regard.

There is little, therefore, in the history or theory of governmental participation in corporate decision making which suggests that it is likely to be an effective means of coping with corporate power in the oil industry or elsewhere.

GOVERNMENTAL ACTIONS OFFSETTING CORPORATE POWER

A common governmental response to problems of corporate power has been to strengthen the hand of certain groups in the society in dealing with corporations about matters in which they have particular concern. This response has been employed, for example, to strengthen politically powerful labor through federal and state laws protecting the right of workers to organize, requiring collective bargaining, setting minimum wages and hours, and standards of safety and health. More recently, the same types of assistance for the consumer are to be found in laws or proposed laws designed to enhance product safety or to insure that the consumer receives effective warranties which correspond with his reasonable expectations when he purchases a product. There have also been proposals for placing consumer advocates within regulatory agencies or even within the corporations themselves. Environmental groups have also been provided with new laws and procedures designed to enhance their ability to deal more effectively with corporations about their environmental concerns. Efforts are made to protect women and ethnic groups against discrimination in employment. More liberal interpretations of the antitrust laws by the courts have enabled corporations, usually but not always those with relatively less economic power, to challenge in treble damage suits discriminatory and predatory behavior of powerful corporations which has injured them in the market place. Small businesses are given preferential treatment in access to loans, government contracts, and other crucial resources of the powerful.

These varied responses of society to corporate power are obviously quite different in their thrust and theoretical justification than the antitrust and regulatory responses discussed in the preceding sections. These responses assume that corporate power can be managed best by chipping away at its various manifestations through the medium of the organizations and groups who are the most affected by the corporate power and therefore the most motivated to prevent that power from being mismanaged.

But we are concerned here not so much with the intent of societal responses to corporate power as with their dynamics. How effective are these attempts likely to be to institutionalize the response to corporate power in the affected groups? And what considerations are likely to determine their effectiveness?

In a summary such as this, little more can be done than to suggest some of these considerations and then to make an intuitive judgment about the overall effect upon corporate power of measures designed to confer offsetting power on groups outside the corporation.

The crucial factors are the ability of the favored group to use effectively the tools the government provides it, the degree of motivation possessed by the group to oppose the power of corporations, the likely attitudes of the governmental agencies which have the responsibility for translating the governmental policy into significant support for the favored group.

Thus, a governmental agency that has as its primary or exclusive mission the strengthening of labor unions or assistance to those who are the subject of discrimination in employment is likely to fight harder for its clients than it would if it had many missions and more diverse constituencies. The clients of a governmental agency, if they are powerful enough politically, will tend to "capture" the agency in the same manner that a regulated industry tends to take over the agency regulating it.

Occasionally, the legislature places powerful weapons directly in the hands of organizations or firms which they can employ against powerful corporations without the necessity of working through an intervening governmental agency. This may occur when the legislature is not even aware of the potential strength of the weapon which it has fashioned. Two notable recent examples have been the successful private suits brought under the antitrust laws and the Environmental Protection Act of 1969 and other environmental laws.

Weaker competitors and industrial customers and franchisees have successfully prosecuted under the antitrust laws multi-million-dollar treble damage suits and significant injunction suits against corporate giants. Imaginative industrial plaintiffs have on occasion stimulated through their own suits governmental enforcement agencies to institute actions against powerful corporations. For example, it was Control Data Corporation's suit against IBM which at least in part stimulated the Antitrust Division to start its own action for monopolization.

In the environmental area, the construction and expansion plans of many powerful businesses, particularly in the energy industries, have been greatly delayed, if not required to be abandoned altogether by the activities of environmental and conservation groups, such as the Sierra Club and the Environmental Defense Council, who, armed with the unexpectedly broad weapons provided by Congress in a burst of protectionist zeal, have found many sympathetic judges to support their opposition to corporate power.

It is quite possible that in the long run the most effective societal response to corporate power will be governmental action aimed at helping less powerful groups and firms to cope with corporations directly. But this will require at a minimum that the government provide assistance under conditions which are likely to bring about meaningful action by those being helped. Too often, complex governmental mechanisms which are designed to increase the power of private groups in their dealings with powerful corporations fail almost completely in their purpose. There is perhaps no better example of this than the unsuccessful efforts over the years by the federal government and others to bolster through the securities laws the power of corporate shareholders in dealing with the management of the companies which the shareholders "own." Whatever the success of public interest groups in recent years in calling public attention by means of stockholder meetings and shareholder proposals to certain socially significant decisions of corporate management, few would assert that any real dent has been made or is likely to be made in corporate power in this manner.

EXHORTATIONS TO INDUSTRY TO ACT "IN THE PUBLIC INTEREST"

One response to corporate power which is often made by governmental officials and private groups, particularly at times of crisis, is to urge management to act "in the public interest." Before formal controls were imposed on wages and prices in 1971, there had been a long period extending back at least to the Truman Administration of "jawboning" to encourage both corporations and unions to be "reasonable" in setting prices and wages. In 1971, just before the federal government "froze" prices and wages, the Committee for Economic Development listed as one of the many ongoing activities of corporations to improve society, "cooperating with the government in developing more effective measures to control inflation and achieve high levels of employment."

How effective is such a response to corporate power? How effective is it likely to be? In order to answer these questions, it is necessary to analyze the dynamics of the relationships between corporations and the society, and particularly the implications of the concept of corporate social responsibility for the exercise of corporate power. In making this analysis, it is not the purpose of this paper to enter into the extensive debates concerning whether corporations should be socially responsible or what constitutes socially responsible behavior.

By way of example, let us turn once more, and for the last time, to the oil industry. Although there is yet much to be known about the way that major American international oil companies make decisions, there seems to be general agreement that these companies have been aware for years that the dependence by the United States upon foreign sources of crude oil would lead to serious shortages if those sources were cut off. They also knew that this threat could be averted by increasing the stocks of oil in the United States, by increasing oil imports, by increasing domestic oil exploration efforts, and by increasing the capacity of United States based refineries. If these measures had been adopted in time, the supply of oil in the United States would have been in jeopardy only if there was a simultaneous boycott of the United States by all oil producing countries, a most unlikely contingency. Knowing all this, the oil companies decided not to make the necessary additions to refining capacity in the United States, because they believed that their profits would be higher if foreign, rather than domestic, refineries were built. Furthermore, major oil companies, at least as late as 1969, fought for the continuation of import quotas to the United States and as late as 1972 chose to import less oil than was permitted under the import quotas. Major oil companies now concede that they erred in their estimate of the extent to which the nation's oil supply was threatened.

Let us suppose that an alert and fully informed government or an alert and fully informed public had urged the oil industry to act in such a way as to insure an adequate supply of oil for industrial and private consumers in the United States regardless of the effect that such a course might have had on the anticipated profits of the companies concerned. Is it at all likely that such an exhortation would or could have had any real impact on the course of events?

There is little in our own experience or in the literature dealing with corporate responsibility to suggest that any industry is likely to respond to such an approach when incentives for the requested action are lacking. On the contrary, there have been numerous, frequently hair raising, accounts of how individual corporations in a variety of industries, including automobile, airplane parts manufacturers, and others, have acted when confronted with a choice between creating products or operating conditions that represent a substantial threat to the health or safety of their customers, employees, or the community at large, and surrendering substantial revenues. What is more, when their actions have been questioned and they have been threatened with governmental intervention which might prevent them from their self-serving course, they often have lobbied vigorously to preserve their autonomy. It has been aptly pointed out that "Few of the leaders of business who have embraced social responsibility have given any sign that they recognize the implications for the lobbying activities of their own firms." "Enterprises generally have been reluctant—if not obstructive—reactors to new social values, instead of innovative leaders in satisfying them." It is unlikely that such enterprises will respond meaningfully to mere exhortations to be responsible.

In operational terms, corporate social responsibility has been an extremely vague and unpredictable basis for corporate action, even when managers assert it as a basis for their decisions. Seemingly irresponsible behavior is often not explained. The specific examples of responsible action which are cited by corporations are frequently the making of expenditures already required by law, as to reduce certain pollutant effects of the corporation's operations on the physical environment. Most corporate executives still equate social responsibility with charitable corporations and aid to higher education. There still do not exist effective mechanisms other than the traditional reporting of corporate earnings to guide corporations in their decision making. The current, rather extensive efforts to develop corporate social accounting are in part designed to supplement existing mechanisms but the embryonic character and the relatively limited scope of the aspirations for social accounting by those seeking to develop it suggest that it will be a very long time before they meaningfully implement the exhortations to corporations to act in the public interest.

CONCLUSION

The societal responses to corporate power which we have examined have not, either individually or in the aggregate, coped with that power. Ever since corporate power developed to the point where it was perceived necessary to counteract it, there has been a constant backing and filling between various courses of action (or inaction). These have involved laissez faire, competition policy, governmental regulation, exhortation, and efforts to establish counterpoises to the corporation. As many students of the American economic and political condition have, in effect, concluded, corporate power remains essentially unchecked, and is likely to remain so in the foreseeable future. Our analysis suggests some of the reasons why this is the case.

One does not relish, of course, the feeling of helplessness engendered by this conclusion. It is inevitable, therefore, that some seek to temper this feeling with assurances that the necessary adjustments will somehow be made in corporate attitudes and behavior or to try their own hand at changing corporate attitudes through exhortations and warnings of the fate that faces corporations if they do not exercise their power in the public interest.

My own view of the matter is closest to the rather pessimistic, but not entirely hopeless statement that follows:

> We are easily misled by the gleaming technology of our age into thinking that we live at a time when men are also highly polished, or would be if only the present institutions were changed for other ones. We might as well believe that the shining armor of the knight encased a person of superior morality as well as strength. . . . As things now stand, the corporation that binds men together by appealing to their acquisitive natures, and the state that binds them together by appealing to their patriotic natures, are the only means we have for ensuring our survival, even if by a terrible irony they are also the institutions by which our survival is most seriously endangered.
>
> . . .
>
> Does this render futile all efforts to achieve corporate responsibility? On the contrary, the very persistence of the corporation gives to the search for responsibility a deeper significance than the remedy of the abuses of the moment. The creation of a responsive and responsible corporation becomes an indispensable step in the creation of a responsive and responsible state—perhaps the central social problem of our age. . . .

QUESTIONS

1. Explain each of Marcus' five major social responses to excessive corporate power. Do you agree with his assessment?
2. Can you think of additional forces in the business environment that operate to restrain business power? Are any of the factors discussed here underestimated?
3. Can you think of any new forces that are likely to arise in the future to restrain business power in American society? Which of the restraints discussed by Marcus will become more powerful? Which will become less important?
4. Do you agree that corporate power is "a condition without a remedy"? If so, is this a deplorable fact?
5. Marcus repeatedly cites the oil industry as an example of less than adequately restrained corporate power. Is the oil industry typical or atypical of all concentrated industries in the American economy?

CORPORATE BIGNESS—FOR BETTER OR FOR WORSE?

ARTHUR A. THOMPSON

Arthur A. Thompson, professor of economics and business administration, Graduate School of Business, University of Alabama, examines the case for and against big business and concludes that the case for corporate bigness is much stronger than might have been anticipated.

Once again corporate critics have succeeded in restoring the "bigness is bad" syndrome to the public spotlight. Bolstered by the grass-roots appeal of consumerism and exposés of alleged corporate mischievousness (ITT's lobbying activities, oil company profits, illegal campaign contributions), the critics have fanned long-standing suspicions of corporate giantism to the point where stepped-up antitrust investigations are a reality and even new legislation may be on the near horizon. At the very least, the IBM, AT&T, and breakfast cereal cases, together with stricter accounting standards and Senator Hart's proposed Industrial Reorganization Act, are serving as debating points for whether new checks and balances are needed to make the private enterprise system work to greater social advantage.

While it is open to dispute whether the real trouble lies with the large corporation or with its critics' perceptions and expectations, few would question that corporate executives are having a frustratingly hard time presenting a convincing case for corporate bigness before the public eye. In essence, the suspicion of corporate bigness emanates from the twin issues of corporate power and the adequacy of competitive forces. The themes of criticism and concern are familiar:

Giant corporations have grown to a point where they are too large and too powerful. Horizontal and vertical integration, diversification, and conglomerate merger have been carried beyond the bounds justified by efficiency considerations.

The size and power of giant firms put them in a position to manipulate markets rather than respond to them. This is evidenced by administered pricing, output restrictions, anticompetitive trade practices, tacit collusion, and conscious parallelism—each of which is the antithesis of free market economics.

Competitive forces are no longer strong enough or reliable enough to protect consumers from inflated prices, excessive profits, and self-serving corporate policies.

Arthur A. Thompson, "Corporate Bigness—for Better or for Worse?" *Sloan Management Review,* Vol. 17, No. 1, Fall 1975, pp. 37–60. Reprinted by permission.

- The oligopolistic structure of corporate-dominated markets diverts competitive rivalry away from price competition (the most desirable competitive form) into nonprice areas—a much less desirable competitive style that encourages overemphasis on persuasive advertising, product proliferation, planned product obsolescence, and cosmetic product improvements.
- Because of the political leverage which goes with bigness and which big firms deliberately cultivate, corporate enterprises are able to gain undue access to government in achieving private economic goals.
- The motives and pressures for improved corporate performance (growth in sales, profits, etc.) have led to questionable mergers and acquisitions, manipulative accounting practices, and financial machinations that have doubtful social or economic value.
- Reforms both from within and without are needed to curb corporate power, enliven competition, and make large firms more responsible and responsive to the general economic welfare of society.

IN THE NAME OF FREE ENTERPRISE

To date, corporate rebuttals to these themes have mostly been couched in the familiar tenets of Adam Smith and his model of laissez-faire capitalism. For example, the image ads of large corporations almost invariably contain euphoric idealizations about freedom of choice, the benefits of a free market, the omnipotence of supply-demand forces, and the necessity of profit as a reward for risk-taking. In 1974, chronic inflation and short supplies of essential commodities prompted a wave of institutional ads emphasizing two other free market principles—namely that (1) price controls are unworkable because unless prices are allowed to fluctuate in response to changes in supply and demand, disincentives and resource misallocation will develop, and (2) higher profits are requisite for providing the money and the motivation to finance expansions and alleviate shortages.

In a less ideological vein, giant enterprise has been defended on grounds that:

- Bigness is not a product of monopoly but of technological necessity and a drive for competitive efficiency.
- Large firms, regardless of size, are subject to strong and unrelenting competitive pressures from rival firms (domestic and foreign), new or substitute products, and the potential entry of new firms into their markets.
- Persuasive advertising cannot sell products which consumers do not like or which repeatedly prove unsatisfactory (thereby validating the doctrine of consumer sovereignty).
- Changes in buying habits, customer requirements, costs, and the balance between supply and demand factors—not corporate whim—are the decisive forces in shaping price policies, product quality, and new product development.

All of these defenses of bigness have roots in the litany of laissez-faire capitalism. All are plainly laced with elements of accuracy. But, just as plainly, the defenders of big business have not carried the day with their free enterprise campaign. Some would say the failure is a mixture of public ignorance of basic supply-demand economics, a reaction against overemphasis on economic materialism, and a liberalist rejection of free enterprise ideology. Perhaps, but an equally plausible explanation relates to the false ring which the free enterprise philosophy has when measured against readily observed economic realities. The average consumer, for example, can scarcely be blamed for turning a deaf ear to claims that corporate-dominated markets are "free" when daily experience and common sense instruct him that giant firms can and do influence the prices of the products he buys. It is one thing to be persuaded that small companies are without influence over prices, but who can seriously believe that General Motors has little to say about the prices of automobiles, or that it is simply market forces, not oil company policies, which govern gasoline prices. Hence, it is understandable why the average person is prone to suspect that corporate arguments for "free market pricing" are prompted more by a desire to stave off government interference than by a strong ideological belief in the efficacy of laissez-faire.

In a similar vein, the size of giant enterprises goes against the consumer's concept of a fair and equal balance of power between buyers and sellers. Inflation (and particularly an inflationary recession) dramatizes to consumers their economic vulnerability as individuals. Their only really effective countervailing weapon against inflated prices is collective action in refusing to buy products whose offer prices are deemed "too high" or whose quality or safety is deemed deficient. However, not many consumers will view "doing without" as a satisfactory device for protesting seemingly unilateral price decisions of producers, especially after a good or service has become ingrained in living standards. Instead, a sizeable segment of the public is certain to call upon government to intervene in a market process which they perceive to be functioning unfairly or to their detriment.

Predictably, corporate attempts (via public relations ads, speeches to civic groups, and so on) to generate broad public support for more free enterprise and less government interference have limited potential for success. Persistent public suspicion of bigness should be clue enough that corporate giantism cannot be sold to the public in the name of free enterprise. The average person is sharp enough to perceive that the principles of free market economics represent "the truth but not the whole truth" about the economics of corporate capitalism and corporate power.

FREE MARKETS AND BIGNESS ARE INCOMPATIBLE

When big business talks about free enterprise it is mainly promoting the concepts of business autonomy and freedom from government interference, but when economists and policy makers advocate free enterprise they are talking about an economic system where consumers are safe from monopoly power and capricious business decisions. The latter commonly interpret adequate safeguards from monopoly to require that the supply side of all markets be comprised of many producers, no one of which has an unduly large market share. Since there are *no* examples of market capitalism where the population of producers is made up of giant corporations, the tendency to link bigness with monopoly is widespread.

Consequently, the received wisdom, both among academics and in regulatory agencies, though acknowledging that large size gives firms better access to production-related economies of scale, persistently focuses on how large size breeds concentration and market power. More specifically, anti-bigness critics urge that oligopolistic corporations, either formally or tacitly, tend to establish monopolistic price structures. Corporate prices are viewed as gravitating either towards a level that yields the greatest collective profit for firms in the industry or towards a price that maximizes the (short-term or long-term) profits of one or more of the largest and most influential firms in a position to impose its preferences, via price leadership techniques, upon the remainder of the industry. The critics of bigness also contend that it is fairly easy for a few giant firms to coordinate their market strategies to mutual advantage, resulting in firms becoming complacent and losing their venturesome spirit. In effect, they contend that such behavior turns corporate-dominated markets into a "shared monopoly" with rival firms enjoying high entry barriers and a "relaxed" atmosphere of nonprice competition that embraces wasteful advertising, brand proliferation, and so on. The FTC complaint against the breakfast cereal firms exemplifies this view.

On balance, say the critics of bigness, the rise to power of giant corporations is inherently in conflict with the requirements of a competitive price system. This conclusion is taken as an article of faith among the true believers in a free market's power to serve the general economic welfare and explains their appeal for the proposed Industrial Reorganization Act or similar deconcentration schemes. It also accounts for why microeconomists, the great majority of whom qualify as "true believers," have had neither interest nor faith in the development of a "theory of corporate capitalism" which accords the giant corporation a legitimate role. The absence of any plausible alternative *competitive* models which accommodate firms of either great absolute or relative size has left the giant corporation hanging in limbo, with no foundation upon which to base a defense of bigness.

Plainly, without a consistent and empirically-validated model of "corporate capitalism," giant firms are at a distinct disadvantage in taking their case for bigness to the public. Legitimacy is crucial to making a favorable impact on the public mind, especially for organizations with so visible a profile as today's corporate giants. Since the substance of legitimacy is rooted in society's ideological concepts and beliefs, the lack of a conceptual framework which justifies bigness has practical as well as theoretical import, especially when the mainstream of economic activity so clearly runs through the doors of giant firms.

HOW CORPORATE CAPITALISM IS DIFFERENT

Corporate capitalism has features which are in marked contrast to those of market capitalism. The modern corporation's organizational complexity, operating scope, market strategies, and competitive modes have little in common with those of the classic entrepreneurial enterprise straitjacketed by market forces beyond its control.

However, the comparison is not altogether simple. This is partly because the oligopolistic character of corporate capitalism spawns a variety of competitive behavior patterns and partly because there are divergent forms of corporate enterprise (each of which can give rise to differences in the competitive environment). Regarding the latter, four *basic* forms of corporate enterprise stand out:

The horizontally-integrated, single product line corporation (Holiday Inn, Delta Airlines, Prudential, Safeway, and McDonald's);
The vertically-integrated, single product line corporation (American Motors, Polaroid, Inland Steel, and Exxon);
The diversified (related product or technology) corporation (General Electric, DuPont, 3M Co., and Eastman Kodak); and
The diversified (unrelated product or technology) corporation (Litton, Textron, U.S. Industries, LTV, and Gulf & Western).

Many firms, of course, do not fit neatly into just one of these categories but embrace, instead, two or more of the basic forms (RCA, ITT, Coca-Cola, Heublein, and AT&T). The vast majority of large manufacturing firms, for example, are now diversified to the extent of over 5 percent of sales, with 181 of the 200 largest manufacturing corporations each operating in at least ten distinguishable product markets.

The significant point to be made here about the several forms of corporate enterprise, though, relates to the variations in the competitive environments confronting giant corporations and, further, to how these contrast with the stereotype of market capitalism. Table 1 highlights these differences. In market capitalism, firms are forced into an essentially rigid competitive mode. Each enterprise has no realistic choice but to compete impersonally against "the market"; any differences among firms with respect to organization, products, market scope, and the like are held to be so subservient to market forces as to have little significance.

On the other hand, competition among giant firms is a complex configuration based upon price-quality-service features, technology and innovation, the promotion of product differences, and the motives for corporate growth. No one form of competitive behavior stands out. Furthermore, studies indicate that the competitive matrix confronting large corporations generates pressures and constraints which vary both in type and degree from firm to firm, industry to industry, and time to time. At any one moment, some giant firms appear to be more sheltered from competition than others, in reflection of their differing successes in carving out a unique market niche for themselves. There seem to be relatively few instances where corporate giants have succeeded in shielding themselves from competition over the long run. The corporate landscape is littered with firms which once enjoyed a position of advantage yet now face rugged competition (for example, Alcoa, U.S. Steel, Birdseye, Coca-Cola, and Standard Oil). Thus, while short-term competitive pressures are admittedly uneven in their impact upon large firms, it is difficult to find many examples where corporate capitalism has utterly failed in generating competitive pressures of one sort or another.

EVALUATING CORPORATE CAPITALISM

Although corporate capitalism obviously lacks many of the essential traits of laissez-faire capitalism, the yardsticks for judging the social worth and legitimacy of large firms continue to revolve around the issues of market power, price levels, and profitability—essentially the same ground rules used for judging small-scale enterprises operating under conditions of "competition among the many." Senator Hart's Industrial Reorganization Act, for example, seeks to use such statically-oriented indices of competitiveness as (1) the prevalence and persistence of price competition, (2) the sizes of market shares, and (3) the rates of return on stockholder's equity in judging whether competition among large corporations is sufficiently vigorous.

The thrust of antitrust rules and regulations has been and still is to try to shoehorn corporate enterprises into an economic model of many small companies competing in a free market environment. The prevailing philosophy seems to be that unless the competitive process allows small companies to compete effectively against big companies . . . the behavior of big companies is anticompetitive.

So long as competitiveness is measured in Adam Smith terms, the large corporation is likely to remain "illegitimate." There is no escaping the fact that when the same ground rules established for small-scale enterprises operating under conditions of "competition among the many" are applied to large corporations, something of an irreconcilable conflict emerges between market capitalism and corporate giantism.

None of this, however, is sufficient to justify taking up the call to pulverize the corporate sector so as to approximate more closely the allegedly desirable conditions of "competition among the many." Some thirty years ago the late Harvard professor Joseph Schumpeter observed that inquiry into the origins of high living standards "leads not to the doors of those firms that

Table 1 Contrasts between Market Capitalism and Corporate Capitalism

Structural Characteristics of Markets and Firms	MARKET CAPITALISM	CORPORATE CAPITALISM Horizontally-Integrated Corporations
Owner-Manager Relationships	Closely held, entrepreneurially-oriented	Investor-owned, professionally managed
Line of Business	Traditionally produces a single product or product line	Usually concentrates on a single product or product line; little diversification
Degree of Product Differentiation	Undifferentiated to weakly differentiated	No clear-cut pattern; anywhere from weak to strong differentiation
Strategy of the Firm	Based upon profit opportunities in a single product or product line	Based upon strengthening the firm's geographic coverage
Market Shares of Firms	Very small	Small to moderate within the industry, but large within a particular locality
Degree of Interfirm Rivalry	Competition is highly impersonal because of large numbers of firms; each firm focuses its competitive energies on "the market" in an effort to survive at the going price	The larger the market shares of major firms, the more intense is the degree of interfirm rivalry

	CORPORATE CAPITALISM	
Vertically-Integrated Corporations	Diversified Corporations	
	Related Products	Unrelated Products
Investor-owned, professionally managed	Investor-owned, professionally managed	Investor-owned, professionally managed
Concentrates upon a single major product line, but with plant investments in many stages of the manufacturing process	Markets many technologically- or market-related products and services	Markets many unrelated products and services
Usually ranges from undifferentiated to weakly differentiated, but occasional strong differentiation (as in autos)	No clear-cut pattern; anywhere from weak to strong differentiation	No clear-cut pattern; anywhere from weak to strong differentiation
Scale economies motivate the firm to integrate forward and/or backward so as to achieve the cost and price reductions requisite for increased market penetration	Aimed at capitalizing upon opportunities in related markets	Aimed at capitalizing upon opportunities in unrelated industries
Substantial, except for competitive fringe firms	Moderate to substantial	Small to substantial
Competition is highly personalized, especially among major firms in the industry	Embraces a substantial degree of interfirm rivalry, but a firm's chief rivals vary from product to product	Degree of interfirm rivalry varies since firms may face competition from a few giants for some products and from a whole host of firms for other products

Table 1—continued

Structural Characteristics of Markets and Firms	MARKET CAPITALISM	CORPORATE CAPITALISM: Horizontally-Integrated Corporations
Ability of One Firm to Influence Prices or Supplies within Its Market Area	Minimal	Moderate to substantial depending on market share
Barriers to Entry	Minimal	Low to moderate barriers depending on degree of product differentiation and size of entry costs
Market Coverage	Firm's growth horizon is usually restricted to local or regional markets; lack of scale economies restrains tendency to expand	Firm is motivated to move progressively into national and international markets as present markets become saturated
Changes in Industry-Wide Supply Capability	Occur mainly via changes in the number of firms (entry and exit) rather than by the growth or decline of existing firms	Occur mainly via changes in the output capacities of existing firms, except in situations where high growth potential stimulates entry

work under conditions of comparatively free competition, but precisely to the doors of the large concerns . . . and a shocking suspicion dawns upon us that big business may have had more to do with creating that standard of life than with keeping it down." Schumpeter's observation, though familiar to economists, has never really been accepted as gospel; the bias against large size and competition among the few has proven too strong. Yet, there is evidence that the long-run competitive performance of corporate

CORPORATE CAPITALISM		
Vertically-Integrated Corporations	Diversified Corporations	
	Related Products	Unrelated Products
Substantial in the case of firms with large or dominant market shares	Moderate to substantial depending on market share	Small to substantial depending on market share
Presence of high barriers usually restricts entry to other giants having the ability to achieve scale economies and overcome high capital investment requirements and high selling costs	Moderate to high barriers, owing to scale economies, product differentiation barriers, R&D and know-how barriers; potential entrants are mainly other growth-oriented corporate giants	Low to moderate to occasionally high barriers, depending on the product in question
The economies of large-scale operation motivate the firm to move progressively into national and international markets	Scale economies and desire to grow cause firms to expand into national and international markets, as well as to add new products	Scale economies and desire to grow cause firms to expand into new market areas, as well as to broaden product lines
Occur mainly via changes in the output capacities of existing firms, except in rare situations where high growth potential induces the entry of other giant firms	No clear-cut pattern; depends on size of barriers to entry and exit in specific product markets	No clear-cut pattern; depends on size of barriers to entry and exit in specific product markets

capitalism is socially beneficial, despite the fact that some key free market traits are missing. Specifically, there are indications that over the long term competition in corporate-dominated markets tends to produce:

Increased rates of technological progress and new product innovation,
Low-cost production efficiency, sustained with above-average productivity gains,

Slower rates of increase in prices (or even declines in prices in cases where costs permit), and
Profit rates comparable to those earned in allegedly "more competitive" industries.

True, the available evidence in support of these claims is neither complete nor entirely consistent. Nonetheless, it is worth a serious look, because if it should turn out that the long-run performance of corporate-dominated markets outweighs any lack of competitive vigor in the short run, then the case for deconcentration is weakened greatly.

TECHNOLOGICAL PROGRESS AND INNOVATION

Although the empirical evidence is not clear-cut and several prominent exceptions can be cited (steel, railroads), competition on the basis of technology and innovation reaches its most intense proportions in markets dominated by giant firms. In fact, a good case can be made that the giant corporation has become the economy's major organizational vehicle for effecting innovation and technological achievement.

Statistics compiled by the National Science Foundation show that as of 1971 firms having 5,000 or more employees accounted for 88.5 percent of the $18.3 billion spent for industrial R&D; firms with 1,000 to 4,999 employees accounted for 6.5 percent; and firms with fewer than 1,000 employees accounted for the remaining 5 percent. Of the 505 companies with 5,000 or more employees, 418 had R&D budgets of $1,000,000 or more and 172 spent more than $10 million for R&D activities. Moreover, in 1972 over 82 percent of the scientists and engineers engaged in R&D were employed in firms with 5,000 or more employees. Very little formal scientific and engineering effort seems to occur in industries where the four largest firms have a combined market share below 15 percent.

R&D outlays, of course, are only an input measure; they do not reflect innovational success or significance. Yet it seems unlikely that innovation will occur as regularly where R&D is haphazard and casual as it will where R&D is organized and sustained. It is more than coincidence that small firms operating in atomistically-structured markets have instigated none of the showcase results of technological superiority and economic achievement.

Nonetheless, once the firm passes some threshold size there is room to question just how supportive bigness is of technical progress. Instances have occurred where companies dominating their markets have been slow innovators but aggressive followers. Sometimes progressiveness is as much the result of technological opportunity and profit potential as it is bigness or market concentration while on other occasions the largest firms' share of significant innovations has been found to be inversely correlated with high market concentration. Furthermore, where large firms are solidly entrenched, there is always the chance that technical progress will be retarded by a restricted number of independent sources of initiative and by a dampened incentive to gain an ever stronger market position through accelerated R&D.

These examples in no way undermine the fact that large corporations, from the standpoints of risk and organizational and financial know-how, are better positioned than small companies to serve as potential pacesetters for implementing profitable technological discoveries and new product improvements. What they do say very clearly is that the large corporation's potential for innovation must be kept activated by competitive pressures if faster technological progress is to result from bigness and oligopoly. No one, however, seriously contends otherwise and such illustrations should not be allowed to confuse the issue.

Much more important than the question of whether giant firms achieve the largest possible rate of technical progress is the question of whether they are still, on balance, more progressive than firms of lesser size. In the final analysis, *an industry composed of many small firms whose rate of technological progress is "slow" will in the long run prove to be less efficient and will make less of a contribution to society's economic well-being than will a competitive industry composed of firms large enough to achieve a higher rate of technological achievement.* This result holds even though the slowly progressing firms start from a position of lower costs and prices. Consider the following situation which illustrates this point.

Assume an industry is composed of 100 small companies, each producing 20 units of output and operating its facilities at peak efficiency. Total industry output would therefore be 2000 units which, let us say, could currently be sold at a price of $5 a unit. Suppose further that (1) new technological innovations raise efficiency and permit the firms to increase production by 2 percent each year using the same amounts of resource inputs and (2) competition causes any cost savings (after allowing for any increases in resource prices) to be passed on to consumers via price reductions of 1 percent annually. At the end of five years, then, industry output will have risen to 2208 units and the market price will have fallen to $4.75.

Now let us assume that this same industry is, instead, composed of four large corporations each producing 475 units of output. Total industry output initially would total 1900 units or 5 percent less than the output under 100-firm market structure. The lesser initial output of these large corporations, assuming identical market demand conditions, will allow them to obtain a higher price, say $5.25. But suppose the large firms invest more heavily in R&D and, because of resulting efficiencies, are able to expand output by 3 percent per year using the same amount of resource inputs. Suppose, too, that competitive pressures are strong enough to force them to pass part of the cost-savings along to consumers in the form of price reductions of 2 percent per year. At the end of five years the total output of the four large corporations will be 2203 units and price will have fallen to $4.75—results that are comparable to the small firm market structure, even though the four corporations started out with a lower total output and higher prices.

Moreover, every year thereafter the corporate market will *outperform* the small firm market on both *price* and *output* by an increasing amount. Corporate prices will fall by 2 percent compared to only 1 percent in the small firm market; corporate output will expand by 3 percent compared to only 2 percent in the small firm market. These results will occur without any economies-of-scale advantage and despite the fact that the large corporations may earn greater profits per unit of output.

This example, although oversimplified, illustrates the importance of long-run performance in evaluating corporate behavior. The rate of technical progress, not prices, profits, or efficiency at some moment of time, ultimately determines the quality and quantity of a product and the impact on the consumer's pocketbook. For this reason alone, it follows that for a market structure to yield socially-optimum results it must not only be competitive enough to protect consumers against abuses of market power but it must also be conducive to technical progress and innovation.

This principle is easily expanded to encompass the importance of technological progress and innovation to the whole economy. As it turns out, what economists call "the static deadweight welfare loss from monopoly power and resource misallocation" is overcome by technologically-induced growth in the GNP in a surprisingly short time. A welfare loss amounting to 2 percent of the GNP is surmounted in just two years if an increased rate of technological progress raises GNP by 1 percent per year. Most estimates place the economy-wide welfare loss from monopoly power at less than 6 percent and even exaggerated estimates go no higher than 12 percent. At the same time, a minimum estimate of the annual average economic welfare gain from innovation and technical change would be in the 1.2 to 1.5 percent range. Consequently, the "worst case" length of time required for innovation-related growth to surmount the adverse effects of monopoly power is about nine years, with a more probable time being one to four years.

The conclusion to be drawn here is straightforward: if a large portion of technological progress is, in fact, attributable to the activities of giant corporations, then the static monopoly welfare loss would have to be much larger than is presently indicated before society could be made better off by breaking large firms up into many small companies.

PRODUCTION EFFICIENCY AND PRODUCTIVITY

Although some studies have found that the sizes of giant firms are not entirely justified by scale economies realized at the manufacturing or plant levels, there is no general indication on an overall production, distribution, and managerial basis that large size hampers the achievement of peak efficiency and low unit costs. On the contrary, good reasons exist why giant firms should be more successful than small companies in containing rising cost pressures, in implementing cost-saving methods of production, distribution, and management, and in realizing above-average gains in productivity. To begin with, the giant firm's debt capacity and capital-raising potential are available for:

Financing the development and implementation of technological innovations, such as automation or computerization, that offset rising costs and reduce human error or drudgery.

Operating a proficient R&D program, keeping a firm on the frontiers of technical know-how and supplied with a reliable stream of new products and product improvement, and exploiting the market potential of innovative ideas.

Withstanding the risk of cyclical downturns, sour investments in a new project, or secular decline in one or more product markets.

Undertaking large-scale capital expansion of production facilities.

Attracting and holding a talented supply of managerial, scientific, engineering, and technical manpower.

Acting both as a miniature capital market and employment agency to reallocate capital and labor to areas with superior potential and need—and to do so with a speed and accuracy exceeding less knowledgeable external market forces.

In addition, there are a number of diverse kinds of operating economies which accrue to large-scale enterprises.

Vertically integrating their operations gives firms increased opportunities to overcome market uncertainties associated with unreliable sources of supply and channels of distribution. If neither substitute inputs nor technical solutions are available, then bringing strategic supplies and costs under internal control via backward integration can reduce the threat to profits from undependable suppliers, volatile input prices, production bottlenecks, and the tactical maneuvers of rival firms regarding raw material supplies. Similarly, unreliable product outlets may prompt forward integration in the form of corporate-owned distribution networks or franchising arrangements with strong dealer controls so as to obtain both the economies of stable production operations and the economies of large-scale distribution.

Large size gives a firm better access to economies in the purchase of raw materials (fixed-price contracts) and in the purchase of mass-media advertising exposure.

To the extent that labor costs tend to rise faster than the costs of capital goods, large capital-intensive firms are able to maintain profit margins with price increases decidedly smaller than firms using more labor-intensive production methods, thus preserving growth opportunities and lessening the pressure for lower-priced substitutes.

Large size allows firms to pursue the diverse range of economies arising from specialization, including those based upon function, product-market relationships, and technological (or capital-deepening) relationships.

Large multiplant firms have somewhat greater ability to locate new production facilities in areas with the most favorable economic advantages—including, if desirable, the location of plants in foreign countries.

Large size gives firms greater motivation and opportunity for developing and experimenting with efficiency-increasing managerial methodologies. Indeed, large corporations have pioneered in the application of a higher order of *managerial technology,* realizing in the process various economies of administration and finance and clearing the way of management-related obstacles to large size.

No one of the foregoing advantages of large size is necessarily decisive in foreclosing smaller firms from being competitive. Yet, taken together they constitute a powerful battery of reasons why bigness may not be bad and why it is possible for giant corporations to outperform smaller enterprises on a sustained basis. Large absolute firm size does make a difference in a firm's long-term ability to compete.

Of course, the advantages of large size vary in significance from firm to firm and industry to industry. Rarely would a large firm be so fortunately positioned as to obtain the benefits of every advantage in the listing above. But it is common for firms to combine several of the advantages of large size into a successful corporate strategy. For example, the success of vertically-integrated firms is founded on (1) technology-related opportunities for manufacturing economies and product improvements, (2) the advantages of specialization based on function, and (3) operating economies associated with insulating the firm from unfavorable developments in either input or product markets. The multiproduct, multidivisional corporation, however, is predicated on the benefits to be gained from (1) spreading risks and sustaining growth via diversification, (2) financial, marketing, and administrative economies that are apart from manufacturing economies, (3) specialization based on similar technologies or market channels, and (4) an ability to capitalize upon new product innovation.

Evidence in support of the foregoing size-efficiency-cost relationships can be inferred from data showing that productivity gains in a number of highly visible, corporate-dominated industries have consistently been above the total private sector average of 3.0 percent over the 1950–1973 period. For example, during the 1947–1972 period the rates of gain in output per man-hour (all employees) averaged 5.7 percent in petroleum refining, 4.0 percent in tires and inner tubes, 4.7 percent in primary aluminum, 5.4 percent in major household appliances (1958–1972), 3.8 percent in motor vehicles and equipment (1957–1972), 6.3 percent in radio and television sets (1958–1972), 7.7 percent in air transportation, 4.0 percent in pulp and paper, and 6.8 percent in gas and electric utilities. On the small-scale firm side of the ledger, the average annual gain in output per man-hour (all employees) was 3.3 percent in canning and preserving (1947–1971), 2.4 percent in bakery products (1947–1972), 1.4 percent in footwear (1947–1972), –0.7 percent in hospitals and clinics (1967–1973), 2.2 percent in ready-mixed concrete (1960–1971), 2.2 percent in gray iron foundries (1954–1972), and 5.3 percent in hosiery (1947–1972).

At the same time, as compared to small-scale firms, corporate employees typically earn above-average wages and have attractive fringe benefit packages. This is partly because larger productivity gains in corporate enterprises have allowed the payment of higher wages and fringes as a matter of course, and partly, no doubt, because strong unions in the corporate sector have been modestly successful in "expropriating" a portion of the corporation's market power and scale advantages for the benefit of rank-and-file employees. Even so, there is scant evidence that greater payroll costs per employee have endangered the giant firm's long-term ability to compete. Indeed, operating losses, low or negative rates of return, and corporate bankruptcy are of an isolated and short-term variety.

CORPORATE PRICES

Despite the lack of separate price index data for giant corporations, several indications of socially-beneficial price behavior can be found in the corporate sector. In a recent study of industrial prices the author found that BLS price indexes for thirty-one product categories where large corporations are the dominant sellers rose more slowly on the average over the 1947–1973 period than did the price indexes of twenty-nine small firm-dominated product groups. Figure 1 depicts a sampling of price behavior in large-firm versus small-firm markets. The charts are based on the annual average index of prices as reported in the Consumer Price Index (panels a and b), the Wholesale Price Index (panels c and d), and the Industry-Sector Price Index Series (panels e and f).

In general, the charts in Figure 1 suggest that consumers may have been victimized by higher prices in the corporate sector no more often and perhaps less often than by higher prices in the small business sector. For the product groups shown, corporate prices, for whatever reason, were somewhat less flexible upward and exhibited a flatter trend, especially for the years prior to 1970. Such giant firm-produced products as household appliances, television sets, drugs and pharmaceuticals, home electronic equipment, and synthetic rubber have actually declined. On the other hand, in the small-firm sector there have been sharp rates of price increase, including an eightfold increase in daily hospital rates for semiprivate rooms between 1947 and 1973 and a 60 percent rise in construction repair and maintenance services between 1964 and 1973.

CPI Values
170
160
150
140
130
120
110
100
90
80
70
60
50
40
TV Sets
Household Appliances
New Automobiles
Laundry Soaps and Detergents
Gasoline
'48 '51 '54 '57 '60 '63 '66 '69 '72
Year

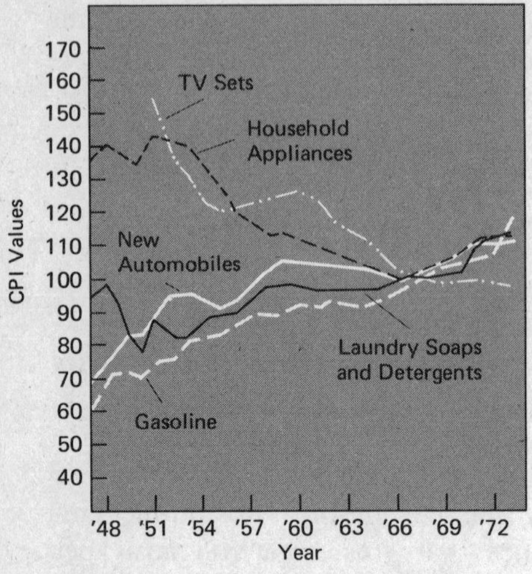

Figure 1a Corporate Price Trends as Reported in BLS Consumer Price Index, 1947–1973

CPI Values
170
160
150
140
130
120
110
100
90
80
70
60
50
40
Daily Hospital Rates, Semiprivate Rooms
Construction Repairs and Maint. Services
Fresh Fruits and Vegetables
Restaurant Meals
Footwear
'48 '51 '54 '57 '60 '63 '66 '69 '72
Year

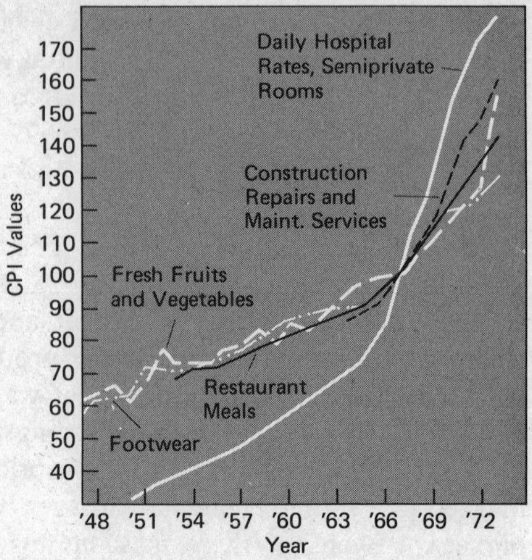

Figure 1b Price Trends in Small-Firm Markets as Reported in BLS Consumer Price Index, 1947–1973

WPI Values
180
170
160
150
140
130
120
110
100
90
80
70
60
50
Refined Petroleum Products
Home Electronic Equip.
Drugs and Pharmaceuticals
Industrial Chemicals
Agricultural Mach. and Equip.
Steel Mill Products
'48 '51 '54 '57 '60 '63 '66 '69 '72
Year

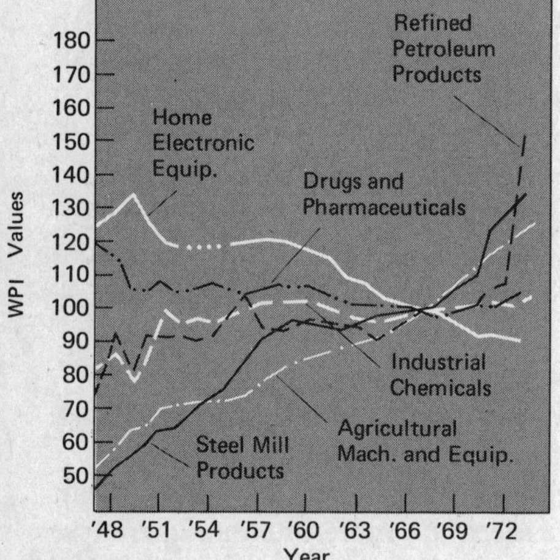

Figure 1c Corporate Price Trends as Reported in BLS Wholesale Price Index, 1947–1973

WPI Values
218.1
180
170
160
150
140
130
120
110
100
90
80
70
60
50
Coal
Meats, Poultry, and Fish
Millwork
Fabricated Structural Metals
Hardware
'48 '51 '54 '57 '60 '63 '66 '69 '72
Year

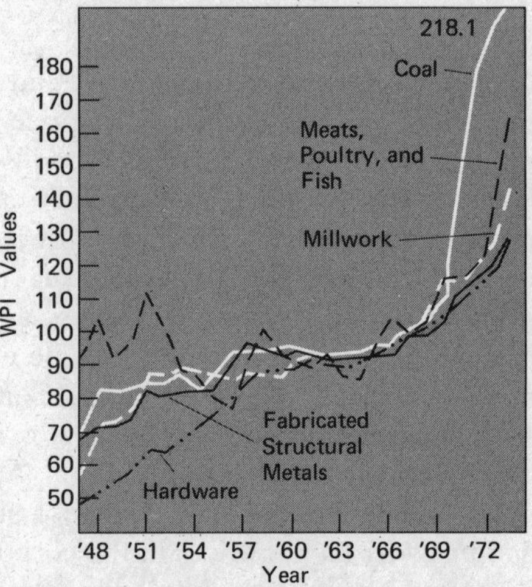

Figure 1d Price Trends in Small-Firm Markets as Reported in BLS Wholesale Price Index, 1947–1973

Figure 1 Comparative Price Trends in Corporate-Dominated and Small-Firm–Dominated Markets

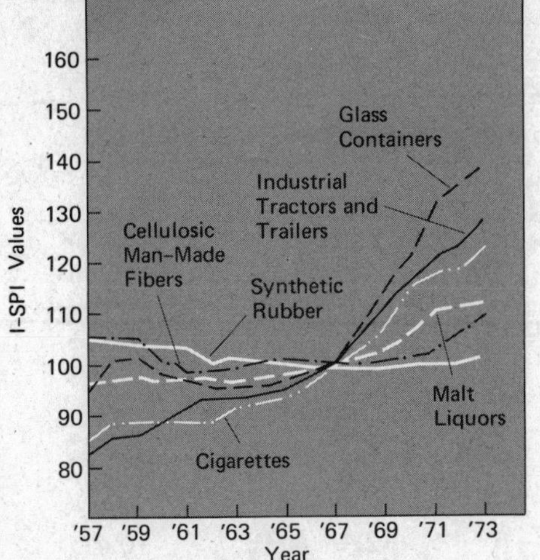

Figure 1e Corporate Price Trends as Reported in BLS Industry-Sector Price Index Series, 1957–1973

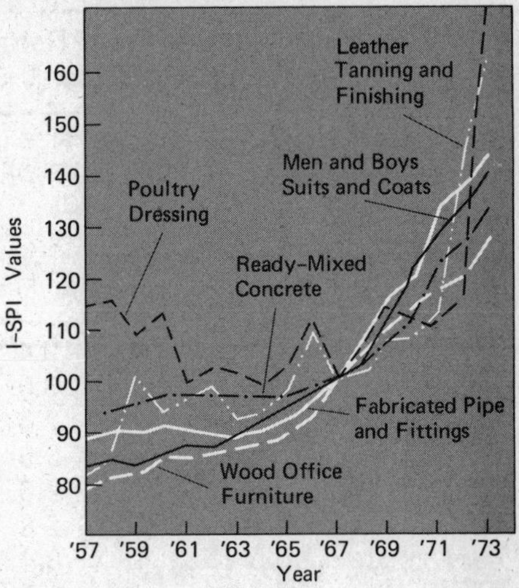

Figure 1f Price Trends in Small-Firm Markets as Reported in BLS Industry-Sector Price Index Series, 1957–1973

The price trends in Figure 1 thus cast doubt on the thesis that giant corporations are disproportionate instigators of inflation owing to their excessive market power. On the contrary, it would appear that many giant firms have been surprisingly successful in containing production costs and holding prices down.

One explanation for superior corporate price performance is that an environment of dynamic uncertainty generates long-term competitive pressures of a nature sufficient to cause large firms to undertake the achievement of secular çost and price reductions. In other words, oligopolistic competition among giant enterprises exhibits a tendency to be "dynamically competitive" even though it is not "statically competitive" to the same extent as market capitalism.

CORPORATE PROFITS

A final measure of the effectiveness of competition in the corporate sector derives from whether large size begets "excess" profits. Certainly, the average citizen is prone to surmise from the headline-capturing dollar amount of profit reported by giant firms that corporate profits are "excessive." On the whole, however, the profit rates of the largest corporations are comparable to the rates of return earned by lesser-sized firms. Table 2 shows that during the 1958–1973 period the after-tax rates of return on stockholder's equity for the *Fortune 500* firms ranged from a low of 9.5 percent to a high of 13.7 percent. This is within the 6.6–14.0 percent range of

Table 2 Profits and Rates of Return for *Fortune's 500* as Compared to All Other Manufacturing Firms, 1958–1973

Year	AFTER-TAX PROFITS AS A PERCENTAGE OF SALES REVENUE		RATES OF RETURN ON STOCKHOLDER'S EQUITY	
	500 Largest Corporations	All Other Mfg. Firms	500 Largest Corporations	All Other Mfg. Firms
1958	5.4	2.4	9.5	6.6
1959	6.1	3.0	11.0	8.9
1960	5.7	2.6	10.1	7.2
1961	5.6	2.5	9.6	7.2
1962	5.9	2.6	10.6	7.8
1963	6.0	2.8	11.1	8.4
1964	6.5	3.4	12.1	10.4
1965	6.7	3.9	13.0	13.0
1966	6.6	4.0	13.2	14.0
1967	6.0	3.5	11.8	11.6
1968	6.0	3.5	12.2	11.7
1969	5.5	3.4	11.5	11.4
1970	4.7	2.8	9.6	8.6
1971	4.7	3.6	9.8	10.7
1972	5.0	3.0	10.9	9.8
1973	5.8	2.7	13.7	10.3

Source: Derived from statistics cited in *The Economic Report of the President*, 1974, p. 336 and *The Fortune Directory of the 500 Largest Corporations*, 1958–1973

return on equity realized by all other manufacturing firms, although the sixteen-year average for the *Fortune 500* firms is slightly higher—11.2 percent to 9.8 percent.

The after-tax profits per dollar of sales revenue for the *Fortune 500* firms have consistently averaged 5.0 to 6.5 cents as compared to 2.5 to 4.0 cents per dollar of sales for all other manufacturing firms (see Table 2). The somewhat larger difference in profits per dollar of sales, but the more equal rate of return on stockholder's equity, stems from large corporations' significantly greater amounts of invested capital per dollar of sales. During the 1958–1973 period, for example, the total invested capital of the *Fortune 500* firms was an average of three times the size of the combined invested capital of the remaining 300,000-plus manufacturing firms. In other words, *Fortune 500* firms had about $1 in invested capital for each $2 worth of goods sold, whereas all other industrial firms had an average investment of only 67¢ for each $2 worth of goods sold.

Figures 2 and 3 provide a more penetrating picture of profit-size relationships. Rates of return on stockholder's equity, though varying by as much as 100 percent from one asset size to another in 1960, have shown a sur-

Figure 2 Rates of Return on Stockholder's Equity for U.S. Manufacturing Firms by Asset Size, 1960–1973

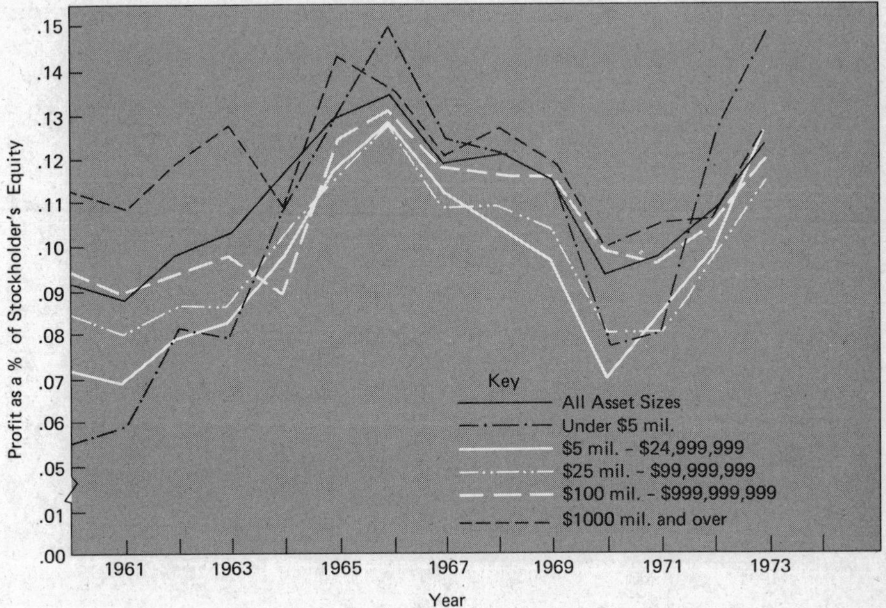

Source: Derived from data in *Quarterly Financial Report For Manufacturing Corporations*, 1960–1973

prising convergence during the last sixteen years to a figure near 12 percent. As of 1973, return on equity was within a narrow 11.5–12.5 percent for all asset sizes with the exception of those firms under $5 million and they, interestingly enough, had an average return on equity in 1973 of nearly 15 percent. If anything, the profit trends in Figure 2 suggest that competition in the corporate sector is becoming more intense and more effective, rather than less so. Otherwise, one would expect to see persistently higher rates of profitability among larger, and allegedly more powerful, firms than among smaller firms—and such does not appear to be the case.

However, it is true, as Figure 3 depicts, that there is a clear and remarkably consistent tendency for profits per dollar of sales to be positively related to a firm's asset size. But even here the range of profitability has been narrowing—from 1.5¢ to 8.1¢ in 1960 to 3.2¢ to 5.8¢ in 1973—rather than widening. Since the returns on equity are so similar among firms of all asset sizes, then the gap between profits/dollar of sales can be attributed to differences in capital intensity rather than to differences in market power. Consequently, according to available profit indices, the competitive forces of corporate capitalism appear on the average to be strong enough to keep corporate profits in line with those earned by firms in supposedly "more competitive" (or atomistic) markets.

Figure 3 Profits as a Percent of Sales for U.S. Manufacturing Firms by Asset Size, 1960–1973

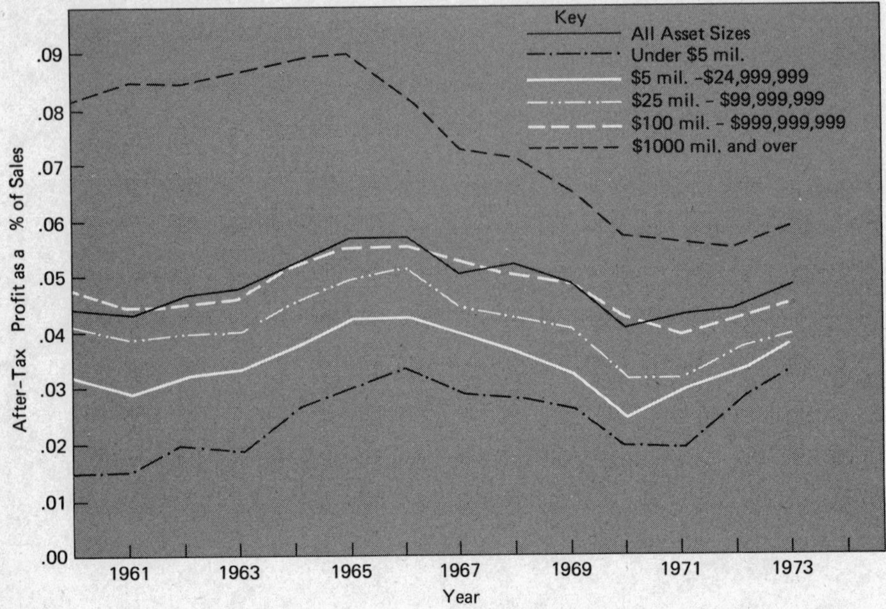

Source: Derived from data in *Quarterly Financial Report For Manufacturing Corporations*, 1960–1973

A PERSPECTIVE VIEW OF GIANT SIZE

In the final analysis, the case for corporate capitalism and corporate giantism boils down to a matter of trade-offs between the short run and the long run. When the standards for judging market performance are geared to the size of profit margins, market share considerations, and the presence of price competition, then there is merit to claims that a more atomistically competitive environment might improve market performance. Certainly, from a short-term perspective, having more competitors with less market power and with more motive to compete on price can yield positive social value.

In industries where technical progress and productivity gains are a function of large size (at least up to some threshold size), then oligopolistic forms of corporate capitalism can offer greater social potential. In such cases, society will be better off over the long term with markets comprised of firms able to exploit the full range of size-related advantages (even if corporate prices do yield above-average profits) than it will be with atomistic competition where markets are "freer" and profit margins thinner. Indeed, the arithmetic of long-term performance makes the argument for bigness quite decisive (despite gaps and contradictions in the accumulated evidence) except for two things. One, large size breeds an uncomfortable, and sometimes politically tenuous, concentration of power and, two, the competitive character of corporate capitalism does not offer society as reliable protection against abuses of market power and anticompetitive practices as does market capitalism.

As a consequence, any public policy "solution" to the problems of corporate power and bigness comes down to whether the long-term advantages of size are deemed sufficient to outweigh the short-term advantages of more competition (as measured by numbers of firms) and deconcentration of markets. As of now, there is no a priori method for predicting which way the economic scales will tilt on this trade-off, nor is a reliable formula-like yardstick in the offing. This is because the advantages of bigness tend to be variable among products and technologies and because, on some occasions at least, oligopoly has proven to be highly competitive even in the short term (as in the semiconductor industry). Legislating across-the-board standards or limits to size such as those proposed in the Industrial Reorganization Act would thus appear to be inferior to a policy of evaluating bigness on a firm-by-firm basis.

The immediate problem, however, rests with developing valid measures of long-term market performance and giving them the credibility and acceptance which the short-term measures of price competition, profits, and market shares have come to have. With the debate over bigness growing, the time is propitious for both corporations and independent analysts to begin to measure and evaluate the contributions of large size to increased technological progress, faster gains in productivity, improved access to scale economies, flatter (or even downsloping) price trends, a higher quality of consumption, and rising living standards. Otherwise, when the time comes in the not too distant future for Congress to once again scrutinize the legitimacy of giant-sized firms, corporate executives may not be armed with the facts necessary to deflect the course of antitrust policy from the path of divestiture and dissolution.

> With the rise of the modern corporation, the emergence of the organization required by modern technology and planning and the divorce of the owner of the capital from control of the enterprise, the entrepreneur no longer exists as an individual person in the mature industrial enterprise. Everyday discourse, except in the economics textbooks, recognizes this change. It replaces the entrepreneur, as the directing force of the enterprise, with management. This is a collective and imperfectly defined entity; in the large corporation it embraces chairman, president, those vice presidents with important staff or departmental responsibility, occupants of other major staff positions and, perhaps, division or department heads not included above. It includes, however, only a small proportion of those who, as participants, contribute information to group decisions. This latter group is very large; it extends from the most senior officials of the corporation to where it meets, at the outer perimeter, the white and blue collar workers whose function is to conform more or less mechanically to instruction or routine. It embraces all who bring specialized knowledge, talent or experience to group decision-making. This, not the management, is the guiding intelligence—the brain—of the enterprise. There is no name for all who participate in group decision-making or the organization which they form. I propose to call this organization the Technostructure.
>
> From the book THE NEW INDUSTRIAL STATE, by John Kenneth Galbraith. Reprinted by permission of Houghton Mifflin Company, Boston.

QUESTIONS

1. What, according to Thompson, are the major criticisms of the power of large corporations? From the readings in the chapter, and your own thinking, what additional criticisms would you suggest can be levied at large corporations? Are they justified?
2. Have the general responses in defense of large companies been effective in combating these allegations?
3. What, according to Thompson, are the major differences between "corporate capitalism" and "market capitalism"?
4. Thompson sets forth major measures of "effective competition." What are they? Do you agree or disagree with them?
5. Argue pro and con the following propositions:
   a. "Effective competition can only exist when concentration is absent in industry."
   b. "Technological innovation and new product innovation are likely to be greater in areas where large corporations are dominant than in areas where they are absent."
   c. "Giant firms tend to be less efficient and productive than smaller ones."

d. "Large companies are a disproportionate source of price inflation owing to their market power."
e. "Profits in large companies are excessive compared with the average manufacturing company."

6. Should we try to return to market capitalism?
7. What is Galbraith's "technostructure"? (See box.) Is there really such a unified and monolithic group that makes decisions in large corporations? (See Neil H. Jacoby, "Professor Galbraith's *The New Industrial State,*" *California Management Review,* Spring 1968; and Irving Kristol, "Professor Galbraith's *New Industrial State,*" *Fortune,* July 1967.)
8. Assuming that Thompson's economic arguments defending large companies are accepted, are there possibly psychological, social, political, or philosophical objections to large enterprises? Argue the case for and against large companies from these points of view.

THE BUSINESSMAN'S SHRINKING PREROGATIVES

PAUL A. SAMUELSON

Paul A. Samuelson, professor of economics, Massachusetts Institute of Technology and the 1970 Nobel prize winner for economic science, briefly explains in the following article how business power is becoming more limited.

It is obvious that in the years ahead, the so-called private corporation will find itself increasingly subjected to external constraints never dreamed of at the Harvard Business School. Not only will the corporation president find he cannot follow policies that will pollute the atmosphere; he will also discover that hundreds of traditional ways of making business decisions will simply no longer be available to him. Society will expand business's responsibilities and take increasing part in deciding how they are to be met.

What will be the new framework within which business decision-making will have to operate? How will the new way of life affect growth in national product and distribution of incomes among the social classes?

Confident and detailed forecasting is quite impossible in so cosmic an area as this. The economist who has studied the econometric patterns of past GNP growth can often predict with some assurance that a particular region is on the brink of a vigorous expansion or is nearing an epoch of relative stagnation. The general laws of technology, despite what you read in the Sunday supplements, are conservative and regular and fairly predictable in their unfoldings. Not so the social environment. It takes a seer and a prophet to pinpoint the changes in this sphere. Alas, even a child's re-reading of history will show the seers and prophets of the past lacked genuine sorcerer's hats. Neither Karl Marx nor Henry Adams nor Oswald Spengler have been at all near the mark in their prognostications.

Although I shall not rush in where they were brave to tread, I think it is useful to speculate, to let hypotheses well up freely, unrestrained by inhibitory criticisms. The critical testings of experience and analysis will reject and elect among the many possibilities.

PROPHET OF DOOM

Almost thirty years ago, Joseph Schumpeter, in his *Capitalism, Socialism and Democracy,* predicted the shape of things to come after the second

Paul A. Samuelson, "The Businessman's Shrinking Prerogatives." Reprinted from *Business and Society Review,* Spring 1972, Number 1, Copyright 1972, Warren, Gorham, and Lamont, Inc. 210 South Street, Boston, Massachusetts.

world war. "Capitalism in an oxygen tent"—that, in a nutshell, was his vision of the timid new world. Such a capitalism, he thought, could linger on for quite a while. But he did not really expect the hospital invalid to perform with the vigor that the youthful capitalism had, in his view, prior to the first world war.

Schumpeter was dead wrong. In the two decades since his death, the modern mixed economy has surpassed in performance classical capitalism at its finest hour. The miracle is not that Japan's economy has been growing for two decades at better than 9 percent per annum in real terms—remarkable as that performance has been. The miracle is that all over the Western world, whether in cynical Austria, effete France, mercurial Italy, or complacent America, real growth rates and average living standards have strongly and steadily outperformed the most daring predictions that could have been made by any objective observer of the years between the two world wars.

The developing countries—once called "backward countries" but which can, in plain truth, be called poor countries—have generally speaking not grown as rapidly economically as the more technologically advanced nations. The widening gap is sad to observe and ominous to contemplate. But it is insufficiently realized that the divergence is not the result of poor performance by the developing nations as compared to either their own pasts or the pasts of the affluent nations at earlier stages of development. Rather it is the mushrooming affluence of the technologically advanced nations that is placing them further out front. Actually, the 1960s saw most of the world's low-income regions grow at rates more rapid than those which generally prevailed in the years of high capitalism, when Queen Victoria reigned in Balmoral Castle and Calvin Coolidge dozed in the White House.

PREMATURE TIMING

Was, however, Schumpeter's error merely a case of premature timing? For there are unquestionably parts of the world where material progress has been slow. Witness the miracle of almost negligible economic growth in Latin America. And not even those most sympathetic to the ideals of socialism can find much to cheer about in the lack of economic progress in societies newly freed from colonial rule. What Nkrumah or Nasser or Nehru were able to accomplish under the banner of rational social planning has, in the short run, been disappointing. To the satirist, it is not a case of business in an oxygen tent as much as business in bedlam.

Although I am not an expert on Latin America, I cannot reject the suggestion that the slow growth of Argentina or of Uruguay (the one-time "Switzerland of South America") or of pre-Allende Chile is related to the fact that these societies are neither fish nor fowl, nor good red herring.

They place social demands on industry that industry simply cannot effectively meet. Antipathy toward the corporation and the bourgeois way of life has served to hamstring performance. It is nonsense to continue to blame the dictator Peron for a stagnation in the Argentinian economy which has prevailed in the decades since he lost office. But it is not nonsense to infer that the populist imperatives upon which Peron so skillfully played have a pivotal role in explaining the miracle of Argentinian stagnation. There is a dictum attributed to Lenin to the effect that we will ruin the capitalist system by debauching its currency. That is not a very intelligent way to hurt an economic system and advance the day of successful revolution. By contrast, there are few better ways to ruin a modern mixed economy than to insist on 40 to 70 percent increases in money wage rates within a brief period of time. This, to a degree, has happened time and time again in the unhappy economic history of Latin America.

SHRINKING BUSINESS PREROGATIVES

It is thus interesting to note some new forces developing in the wealthier nations. New demands for greater social responsibility are being made of business. At the same time, the principal old demands—ever greater productivity and higher living standards for all—continue to be strongly pressed, perhaps even more so than at any time in the past.

In the face of the rising tide of social concern, some business strengths may be lost. Of course, there will always be sacrifices that are well worth making if on balance the common good is advanced. I am not concerned with the fact that zoning ordinances and taxes on effluence will undoubtedly prevent the corporation of the future from polluting the environment. Of course that will happen. But when it does, it will not be so much a case of losing old legitimate corporate freedoms as being required for the first time to follow good practices. Society and the Promethean business giants will be the better for such fetters.

I am interested, however, in contemplating the restrictions which may be placed on the exercise of previously accepted prerogatives. For example, in the United States, management cannot always shut down an unprofitable textile plant and throw its labor force out of work so that the firm can move to a more congenial environment where net labor costs are lower. In Northern Italy, corporations are not always free to trim their labor forces as their efficiency experts would desire. Collective bargaining takes place over the numbers to be employed as well as wage rates, fringe benefits, and severance pay. There may be a problem here. It is not that my heart bleeds for the corporation, but that one realizes that consumers and the earners of real wages also have a stake in the avoidance of dead-weight-loss practices.

SOCIETY'S POWER

At any rate, the line between rational concern and paranoia is a fine one. I have no wish to conjure up hobgoblins to terrify the denizens of the executive suite. I shall content myself with one last example of new pressures on corporations.

Ralph Nader is a social force of primary significance. The movement with which his name is associated represents much more than "mere consumerism," although that movement will itself be of increasing importance in the years to come. Naderism involves participatory democracy on the part of the workers and the public interest. You are naive if you look only at the number of proxy votes the Nader movement is able to mobilize against management. Even if foundations and universities are increasingly persuaded to cast their votes against management, it will be scores of years before opposition votes now 3 and 5 percent become majority votes of 51 percent.

The leverage of such movements is not to be found inside the corporate ballot box, but in the minds of men. Once the public comes to believe that what is deemed good by General Motors is no longer good for the public, they will not wait for victory in the voting of shares and proxies. *They will strike directly by legislation.*

Let me illustrate. A group at the Yale Law School recently came up with the ingenious suggestion presented in an article in the *Yale Law Journal,* that the antitrust division of the Justice Department prevent by legal action the large auto companies from introducing substantial annual or semiannual model changes. This pattern of contrived obsolescence, which Alfred P. Sloane Jr. innovated to help bring General Motors to its present size and prominence, is said by the Yale reformers to constitute unfair competition and to promote monopolistic imperfection of markets.

At first glance, one might tend to dismiss such proposals as utopian and no real threat to existing corporate hegemony. But often, quite often, criticism prompts some governmental response which can lead to change—even if only through the reaction of an industry to such attention.

I can recall that years of criticism by economists like myself of the monopolistically imposed minimum brokerage rates of the New York Stock Exchange got absolutely nowhere. Yet when the Department of Justice entered the fray with an announcement that it intended to bring antitrust suits against this anomalous practice, it was only a short time until the New York Stock Exchange and the Securities and Exchange Commission drastically modified the industry's practices.

We must resolve many competing demands. Business is being challenged and society shapes business's ability to respond. Can we tread a path that will avoid the excesses of private greed and narrow-minded management on the one hand and the debilitating destruction of all business prerogatives on the other? We have within our grasp a system that can meet the legitimate demands made upon it now and in the future.

4 CHANGING SOCIAL VALUES AND THE BUSINESS ROLE

BUSINESS AND THE CHANGING SOCIETY

GEORGE CABOT LODGE

George Cabot Lodge, professor of business administration, Harvard Business School, believes that

> we are in the process of changing a number of the fundamental ideologies and values underlying our socio-economic system and that business managers must be aware of them.

His views on this subject are contained in the following article. For a more complete treatment of this subject, see his book *The New American Ideology* published by Alfred A. Knopf, New York, 1975.

The United States is in the midst of one of the great transformations of Western civilization. Like many other managers, the chief executive of General Motors [Richard C. Gerstenberg] feels the quakes:

> I am concerned about a society that has demonstrably lost confidence in its institutions—in the government, in the press, in the church, in the military —as well as in business.

What is happening is that the old ideas and assumptions, which once made our great institutions legitimate, authoritative, and confident, are fast eroding. They are slipping away in the face of a changing reality and are being replaced by different ideas and different assumptions, which are as yet ill-formed, contradictory, and shocking. The transition is neither good nor bad; there is the possibility of plenty of both. The point is that it is taking place.

It it hard for managers, especially those in large corporations, to operate in an environment in which the old ideas no longer seem to work. If these new ideas were well defined, it would be difficult enough for managers—and for all of us—to cope with them; but since they are still plastic, unfamiliar, and disruptive, we are baffled—and perhaps afraid.

We need to stand back and look at the whole body of our problems and not merely at the dilemmas and questions each one presents to us individually —we must look at the forest, now, instead of the trees. It behooves managers to clear their heads, to inspect all old assumptions, to identify as precisely as possible what is happening and what new ideas and definitions of values are germinating, and then to look objectively at the choices that remain.

This is not an easy thing to do. The old ideas are hard to let go; they have

George Cabot Lodge, "Business and the Changing Society," *Harvard Business Review,* March–April 1974, pp. 59–72.

glorious associations for us, springing as they have from the revolutions against hierarchical medievalism of the sixteenth and seventeenth centuries. It is difficult also because the old ideas are what in many cases have made legitimate the seats of power. They justify the status quo. Nobody likes to look at the weakness beneath him.

But the stakes are high. Some institutions may be able to adapt to the incoming ideology, and survive and prosper. Others may have to look outside the United States for more hospitable surroundings where the old ideas are still acceptable. Still other institutions will be shaken apart, and they are beginning to know it; but they are paralyzed, unwilling or unable to change or move. Why?

OUR INSTITUTIONS ARE SPINNING THEIR WHEELS

As I write this, the nation's economy is at full throttle. Sales, profits, and production have never been greater. But there is an unease, a certain absence of control and direction with which the economists cannot reckon. We have lost confidence in ourselves and the world knows it:

The decline of the dollar is a measure of our loss.
Food and fuel are in short supply.
The malaise on the assembly line continues.
The trade-off mechanisms through which we balance energy, policy, technology, transportation, economic growth, and ecological integrity are not functioning.
The structures of government are bloated and inefficient, manipulated by powerful interest groups whose clear-cut ends seem to justify any means.
Opinion polls confirm Gerstenberg's perception of declining confidence in our political leadership; and each day's newspaper brings to each of us new revelations of illegality by business and government leaders.

Thus an ominous self-doubt prevails, a fear that we are moving inexorably away from old, familiar moorings and sailing off, for all we are worth, into an unknown sea of storms. We need a chart, a plan, to find our way. But whom can we trust to draw the plan and mark the course?

There is a propensity in times like these to blame the devils and praise the angels. Some are even tempted to welcome the ruin and destruction of the old, blindly hoping to find the good and reliable in the purity of the ashes.

But neither praise nor blame nor ruin is the answer. We need new social and political constructs that (a) clearly embrace our economic and technological activities and (b) allow for the development of a new sense of community. But what should these constructs be?

In essence, they must weave together for us a new system of definitions for the ancient values—survival, justice, creativity, self-respect, and the like. All communities everywhere have treasured these values; they are timeless and essentially noncontroversial. It is the definitions of such values that vary from time to time and place to place.

For example, in ancient Egypt, justice and self-respect involved lugging stones to memorialize Pharaoh's transition to the next life. And in modern China, these same values are fulfilled by total service to the community and the nation.

Our own definitions are quite different; but they are also fuzzy and contradictory. The proof of this statement is the fact that we have lost our sense of what "ought to be"—we have lost the sense of direction that would allow us to answer the questions being raised about our society today:

> By what criteria will we measure our progress?
> What is the good community?
> How many people should it have?
> Where should they live?
> What do they need?
> What are their rights?

There are no pragmatic answers to questions such as these. Ad hoc experimentalism of the kind to which we have become addicted constitutes floundering from crisis to crisis. The need for broad conceptions has become essential.

They may come, as they have so often in the past, with cruelty, bloodshed, repression, and waste. They may come humanely, efficiently, and with a maximum of liberty, as they have relatively seldom. If we perceive the nature of our crisis sooner rather than later and do not shrink from its implications, however threatening to existing assumptions and interests those implications may be, the chances will increase that our transition from our old ideology to a new ideology will be relatively benign.

But if we wait, confident of somehow muddling through, we shall lurch from crisis to crisis until large-scale depression and disruption cause us to welcome the orderly relief of dictatorship.

IDEOLOGY AS CONNECTIVE TISSUE . . .

One great difficulty we have in facing up to this problem of ideological transition is that we have always thought of ourselves as a pragmatic people that does what needs to be done to meet the requirements of the time. We have supposed that ideology is something we left behind in Europe with our ancestors—a theoretical bag of confusion that trammeled up socialism and communism and the other "isms," from which hardheaded Americans are happily free.

This, of course, is nonsense. We are just as deeply imbued with ideology as any other community—probably more so. We sometimes call it Americanism. It is the basis of our motivation, our national "collective unconscious." To assert that we are free of it is as absurd as to assert that a true man exists who does not have a subconscious mind.

. . . IN THE OLD BODY

Our traditional ideology is not at all hard to identify. It is composed of five great ideas that first came to America in the eighteenth century, having been set down in seventeenth century England as "natural" laws by John Locke, among others. These ideas found a particularly fertile soil in the vast, underpopulated wilderness of America and served us well for a hundred years or so. They are now in an advanced state of erosion.

INDIVIDUALISM

This is the atomistic notion that the community is no more than the sum of the individuals in it. It is the idea that fulfillment lies in an essentially lonely struggle in what amounts to a wilderness where the fit survive—and where, if you do not survive, you are somehow unfit. Closely tied to individualism is the idea of *equality,* in the sense implied in the phrase "equal opportunity," and the idea of *contract,* the inviolate device by which individuals are tied together as buyers and sellers. In the political order in this country, individualism evolved into *interest group pluralism,* which became the preferred means of directing society.

PROPERTY RIGHTS

Traditionally, the best guarantee of individual rights was held to be the sanctity of property rights. By virtue of this concept, the individual was assured freedom from the predatory powers of the sovereign.

COMPETITION

Adam Smith most eloquently articulated the idea that the uses of property are best controlled by each individual proprietor competing in an open market to satisfy individual consumer desires.

THE LIMITED STATE

In reaction to the powerful hierarchies of medievalism, the conviction grew that the least government is the best government. We do not mind how big government may get, but we are reluctant to allow it authority or focus. And whatever happens the cry is, "Don't let it plan—particularly down there in Washington. Let it just be responsive to crises and to interest groups. Whoever pays the price can call the tune."

SCIENTIFIC SPECIALIZATION & FRAGMENTATION

This is the corruption of Newtonian mechanics which says that, if we attend to the parts, as experts and specialists, the whole will take care of itself.

There are a number of powerful American myths associated with these ideas: John Wayne as the frontiersman; rags to riches with Horatio Alger; and, most fundamentally, *the myth of material growth and progress.*

Implicit in individualism is the notion that man has the will to acquire power, that is, to control external events, property, nature, the economy, politics, or whatever. Under the concept of the limited state, the presence of this will in the human psyche meant the guarantee of progress through competition, notably when combined with the Darwinian notion that the inexorable processes of evolution are constantly working to improve on nature.

Scientific specialization has been part of this "progress," fragmenting knowledge and society while straining their adaptability. This splintering has brought us at least one hideous result: an amoral view of progress "under which nuclear ballistic missiles definitely represent progress over gunpowder and cannonballs, which in turn represent progress over bows and arrows." This treacherous myth places no apparent limit on the degree to which man can gain dominion over his environment, nor does it stipulate any other ideological criteria for defining progress.

If we consider the past 6,000 years of human history, we are struck by the extent to which this atomistic, individualistic ideology constitutes a fundamental aberration from the historically typical communitarian norm. It stands as a radical experiment that achieved its most extreme manifestation in America in the nineteenth century. Since that time it has been steadily deteriorating in the face of various challenges—wars, depressions, new economic and political systems, the concentration and growth of populations, and institutional as well as environmental degeneration.

. . . & IN THE NEW

Institutions that depended on the traditional ideas for their legitimacy—notably the large corporations—have thus become unmoored. It is now important to determine what new ideas are moving in as "legitimizers" so that more fitting institutional forms and structures can be created. Here are my own impressions.

1

Individual Fulfillment Occurs Through Participation in an Organic Social Process. The community as conceived today is indeed more than the sum of the individuals in it. It has special and urgent needs, and the survival and the self-respect of the individuals in it depend on the recognition of those needs. There are few who can get their kicks à la John Wayne, although many try. Individual fulfillment for most depends on a place in a community, an identity with a whole, a participation in an organic social process. And further:

If the community, the factory, or the neighborhood is well designed, its members will have a sense of identity with it. They will be able to make maximum use of their capacities.

If it is poorly designed, people will be correspondingly alienated and frustrated.

In the complex and highly organized America of today, few can live as Locke had in mind.

Both corporations and unions have played leading roles in the creation of the circumstances which eroded the old idea of individualism and created the new. But invariably they have been ideologically unmindful of what they have done. Therefore, they have tended to linger with the old forms and assumptions even after those have been critically altered:

A central component of the old notion of individualism is the so-called protestant ethic: hard work, thrift, delayed gratification, and obedience to authority. Business has extolled these virtues on the production side of things even as it has systematically undercut them on the marketing side. Advertising departments spend millions reminding us that the good life entails immediate gratification of our most lurid desires, gratification which we can buy now and pay for later. Leisure and luxury are touted as the hallmark of happiness.

Similarly, the assembly worker has been led to believe by management, parents, and TV that the old idea of individual fulfillment is valid. But he finds himself constrained in an inescapable work setting dramatically unlike anything that he has been led to expect. He is liable to strike out, perhaps violently. Or he may join the absentee lists, taking Fridays and Mondays off to eke out some spurious individualism via drugs, drink, old movies, or—if he is lucky—a walk in the hills.

Paradoxically, such behavior puzzles both management and unions. They linger with the traditional individualistic idea of the contract long after the contract has ceased being individualistic and has become "collective," unmindful of the irrelevance of the individual labor contract to the communitarian problems at hand.

Our former social policy attempted to guarantee that each worker have equal opportunity. The young lawyers enforcing equal employment legislation, however, have taken quite a different tack. In the case of AT&T, for example, they argued that discrimination had become institutionalized; it

> had become endemic to the AT&T community, and women, for example, had been slotted into certain tasks.

When this kind of argument is being accepted, it is no longer necessary to prove individual discrimination in order to get redress.

The government then moved to change the makeup of the whole of AT&T so as to provide, in effect, for *equality of representation* at all levels. Without any specific charge having been brought, the company in turn agreed to upgrade 50,000 women and 6,600 minority group workers and—perhaps most significantly—to hire 4,000 men to fill traditionally female jobs such as operator and clerk. The company also agreed to pay some $15 million in compensation. Thus the issue became one of *equality of result* not of opportunity; a communitarian idea had superseded an individualistic one.

Given this definition of the issue, the company's task was to redesign itself according to certain overall criteria, in recognition (a) of the fact that individuals are unequal in many important respects and (b) of the dictum that the good organization is one which adapts itself to those inequalities to assure equality of result.

Needless to say, the union at AT&T protested bitterly, since the government's action was a direct threat to the contract which previously had been the device used to resolve inequities in seniority and promotion policies. The company itself has had commensurate difficulty in meshing its old thinking with the specific steps demanded by the representatives of the new ideology. Yet the changes are being forced forward, in one fashion or another, nonetheless.

2
Rights of Membership Are Overshadowing Property Rights.

A most curious thing has happened to private property—it has stopped being very important. After all, what difference does it really make today whether a person *owns* or just *enjoys* property? He may get certain psychic kicks out of owning a jewel or a car or a TV set or a house—but does it really make a difference whether he owns or rents?

Today there is a new right which clearly supersedes property rights in political and social importance. It is the right to survive—to enjoy income, health, and other rights associated with membership in the American community or in some component of that community, including a corporation. As of January 1, 1974, for example, all U.S. citizens who are 65 years old, or blind, or disabled, have had an absolute right to a minimum income of $140 a month. President Nixon's Family Assistance Plan would have guaranteed an income to all. Health legislation guaranteeing medical care to all is likely.

This right derives not from any individualistic action or need; it does not emanate from a contract. It is a communitarian right that public opinion holds to be consistent with a good community. It is a revolutionary departure from the old Lockean conception under which only the fit survive. President Nixon, apparently unaware of what is happening, said once: "If you underwrite everybody's income, you undermine everybody's character." Well, of course, that depends on the definition of self-respect.

The utility of property as a *legitimizing* idea has eroded as well. It is now quite obvious that our large public corporations are not private property at all. The 1,500,000 shareholders of General Motors do not and cannot control, direct, or in any real sense be responsible for "their" company. Furthermore, the vast majority of them have not the slightest desire for such responsibility. They are investors pure and simple, and if they do not get a good return on their investment, they will put their money elsewhere.

Campaign GM and other similar attempts at stockholder agitation represent heroic but naïvely conservative strategies to force shareholders to behave like owners and thus to legitimize corporations as property. But such action is clearly a losing game. And it is a peculiar irony that James Roche, as GM chairman, branded such agitation as radical, as the machinations of "an adversary culture . . . antagonistic to our American ideas of private property and individual responsibility." In truth, of course, *GM is the radical;* Nader et alia were acting as conservatives, trying to bring the corporation back into ideological line.

But, the reader may ask, if GM and the hundreds of other large corporations like it are not property, then what are they? The best we can say is that they are some sort of collective, floating in philosophic limbo, dangerously vulnerable to the charge of illegitimacy and to the charge that they are not amenable to community control. Consider how the management of this nonproprietary institution is selected. The myth is that the stockholders select the board of directors which in turn selects the management. This is not true, however. Management selects the board, and the board, generally speaking, blesses management.

Managers thus get to be managers according to some mystical, circular process of questionable legitimacy. Under such circumstances it is not surprising that "management's rights" are fragile and its authority waning. Alfred Sloan warned us of this trend in 1927:

> There is a point beyond which diffusion of stock ownership must enfeeble the corporation by depriving it of virile interest in management upon the part of some one man or group of men to whom its success is a matter of personal and vital interest. And conversely at the same point the public interest becomes involved when the public can no longer locate some tangible personality within the ownership which it may hold responsible for the corporation's conduct.

We have avoided this profound problem because of the unquestioned effectiveness of the corporate form per se. In the past, when economic growth and progress were synonymous, we preferred that managers be as free as possible from stockholder interference, in the name of efficiency. But today the definition of efficiency, the criteria for and the limitations of growth, and the general context of the corporation are all much less sure. So the myth of corporate property is becoming a vulnerability.

There is no doubt that some means will be found to legitimize the large corporation and to make it responsive to community demands. Several options seem possible:

Effective shareholder democracy might work in small companies.

More comprehensive and intelligent regulation by the state might be a possibility, with respect to public utilities.

Self-management schemes such as those in Europe are being tried by some U.S. companies.

Federal corporate charters that define corporate purpose, management rights, and community authority might be successful "legitimizers."

Finally, there is nationalization, perhaps the most brutish and inefficient way to legitimization. If managers do not take leadership in rebuilding their base of legitimacy, and do it artfully and well, they might as well contemplate the worst of the possibilities.

3
Community Need to Satisfy Consumer Desires Is Replacing Competition as a Means for Controlling the Uses of Property.

It was to the notion of community need that ITT appealed in 1971 when it sought to prevent the Justice Department from divesting it of Hartford Fire Insurance. The company lawyers said, in effect: "Don't visit that old idea of competition on us. The public interest requires ITT to be big and strong at home so that it can withstand the blows of Allende in Chile, Castro in Cuba, and the Japanese in general. Before you apply the antitrust laws to us, the Secretary of the Treasury, the Secretary of Commerce, and the Council of Economic Advisers should meet to decide what, in the light of our balance-of-payments problems and domestic economic difficulties, the national interest is."

Note that here again it was the company arguing the ideologically radical case. The suggestion was obvious: ITT is a partner with the government—indeed with the Cabinet—in defining and fulfilling the communitarian needs of the United States. There may be some short-term doubt about who is the senior partner, but partnership it is. This concept is radically different from the traditional idea underlying the antitrust laws—namely, that the public interest emerges *naturally* from free and vigorous competition among numerous aggressive, individualistic, and preferably small companies attempting to satisfy consumer desires.

In the face of the serious pressures from Japanese and European business organizations, which emanate from ideological settings quite different from our own, there will be more and more reason to set aside the old idea of domestic competition in order to organize U.S. business effectively to meet world competition. Managers will probably welcome if not urge such a step; they may, however, be less willing to accept the necessary concomitant: if, in the name of efficiency, of economies of scale, and of the demands of world markets, we allow restraints on the free play of domestic market forces, then other forces will have to be used to define and preserve the public interest. These "other forces" will amount to greater regulation by the political order, in some form or other.

4
The Role of Government Is Inevitably Expanding.

It follows that the role of the state is changing radically—it is becoming the setter of our sights and the arbiter of community needs. Inevitably, it will take on unprecedented tasks of coordination, priority setting, and planning in the largest sense. It will need to become far more efficient and authoritative, capable of making the difficult and subtle trade-offs which now confront us—for example, between environmental purity and energy supply.

Government is already big in the United States, probably bigger in proportion to our population than even in those countries which we call "socialist." Some 16% of the labor force now works for one or another governmental agency, and by 1980 it will be more. Increasingly, U.S. institutions live on government largess—subsidies, allowances, and contracts to farmers, corporations, and universities—and individuals benefit from social insurance, medical care, and housing allowances. The pretense of the limited state, however, means that these huge allocations are relatively haphazard, reflecting the crisis of the moment and the power of interest groups rather than any sort of coherent and objective plan.

The web of interrelated factors which together constitute the energy crisis is the direct result of governmental "ad hocism" and the lack of an integrated plan.

Significantly, like Franklin Roosevelt before him, President Nixon cloaks his departures from the limited state in the language of the traditional ideology. Seeking to make his massive and increasing (but uncertain) interventions palatable, he has tried to make his motives appear pragmatic, not ideological. But he, like ITT, is the radical in the case: even as he has regularly called us to loyalty to what he terms cherished values (essentially, the Lockean five), he has deliberately acted to subvert these very notions. This is worse than merely confusing because it delays the time when we will recognize the planning functions of the state for what they are and must be.

If the role of government were more precisely and consciously defined, the government could be smaller in size. To a great extent, the plethora of bureaucracies today is the result of a lack of focus and comprehension, an ironic bit of fallout from the old notion of the limited state.

The greatest significance of Watergate is perhaps that it has set back the inevitable trend toward increased executive power and efficiency at a time when we need strong, sound executive leadership more than ever. It is ironic that at this junction Sam Ervin, as pure and noble an embodiment of the Lockean faith as one could imagine, is a national hero. There has not been a hero in America since the turn of the century, and there probably will not be again.

Watergate, however, will have served a most useful purpose if it alerts us to the need for strict and explicit statutory limitations on executive power as we go into a time when that power will necessarily grow.

5
Reality Now Requires Perception of Whole Systems, Not Only the Parts.

Finally, and perhaps most fundamentally, the old idea of scientific specialization has given way to a new consciousness of the interrelatedness of all things. Spaceship earth, the limits of growth, the fragility of our life-supporting biosphere have dramatized the ecological and philosophical truth that everything is related to everything else. Harmony between the works of man and the demands of nature is no longer the romantic plea of conservationists. It is an absolute rule of survival, and thus it is of profound ideological significance, subverting in many ways all of the Lockean ideas.

THE DILEMMA OF PROTEST

But introducing cohesive and organic order into our fractionated world is not painless. It is difficult even for those most intimately involved in the process to see clearly what the real problems are. For example, consider the decline in youth protest—many have remarked on it. What really happened?

The so-called counterculture was rooted in an ideological contradiction which it diligently avoided resolving. It voiced a traditional (if extreme) cry for the full promises of the Enlightenment, individualistic and romantic: "Do your own thing, now, no matter what." It was also, however, a radical call for new communitarian norms governing income distribution, inheritance, harmony with nature, and a new political order. Young people, not surprisingly, were unable to live with such contradiction.

And educational institutions gave them little help in understanding or coping with it. Academic bureaucracies, based on the old idea of specialization, constitute a series of long dark tunnels called disciplines. The best man in each field is at the end of his tunnel, digging an ever-narrowing trench of new knowledge. "If you are diligent you may find him," the student is told, "and if you are persistent you may get him to raise his head and mumble."

Whatever the ultimate value of academic research may be, the student has come to wonder whether this kind of education is what he needs to understand the world—whether, in fact, what is truly important is not what ties the tunnels together and how they are related to one another. What, for example, are the implications of genetics, biology, or psychology for political science, philosophy, and sociology?

If he tries to find out, there are only a few mavericks to hold his hand. It is no wonder that increasing numbers of college seniors have no conception of where they are going to fit. It is also no wonder that increasing numbers of students are dropping out to seek their own integration through direct experience in the world.

Understandable as this reaction may be, it is woefully inefficient. Realizing this fact, the educational bureaucracies are beginning to budge—but no more than that. And hierarchies of the business world are not doing much better.

An Autopsy on Industry

Once General Motors was beautifully harmonious with the community. In 1910, what were to become GM's components were clearly owned by entrepreneurs: Louis Chevrolet and his counterparts at Buick, Oldsmobile, Hyatt Roller Bearings, and so on. Their authority and legitimacy were clear. Young men came out of the hills hungry for work in Detroit; thousands massed outside the hiring gates. Survival was at stake. The rights of property were secure, and the contract which followed from them was authoritative. Mr. Chevrolet offered the terms, and workers took them or left them.

Time passed, and workers demanded more power. They submerged their individualism into an interest group, the United Automobile Workers. Management, acting out of a sense of property rights, resisted. Violence ensued. The UAW finally won, and the contract became collectivized—almost a contradiction in terms, if one thinks of the contract in its pure, individualistic form.

Also, property rights were themselves eroded by becoming a subject for bargaining in an adversary procedure. These rights were further diluted by the emergence of an entirely different type of management, one divorced from ownership. Nevertheless, the structure worked efficiently, and the United States accepted it because of its respect for the automobile and for material growth per se.

Then in the 1960s, the UAW started to splinter, individual locals and individual workers within locals feeling needs which could not be embraced by the already bloated contract. Survival having been assured by the community, the workers began to demand avenues to individual fulfillment in a communitarian setting where it could not be found.

By this time, too, the ownership of GM had become immensely diluted; and today the legitimacy of its function is increasingly suspect. In 1964, Sloan wrote of flying over the countryside, delighting in the "splash of jewel-like color presented by every parking lot." Such a lyrical description falls a bit flat today.

So the legitimacy and power of management, on the one hand, and of the labor contract and thus the union, on the other, have deteriorated. But the hierarchies have barely budged. For a while, company management's answer was to pay workers more for their unhappiness, a recourse suitable to the contractual form. The union hierarchy, on their side, had roughly the same idea—a fatter contract. Absenteeism, sabotage, and lowering productivity have continued, however. Meanwhile, at Toyota, when the night shift goes off duty, it cheers the day shift on to harder and harder work.

This whole syndrome is generic to U.S. industry. Its root is simply that we have outgrown the old ways of doing things. We must now find a new way of doing things, one that accords with present realities and new definitions of values.

THE MANAGER'S MIND

Let me now consider what these five transformations imply for managers—in particular, managers of large, publicly held corporations.

In simplest terms, the manager must form a certain attitude of mind, a willingness to confront manifold change openly and with breadth of vision, not with the heels dug in and the old blinders on. More than ever, he must see his task as a general not a specialized one. He is not an expert; he is an integrator, a synthesizer, responsible for the whole and capable of perceiving the whole, within and without; and he had better recognize the fact.

This requires both courage and hope:

It requires courage, to rinse out the mind and inspect all the assumptions (especially those that underlie his power and legitimize it); to consider the interests of the whole and not merely his own momentary bureaucratic status and prerogatives; to think the unthinkable and discuss it.

It requires hope, not for "the good old days" to return, nor for more ad hoc solutions, but for the potential value of the future. It requires the hope of those who "see and cherish all forms of new life and are ready at every moment to help the birth of that which is ready to be born."

Once the manager has opened his mind fully, he can consider two sets of problems which the changing ideology raises for the large corporation. The first has to do with the internal organization of the corporation and concerns matters of ownership, accountability, and contract. The second has to do with the relationship between the corporation and the communities which it affects: the neighborhood, the city, the state, the nation, and the world.

Then he can focus on the questions that all these problems raise:

Which problems should the corporation resolve and which must be decided by the community?

With respect to community decisions, how are they best made—by government, by consumers, or by interest groups?

If by interest groups, then *how*—by direct (perhaps radical) action, through legislative and legal pressure, or through leverage on the executive branch, as has ITT?

To what extent is dispersion of power a desirable thing politically? As the legitimacy of management has declined, the central government has moved in to control increasing segments of corporate operation. Should corporations try to regain what political edge they have lost?

If dispersion of power is a good thing (which I think it is), how should the corporation encourage the design of more dispersed forms of community legitimization and control, within its own framework and outside it?

This is a valuable exercise, not so much because the manager can always influence the answers directly, but because it helps the manager set out the possibilities for himself. (*Exhibit I* diagrams the context of these questions.)

Directions to Consider

Industry has taken some hesitant steps of its own toward resolving its ideological confusions, some of which are oriented toward minimizing or eliminating the labor contract and replacing it with institutionalized consensus. Somewhat like its Japanese and European counterparts, the U.S. corporation is moving away from the adversary-contractual structure toward a consensual, collective form in which, to put it simply, no one feels left out of anything. As this change occurs, alternatives to property rights are emerging as the way to provide legitimacy and thus authority to management. Here are some vignettes of the change.

FOOD PROCESSING

A plant manufacturing pet food in Topeka, Kansas, is organized into self-managed work teams which are given collective responsibility for large parts of the production process. To accommodate the capabilities and needs of individual workers, assignments of individuals to tasks are subject to team consensus. There is a deliberate attempt to break down division of labor and specialization: "Pay increases are geared to an employee mastering an increasing proportion of jobs first in the team and then in the total plant." All signs are that this plant is extremely productive and profitable.

Note the radical implications of this experiment. In a real sense, the legitimacy and thus the authority of the management of the Topeka plant comes from the workers as a whole, not from some outworn conception of property rights. This fact feeds the workers' sense of fulfillment and thus contributes to the high productivity and profits of the operation.

Exhibit 1 Internal and External Questions Relating to Large Public Corporations

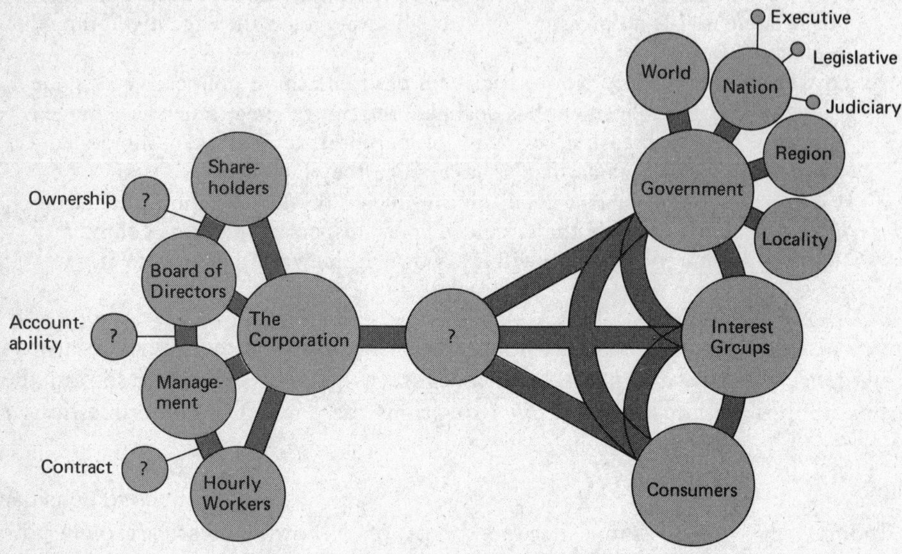

Internal

Traditional ideology has it that the corporation is property; that it is owned by its shareholders; that the owners elect the board of directors; that the board names the managers; that the managers thus have the rights associated with property by "natural" law and, therefore, the right to contract for labor. The contract between management and the union that was once individualistic is now, in general, collective. Every aspect of this sequence is vulnerable.

External

Traditional ideology has it that the fundamental control on the corporation is that exerted by individual consumers in an open market. Circumstances, however, have required the intervention by government into this essential relationship. Traditional ideology, however, has fostered the development of interest groups to pressure government and, lately, as a result of declining confidence in government, to act directly on the corporate-community relationship.

The top management of the company thus faces some excruciating questions:

"Do we extend this idea to other plants—maybe to headquarters itself—to increase ROI, even though it will undercut our jobs?"

"If we do it anyway, what happens to the myth that we are answerable to the board of directors, who represent the shareholders?" (The answer to this one is complicated by the fact that shareholders appear to be getting a better return on their investment from Topeka. Perhaps the management hierarchy, or part of it, *should* be dispensed with.)

It is indeed difficult to open one's eyes to the possibility—the mere possibility—of extinction.

Also, note the threat to the idea of equality when an organization moves to consensus from contract. Each team is responsible for hiring replacements; presumably it selects those who will get along well with the group. If the group objects to certain persons, they will not be hired. Race might be involved. My point is that collectivism can be dehumanizing unless it is controlled by a definite social theory—an ideology.

Moving from contract to consensus obviously threatens unions as well. The Topeka plant is small and new, with an innovative management and no union. To apply the same principles in the automobile or steel or utilities industries, however, raises many problems. All these industries are trying, although in somewhat different ways.

THE AUTO INDUSTRY

The automobile industry is introducing job enrichment and organizational development programs. Union leaders have criticized these efforts as elitist nonsense, as paternalistic attempts to divide the worker from the union. "The better the wage, the greater the job satisfaction," says William Winpisinger, general vice president of the International Association of Machinists. "There is no better cure for blue-collar blues." Company industrial relations officials join Leonard Woodcock of the UAW in attributing "the alienation problem" to academics who do not know what they are talking about.

It is not surprising that labor relations bureaucrats on both sides eye any threat to the contract anxiously, since it is the idea that supports their bureaucracies. Their resistance testifies both to the ideological nature of the problem and to the difficulty of solving it in situations where rigid hierarchies are unwilling to inspect the assumptions beneath them.

STEEL

The steel industry appears to be following a somewhat different route to establishing a basis for consensus. Industry labor relations officials and union leaders have worked out a peace agreement involving a no-strike clause and binding arbitration in the face of the common interest—namely, making U.S. goods more competitive against foreign imports. Although neither side is likely to admit it, such an arrangement is a step toward replacing the idea of contract with that of consensus.

This scheme may have more promise than the organizational development and job enrichment schemes of the automobile industry because it protects directly *all* of those whose power is threatened. Its weakness is that, in itself, it does nothing to give a greater sense of participation to workers on the shop floor. But a recent HEW task force notes that this may be a serious shortcoming: "What workers want most, according to more than 100 studies made in the past 20 years, is to become masters of their immediate environments and to feel that their work and they themselves are important—the twin ingredients of self-esteem."

If consensual systems are going to work, it will be necessary to educate young people according to the new ideology rather than the old. It will also be necessary to hire people who want to become part of a certain whole. No matter how consensual a collective may get, there are going to be boring jobs which will not provide the necessary sense of fulfillment to college graduates, for example. Workers will have to be screened for jobs with the idea of weeding out those whose capacities are *more* as well as *less* than the work requires. This prospect raises ominous specters of Orwellianism and deserves careful watching.

ELECTRIC UTILITIES

For years, the utility companies have tried—successfully—to keep government regulation diffuse. Government has responded by steadfastly failing both to manage our nation's energy needs and to plan a procedure to fulfill them. The result is that many utilities find themselves in a devil of a mess: rates fixed by state agencies, taxed by the cities, partly regulated by the Federal Power Commission, and affected by the Atomic Energy Commission and a host or other local and national governmental entities.

At the same time, the environmental interest groups are grabbing for the utility companies' throats. The Scenic Hudson Preservation Society, for example, successfully kept Consolidated Edison Company of New York from building its pump storage power station at Cornwall on the Hudson River for ten years, and the battle is not entirely over yet. Like great dinosaurs, many public utilities are being bitten to death in a swamp partly of their own making.

The need for federal intervention to plan the future of electric power seems plain. Regional power production jurisdictions should be planned; research on new technologies needs to be increased; technology and site decisions must be made. The problem is far too big and too national in scope to leave to a scattering of private companies.

But this does not mean that these companies should be nationalized. That will be the inevitable result, however, unless more intelligent steps are taken soon. These companies must realize what government, and *only* government, can and must do: plan the allocation of resources and make the critical judgments of costs and benefits. To do this it must intervene with authority and coherence.

ONE'S OWN RESPONSIBILITY

The viewpoint I have laid out in this article has, I hope, triggered some thoughtful responses in the reader. Even if he argues with the way I diagnose our problems, I do not believe he can deny their omnipresence, their interrelation, and their seriousness.

If he can inspect his own ideological assumptions objectively, he may find himself reasoning out a new personal position of his own, one that accords more closely with the realities of the world we live in today than does the hodge-podge of quasi-official ideological notions we have inherited from our ancestors.

Most importantly, this may enable him to perceive more clearly the nature of the crises which abound. The quick and accurate perception of crisis is crucial because it is through the intelligent use of crisis that change occurs most effectively. The central managerial task of the future may well be the use of minimum crisis to cause maximum change with least waste and violence.

Ideological analysis and contemplation also will allow managers to consider how what is best and dearest in the old ideology may be preserved. One ideology obviously builds on another. The glories of the old—the rights of the individual, his dignity, the beautiful efficiency of competition in many areas, the incentives of enterprise and invention—are all in jeopardy. The best of them can be preserved only if we consciously design them into what is coming.

Broad reading can help to provide an understanding of what paths we might take. I also stress that *no* amount of reading, automatically pursued, will broaden the hidebound. The old preconceptions and prejudices must be washed away first, by a conscious effort of a person's will, before he can appreciate, weigh, and evaluate the myriad alternatives we might pursue—alternatives that are, in fact, often articulated by champions of special causes or of ideologies that are foreign, even hostile, to our own.

Why should managers bother? Because they lead corporations, collectively an immensely powerful force. What managers believe affects the way they lead. The effect of a manager's mind on the corporation he works for may be subtle or obvious, but it is always there, directly and indirectly.

Also, managers, taken as a class, are an important and influential group of citizenry. Perhaps the ultimate question they must consider now is whether or not our current procedures for producing political leadership and a vision of the community are sufficient. Can we rely on the Republican and Democratic parties to call forth the leadership this country needs now and in the future? Or do we need a new political movement—avowedly radical—to address openly and forthrightly the unquestionably radical problems of ideological transformation which we confront and to reestablish the confidence which Mr. Gerstenberg rightly says has been lost?

THE EXPECTATION-REALITY GAP

Let us consider the nature of a "social problem." In January 1969 the distinguished Panel on Social Indicators appointed by the Secretary of Health, Education and Welfare reported that, by nearly all measures, the well-being of the American people had improved materially since World War II. Yet it found that public disaffection had also risen markedly. The reason was, it wisely observed, that *people's expectations had risen faster than reality could improve.*

The phenomenon noted by the Panel on Social Indicators was the same as that observed by de Tocqueville in 18th-century France: "The evil which was suffered patiently as inevitable, seems unendurable as soon as the idea of escaping from it crosses men's minds. All the abuses then removed call attention to those that remain, and they now appear more galling. The evil, it is true, has become less, but sensibility to it has become more acute." (See *Toward a Social Report,* U.S. Department of Health, Education and Welfare, Washington, 1969, pp. xi and xii.)

A social problem, then, may be defined as a gap between society's expectations of social conditions and the present social realities. Social expectations are the set of demands and priorities held by the people of a society at a given time. Social realities mean the set of laws, regulations, customs, and organizations, along with the appurtenant economic, political, and social processes, that prevail at a given time.

Social problems are created by public awareness of, or belief in, the existence of an expectation-reality gap. They are basically psychological phenomena—ideas held in the minds of people—about the size of the disparity between what should be, and what is, in our society. Social problems are not definable solely in physical or biological terms, such as so many calories of food intake per day, or so many square feet of housing per capita. They must be defined in terms of the size of the expectation-reality gap.

One may illustrate the independence of a social problem from any particular social condition by considering the example of poverty. Poverty is now perceived by Americans to be an important social problem in the United States, because in 1970 11 percent of the population had incomes under the official poverty level (about $3,500 per year for a family of four), whereas Americans generally believe that no one should live under the poverty line. Poverty was not perceived to be an important social problem in 1947, although 27 percent of the population then lived under the poverty line by 1970 standards. Despite an astonishing gain in the real incomes of those in the lowest brackets, public expectations outraced realities. Hence the expectation-reality gap with respect to poverty is wider today than it was in 1947. The problem of poverty has become more serious at the same time that the incidence of poverty has been cut 60 percent and continues to decline!

Neil H. Jacoby, in George A. Steiner, ed., *Issues in Business and Society.* New York: Random House, 1972, pp. 71–72.

CHANGING MANAGERIAL PRACTICES

There is no doubt that the ways in which things are done in business today, especially in the larger companies, are different from the past because of the changing environment in which business finds itself. Many of the current trends will accelerate. In my presidential speech before the Academy of Management (August 1972) I expressed my position in this regard as follows: ". . . future managerial practices and theory will have changed drastically in response to society's new demands that business improve the quality of life. However, the changes will be evolutionary—rapidly evolutionary—but not revolutionary. We today would recognize the changes in management practices and theories which will take place over the next few decades. The total picture, a decade or two in the future, however, will be substantially different from that of today."

The following table shows a few of the major business practices which are undergoing change and the direction in which they point.

Recent Past Versus Future Managerial Practices

RECENT PAST	TOWARD FUTURE
Assumption that a business manager's sole responsibility is to optimize stockholder wealth	Profit still dominant but modified by the assumption that a business manager has other social responsibilities
Business performance measured only by economic standards	Application of both an economic and social measure of performance
Emphasis on quantity of production	Emphasis on quantity *and* quality
Authoritarian management	Permissive/democratic management
Short-term intuitive planning	Long-range comprehensive structured planning
Entrepreneur	Renaissance manager
Control	Creativity
People subordinate	People dominant
Financial accounting	Financial and human resources accounting
Caveat emptor	Ombudsman
Centralized decision-making	Decentralized and small group decision-making
Concentration in internal functioning	Concentration on external ingredients to company success
Dominance of solely economic forecasts in decision-making	Major use of social, technical, and political forecasts as well as economic forecasts
Business viewed as a single system	Business viewed as a system of systems within a larger social system
Business ideology calls for aloofness from government	Business-government cooperation and convergence of planning
Business has little concern for social costs of production	Increasing concern for internalizing social costs of production

From George A. Steiner, *Business and Society,* 2nd ed. New York: Random House, 1975, p. 104.

QUESTIONS

1. Do you find Lodge's argument that our old values are slipping away convincing? Is this phenomenon a continuing one or a new one?
2. If Lodge is correct, should we be alarmed by the erosion of traditional values or see the process as a beneficial one? Are there certain values that we should be concerned about retaining and others that are more expendable?
3. Can you think of other values not mentioned by Lodge that will have an important impact on business practices when and if they alter?
4. What changes in the structure and/or function of capitalism will likely come about because of the value changes discussed here?
5. Do you agree with Jacoby's definition of a social problem?
6. If Jacoby is correct does this mean that business is likely to be faced with unrealistic expectations?
7. In your judgment do the underlying forces leading to the changing managerial practices (see p. 151) really constitute a new set of "rules of the game" for business?
8. Would you go so far as to say that if businesses really are changing practices (see p. 151), the net result will be a dramatically different functioning of businesses than that of only a few years ago? Explain.

THE QUALITY OF WORKING LIFE

JAMES C. TAYLOR

James C. Taylor, assistant professor of Socio-Technical Systems, Graduate School of Management, University of California at Los Angeles, examines in the following article changing ideas about the quality of working life and implications for managers of organizations.

Interest in improvement of the quality of working life has emerged recently as a dual area of concern. On the one hand, it represents a concern for the need to further increase operational effectiveness, a goal that although prominent in industry for many years has taken on a new dimension recently as our current position in world markets is under challenge. The goal of operational effectiveness has achieved prominence in government as well. On the other hand, quality of working life represents a recently seen need to avoid the waste of talent in the American labor force. Attention to enhancing the quality of the experience of work seems destined to join other organizational requirements such as: to optimize returns to owners or to reduce costs to taxpayers, to satisfy consumer needs or client needs, and to minimize the ecological impact of industrial and organizational activity.

The severity of the need to increase the quality of working life is only beginning to become apparent but the signs are clear. Three sizable groups in the American labor force are exhibiting unhappiness with their quality of work and are exhibiting signs of alienation from work as it presently exists. These three groups are young people, women, and ethnic and racial minorities. Together they are an increasingly important element in the labor force and their impact will increase in the future. In general they are questioning the quality of their working life—their experience at work. What this means is that we cannot replace the work force that is now nearing the end of its course for the same or greater productivity if we continue offering the jobs and work they've had. The work force replacing it is increasingly unwilling to take or hold those jobs as presently designed.

The first group in this vanguard work force are younger people. Young people, according to recent polls, are less willing to accept authority for its own sake, and they are less interested in seeking work that will provide only economic security. This generation of workers, now entering the labor force, is unmoved by the specter of economic depression. Issues for them in taking jobs are challenge and interest in the activities involved and involve little, if any, concern for economic security. Many young men look at white collar

James C. Taylor, "The Quality of Working Life," *Changing Business-Society Interrelationships,* George A. Steiner (ed.), Los Angeles, California: Graduate School of Management, UCLA, 1975. Updated and slightly revised March 1976. Reprinted by permission.

or "good" factory work jobs their fathers held and decide that the *security of any job at all* is not worth doing a job which does not directly allow continued growth and learning, which does not utilize a large portion of their skills and abilities, and which does not allow dignity.

The bitter 1971 strike at the Vega assembly plant at Lordstown, Ohio, is seen by many as a signpost in this shift of values and attitudes on the part of young workers. General Motors' management, however, vigorously denies that workers' youth plays any role here. They do admit, however, that Lordstown workers are younger, and that Lordstown reaction is more severe than other Chevrolet and Fisher Plant takeovers by their GM Assembly Division elsewhere. In 1972, the UAW emphasized the line speed-up, not youth, as the primary reason for the strike. Regardless of the "truth" in the complex Lordstown case, youth tells us either that it's sad that their fathers had to do factory jobs just to keep from starving—or they tell us we must have been crazy to have liked these jobs. They also tell us that the reason they work four days a week is that they can't afford to work only three days.

In addition to the forces already noted, other more general theories of what is happening to the younger worker can be mentioned. We have, for example, experienced a shift in family and child raising patterns during the last three decades. The newer patterns are less authoritarian, less patriarchal, and more sensitive to the child's own needs and individuality. Education is considered by many to be another potent force. In it, our system of democracy and its values are taught. Feelings of self-worth and the power of participation are central to these values. In addition, teaching methods have become more child-centered and students are becoming more involved in decision-making in school.

The second group in the quality of work vanguard is women workers. Increasingly, women are becoming permanent, rather than temporary, members of the labor force. Furthermore, they are becoming full-time rather than part-time. They are increasingly combining work and family activities in order to maximize their work experience. However, as women enter what has traditionally been considered men's work, especially administrative, managerial positions and professional positions, they are rejecting many of the characteristics of that work as psychologically stressful—or that these jobs demand more than people should reasonably be expected to provide. Examples of such demands are unswerving loyalty to the job over and above family and home, the necessity for working compulsory overtime, or the rigorous demands for work as an all-encompassing but an inflexible role, vis-a-vis other life activities.

Women are coming to think of themselves as qualified for many of the same jobs as men, and at the same pay. But as their expectations have risen, so have their standards for what is good work. Many women in higher level professional and managerial positions are questioning the right of employers to expect the blind loyalties, the dominance of competition over cooperation, and the interference of work into family and leisure time. They, like young people and minorities, are seriously questioning what their respective predecessors accepted without question. This pattern is similar also to that of the better educated who won't work night shift or overtime because family is more important to them than their jobs.

The third category of workers reacting against the present quality of working life includes minority ethnic or racial groups. As people in these minorities enter work and jobs traditionally held by white males, they are discovering that the alternative activities they know are more attractive than the work engagements. For example, the hard-core unemployed being given entry-level jobs in the automotive industry rejected that work on the basis of its being uninteresting, unchallenging, and hazardous. These people had been given jobs we might consider "honest factory work." But most of them quit within six weeks. They say that if this is work and if "whitey" has been doing this for all these years, he must be crazy. The only way found to keep these people with these companies is to change the work and make it more responsible and challenging.

In effect, young people, women, and minorities are saying "if this is work, you can have it." To the degree that the national interest is to increase ratios of worker participation rates from the segments of young people, from women, and from racial minorities, jobs and work will have to be redesigned. Young people, women, and minorities are responding to poor quality of working life with absenteeism, increased job mobility, violence, sabotage, or by dropping out of the labor force entirely.

It is also becoming apparent that even the great mass of American workers, whether in the private or public sector, are beginning to demand satisfaction of needs in work in addition to wages, hours, and working conditions. Some examples of how more conventional American workers have protested low quality of working life in more conventional ways are presented below.

As early as 1965 in the GM assembly plant at Willow Run, Michigan, workers were unwilling to ratify a national "cents-per-hour" agreement without including some element of more human work life such as stalls and doors around toilets and lunch away from the assembly line. This was the first time a major local union component had done more than grumble about what the national union wasn't doing for them in the area of human dignity.

The 1967 wildcat strike at Sinclair's East Chicago Refinery was over compulsory overtime agreements. Per contractual agreement, compulsory overtime could be called within an eight-hour work day. Management could excuse workers on an individual basis, but foremen were not allowed to do this (as it was felt that they might side with the men). A man was given a disciplinary suspension for telling his foreman—rather than asking the superintendent—that he wanted not to work overtime. The sentiment of other workers at the plant was right, and a walkout occurred at change of shift in opposition to this disciplinary layoff. Both management and union urged the men to obey the court injunction because, in effect, obtaining permission to maintain one's off-work activities was implicit in the contract.

In 1973 the United Auto Workers took what I consider the first formal step organized labor has made toward improving quality of working life, beyond the more traditional but clearly important areas of wages, hours, and working conditions. In the agreement with the auto companies signed last year, the UAW included first an agreement to eliminate compulsory overtime, substituting a voluntary arrangement, and, second, union and management agreed to set up a joint committee to study broad quality of work life issues in the auto companies. According to a union official, the impetus for this change to voluntary overtime came indirectly from the changing composition of the labor pool in the auto industry. In particular, it was the younger, unmarried workers who protested overtime most vocally. They, it seems, would rather lose some added pay than lose a "hot date." Married men, it was found, vigorously supported their unmarried brethren when the issue was raised, just as workers had supported the idea with the wildcat strike in the refinery case described above.

These cases deal with issues of dignity of self and increased privatization of home and family life. The ability of an organization, for example, to demand and get mandatory overtime on short notice is becoming increasingly difficult. The traditional, older American labor force in the private sector is beginning to respond by more traditional methods; specifically, refusal to ratify national agreements that don't include issues of dignity of work, or unauthorized strikes for more human work. Finally, however, the traditional American labor force is beginning to listen to dissident elements on the factory floor and in the office. And the call for higher quality of working life is becoming stronger as a result.

HOW THE CURRENT ISSUE IS DEFINED

Historically, the idea of quality of working life has included only the issues of wages, hours, and physical working conditions. These elements have been the prime concern of organized labor and have been well served by it. Wages, hours, and working conditions are still included in any definition of quality of working life, but the concept is expanding to include much more. Industrial organizations are experiencing a phenomenon of worker alienation that results in high absence and turnover despite the tight job market. Business also claims that even when employees are on the job and working, they are reluctant to work with the intensity or dedication that American management once believed it could expect from its workers. Societal interest in the broader implications of quality of life has influenced government concern for all aspects of its citizens' experiences—including work experiences. At the individual level, a current social trend toward personal freedom, on the job as well as off, has resulted in employees who increasingly demand more relevance and involvement in their work.

I define quality of working life as the *phenomenological experience of people at work,* and refer primarily to the quality of working life from the point of view of the individual employee. It is not motivation, nor is it productivity. It is no more these things than concern with consumerism *is* higher sales figures, or interest in improving ecological balance *is* increased public campground use. Quality of working life is not yet a management issue, but "worker alienation" is. What is the difference in this context?

From my point of view, the difference is one of emphasis. Quality of working life talks about a positive experience—enhancing employee options in individual growth, control, and participation. Reducing alienation on the other hand talks about reducing the negative aspects of the job, or the work place. By this logic, reducing alienation may return us to levels of employee motivation we experienced in decades past, while enhancing quality of working life leads in uncharted directions. By all signs, management generally has been interested in returning to prior levels of employee motivation and productivity as opposed to exploring the potential of new employee engagements with jobs and work.

Quality of working life as an issue has been recently defined and described in a number of places outside of academia, most importantly perhaps is the recent and continuing interest in the federal government. The book, *Work in America,* published in 1973 by MIT Press (followed this year by a supporting collection of individuals' papers), is the report issued in 1972 by the Department of Health, Education and Welfare on the urgency to consider the effects of present jobs and work on the American labor force. The Congressional Bill No. S.3916 introduced by Edward Kennedy and others during recent sessions of Congress addresses the problem of increasing worker alienation as a serious one. Government research money has been available for investigation in this area in spite of the considerable attention redirected recently by the Watergate scandal, international détente and conflict, the energy crisis, and our serious economic problems.

The mass media of course have had plenty of copy recently with the above issues, but they have played, and continue to play, an important role in increasing the visibility of quality of working life issues. Worker alienation and the design of jobs and work have been featured stories in *Atlantic Magazine* and *Newsweek,* among others as well as a national television network documentary.

Another recent event marking current interest in quality of working life was the 43rd American Assembly which met in late 1973 with the theme "The Changing World of Work." The book which resulted from this assembly, *The Worker and the Job,* emphasized the importance of job and work design in quality of working life as well as the need for timely and relevant information about the new developments in the area.

Some of these various sources of interest and concern choose to emphasize the work place and job elements seen to be associated with worker responses, while others of these have focused merely on the employee reactions themselves. As a rule, the former sources start from one of two initial positions. Either they begin with statements by social scientists who believe that a confluence of forces, technological as well as cultural, lead us to new job and *work systems;* or they begin with reports of new organizational forms for jobs and work, which are either planned or accidental. The sources of information and definition which emphasize worker response alone as the issue are as a rule more interested in the meaning and measures of worker alienation and satisfaction. These sources in turn, do not necessarily conclude that jobs and work design are at the heart of this worker response; although they frequently do so.

In spite of the fact that worker's response is important in determining what in the industrial system has gone wrong, I maintain that we cannot count on our measures of job satisfaction alone for this.

DRAWBACKS WITH THE JOB SATISFACTION DEFINITION

Studies of job satisfaction done within the last two or three years show the same basic results as did similar surveys twenty years ago. An overwhelming proportion of American workers state they are at least "not dissatisfied" with their jobs and work. Yet at the same time, for major corporations like General Motors and General Electric, absenteeism has increased dramatically over the past decade—for instance, in the auto industry absenteeism increased 100 percent over the ten-year period 1962–72, and the high rates of part-week absenteeism (Monday–Friday absenteeism) continued into late 1975.

If we can agree that these problems of apparent work alienation are significant, then how can we explain the fact that morale surveys continue to show that the American labor force is satisfied with its work. I would maintain that the major reason why, is because definitionally and methodologically, job satisfaction is an improper measure of the quality of the work experience, and is a better measure of the ability of employees to adapt or adjust to basically unsatisfactory labor and working conditions.

The definition of job satisfaction as need-satisfaction is commonly encountered in the literature. Need-satisfaction, however, is very narrow. It is an attempt to tie fixed (or apparently fixed) human needs to measures or statements of satisfaction with the job. It is, for example, possible to maintain that everyone needs some basic physical characteristics or elements. We can say (as Abraham Maslow does) that everyone needs security. However we may agree with that in general, we may disagree in regard to the specific level at which any one of us desires security, or at the basic level that our security needs are satisfied. We may all have security needs but those security needs may be satisfied with different degrees of the same element on the job.

The other general definition of satisfaction is basically the notion of job satisfaction as an attitude, or likes and dislikes. It is not the satisfaction of needs concerning us here, but the satisfaction of wants. As the definition above is too narrow, this definition is very ambiguous. And I would maintain that the definition of this is ambiguous because the definition relies on liking what is known. That is, we may not want something and therefore not be dissatisfied or frustrated—until we know about it or until we know that it exists or know it is available.

The problems of interpreting job satisfaction data become further complicated with consideration of measurement errors. A critical measurement issue rests with the fact that satisfaction can be reflected in one's ability to adjust to a given work situation, or to modify that situation to one's needs. In other words, workers may report general satisfaction with a job to which they have specifically adjusted their needs or requirements, irrespective of the real quality of that job or of their working life. On the other hand, people can adjust jobs and work to suit themselves instead of adjusting themselves to the job. Recent examples of such adjustment are soldiering on the job, and sabotage of both product and plant which represent workers' attempts to modify the job or work place to suit their own needs. A frustrated operator might say that the job is satisfactory or satisfying if he can safely do mischief to the organization by these means.

Thus, when we get out to measure satisfaction, we are never certain whether the respondent or employee knows that there is something better the employee can evaluate his job in terms of how well *he* is able to adapt to it (even if it is a lousy job), or how well he is able to adapt it in ways to suit some wants created by certain frustrations on the job.

So, job satisfaction, as measured, remains high, but the signs and products of alienation keep going up—sabotage, pilferage, absenteeism, soldiering, constant testing of minimum production levels, and turnover in a tight labor market.

Foremen have told us for several years now that their single biggest problem is that workers won't take orders like workers used to. In effect, they were saying that workers are no longer motivated by fear. For a whole host of reasons, such as changes in child rearing patterns, educational methods and content, and sustained relative economic prosperity, fear as a motivator is gone or is going; and unless we have another great famine, depression, or world war, it is unlikely to return.

WHAT SPECIFICALLY HAVE WE FOUND TO BE THE QUALITY OF WORKING LIFE?

CASES

If employers no longer can motivate by fear, and if workers want more dignity of self, more control, more privatization, and more challenge in work, then changes in the work system itself can be seen as one important (and perhaps the most important) element in improving this situation. This is what we see when we consider the similarity of recent cases of work system design which extends internationally and has extended without a network, a fad, or an industry publication.

These current cases include the following countries and industries:

Country	*Industry*
Netherlands	Electronics Mfg (Philips)
Sweden	Auto Mfg (Saab, Volvo)
Norway	Chemical Fertilizers (Norsk Hydro)
Canada	Aluminum (ALCAN)
United Kingdom	Oil Refining (Shell)
Italy	Office Machine Mfg (Olivetti)
Japan	Electronics Mfg (Sony)
United States	Non Durable Consumer Prod. (P&G)
	Pet Food Mfg (General Foods)
	Auto Parts Mfg (Donnelly; Harmon)
	Oil Refining
	Paper Goods Mfg (Mead Corp.)
	Mining (Rushton)

Common elements among these cases include broader job classification including multiple skill requirements (and frequently, pay based on number of skills held), worker participation in deciding on work rules and setting group targets, diminution of status differences within plants, development of work team organization around meaningful group tasks, and a shift of foreman roles from supervision, to liaison with other organizational units. The reported results for these cases all include more harmonious work relationships, little evidence of alienation, and improved effectiveness. Each case is unique of course. Some of the above characteristics are more evident or more fully developed than others, although they each share this reorganization of work to increase autonomy, power, and responsibility of employees in a task group setting.

These cases also differ in the individual change setting and strategy. For instance, some of these plants were non-union, some were organized. Some were small companies, some were large. Some of these had parent company support, some had only grudging acceptance. Unfortunately, they are all manufacturing. We have yet to uncover a current case in the same sense in white collar or service organizations. There is evidence of individual job enrichment in the white collar sector, but no work organization cases such as the above. This material does tend to support the above conclusion, however, that improving the nature of work (as defined in this case by individual jobs) is related to reducing worker feelings of alienation and frustration.

Most of these cases have been referred to in the book, *Job Power,* by

David Jenkins. In addition, many of them are fully reported in a collection of cases published in 1975 entitled *Quality of Working Life: Cases and Commentary,* and edited by Louis E. Davis, Albert B. Cherns, and Associates.

LITERATURE REVIEW

Although the number of cases is increasing all the time, the overall number is woefully small. In an attempt to more fully reveal the "state of the art" in research on what I'm calling the quality of working life, several of us reviewed the empirical research available in the English language, presented in professional journals, books, and unpublished reports during the fifteen-year period 1957–72. We searched this literature for the appearance of one or more specified quality of working life criteria, together with some (unspecified) correlate or causal variable such as organizational, job, or personal characteristics. This search and review, under Department of Labor sponsorship, resulted in an annotated bibliography on the quality of working life.

We excluded a large portion of the available literature as being "morale studies" (containing no behavioral measures of the quality of working life criteria) for the reasons of definitional and methodological ambiguity as discussed above. Much literature still remained to be summarized, however, if we were to look at fifteen years of publications. We, however, tested eleven categories that we felt would cover the major resultant or outcome variables, that could also be operationalized in behavioral terms, and that consciously excluded attitudes per se. These eleven quality of working life criteria are as follows:

Alienation
Health and safety
Economic security
Self-esteem
Self-actualization
Work environment
Control and influence
Organizational inclusion (or enclosure)
Career aspirations
Extra-work activities
Home and family

I fully realize that these categories are not perfect, but our informal tests established that they were at least useful for the task at hand. This list of criteria or parameters, of course, aids in further refining our definition of the quality of working life, since all of these criteria are part of the individual experience of people at work.

During the past two decades, the quality of working life has not been studied systematically, but much research has been done on "human relations" at work. At this point in our collective experience we need to summarize what has been done, evaluate how well it has been done, and identify the gaps in this knowledge base.

The state of the art, as represented by the research we reviewed for the period 1957–72, is characterized by large-scale, static investigations; over time, they show increasing concern for the dignity of the individual. One major segment of research has examined job and work demands; more recent studies in this area are beginning to illustrate some effects of job design on employee behavior.

Quality of working life as related to issues of concern to the society as a whole is less well represented in the literature. Most of such evidence is to be found in British and Scandinavian studies. It is encouraging, however, to note an increasing tendency to report research on issues of dignity, development, and concerns of the whole person.

There is also a trend toward explaining quality of working life (QWL) phenomena in terms of multiple causes; mediating and contingency variables have begun to replace simple, two-element models of cause and effect.

Otherwise, however, the research conducted during the past fifteen years is deficient in field investigations that are both intensive and systematic. Few cases evaluate change over time, although longitudinal studies are becoming more frequent.

Although our bibliographic search was undertaken specifically to review studies that measured the quality of working life, or its immediate outcomes, in terms of behaviors, we found the shortage of quantifiable behavioral measures of QWL to be so acute that we were forced to include some studies of employees' attitudes toward elements of the work life setting. If we are to learn effectively from studies now in progress or about to begin, this lack must be overcome. Our findings support the strong concern, recently expressed in various quarters, for standardization of measurement in QWL research.

In the journals and books reviewed for the bibliography, a relatively large number of studies have investigated such QWL criteria as worker alienation, worker turnover, self-esteem, pay-related issues, discretion, control and influence, and the social working environment. On the other hand, there has been relatively very little investigation of the impact of working on home and family and on such extra-work activities as consumption, creation, and community-citizen involvement.

Looking at the variables associated with quality of working life, we found that occupational and job characteristics account for a nominally greater proportion (44 percent of the total associations with QWL criteria than do either organizational variables (31 percent) or individual respondent characteristics (25 percent) (this difference is significant at the 10 percent level of confidence).

Although fifteen years is not a particularly long time span in social sciences literature, it is a comparatively long period for considering issues in the experience of work. For that reason, examining the literature for that period in five-year sections has the potential for revealing some interesting trends in the quality of working life parameters that were studied. The totals for the three five-year time periods, 1957–61, 1962–66, and 1967–72, reveal a significantly increasing number of studies in the literature as we go from the earliest period to the latest one. Approximately 14 percent of all studies in the bibliography belong to the five-year period from 1957–61; 28 percent are from 1962–66; and 58 percent became available between 1967–72.

Analysis of trends over time shows clearly that the absolute number of appearances of "our" QWL criteria is increasing at a rapid rate in the literature. Reviewing the specific percentages of individual cell entries, however, suggests that the studies dealing with "self-esteem," "actualization," and "control and influence," do not significantly increase relative to studies dealing with "health and safety," and "economic security."

A comment that must be made about the literature on the quality of working life published during the past fifteen years is that it is not systematic, it is not very rich from the standpoint of new directions, and it contains few surprises.

Some 365 studies are reported in the annotated bibliography. Although the bibliography does not encompass all relevant studies, it does nonetheless cover the vast majority of those concerning QWL criteria which were to be found in the published journals and books and the unpublished reports and cases which were scanned during the annotation process—sources that must cover the majority of such studies in the English-language literature. The research that has been published in the past fifteen years reflects a growing balance of concern between the traditional quality of working life parameters (wages, hours, and working conditions) and the more contemporary issues, from the individual viewpoint, of self-esteem and actualization. Interest in control and influence as an important dimension of the quality of working life has apparently remained high throughout the period.

The point of view of the individual of the quality of working life is coming into its own. The measures of alienation, self-esteem, self-actualization, and influence are neither standardized nor consistent, and the results of relationships with them are inconsistent. But the number of studies in this area is doubling every five years, and the consistency of results is increasing. This consistency is obscured somewhat by a shift from more simplex causal models to the use of mediating and conditioning variables in more complex models. Of the major trends in the area of quality of working life for the individual, increased interest in investigating job characteristics and job demands, and renewed interest in work group dynamics, loom large.

From the standpoint of quality of working life for the organization, the characteristics or parameters of organizational motivation or inclusion appear to be suitably measured and seem to be related to many of the same causal or correlate variables as are the other quality of working life characteristics. Such causal variables are organizational climate and hierarchy, organizational reward structure, the types and demands of organizational and job characteristics, supervisory characteristics, work groups, status and prestige, and technology, as well as some member characteristics such as age and job tenure. Personality, needs and expectations, and personal experiences are also important in relation to the organizational inclusion measures.

By contrast, the more societally relevant dimensions—work-related effects on employees' extra-work life roles—have been studied very little but are just beginning to emerge. Research on quality of working life from a societal point of view has been especially scant, except for some studies done in Europe, particularly in Scandinavia. The research undertaken in the United States and reported in English-language journals virtually ignores the relationships between work and extra-work characteristics, behavior, activities, and attitudes.

Overall, the gross frequency measures reveal a large number of studies dealing with economic security and human relations concerns of the social working environment. Studies examining (at least tangentially) self-esteem and actualization, control and influence, and alienation also are numerous, and these measures are more representative of the quality of working life as, it appears, it is becoming defined.

A review of the characteristics causal to the quality of working life confirms the suspicion that, in the fifteen years of research reviewed, a great deal of effort has been devoted to investigating the characteristics of workers and organizations, whereas little research has investigated work groups or technology variables as they relate to the quality of working life. It is to the credit of social sciences research during that period, however, that a relatively large number of studies have investigated job demands, as well as job types in general.

We can therefore report that the variable, job demands, has recently become important, perhaps as a function of Herzberg's ideas of job enrichment. Of the rather large number of studies in the bibliography which deal with job demands and alienation, for example, a good number (about half) tend to report a particular pattern of findings that can be summarized as "alienation/job dissatisfaction follow from job context." The other half, dating from somewhat later in the period studied here, tend to report a different pattern: "alienation/absence and turnover follow from job content." Both job content and context are doubtless important, and the discrepancies in the literature may perhaps best be seen as a shift in the application of particular dependent variables, rather than as a theoretical inconsistency. It is important to note, however, that the shift in emphasis is from job context to job content, and not the reverse.

Other studies reported in the bibliography show increasing support for the idea of mediating or contingency variables operating between causal variables and quality of working life parameters. For example, the relationship between hierarchical level and degree of influence may be mediated by such things as line vs. staff assignment, amount of pay, and degree of expert knowledge.

CONCLUSION

As defined, quality of working life is a significant social goal for the present decade. People (our labor force) are changing faster than the jobs, and work they do, provide for those changes. This period of dislocation may be prolonged, although I would maintain that there are ways and signs to guide us through it more quickly. Among these is the consideration that quality of working life begins with the work itself, and is no longer defined solely by wages, hours, and working conditions. Further, defining quality of working life by the amount of job satisfaction is inappropriate since job satisfaction itself has such ambiguous referent. If, however, it is used in its usual form, job satisfaction is intended to measure the satisfaction of individual *needs.* Designing jobs and work solely on the basis of individual needs has the danger of suboptimizing the organizational, technical, and even social elements in the work setting. As in the past, the design of individual jobs leaves the coordination and communication up to management, as examination of the scientific management measurement so clearly shows. It is ironic that a job redesign effort based solely on individual human needs should result in the same effect as a job design effort based solely on technological requirements. In both, however, management must take responsibility of the process of coordination and integration.

If all production technology was the same today as it was forty years ago, the choice of management to coordinate and control the work place would be easier. But technology as it has evolved makes possible more alternative organizational designs. By absorbing routine activities into machines rather than leaving them for people, and by leaving only the role of regulator and controller for the human in the system, even greater pressure is applied for management to relinquish the superstructure's dominant role in integration and regulation. New sophisticated technology requires skills related to regulation, skills in monitoring and diagnosing, and skills in the adjustment of the process.

This is becoming as true of white collar organizations as it is for blue collar organizations with the primary differences being one of time lag, in which the demands of new technology can still be translated into ever more meaningless fractionation of individual jobs in the white collar case. The naive assumption that the shift from manufacturing, to service, administration, and other white collar work would bring with it a high quality of working life is now revealed as an unfounded expectation as white collar work is increasingly organized on the principles of earlier production technology.

If we are to simultaneously meet the changing values of our labor force for a more challenging and responsible experience at work, as well as technological demands for new skills and abilities on the part of operators, something more than the mere redesign of individual jobs is required. A total organizational approach, which will take into account and jointly optimize social, technical, and individual requirements may be considered. The em-

5 BUSINESS SOCIAL RESPONSIBILITIES

THE SOCIAL RESPONSIBILITY OF BUSINESS IS TO INCREASE ITS PROFITS

MILTON FRIEDMAN

Milton Friedman, professor of economics at the University of Chicago, presents in this article a strong defense of the view that the only social responsibility of business is to maximize its profits.

When I hear businessmen speak eloquently about the "social responsibilities of business in a free-enterprise system," I am reminded of the wonderful line about the Frenchman who discovered at the age of 70 that he had been speaking prose all his life. The businessmen believe that they are defending free enterprise when they declaim that business is not concerned "merely" with profit but also with promoting desirable "social" ends; that business has a "social conscience" and takes seriously its responsibilities for providing employment, eliminating discrimination, avoiding pollution and whatever else may be the catchwords of the contemporary crop of reformers. In fact they are—or would be if they or anyone else took them seriously—preaching pure and unadulterated socialism. Businessmen who talk this way are unwitting puppets of the intellectual forces that have been undermining the basis of a free society these past decades.

The discussions of the "social responsibilities of business" are notable for their analytical looseness and lack of rigor. What does it mean to say that "business" has responsibilities? Only people can have responsibilities. A corporation is an artificial person and in this sense may have artificial responsibilities, but "business" as a whole cannot be said to have responsibilities, even in this vague sense. The first step toward clarity in examining the doctrine of the social responsibility of business is to ask precisely what it implies for whom.

Presumably, the individuals who are to be responsible are businessmen, which means individual proprietors or corporate executives. Most of the discussion of social responsibility is directed at corporations, so in what follows I shall mostly neglect the individual proprietor and speak of corporate executives.

. . .

In a free-enterprise, private-property system, a corporate executive is an employe of the owners of the business. He has direct responsibility to his employers. That responsibility is to conduct the business in accordance with their desires, which generally will be to make as much money as possible while conforming to the basic rules of the society, both those embodied in

The New York Times Magazine, September 13, 1970, pp. 33, 122–126.

law and those embodied in ethical custom. Of course, in some cases his employers may have a different objective. A group of persons might establish a corporation for an eleemosynary purpose—for example, a hospital or a school. The manager of such a corporation will not have money profit as his objective but the rendering of certain services.

In either case, the key point is that, in his capacity as a corporate executive, the manager is the agent of the individuals who own the corporation or establish the eleemosynary institution, and his primary responsibility is to them.

Needless to say, this does not mean that it is easy to judge how well he is performing his task. But at least the criterion of performance is straightforward, and the persons among whom a voluntary contractual arrangement exists are clearly defined.

Of course, the corporate executive is also a person in his own right. As a person, he may have many other responsibilities that he recognizes or assumes voluntarily—to his family, his conscience, his feelings of charity, his church, his clubs, his city, his country. He may feel impelled by these responsibilities to devote part of his income to causes he regards as worthy, to refuse to work for particular corporations, even to leave his job, for example, to join his country's armed forces. If we wish, we may refer to some of these responsibilities as "social responsibilities." But in these respects he is acting as a principal, not an agent; he is spending his own money or time or energy, not the money of his employers or the time or energy he has contracted to devote to their purposes. If these are "social responsibilities," they are the social responsibilities of individuals, not of business.

What does it mean to say that the corporate executive has a "social responsibility" in his capacity as businessman? If this statement is not pure rhetoric, it must mean that he is to act in some way that is not in the interest of his employers. For example, that he is to refrain from increasing the price of the product in order to contribute to the social objective of preventing inflation, even though a price increase would be in the best interests of the corporation. Or that he is to make expenditures on reducing pollution beyond the amount that is in the best interests of the corporation or that is required by law in order to contribute to the social objective of improving the environment. Or that, at the expense of corporate profits, he is to hire "hard-core" unemployed instead of better-qualified available workmen to contribute to the social objective of reducing poverty.

In each of these cases, the corporate executive would be spending someone else's money for a general social interest. Insofar as his actions in accord with his "social responsibility" reduce returns to stockholders, he is spending their money. Insofar as his actions raise the price to customers, he is spending the customers' money. Insofar as his actions lower the wages of some employes, he is spending their money.

The stockholders or the customers or the employes could separately spend their own money on the particular action if they wished to do so. The executive is exercising a distinct "social responsibility," rather than serving as an agent of the stockholders or the customers or the employes, only if he spends the money in a different way than they would have spent it.

But if he does this, he is in effect imposing taxes, on the one hand, and deciding how the tax proceeds shall be spent, on the other.

This process raises political questions on two levels: principle and consequences. On the level of political principle, the imposition of taxes and the expenditure of tax proceeds are governmental functions. We have established elaborate constitutional, parliamentary and judicial provisions to control these functions, to assure that taxes are imposed so far as possible in accordance with the preferences and desires of the public—after all, "taxation without representation" was one of the battle cries of the American Revolution. We have a system of checks and balances to separate the legislative function of imposing taxes and enacting expenditures from the executive function of collecting taxes and administering expenditure programs and from the judicial function of mediating disputes and interpreting the law.

Here the businessman—self-selected or appointed directly or indirectly by stockholders—is to be simultaneously legislator, executive and jurist. He is to decide whom to tax by how much and for what purpose, and he is to spend the proceeds—all this guided only by general exhortations from on high to restrain inflation, improve the environment, fight poverty and so on and on.

The whole justification for permitting the corporate executive to be selected by the stockholders is that the executive is an agent serving the interests of his principal. This justification disappears when the corporate executive imposes taxes and spends the proceeds for "social" purposes. He becomes in effect a public employe, a civil servant, even though he remains in name an employe of a private enterprise. On grounds of political principle, it is intolerable that such civil servants—insofar as their actions in the name of social responsibility are real and not just window-dressing—should be selected as they are now. If they are to be civil servants, then they must be selected through a political process. If they are to impose taxes and make expenditures to foster "social" objectives, then political machinery must be set up to guide the assessment of taxes and to determine through a political process the objectives to be served.

This is the basic reason why the doctrine of "social responsibility" involves the acceptance of the socialist view that political mechanisms, not market mechanisms, are the appropriate way to determine the allocation of scarce resources to alternative uses.

On the grounds of consequences, can the corporate executive in fact discharge his alleged "social responsibilities"? On the one hand, suppose he could get away with spending the stockholders' or customers' or employes' money. How is he to know how to spend it? He is told that he must contribute to fighting inflation. How is he to know what action of his will contribute to that end? He is presumably an expert in running his company—

in producing a product or selling it or financing it. But nothing about his selection makes him an expert on inflation. Will his holding down the price of his product reduce inflationary pressure? Or, by leaving more spending power in the hands of his customers, simply divert it elsewhere? Or, by forcing him to produce less because of the lower price, will it simply contribute to shortages? Even if he could answer these questions, how much cost is he justified in imposing on his stockholders, customers and employes for this social purpose? What is his appropriate share and what is the appropriate share of others?

And, whether he wants to or not, can he get away with spending his stockholders', customers' or employes' money? Will not the stockholders fire him? (Either the present ones or those who take over when his actions in the name of social responsibility have reduced the corporation's profits and the price of its stock.) His customers and his employes can desert him for other producers and employers less scrupulous in exercising their social responsibilities.

This facet of "social responsibility" doctrine is brought into sharp relief when the doctrine is used to justify wage restraint by trade unions. The conflict of interest is naked and clear when union officials are asked to subordinate the interest of their members to some more general social purpose. If the union officials try to enforce wage restraint, the consequence is likely to be wildcat strikes, rank-and-file revolts and the emergence of strong competitors for their jobs. We thus have the ironic phenomenon that union leaders—at least in the U.S.—have objected to Government interference with the market far more consistently and courageously than have business leaders.

The difficulty of exercising "social responsibility" illustrates, of course, the great virtue of private competitive enterprise—it forces people to be responsible for their own actions and makes it difficult for them to "exploit" other people for either selfish or unselfish purposes. They can do good—but only at their own expense.

Many a reader who has followed the argument this far may be tempted to remonstrate that it is all well and good to speak of Government's having the responsibility to impose taxes and determine expenditures for such "social" purposes as controlling pollution or training the hard-core unemployed, but that the problems are too urgent to wait on the slow course of political processes, that the exercise of social responsibility by businessmen is a quicker and surer way to solve pressing current problems.

Aside from the question of fact—I share Adam Smith's skepticism about the benefits that can be expected from "those who affected to trade for the public good"—this argument must be rejected on grounds of principle. What it amounts to is an assertion that those who favor the taxes and expenditures in question have failed to persuade a majority of their fellow citizens to be of like mind and that they are seeking to attain by undemocratic procedures what they cannot attain by democratic procedures. In a free society, it is hard for "good" people to do "good," but that is a small price to pay for making it hard for "evil" people to do "evil," especially since one man's good is another's evil.

I have, for simplicity, concentrated on the special case of the corporate executive, except only for the brief digression on trade unions. But precisely the same argument applies to the newer phenomenon of calling upon stockholders to require corporations to exercise social responsibility (the recent G.M. crusade, for example). In most of these cases, what is in effect involved is some stockholders trying to get other stockholders (or customers or employes) to contribute against their will to "social" causes favored by the activists. Insofar as they succeed, they are again imposing taxes and spending the proceeds.

The situation of the individual proprietor is somewhat different. If he acts to reduce the returns of his enterprise in order to exercise his "social responsibility," he is spending his own money, not someone else's. If he wishes to spend his money on such purposes, that is his right, and I cannot see that there is any objection to his doing so. In the process, he, too, may impose costs on employes and customers. However, because he is far less likely than a large corporation or union to have monopolistic power, any such side effects will tend to be minor.

Of course, in practice the doctrine of social responsibility is frequently a cloak for actions that are justified on other grounds rather than a reason for those actions.

To illustrate, it may well be in the long-run interest of a corporation that is a major employer in a small community to devote resources to providing amenities to that community or to improving its government. That may make it easier to attract desirable employes, it may reduce the wage bill or lessen losses from pilferage and sabotage or have other worthwhile effects. Or it may be that, given the laws about the deductibility of corporate charitable contributions, the stockholders can contribute more to charities they favor by having the corporation make the gift than by doing it themselves, since they can in that way contribute an amount that would otherwise have been paid as corporate taxes.

In each of these—and many similar—cases, there is a strong temptation to rationalize these actions as an exercise of "social responsibility." In the present climate of opinion, with its widespread aversion to "capitalism," "profits," the "soulless corporation" and so on, this is one way for a corporation to generate good will as a by-product of expenditures that are entirely justified in its own self-interest.

It would be inconsistent of me to call on corporate executives to refrain from this hypocritical window-dressing because it harms the foundations of a free society. That would be to call on them to exercise a "social responsibility"! If our institutions, and the attitudes of the public, make it in their self-interest to cloak their actions in this way, I cannot summon much indignation to denounce them. At the same time, I can express admiration for those individual proprietors or owners of closely held corporations or stockholders of more broadly held corporations who disdain such tactics as approaching fraud.

Whether blameworthy or not, the use of the cloak of social responsibility, and the nonsense spoken in its name by influential and prestigious businessmen, does clearly harm the foundations of a free society. I have been impressed time and again by the schizophrenic character of many businessmen. They are capable of being extremely far-sighted and clear-headed in matters that are internal to their businesses. They are incredibly short-sighted and muddled-headed in matters that are outside their businesses but affect the possible survival of business in general. This short-sightedness is strikingly exemplified in the calls from many businessmen for wage and price guidelines or controls or incomes policies. There is nothing that could do more in a brief period to destroy a market system and replace it by a centrally controlled system than effective governmental control of prices and wages.

The short-sightedness is also exemplified in speeches by businessmen on social responsibility. This may gain them kudos in the short run. But it helps to strengthen the already too prevalent view that the pursuit of profits is wicked and immoral and must be curbed and controlled by external forces. Once this view is adopted, the external forces that curb the market will not be the social consciences, however highly developed, of the pontificating executives; it will be the iron fist of Government bureaucrats. Here, as with price and wage controls, businessmen seem to me to reveal a suicidal impulse.

The political principle that underlies the market mechanism is unanimity. In an ideal free market resting on private property, no individual can coerce any other, all cooperation is voluntary, all parties to such cooperation benefit or they need not participate. There are no "social" values, no "social" responsibilities in any sense other than the shared values and responsibilities of individuals. Society is a collection of individuals and of the various groups they voluntarily form.

The political principle that underlies the political mechanism is conformity. The individual must serve a more general social interest—whether that be determined by a church or a dictator or a majority. The individual may have a vote and a say in what is to be done, but if he is overruled, he must conform. It is appropriate for some to require others to contribute to a general social purpose whether they wish to or not.

Unfortunately, unanimity is not always feasible. There are some respects in which conformity appears unavoidable, so I do not see how one can avoid the use of the political mechanism altogether.

But the doctrine of "social responsibility" taken seriously would extend the scope of the political mechanism to every human activity. It does not differ in philosophy from the most explicitly collectivist doctrine. It differs only by professing to believe that collectivist ends can be attained without collectivist means. That is why, in my book *Capitalism and Freedom,* I have called it a "fundamentally subversive doctrine" in a free society, and have said that in such a society, "there is one and only one social responsibility of business—to use its resources and engage in activities designed to increase its profits so long as it stays within the rules of the game, which is to say, engages in open and free competition without deception or fraud."

QUESTIONS

1. Do you accept Friedman's thesis that an executive in a large company is the employe of the owners?
2. Do you accept Friedman's views that social responsibilities refer to actions taken by executives that result in the expenditure of money in a different way than stockholders, customers, or workers would choose to spend the money?
3. Do you think that Friedman is correct when he says that spending money for social responsibilities raises a major political issue, namely, taxation without representation?
4. What do social responsibilities of business mean to you?
5. If an executive chooses to assume social responsibilities, there is no clear formula for telling him what he can or should do like that of the old MR = MC rule. Does the absence of such a formula necessarily mean that a businessman should assume no social responsibilities?
6. Is the business system more likely to collapse if it follows Friedman's rigid doctrine of absolutely no business social responsibilities (except to use resources efficiently to maximize profits) or if it follows a moderate program to adapt its activities to social needs while still retaining a primary economic objective?

A CASE FOR SOCIAL RESPONSIBILITY

DOUGLAS A. HAYES

Douglas A. Hayes, professor of finance, Graduate School of Business Administration, University of Michigan, presents several reasons why he is in favor of modifying the classical economic optimal decision-making concepts and why vigorous programs to meet social needs are not incompatible with long-run business profit goals.

It is difficult to argue with the proposition that the basic objective of corporate business in the private sector is to maximize the long-term return opportunities for the shareholders within the constraints imposed by law and generally accepted ethical standards. However, as certain problems have become more complex and more critical in their implications for the long-run future of society, it no longer seems sufficient to hold that the operational policies instituted to implement this objective should be based on the simplistic notion of earnings potentials in relation to risks assumed. This notion is specifically incorporated into the capital budgeting models used in business school finance courses and as a guide for resource allocation by many industrial corporations. Therefore, at the outset I confess to being a heretic. The heresy, however, is finding support. For example, an increasing number of corporations are taking the view that satisfactory pollution control policies are desirable, if not essential, despite the fact that the diversion of scare resources to these ends may promise lower returns than alternative uses.

The rationale for policies which are nonoptimal from an economic standpoint but are designed to contribute to the solution of environmental and social problems can be based on the view that corporations have instituted social welfare goals that are completely independent of the profit goals. Indeed, some academic behavioral scientists have advanced this notion as exemplified by the following statement:

> The norms and roles of big business include a conglomeration of profits, efficiency, democratic human relations, freedom and justice. Big business is not cast in the simple molds of profit maximization or of pursuit of public welfare.

However, because managerial performances are largely evaluated in terms of their current results and long-term prospects, it is doubtful if purely "public welfare" considerations bulk large in their decision-making process beyond a

Douglas A. Hayes, "Management Goals in a Crisis Society," Vol. 22 (November 1970), 7–11. Reprinted by permission from the November 1970 issue of the *Michigan Business Review,* published by the Graduate School of Business Administration, The University of Michigan.

modest concern with a favorable "public relations" image. A possible exception may be those unusual corporations that have been highly successful because of a unique product line or for other reasons. In these cases, even if significant resources are diverted to social purposes, their stockholders and employees may still enjoy returns well above average. Xerox Corporation, for example, is well known for its concern and expenditures on educational and cultural programs, but its exceptional growth and profitability give its management a degree of flexibility not enjoyed by most private sector firms. It is particularly known for sponsorship of public interest television programs at prime time costs with probably less than commensurate marketing rewards.

A second rationale advanced to justify policies that are socially rather than profit oriented is that they are a necessary defensive reaction to pressures from governments and organized public interest groups. The public sector, it is noted, have assumed an increasingly aggressive posture in their attitudes toward the apparent deficiencies of corporate enterprises, particularly large companies. Therefore, it is argued, in order to avoid punitive regulations which might seriously erode profit potentials, it is necessary to introduce some policies aimed at the mitigation of social problems, although reluctantly and minimally as they are essentially regarded as conflicting with the main goals of the corporation.

Probably some managements are oriented to the defensive view of those policies which commit corporate resources to projects not directly related to immediate profit potentials. But a third rationale is also possible. It is that the long-term profit prospects of many, if not most, corporations may be eroded unless adequate solutions are found within a reasonable time to the pressing environmental and social problems. For example, as a major segment of corporate resources is committed to large metropolitan areas, the preservation of the value and productive usefulness of these resources may well depend on maintaining a stable society and tolerable environmental conditions in these areas. It has become apparent that urban decay has seriously impaired the progress of many companies, particularly where both employees and customers are largely concentrated in these areas.

Enterprises dependent on urban markets, such as retailers and banks, would seem particularly exposed to deterioration in the condition of the cities. Therefore, it is not surprising that Mr. Charles Lazarus, the head of a leading department store chain, made the following statement concerning the need for enlightened social policies:

> . . . whether you are a part of a national, a regional or a local business, the great urban center—whatever its name—is where most of our business is done. The city is where, when we speak of the future, we will either grandly win or meanly fail. That will depend, more than perhaps on any other group, on the business leaders, and particularly the retail leaders, of each great urban community.

The clear recognition that policies instituted to alleviate environmental and social decay are not dictated by a peripheral concern for "public welfare" outside the mainstream of corporate goals would seem salutary rather than deplorable. If corporate managements generally accept the view that such policies are not only compatible with, but may be essential to, their goals of long-term profit maximization, then they will probably be more forcefully conceived and implemented. Until recently, there seemed to be no more than a rather vague conceptual justification for policies not related directly to earnings performance. These policies were, therefore, often tentative and minimal in character. The concept that long-term profit goals may depend on solving problems ordinarily considered beyond the concern of individual private companies may seem a self-serving approach, but it might well provide the incentive to more dedicated action with respect to these problems than has been evidenced in the past.

As my major direct interest in teaching and research is banking, let me observe that large metropolitan banks have reason to be particularly sensitive on this score. While most have penetrated into regional, national, and even international markets, a substantial proportion of their business is still generated locally. They have, therefore, a substantial stake in the maintenance of a viable metropolitan community. In addition, because they have been given the privilege of providing society with its major monetary mechanism, demand deposits, they are subject to special public regulation by both State and Federal jurisdictions. Favorable political relations are highly important to banks. As a result, clear evidence of operational policies concerned with the social problems of their communities would seem desirable, if not imperative, in order to preserve the economic base of their major markets and to convince political bodies that their activities are positively in the public interest and not insensitive to it. For example, vigorous programs to render financial and even management aid to businesses operated by minority groups in the inner-city would seem particularly relevant for major urban banks.

Therefore, despite the increasingly serious environmental and social problems plaguing society, it is arguable that the basic management goals remain intact. These are (1) maximizing long-term total returns to the shareholders and (2) maintaining the integrity of their investment. However, the policy spectrum related to achieving these goals has changed. Whereas a decade or so ago, most policy decisions might have been based almost entirely on their probable effects on earnings relative to risks assumed, the policy parameters now appear more complex. For large urban corporations, the additional dimension of the impact of policies on the environmental and social quality of their communities should become, if it has not already, a more important factor in future policy decisions.

It should not be concluded that major corporations in the past have lacked any concern for the social problems of their communities. Most have cooperated in civic charitable and developmental projects, but these activities have usually been peripheral to the mainstream of corporate activities. Trade-offs between socially oriented policies and earnings oriented policies have not been typical, but looking ahead to the remaining decades of the twentieth century, a real question can be raised as to whether such trade-offs might not become increasingly necessary in order to preserve large corporations as viable private sector institutions.

But in view of their obligations to their stockholder constituents, some managements hold that corporate enterprise cannot make major sacrifices in their earnings potentials in order to solve these problems. Consequently, it is further argued, to achieve the massive resource commitments, social and environmental programs should include the profit motive in their program parameters; otherwise, it is doubtful if the real and managerial resources will be made available on the scale required.

Mr. Tilford Gaines, senior economist of a New York bank, argued in this vein as follows:

> Programs of the type proposed in the Master Plan must be heavily weighted with government participation, since many are by their nature essential functions of government. At the same time, the compatibility of the overall programs with the economic and social structure of the country and, therefore the likelihood of success for the program demand that private enterprise should be employed wherever possible. To enlist *maximum* [italics mine] support from private industry, it will be necessary that there be a realistic prospect of profits and a minimum of interference from government in the form of surveillance, unnecessary requirements, and an atmosphere of suspicion toward the motives of private business.

While one might agree in principle with these comments, it is probably sanguine to expect that they will be fully implemented in practice. Since the Great Depression, it has been fashionable in liberal political circles, and to some extent in the communications media, to regard the "profit motive" as crass and somewhat suspect. To expect politically oriented policies to embrace the efficacy of profit incentives solving the pressing problems of society may prove to be a difficult proposition. Despite the logic of the matter, politically initiated programs have tended to emphasize compulsory controls to achieve the necessary resource allocations rather than indirect inducements through profit prospects.

Clearly, it would be intolerable for behavioral biases to interfere with the solutions to these problems, because they must be solved one way or another if existing social and economic structures are to persist. Compromise would seem essential and this might suggest two courses of action. First, corporate goals and related policies, particularly those of large corporations, should be made compatible with the vital goals of society at large. Second, because it would seem highly inequitable to allow a minority of insensitive managements to ignore their responsibilities and thereby enjoy a competitive cost advantage, public controls to achieve the necessary resource allocations and to distribute costs in an equitable manner should be welcomed and even initiated rather than reluctantly accepted.

One further point, implicit in the above comments, should be emphasized. An increasing number of active, concerned, and intelligent groups, including the communications media, are constantly evaluating the performance of the private sector on these matters. As a result, corporations would be well advised not to yield to the temptation of making the rhetoric of their public relations statements in excess of true performance. The media and the public are becoming increasingly sensitive to "credibility gaps," and the corporate sector must expect that any differences between their public statements and operational policies are likely to be critically exposed to public view. A serious "credibility gap" could prove disastrous. This would invite public support, if not agitation, for punitive regulations and controls on the grounds that corporations cannot be trusted to act voluntarily in a socially responsible manner, and in fact will attempt to evade their responsibilities through hypocritical smoke-screens.

Thus it is my opinion that vigorous programs to meet the crucial social and environmental problems of our society are not incompatible with the long-run profit goals of business. Such programs may, however, require significant near-term sacrifices of optimal resource allocations. But unless these sacrifices are made, the corporate sector can expect increasingly hostile responses from activist groups and ultimately the free enterprise system itself may be endangered. Some argue that these matters are largely the concern of the government and that the private sector should merely cooperate with governmental programs. Now hopefully, some of the real costs involved in allocating scarce resources to these programs can be met partially through a shift in government spending priorities, particularly through a massive shift in expenditures from defense and subsidy programs to social programs. But to default leadership on these matters to the government would be, in my opinion, a serious mistake; it would suggest that the private sector is for all practical purposes inept in responding to the basic problems of society.

There is no doubt that under a competitive free enterprise system, a creative and industrious people will maximize the traditional measures of economic performance, such as per capita output and growth thereof. The question is whether such a system can adapt itself to other measures of performance, such as preserving the quality of the environment and alleviating urban decay. If it cannot, then the critics who argue [that] the system is out of control may be right. But the system has proven to be remarkably adaptable in the past and I feel that management goals will increasingly recognize the need for enlightened long-term policies in order to avoid self-destruction. But it will not be easy, because such policies will require major changes in the traditional patterns of management decision-making that will be difficult to bring about. Therefore, it is not a time for complacency. Unless the system is responsive, history may show that the last half of the twentieth century witnessed the demise of the free enterprise system as we know it, and this would be a tragic event.

QUESTIONS

1. Do you agree with the rationale that Hayes presents to support business decisions that are "nonoptimal"? Explain your position.
2. It is argued that current socially oriented business activities may be justified because they will result in long-range profit maximization. Is this really justified if the connection between the action today and the long-range profit maximization of a company is not clear? For example, can a corporation trace the future impact on its profits of a current decision to increase its community welfare contributions?
3. What limits does Hayes put on the assumption of social responsibilities by a business? Do you accept them as appropriate for this day and age?

FIVE PROPOSITIONS FOR SOCIAL RESPONSIBILITY

KEITH DAVIS

Keith Davis, professor of management, College of Business Administration, Arizona State University, and a well-known writer in the field of business-society relationships, explains in the following article five important guidelines that have evolved over the past twenty-five years of controversy to help guide the pursuit of social programs by individual business firms.

Business's need for social response and social responsibility has been discussed loudly and at length. What does it all mean? One way to understand the issues is to examine the basic propositions offered in the social responsibility debate.

Modern society presents business with immensely complicated problems. Technology has advanced to a level that tests intellectual capacities, markets have become more complex and international in scope, and difficult new problems of social issues and social responsibility have arisen. In earlier periods, the mission of business was clear. It was strictly an economic one—to produce the best quality of goods and services at the lowest possible price and to distribute them effectively. The accomplishment of this mission was remarkably effective, so effective that large numbers of the population found their minimum economic needs reasonably satisfied and began to turn their thoughts toward other needs.

Beginning in the 1950s, the public's mood shifted sharply toward social concerns, and this mood was reflected in extensive social demands made on institutions. Since business interacts extensively with all of society, perhaps more of these demands were made on business than on any other institution. By sticking strictly to its economic role in the past, business had left the social side of its activities largely untended and was unprepared to deal effectively with social issues. However, the public also was unprepared for its new role as social protagonist, and, as a result, churning and ferment have marked discussion of social priorities, how they are to be accomplished, and what role business should play in this accomplishment.

After more than twenty years of controversy, the debate over business and social issues has now reached some maturity. Out of this maturity, a degree of uniform support is developing for certain social propositions to guide the conduct of business as well as of other institutions. These guidelines apply to a greater or lesser degree according to individual circumstances, but the important point is that they do apply. Intelligent businessmen will take heed of these guidelines if they wish to avoid unnecessary confrontations with

Keith Davis, "Five Propositions for Social Responsibility," *Business Horizons,* June 1975, pp. 19–24. Reprinted by permission.

society. This article examines five of these guidelines which are supported by a degree of consensus. These guidelines collectively will be called the social responsibility mode.

SOCIAL RESPONSIBILITY AND POWER

One basic proposition is that *social responsibility arises from social power.* Modern business has immense social power in such areas as minority employment and environmental pollution. If business has the power, then a just relationship demands that business also bear responsibility for its actions in these areas. Social responsibility arises from concern about the consequences of business's acts as they affect the interests of others. Business decisions do have social consequences. Businessmen cannot make decisions that are solely economic decisions, because they are interrelated with the whole social system. This situation requires that businessmen's thinking be broadened beyond the company gate to the whole social system. Systems thinking is required.

Social responsibility implies that a business decision maker in the process of serving his own business interests is obliged to take actions that also protect and enhance society's interests. The net effect is to improve the quality of life in the broadest possible way, however quality of life is defined by society. In this manner, harmony is achieved between business's actions and the larger social system. The businessman becomes concerned with social as well as economic outputs and with the total effect of his institutional actions on society.

Business institutions that ignore responsibility for their social power are threatened by what Keith Davis and Robert L. Blomstrom call the Iron Law of Responsibility: "In the long run, those who do not use power in a manner which society considers responsible will tend to lose it." The record of history has supported operation of this law as one institution after another has found its power either eroded or overthrown when it fails to use power responsibly. The implication for business is that, if it wishes to retain its viability and significance as a major social institution, then it must give responsible attention to social issues.

The fundamental assumption of this model is that society has entrusted to business large amounts of society's resources to accomplish its mission, and business is expected to manage these resources as a wise trustee for society. In addition to the traditional role of economic entrepreneurship, business now has a new social role of trusteeship. As trustee for society's resources, it serves the interests of all claimants on the organization, rather than only those of owners, or consumers, or labor.

The history of business responsibility in economic and social areas has evolved gradually. In the beginning, business accepted little responsibility of any kind. It operated strictly according to the rules of pure competition so ably described by Adam Smith in 1776. Then business gradually began to accept some responsibility—and credit—for providing jobs in the community. It properly claimed that providing jobs was a valuable community service and that business was the institution that could best provide this service.

Over a period of time, concern for jobs expanded to become concern for the full economic impact of business on its community, whether in terms of job, taxes, or something else. Business was seen as part of a whole economic community with responsibilities for playing its proper role in that complex system. Then business began to accept responsibility for philanthropic gifts in areas less directly connected to its economic function, and the door gradually was opened to recognition of business's social power and responsibility along with its economic power and responsibility. This recognition was hastened by the rise of consumerism, civil rights issues, and environmental pollution.

AN OPEN SYSTEM INTERFACE

A second basic proposition is that *business shall operate as a two-way open system with open receipt of inputs from society and open disclosure of its operations to the public.* An open interface in both directions is essential. Business has been charged with consistently turning a deaf ear toward many of the inputs directed toward it. The executive suite has been geared to send messages but not to receive them. Under the best of conditions, business has offered an untrained ear to social inputs so that it misunderstood the message or heard only selected parts.

The social responsibility model expects business to turn both a sensitive and a trained ear to social needs and wants. If these inputs do not flow freely from society, perhaps because of society's past frustrations with communication efforts, business will seek them just as avidly as it seeks market information for traditional economic purposes. Business must know what is going on in society if business is to respond to social needs.

With regard to business communication outputs, the charge is that most outward communication has been a public relations facade, usually revealing the good but rarely the bad about business products or operations. The social responsibility model, however, postulates a policy of full disclosure in which both product and social data about a firm are available in the same way that economic data are now available. To accomplish the objective of full disclosure the social audit is proposed. Such an audit would serve the same purpose in social areas that an accounting audit serves in economic areas. It is a necessary instrument to determine whether a business has been using its social assets responsibly. It shows where progress has been made and where deficiencies remain. It is a useful guide to management for improving its performance, a check and balance on mismanagement of resources, and an open disclosure to those with a bona fide interest in social performance.

The model of the social audit is, of course, an ideal. At the present, it is hardly operational and decades may pass before it reaches the proficiency of today's accounting audits, but it is a justifiable model in support of an open business system. Though the ideal of open communication probably can never be reached fully because of inherent difficulties in the communication process, the social responsibility model postulates that considerable improvement is both possible and necessary.

Some aspects of consumerism are examples of the beginning of open disclosure. For example, the public has insisted that installment debt charges be fully disclosed, that grocery prices allow comparative price shopping, that containers not be misleading, and that labels disclose the dangers of products.

CALCULATION OF SOCIAL COSTS

A third basic proposition is that *social costs as well as benefits of an activity, product, or service shall be thoroughly calculated and considered in order to decide whether to proceed with it.* In the past, business has been required to consider only two factors in deciding whether to proceed with an activity. These factors were technical feasibility and economic profitability. If they were favorable, the activity was launched. Now business has a third factor to consider—the social effect of an activity. Only if all factors are favorable is it safe to proceed.

In making these kinds of decisions, both short- and long-run costs must be considered. For example, a firm that builds row upon row of look-alike houses may be saving $500 on each house and passing along $400 of the saving to each buyer, thus serving consumer interests. In the long-run, however, this kind of construction may encourage the rapid development of a city slum. In this instance, the lack of a long-range outlook may result in serious social costs.

Long-run cost data need to be diligently sought; business cannot assume that if nothing negative is evident, there is no problem. The automobile industry, for example, is faulted for the myopic vision that prevented it from perceiving the serious environmental problems that developed from automobile emissions. Even though it was a transportation expert on which the public depended, the industry was unable to foresee and prevent the environmental degradation that resulted from its products. Similarly, the chemical industry did not foresee the health-damaging effects of vinyl chloride gas even though it was known as a powerful chemical.

If better forecasting cannot be developed, then is it worthwhile to initiate potentially damaging activities even when they bring short-run benefits? In the future, for example, extreme caution may be required for introduction of new products from dangerous chemical families.

In sum, the expectation of the social responsibility model is that a detailed cost/benefit analysis will be made prior to determining whether to proceed with an activity and that social costs will be given significant weight in the decision-making process. Almost any business action will entail some social costs. The basic question is whether the benefits outweigh the costs so that there is a net social benefit. Many questions of judgment arise, and there are no precise mathematical measures in the social field, but rational and wise judgments can be made if the issues are first thoroughly explored.

For major business projects, such as the doubling of a plant's capacity and employment in a suburban area, the social responsibility model implies that society may eventually require social impact statements comparable with today's environmental impact statements. Then affected parties could become involved in considering a project before decisions have been made. In other instances, such as the introduction of new drugs, the public wants the government to act in the public's interest through regulatory agencies.

What is being threatened is the business decision-making process itself. Business is expected to make responsible decisions based on thorough examination of costs and benefits and, if necessary, only after those groups affected have been involved, such as a community. If business cannot establish a track record of responsible decisions, then the Iron Law of Responsibility will force business to share its decision-making powers with government and representatives of affected interest groups. Business will have a less free hand in making decisions with a social impact.

THE USER PAYS

A fourth basic proposition is that the *social costs of each activity, product, or service shall be priced into it so that the consumer (user) pays for the effects of his consumption on society*. This philosophy holds that a fair consumer price for a product or service is one that includes all costs of production, including social costs. Historically, society or someone else has had to bear these social costs while the consumer benefited from reduced product prices.

Consider the case of the environment. For the most part, the environment has been an economic free good that a business could use, passing much of the saving on to the consumer. It was a public common available to all without substantial charge. The strip miner could mine coal without the cost of restoring the topsoil, thus providing cheaper electricity for consumers. The steelmaker could use oxygen from the air for his blast furnace without paying society a penny for it, and he also could use the air as a dumping ground for his wastes. Similarly, he could draw water from the river and discharge his wastes into it without paying for this service.

Society placed no economic value on these public commons. They were free goods. Therefore, both the businessman and his customers avoided paying for degradation of the common, and these costs were transferred to society as social costs. This was not a serious problem as long as the load on the common was light, but when it became heavy, society found itself burdened with costs that it did not wish to bear. The social responsibility model assumes that generally society should not bear these costs. The consumer should pay for his consumption, including social costs of preventing pollution. That is a fair price; any other would be unfair to the public or to innocent third parties.

The philosophy that the user pays is a general guide, not a hard and fast rule. There will be many exceptions including instances when the costs are unknown at the time the user makes his purchase or when the costs are so minimal that they will be ignored. In other cases, a remedy may not be technologically feasible and so no costs are established, for example, the removal of sulfate chemicals from the stacks of coal-burning electrical generating stations. Technology is not available for the complete removal of these pollutants, so some are allowed and no additional charge is transmitted to the customer. Thus he buys his electricity more cheaply than he could if total removal were technologically feasible and the removal equipment required. In other instances, the government may underwrite part of the costs in the name of the public interest, passing costs on to taxpayers rather than to users of that particular product or service.

Nevertheless, the general philosophy that the user pays still applies. The reasoning is that since his consumption incurs the social cost, he should bear as much of it as possible. If the added costs discourage his consumption, the result is still beneficial because certain social costs are avoided.

SOCIAL RESPONSIBILITIES AS CITIZENS

A fifth basic proposition is that *beyond social costs business institutions as citizens have responsibilities for social involvement in areas of their competence where major social needs exist*. The four preceding propositions concern social costs directly caused by business. In the fifth proposition, business actions are only indirectly related to certain social problems, but nevertheless business is obliged to help solve them.

The fifth proposition is based essentially on the reasoning that business is a major social institution that should bear the same kinds of citizenship costs for society that an individual citizen bears. Business will benefit from a better society just as any citizen will benefit; therefore, business has a responsibility to recognize social problems and actively contribute its talents to help solve them.

Such involvement is expected of any citizen, and business should fulfill a citizenship role. Business will not have primary responsibility for solving problems, but it should provide significant assistance. For example, business did not directly cause educational problems, but it does stand to gain some benefit from their solution; therefore, it has some responsibility to help develop and apply solutions.

A MATTER OF HARMONY

The thrust of the foregoing propositions is that business, like any individual, needs to act responsibly regarding the consequences of its actions. The socially responsible organization behaves in such a way that it protects and improves the social quality of life along with its own quality of life. In essence, quality of life refers to the degree to which people live in harmony with their inner spirit, their fellow man, and nature's physical environment. Business has a significant effect on each of these, particularly the last two. It can support harmony among people as well as in the environment if it will take the larger system's view.

Although quality of life embraces harmony, it is not a static concept that seeks to preserve a utopian status quo. Rather, it is a dynamic concept in which people live harmoniously with the changes occurring in nature and in themselves. It is, however, a utopian concept in the sense that most people use it as an ultimate goal that they realize probably will never be obtained absolutely. It is essentially a set of criteria by which judgments may be made about social progress. The social responsibility model seeks to improve the quality of life through its five propositions.

Certain observations can be made concerning the implementation of the social responsibility model.

First, it applies to all organizations. Although this discussion has been presented in the context of business, the social responsibility model does not single out business for special treatment. All organizations have equal responsibilities for the consequences of their actions.

Similarly, social responsibility applies to all persons in all of their life roles, whether employee, camper, renter, or automobile driver. An individual who tosses his rubbish along a roadside is just as irresponsible as a business that pours pollutants into a river. The individual may argue that his offense is less in magnitude, but when his rubbish is added to all the rest, it becomes a massive offense against the public interest.

As a matter of fact, quality of life will be improved less than people expect if only business is socially responsible. Substantial improvement will be achieved only when most organizations and persons act in socially responsible ways.

Second, the movement toward greater social responsibility is not a fad but a fundamental change in social directions. Business executives will do their organizations grievous damage if they assume social responsibility is merely something to be assigned to a third assistant with action to be taken only when absolutely necessary and when the organization is backed into a corner.

Social responsibility is here to stay despite its intangibles and imponderables. As stated earlier, business probably has been a significant cause of the rise of social responsibility ideas because it did its economic job so well that it released people from economic want, freeing them to pursue new social goals.

Third, social response by business will increase business's economic costs. Social responsibility is not a free ride or a matter of simple goodwill. Actions such as the reduction of pollution take large amounts of economic resources. The costs are there. It is true that some of these costs are transferred from other segments of society, so society as a whole may not bear higher costs for some actions; however, these costs are brought into the business system and, in most instances, will flow through in the form of higher prices.

This situation is likely to put further strain on business-consumer relations. It may even lead to consumer demands for less social involvement in the short run, but the long-run secular trend toward more social involvement is likely to remain.

QUESTIONS

1. Are these five propositions useful guidelines for managers in concrete situations where action is required? Why or why not?
2. Examine each proposition. What federal laws and regulations attempt to impose each on the business community? What proposals might arise in the near future to bring about more stringent accountability to the dictates of each of Davis' propositions?
3. Can you think of any other basic propositions that might be added to those in the article?

INSTITUTIONALIZING CORPORATE SOCIAL DECISIONS

GEORGE A. STEINER

George A. Steiner in the following article discusses the many different methods being employed by individual business firms to institutionalize the social point of view in organizational decision-making processes.

In recent years there has been a significant change in the role of business in society. Succinctly, it is that effective social action by individual enterprises is becoming an integral part of business operations. Not all corporate managers accept this role but more and more do, especially those in larger corporations. This concept will become considerably more predominant in the future and it will be of increasing importance to managers as they move through their business careers. Furthermore, how managers respond to it will have much to do with the survival and vitality of the business system as we know it.

Many thoughtful people fear that the acceptance of an expanding social role by business will produce unfortunate consequences for business and society. I believe the results will be just the reverse. An appropriate blending of the social and economic performance of business will strengthen each and permit business to respond much better to the aspirations of people for a better life. Every manager should have in his or her intellectual tool kit some understanding of the forces at work which relate to the new social role of business in society. The purpose of this article is not only to provoke thinking along these lines, but also to suggest policies for action which will benefit not only companies but the careers of managers.

NEW DEMANDS ON BUSINESS PERFORMANCE

Just as our physical environment is rapidly changing, values in society are changing, and are placing new demands on business. Peter Drucker caught the essence of the change when he said, "The new demand is a demand that business and businessmen make concern for society central to the conduct of business itself. It is a demand that the quality of life become the business of business." This does not mean that business is relieved of its past social obligation to be efficient in the use of resources at its disposal. Society still wants that, but also something more: society wants corporations to help people improve the quality of their lives.

George A. Steiner, "Institutionalizing Corporate Decisions," *Business Horizons,* December 1975.

However, there is no concensus about what quality of life means or what individual companies should be doing about it. At a high level of abstraction there is agreement that improvements in our society would include a high and rising level of minimum personal income for everyone, progress in human equality, an opportunity for individuals to achieve self-fulfillment, a pollution free environment, resolution of major socio-economic problems, and more satisfied consumers. There is a broad acceptance of the view that corporations ought to help achieve these conditions, but at that point agreement ends.

Individuals and groups can, of course, be very specific about programs which they expect business to pursue in their social interest. The list of programs which corporations are expected to pursue is lengthening. Even the Committee for Economic Development, a group of prominent businessmen, in a milestone report on the social obligations of business, said a few years ago that ". . . the corporate interest broadly defined by management can support involvement in helping to solve virtually any social problem . . ." It should be added that a number of opinion polls have shown that many public expectations of business social action are well beyond reality. For instance, to take an extreme case, one poll showed that 68% of the respondents expected business to take leadership in reducing the threat of war.

Society's demands for corporate social action can be met in three ways. First, society can dictate corporate social programs through government legislation. Second, powerful individuals and groups can exert pressure directly on corporations. Third, corporations can respond voluntarily to changing social attitudes. It is the latter category of actions which we shall address. These actions can be viewed in different ways. The Committee for Economic Development, for instance, says that the corporate response to society's demands has widened in three expanding circles. First is the inner circle which embraces responsibility for the efficient execution of a business's basic economic function in producing goods and services, providing jobs, and assuring economic growth. Next is an intermediate circle which encompasses responsibility to use this economic function with a sensitive awareness of changing social demands—for example, by conserving scarce resources, employing disadvantaged minorities, and giving consumers more information about products. The third circle includes emerging responsibilities that business should accept to help society achieve the objectives it sets for itself.

The U.S. Chamber of Commerce looks at the matter from a slightly different perspective. It says that the area of voluntary social action can be viewed at four levels. The first is conforming to existing legal requirements in fulfilling the economic function; second, is meeting recognized public expectations and social demands; third, is anticipating new social demands and preparing in advance to meet them; and fourth, is serving as leaders in setting new standards of business social performance.

There is no doubt that new demands on business for social performance are being added to old economic demands. Business is indeed responding, and the result is a new role which is distinctly different from the past. Business today must be successful as an economic entity but at the same time it must serve social needs. The ability to achieve this dual purpose may distinguish the successful from the unsuccessful business. Richard Gerstenberg, former chairman of General Motors, captured this thought when he said, "The most successful business in the years ahead will be the one that not only offers quality products at competitive prices, but also succeeds in matching its resources to society's changing demands, the business that is best able to give creative response to the social aspirations of the people it serves. Conversely, the business that fails in the years ahead will be the one that fails to understand how it is related to the society around it and will, therefore, overlook opportunities for service, for growth and for profit."

Though there is no way to measure the strength of the pressures on business to undertake voluntary social programs, they appear to be very strong. They spring from a new motivation in society, namely, a coalescence of individual personal values which reach for a better quality of life. This new driving force is so powerful that it is challenging other traditional societal motivating forces such as increased technology and economic growth. This new force has weakened a bit with the recent economic downturn, but it will gain new strength as economic problems are resolved.

HIGHLIGHTS OF THE DEBATE

Not everyone accepts the idea that business has social responsibilities. One reason is that the concept of social responsibility is subject to various interpretations, and there are those who can always find a new spark to rekindle the argument. For this reason, a few of the highlights of the debate should be kept in mind.

A well-known opponent of businesses' assumption of social responsibilities is Milton Friedman, a distinguished professor of economics. His position is clearly expressed in the following passage: ". . . there is one and only one social responsibility of business—to use its resources and engage in activities designed to increase its profits so long as it stays within the rules of the game, which is to say, engages in open and free competition without deception or fraud. Few trends could so thoroughly undermine the very foundations of our free society as the acceptance by corporate officials of a social responsibility other than to make as much money for their stockholders as possible. This is a fundamentally subversive doctrine."

Friedman's position is not taken without reason. He argues that if funds are diverted to social programs without stockholders' approval, the effect in essence is taxation without representation. Also, if business pursues too much social activity, its performance may eventually be measured by social rather than economic criteria. This, in turn, may lead to less economic efficiency and produce consequences which could be to the disadvantage of all society. Finally, business capability lies in economic, not social, programs. Those of Friedman's persuasion would prefer to let government deal with the social aspirations of the community.

Strong voices opposing this philosophy emanate from both the business and academic worlds. The Committee for Economic Development, for example, advanced the doctrine in the policy statement noted earlier that "It is in the 'enlightened self-interest' of corporations to promote the public welfare in a positive way." This is so, the CED added, because ". . . people who have a good environment, education, and opportunity, make better employees, customers, and neighbors for business than those who are poor, ignorant, and oppressed."

Another argument in favor of corporate social action, not entirely separate from the self-interest doctrine, is that corporations are institutions sanctioned by society and when society's expectations about their functions change, corporate actions should change. Gerhard Bleichen, chairman of the board of John Hancock Mutual Life Insurance Company, put it this way: ". . . it never occurred to me that there was a time when American business was at liberty to operate in conflict with the interests of society." Others believe that business should fulfill social obligations to avoid or delay government legislation. Obviously, businessmen are citizens, and as such, many feel an obligation to use their resources to meet needs for social action.

ASSESSING THE ARGUMENTS

Those with a laissez-faire attitude are on weak ground for two major reasons. First, they overstate the trend and ultimate magnitude of business's voluntary assumption of social responsibilities. As Friedman says, corporations should comply with the rules of the game, which include legislation, so there is no argument about a business's obligation to assume social responsibilities which are dictated by government. But the social responsibilities which businesses voluntarily assume today are not, nor are they likely to be, so large as to result in any serious erosion of economic standards as measures of performance. We are moving into an era in which corporate social performance will be more and more the subject of measurement, but this will complement economic performance measurement, not replace it. A second major weakness of those opposing business social action is that they ask corporations to ignore society's demands, which is something they simply cannot do.

We should not conclude that the arguments against social actions by corporations are groundless and have no substance. They do contain warning signals that caution against excessive thrusts away from economic motivations and economic measures of performance. They warn that private businesses should not assume excessive burdens which are rightfully the responsibility of government or private citizens. They warn that unrealistic expectations can lead to widespread discontent with business, which would not be in the best interests of business or the public. To prevent expectations from getting out of bounds, a set of realistic limitations on the corporate assumption of social responsibilities should be agreed upon.

WHAT IS BUSINESS DOING?

At the present time there seems to be a paradoxical trend regarding business social responsibilities. On the one hand, the rhetoric which hit rather high decibles a year or so ago has noticeably diminished. On the other hand, empirical observations and surveys suggest that social involvement of American businesses is increasing. We shall discuss changing managerial philosophies, and how firms can formulate and implement social action programs which are appropriate to particular companies.

CHANGING MANAGERIAL PHILOSOPHIES

Classical business philosophy teaches that the only responsibility of managers is to use the scarce resources at their disposal as efficiently as possible to produce the goods and services that people want, at prices they are willing to pay. Economists reasoned that if businessmen did this job well, they would maximize profits.

The first major break from this view occurred in the early 1930s, when managers of very large corporations took the position that they were not solely responsible to common stockholders, but had an obligation to consider all those with a major interest in the enterprise, including employees, customers, suppliers, and the general public, in addition to stockholders. If this were done well, it was reasoned, the long-range interests of stockholders would be best served. This is the balanced-interest managerial philosophy.

The second major break with classical philosophy is now taking place. It is what might be termed the socioeconomic managerial philosophy. It asserts that managers have responsibilities to stockholders and also to the larger community in reacting positively to its demands for social programs which will improve the quality of life. It is a recognition that corporations must react not only to economic forces in their environment but also to social forces. The new socioeconomic view is epitomized by Edward Cole, former president of General Motors, in these words: "The big challenge to American business—as I see it—is to carefully evaluate the constantly changing expressions of public and national goals. Then we must modify our own objectives and programs to meet—as far as possible within the realm of economic and technological feasibility—the new demands of the society we serve."

These three managerial philosophies—the classical, the managerial, and the socioeconomic—are not sequential. Among managers, the public, government officials, and students of business, each can be found today and each is being used to justify particular types of social actions and thoughts. More managers are accepting the socioeconomic managerial philosophy and the trend will probably continue. While no two companies have taken the same identical actions to implement this philosophy, a number of specific practices are somewhat indicative.

STANDARDS FOR MANAGERIAL PROMOTION

More and more companies are making it clear that those who aspire to the top levels of management must be aware of changing social needs and demands, and be capable of directing the company's activities to meet them in an acceptable fashion. For example, A. W. Clausen, president and chief executive officer of Bank of America National Trust & Savings Assn., set forth several criteria which are to be used in selecting senior management people at the bank. One of them is *sociopolitical sensitivity*. Clausen says, ". . . it is imperative that the senior corporate manager understand . . . sociopolitical forces. While there are many of these forces, if I were asked today to rank them in terms of their importance . . . I would suggest this order: consumerism, demands of minorities, demands of women and the crisis of the environment. We do not feel that anyone can aspire to a senior management position in BankAmerica . . . without an acute awareness of the impact these forces may have on our operations."

Closely associated with the sociopolitical sensitivity standard is a second one concerning *awareness of people* which reads: ". . . the senior manager today and tomorrow must understand in both mind and heart that new philosophical forces are changing the value systems of today's work force. The manager must see the reality behind the rising cry for job enrichment. There must be increased awareness of the growing demand, particularly from younger members of the work force, for greater freedom of action, for greater responsibility, or both." The final criterion for prospective BankAmerica managers is *profit consciousness,* and regarding that standard, Clausen said, in part, "I have deliberately placed the most important dimension last. I have left it until last because each of the other characteristics we seek in a senior manager is necessary to preserve, protect and enhance our ability to generate a profit. It is our considered judgment . . . that without the other dimensions, a management may run grave risks of having some good profit years and then some bad ones."

POLICIES CONCERNING SOCIAL RESPONSIBILITIES

Increasingly, companies are formulating policies to govern their social actions. To illustrate, the Occidental Life Insurance Company of California adopted the following policy: "To commit a reasonable portion of our human and financial resources to the improvement of the quality of human life of our various publics, giving priority to those areas where our special competence can make a significant contribution and those areas which have the most direct immediate effect upon the consumer of our services. To accumulate and maintain a body of knowledge that represents the current 'state of the art' in corporate social responsibility. (To) include in the body an annual inventory of our current activities that contribute to improvement in the quality of human life." The company also created machinery to implement that policy.

In developing policies governing social actions, companies are reexamining their profit concepts. The following profit objective statement is suggested for companies which are reevaluating their responsibilities:

> It is the policy of the company to take actions in the name of social responsibilities but not at the expense of that required level of rising profits needed to maintain the economic strength and dynamism desired by top management. Actions taken in the name of social responsibility should enhance the economic strength of the company and/or the business community. The over-all mission of the company is two pronged, as follows: to set forth and achieve corporate objectives which meet specified social challenges ranging from product quality to the quality of life requirements, both internally and externally, and to increase the company's earnings per share at a rate required to meet shareowner/profit expectations *and* these new requirements.

A number of companies have adopted similar profit policy statements.

SURVEYS OF NEEDS AND DEMANDS

Within the past few years several large companies began to systematically survey the needs and/or demands of their constituents; General Electric was one of the first to undertake such a survey. Their study identified ninety-seven specific needs, demands, and threats which were of concern to the company. The list is used to determine which interests have the highest priority for action, and the strategic planning process of the company is affected accordingly. Any company that wants to address itself to social obligations ought to have some concept of the needs and demands of its constituents. This is not easy to determine, but it is desirable, and more companies in the future will be following in GE's footsteps.

ESTABLISHING COMMITTEES

Many companies establish committees from their boards of directors to determine which social programs the company should undertake. In 1970, for instance, General Motors created a Public Policy Committee composed of five members of the GM board. The committee meets once a month to make recommendations to GM's top management. Other companies which use board members in this way are Ford Motor Co., IBM Corp., Kimberly-Clark Corp., and Philip Morris, Inc.

Firms also have changed their organizational structures so that social action programs are the responsibility of one individual, a department, or a committee. The power and scope of these individuals and groups vary, of course, but the point is that companies have specifically assigned responsibility for social programs.

MANAGERIAL IMPLEMENTATION SYSTEMS

If the social point of view is to be institutionalized in the decision-making process, much more needs to be done than to establish a broad policy or a committee. Goals, detailed policies, and specific procedures must be established, as well as information and feedback systems, rewards and punishments, and a commitment to achieve objectives. In other words, a managerial system must be created which plans for social activities and controls the effort. Such systems must be developed if top managers are to be sure that their companies comply with social policies, whether formulated in response to laws or established voluntarily.

The last managerial instrument noted here is the social audit, which was widely discussed in the late 1960s and early 1970s, when demands for it increased from groups outside of business. Since then the clamor for corporate social audits has declined but, paradoxically, more companies are making them. A social audit is a report on the social performance of a business in contrast, for instance, to its financial performance. No standards for making a social audit are widely accepted. Audits range from lengthy annual publications such as that of General Motors called *Report on Progress in Areas of Public Concern* to a short statement about social activities in an annual financial report. Some companies make social audits only for internal use.

The trend seems to be toward more disclosure of social performance. The Securities and Exchange Commission has conducted hearings on the subject and some requirements governing such disclosures may be set. The business community seems to expect more pressure for disclosure. In a recent CED survey, respondents were asked whether they thought social audits would be mandatory in the future. Surprisingly, 46% said yes, and most of those respondents indicated a mandatory social audit was acceptable to them.

Today in the United States, there exists a powerful move to seek continued improvement in the quality of life for the entire population. All institutions, including business firms, are expected to participate in achieving this end. Thus, the corporations must pursue social goals as well as traditional economic objectives. Many see an inconsistency and conflict between these two roles, but corporations are demonstrating that the two roles can complement one another. The great challenge ahead for managers of corporations is to establish policies and programs which will pursue both economic and social goals which will be mutually supportive.

QUESTIONS

1. It is argued that "an appropriate blending of the social and economic performance of business" will strengthen the business system and boost social welfare. What arguments does the author advance to substantiate this claim?
2. Does the author give an objective assessment of the pros and cons of the social responsibility debate?
3. In his "Assessing the Arguments," Steiner asserts that corporations simply cannot ignore society's demands. Do you agree? Do business executives agree?
4. Are the policies suggested for coping with the changed managerial environment adequately compelling to reach the state of responsiveness Steiner feels is desirable? Can you think of others that may be equally or more effective or appropriate?

THE SOCIAL AUDIT

JOHN J. CORSON AND
GEORGE A. STEINER

John J. Corson, retired chairman of the board of Fry Consultants, Inc., and former professor of political science, Princeton University, and George A. Steiner discuss major issues relating to the social audit.

CONCEPTS OF THE SOCIAL AUDIT

There are many different ideas about what a social audit is, and consensus on the subject is limited to the agreement that, at a high level of abstraction, the social audit is concerned with the social performance of a business in contrast to its economic performance as measured in the financial audit. Since all the definitions cannot be presented here, five basic types will be described.

First, some businessmen have concentrated on identifying and totaling expenditures for social activities. This concept, described as the "cost or outlay approach," involves the recognition of costs and the search for ways to reduce such costs. The application of this concept poses difficult problems of cost allocation. For example, what part of the cost of orienting and training a new employee should be attributed to the regular costs of doing business, and what part, such as the reduction of unemployment among black youths, should be attributed to the employer's undertaking of a social activity? The cost approach concentrates on inputs and makes no attempt to measure outputs—that is, how much social good and/or favorable public reaction toward the corporation have the dollars expended actually produced? It provides information needed to guide operating officials within the corporation but offers no measures of accomplishment that will satisfy the demands for information by consumers, the public at large, and government.

Second, the "human asset valuation approach to the social audit" is designed to measure the "value of the productive capability of the firm's human organization" and the "value of shareholder loyalty, banker and finance community goodwill, customer loyalty, supplier loyalty, and loyalty in the communities where plants or offices are located." That these factors have values and that these values are influenced by the corporation's social behavior (e.g., the environment the firm provides for employees; the reputation for integrity it builds with customers, suppliers, and financiers; and the image it establishes in the minds of citizens) are ideas that are generally accepted. Hence, some students of the idea of a social audit propose the

From John J. Corson and George A. Steiner, *Measuring Business's Social Performance: The Corporate Social Audit*. New York: Committee for Economic Development, 1974, pp. 18–20, 40, 41, 45, 46, 49–52, 59–63. Reprinted by permission.

fulfillment of these values as a justification for the costs of social activities that the corporation carries on.

Those espousing this concept contend that it offers a "positive evaluation" of the worth of social activities and is preferable to a negative approach that focuses on costs and perhaps measures of what is done (e.g., number of women promoted above the supervisory level or the abandonment of billboard advertising). Critics of this concept, while accepting it as an aid to executive decision making and stockholder understanding, fault this approach on the grounds that it measures social accomplishments in terms that are not meaningful to constituents outside the corporation.

A third concept of the social audit has been described as the "program management approach," which focuses on measuring only those activities in which a particular company is involved largely for social reasons. With respect to each such activity (e.g., the student loan program of a bank or the provision of scholarships for the children of employees of a corporation) this approach would involve (1) an approximation of the costs and (2) an evaluation of the effectiveness of the activity. The Bank of America has used this approach in assessing its activities, and its spokesmen argue for this concept in very pragmatic terms: Such "an audit appraises what can be appraised." Thus, this kind of social audit serves the needs of corporate officials and provides some measures of accomplishment that meet the demands of certain external constituents.

A fourth concept, generally called the "inventory approach," involves the cataloging and narrative description of what the corporation is doing in each area where it recognizes that society (or articulate segments of society) expects it to do something. The results of this approach may be a massive descriptive listing of the corporation's activities with little or no analysis of results or costs. This approach does not provide a measure of the aggregate costs entailed; of the value to the company in terms of morale, goodwill, and public image; or of the benefits contributed to the society. It serves to inform the corporation's management and directors but provides less than is required to meet the demands of many outside the company who seek an evaluative accounting.

A fifth concept of the social audit can be called the "cost/benefit approach." There are a number of possible types of cost/benefit analysis. One may be called the "balance sheet approach." This tries to quantify values contributed to society (assets) and detriments to society for actions taken or not taken (liabilities) and arrays them in a fashion comparable to the typical financial balance sheet. This is fundamentally an accounting approach to making a social audit and entails difficult and costly calculations. Very few companies have tried this approach. Another, simpler approach is to calculate costs of social programs and benefits, to the company and/or society, for programs undertaken, in either quantitative or qualitative terms. A number of companies have done this.

In actual practice, we have found no type of social audit that predominates either conceptually or operationally. There are combinations of approaches ranging from highly simplified descriptive statements to substantial documentation and quantification. The pressures for accountability suggest that a concept of the social audit that most businessmen may accept will likely evolve and that a standard operational format will be developed. That time, however, is far off.

Nonetheless, a surprising amount of interest and activity about the social audit is found in American business today, especially among the larger corporations. This is revealed in a survey of the business social audit completed in late 1973 by the authors . . .

THE LOGIC, SCOPE, AND FEASIBILITY OF THE CORPORATE SOCIAL AUDIT

Is the social audit to become common corporate practice, or is it a fad to be abandoned in the years to come? To determine if the social audit is a valid concept requires consideration of three precedential questions.

1. Is the concept of the social audit founded on logical reasoning with regard to the relationship that does, or should, obtain between the corporation and the society?

It is most probable that less than one-fifth of all American corporations have as yet attempted to assess their social activities currently in terms of society's expectations. An indication that the very idea of responsibility to society for the performance of social activities is held by few corporate executives is suggested by the respondents' answers to two survey questions. When asked what purpose or purposes led management to undertake a social audit, a small minority attributed their action to the felt need for public disclosure or to their desire to "meet public demands for corporate accountability." . . . When asked to whom the results of their audits were disclosed, the responses indicated that less than half these companies made their findings available to their stockholders and the public. . . . Yet almost half the corporations undertaking such audits voiced the belief that all corporations will be required to submit to social audits in the future. . . .

2. If a social audit is to be made, what activities should be evaluated? What should be the scope of the audit?

A substantial majority of all corporations surveyed assumed responsibility for a variety of social activities, but there is no consensus as to what a social audit should include. Some of the possibilities are:

All social activities being performed, *or* those the corporation deems it advantageous to report on because of special accomplishments or because of special public concern at the moment

Only those activities the corporation is legally obligated to perform, *or* only those undertaken of its own volition

Activities of clear social utility without prospect of profit (e.g., the operation of a day-care center for the children of women workers), *or* activities of equal social utility that are operated for profit (e.g., the operation of schools)

3. Is the making of a social audit feasible? More specifically, can the performance of social activities be measured? Is quantification of performance essential for evaluation?

Survey respondents reported that the inability to measure accomplishments in some or all social activities constituted a principal obstacle to making a social audit. Other respondents, confronted with the problem of quantifying achievements, shied away from use of the term audit. Some suggested the alternative term social report for a statement that would describe but not measure. Still others hold that when you cannot measure what you are speaking about, when you cannot express it in numbers, your knowledge is of a meager and unsatisfactory kind. Can the demand for accountability be met despite the current difficulty of measurement?

. . .

SCOPE OF THE SOCIAL AUDIT

Historically, the primary *social* responsibility of the corporation has been to discover and develop goods and services that satisfy the needs of people. The accomplishment of that end—the production of an increasing abundance of steadily improving goods and services—has long been regarded as of such great value to the society as to warrant the earning of profits.

As the basic wants for food, clothing, shelter, and health care of most members of American society have been satisfied, society's expectations have grown to include not only new and better goods and services but other things as well. For example: (1) services of clear social utility that were once provided by government and are now provided by corporations at a *profit;* such services include postsecondary education (e.g., the schools and educational services marketed by Bell and Howell Company) and providing food services for school programs and for aged and invalid persons in their homes; (2) a widening range of amenities, services, and information for employees, consumers, shareholders, and the community, without prospect of profit and at the cost of the corporation.

If the social audit is to catalogue all such activities, verify the costs entailed, and evaluate the benefits produced, it becomes an evaluation of everything a corporation is doing. When the scope is thus defined, it becomes impractical to accomplish a social audit and, indeed, the information it would present would likely be too massive to be useful.

If, on the other hand, the scope of the audit—that is, the activities to be catalogued, verified, and evaluated—is limited, it will not demonstrate to the constituencies the extent to which the corporation's social performance measures up to what the constituents expect. For example, the social audit will not perform this principal function if it is limited to (1) those activities for which a corporation's executives are particularly concerned about accomplishments and/or costs incurred; (2) those activities about which information is publicized to better the corporation's public image.

Therefore, the scope of the social audit (like the scope of the financial audit) is determined by the informational needs of those it is designed to serve—employees, consumers, concerned shareholders, the general public, and those who influence the shaping of public opinion. In the course of time those needs will undoubtedly change, but in the main they will include the need for information about: (1) statutorily required activities (e.g., the provision of equal employment opportunities for minority group members); (2) voluntary activities (e.g., the making of contributions to health, educational, and cultural agencies and the "adoption" of a local high school); and (3) socially useful activities undertaken for the making of profits (e.g., contracting to provide teaching services in the schools).

The key task for the corporation is to specify what activities are of concern to its constituencies at a particular time. It is a difficult task, and new ways and means must be developed to accomplish it.

HOW TO DETERMINE THE SCOPE OF THE SOCIAL AUDIT

Few social audits made today embrace the categories of activities that fall logically within its scope as suggested here. The scope of few if any of these audits is determined by the standard of social expectations that has been proposed. The failure to attain this ideal is to be expected at this early stage in the evolution of this form of appraisal. A methodology for identifying social expectations and appraising corporate social performance is still being developed. To indicate the point that has been reached, we will describe ways of determining what society expects of the corporation and examine existing yardsticks for measuring the corporation's performance of various social activities.

. . .

THE MEASUREMENT PROBLEM

Presuming that the scope of a social audit can be determined, what yardsticks are available to measure the cost and accomplishments of activities included in the social audit? Without credible measures of business's social performance the social audit will make little progress. Many business executives hold views similar to that expressed by one respondent to the survey, who stated: "Most of the elements involved cannot be quantified in any meaningful way and . . . a balance sheet would result only in an oversimplified representation which might lend itself to puffery." Measures of accomplishment for many activities, as this respondent has accurately pointed out, do not yet exist, and the identification of costs is sometimes difficult. The problems involved in developing measures of accomplishment and in identifying relevant costs are substantial, yet the development of useful measures is progressing.

The financial auditor has numerous acceptable yardsticks for evaluating the financial operations of a business enterprise. They include unit production costs, the ratio of each category of costs to the sales dollar, the current ratio, inventory turnover, the aging of receivables, cash flow analyses, the ratio of net earnings to interest on debt, and others. The social auditor is at an early stage in forging similar yardsticks and faces formidable obstacles in perfecting measures for a number of social activities.

THE BOGEY OF QUANTIFICATION

The development of the social audit today is hobbled, as our survey indicates, by confusion as to purpose as well as by difficulties confronted in striving to measure costs and accomplishments. If the social audit is to inform insiders alone, one set of measures focusing on costs and efficiency of performance is needed. If the social audit is designed to meet the demands of outsiders for an assessment of social performance, a different set of measures is required.

If we assume that both needs must be served, the problem of measurement still remains. By definition an audit is a "methodical examination and review," but many businessmen view an audit as necessarily involving quantification, and, as we have stated, the quantification of costs and accomplishments is difficult, the latter more so than the former.

The costs involved in many social activities, although not all, are difficult to isolate. The benefits received by the company itself or those contributed to society are difficult to appraise. For example, what cost/benefit is involved in the maintenance by corporations of deposits in minority-owned and -operated banks? In increasing the proportion of blacks in the corporate work force? If the cost of building a plant in the inner city rather than moving it to the suburbs can be identified, how can the auditor measure the benefits produced for the company? For the community? What is the value to society of contributions to the support of black colleges and universities? Of the service of corporate employees on leave to teach in universities? Of the stimulation of interest in liturgical music?

The quantification that is involved in the financial audit (which conditions thinking as to the nature of a social audit) evolved over many years. Gradually accountants have found ways of quantifying concepts that at an earlier time were dealt with only or primarily as subjective judgments (e.g., cash flow). But even today some important concepts of costs and value are difficult to quantify and are treated in descriptive footnotes to corporate financial statements.

Methods for quantifying accomplishments of social activities are being developed. For those activities that are now required by government, some yardsticks that quantify what is expected have been established; for example, state and federal governments have established air quality and water quality standards. Yardsticks are evolving for some activities that are generally accepted by corporations as responsibilities they should bear, for example, the proportion of net income the corporation contributes to charitable, educational, religious, and welfare institutions. For many activities that corporations have undertaken, no yardsticks of accomplishment are yet available. To illustrate, there are no yardsticks to measure the performance of a company in helping society to improve its transportation systems or to preserve animal life or to recycle materials. . . . Gradually ways must and, hopefully, will be found to evaluate the worth as well as the cost of many activities that are now unmeasurable.

TO WHOM SHOULD THE SOCIAL AUDIT BE MADE AVAILABLE?

One-half of the companies responding to our survey stated that they made the results of their audit of social activities available only to the company's executives and directors. Less than half the respondent companies made the results available to stockholders and to the public. Do these practices constitute the kind of accountability being called for?

When one assesses the demands from constituents and the breadth of the social audits being made by the pioneering companies, the answer must be "No." Yet, an increasing number of corporations are now including statements in their annual and quarterly reports to stockholders describing what they have done in particular fields of social activity. A few corporations use newspaper advertising to tell the general public about social activities they are engaged in, and some others have prepared special reports describing rather comprehensively their activities and have made them generally available.

Examples of such special reports are those made in 1972, 1973, and 1974 by the General Motors Corporation entitled *Report on Progress in Areas of Public Concern.* These reports explain what General Motors did in these years to meet the problems of automobile pollution and automobile safety. They refine and make more generally known the corporation's policy relative to investments in South Africa, its policy and accomplishments in hiring members of minority groups, its efforts to assist minority group members to conduct their own businesses, and its efforts to seek the views of the consumers of its products and act upon their complaints.

EVOLUTION OF A SOCIAL REPORT

. . . As trends of recent years indicate, pressure is growing for both social performance and accountability for that performance, and executive "feel for the situation" will no longer be the only criterion for determining a corporation's involvement. In fact, it would be appropriate to assume that in the future all corporations will be required to submit a social audit to the public. (Forty-six percent of the respondents to the survey made this assumption.)

If this forecast is valid, how are corporations likely to meet this demand for accountability? An accounting maxim specifies that "the uses to which information will be put should govern both the conceptual and procedural bases on which information is prepared and disseminated." This suggests that to satisfy the demand for accountability, corporations will continue, by trial and error, to develop ways of assessing and reporting on social performance in forms that will provide constituents with information as to how the corporation is responding to society's expectations and how it compares with other corporations in the same geographical area and/or the same industry.

To make information available that would permit an informed evaluation of a corporation's response to society's expectations by those who demand accountability, we suggest the social auditing/reporting model illustrated in Exhibit 1. This model does not provide a response to every demand that is voiced nor does it provide a single measure of a corporation's aggregate social performance. Rather, it presents a comprehensive report of what the corporation is doing and has done, and places the burden of evaluation on readers of the report.

The model presumes that the corporation, by such methods as it chooses, has identified society's expectations, has determined the priority each deserves, and has accepted responsibility for some or many. Once the corporation has taken these steps, the model proposes that it report which expectations it recognizes, which expectations it can and is responding to, and the results of an assessment of its performance in each activity it is conducting. This effort would involve the steps given in Exhibit 1.

MAKING CREDIBLE A SOCIAL REPORT

If the model for auditing and reporting outlined above is used, the nature of the corporation's social commitment could be effectively judged by the corporation's choice of the social expectations it will respond to, its definition of objectives and goals, the activities it undertakes, the resources it commits, and the accomplishments it reports. The report should provide sufficiently detailed information to enable readers—executives within the corporation or members of the public outside it—to compare the corporation's social program with those of other corporations operating in the same locality or the same industry. As yardsticks for the measurement of accomplishment gradually gain acceptance, or are mandated by government, they can be utilized to add specificity to the report and to facilitate comparison.

In the absence of consensus about what social responsibilities the corporation is obligated to discharge and about the standards of performance that should prevail with respect to each social activity undertaken (e.g., what

Exhibit 1

A MODEL FOR SOCIAL AUDITING/REPORTING

1. An Enumeration of Social Expectations and the Corporation's Response	A summary and candid enumeration by program areas (e.g., consumer affairs, employee relations, physical environment, local community development) of what is expected, and the corporation's reasoning as to why it has undertaken certain activities and not undertaken others.
2. A Statement of the Corporation's Social Objectives and the Priorities Attached to Specific Activities	For each program area the corporation would report what it will strive to accomplish and what priority it places on the activities it will undertake.
3. A Description of the Corporation's Goals in Each Program Area and of the Activities It Will Conduct	For each priority activity, the corporation will state a specific goal (in quantitative terms when possible) and describe how it is striving to reach that goal (e.g., to better educational facilities in the community it will make available qualified teachers from among members of its staff).
4. A Statement Indicating the Resources Committed to Achieve Objectives and Goals	A summary report, in quantitative terms, by program area and activity, of the costs—direct and indirect—assumed by the corporation.
5. A Statement of the Accomplishments and/or Progress Made in Achieving Each Objective and Each Goal	A summary, describing in quantitative measures when feasible and through objective, narrative statement when quantification is impracticable, the extent of achievement of each objective and each goal.

proportion of its net income should a corporation contribute to the support of educational and health institutions), the credibility of a corporate social audit rests on the comprehensiveness and candor with which results are reported. Two courses of action will lend assurance that such comprehensiveness and candor will be achieved.

The first step is the retention of an independent analyst to examine the corporation's performance and to prepare and certify the report. Qualified independent analysts are scarce, but a few of the national management consulting firms, a few of the national accounting firms, and a few members of the faculties of graduate schools of business possess the requisite competence.

The second step is to have a committee composed of members of the board of directors (including public directors) review and approve the social report. A few companies have established board committees to consider issues of social responsibility.* These committees, often called the public affairs committee, the urban affairs committee, or the social policy committee, are . . . composed of some (or all) public directors. Moreover, these committees logically include those directors that bring to their deliberations a broad understanding of the society and its needs. For example, Vernon E. Jordan, executive director of the National Urban League, serves on the Celanese committee; James R. Killian, former president of the Massachusetts Institute of Technology, serves on the General Motors committee; and J. George Harrar, former president of the Rockefeller Foundation, serves on the analogous committee of Kimberly-Clark's board of directors. The committee's review and approval of the independent report would be essentially analogous to the action of the corporate audit committee, which in many corporations meets with the independent accountants, reviews a draft of their financial report, and approves this report before it is promulgated to the stockholders and to the public.

The CED statement on the *Social Responsibilities of Business Corporations* issued in June 1971 declared: "Business functions by public consent, and its basic purpose is to serve constructively the needs of society—to the satisfaction of society." The demands for information voiced by reformers, consumers, investors, government, and the public in general constitute a continuing and expanding effort to appraise how well business is serving the needs of society. The corporate social audit is, for those companies that have pioneered in the making of such assessments of their own social performance, a tool by which they can demonstrate how constructively and how comprehensively they are serving the needs of the society. . . .

QUESTIONS

1. Identify the five major concepts of the social audit, according to Corson and Steiner. Which do you think are the most appropriate for business?
2. Is the concept of the social audit a logical one? Explain.
3. What is the measurement problem in making the social audit? Is this problem one that makes the social audit impractical?

* Such committees have been established, for example, by ARA Services, Celanese Corporation, Ford Motor Company, General Motors Corporation, International Business Machines Corporation, Kimberly-Clark Corporation, and Philip Morris.

4. What advantages accrue to the business that undertakes a social audit? What disadvantages might arise?
5. If a company makes a social audit, should it always be made public? Under what circumstances might it better be considered proprietary?
6. Is the audit model outlined here adequate in light of today's demands for accountability? Why or why not? Explain your position.
7. What do you think the social audit may look like in a typical large corporation in the year 2000?

CORPORATE SOCIAL RESPONSIBILITY PRECISELY DEFINED AT SHELL

The impact of business on people and their physical and social environment is a major public issue—popularly known as "corporate social responsibility." While generating a good deal of public debate, these "buzz words" have not acquired an accepted definition.

Shell executives decided some time ago that rather than be guided or judged by an undefined concept, they would manage social concerns as they do other dimensions of their business: by using objectives and principles as a guide for consistent action. Since Shell executives believed the company's record of social performance was positive and substantial, they decided to derive from this experience a corporate social objective and managing principles as a guide for Shell people. The resulting document is the Shell Social Performance Guidelines.

"Our overall corporate objective," the guidelines state, "is to operate our business successfully, that is, profitably and in perpetuity. An integral part of this involves the effect our business has on people and their varying interests. We express this factor in terms of a social objective. Briefly stated, our social objective is to enhance the well-being of the people we affect, as an integral part of managing our business successfully."

Following are summaries of the guidelines:

(1)

Delineate the social dimensions of our business and establish priorities.

Primary attention is directed at problems where Shell is a party or can make a meaningful contribution within its competence and resources. Some current examples are environmental protection, energy supply, energy conservation, consumer protection, equal opportunity, and occupational safety and health.

Other social problems are those "related to Shell's business" (e.g., minority economic development, highway and urban mass transit) and those "of general concern to Shell" (e.g., local education and government services). While the legitimate role business has in helping resolve such problems is open to question, Shell looks for the coincidence of social and business needs where special initiatives taken in its business operations can help solve both. Examples are Shell Minority Vendor, Banking and Dealer Development Programs.

From Trends, Nov.–Dec., 1975, pp. 18–19.

There are other important problems, such as military policy and birth control, where Shell has no specific expertise and thus believes the corporation should not be involved.

(2)

Assign authority to deal with the social dimensions of our business.

The president and other general executive officers are responsible for overall performance consistent with the Shell social objective. Vice presidents and their managers are similarly responsible for their organizations and departments, and each individual for his or her performance.

(3)

Adhere to legal and ethical behavior.

Shell regards legal and ethical business practices as the foundation of socially desirable corporate performance. Adherence to legal obligations and ethical behavior in every aspect of business performance has an overriding effect on corporate well-being and reputation. This guideline provides that Shell people are responsible for conducting business in the forefront of ethical business practices.

The guideline also discusses complex questions such as this quotation regarding "legal vis-a-vis ethical considerations": "Law in our society proscribes socially intolerable conduct and prescribes the minimum obligation that is legally required. Law does not prescribe what society regards as desirable conduct by individuals or corporations. As a result, business problems occur in which decisions must be made where what is legally permitted may be unacceptable in terms of changing public attitudes. Consequently, for a manager to regard what is legal as acceptable can cause his actions to be regarded as unethical."

(4)

Give conscious attention to the people and interests we affect.

This guideline identifies the breadth of public interest in Shell. Those directly involved in Shell's business performance include retail and commercial customers, shareholders and investors, employees, suppliers and contractors, dealers and jobbers, and government regulatory officials. Those concerned with the company's business performance include legislatures, the judiciary, the media, competitors, Shell pensioners, the financial community, industry associations, the educational community, private welfare and religious organizations and special-interest groups such as those concerned with consumerism, ecology, and the rights of minorities, women, youth and older persons. While recognizing the diverse and conflicting viewpoints of these "constituencies," Shell recognizes that the interests of each must be considered in decision-making.

(5)

Integrate social considerations into our managing process.

This guideline stresses that social as well as economic and technical factors must be integrated into the corporate managing process of planning, operating, and evaluating results.

Since social factors are often difficult to assess and their impact may be extensive, managers are responsible to seek advice from their higher management. The guideline points out that this is necessary when corporate-wide perspective is needed to resolve problems such as incurring significant added costs, foregoing short-term profitability, and resolving conflicting ethical considerations.

(6)

Participate in the public process of formulating relevant laws and regulations.

This guideline recognized that all components of society are concerned with quality government and that one way to help achieve this is to participate in the process of establishing laws and regulations. While recognizing that corporation managements have no mandate to set society's goals, Shell believes that they are a legitimate participant in the public process of formulating laws and regulations relevant to business affairs.

The guideline also points out that some difficulties occur from participating in the public policy process. For example, the need to respond to extreme but relevant legislative or regulatory proposals can create the impression of an anti-social posture.

(7)

Make public disclosure of company information with a minimum of constraint.

This guideline proclaims that increasing interest in corporate performance is leading to disclosure of a good deal of information which corporate managements previously considered confidential or proprietary. It states that: "Openness and disclosure of relevant information is an important element of credibility and public confidence. This is based on the widely held opinion that decisions and actions which are subject to external scrutiny are more likely to be in the public interest."

Beyond the many legal requirements to disclose corporate information, Shell voluntarily responds to government, media and bona fide public inquiries in a positive way and with a minimum of constraint. The principle of disclosure followed is to provide information which is requested in a form, frequency and amount practicable to assemble and which would not:

a. Lead to violation of any laws (e.g., antitrust) or proper contractual provision (e.g., secrecy agreements in negotiating documents).
b. Abridge individual privacy (e.g., employee health records, undocumented customer credit references).
c. Give competitors or others an unfair commercial or economic advantage (e.g., proprietary technical, trade secret, customer data, or other sensitive financial or commercial information).
d. Be misleading in the absence of supplemental information not disclosed for the foregoing reasons.

The ability to manage social concerns successfully is important beyond the present need for socially acceptable performance. By learning to cope with contemporary problems, future Shell senior managers should be better prepared to harmonize the complex social, technical, and economic factors they will face in the years ahead.

If in response to a specific request, disclosure involves "material information" (e.g., as contemplated by Federal securities laws) such information is concurrently disclosed to the public at large.

Shell executives recognized that merely announcing the Social Performance Guidelines would not result in social performance in tune with public expectations and government requirements. Therefore, they recently began testing a process which includes the application of the Social Performance Guidelines and the incorporation of social performance goals or projects in their regular business planning and review activity.

This test provides that each Shell organization and its component units develop specific goals or projects and review progress related to one or more of the following social performance areas:

Consumer Relations
Environmental Protection
Occupational Safety and Health
Employee Development and Effectiveness
Stability of Employment
Equal Opportunity for Minorities and Women
Communication with "Constituents"
Community Relations

QUESTIONS

1. Is this policy comprehensive? What additional items, if any, should be included?
2. What problems may Shell encounter within its organizational structure in attempting to implement this social responsibility agenda? What techniques exist to measure progress toward full compliance throughout the corporation?
3. In your opinion, can a policy such as this be successfully administered in a constructive way?

6

WHAT IS THE PROPER ROLE OF PUBLIC DIRECTORS?

PUBLIC DIRECTORS MERIT A TRY

CHRISTOPHER D. STONE

Christopher D. Stone, professor of law, University of Southern California, argues for "limited public directors" who would provide special representation for the public in special situations such as "demonstrated delinquency" (repeated violations) and "generic industry problems" (industrial social problems that are not necessarily violations of the law).

With the country's temper over corporate misconduct running so high, there is fresh life in the notion of sticking some public presence into the boardroom. It is disappointing, though, that the various proposals—for directors elected by the public at large, for women, blacks, and consumer advocates—should be bandied about so vaguely and so unmindfully of all the reasons to be skeptical. Not that the notion is empty. Some recent SEC settlements (discussed herein) have already brought about one manner of public directorship in everything but name. I myself believe that further reaches should and almost certainly will be made.

But if a workable arrangement is to emerge (one that is more than cosmetic, yet less than fractious), it has to account for the sobering, if limited lessons available from public directorship experiences at home and abroad—and salt in just a bit of common sense.

It should be obvious, for example, that even the best-staffed directors are too removed from day-to-day operations to expect reform at the board level to touch—much less cure—most of the problems which trouble would-be reformers.

We know, too (from the brief but unpromising experiment with public directors on the Union Pacific Railroad in the nineteenth century), that a public director, if he is to know where to begin, needs a more modest, manageable, and detailed commission than "the public's interest."

There are indications that the effectiveness of any public director would gain, too, the more there were a specific and evident reason for his having been thrust onto the board, the more carefully he were integrated into systems of information and authority—both downward into the corporation and outward into key areas of the corporation's environment—and the more he should have (like the board representative of a major creditor) some "outside" power to backstop his judgments.

Christopher D. Stone, "Public Directors Merit a Try," *Harvard Business Review,* March–April 1976, pp. 20–22, 26–34, 156.

SPECIAL REPRESENTATION . . .

Considerations such as these suggest that if society is heading in the direction of public board representation—as well it might—we best consider what I call "limited public directors," at least as a first step. Instatement of a public director would not depend simply on the size and influence of the company.

Instead, his appointment would be reserved for two restricted situations, both of which contain special circumstances that make a strong case for some form of government intercession into the corporate decision-making process. The first I call the "demonstrated delinquency situation"; the second, the "generic industry problem."

. . . FOR 'DEMONSTRATED DELINQUENCY'

This situation involves the company which has been afoul of the law so repeatedly that further trust in existing corporate control measures seems misplaced; as a last resort, the limited public director would become a sort of in-house probation officer.

If this seems farfetched, remember that it would be only a step toward empowering the law with the same hold it has over the ordinary human—a less formidable quarry. When a flesh-and-blood mortal wanders repeatedly outside the law, we have as an alternative not only probation, but a prison to clap him in as well.

But with the corporation, the more severe remedy is not, in any literal sense, available. We can fine it, but the fines that "the company" suffers land, as we know, on the shareholders, not on those who are calling the shots. And while, from time to time, personal judgments may be levied against the men at the top, the real brunt is almost inevitably deflected by indemnification and legal liability insurance.

This is not to deny all force to the law in keeping its corporate actors in check; we have to allow, though, that a giant corporation can put between itself and the law's taunts a far thicker skin than can the ordinary human. And while the indifference will surely yield if we keep at it long enough (higher and higher fines might work), a lot of mischief can be set in motion in the meantime.

In circumstances—rare perhaps, but real—when a specific company has established itself as a recidivist (a "repeater"), whose continued failure to put its own house in order may do us irreparable harm, I suggest that the law needs a fall-back position to augment its present remedies: the power to appoint a limited public director to the company's board. How such a director would be selected and what his precise functions and powers would be are matters to which I shall return. Let me first proceed to the other situation which calls for a limited public director.

. . . FOR GENERIC INDUSTRY PROBLEMS

This situation involves matters of serious concern that can be associated with a particular industry. Unlike the demonstrated delinquency situation, the companies involved are not necessarily violating the law.

Indeed, typically the problem will be one not covered by present law for the very reason that it is not satisfactorily amenable to any of the traditional legal solutions. Such a failure can occur for a number of reasons. For example, the government may be aware that a problem exists, yet lack adequate information on which to legislate sensibly; absolutely eliminating the activity through traditional measures (e.g., fines, injunctions) may carry costs that far exceed the benefits; it is often difficult to frame what the society wants the corporations to do into legally enforceable language; and so forth.

An illustration may be the tragic worker-health situation in the asbestos industry, which has recently come to light. Similarly, we know that plastic workers are susceptible to liver cancer. Paper mills and steel companies create vast amounts of water pollution. Oil refineries are typically air polluters. Multinationals present special problems relating to our foreign relations and monetary stability. Companies that produce and utilize nuclear energy present obvious risks of their own. In many such areas, a limited public director could be appointed with appropriately tailored mandates and functions.

APPOINTMENT PROCESS

How would one go about placing an appropriate public director on a board? In the case of demonstrated delinquency, the company will be before a court or agency, and not for the first time. In this situation, the appointment could be by the court with the advice and consultation of the company, the prosecuting authority, the court's own probation staff, and perhaps (for reasons that will be clearer as my discussion progresses) a management-organizational specialist.

The possibility of a court appointing such a director is not as remote as it may sound. Even today, many state corporation codes provide for court appointment of directors, although the power is generally reserved for the corporation's shareholders (as in the case of deadlock) rather than for its consumers or neighbors. Courts are similarly empowered to appoint high-level management when a company is in bankruptcy or reorganization.

Recently, though, there have been signs of more far-reaching incursions into the traditional board selection process. One avenue for change is almost certainly coming through the shareholder's derivative action. Typically, the relief asked in these suits has been for the directors to reimburse the company for losses their negligence or willful mismanagement has caused. (Typically, too, the whole affair is chummily terminated with a bounty to the plaintiff's attorney and some even cheaper promises to be more careful henceforth.)

But in a shareholder's derivative suit against Northrop, Inc. (arising out of bribery disclosures), the Los Angeles-based Center for Law in the Public Interest insisted not only on replacing the president, but also arranged the instatement of four new directors from a joint slate proposed half by it and half by the company and approved by the court. Three of the new appointees were constituted a majority of the executive committee, which was then given the special mandate to investigate and report on the bribery (with the aid of a special counsel brought in for the purpose, Wilmer, Cutler & Pickering). Other "private" suits asking comparable relief are, I know, in the works.

Meanwhile, the SEC occupies the forefront. It possesses an ill-defined "general equity" power to set corporate wrongdoing, once exposed, in the right. How far onto the board table these powers can be elbowed, no one knows, but the commission is enjoying finding out. Consider:

In the Westgate-California mess (involving the collapse of C. Arnholt Smith's paper empire in San Diego in 1973), five new directors were approved by the SEC and the court.

In August 1974, in settling a civil fraud action against Mattel, Inc. (growing out of improper financial reporting), the SEC forced the giant toy manufacturer to appoint two additional directors to its board, neither of whom was to have any other affiliation with Mattel. Their selection was made subject to SEC and court approval.

Soon thereafter, when it appeared that the Mattel situation ran deeper than had been first imagined, the court ordered that an absolute majority of special outsiders be arranged and required the establishment of two special board committees—one on financial controls and audit, the other on litigation and claims. The functions of the committees are not left to the company to define—as is traditional—but are provided for by the public through the court, in detail.

In both the Westgate and Mattel situations, as in some other recent SEC settlements, it was the shareholders and creditors who inspired this extra measure of court-ordered protection. The Northrop settlement was a sort of hybrid. As a derivative suit, the form of the action constrains the lawyers to speak of the investors' claims, but there can be no doubt whatsoever that broader public interests were feeding the fires.

And why not? In extreme cases of corporate wrongdoing, why shouldn't public directors be appointed and board committees established whose primary concern is to achieve compliance with the law where people other than investors are being put at a risk?

In the generic industry situation, when the companies involved will not typically be before any court or agency, the original impetus for appointment would presumably come from the regulatory bodies with primary concern over the industry or problem. Thus in a situation like that in the asbestos industry, if a government information-gathering source (e.g., the National Institute of Occupational Safety and Health) were to become aware of the possible hazards, it would then apply to a federal court (under legislation easily drafted) for a hearing on the appointment of a limited public director.

At such a hearing, the court would call trade associations and corporate representatives to discuss the problem, and to deal with the likelihood and mechanics of its being ameliorated by a special director. One possible outcome of the hearing—other than dismissal of the motion—might be to compromise on the appointment of, say, a corporate vice president or even a division executive, as distinct from a director.

Indeed, if public or quasi-public appointments are to be made, it may often be preferable to instate someone closer to the action than a director. But if, in a particular instance, appointing a director were deemed advisable, his functions would be proposed and (as in the appointment of a trustee in bankruptcy), those interested, including the company, would submit recommendations for the post—subject to final approval of the court.

TAILORED TASKS

For obvious reasons, the functions of the limited public director would have to be developed so that his actual vote was not being banked on. (One or two public directors can always be out-voted.) Instead, we might expect from him the following tasks, tailored to meet the exigencies of the situation that led to his appointment.

'SUPEREGO' FUNCTION

Although we ultimately have to define the public director's specific role, his first function is admittedly loose. It has to do with the creation of an atmosphere that an "outsider" (through his very presence, as well, of course, as his questioning) can contribute to. This translates into inducing the body to consider, before the company acts, a broader range of consequences than are currently being worried about: getting the others to reflect a little more on alternatives; extending the company's time horizon; introducing into the board's analysis more of the categories of judgment that inhabit the outside world.

What reason is there to hope that the concept of a public director, doggedly pressing such a "super-ego" function, might hold some promise today, even though the notion had such little success in the Union Pacific experience? First is an evolution in the self-image of business leaders over the years.

More importantly, the public director would carry with the board the weight of special expertise. That is, if the appointment had been occasioned by water pollution problems, we would expect the director to be a sanitary engineer; in the asbestos industry, a doctor or a public health figure. In his area, his questions and recommendations would be received in the way a well-meaning generalist's would not.

Then, too, it is not likely that the board would give the outsider short shrift, in light of the fact that its company would have been singled out for a limited public director, would be on notice that failure to account adequately for his input may increase the board's own, as well as the company's, liability.

Putting such a person on the board may give a useful "lift," too, to those employees throughout the organization who can identify with him professionally. Placing an environmental engineer on the board of a paper manufacturer, for example, would signal to the entire organization that in terms of the organization's values, from now on the environment was to be taken into account seriously—and that those throughout the organization who were engaged in that effort were to be given special recognition.

LAW COMPLIANCE ASSURANCE

To be effective, the public director will need to have his functions more narrowly defined than just "contribute to a responsible atmosphere." One of these would be to ensure that the laws in his special area were being obeyed in good faith. I am not referring now to the sporadic and unpredictable law violations that any huge enterprise becomes involved in, merely because of its many points of contact with society. The director would be concerned with violations and circumventions that are chronic to the organizational system itself, such as those arising from its established ways of marketing, its patterns of employee compensation and advancement, and the "accepted practices" of the industry.

To establish where compliance was in doubt, the public director and his staff would undertake "legal audits" in association with the corporation's legal counsel, and, where appropriate, with the outside law firm that handles the corporation's affairs. (Such a measure would be in a class with the Northrop case and with the recent SEC-prompted report by Gulf Oil Corporation, prepared under the direction of an outside attorney, on that company's "political activities.")

Where "soft spots" were located, it would be the duty of the legal audit crew to propose or review plans that provided reasonable assurances of remedial action. If some area of product defect were suspected, a remedial plan might include placing a top-quality control person at a key production point, and making him report directly to the director's staff. The existence of the problem area, the remedial plan, and periodic reports on actions taken under the plan would all be matters that the public director would regularly report to the entire board, and, where appropriate, to the agencies that made and/or moved for his appointment.

LEGISLATIVE PROCESS LIAISON

One shortcoming in our society is that information signaling the need for remedial action is often available in (or can be readily developed in) the corporate sector long before it gets to the legislatures and agencies.

For example, when the media announce that a pesticide is seriously injuring farm workers, can one doubt that there were clues in the producing company's laboratories—or even its packing areas—which, if systematically pursued, would have brought the dangers to light several years and hundreds of injuries earlier?

Especially in the generic industry situations, the limited public director, who would be gathering the relevant data, could act as a conduit to public agencies in proposing and reviewing administrative standards. He could be available, too, for comment on pending legislation.

The advantage of this to industry—the quid pro quo for his acceptance by the corporate sector—is that he would be able to do so sensitive, from the industry's viewpoint, to the costs as well as the benefits of various alternatives.

And in laying out the "private interest," he would carry a degree of credibility that the ordinary pro-forma industry lobbyist lacks.

INTERNAL SYSTEM AUDITING

One cannot expect any director, however well staffed, to keep abreast of everything that is going on in the corporation, even within a designated area. But as all managers know, the workings of a corporation need not be understood in terms of its acts alone. The organization is also a composite of systems, some of which are oriented toward R&D, others toward production, some others toward the maintenance of internal authority, and still others toward the gathering and transmission of data.

Even if it is impossible to keep tabs on everything that is happening in the company, it is not impossible to audit the effectiveness of all the various systems. This one would expect the public director to do.

For example, are corporate health records being preserved in a manner conducive to the statistical sampling needs of the National Institute of Occupational Safety and Health, the National Cancer Institute, the Office of Technology Assessment? Where environmental degradation has led to the public director's appointment, is ecological monitoring being carried out, and are the results landing on the right desks for action?

'HOT LINE' FUNCTION

The director and his staff would be designated to receive, from anyone within (or outside) the organization, notice of anything seriously wrong in the corporation that the ordinary organizational systems for detection were not uncovering. I cannot overemphasize the importance of this function. In almost all the problem cases analyzed by a task group under my direction at USC, it turned out that someone down in the corporate hierarchy was aware that the company was headed for trouble. But those in high authority were never warded off.

Is there no way to get such information to people who have both the interest and the power to set things right? It is not easy. All the psychology of the organization discourages contact between the operating levels and management high above them, and all the more so if the news is "bad." And it is not just manners; the employee must reckon with the possibility that his immediate superiors will retaliate.

In this context, it should be obvious that the ordinary outside director, whose primary employment lies elsewhere, is too distant in every sense—not only physically and hierarchically, but even in terms of what the employee presumes him to be concerned about—to be "bothered."

In part, then, the answer must be to change the protocol. Where a limited director is serving, he and his staff would be expressly authorized to receive "bad news." If this were done; (a) there would be some higher-up to whom, in the regular course of events, personnel aware of developing trouble areas could turn; (b) the person to whom they would be turning would be someone not so closely identified with "the organization" and its ethos as to be angry with them; and (c) he would be someone who was high enough in the organization both to right the situation and to protect the source from harassment.

In at least one way this is a more promising system to foster than ordinary "whistle-blowing"—encouraging workers to go to the outside world in the first instance. Giving insiders the alternative of bringing their misgivings to the public director would promote responsible in-house investigations, so that malicious and mistaken charges could be screened before they caused unjust damage.

IMPACT STUDY DIRECTION

One of the major problems facing corporations is that neither they nor the agencies which oversee them are able to anticipate the impact contemplated corporate action is likely to have. Did any of the soap companies undertake to examine, in advance, the effect their detergents were going to have on streams? Or the pesticide manufacturers, what their products would do to the ecological cycle?

The more that society becomes technologically interdependent, the more such problems will increasingly become a concern. And the more that goods and services are produced on a mass scale, the longer the time lag will become between planning and production (which increases organizational resistance to adaptation in the face of trouble).

In areas in which an industry or company is "on notice" that dangers of an as yet unassessed intensity may exist, the company or companies could be required to make impact findings under the direction of the limited director and his staff.

INFORMATION SYSTEM INTERFACE

Viewed from one perspective, the corporation is an information system that consumes, digests, and produces data. How adequately the corporation discharges its social functions depends, in part, on the validity of the information it turns out.

But the adequacy of the information system depends on a lot more than truth and falsity. It also depends on where in its environment the corporation reaches to gather information; what categories of abstraction it employs (i.e., what it "looks for"); where, within itself, it dispatches the gathered items; how it "translates" data as they move from one subunit to another; which items it stores for recall; and which items it remits to the outside world and in what form.

Depending on the situation, the limited director could be charged with the details of the information processes. As part of a "window-out" function, he would gather, verify, and disseminate agreed-on categories of information that are crossing the boundary to the outer world.

As a "window-in," he would see to it that the corporation was getting the information the society wants it to have. In his function, the director could be used as a conduit by agencies to bring to the corporation's attention (for relaying, for example, to the corporation's R&D people) matters that it ought to know about—and for which the society at large is as much the ultimate beneficiary as the corporation.

SPECIFIC POWERS

Let me sketch out some of the powers the public directors ought to have if they are to be effective:

1. They should serve with the company on a full-time basis, although for a limited period in time. (For example, if the director's appointment were a condition of corporate probation, he might serve until the probationary period had run.)
   For reasons that are symbolic as well as fair, they ought to be paid in part by the company and in part by the public.
2. They should have the power to hire their own staffs, paid on a similar basis and serving the limited public directors responsibly in their duties. In addition, they should have the power to retain outside expertise, as they may need it from time to time. Indeed, I doubt that really qualified people would step into such posts without the assurance of some special counsel or other staff.

3. They should have the power to inspect all corporate books and records related to their work and to requisition from general corporate staff appropriate surveys, reports, and so on that are not otherwise on hand.
4. There should be the right to be seated on all corporate committees whose work is relevant to the furtherance of their functions, and the right to stay the firing (or any other punishment) of an employee on account of his cooperation with the public director and his staff.
5. In the event of management's recalcitrance in carrying out board orders, or obstruction of the limited director in the performance of his duties, they should be authorized to go directly to court to seek an order citing noncompliance, which would be punishable by contempt. The order should run not against "the corporation" (which is often small intimidation to management), but against the specific corporate individuals whose obstructionism the director identifies.

The specific powers of the public director should not be exercised without constraint. Certainly both the board and management have a right to object if the director's budget is getting out of line or if his particular demands on corporate staff are interfering with the balance of their expected duties, or if he is stepping beyond his powers. Disputes of this sort may arise, and resolving them will not be easy.

In the Mattel situation, the parties have to return to court in the event of disagreement. The courts often feel, rightly, that theirs is not the forum for resolving differences that are so heavily flavored with managerial business discretion. Tom Loo, who is serving as one of the Mattel "additional directors," has suggested to me that at the time of appointment of any limited director, the court might also appoint an advisory panel of businessmen to arbitrate these conflicts.

ULTIMATE SUCCESS?

It does not seem to me, as it has to some commentators, that "special interest" representation would inevitably reduce the boardroom to a factionalist brawl. All sorts of public bodies (e.g., Parliament and Congress), though constituted factionally, muddle along fairly nicely. And it is hard to resist the thought that some new degree of factionalism would be preferable to the present degree of clubbiness.

Besides, whatever scenarios of hostility can be worried up in theory, those who have examined special interest participation in actual practice (e.g., as with worker representation in Europe) seem to suggest the very opposite result; co-option is at least as likely.

There is, in any event, a valid point underlying these diametric scenarios: the ultimate success of such a system would depend on the social (as distinct from the strictly legal) interaction between the special representative and the balance of the company. This is not a profound point, nor is there anything special about corporations.

On the contrary, one should anticipate the corporation putting up the same reaction to a public director as would any organization to a comparable "intruder." No community shares its autonomy gladly, especially when the outsider seeks to introduce "foreign" and discordant aims. (Consider the problems the law has in getting the police—whose orientation is toward collaring wrongdoers—to implement due-process considerations.)

In such a fashion, we should expect that the more the operations of the public director and his staff are viewed as inconsistent with the organization's independently established goals (i.e., the more, in a way, he threatens to succeed), the more his environment will turn upon him with its subtle array of threats, concealments, bribes, and snubs.

It is almost inevitable, too, that the public director and his staff will bring with them their own bureaucratic complications. For example, an environmental control appointee, knowing that he will be on the carpet if there is, say, another damaging spill, will continually press for a larger staff and more authority. Defining rules for his staff's containment will be a constant source of friction and negotiation.

Of course, the magnitude of these problems is a matter of degree, and the degree will vary with the stature of the public director. Considering the corporation's culture of expertise, a man who is seen as competent will be able to press more successfully than someone who is adjudged a "turkey."

But then, how many well-qualified people can there be who are not already nailed down? If for no other reason, the limited supply of talent would compel one to approach public directorship on a restricted case-by-case basis.

But in spite of my misgivings, I think that the chances of success are large enough to begin experimenting with such appointments on a limited basis. And I believe they would succeed precisely because the corporations would come to acknowledge, if only begrudgingly, that, as a way of dealing with an increasingly significant range of problems, the idea has something in it for them as well as for the public.

This may sound odd. But what is most evidently missing today and needs to be restored, is a measure of mutual trust and respect. As things stand, we are settling into a cycle in which the laws wielded against corporations are products of little more than mutual frustration, a cycle which is giving the businessman fits, and the public little to show for it.

When the evidence points to an acute problem like work-related cancer, society, distrustful of what is going on within the corporation's walls, and kept at arm's length from the loci of corporate decision making, sees little choice but to slap together a battery of new regulations even before it is adequately informed. There are obvious costs to both sides.

In a context like this, some systematic integration of the "inside" with the "outside" could lead—may be the only way to lead—to bases for new, more productive patterns of cooperation. Public director appointments would bring with them their own red tape; but one could hope for reductions elsewhere in the inevitable paper work associated with second-guessing from a distance, and with blanket, across-the-board applications of restraints that might more profitably be focused on a narrower range of targets.

If the limited public director approach did not lead to a net reduction in bureaucratic overview, I should at least expect it to redistribute the paper work more satisfactorily, from the view both of the regulators and of their quarry. As society grows more complex and more and more dependent on corporations as the dominant form for social action, that may be about the best one can hope for. It merits a try.

QUESTIONS

1. Stone argues that public directors have "special expertise" relating to salient company problems. If problems were moral ones, however, what kind of background or skill would qualify a public director?
2. How would a "typical" director on a traditional board view Stone's arguments? Do you think business executives would agree, for example, that corporations are "the dominant form for social action" in American society?
3. If business executives were hostile or indifferent, could a public director—even one with significant formal authority—be effective? (See, for example, "Arthur Goldberg on Public Directors" in *Business and Society Review/Innovation,* Spring, 1973.)
4. On balance, are you in favor of Stone's proposals or against them? Why?

BUSINESS ETHICS AND MORALITIES: UNIVERSAL ASPECTS

IS THE GOLDEN RULE A USEFUL GUIDE TO BUSINESS DECISION MAKING?

CRAIG C. LUNDBERG

Craig C. Lundberg, associate professor of behavioral science and administration, Southern Methodist University, analyzes the applicability of an ancient rule for ethical conduct to today's business behavior.

As I have talked with business managers I have been impressed that the vast majority of these men propose the Golden Rule as the most important guide for organizational behavior. Certainly this maxim is well-known as a guide for human conduct, yet regardless of its popularity we might question its adequacy as a business policy. Let me focus this paper by contrasting two sets of reasoning:

The Golden Rule is the best general prescription for regulating human relationships, therefore, it is a good maxim for behavior in business especially within complex modern organization settings.

The Golden Rule is a guide for human relations which is very limited in its applications in modern society. It must be applied with caution or not at all in contemporary business practice.

In the pages to follow I will note how the reasoning supporting the first assertion is generally believed, but will rely on my frame of reference as a social scientist to argue in favor of the second position. To do this I will differentiate between the Golden Rule as a religious norm and as a guide to ethical fairness in exchange relationships. Then I will examine some assumptions implicit in the rule and underline aspects which are simply unclear.

RELIGIOUS UNIVERSALITY OF THE GOLDEN RULE

While familiar the Golden Rule is stated in numerous forms. The book of Matthew, for instance, states that: "All things whatsoever ye would that men should do to you, do ye so unto them: for this is the Law and the Prophets." The medieval Biblical injunction, "Love thy neighbor as thyself" has of course been most commonly interpreted wtih the contemporary maxim, "Do unto others as you would like them to do unto you."

Craig C. Lundberg, "The Golden Rule and Business Management. Quo Vadis?" *Journal of Economics and Business,* formerly the *Economic and Business Bulletin,* 20 (January 1968), 36–40. Reprinted by permission.

We should not assume that the Golden Rule is primarily associated with Christianity for most other religions carry some version of it. In the Talmud, for example, we find, "What is hateful to you, do not do to your fellow man. That this is the entire law; all the rest is commentary." Confucianism, too, in the Analects has, "Surely it is the maxim of loving kindness: do not unto others that you would not have them do unto you." Buddhism in the Udana-Yarga says, "Hurt not others in ways that you yourself would find hurtful." Islam joins the chorus with, "Not one of you is a believer until he desires for his brother that which he desires for himself." And in the Mahabharata the Brahman injunction says, "This is the sum of duty: do not do unto others which would cause you pain if done to you." And so we see that the Golden Rule exists throughout the major religions of mankind.

THE RULE AS A GUIDE FOR EXCHANGES

We must at this point distinguish between the Jewish-Christian norm of brotherly love and the Golden Rule of fairness-ethics. The Biblical

> Love thy neighbor as thyself,

is a norm of Jewish-Christian brotherly love; it means love your neighbor, that is, to feel responsible for and at one with him. The Golden Rule as interpreted today is quite different. Perhaps it is no accident that the Golden Rule has become one of the most popular religious maxims of today because it can be interpreted in terms of fairness-ethics, which sounds a great deal like the religious maxims, but which in fact has quite a different meaning, namely, be fair in your exchanges with others. Contrast with the religious norm is complete for fairness-ethics means do not feel responsible and at one, but feel distant and separate; respect the rights of your neighbor, but do not love him. This differentiation between religious norm and a maxim of fairness-ethics is made so that we can focus on the latter, which is the principle or generalization in the fields of human relations as conceived by business management today.

DISTORTIONS AND CHANGES IN MEANING

The Golden Rule is very well known in western culture; it is a fairness-ethics injunction; and it is usually accepted unquestioningly. Although probably the most revered of common sense generalizations handed down by our industrial forbears, the Golden Rule has not gone unthought about or completely unchallenged. As our society has become more liberal and the value of individual work has been widened to include a value of individual differences, the Golden Rule has been revamped. The playwright Bernard Shaw, for instance, has rewritten the Golden Rule:

> Don't do unto others as you would have them do unto you because their tastes may be different.

Even Shaw's version has been altered. A well-known psychologist has rephrased the Golden Rule to serve as a guide for ethical conduct or as a guide for amiable relations among men:

> Do unto others as you would have them do unto you if you were they.

This last statement of the rule seems to take Shaw's point that one man's meat is another man's poison, and adds the contemporary concern we have for empathy, the usefulness of putting ourselves in another person's place so we can appreciate how he thinks and feels.

In a recent graduate course and in a recent executive development program for middle managers, I asked participants to write out the versions of the Golden Rule known to them. The response was overwhelming and reflects and shows how far the Golden Rule has pervaded the mainstream of our business culture, everything from "an eye for an eye, a tooth for a tooth" to "every girl has a father"; from "You pat my back, I'll pat yours but you pat me first" to "drive carefully, the life you save may be your own"; from "The only way to have a friend is to be one" to "owe no man anything." Variations are reported implicit in our everyday petitions for help, such as "Share the United Way" or "Give blood, the gift of life"; and we find variations in advertising such as one card manufacturer who asks that you give his card to show you care enough to send the very best, and of course there are even business philosophies such as the Murray D. Lincoln's "Intelligent selfishness."

We often hear people talk about the imperatives of life, and of course the Golden Rule is often promoted in just that way. It was the German-Scottish philosopher Immanuel Kant who conceived of the categorical imperative, the unconditional command of nature. It, too, sounds much like the Golden Rule:

> Act so that the principle of your action could be made a universal law.

When men act on the Golden Rule as if it were such an imperative, . . . then we can expect confusion and perhaps even injustice to occur.

ON APPLYING THE GOLDEN RULE

We see that from a religious origin strained through the web and woof of an industrial society the Golden Rule has come to reside in humor, in philosophy, and common sense, in fact nearly all arenas of contemporary life. The question still remains, however, is it a useful imperative? Can we take it as a generalized principle of, or guide for, human relationships? Let us now examine a few simple situations which, while hypothetical, could very well exist, and as we look at them let us ask ourselves about the utility of applying the Golden Rule in each case.

Picture a janitor and the president of a major corporation approaching the lobby doors of the corporation's downtown headquarters building. The two men approach the doors simultaneously. Who will open the door for whom and with what effects on the men?

Consider the marketing vice president of a major American business firm promptly arriving at the stated time for an appointment with an executive of potentially the largest purchaser of his product in Venezuela. After an hour and a half of waiting the v.p. actively considers leaving.

Consider the personnel manager of a local company picking up his telephone to hear his counterpart in a competitor's firm asking if he would provide a summer job for the other man's high school age son.

Picture a computer expert who is new to a business deciding not to include certain critical information in his first report to his superior because he thinks it might jeopardize the existence of his function in the firm.

In the hypothetical examples above the parties have represented different organizational statuses, different cultures, different personal needs and capabilities for action, and different constraints on their behavior. In each example a literal application of the Golden Rule would be rather difficult for most reasonable people—they would feel the pressures of expectations and no doubt worry about the consequences to their responses to these situations. Perhaps these examples force us to wonder as to the universal application of the rule, and perhaps to question the assumption on which it is based. Let us now turn to this latter aspect.

ASSUMPTIONS BEHIND THE GOLDEN RULE

One assumption in the Golden Rule is that the "others" in an exchange situation are in fact capable of reciprocating the behavior. We quickly remember that persons are not equal in terms of abilities, at least adults, and clearly are not equally capable in terms of the organizational power they command. You might go on with this assumption and ask whether the "others" are in fact motivated to reciprocate, that is, whether they would want to return similar behaviors if it were possible to. A second assumption would be that either party to an exchange really understands the consequences to the behavior—how, in fact, will the others really feel and think. This if of course contingent on their having similar goals or aims, and in most cases this seems extremely unlikely. A third major assumption is that the Golden Rule assumes that other rules are not being violated whether they be formal, explicit rules or other implicit perhaps informal ones, such as custom. Take the privilege and duty which come with certain statuses in our society, perhaps illustrated in the first example above. Today, too, we have a widespread understanding that business practice should not include reciprocity in regard to purchasing, for example, and this may in certain instances conflict with the Golden Rule injunction. A fourth assumption has to do with the assumed similarity of preference or taste of the parties to the Golden Rule. One could confuse or sadden, hurt, or disadvantage another who did not have somewhat similar preferences or tastes, that is, values and interests like ours. Cross cultural examples often make this point clearly.

Let us now examine the Golden Rule in terms of its clarity. Unless it is specific and explicit it becomes a maxim hard to follow. We might begin by asking about the unit of action. Are the actions implied in the rule a person or persons, groups or some larger social? Are you and the others in the Golden Rule to be seen as representatives of various social units or as independent citizens or persons in their own right, or does it make a difference? Of course the word "do" in the Golden Rule can mean many things too, and as usually interpreted all behaviors are included. Another thing which is not too clear has to do with the adequacy of resources. In most human situations there is a scarcity of resources. A major unclear aspect of the Golden Rule has to do with the amount and/or frequency of the exchange. Most people read the Golden Rule as implying some kind of equality. It would seem in our discussion of assumptions above that people are not equally capable or motivated to enter into an equal kind of exchange. In fact, we know from the new field of equity theory that the equality of exchange is almost never really expected. The act implied in the Golden Rule is of course conditioned by perception of the parties, and we know from the research in psychology that emotional and situational factors, among others, can alter and distort what is perceived to be done to oneself, this seemingly inviting considerable creative distortion and error. And of course the Golden Rule is not very clear as to how one measures the consequences which arise by using it. Do we look at both mental and physical consequences, how does the time dimension come in, and so on?

EVALUATION OF THE GOLDEN RULE

We have seen that the Golden Rule, at least as a maxim of fairness-ethics, is extremely popular, and widely applied in our industrial society. By means of some hypothetical illustrations and by examining more directly the assumption behind and the lack of clarity in the Golden Rule we have also been able to offer some comment on the adequacy of this rule as a general principle of organizational behavior. I believe that we have demonstrated that the Golden Rule cannot be taken as a categorical imperative, that in fact one would have to be extremely careful in applying it in business and other human affairs. I do not want to appear as relegating all common sense knowledge to the dustbin for in fact the scientific study of human relations is able to confirm a lot of the tried and true folklore and rules of thumb. It is crucial, however, to know when injunctions from the past are no longer applicable or to be able to identify the conditions when they do not apply. Such has been our intent in examining the Golden Rule's validity for contemporary business management.

QUESTIONS

1. What is your own interpretation of the meaning of the Golden Rule? Trace the historical development of this rule as a guide for organizational behavior.
2. Critically analyze and evaluate the major assumptions behind the Golden Rule.
3. Can business executives apply the Golden Rule to their decisions? Explain your position.

IS BUSINESS BLUFFING ETHICAL?

ALBERT Z. CARR

Albert Z. Carr, a former consultant to businesses and now a full-time writer, says in this controversial article that the ethics of business are not those of society but rather those of the poker game.

A respected businessman with whom I discussed the theme of this article remarked with some heat, "You mean to say you're going to encourage men to bluff? Why, bluffing is nothing more than a form of lying! You're advising them to lie!"

I agreed that the basis of private morality is a respect for truth and that the closer a businessman comes to the truth, the more he deserves respect. At the same time, I suggested that most bluffing in business might be regarded simply as game strategy—much like bluffing in poker, which does not reflect on the morality of the bluffer.

I quoted Henry Taylor, the British statesman who pointed out that "falsehood ceases to be falsehood when it is understood on all sides that the truth is not expected to be spoken"—an exact description of bluffing in poker, diplomacy, and business. I cited the analogy of the criminal court, where the criminal is not expected to tell the truth when he pleads "not guilty." Everyone from the judge down takes it for granted that the job of the defendant's attorney is to get his client off, not to reveal the truth; and this is considered ethical practice. I mentioned Representative Omar Burleson, the Democrat from Texas, who was quoted as saying, in regard to the ethics of Congress, "Ethics is a barrel of worms"—a pungent summing up of the problem of deciding who is ethical in politics.

I reminded my friend that millions of businessmen feel constrained every day to say *yes* to their bosses when they secretly believe *no* and that this is generally accepted as permissible strategy when the alternative might be the loss of a job. The essential point, I said, is that the ethics of business are game ethics, different from the ethics of religion.

He remained unconvinced. Referring to the company of which he is president, he declared: "Maybe that's good enough for some businessmen, but I can tell you that we pride ourselves on our ethics. In 30 years not one customer has ever questioned my word or asked to check our figures. We're loyal to our customers and fair to our suppliers. I regard my handshake on a deal as a contract. I've never entered into price-fixing schemes with my competitors. I've never allowed my salesmen to spread injurious rumors

Albert Z. Carr, "Is Business Bluffing Ethical?" *Harvard Business Review,* January–February 1968.

about other companies. Our union contract is the best in our industry. And, if I do say so myself, our ethical standards are of the highest!"

He really was saying, without realizing it, that he was living up to the ethical standards of the business game—which are a far cry from those of private life. Like a gentlemanly poker player, he did not play in cahoots with others at the table, try to smear their reputations, or hold back chips he owed them.

But this same fine man, at that very time, was allowing one of his products to be advertised in a way that made it sound a great deal better than it actually was. Another item in his product line was notorious among dealers for its "built-in obsolescence." He was holding back from the market a much-improved product because he did not want it to interfere with sales of the inferior item it would have replaced. He had joined with certain of his competitors in hiring a lobbyist to push a state legislature, by methods that he preferred not to know too much about, into amending a bill then being enacted.

In his view these things had nothing to do with ethics; they were merely normal business practice. He himself undoubtedly avoided outright falsehoods—never lied in so many words. But the entire organization that he ruled was deeply involved in numerous strategies of deception.

PRESSURE TO DECEIVE

Most executives from time to time are almost compelled, in the interests of their companies or themselves, to practice some form of deception when negotiating with customers, dealers, labor unions, government officials, or even other departments of their companies. By conscious misstatements, concealment of pertinent facts, or exaggeration—in short, by bluffing—they seek to persuade others to agree with them. I think it is fair to say that if the individual executive refuses to bluff from time to time—if he feels obligated to tell the truth, the whole truth, and nothing but the truth—he is ignoring opportunities permitted under the rules and is at a heavy disadvantage in his business dealings.

But here and there a businessman is unable to reconcile himself to the bluff in which he plays a part. His conscience, perhaps spurred by religious idealism, troubles him. He feels guilty; he may develop an ulcer or a nervous tic. Before any executive can make profitable use of the strategy of the bluff, he needs to make sure that in bluffing he will not lose self-respect or become emotionally disturbed. If he is to reconcile personal integrity and high standards of honesty with the practical requirements of business, he must feel that his bluffs are ethically justified. The justification rests on the fact that business, as practiced by individuals as well as by corporations, has the impersonal character of a game—a game that demands both special strategy and an understanding of its special ethics.

The game is played at all levels of corporate life, from the highest to the lowest. At the very instant that a man decides to enter business, he may be forced into a game situation, as is shown by the recent experience of a Cornell honor graduate who applied for a job with a large company:

> This applicant was given a psychological test which included the statement, "Of the following magazines, check any that you have read either regularly or from time to time, and double-check those which interest you most. *Reader's Digest, Time, Fortune, Saturday Evening Post, The New Republic, Life, Look, Ramparts, Newsweek, Business Week, U.S. News & World Report, The Nation, Playboy, Esquire, Harper's, Sports Illustrated."*
>
> His tastes in reading were broad, and at one time or another he had read almost all of these magazines. He was a subscriber to *The New Republic,* an enthusiast for *Ramparts,* and an avid student of the pictures in *Playboy.* He was not sure whether his interest in *Playboy* would be held against him, but he had a shrewd suspicion that if he confessed to an interest in *Ramparts* and *The New Republic,* he would be thought a liberal, a radical, or at least an intellectual, and his chances of getting the job, which he needed, would greatly diminish. He therefore checked five of the more conservative magazines. Apparently it was a sound decision, for he got the job.
>
> He had made a game player's decision, consistent with business ethics.

A similar case is that of a magazine space salesman who, owing to a merger, suddenly found himself out of a job:

> This man was 58, and, in spite of a good record, his chance of getting a job elsewhere in a business where youth is favored in hiring practice was not good. He was a vigorous, healthy man, and only a considerable amount of gray in his hair suggested his age. Before beginning his job search he touched up his hair with a black dye to confine the gray to his temples. He knew that the truth about his age might well come out in time, but he calculated that he could deal with that situation when it arose. He and his wife decided that he could easily pass for 45, and he so stated his age on his résumé.

This was a lie; yet within the accepted rules of the business game, no moral culpability attaches to it.

THE POKER ANALOGY

We can learn a good deal about the nature of business by comparing it with poker. While both have a large element of chance, in the long run the winner is the man who plays with steady skill. In both games ultimate victory requires intimate knowledge of the rules, insight into the psychology of the other players, a bold front, a considerable amount of self-discipline, and the ability to respond swiftly and effectively to opportunities provided by chance.

No one expects poker to be played on the ethical principles preached in churches. In poker it is right and proper to bluff a friend out of the rewards of being dealt a good hand. A player feels no more than a slight twinge of sympathy, if that, when—with nothing better than a single ace in his hand—he strips a heavy loser, who holds a pair, of the rest of his chips. It was up to the other fellow to protect himself. In the words of an excellent poker player, former President Harry Truman, "If you can't stand the heat, stay out of the kitchen." If one shows mercy to a loser in poker, it is a personal gesture, divorced from the rules of the game.

Poker has its special ethics, and here I am not referring to rules against cheating. The man who keeps an ace up his sleeve or who marks the cards is more than unethical; he is a crook, and can be punished as such—kicked out of the game, or, in the Old West, shot.

In contrast to the cheat, the unethical poker player is one who, while abiding by the letter of the rules, finds ways to put the other players at an unfair disadvantage. Perhaps he unnerves them with loud talk. Or he tries to get them drunk. Or he plays in cahoots with someone else at the table. Ethical poker players frown on such tactics.

Poker's own brand of ethics is different from the ethical ideals of civilized human relationships. The game calls for distrust of the other fellow. It ignores the claim of friendship. Cunning deception and concealment of one's strength and intentions, not kindness and openheartedness, are vital in poker. No one thinks any the worse of poker on that account. And no one should think any the worse of the game of business because its standards of right and wrong differ from the prevailing traditions of morality in our society.

DISCARD THE GOLDEN RULE

This view of business is especially worrisome to people without much business experience. A minister of my acquaintance once protested that business cannot possibly function in our society unless it is based on the Judeo-Christian system of ethics. He told me:

> I know some businessmen have supplied call girls to customers, but there are always a few rotten apples in every barrel. That doesn't mean the rest of the fruit isn't sound. Surely the vast majority of businessmen are ethical. I myself am acquainted with many who adhere to strict codes of ethics based fundamentally on religious teachings. They contribute to good causes. They participate in community activities. They cooperate with other companies to improve working conditions in their industries. Certainly they are not indifferent to ethics.

That most businessmen are not indifferent to ethics in their private lives, everyone will agree. My point is that in their office lives they cease to be private citizens; they become game players who must be guided by a somewhat different set of ethical standards.

The point was forcefully made to me by a Midwestern executive who has given a good deal of thought to the question:

> So long as a businessman complies with the laws of the land and avoids telling malicious lies, he's ethical. If the law as written gives a man a wide-open chance to make a killing, he'd been a fool not to take advantage of it. If he doesn't, somebody else will. There's no obligation on him to stop and consider who is going to get hurt. If the law says he can do it, that's all the justification he needs. There's nothing unethical about that. It's just plain business sense.

This executive (call him Robbins) took the stand that even industrial espionage, which is frowned on by some businessmen, ought not to be considered unethical. He recalled a recent meeting of the National Industrial Conference Board where an authority on marketing made a speech in which he deplored the employment of spies by business organizations. More and more companies, he pointed out, find it cheaper to penetrate the secrets of competitors with concealed cameras and microphones or by bribing employees than to set up costly research and design departments of their own. A whole branch of the electronics industry has grown up with this trend, he continued, providing equipment to make industrial espionage easier.

Disturbing? The marketing expert found it so. But when it came to a remedy, he could only appeal to "respect for the golden rule." Robbins thought this a confession of defeat, believing that the golden rule, for all its value as an ideal for society, is simply not feasible as a guide for business. A good part of the time the businessman is trying to do unto others as he hopes others will *not* do unto him. Robbins continued:

> Espionage of one kind or another has became so common in business that it's like taking a drink during Prohibition—it's not considered sinful. And we don't even have Prohibition where espionage is concerned; the law is very tolerant in this area. There's no more shame for a business that uses secret agents than there is for a nation. Bear in mind that there already is at least one large corporation—you can buy its stock over the counter—that makes millions by providing counterespionage service to industrial firms. Espionage in business is not an ethical problem; it's an established technique of business competition.

"WE DON'T MAKE THE LAWS"

Wherever we turn in business, we can perceive the sharp distinction between its ethical standards and those of the churches. Newspapers abound with sensational stories growing out of this distinction:

> We read one day that Senator Philip A. Hart of Michigan has attacked food processors for deceptive packaging of numerous products.

The next day there is a Congressional to-do over Ralph Nader's book, *Unsafe At Any Speed,* which demonstrates that automobile companies for years have neglected the safety of car-owning families.

Then another Senator, Lee Metcalf of Montana, and journalist Vic Reinemer show in their book, *Overcharge,* the methods by which utility companies elude regulating government bodies to extract unduly large payments from users of electricity.

These are merely dramatic instances of a prevailing condition; there is hardly a major industry at which a similar attack could not be aimed. Critics of business regard such behavior as unethical, but the companies concerned know that they are merely playing the business game.

Among the most respected of our business institutions are the insurance companies. A group of insurance executives meeting recently in New England was startled when their guest speaker, social critic Daniel Patrick Moynihan, roundly berated them for "unethical" practices. They had been guilty, Moynihan alleged, of using outdated actuarial tables to obtain unfairly high premiums. They habitually delayed the hearings of lawsuits against them in order to tire out the plaintiffs and win cheap settlements. In their employment policies they used ingenious devices to discriminate against certain minority groups.

It was difficult for the audience to deny the validity of these charges. But these men were business game players. Their reaction to Moynihan's attack was much the same as that of the automobile manufacturers to Nader, of the utilities to Senator Metcalf, and of the food processors to Senator Hart. If the laws governing their businesses change, or if public opinion becomes clamorous, they will make the necessary adjustments. But morally they have in their view done nothing wrong. As long as they comply with the letter of the law, they are within their rights to operate their businesses as they see fit.

The small business is in the same position as the great corporation in this respect. For example:

In 1967 a key manufacturer was accused of providing master keys for automobiles to mail-order customers, although it was obvious that some of the purchasers might be automobile thieves. His defense was plain and straightforward. If there was nothing in the law to prevent him from selling his keys to anyone who ordered them, it was not up to him to inquire as to his customers' motives. Why was it any worse, he insisted, for him to sell car keys by mail, than for mail-order houses to sell guns that might be used for murder? Until the law was changed, the key manufacturer could regard himself as being just as ethical as any other businessman by the rules of the business game.

Violations of the ethical ideals of society are common in business, but they are not necessarily violations of business principles. Each year the Federal

Trade Commission orders hundreds of companies, many of them of the first magnitude, to "cease and desist" from practices which, judged by ordinary standards, are of questionable morality but which are stoutly defended by the companies concerned.

In one case, a firm manufacturing a well-known mouthwash was accused of using a cheap form of alcohol possibly deleterious to health. The company's chief executive, after testifying in Washington, made this comment privately:

> We broke no law. We're in a highly competitive industry. If we're going to stay in business, we have to look for profit wherever the law permits. We don't make the laws. We obey them. Then why do we have to put up with this "holier than thou" talk about ethics? It's sheer hypocrisy. We're not in business to promote ethics. Look at the cigarette companies, for God's sake! If the ethics aren't embodied in the laws by the men who made them, you can't expect businessmen to fill the lack. Why, a sudden submission to Christian ethics by businessmen would bring about the greatest economic upheaval in history!

It may be noted that the government failed to prove its case against him.

CAST ILLUSIONS ASIDE

Talk about ethics by businessmen is often a thin decorative coating over the hard realities of the game:

> Once I listened to a speech by a young executive who pointed to a new industry code as proof that his company and its competitors were deeply aware of their responsibilities to society. It was a code of ethics, he said. The industry was going to police itself, to dissuade constituent companies from wrongdoing. His eyes shone with conviction and enthusiasm.
>
> The same day there was a meeting in a hotel room where the industry's top executives met with the "czar" who was to administer the new code, a man of high repute. No one who was present could doubt their common attitude. In their eyes the code was designed primarily to forestall a move by the federal government to impose stern restrictions on the industry. They felt that the code would hamper them a good deal less than new federal laws would. It was, in other words, conceived as a protection for the industry, not for the public.
>
> The young executive accepted the surface explanation of the code; these leaders, all experienced game players, did not deceive themselves for a moment about its purpose.

The illusion that business can afford to be guided by ethics as conceived in private life is often fostered by speeches and articles containing such phrases as, "It pays to be ethical," or, "Sound ethics is good business." Actually this is not an ethical position at all; it is a self-serving calculation in disguise. The speaker is really saying that in the long run a company can make more money if it does not antagonize competitors, suppliers, employees, and customers by squeezing them too hard. He is saying that oversharp policies reduce ultimate gains. That is true, but it has nothing to do with ethics. The underlying attitude is much like that in the familiar story of the shopkeeper who finds an extra $20 bill in the cash register, debates with himself the ethical problem—should he tell his partner?—and finally decides to share the money because the gesture will give him an edge over the s.o.b. the next time they quarrel.

I think it is fair to sum up the prevailing attitude of businessmen on ethics as follows:

We live in what is probably the most competitive of the world's civilized societies. Our customs encourage a high degree of aggression in the individual's striving for success. Business is our main area of competition, and it has been ritualized into a game of strategy. The basic rules of the game have been set by the government, which attempts to detect and punish business frauds. But as long as a company does not transgress the rules of the game set by law, it has the legal right to shape its strategy without reference to anything but its profits. If it takes a long-term view of its profits, it will preserve amicable relations, so far as possible, with those with whom it deals. A wise businessman will not seek advantage to the point where he generates dangerous hostility among employees, competitors, customers, government, or the public at large. But decisions in this area are, in the final test, decisions of strategy, not of ethics.

THE INDIVIDUAL AND THE GAME

An individual within a company often finds it difficult to adjust to the requirements of the business game. He tries to preserve his private ethical standards in situations that call for game strategy. When he is obliged to carry out company policies that challenge his conception of himself as an ethical man, he suffers.

It disturbs him when he is ordered, for instance, to deny a raise to a man who deserves it, to fire an employee of long standing, to prepare advertising that he believes to be misleading, to conceal facts that he feels customers are entitled to know, to cheapen the quality of materials used in the manufacture of an established product, to sell as new a product that he knows to be rebuilt, to exaggerate the curative powers of a medicinal preparation, or to coerce dealers.

There are some fortunate executives who, by the nature of their work and circumstances, never have to face problems of this kind. But in one form or another the ethical dilemma is felt sooner or later by most businessmen. Possibly the dilemma is most painful not when the company forces the action on the executive but when he originates it himself—that is, when he has taken or is contemplating a step which is in his own interest but which runs counter to his early moral conditioning. To illustrate:

The manager of an export department, eager to show rising sales, is pressed by a big customer to provide invoices which, while containing no overt falsehood that would violate a U.S. law, are so worded that the customer may be able to evade certain taxes in his homeland.

A company president finds that an aging executive, within a few years of retirement and his pension, is not as productive as formerly. Should he be kept on?

The produce manager of a supermarket debates with himself whether to get rid of a lot of half-rotten tomatoes by including one, with its good side exposed, in every tomato six-pack.

An accountant discovers that he has taken an improper deduction on his company's tax return and fears the consequences if he calls the matter to the president's attention, though he himself has done nothing illegal. Perhaps if he says nothing, no one will notice the error.

A chief executive officer is asked by his directors to comment on a rumor that he owns stock in another company with which he has placed large orders. He could deny it, for the stock is in the name of his son-in-law and he has earlier formally instructed his son-in-law to sell the holding.

Temptations of this kind constantly arise in business. If an executive allows himself to be torn between a decision based on business considerations and one based on his private ethical code, he exposes himself to a grave psychological strain.

This is not to say that sound business strategy necessarily runs counter to ethical ideals. They may frequently coincide; and when they do, everyone is gratified. But the major tests of every move in business, as in all games of strategy, are legality and profit. A man who intends to be a winner in the business game must have a game player's attitude.

The business strategist's decision must be as impersonal as those of a surgeon performing an operation—concentrating on objective and technique, and subordinating personal feelings. If the chief executive admits that his son-in-law owns the stock, it is because he stands to lose more if the fact comes out later than if he states it boldly and at once. If the supermarket manager orders the rotten tomatoes to be discarded, he does so to avoid an increase in consumer complaints and a loss of good will. The company president decides not to fire the elderly executive in the belief that the negative reaction of other employees would in the long run cost the company more than it would lose in keeping him and paying his pension.

All sensible businessmen prefer to be truthful, but they seldom feel inclined to tell the *whole* truth. In the business game truth-telling usually has to be kept within narrow limits if trouble is to be avoided. The point was neatly made a long time ago (in 1888) by one of John D. Rockefeller's associates, Paul Babcock, to Standard Oil Company executives who were about to testify before a government investigating committee: "Parry every question with answers which, while perfectly truthful, are evasive of *bottom* facts." This was, is, and probably always will be regarded as wise and permissible business strategy.

FOR OFFICE USE ONLY

An executive's family life can easily be dislocated if he fails to make a sharp distinction between the ethical systems of the home and the office—or if his wife does not grasp that distinction. Many a businessman who has remarked to his wife, "I had to let Jones go today" or "I had to admit to the boss that Jim has been goofing off lately," has been met with an indignant protest. "How could you do a thing like that? You know Jones is over 50 and will have a lot of trouble getting another job." Or, "You did that to Jim? With his wife ill and all the worry she's been having with the kids?"

If the executive insists that he had no choice because the profits of the company and his own security were involved, he may see a certain cool and ominous reappraisal in his wife's eyes. Many wives are not prepared to accept the fact that business operates with a special code of ethics. An illuminating illustration of this comes from a Southern sales executive who related a conversation he had had with his wife at a time when a hotly contested political campaign was being waged in their state:

> I made the mistake of telling her that I had had lunch with Colby, who gives me about half my business. Colby mentioned that his company had a stake in the election. Then he said, "By the way, I'm treasurer of the citizens' committee for Lang. I'm collecting contributions. Can I count on you for a hundred dollars?"
>
> Well, there I was. I was opposed to Lang, but I knew Colby. If he withdrew his business I could be in a bad spot. So I just smiled and wrote out a check then and there. He thanked me, and we started to talk about his next order. Maybe he thought I shared his political views. If so, I wasn't going to lose any sleep over it.
>
> I should have had sense enough not to tell Mary about it. She hit the ceiling. She said she was disappointed in me. She said I hadn't acted like a man, that I should have stood up to Colby.
>
> I said, "Look, it was an either-or situation. I had to do it or risk losing the business."
>
> She came back at me with, "I don't believe it. You could have been honest with him. You could have said you didn't feel you ought to contribute to a campaign for a man you weren't going to vote for. I'm sure he would have understood."
>
> I said, "Mary, you're a wonderful woman, but you're way off the track. Do you know what would have happened if I had said that? Colby would have smiled and said, 'Oh, I didn't realize. Forget it.' But in his eyes from that moment I would be an oddball, maybe a bit of a radical. He would have listened to me talk about his order and would have promised to give

it consideration. After that I wouldn't hear from him for a week. Then I would telephone and learn from his secretary that he wasn't yet ready to place the order. And in about a month I would hear through the grapevine that he was giving his business to another company. A month after that I'd be out of a job."

She was silent for a while. Then she said, "Tom, something is wrong with business when a man is forced to choose between his family's security and his moral obligation to himself. It's easy for me to say you should have stood up to him—but if you had, you might have felt you were betraying me and the kids. I'm sorry that you did it, Tom, but I can't blame you. Something is wrong with business!"

This wife saw the problem in terms of moral obligation as conceived in private life; her husband saw it as a matter of game strategy. As a player in a weak position, he felt that he could not afford to indulge an ethical sentiment that might have cost him his seat at the table.

PLAYING TO WIN

Some men might challenge the Colbys of business—might accept serious setbacks to their business careers rather than risk a feeling of moral cowardice. They merit our respect—but as private individuals, not businessmen. When the skillful player of the business game is compelled to submit to unfair pressure, he does not castigate himself for moral weakness. Instead, he strives to put himself into a strong position where he can defend himself against such pressures in the future without loss.

If a man plans to take a seat in the business game, he owes it to himself to master the principles by which the game is played, including its special ethical outlook. He can then hardly fail to recognize that an occasional bluff may well be justified in terms of the game's ethics and warranted in terms of economic necessity. Once he clears his mind on this point, he is in a good position to match his strategy against that of the other players. He can then determine objectively whether a bluff in a given situation has a good chance of succeeding and can decide when and how to bluff, without a feeling of ethical transgression.

To be a winner, a man must play to win. This does not mean that he must be ruthless, cruel, harsh, or treacherous. On the contrary, the better his reputation for integrity, honesty, and decency, the better his chances of victory will be in the long run. But from time to time every businessman, like every poker player, is offered a choice between certain loss or bluffing within the legal rules of the game. If he is not resigned to losing, if he wants to rise in his company and industry, then in such a crisis he will bluff—and bluff hard.

Every now and then one meets a successful businessman who has conveniently forgotten the small or large deceptions that he practiced on his way to fortune. "God gave me my money," old John D. Rockefeller once piously told a Sunday school class. It would be a rare tycoon in our time who would risk the horse laugh with which such a remark would be greeted.

In the last third of the twentieth century even children are aware that if a man has become prosperous in business, he has sometimes departed from the strict truth in order to overcome obstacles or has practiced the more subtle deceptions of the half-truth or the misleading omission. Whatever the form of the bluff, it is an integral part of the game, and the executive who does not master its techniques is not likely to accumulate much money or power.

QUESTIONS

1. Henry Taylor has pointed out that "falsehood ceases to be falsehood when it is understood on all sides that the truth is not expected to be spoken." Critically analyze and evaluate this statement, and present your own views on this subject.
2. Carr believes that "the ethics of business are game ethics, different from the ethics of religion." What is he trying to say? Do you agree? Why or why not?
3. Where and how can one draw the line between ethics and normal business practices? Justify and illustrate.
4. Do you believe that we can learn a great deal about the nature of business by comparing it with poker? How and why?
5. Do you agree or disagree with Carr's views on the subject of business ethics? Why or why not? What are your own feelings on this subject? (See readers' comments on Carr's article in "Showdown on 'Business Bluffing.'" *Harvard Business Review,* 40 (May–June 1968), 162–170. Also note the following article by Norman C. Gillespie, which takes sharp issue with Carr's thesis.)

THE BUSINESS OF ETHICS

NORMAN C. GILLESPIE

Norman C. Gillespie, assistant professor of philosophy, University of Texas, Austin, in the following article rejects Carr's thesis that business ethics is like bluffing at poker and asserts that ordinary moral standards do apply to business decisions.

> It is the business of ethics to tell us what are our duties, or by what test we may know them.
>
> John Stuart Mill
> *Utilitarianism*

The public image of business does not always inspire public confidence, since it is often assumed that talk of ethics in business is only talk, not something that makes a difference in practice. Business executives are pragmatic individuals, accustomed to dealing with their environment as they find it and not inclined to question how things ought to be. That frame of mind reinforces the public image of business as impervious to moral imperatives. That image is only confirmed by such articles as those of Albert Carr, which embrace the purest kind of moral conventionalism: that which is generally done in business sets the standard of ethical conduct, so that an executive acts ethically as long as he conforms to the general practice. Carr goes so far as to maintain that misrepresentation in business is as ethical as bluffing in poker, and that only needless concern and anxiety will result from applying the ordinary moral standards of society to the conduct of business. On this score, I believe Carr is completely mistaken. This paper will argue that ordinary moral standards do apply to business decisions and practices and will explain *how* they apply. This should result in a clearer picture of the relationship between business and ethics—what it is now and what it ought to be.

Carr, in setting forth the conventionalist position, argues:

(1) Business, like poker, is a form of competition.
(2) In this competition, the rules are different than they are in ordinary social dealings.
(3) Anyone who abides by ordinary moral standards instead of the rules of business places himself at a decided disadvantage. Therefore,
(4) It is not unethical or immoral to abide by the current rules of business. (These rules are determined in part by what is generally done in business and in part by legal statutes governing business activities.)

Reprinted by permission from the November 1975 issue of the *University of Michigan Business Review*, published by the Graduate School of Business Administration, The University of Michigan.

In support of this position, three "rules" might be offered: (1) If a business practice is not illegal, it is thereby ethically acceptable. (2) If a businessman does not take advantage of a legal opportunity, others will surely do so. (3) If a practice is so widespread as to constitute the norm, everyone expects conformity. The "rule" that it is ethically correct to do something because it is not illegal is, of course, one of the conventionalist's weakest arguments, since it should be obvious that legality does not establish morality—it may not be illegal for a teacher to favor some students over others for non-academic reasons, yet it is clearly unethical. When one speaks of ethics in business, it is to establish what business practices *ought* to be. The law, as written, does not settle that issue. The other two "rules," however, may appear to have some merit and require more detailed analysis.

BUSINESS AS A GAME

Suppose that such things as industrial espionage, deception of customers and shading the truth in published financial statements are common enough to be of broad concern, in effect comprising some *de facto* state of business affairs. What bearing would such a state have upon what is moral or ethical in conducting business? Would the existence of such "rules of the game" relieve owners, managers and employees of otherwise appropriate ethical obligations? Or, would such behavior merely be a matter of business strategy and not a matter of ethics?

The obvious fallacy in the "business-as-a-game" idea is that, unlike poker, business is *not* a game. People's lives, their well-being, their plans and their futures often depend upon business and the way it is conducted. Indeed, people usually exchange part of their lives (i.e., the portion spent earning money) for certain goods and services. They have the right not to be misled or deceived about the true nature of those goods or services. Similarly, elected officials have a duty to legislate and act for the good of their country (or state). It can hardly be right for business executives to frustrate them in the performance of that duty by providing them with evasive answers or by concealing relevant facts.

THE PRICE OF DUTY

So, the poker analogy, while informative of the way things *are,* seems to have no bearing at all on the way they *ought* to be in business. Why, then, do so many people adopt the conventionalist position that "business is business and, when in business, do as the others do"? Some take that position for essentially the same reason Yossarian offers to justify his conduct in the novel, *Catch 22*. Yossarian has refused to fly any more combat missions and when asked, "But suppose everybody on our side felt that way?" he replies, "Then I'd be a damn fool to feel any other way. Wouldn't I?" If everyone were refusing to fly, Yossarian says, he would be a fool to fly. In business, the position would be: if everyone is bluffing, an individual would be a fool not to do the same. On this point, Yossarian and the conventionalist are correct, but not because there are special rules (or special ethics) for airplane gunners and people in business. The reason, instead, is that our ordinary moral reasoning does, indeed, make allowance for just such cases. In other words, the idea that there is something ethically distinctive about a situation in which a person in business may find himself is sound. But it is sound because ordinary moral reasoning allows for such circumstances, not because there are special ethical rules for people in business comparable to the rules of poker.

The sort of considerations I have in mind all involve the *cost* of doing what would normally be one's duty. There are at least three ways in which a normal or ordinary duty may cease to be so because the cost is too high. The first of these is widely recognized: sometimes the *moral cost* of obeying a standard moral rule is too great, so one must make an exception to that rule. If the only way to save someone's life is by telling a lie, then one should normally lie. If treating an accident victim involves breaking a promise to meet someone on time, then one should normally be late. In a variety of circumstances, obeying a moral rule might require breaking some other, more urgent, moral duty. In these circumstances, the more urgent duty dictates an exception to the lesser rule.

The second way in which an ordinary duty may cease to be a duty is when the *cost to the individual* of fulfilling that duty is too high. For example, when driving an automobile, one normally has the duty not to run into other cars, and one also has the general duty not to harm or injure other persons. But suppose one is driving down a steep mountain road and the brakes fail. One might have a choice among options: cross into the oncoming lane of traffic, go off the cliff on one's right, or drive into the car in front. In such a case, a driver would not act wrongly if he chose the third option, even though there is a way in which he can meet his duty of not injuring others and not driving into other peoples' cars, namely, by going off the cliff. In these circumstances, the cost to the individual of meeting his duty is simply too high, and virtually no one would blame him or condemn his action as morally wrong if he drove into the back of the car in front of him rather than going off the cliff.

The third way in which a normal duty may turn out not to be a duty is the kind of situation described by Yossarian. If everyone else is not doing what ought to be done, then one would be a fool to act differently. This third consideration does not obviate all duties, e.g., just because everyone else is committing murder does not make it right for you to do so, but it does apply to those cases in which the *morally desirable state of affairs can be produced only by everyone, or virtually everyone, doing his part.* With respect to such a duty, e.g., jury-duty, one person by himself cannot accomplish anything; he can only place himself at a disadvantage *vis-à-vis* everyone else by doing what everyone ought to do but is not doing. This sort of situation can be described as a "state of nature situation," and by that I mean a situation in which certain moral rules are generally disobeyed either by everyone or by the members of a well-defined group.

In dealing with such situations, the fact that other people can be expected to act in certain ways is morally relevant in that it creates a special sort of moral dilemma. If one does what everyone ought to do but is not doing, then one will, in all likelihood, be at a disadvantage. The morally questionable behavior of others creates the circumstances in which one finds oneself, and in those circumstances it may be necessary to fight fire with fire and to resist deception with deception. But replying in kind only prolongs the state of nature situation, so one's primary goal should be to attempt to change the situation. No one ought to take unfair advantage of others, but no one is obligated to let others take unfair advantage of him.

It is absolutely essential to note, in connection with such situations, that people are not doing what they ought to be doing. The conventionalist recognizes that simple application of ordinary moral rules to such situations is inadequate. But it is a mistake to conclude (1) that ordinary rules do not apply *at all* to such cases, and (2) that business has its own distinctive set of rules that determines one's duties in such circumstances. Both points are incorrect because (1) the ordinary rules help define the situation as one in which people are not doing what they ought to be doing (we apply the ordinary moral rules to such cases and find that they are not being generally observed), and (2) the considerations that are relevant in determining one's duties in such circumstances do not constitute a special set of factors that are relevant only in business. The mitigating considerations apply generally and are an important part of ordinary moral reasoning.

When virtually everyone is not doing what ought to be done, it affects what we can morally expect of any one individual. He does not have a duty to "buck the tide" if doing so will harm him substantially or not do any good. But he, in conjunction with everyone else, *ought to be* acting differently. So the tension he may feel between what he does and what he ought to do is quite real and entirely appropriate.

In the conventionalist argument, these two considerations—the cost to the individual and what everyone else is doing—recur again and again: It is right to lie about one's age and one's magazine preferences when doing otherwise will prevent you from getting a job; right to engage in industrial espionage because everyone else is doing it; right to sell a popular mouthwash with a possibly deleterious form of alcohol in it because cigarettes are sold to the public; and right to sell master automobile keys through the mails (to potential criminals) because guns are sold.

Of these four examples, the last two seem to me to be clearly wrong since neither the high cost to the individual of doing otherwise nor the existence of a general practice has been established. Industrial espionage, however, is a good illustration of a "state of nature situation," and if (1) one does it to others who are doing the same, and (2) it is necessary to "fight fire with fire" for the sake of survival, then it would not be morally wrong. For the job applicant, the conditions themselves are morally dubious, so here, too, it may be a case of fighting fire with fire for the sake of personal survival. But notice, in each of these examples, how distasteful the action in question is; most of us would prefer not to engage in such activities. The point is that conditions may be such that the cost of not engaging in them may be so great that an individual caught in such circumstances is blameless. At the same time, however, we do feel that *the circumstances* should be different.

The second consideration, distinct from the cost to the individual, is that one person doing what everyone ought to do (but is not doing) will accomplish nothing. This can be the case even where the individual cost is insignificant. To take a homely example, suppose there were a well-defined path across the local courthouse lawn as the result of shortcuts taken across it. It would not cost anyone very much to walk around instead of across the lawn, but if one knows his fellow citizens and knows that the path is there to stay, then walking around will accomplish nothing. So one may as well take the path unless, of course, one decides to set an example of how others ought to be acting. Since it costs so little, it might well be a good idea to set such an example. This would be one small way at least of trying to change the situation.

Although one's primary goal ought to be to change the situation, that statement, like all claims about what one ought to do, is subject to the moral precept that individuals have a *duty* to do only what they *can* do. So, if it is impossible for one individual to change the situation, he does not have a duty to change it. What is true is that *the situation* ought to be different but to make it so may require the combined efforts of many people. All of them collectively have the duty to change it, so this is not a duty that falls solely or directly on the shoulders of any one person. For the individual executive, then, the question is primarily one of what he, in conjunction with others, can accomplish. Secondarily, it is a question of the likely personal cost to him of instituting or proposing needed changes.

A ROLE FOR THE INDIVIDUAL EXECUTIVE

At the very least, executives should not *thwart* the impetus for change on the ground that business sets its own ethical standards. Everyone has a legitimate interest in the way business is run, and Better Business Bureaus and legislative inquiries should be viewed as important instruments serving that interest. We know on the basis of ordinary moral rules that in certain business environments a new way of acting is a desirable goal. If no one else will join in the promotion of that goal, then the individual executive can, as the poet said, "only stand and wait." But according to that same poet, John Milton, "They also serve who only stand and wait."

The essential difference between the conventionalist position and ordinary moral reasoning comes out most clearly in the following example, provided by Carr in defense of his position. A businessman, Tom, is asked by an important customer, in the middle of a sales talk, to contribute to the election campaign of a candidate Tom does not support. He does so, and the talk continues with enthusiasm. Later, Tom mentions his action to his wife, Mary, and she is furious. They discuss the situation, and the conversation concludes with her saying, "Tom, something is wrong with business when a man is forced to choose between his family's security and his moral obligation . . . It's easy for me to say you should have stood up to him—but if you had, you might have felt you were betraying me and the kids. I'm sorry you did it, Tom, but I can't blame you. Something is wrong with business."

Carr comments that, "This wife saw the problem in terms of moral obligation as conceived in private life; her husband saw it as a matter of game strategy." Those who would refuse to make the contribution "merit our respect—but as private individuals, not as businessmen."

What Tom did was not morally wrong in those circumstances but not for the reasons cited in Carr's paper. There is something wrong with *the situation* in which Tom found himself. It *ought not be the case* that one has to choose between his family and being honest about his political preferences. Carr fails to recognize this, and either misses or ignores entirely the fact that Mary makes precisely this point: she does not blame her husband, or say that he did the wrong thing in those circumstances; what she says, instead, is that *something is wrong with business* when a person has to act as her husband did. It is business and the way it is conducted that ought to be changed. The conventionalist position simply blocks out such an issue: it nowhere considers how business ought to be. It merely says that "the way it is" is all that need be taken into account in deciding what would be ethical.

An analogous situation exists in connection with the financing of political campaigns. No one blames candidates for taking contributions from lobbyists and other individuals, since they need the money to run for office. But many people do think that *the system ought to be changed.* In other words, the current practices are not as honest or ethical as they ought to be. Now, how can the conventionalist handle such a claim? It seems obvious that he cannot, since he systematically rules out applying ordinary moral standards to business practices. But the correct position is that these standards do apply, and sometimes we find they are not being practiced. In precisely those cases, the general practice ought to change.

THE NEED FOR CHANGE

There is a most important difference, then, between asking, "What are the individual duties of a person doing business?" and "What are the ways in which business ought to be conducted?" Both are an essential part of the ethics of business but the conventionalist simply ignores the second question in attempting to answer the first. The answers to the second question can be found, for the most part, by consulting our ordinary moral standards of how people ought to act *vis-à-vis* one another. When we find that business is not as moral as we would like it to be, that *does* have some bearing upon the answer to the first question. But, as I have argued in this paper, ordinary moral reasoning is prepared to take those facts into account. It is not at all necessary to postulate a special ethical outlook or a distinctive set of ethical rules for business in order to explain the ethical relevance of such phenomena to the individual businessman.

Ordinary moral reasoning, then, is far richer than mere conventionalism, and the factors it takes into account are relevant in many managerial and executive decisions. Ethics can be subtle, as well as realistic, and conventionalism is unrealistic when it obscures the moral imperative for change.

QUESTIONS

1. Gillespie asserts that "unlike poker, business is *not* a game." Argue that, in rejecting Carr's basic assumptions, Gillespie has simply substituted one set of rules for another.
2. Does Gillespie's rebuttal of Carr leave business executives with a clearer conception of adequate ethical behavior than Carr's? Does it leave them with a more elevating standard for conduct?

MAJOR FORCES UPGRADING AND DOWNGRADING BUSINESS ETHICAL BEHAVIOR

JOHN F. STEINER

There are many forces that serve to upgrade business ethical behavior. And there are many forces that help to downgrade it. In this brief comment, John F. Steiner presents what he thinks are some major forces.

Although it is easy to be pessimistic in the wake of Watergate and Equity Funding, the outlook for resolving the ethical problems reflected there and elsewhere is good. Business ethics is not the desperate problem we think it is.

We need not expect moral uplift in business leaders to occur spontaneously. Rather, we need to appreciate more the operation of impersonal forces in the business environment which are likely to lead to rising levels of business ethics in the future. These forces have upgraded ethical behavior in the past and will continue to do so. They include the following.

FORCES IN UPGRADING ETHICAL BEHAVIOR

1. The periodic impact of episodic moral indignations which raise public expectations of business performance during periods such as the Agrarian revolt, the Progressive era, the Depression era and the post-Watergate years.
2. The increased professionalization of today's managers who place the dignity of an occupation and its service duties above naked personal gain.
3. A leadership selection process in large corporations which weeds out the most predatory and ruthless individuals before they get to the very top.
4. A growing climate of affluence which gives businessmen the luxury to respond to higher public expectations.
5. The ascendance of powerful opposition groups which have acted in the policy-making process to control the voraciousness of businessmen.
6. Continuing government surveillance of business and an increased blurring of the public-private distinction.
7. Rising individual and societal expectations of business's behavior.
8. An increasingly educated and informed populace growing out of the predicted knowledge revolution of post-industrial society.
9. Increasing attention to ethical matters in professional schools.
10. Development of a conservation ethic which is higher than a consumption ethic as the full impact of our finite resource base is realized.

John F. Steiner, "The Perfection of Ethics in Business," Comments From Readers, *Los Angeles Business and Economics,* Spring 1976, p. 2.

11. Continued democratization and increased accountability of large private institutions to society-at-large.
12. A yielding of the classical profit maximization ideology to the doctrine of social responsibility.
13. The institutionalization of social responsiveness in corporate bureaucracies and the increasing attention of top executives to the subject.
14. New considerations of social and ethical performance in the selection of chief executive officers in large corporations.
15. More external restraints on management through new laws such as federal charters for corporations.
16. More stringent disclosure requirements which limit corporate secrecy.
17. An increasingly litigation-prone public.
18. Achievement of popular consensus for increasingly humane public policy goals such as floors on income and welfare.
19. Increasing realization of the interdependence of public and private institutions in solving the great social problems of the 20th century.
20. Increased attention to forecasting and planning of the social impacts of business by experts in business and government.
21. Increasingly humanitarian-oriented scientific and technological endeavors focused on problems of human survival and personal fulfillment.
22. Emergence of political leadership to direct public values away from traditional materialism and toward visions of a more fulfilling life linked to inner rewards.
23. Changing social values which feature declining emphasis on materialism and increased emphasis on the quality of life.
24. The development of new participatory and democratic personnel practices in large corporations.
25. Increasingly organized and sincere efforts by large corporations to allay public cynicism by improving their behavior in many areas.

FORCES WHICH MAY DOWNGRADE BEHAVIOR

It should be recognized, of course, that the social setting of business is complex and can be expected to contain some contrary forces which may act to downgrade the behavior of businessmen. These include the following.

1. The problematic aspects of technological innovation. Computer criminals and electronic eavesdropping, for example, are indications of new and sophisticated business criminality.
2. The decentralizing trends in large-scale business bureaucracies which make it easier to hide moral turpitude from the highest echelons and more difficult to fix responsibility for wrongdoing anywhere.
3. Economic problems such as inflation, competition, government regulation, and such, which may make it more difficult for some companies to maintain acceptable levels without resorting to morally questionable behavior.
4. The growing tendency, nurtured by many forces, for individuals to take advantage of the law and of others.

5. The decline in the acceptance of rigid religious standards and the re-examination of traditional values such as the work ethic by large numbers of people.
6. The regulation of businesses by distant and unresponsive government bureaucracies which may lead to inequities and injustices.
7. The presence of rising and unfulfilled expectations among important groups.
8. The continued existence of a political system which, despite some reforms, remains responsive to organized special interests which work in undisclosed ways out of the limelight.
9. The continued resistance of some managers to doctrines of social responsiveness and accountability.
10. The immutability of human nature and the continued existence of those baser emotions which motivate unethical business behavior.

In my opinion the more powerful and numerous factors operating to upgrade business ethics will lead to the continuation of a positive trend. We should not let periodic scandals such as the Watergate-related ones blind us to the continuing progress of business toward higher moral standards. Abuses will continue but we should not lose our confidence yet. The "problem" of business ethics is not an impossible one.

QUESTIONS

1. Do you have any major forces to add to this list?
2. Looking back over business history, say for one hundred years, do you think that the level of business ethics has risen or fallen?
3. Do you believe that business executives today, generally, are more ethical than they were one hundred years ago? Or is human nature fundamentally the same but seems to be improved because of new laws and social pressures?
4. Are business executives any more or less ethical than anyone else given the same set of circumstances surrounding their actions?

BUSINESS ETHICS AND MORALITIES: FOREIGN "PAYOFFS" AND RECOMMENDED SOLUTIONS FOR UNETHICAL BEHAVIOR

REFORM OF BRIBERY ABROAD INVOLVES U.S. POLICY

MILTON S. GWIRTZMAN AND ALAN R. NOVAK

Milton S. Gwirtzman, an international lawyer with offices in Washington, D.C., and Paris, and Alan R. Novak, a lawyer and businessman, formerly executive assistant to the Undersecretary of State, in the following article survey practices abroad concerning inducements to do business, point out dilemmas facing American business executives, and raise fundamental issues regarding ethics in international transactions.

This has not been an easy year for American business. Still struggling to recover from the worst sales decline in 30 years, the business community has been hit with sweeping new regulations of its products and advertising by the government, and with increasing complaints about high prices and defective merchandise by a public whose faith in the free-enterprise system, according to recent polls, has sunk to a new low.

In this already embattled atmosphere, some of the big multinational firms have been targets of a highly publicized series of revelations concerning bribery and payoffs abroad. Some of the country's flagship corporations—Exxon, Lockheed, Northrop, Gulf, United Brands—have admitted funneling massive amounts of cash to officials of foreign governments and hiding the transactions from their shareholders and directors. With their ethics as well as their profits under attack, many businessmen view themselves as Job beset by a plague of boils.

Of all the tribulations, the exposure of shady foreign business practices was the most unexpected, concerning as it does a practice that has existed at least since the 1600's, when the British East India Co. won duty-free treatment for its exports by giving Mogul rulers "rare treasures," including paintings, carvings and "costly objects made of copper, brass and stone."

Nations like Britain and Sweden, whose standards of government ethics are a good deal stricter than our own, take it for granted that their businessmen will pay bribes when operating abroad, especially in developing countries. "Without it," says The Financial Times of London, "business simply would not get done." The only difficulty such bribes pose for British firms, according to a recent survey by The Financial Times, is one of morale. Some British executives feel unfairly treated when comparing their own modest and highly taxed salaries with what The Times calls "the large, tax-free rewards going to an assortment of foreign middlemen."

Milton S. Gwirtzman and Alan R. Novak, "Reform of Bribery Abroad Involves U.S. Policy," *New York Times Magazine,* October 5, 1975.

But in the United States, this traditional way of doing business abroad has become food for scandal because of the new climate of openness and honesty that former Vice President Agnew ruefully and accurately called in his resignation speech the "post-Watergate morality."

It was largely corporate funds, laundered in foreign countries and returned to the United States in black satchels, that financed the Watergate break in and the subsequent illegal payoffs to cover it up. In the course of its investigations, the Special Prosecutor's Office found in the possession of Richard Nixon's personal secretary a list of firms that had made illegal corporate contributions to President Nixon's campaign.

The Securities and Exchange Commission, which protects shareholders by requiring companies to disclose material facts of their activities, went after the firms for failure to report these contributions to their owners. Further probing revealed that some of the devices used to hide illegal contributions had also been used to hide the bribery of foreign officials from the companies' shareholders, and even from their own auditors. The SEC then moved to require disclosure of the questionable overseas practices, arguing that, while there is no law against such payments, the amounts of the bribes and the names of the recipients were important facts that present and prospective shareholders had a right to know.

Firms caught up in these proceedings feel as if they have been hit by a ton of bricks.

When the facts began to unravel about a $1.25-million bribe paid by United Brands to the former president of Honduras to reduce the tax on the production of bananas, the company's president committed suicide, its stock dropped 40%, its holdings in Panama were expropriated and its tax and tariff concessions in Honduras were revoked.

The Internal Revenue Service is investigating more than 100 corporations for improperly deducting payoffs and political contributions on their tax returns. (A bribe is not a legitimate business deduction. An agent's fee is.) A series of hearings by the Senate subcommittee on multinational corporations, led by Sen. Frank Church of Idaho, has fueled a push for new legislation, ranging from compulsory disclosure of such payments, to their criminal prosecution, to a requirement that the State Department keep watch on American businessmen and report all suspicious activities to the appropriate U.S. authorities.

All of this presents the American businessman operating abroad with a seemingly cruel dilemma. If he keeps paying foreign officials, he runs afoul of the post-Watergate morality in all its fury. If he is prevented from making these payments, either by law or by the chilling effect of disclosure, he risks the loss of important sales and investment opportunities to foreign competitors, who can apparently continue to pass bribes without embarrassment.

The Lockheed case presents the most dramatic example of this predicament. Despite considerable initial pressure from Congress and the SEC, the company refused to reveal the names of the recipients of the $25 million to $30 million in bribes it admitted having paid in the last five years.

The firm, represented by former Secretary of State William Rogers, argues that if the whole truth were known about what it did to secure orders from certain foreign governments, the orders could well be canceled, the company ruined, and the $200 million in loans the government has made to keep Lockheed afloat would be lost for good. Lockheed did agree to pass no more bribes, and it subsequently lost a jumbo-jet contract in India to a French company that, Lockheed alleges, had contributed $1.5 million to the ruling Congress party.

American business activities abroad generate 15% of the gross national product, 30% of the total profits of the nation's corporations and an estimated 10 million American jobs. In large measure, the preservation of our current fragile economic health depends upon profits from foreign investment and dollars earned through overseas sales. It is important, therefore, to consider the true extent of the problem of foreign bribery, and its underlying causes, in order to decide what might be done about it.

The bigger payoffs are made by the large multinational companies, and they are part of a broader tendency to place the corporations' interests ahead of those of the countries in which they operate. Some multinationals can, and have, moved factories from country to country with little regard for the workers involved, and shifted profits earned in one country to others where the tax systems are more indulgent.

Studies have shown that the ability of multinational firms to transfer large sums of money from one currency to another at a profit played an important role in the devaluation or revaluation of each of the world's major currencies over the past seven years, and the resultant breakdown in the world monetary system that had previously been based on fixed parities between national monies. (When former President Nixon blamed the devaluation of the dollar on "international speculators," he was speaking of some of his heaviest campaign contributors.)

When firms routinely engage in these kinds of maneuvers, concepts of moral ethics as well as national allegiance tend to blur.

Top managers of these companies often follow a lifestyle that tends to encourage unethical practices. Some heads of multinational companies have virtually unrestricted power. Jetting around the world in their personal planes, whisked from one meeting to the next by limousine, with immediate access to millions of dollars to spend as they see fit, they are driven by one overriding goal—to improve the company's earnings.

This style of management has some advantages, but time for ethical reflection is not among them. These multinational managers are neither grafters nor thieves, but somewhere in the frenzy of travel, pressure and ambition they may lose their ability to balance the needs of their shareholders with the accepted standards of moral behavior.

Nor can they always look for help to their shareholders and directors. At the annual meeting of United Brands in August, the majority of shareholders were far more concerned with the company's passing its common dividend than with its massive bribes in Central America. They cheered a statement by one of their number that bribery was "essential in doing business in many parts of the world." At the annual meeting of Exxon, a resolution to require disclosure of the firm's payments abroad was defeated.

Despite the devastating publicity suffered by Ashland Oil for payoffs in four countries and illegal contributions to scores of U.S. politicians, its directors recommended against firing its chief executive, Orin Atkins (who was directly responsible for most of the payments), on the ground that since he had taken over, the corporation's net income had grown from $31 million to $113 million.

(Such activities are not universal. Several large U.S. multinationals, as a matter of corporate policy, prohibit foreign political contributions and come down hard on suspected bribes. Among them are RCA, IBM and Bendix. W. Michael Blumenthal, president of Bendix, says his company prefers to pass up increased profits and occasionally an entire national market rather than engage in the ethical compromises and deceptions such practices necessarily involved. It is, of course, easier for a firm that has a virtual monopoly of its product line like IBM to stay pure.)

If corporate bribery abroad has offended the post-Watergate morality, the companies implicated have nevertheless taken a greater share of the blame than they deserve. Bribery abroad is not exactly the corruption of innocents. Several of the incidents spotlighted by the Senate hearings smack more of protection and extortion than of simple bribery. In the most outrageous case, the chairman of the ruling party in South Korea threatened to close the $300-million operation of Gulf Oil in that country unless the company made a donation of $10 million to his party's presidential campaign. Gulf's chairman, Bob Dorsey, was able to shave the demand down from $10 million, which he considered "not in the interests of the company," to $3 million, which he said was.

The reasons multinationals must do business amid a profusion of outstretched hands go deep into the history and structure of the lands in which they operate. In much of Asia and Africa the market economy as we know it, in which the sale of goods and services is governed by price and quality competition, never has existed. What has developed in its stead are intricate tribal and oligarchic arrangements of social connections, family relations and reciprocal obligations, lubricated by many forms of tribute, including currency.

In a meeting at the Department of Defense in 1973 (a report of which was subpoenaed from the files of the Northrop Corp.) Adnan Kashogghi, one of the most successful middlemen in the Middle East, justified his enormous sales commissions—$45 million on a single deal for fighter planes—by his need to cover his operating expenses and also take care of his pecuniary "loyalties" to Saudi Arabia's royal family.

Another memo explained Northrop's loss of a contract to build a communications system by noting that Saudi officials wished to help out the local agent of a Northrop competitor, one Ibriham el-Zahed. "They felt," the memo said, "that by awarding a contract to his principals, he will make enough money to pay off his debts. This may sound like an amazing reason to people sitting in Century City (Northrop's California headquarters), but can be a very valid one in Saudi Arabia."

In most developing countries, civil service salaries are deliberately low —the average Indian bureaucrat makes $1,650 a year—on the assumption they will supplement their salaries by taking money where they can find it. Where political instability is the rule, the tenure of high officials is always uncertain and often short. Bribes provide a form of retirement fund. It is considered far more patriotic to take the money from rich foreign corporations than out of one's own country.

The responsibility for present practices must also be shared by the U.S. government, which not only encouraged investment in countries whose ethical standards differ from ours, but also in many respects, set the pattern for the graft under censure today. American intelligence agencies have regularly dealt in bribery and payoffs wherever they seemed to be useful tools in strengthening American influence abroad and frustrating the designs of Communist nations. Bribes have been used not just to acquire useful information, but to restore the Shah to power in Iran, to purchase votes in international organizations against Cuba and to "destabilize" the Allende government in Chile.

Armaments sales provide the most dramatic and dangerous example of corporate profit-seeking, foreign customs and U.S. policy goals combining to create a massive network of bribery. As cutbacks in Western defense budgets have dried up domestic markets for arms, purchases by Third World countries have increased. In addition to maintaining domestic employment and lowering the unit cost of arms produced for our own defense, such exports were considered by Washington to be the most effective way of cementing diplomatic relations. Recipient countries, it was argued, would find it difficult to stay out of the U.S. orbit if they depended upon us for their military hardware, its maintenance and spare parts and the training of personnel in its use.

When the war in Vietnam wound down, the most important market for armaments became the Middle East. For a generation, the United States and the Soviet Union, as well as Britain and France, have tried to strengthen their influence in that region by catering to the Arab rulers' fears of Israel and each other.

The sharp rise in the price of OPEC oil gave the Arabs the means to buy the most sophisticated modern weaponry. Such sales have become a vital element of the "recycling" procedure, by which Western countries try to earn back some of their petrodollars.

From less than $1 billion in 1966, the total arms imports of Mideast nations, including Israel, have rocketed to over $9 billion in 1974. Last year, the United States alone sold $6.5 billion worth of armaments, more than half of them going to Iran, where the Shah has expressed a keen interest in purchasing aircraft capable of delivering nuclear weapons.

Given the stiff competition from other countries and the way business is done in that region, the Mideast arms race was bound to generate millions of dollars in graft. Under recent Saudi Arabian law, no foreign company could do business without a local agent. When Northrop, with strong encouragement from the Pentagon, undertook to sell its F–5 fighter plane there, the Saudi minister of defense told Northrop's "international consultant," Kermit Roosevelt, to advise the firm to hire Adnan Kashogghi, who had previously been the agent for Lockheed and Raytheon. To get the sale approved, the firm fattened Kashogghi's fee to include $450,000 for two Saudi air force generals who were threatening to hold up the deal.

Northrop president Thomas Jones says he knew nothing about this, but admits that on a quick trip to Jidda, the graft question was raised, and he told Kashogghi that "Northrop is a company that meets its obligations." The bribe money was deducted from Northrop's income tax and included as a reimbursable cost in its bill to the Department of Defense. Since the recent scandals, both claims have been withdrawn.

For all these reasons, it would be unwise, as well as unfair, simply to write off bribery abroad to corporate lust. It is a symbol of far deeper issues that really involve America's role in the world. For the past 30 years, from Dean Acheson to Henry Kissinger, the governing principle of U.S. foreign policy has been that a Communist threat to our nation's vital interests exists, sufficient to require a major American presence throughout the world and whatever means are necessary to maintain U.S. influence.

Since our multinational companies, like government agencies, are important instruments of our nation's global power, it is argued that they should not be hobbled by home-bred notions of business morality.

There is, of course, a growing force of opinion in this country that holds such a view of our past foreign policy to be both obsolete and dangerous, arguing that bribery abroad goes hand in hand with coziness with dictators, the excesses of the CIA and everything else that has put us on the defensive in so many parts of the world. A foreign policy that at one stroke can justify bribes, the purchase of influence, the overthrow of governments and assassinations of foreign leaders subverts not just the free-enterprise system, but all our national ideals.

These opposite views of American foreign policy cannot be resolved by argument. With the right pair of candidates, they may be a central issue in next year's presidential election. One thing is certain, however: To implement this last view will require far greater changes in how our country acts abroad than the mere cessation of graft. If that is all that changes, business will be handicapped in many foreign countries and our economy may suffer as a result.

Yet this may be exactly what occurs. The investigations by Congress and the SEC have enjoyed a remarkable staying power on the front pages of the nation's press. The revelations undoubtedly have struck a sensitive national nerve. A sufficient head of steam exists in Congress to push through new laws outlawing both bribery and political contributions abroad. Whether such a law is sensible or even enforceable, is another question.

It would be far better if reform could be coordinated with other countries and with international organizations. Since the United States puts up such a large share of the capital of the World Bank and the Inter-American Development Fund, we could ask that these agencies strengthen their procedures against payoffs on projects financed with their loans.

The best place to initiate common reform may be in the Organization for Economic Cooperation and Development, whose membership comprises all the Western industrialized nations, and which is now working on guidelines for the conduct of both multinational companies and the countries in which they operate. If the United States were to insist on strong prohibitions against bribery in this document, member nations might, in concert, adopt such strictures for themselves.

Yet even if we have to act alone, it will not be the first time. Last year, we were ready to impeach a President for actions that are accepted practices abroad. Watergate showed not that America was the most corrupt of nations, but that it was the most sensitive.

The truth is that we have stood for worthy ideals even while playing international hardball. The export of Marshall Plan aid, Food for Peace and the Peace Corps volunteers were actions others admired and then followed. One of our ideals is that we are an open society that lets its conduct hang out for ethical inspection. Perhaps the export of the new morality born of the Watergate tragedy would not hurt us in this wearied world.

RESULTS OF A SURVEY OF PAYOFFS

JAMES R. BASCHE, JR.

James R. Basche, Jr., a member of the Conference Board research staff, conducted a survey among international executives regarding so-called payoffs, the results of which are summarized here by the editors of this book.

The Conference Board asked 73 international executives this question: "Do you believe that American companies should adopt the commercial modes and moral standards of countries in which they do business or should they adhere to U.S. standards?" Fifty-two percent supported adherence to U.S. standards and the remainder thought U.S. companies should adopt the standards of the countries in which they are operating.

One executive supporting adherence to U.S. standards said that if companies did not follow this policy sooner or later it would become known and cause embarrassment to the country, the country's officials, and to the company. Furthermore, he said, it would shake faith in the free enterprise system "whose preservation, we believe, is more important than any immediate advantage that can be gained from payoffs."

The president of another firm said: "America cannot set itself up as the high priest of the world's business morals without serious consequences in our export trade. It would be well for us to remember that there are civilizations much older than our own in which the concepts of moral conduct are vastly different from our own ethics. I dare say that if we were extreme enough in our zealous approach to eradicate corruption from the world's business, we would damage our international trade position severely in certain countries."

Several executives felt that there was no significant difference between business standards and moral codes in the U.S. and foreign countries. Another executive said that costs to influence business in the United States—trips, vacations incentives, entertaining, lobbying, etc.—were less than overseas as a percent of the sales dollar. Another thought that because of scandals in the United States in the highest political offices that our corporations were in no position to try to reform business morality throughout the world.

Adapted by George A. Steiner from James R. Basche, Jr., *Unusual Foreign Payments: A Survey of the Policies and Practices of U.S. Companies.* New York: The Conference Board, Inc., 1976. Reprinted by permission.

THE BASICS OF BRIBERY

EDITORS OF
THE WALL STREET JOURNAL

In the following editorial, the editors of *The Wall Street Journal* raise some provocative questions about the justification of bribery payments by American companies to foreign politicians and other business executives.

Through much of history, and in places as diverse as the county court house or the Palace of Versailles, there has been dubious money dealing between businessmen and politicians.

It is optimistic to expect the world to be transformed in response to Senator Church's shocking revelations about the favors Lockheed et al. have bestowed on the likes of Yoshia Kodama. But that does not mean such matters should be looked upon with tolerance. There is a possibility of more effective control, provided there is a better awareness of what is at stake.

It is encouraging, for example, that the United States is working through the Organization for Economic Cooperation and Development in Paris to get international adoption of a code of ethics designed to discourage business bribery. It will be even more encouraging if the nations adopting the code signify that they intend to tighten up on procedures for policing their own bureaucracies as well as the international corporations which do business with them.

But for everyone dealing with this problem, there should be a better understanding of why the great market economies cannot afford to tolerate business-government bribery. It is not very helpful to say that only the weak companies attempt bribery or that extortion is a better description, thereby excusing the business majority. Nor is it accurate, on the other side, to say that bribery reflects the underlying corruption in the capitalist system, however much the critics of multinational corporations would like to use that argument.

In fact, few economic systems have a greater experience with under-the-table dealing than the Soviet Union. It is common practice for factory managers to do special favors for suppliers in order to get what they need to meet their quotas. That isn't too much different from a Lockheed salesman passing along baksheesh to try to make his sales quota.

The primary difference is in result. The Soviet deal, taking place in a centrally planned economy that is fundamentally inefficient, may sometimes —although not always—actually improve efficiency of production and distribution and thereby benefit the public. But in market economies, which are highly efficient when the market is functioning properly, bribery represents a market interference. The cost of self-dealing falls on the public.

The money used to bribe politicians is an extra cost borne mainly by the constituents of those politicians. In the case of military aircraft the matter is even more serious, since national security may be at stake. The public of any country knows this, which is why no constituency is tolerant of politicians on the take, or of the companies who make the offers.

In international trade, the situation is altered a bit, but not much. It might be argued that Americans are the winners if Lockheed uses a bribe to beat out Dassault for a Saudi contract. At stake are U.S. aircraft industry jobs, economies of scale that reduce costs of military hardware bought by the U.S. itself, the maintenance of a production capability vital to U.S. defense and exports that are important to the soundness of the U.S. dollar.

Such considerations salve the consciences of American businessmen who engage in bribery abroad. But at best they only represent an argument for an international attack on the problem. They have nothing at all to do with the fundamental morality.

To argue that Americans should tolerate—because it might be in their own interests—the victimization of the people of Japan or Italy is to apply a dangerous double standard. It is dangerous because the higher of two standards almost always sinks to the level of the lower one. It isn't long before the practices winked at abroad are used at home as well. It is dangerous also because it fails to recognize the essential interdependence of the market economies both in an economic and political sense.

Ethical codes cannot, of course, revolutionize the mores of the world. But when the U.S. becomes a nation with no standards to offer it will no longer be the leader of the non-socialist bloc. The ethic it must support to survive is the ethic of the free market and it is essential to the free market that governments enforce honest competition.

If that position is clearly understood as a result of the Church committee revelations and the OECD deliberations, there will indeed have been a worthwhile accomplishment.

WHAT TO DO ABOUT CORPORATE CORRUPTION

RALPH NADER AND MARK GREEN

Ralph Nader, the well-known consumer advocate, and Mark Green, a lawyer in Ralph Nader's organization, ask in the following article why criminal penalties ought not be higher for corporate crimes? They think they should be and prescribe ways to reduce corporate corruption.

Not perhaps since the robber baron era, and certainly not since the 1930s —when New York Stock Exchange president Richard Whitney was convicted of stock theft and utility mogul Samuel Insull escaped prosecution by fleeing abroad dressed as a woman—has America witnessed such an epidemic of corporate corruption.

The evidence to support this claim appears daily on newspaper business pages and front pages—from Lockheed's spectacularly indiscreet millions in bribes to high officials in the Japanese government to government contractors entertaining Pentagon procurement officials in their private duck-hunting retreats.

Are all these, at worst, just a clutch of rotten apples—or is much of the business barrel rotten? The presumption is strong that these illegal practices are common.

When Archie Carroll of the University of Georgia surveyed 238 business managers last year, 60% agreed that the go-along ethic of CREEP's junior members "is just what young managers would have done in business." A survey of 531 top and middle managers by the Opinion Research Corporation in July, 1975 found 48% agreeing that foreign bribes should be paid if such practices were prevalent (even though illegal) in that foreign country. Indeed, the justification of many exposed executives was that "everyone does it."

Joe Sims, an Antitrust Division official, complained recently that based on his agency's record number of grand jury investigations and actual indictments, "price-fixing is a common business practice."

The rationales for such behavior deserve attention:

PAYOFFS ARE COMMON PRACTICE ABROAD

Perhaps common practice, but still illegal in virtually all countries. That X can always cite a Y who violates the law can hardly exculpate X's illegality —unless law enforcement is to sink to the lowest common denominator.

From *The Wall Street Journal,* March 12, 1976.

WE DID IT FOR OUR SHAREHOLDERS

A company may indeed persuade itself that only payoffs can win a lucrative contract, but what of the potential long run costs? An extortionist invariably comes back for more, and other governmental officials may make additional demands when they perceive a company is known to be responsive.

There is the risk of local law enforcement—an ITT director was convicted in Belgium of bribing a high official for an equipment contract—and the risk of exposure in the U.S., with adverse publicity and SEC, Justice Department, IRS and shareholder suits ensuing.

One can hopefully assume that Lockheed, 3M and Northrop, if they could do it all over again, wouldn't.

RECENT BUSINESS VIOLATIONS RESULT FROM TOO MANY LAWS

No, this is not an Art Buchwald parody but the earnest claims of Murray Weidenbaum and The Wall Street Journal.

According to Mr. Weidenbaum, a former assistant secretary of the Treasury, "the fundamental cause of the lawbreaking can be seen to be the tremendous and often arbitrary power that society has given the federal government over the private sector."

The Journal editorialized that recent disclosures in part reflect "the number of new laws, inspired partly by folks like Mr. Nader and Mr. Udall, that businessmen can potentially run afoul of." Laws like those against bribery, domestic payoffs, pollution, and monopoly? This logic has some interesting applications: The only thing wrong with serious consumer fraud or wife-beating are those bothersome consumer protection and assault laws.

BUSINESS ILLEGALITY IS NOT ALL THAT RELATIVELY SERIOUS

Many of these costs of corporate crime, to be sure, are often invisible to the public's eye. There are no burned out buildings or rioters to flash on the evening news. This comparative lack of visible drama has misled even Harvard professor James Q. Wilson. "Unlike predatory street crime," he asserts, these economic violations don't make "difficult or impossible the maintenance of basic human communities." Which confirms Nicholas Murray Butler's observation that "An expert is one who knows more and more about less and less."

Whatever the damage caused by street criminals, suite criminals exact a substantial tribute from society in the form of higher prices, death and injury due to pollution and product hazards, and corrupted government. The latter, exploiting the faith people have in business leaders, violates our trust —and hence inspires mistrust.

"If the word 'subversive' refers to efforts to make fundamental changes in a social system," sociologist Edwin Sutherland wrote in his 1949 classic "White Collar Crime," "the business leaders are the most subversive influence in the United States."

The exposure of corporate crime must rest on more than the confluence of such spectacular events as Watergate and the death leap of United Brands' Eli Black. And the way to deter such violations requires more than wrist slaps as penalties.

Fines imposed by judges in antitrust cases almost invariably are trivial compared to the amounts illegally garnered. The average fine paid by firms successfully prosecuted by the Watergate Special Prosecutor is about $7,000. The SEC and Antitrust Division often conclude their cases with consent decrees by which defendants deny they violated the law but promise to obey it in the future—an obligation they presumably labored under before the decree. Most business officials named in the Special Prosecutor's and SEC's lawsuits still work in their same executive suites.

With these failures in mind, any program of sanction and deterrence must appreciate the two special qualities of corporate crime. First, unlike the tempestuous and murderous spouse or the impoverished and desperate mugger, suite criminals are sophisticated and deliberative businessmen who engage in crime only after carefully calculating the benefits and costs.

And second, as law professor Christopher Stone has written in "Where the Law Ends," "we have arranged things so that the people who call the shots do not have to bear the full risks"; i.e., it is difficult to pinpoint and punish *individual* violations within that *collective* body called the corporation.

If the likelihood of personally getting caught and the penalties for getting caught are sufficiently great, potential business-law violators should be able to literally calculate that crime doesn't pay. If otherwise, profit-lorn businessmen may consider illegality a very logical option.

The following proposals can help ensure that the potential costs of corporate crime outweigh its perceived benefits:

Ideally, the Justice Department should create a separate Division on Corporate Crime. This division should be delegated authority to investigate and prosecute a wide range of business crimes, from mail fraud to regulatory offenses to the illegal distribution of political contributions or bribes, here or abroad, by corporate officers or their agents. (Antitrust enforcement would remain within the Antitrust Division.) The complexity and pervasiveness of corporate crime, as well as the ingenuity of its perpetrator, justify that the Justice Department create a special division to focus on this area—rather than deal with it piece-meal, if at all.

It should be evident that foreign bribes are an "unfair trade practice" under the Federal Trade Commission Act. But since it is not to many observers, federal law should explicitly make such payments illegal.

Given the reality that our prisons are places of cruelty and breeding grounds for recidivism, serving time does not often lead to rehabilitation. Still, it is discriminating to send pick-pockets and check-bouncers to prison but not convicted businessmen. In the first 82 years of the Sherman Act, which is both civil and criminal, there were only four instances when businessmen actually went to jail for their criminal violations; in hundreds of other cases, sentences were suspended.

THE INCARCERATION DETERRENT

The law must punish violators equitably, not according to their rank in society. The threat of incarceration may be the most powerful deterrent to middle and upper class business managers—as the Antitrust Division came to appreciate immediately after the imprisonment of several executives in the 1961 electrical equipment cases.

In order that punishment falls on those individuals responsible, officers convicted of willful corporate-related violations should be disqualified from serving as an officer or director in any American corporation or partnership for five years after a conviction, guilty plea or nolo contendere plea. This is only logical. One does not reemploy an embezzler as a bank teller.

Fines should be calibrated to the size of the firm and the "size" of the violation. Business crime has its own cost curve. If companies are punished with insignificant penalties, the result is predictable. Instead of absolute fines, there would be percentage fines based on gross sales—so the fine would fit the crime.

This approach has some modest precedent. Judge William H. Mulligan fined IBM for failure to produce documents in the Justice Department's current antitrust proceeding. He analyzed the size and resources of IBM and then settled on a fine of $150,000 a day—one appropriate to IBM but not to a small firm or a street-walker. In Common Market nations such as West Germany, antitrust and other laws now impose fines on the basis of a percentage of the gross annual sales or profits of the firm.

There is also the problem of how to deal with corporations which repeatedly violate the law. In addition to percentage fines, penalties for a particular law violation should increase for corporate recidivists—since by definition the company has not been successfully deterred.

Defendants in cases of corporate wrongdoing are often enjoined from future violations but are rarely required to pay restitution. Shareholder suits may seek and obtain restitution, though this does not invariably occur. Ideally, agencies like the SEC and Justice Department, as a part of any relief, should insist on restitution being made by those culpable to their victims or their company.

Autocratic chief executive officers, whose handpicked "inside directors" dominate their boards of directors, lack the kind of external accountability that encourages responsible and lawful decision making. To accomplish this goal, which was the original concept of the board, requires a full-time board comprised of "outside" directors. Such an independent authority should help make executives think twice before casually approving millions of dollars in illegal payments to foreign agents.

Company indemnification and insurance plans often provide for reimbursement to officials who plead nolo contendere in criminal cases or who are found liable in, or agree to settle, a civil lawsuit—if they thought they were acting "in the best interests of the company." Such provisions should be prohibited.

REGULAR REPORTS NEEDED

Finally, federal agencies should maintain and release regular compliance reports which could contain the following:

—The laws enforced by the agency, the resources given it, and the remedies available to it—e.g., recall, repair, fines, warning letters, referrals to Justice for prosecution, etc.;

—A list by company of each violation established and the corrective action required and taken;

—A statement of what additional tools are needed—e.g., subpoena power, increased penalties, more statutory authority, increased staff—for the agency to perform its mission adequately;

—An analysis of the cost to citizens and the economy of the level of violations uncovered and the cost of the level of estimated violations.

With all such information in one report, federal regulators and their congressional monitors can better appreciate the costs of regulatory violation and better deter them. As in so many other areas of government regulation over business, knowledge is power.

QUESTIONS

1. The authors argue that "Not perhaps since the robber baron era . . . has America witnessed such an epidemic of corporate corruption." Have levels of moral behavior in business been rising or falling over the past hundred years? What evidence exists to support your view?
2. Can you think of additional reforms, aside from those mentioned here, that might be effective in curbing corporate crime and immorality?
3. In what sense are the "corporate crimes" criticized by the authors really crimes? Who are the "corporate crimes" committed against? Are corporate officials who decide to commit many of the "corporate crimes" inveighed against in the article always aware that they are engaging in criminal or dishonest activity? Is there room for two points of view?
4. Nader and Green advocate the imposition of fines for companies based on the size and resources of defendant companies. Is this suggestion a violation of traditional fairness doctrines in Anglo-Saxon jurisprudence, which state that the punishment should fit the crime?

THE FAILINGS OF BUSINESS AND JOURNALISM

LOUIS BANKS

Louis Banks, visiting professor at Harvard University, Graduate School of Business Administration, and former managing editor of *Fortune*, explains why business executives may be reluctant to be interviewed by anyone who wants to talk with them. He also says business executives should speak out, especially about business wrongdoing. Also, he says, we need a better perspective in judging business action.

In baseball, a sports reporter can sense the meaning of an outfielder's single step to the left or right as a new man comes to bat, and he would be thumbed out of his job in two days if he patently did not know what he was writing about. Ditto the drama critic or the police reporter. Yet general-assignment reporters plunge into issues that mean life or death for management, employees, customers—even a community—without the slightest sense of business perspective.

The procession of stories that make the front page or 60 seconds on network television constitutes the daily brush between the run-of-the-mine reporter and the run-of-the-mine businessman, with the latter caught in the glare of the spotlight. Here is where we are fed a daily diet of authoritative ignorance, most of which conveys a cheap-shot hostility to business and businessmen. Here is where the nation sees a persistently distorted image of its most productive and pervasive activity, business. The fact is most general reporters and editors are woefully ignorant of the complexities and ambiguities of corporate operations and thus are easy targets for politicians or pressure-group partisans with special axes to grind at the expense of business.

Some of these newsmen are like kids with loaded pistols, prowling through the forests of corporate complexity to play games of cowboys and Indians or good guys and bad guys. Their only interest in business is to find a negative story that will get them promoted out of business into Woodward and Bernstein. And by and large this is what too many of their editors also want.

Every businessman has his own tale of horror in this matter, and here are only a few:

At the time of a critical issue of securities, the chief financial officer of AT&T is challenged on his financial policies by a wire-service reporter

Louis Banks, "The Failings of Business and Journalism," *Time,* February 9, 1976, pp. 78–79. Reprinted by permission from TIME, The Weekly Newsmagazine; Copyright Time Inc.

who, it turns out, does not know the difference between a stock and a bond.

The chairman of Exxon explains his company's policy in the Middle East for 45 minutes to network television, only to see it compressed to a meaningless 30 seconds.

A progressive and socially oriented corporation, caught in a long, involved controversy with a small group of employees, has to start all over again on each day's development with a new reporter who has no knowledge except a clipping of the last story.

Students at a Harvard Business School seminar will not soon forget the words of a visiting editor of a metropolitan daily who frankly stated that his happiest moment comes when he has brought a businessman to his knees.

In spite of all this, business and journalism may well deserve each other. Why? Because something serious and menacing has been added to the equation over the past year or so—and is still being added—that makes me cherish the independent, critical coverage of business in whatever form. It is something that, to my mind, shifts the burden of responsibility to the other side.

That something can loosely be described as the post-Watergate disclosures about corporate custom and practice. The net message of the headlines is that chief executive officers of some of the nation's best-known corporations have tolerated practices that range from illegal political payoffs to the subornation of foreign governments, to secret Swiss bank accounts and laundered funds, to colossal short weight in grain sales, to deceiving boards of directors and so on. These are not tawdry little games that can be explained away with a wink but transactions that trespass against the soul of trust in the modern, publicly held corporation: rigging the market and doctoring the books.

How does business respond? A tiny number of businessmen mutter that there is nothing new about all this, and it is just the fault of the goddamned press and TV for stirring things up again. The responsible business community wholeheartedly rejects and repudiates this style of doing business.

But for a long time this business attitude was the world's best kept secret. We did see some management changes—some real and some that looked like window dressing. Then the headlines exploded with the Gulf story. Faced with the evidence of some $12 million in secret payments to politicians in the U.S. and abroad, the Gulf board, at the behest of its outside directors, fired the chairman and two other top executives and demoted a third. We do not yet know the whole story, nor the sum of the damage to the reputation of one of the world's greatest companies—the crown jewel in the constellation put together by the Mellon interests of Pittsburgh.

Even so, it is strange that only two or three members of the business community—among them Irving Shapiro, the chairman of Du Pont, and

W. Michael Blumenthal, chairman and president of Bendix—have spoken out on behalf of all business to challenge the lengthening public record, let alone formulate a code of professionalism or ethics to guide future practice. Yet a personal friend, who has helped build one of the world's most successful corporations—one that has never, to his knowledge, passed an illegal coin in order to do business in any of the dozens of countries where it operates—reports that there has been a kind of informal retribution. He says the executives whose names the public has been reading in the headlines and whose faces have been on the tube have become, in fact, "corporate zombies," all but shunned by their business friends. If so, perhaps this is all the retribution we need. But this attitude may be caused more by the implied ethical standards of critical journalism—good, bad and indifferent—than by anything the business community has yet said or done.

If it is true that in the present state of affairs business and journalism deserve each other, the rest of us deserve much better from both of them. And we all deserve better of ourselves. The basic fact about the U.S. is that we are a business society, perhaps a business civilization. Daniel Yankelovich, the attitude researcher, reported with some astonishment over a year ago that 93% of Americans—"just about a consensus—express their willingness to 'make personal sacrifices, if necessary, to preserve the free-enterprise system.' " It might be hard to muster such a consensus even on behalf of the First Amendment. What this indicates is that business leaders must realize that their every decision and action have social and political, as well as economic, implications. Business, in sum total, focuses the major effort of this country, defines the quality of its national life and determines what our children will ultimately think of these times.

Against that 93% consensus for the free-enterprise system, Yankelovich put the more familiar finding that only about 30% of the people have confidence in business leadership. How to explain the difference? Perhaps one could argue that the spread between the 93% and the 30% measures the gap between corporate performance and public expectation in these matters. We do deserve better.

For journalists, the message is much the same. Television and the press powerfully influence our sense of what we ought to do next. We need, value and trust the competent, informed, honest, independent criticism that is implied in the First Amendment, and we have proved its worth over and over again. But today we are drowning in criticism, informed and otherwise. What we need now is the recognition of achievement as well. The late Abraham Maslow, the distinguished psychologist and philosopher, offered a very trenchant warning. He wrote: "If you demand a perfect leader or a perfect society, you thereby give up choosing between better and worse. If the imperfect is defined as evil, then everything becomes evil, since everything is imperfect."

And he went on: "The demonstration that wonderful people *can* and do exist—even though in very short supply and having feet of clay—is enough to give us courage, hope, strength to fight on, faith in ourselves and in our own possibilities for growth."

QUESTIONS

1. Although many inexperienced reporters may be assigned to business beats, so are many experienced finance and business writers. How do you assess Banks's indictment?
2. Does much of the reporting problem lie in lack of disclosure and secretiveness on the part of business executives? Or are deliberate exaggerations by journalists more significant?

STANDARDS FOR BUSINESS CONDUCT

BUSINESS ETHICS ADVISORY COUNCIL

The Business Ethics Advisory Council, organized by the U.S. Department of Commerce, prepared the following set of questions, which, it was hoped, business executives would ponder and answer in such a fashion as to improve the ethical levels of business conduct.

A STATEMENT ON BUSINESS ETHICS AND A CALL FOR ACTION

The ethical standards of American businessmen, like those of the American people, are founded upon our religious heritage and our traditions of social, political, and economic freedom. They impose upon each man high obligations in his dealings with his fellowmen, and make all men stewards of the common good. Immutable, well-understood guides to performance generally are effective, but new ethical problems are created constantly by the ever-increasing complexity of society. In business, as in every other activity, therefore, men must continually seek to identify new and appropriate standards.

Over the years, American businessmen in the main have continually endeavored to demonstrate their responsiveness to their ethical obligations in our free society. They have themselves initiated and welcomed from others calls for the improvement of their ethical performance, regarding each as a challenge to establish and meet ever-higher ethical goals. In consequence, the ethical standards that should guide business enterprise in this country have steadily risen over the years, and this has had a profound influence on the performance of the business community.

As the ethical standards and conduct of American private enterprise have improved, so also has there developed a public demand for proper performance and a keen sensitivity to lapses from those standards. The full realization by the business community of its future opportunities and, indeed, the maintenance of public confidence require a continuing pursuit of the highest standards of ethical conduct.

Attainment of this objective is not without difficulty. Business enterprises, large and small, have relationships in many directions—with stockholders and other owners, employees, customers, suppliers, government, and the public in general. The traditional emphasis on freedom, competition, and progress in our economic system often brings the varying interests of these groups into conflict, so that many difficult and complex ethical prob-

U.S. Department of Commerce, Business Ethics Advisory Council, *A Statement on Business Ethics and a Call for Action* (Washington: Government Printing Office, 1962).

lems can arise in any enterprise. While all relationships of an enterprise to these groups are regulated in some degree by law, compliance with law can only provide a minimum standard of conduct. Beyond legal obligations, the policies and actions of businessmen must be based upon a regard for the proper claims of all affected groups.

Moreover, in many business situations the decision that must be made is not the simple choice between absolute right and absolute wrong. The decisions of business frequently must be made in highly complex and ever-changing circumstances, and at times involve either adhering to earlier standards or developing new ones. Such decisions affect profoundly not only the business enterprise, but our society as a whole. Indeed, the responsible position of American business—both large and small—obligates each participant to lead rather than follow.

A weighty responsibility therefore rests upon all those who manage business enterprises, as well as upon all others who influence the environment in which business operates. In the final analysis, however, the primary moral duty to establish high ethical standards and adequate procedures for their enforcement in each enterprise must rest with its policymaking body—its board of directors and its top management.

We, therefore, now propose that current efforts be expanded and intensified and that new efforts now be undertaken by the American business community to hasten its attainment of those high ethical standards that derive from our heritage and traditions. We urge all enterprises, business groups, and associations to accept responsibility—each for itself and in its own most appropriate way—to develop methods and programs for encouraging and sustaining these efforts on a continuous basis. We believe in this goal, we accept it, and we encourage all to pursue its attainment.

SOME QUESTIONS FOR BUSINESSMEN

The following questions are designed to facilitate the examination by American businessmen of their ethical standards and performance. They are intended to illustrate the kinds of questions that must be identified and considered by each business enterprise if it is to achieve compliance with those high ethical standards that derive from our heritage and traditions. Every reader will think of others. No single list can possibly encompass all of the demands for ethical judgments that must be met by men in business.

1. General Understanding

Do we have in our organization current, well-considered statements of the ethical principles that should guide our officers and employees in specific situations that arise in our business activities, both domestic and foreign? Do we revise these statements periodically to cover new situations and changing laws and social patterns?

Have those statements been the fruit of discussion in which all members of policy-determining management have had an opportunity to participate?

Have we given to our officers and employees at all levels sufficient motivation to search out ethical factors in business problems and apply high ethical standards in their solution? What have we done to eliminate opposing pressures?

Have we provided officers and employees with an easily accessible means of obtaining counsel on and resolution of ethical problems that may arise in their activities? Do they use it?

Do we know whether our officers and employees apply in their daily activities the ethical standards we have promulgated? Do we reward those who do so and penalize those who do not?

2. Compliance with Law

Having in mind the complexities and ever-changing patterns of modern law and government regulation:

What are we doing to make sure that our officers and employees are informed about and comply with laws and regulations affecting their activities?

Have we made clear that it is our policy to obey even those laws which we may think unwise and seek to have changed?

Do we have adequate internal checks on our compliance with law?

Have we established a simple and readily available procedure for our officers and employees to seek legal guidance in their activities? Do they use it?

3. Conflicts of Interest

Do we have a current, well-considered statement of policy regarding potential conflict of interest problems of our directors, officers and employees? If so, does it cover conflicts which may arise in connection with such activities as: transactions with or involving our company; acquiring interests in or performing services for our customers, distributors, suppliers and competitors; buying and selling our company's securities; or the personal undertaking of what might be called company opportunities?

What mechanism do we have for enabling our directors, officers and employees to make ethical judgments when conflicts of interest do arise?

Do we require regular reports, or do we leave it to our directors, officers and employees to disclose such activities voluntarily?

4. Entertainment, Gifts, and Expenses

Have we defined our company policy on accepting and making expenditures for gifts and entertainment? Are the criteria as to occasion and amount clearly stated or are they left merely to the judgment of the officer or employee?

Do we disseminate information about our company policy to the organizations with which we deal?

Do we require adequate reports of both the giving and receiving of gifts and entertainment; are they supported in sufficient detail; are they subject to review by appropriate authority; and could the payment or receipt be justified to our stockholders, the government, and the public?

5. Customers and Suppliers

Have we taken appropriate steps to keep our advertising and sales representations truthful and fair? Are these steps effective?

How often do we review our advertising, literature, labels, and packaging? Do they give our customers a fair understanding of the true quality, quantity, price and function of our products? Does our service as well as our product measure up to our basic obligations and our representations?

Do we fairly make good on flaws and defects? Is this a matter of stated policy? Do we know that our employees, distributors, dealers and agents follow it?

Do we avoid favoritism and discrimination and otherwise treat our customers and suppliers fairly and equitably in all of our dealings with them?

6. Social Responsibilities

Every business enterprise has manifold responsibilities to the society of which it is a part. The prime legal and social obligation of the managers of a business is to operate it for the long-term profit of its owners. Concurrent social responsibilities pertain to a company's treatment of its past, present and prospective employees and to its various relationships with customers, suppliers, government, the community and the public at large. These responsibilities may often be, or appear to be, in conflict, and at times a management's recognition of its broad responsibilities may affect the amount of an enterprise's immediate profits and the means of attaining them.

The problems that businessmen must solve in this area are often exceedingly perplexing. One may begin his reflections on this subject by asking—

Have we reviewed our company policies in the light of our responsibilities to society? Are our employees aware of the interaction between our business policies and our social responsibilities?

Do we have a clearly understood concept of our obligation to assess our responsibilities to stockholders, employees, customers, suppliers, our community and the public?

Do we recognize and impress upon all our officers and employees the fact that our free enterprise system and our individual business enterprises can thrive and grow only to the extent that they contribute to the welfare of our country and its people?

QUESTIONS

1. Critically analyze and evaluate the council's proposals concerning the ethical conduct of American business. What are the fundamental strengths and weaknesses of such proposals?

2. What would you suggest to strengthen the council's proposals?
3. From your own personal observations, compare the level of ethics between typical large and small companies, business generally and the executive branch of the federal government, business generally and the Congress, a large company and a local city government, and a small business and a lawyer.
4. Do you believe that the council's proposals are adequate for overseas operations of multinational enterprises? Can one company insist on high levels of ethical conduct and stay in business when other companies from other countries engage in questionable payment practices?
5. Arjay Miller, dean of the Graduate School of Business, Stanford University, and former president of the Ford Motor Company, in speaking about codes of conduct for multinational companies proposed a simple test: "Do that which you would feel comfortable explaining on television." Do you think this is enough?
6. You are asked by the United Nations to recommend a code to curb foreign payoffs of multinational companies. What do you suggest?

THE PROSPECT OF ETHICAL ADVISORS FOR BUSINESS CORPORATIONS

JOHN F. STEINER

John F. Steiner in the following article summarizes the arguments for and against the hiring of ethical advisors to help top executives of organizations make more ethical decisions.

American culture does not automatically spawn perfectly moral executives. Human nature being what it is, men become businessmen and not business angels. Reformers who have issued prescriptions for more ethical behavior have relied upon business schools and religious institutions to imprint more moral behavior patterns upon individuals. The executive, in the view of the majority, is supposed to embody the highest standards of American society and accept responsibility for his actions. He is a professional and his responsibilities include moral rectitude.

Today, however, as the corporation adopts advanced technologies, communicates and transacts across the globe, and is called upon to solve social problems and improve the quality of life, the ethical problem is becoming far more complex. Can individual businessmen, particularly those in giant, complex corporations, cope adequately with demands for moral behavior by relying upon their own instincts? Is help needed? If so, one approach may be to appoint ethical advisors. This essay will explore some of the implications of this idea.

Father Theodore V. Purcell, a professor at Loyola University, Chicago, has suggested that managers should have " 'ethical advocates' or 'consultants' to identify the generic questions of an ethical nature that should routinely be asked along with the usual legal, financial, and marketing questions." In the May-June 1975 issue of the *Harvard Business Review* William Gossett, a past president of the American Bar Association and a director of several major corporations, suggested that corporate legal counsel is uniquely situated and prepared to act as an arbiter to social conflict between the corporation and society and also to lend "a deep sense of personal morality" to this task. And Los Angeles executive Jan J. Erteszek, president of the Olga Company, has stated the belief that "the chief executive could use a man with knowledge in this area as a sounding board and as a spiritual counselor. The advisor should be a compassionate man who understands the problems and trials and tribulations of a chief executive who is often very lonely."

It may be a shortcoming of the modern business organization that al-

John F. Steiner, "The Prospect of Ethical Advisors for Business Corporations," *Business and Society,* Spring 1976. Reprinted by permission.

though chief executives have functional advisors in areas such as marketing, production, finance, and public relations they have no ready wellspring of advice on ethical issues. Ethical ramifications crop up in all major business decisions. And they may be just as complex as issues in other areas.

America is a business oriented country. And if business assumes some leadership of society we should be deeply concerned with the moral implications of market decisions. Would it be desirable—or even possible—to install moral iconoclasts in the corporate inner sanctum?

There are a number of persuasive arguments in favor of ethical advisors. *First,* the presence of an ethical advisor would institutionalize an ethical input in corporate decision-making. Ethical considerations could assert themselves with a new force which would presage rising levels of business ethics. An ethical advocate might, for example, question the impersonal nature of committee decision-making which blurs responsibility for corporate actions. He might see problems that even top executives with the highest and most noble objectives could overlook under the pressures of all the converging forces to which they are subjected. With an ethical advisor on his staff a top executive could test his convictions in a nonjudgmental environment before making a final decision.

The presence of a functional officer in charge of ethical matters might even lead to moral audits of the firm. Many businesses, including large firms such as General Motors, Arco, and Bank of America, are now undertaking social audits to report social, as distinct from financial, performance. And some companies might seek to demonstrate ethical activity using a similar format of disclosure even if precise quantification [were] impossible. An ethical audit might be undertaken not only to disclose information about company behavior, but to inject ethical performance standards into the thinking of managers at all levels within the company. Performance measurement, even if crude, would be an effective way of raising general levels of moral awareness among managers.

Second, a growing awareness of ethical considerations would help large corporations adapt to a changing business environment. As society has become increasingly plural so it has also become morally complex as new interrelationships and situations of reciprocal authority, obligation, and expectation arise. A business with a built-in ethical awareness would be a step ahead of its competitors in meeting new public demands. The concept of Goodness, in terms of all human behavior—including business behavior—does not characterize what is or has been, but what ought to be. Sometimes what ought to be is, but more often is not. Today the necessity of choice between old ways and new ways is a fact of life and traditional moral behavior should be seen in contrast with new possibilities. An ethical advocate could crystallize constructive thought about alternative ways of responding to social and moral pressures.

Third, the very presence of ethical advisors would serve to bolster public confidence in the business system. People might be led to assume that decisions in the hands of powerful, faceless men would increasingly be made with the public welfare in mind. And as Americans become more and more cynical of their business and governmental institutions any action to arrest the tide of condemnation should be highly valued. Although levels of cynicism are high, there is reason to believe that a great reservoir of public respect for the business institution continues to exist and should be tapped. An institutionalized consideration of corporate morality would pave the way for greater public respect.

Fourth, the presence of ethical advisors could provide a different philosophical foundation for business decisions which they now lack. Such a philosophical foundation would be a needed counterweight to the dominance of allegedly "scientific" and technical data in decision-making which purports to quantify human welfare into digits and dollars. Decisions based on philosophical or theological foundations would be more consistent than decisions based on the less enduring values of calculated opportunism and avarice.

And *fifth,* the consistent application of ethical guidelines in corporate decision-making would appeal to the spiritual needs of men as well as their material needs. Businessmen would be able to minister to the spirit of society as well as its material appetite.

In a widely read 1955 *Harvard Business Review* article entitled "Skyhooks," O. A. Ohman argued persuasively on the superiority of corporate effort that had a moral purpose and appealed to the "true nobility of spirit of which we are capable." He contended that business activity would fail to provide meaning for the lives of those who engaged in it when it was based solely on self-interest and economic gain as motivators. To illustrate, he said that:

> If, for example, my personal goal is to get ahead in terms of money, position, and power; and if I assume that to achieve this I must beat my competitors; that the way to do this is to establish a good production record; that my employees are means to this end; that they are replaceable production units which must be skillfully manipulated; that this can be done by appealing to the lowest form of immediate selfish interest; that the greatest threat to me is that my employees may not fully recognize my authority nor accept my leadership—if these are my values, then I am headed for trouble —all supervisory techniques notwithstanding.

Ohman pointed to the need for "skyhooks," or the enduring concern for moral principles which give life meaning—in or out of the corporation. If Ohman is correct in pointing to this need, a system of moral advisors might serve to allay worker discontent and executive frustration partially based on hunger for moral and spiritual meaning. Such an achievement would contribute significantly to improved morale and efficient operation.

There are, conversely, some problems inherent in the use of ethical advisors. While such individuals would undoubtedly be a humane and elevating influence they would also complicate a sensitive decision-making mechanism not designed to give primacy to moral considerations. Five areas of difficulty are apparent.

First, the injection of ethical values into market decisions might lead businessmen to confuse their economic mission with altruistic concerns so that they fail to fulfill the basic business function of producing goods and services efficiently.

For example, the medieval Church ultimately did not fare well at regulating business enterprise. Early Christian doctrine condemned usury as sinful, a position which remained the official doctrine of the Church for centuries. Another Church-fostered medieval notion was that of the "Just Price," according to which a man could sell a product for a moderate or "reasonable" profit which would keep him and his family at a decent level of comfort matched to his station in the social hierarchy. Any profit above and beyond this was heresy. Even prior to the growth of favorable business conditions in the 16th century, however, these doctrines proved unenforceable in practice. The Church, gradually and unofficially, had to recede from such untenable positions or risk becoming irrelevant to commercial activity.

In Calvin's Geneva all business was regulated in minute detail by the Consistory, a group of clergy and laymen who had the authority to regulate commerce and morality. Despite their ascetic standards and threats to excommunicate usurers, the Calvinists failed to repress business enterprise. Ironically, many wealthy businessmen of the day embraced Calvinist dogma and the rise of Calvinist attitudes may be seen as an early proximate cause of the rise of capitalism.

Today it is not appropriate to inject this type of religious conscience into economic decision-making. Moral advocates would have to accept this fact.

Second, ethical problems cannot be precisely defined or quantified and problems of developing standards would arise. How is justice defined and what, precisely, is ethical in a given situation? Men consistently disagree on sources of ethical guidance. Plato found his criteria of goodness in the knowledge of the Forms, or patterns of perfection which have a real existence independent of human thought or action. St. Augustine suggested that virtue came from an interior illumination which was a gift of God. Wittgenstein finds virtue embodied in socially established practice. And there are countless other criteria for determining what is moral and what is not, including the existentialist belief that absolute ethical standards can never be justified because the human situation is non-rational.

Even if a criterion for ethical behavior could be found, well-intentioned men might disagree. It is probably correct that the great majority of ethical controversies are not about grandiose alternatives but about the implementation of widely accepted dicta. Even the culturally universal standard of the Golden Rule is controversial. As George Bernard Shaw admonished, "Don't do unto others as you would have them do unto you because their tastes may be different." An ethical advisor could not solve the basic and deeply rooted problem of providing universal agreement about the application of standards of justice to specific situations. Hence, even if broadly acceptable criteria existed businessmen would still be accused of having no standard of justice apart from dominant practice, no criteria of virtue apart from success.

Third, the methods of ethical advisors are antithetical to contemporary business management techniques. Philosophy and religion are ontologically at odds with the allegedly "scientific" techniques so popular today. Indeed, science and philosophy do not always address similar questions. The scientist may ask how something works whereas the moralist may question its right to exist irrespective of how it works. An ethical advisor might not interact in a synergistic way with marketing, production, finance, and public relations advisors who are wedded to traditional tenets of scientific method and technical expertise. Similarly, accountants might rebel if forced to look at their ledgers through spectacles of stained glass. Science ponders those questions which are amenable to rational and systematic inquiry. It does not deal with final causes such as the why of existence of the irrational in human nature as do moral inquiry and theology. The contrasting elements of science and philosophy may not be freely compatible if both are given serious attention.

Fourth, there is a danger that ethical advisors might tyrannize a business organization—assuming they had the power to do so—with perfectionist moral standards. Existing as it does in an imperfect world of unpredictable complications, the business organization must often be compelled to make less than ethically optimum decisions to insure survival. An ethical advisor of great conviction, however, might easily value moral purity over the survival of the firm. This situation would not long be tolerated.

An additional difficulty might arise if moral advisors could not stomach prevailing corporate policies and resigned in protest. This could, deservedly or not, damage a company's image. In 1972, for example, former Supreme Court justice Arthur Goldberg resigned from his appointed position as a public director on the TWA board. In an interview with *Business and Society/ Innovation* he indicated that the resignation hinged on his inability as an outside director to perform "moral and legal responsibilities." Public service minded individuals appointed as ethical advocates might be frustrated like Goldberg if ineffective in challenging company policy regarded as morally questionable.

Today there is already a tendency in American culture to stigmatize businessmen for their moral pragmatism. When operational business ethics are shown to fall short of perfectionist moral standards people tend to react with indignation. For years Americans have expected their politicians to be secular saints, while simultaneously subjecting them to intense and conflicting pressures. Similarly, businessmen have been expected to adhere to the highest morality while also safeguarding the existence of their firms in a setting not so far removed from the imaginative descriptions of Herbert Spencer.

The recent hearings of the Senate Foreign Relations Subcommittee on Multinational Corporations are a case in point. In these well-publicized hearings executives of Gulf Oil, Ashland Oil, Lockheed, Northrop, and United Brands admitted they made payments to foreign governmental officials and businessmen as part of their on-going commercial effort. These revelations have been followed with interest and have evoked much public outcry. On June 6, 1975, for example, the *Los Angeles Times* editorially condemned "inexcusable foreign bribes and payoffs." "Honesty is good," the *Times* admonished, "and bribes are bad."

But critics of the hearings from both government and business contend that excessive candor may damage the effectiveness of the American firm as a competitor abroad. If disclosure of foreign bribes, payoffs, and campaign contributions prevents firms from engaging in commonly undertaken business practices they may be at a competitive disadvantage to firms that do. A company might have difficulty ingratiating itself with foreign officials. And foreigners themselves might avoid American connections for fear of exposure damaging to their reputations. If a moral advisor insisted that such payments be avoided would he seriously impair the economic performance of the firm?

And *fifth,* there would be difficulties in finding and placing personnel in positions of such moral rectitude. There would certainly be a shortage of qualified advice givers. Society has not greatly encouraged development of the art of moral decision-making as a discipline.

It is not at all clear, assuming that businessmen would accept ethical advisors, who would be most appropriate. Some people think that theologians might be best. But there are many who say that the ethics of the Church simply do not and should not apply to business. Religious ethics are too rigorous and ethereal for business.

Purcell and Gossett suggest that company lawyers are a ready pool of "ethical advocates." Yet Watergate-related events have given lawyers a tarnished public image—at least for the time being. Furthermore, the legal profession is criticized for the failure of its members to inject their own conceptions of justice and morality into the representation of client's interests. The traditional position of the lawyer has been to temper or forego moral judgments once the decision has been made to represent a client and to rely on the adversary system of justice to insure a virtuous final outcome. The history of the legal profession has been one of escape from moral judgment and the depersonalization of justice in the advocacy system of Anglo-American jurisprudence.

It seems likely that no pool of individuals with both moral training and insight into the arcane world of top management exists to be tapped by executives who want ethical advisors. There are, presumably, enough individuals to meet the present demands.

After reviewing these positive and negative aspects of a system of ethical advisors it is not difficult to conclude that such a development is not immediately likely. Yet we live in a climate of new public demands on business. It has become legitimate in this generation to make social and otherwise nontraditional demands on the corporation, and the public presently is asking for a higher level of ethical behavior. One mark of this sentiment is the growing participation of church groups such as the World Council of Churches in proxy battles and the growing interest of investors in socially and morally superior companies.

In light of on-going social change and public pressure, proposals for ethical advisors are worthy of consideration. The corporation which is best adapted to the socio-ethical climate may be best adapted to the overall business environment. This may be particularly true with multinational firms which operate in a variety of moral climes. In order to be effective in multinational commerce the firm must avoid both sanctimony and immorality.

Large organizations do have a major impact on societies where they do business. If they raise ethical standards in their dealings they will also raise ethical standards generally. If moral advocates contribute to rising levels of business ethics, a positive service will have been performed. Clearly, ethical advisors to chief executive officers of companies such as Equity Funding, Penn Central, and Franklin National Bank probably could have avoided the scandalous conduct of some executives in these firms.

QUESTIONS

1. How would business executives react to the idea of ethical advisors for their company? How likely are business executives to accept the idea?
2. Assume that you have been hired as an advisor on moral matters by a large multinational company. Outline the steps you would go through in developing moral guidelines for company behavior and the types of resistance you might find developing to the implementation of your guidelines.
3. Are there additional arguments, either pro or con, that might be advanced on this subject?

CORPORATIONS: MULTINATIONAL GOOD OR BAD FOR HOST COUNTRIES?

THERE'S NO LOVE LOST BETWEEN MULTINATIONAL COMPANIES AND THE THIRD WORLD

LOUIS TURNER

Louis Turner, research specialist at the Royal Institute of International Affairs, London, explains a number of economic, social, and political complaints of the lesser-developed countries of the world about the operations of multinational enterprises.

Managers of multinational corporations excel at such tasks as transferring products, technology, and advanced management thinking to all quarters of the globe. In doing so, they tend to assume that the problems of New Delhi, Lagos, or Rio de Janeiro can be solved by hardware and concepts developed in Frankfurt or Detroit. Critics deny this. They argue that the impact of such corporations in the Third World is, in fact, harmful in that they exacerbate the tensions found within such societies and help create the kind of tragically polarized societies which we can see throughout Latin America. What is good for General Motors is probably, in the long run, not so good for Gabon and Guatemala.

To take a simple example: The Swiss company, Nestlé, introduced powdered milk as a baby food into West Africa as an alternative to breast feeding. Emulating Western fashion, local mothers adopted bottle feeding wholeheartedly. The result was increased infant mortality: To combat their extreme poverty, mothers were diluting the milk to the point that a bottle had virtually no nutrition. Also, the new fashion involved the use of bottles in societies with inevitably primitive hygiene, thus exposing the children to a range of germs they would not have faced if they had been breast-fed in the traditional manner. Similarly, the Zambian government banned advertisements for Fanta after learning that ever-enthusiastic mothers were weaning their children onto this glamorously Western, but not particularly nutritious, drink.

In earlier times, few managers worried about such niceties. The bulk of corporations in the Third World were looking for minerals or tropical produce which they would ship back to the industrialized world as fast as possible. Rather than contribute to the wider development of the societies in which they found themselves, they created "enclaves," virtual states-within-

Louis Turner, "There's No Love Lost Between Multinational Companies and the Third World." Reprinted from *Business and Society Review,* Autumn 1974, Number 11.

states, in which their rule was law. Due to their influence, some countries with diversified agricultural economies became dependent on single crops; the Central American "banana republics" and the rubber economies of Malaya and Liberia are examples. Even if such countries were formally independent, they were in fact shackled by their nearly total dependence on the benevolence of companies such as Firestone and United Fruit. Political leaders and local entrepreneurs either flourished or were overthrown at the whim of these companies, thus stifling the development of local economic and political initiative. On occasions, the companies even tried to redraw political boundaries, as when the Belgian mining company, Union Minière, helped finance the attempted breakaway of Katanga soon after the ex-Belgian Congo (now Zaire) attained independence.

Today, despite the abortive coup attempts of ITT in Chile, the situation is less stark. As Third World economies have grown, they have become more diversified, reducing their dependence on single companies and forcing managements to become more circumspect in their outward behaviour. In the aftermath of the Independence Era, governments have been growing in self-confidence and experience, and they are now willing to attack corporations which get out of line. Obviously the example of OPEC (Organization of Petroleum Exporting Countries) has been extremely important, as it has shown how relatively powerless the oil giants actually are; but one should not ignore the campaigns of copper producers like Zambia, Zaire, Peru, and Chile to get control of their industries in the 1960s, nor the formation of the Andean Pact, a central goal of which was to tame the multinationals. Since the oil producers began their onslaught, the bauxite producers have started to follow suit, with significant actions also coming from the governments of Malaysia (rubber) and Morocco (phosphates). However, despite this Third World militancy, the multinationals remain formidable adversaries.

SQUEEZING OUT LOCAL ENTREPRENEURS

For one thing, the multinationals are still very large by Third World standards. They possess the technical and marketing skills that countries trying to industrialize desperately need. The result is often a dependence on foreign companies to a degree embarrassing to see. Take the case of Unilever's subsidiary in Nigeria, the United Africa Co. (UAC), which originally entered that country to produce palm oil needed for the manufacture of margarine. By natural expansion it diversified into shipping and a general import-export trade aimed at the Nigerian market. As the country grew, so did the UAC, establishing itself in all the new markets created by Nigeria's fledgling industrialization. By the mid-1960s, it was four times the size of the next largest company, and one could almost claim that the industrialization of Nigeria was the industrialization of UAC. From its start as an agricultural and trading company, it moved into textiles, sugar, beer, cement, cigarettes, building contracting, radio assembly, plastic products, bicycle and truck assembly, etc. In any sector which mattered, the company was involved.

UAC is generally credited with having used its power responsibly; but, in microcosm, its history reflects what has been happening throughout the Third World. In the case of Latin America, foreign industrialists were squeezing local competitors out of all key industries as early as the nineteenth century. Every time there was a slump, it would be the undercapitalized local businessmen who would go to the wall, leaving the multinationals to emerge ever more dominant. Only during the two world wars, when European and American companies had other things on their minds, did local entrepreneurs have a chance to flourish—but this was not enough. Today, it is virtually meaningless to talk [of] Third World entrepreneurship in the sense in which Carnegie or Rockefeller were entrepreneurs. What we find instead is Third World planners and businessmen passively accepting technologies which have been developed by the multinationals, perhaps modifying them slightly for local needs, but certainly not trying to produce innovations which might challenge the foreigners' sway. This approach has probably contributed to the long-term political stagnation found in many Third World countries. Furthermore, it is culturally dangerous in that it assumes that products produced by the multinationals are suitable for Third World needs. In many cases, this is blatantly untrue.

The vast majority of multinationals are just not interested in the Third World except as a convenient residual market in which extra profits can be made once a product has proved itself in the American and European arenas. I once tested this belief by reading a couple of hundred company reports, looking for examples of involvement with the Third World which the companies might want to emphasize. It was a depressing experience. The majority of companies gave Third World activities no coverage at all, instead stressing things like the companies' contribution to the American space program. Otherwise, apart from CPC (the Corn Products Corp.), which had its chairman pictured knee-deep in a paddy field, the reports boasted of products like refrigerator fronts of Formica-based laminate (American Cyanamid in Argentina), car radios (Bosch in Brazil), or the lighting, traffic lights, and [illuminated] fountains along eighteen miles of road in the oil-rich Trucial States (Philips). Nothing about searches for nutritionally enriched forms of tropical fruits and vegetables; virtually nothing about the search for cures for tropical diseases; nothing about the search for labor-intensive industries which might well mop up the vast armies of the unemployed found everywhere in the poor countries. Instead, the companies listed trivial products which can contribute nothing to the long-term development of the Third World, but which are symptomatic of the overall corrupting effect which the multinationals tend to have on Third World elites.

CORRUPTING THE ELITE

These elites should be concerned with the majority of their countrymen who are still in the countryside working outside the market economy (if working at all—only some 2 percent of Nigeria's 63 million population is earning a wage or salary). They ought to be thinking of ways to cope with spiraling urban unemployment (some estimates suggest that 20 percent of the world's potential work force is without a job). Above all, they ought to be preaching austerity, since the task of pulling the world's poorest 40 percent above their current near-starvation level is one which will take decades, if not centuries.

The multinationals have very little constructive to offer. What they are good at is identifying and filling gaps in the markets of industrialized consumer societies; but, as Galbraith has pointed out, private enterprise does not lead automatically to the satisfaction of wider social needs. A dynamic auto industry, for instance, does not guarantee a good educational or health system; in the Third World, such an industry may even harm the interests of the bottom 40 percent of the population, since the elites will divert precious resources to building the roads and importing the gasoline which a flourishing auto industry demands. Thus the inequality of such societies increases, precisely the danger which the World Bank under Robert McNamara is starting to warn against. It contends that social inequality is growing noticeably within the Third World, even within rapidly growing economies like Brazil's. And it is starting to argue that the classic measurement of growth, G.N.P., is (by itself) a misleading indicator of development, that slower growing countries which put more stress on reducing social inequalities may well produce stabler societies in the long run.

The multinationals, whether they know it or not, are firmly on the side of inequality, forming a deadly alliance with corruptible Third World elites. The latter have been brought up to believe that one should envy the slick consumer society of the West, and they see the multinationals as the organizations which will deliver the goods. The elites want record players, refrigerators, cars, television, telephones, etc., and the multinationals are only too happy to deliver them. There are some managers who are aware that none of this is helping the starving and unemployed at the bottom of the pile. Sometimes they make token protests, but the elites prevail, since national pride tells them that their country is not modern unless it has things like an airport, an airline, a car industry, and a Hilton hotel. They can be extremely insistent on getting them. For instance, a Fiat manager once told me of the efforts they made in the late 1960s to persuade various national governments that truck plants were far better investments than car plants for countries at a low level of development. The technologies involved in assembling trucks are simpler, less import-intensive and more labor-intensive, and produce products which are of direct use in activities like farming and civil engineering. Their arguments were to no avail; the government officials insisted on having a car plant.

While the multinationals are not all to blame, clearly they are a vital part of the process which corrupts the elites. Hollywood films, television programs, and advertising are all instrumental in creating a certain image of Western society. The expatriate managers of multinational subsidiaries are a flesh and blood demonstration of this way of life. Highly paid (by local standards), they provide a model to the indigenous managers (who are increasingly replacing them) and to local officials. Their replacement can cause problems. In Africa, for instance, local replacements have been expecting not only similar levels of pay to those of the expatriate managers, but even some of the latters' "perks," like the free trip to Europe every eighteen months. From the start, local managers have expectations which can be satisfied only at the expense of the less powerful in their societies. In East Africa they have coined the name *Wa-Benzi* for the African elite which rides about in Mercedes-Benzes while the peasants and unemployed starve.

Another insidious effect arises from tourism, an industry in which multinationals are playing an increasing role. Tourists are flying more and more to exotic (i.e., poor) Third World destinations like the Pacific Islands, the Caribbean, and North and East Africa. Although many tourist resorts are "golden ghettos," located away from the centers of population, the social harm done by this industry is extraordinarily difficult to avoid. The local population learns to despise and cheat tourists, whose wealth appears limitless and who normally have no clear idea how much anything costs. Prostitution springs up, as seen in the Boy's towns, like Tijuana, along the U.S.-Mexican border. Even more grotesque are government attempts to build an image of friendliness toward tourists, launching "Be-Nice" campaigns and going so far as to have school children taught that tourists are friends who must be smiled at and treated well. Such campaigns are necessary in the sense that expressions of hostility may keep tourists from returning. But there is something intensely degrading about nations like Jamaica, Barbados, and the Bahamas launching such programs, particularly when they are part of a culture steeped deeply in the slave trade, with all its connotations of black servitude.

A further consequence of tourism is that it leaves the host country particularly open to the attentions of organized crime, which has always been strong in hotels and the gambling and entertainment worlds—the heart of a successful tourist industry. Perhaps it is a bit unfair to multinational companies to call the Mafia one, but it certainly has the vision and the global reach to make most of them a bit envious. It has concentrated on Caribbean tourism, working from Miami. It was strong, for instance, in pre-revolutionary Cuba, with Meyer Lansky flying out on the same night as Batista. Then it turned its attention to the Bahamas, which has been one of its bases for "front" corporations.

REAL DEVELOPMENT DOES NOT PAY

Despite everything, we should not be too harsh on the multinationals, since they are merely symbols for the general capitalist system, of which most of us are just as much a part. Asking them to contribute positively to the development of the Third World is to ask them to perform a task for which they were not designed. They are motivated by money, and yet we critics are asking them to develop goods for part of the world which is still predominantly outside the market economy. A bank, the Barclay's, lost $4.2 million in the early 1960s when its managers in West Africa were instructed to lend much more adventurously in rural areas. They managed to pull in small savings, but the amounts were so small, and so expensive to collect, that normal banking practices seemed almost irrelevant. Undoubtedly there was an overall social gain for Nigeria in the attempts to attract rural savings into productive investments, but a profit-oriented institution was obviously not the right vehicle for extending the experiment. Likewise, tractor manufacturers are searching for a mini-tractor which can compete effectively with the traditional ox and plough. Ford, for instance, spent at least six years trying to develop a simple, one-speed, seven-horsepower, rope-started model which could be easily assembled by local dealers, but after field-testing in Jamaica, Mexico, and Peru, and market-testing in Jamaica, they finally concluded that the returns were not going to be enough to justify their utilizing a disproportionately high number of their executives on this product. Both they and General Motors have settled for a basic utility vehicle directly competitive with models the Japanese have been selling in Asia. These simple, jeep-like vehicles can be used for a variety of purposes, but they are still products which the vast majority of rural inhabitants will be totally unable to buy. The polarization of the countryside into rich and poor, which became very noticeable during the so-called Green Revolution, will thus be heightened. Supplies like fertilizers and irrigation and mechanized equipment can be afforded only by rich farmers. In the meantime, the poor stay that way.

One is tempted to argue that there is little that the multinationals can do in key fields like population control, tropical diseases, and tropical agriculture—just the areas which would do most for that bottom 40 percent of the Third World. This is simply because on the scale on which most multinationals work, there just is not sufficient money to be made, and the risks are horrendous. So a pharmaceutical company will always choose to investigate a possible cure for arthritis, rather than a simple, self-administered, long-action contraceptive using materials indigenous, say, to India. A cure for arthritis would be an instant gold mine; a long-action contraceptive for India would run the risk that the company might have to sell to the Indian government at a loss, or might have its patents ignored. Either way, the product aimed at the Third World is just not an acceptable risk. It was probably no accident that the breakthroughs in the search for new, high-yielding wheats and rice were achieved in nonprofit institutions in Mexico and the Philippines. Undoubtedly the seed companies could have come up with their own successful varieties, but the complexities of distribution would have made profitability highly questionable.

The multinationals play safe. They develop products for the U.S. and Europe and are pleasantly surprised if they find Third World markets as well. Obviously, the formula sometimes works well for the poor. The discovery of DDT, for instance, did, with all its side effects, eradicate malaria. On balance, though, the multinationals are happiest doing business with urbanized, westernized elites—the soldiers who will buy their weapons, the managers who will buy their consumer goods. It would be nice if all the people of the Third World were as rich as those of Rio de Janeiro and Sao Paulo; unfortunately, they are not. Multinationals have a lot to contribute to these cities, but virtually nothing for the peasants living in grinding poverty in Brazil's northeast.

THE EVILS OF "DEPENDENCIA"

Finally, if we are looking at the cultural impact of multinationals, we must examine arguments stemming from Latin America about "Dependencia"—the contention that many of the ills of that continent can be blamed on the polarization of societies by overdependence on foreign markets, technology and culture. If this is indeed true of Latin America, what chance have the less developed continents of Africa and Asia?

This argument is difficult to substantiate conclusively, but it is not dissimilar to the charges raised by Ralph Nader and Mark Green about the effect of corporate domination of U.S. communities. They have written that when a community's economy is controlled by national or multinational conglomerates, the overall well-being of the community is threatened. Civic leadership suffers since corporate officials do not identify with communities which are merely one step on the career ladder. The independent middle classes are eliminated and income becomes less equitably distributed. Local society becomes more polarized. They cite the words of C. Wright Mills: "Big business tends to depress, while small business tends to raise the level of civic welfare."

On the international level, one can make a similar argument. Multinationals certainly prefer to do business with authoritarian regimes, which can guarantee a "secure" investment climate. They are happier investing in Brazil or Spain than in radical states like Allende's Chile or Nyerere's Tanzania. Nor do they show much sympathy toward democracies like Italy and India where underlying social tensions interfere with the smooth running of the economy. Governments encourage multinationals to invest by repressing potential troublemakers. Taiwan, Singapore, and Malaysia vie with each other by guaranteeing foreign investors freedom from trade union activities.

On a deeper level, reliance on multinationals saps a nation's vitality. Multinationals do not encourage indigenous research and development, almost always choosing to locate these facilities in North America or Europe. Local businessmen become mere intermediaries, adapting foreign technologies (if at all) to local conditions. On a more strictly cultural level, intellectuals and artists tend to mimic their business compatriots by taking their ideas and artistic models from the West. Throughout society there is a gradual drying up of the creativity needed to solve domestic problems. Europe escaped the worst of this, because it was already industrializing before U.S. investment became a significant factor. So, although Ford and G.M. established themselves in Europe early in this century, independent national companies like Volkswagen and Fiat were able to coexist without much difficulty. The situation in the Third World is completely different. Where countries are industrializing, multinationals move in to snuff out local competition before it has any chance of getting established.

THE AMERICAN LESSON

The degree of dominance exercised, however benevolently, by companies like UAC in Nigeria is a phenomenon which no Western commentator is entitled to gloss over. It is totally unlike anything in the history of the United States or Europe. To begin to comprehend it, imagine the United States as a Third World country winning its independence from a technically sophisticated Great Britain whose per capita GNP was ten times as great as that of ours, and which possessed companies fully capable of operating in the American market. The first result would have been that the incredible flowering of American entrepreneurial talent in the nineteenth century would have been nipped in the bud. Cyrus McCormick, Francis Cabot Lowell, Cornelius Vanderbilt, John D. Rockefeller, and J. P. Morgan would, at best, have ended up as talented managers for some British conglomerate. After all, who would need to design an American reaper when perfectly adequate British designs already existed and could be imported or assembled under license? Public ire in the late nineteenth century would not have focused on "the trusts," but would have vented itself against a handful of British giants, one of which might well have owned not just the oil industry, but the key American railroads and transatlantic shipping lines as well. Congress would have been in the pay of the British, and independent presidents would have invited bombardment by the British navy or coups from the British intelligence service.

This is a fair picture of what multinational investment has meant to many Third World countries. Clearly, the American political tradition would have been totally different had it sprung from such a background. For one thing, political divisions would have been far deeper than they are. Labor disputes and left-wing politics would be tinged with greater intensity, for there would be a xenophobic element to all controversies. Radical critics would face a much less powerful middle class, since the entrepreneurial element of U.S. society would be much smaller. Above all, the unifying belief in the American dream would not exist. How could there be a feeling of hope and optimism in a society where material "success" means working for some giant foreign company? The forces of the left would thus be relatively strong, forcing foreign corporate interests into relatively extreme defensive action. The likelihood of coups, armed repression, and terrorist tactics would be high.

So, we come to the harsh conclusion that multinational investment in the Third World has long-term harmful social and cultural effects. The multinational managers who complain about political chaos in Latin America are deluding themselves, since they are an integral part of the problem. This is not to claim that the majority of such managers are not perfectly well-meaning citizens; nor is it to deny that many of the products of their companies are of vital importance to the Third World. But we would do well to look more sympathetically at alternative approaches to development, while agreeing sadly with the words of George Bernard Shaw:

> Capitalism is not an orgy of human villainy, but a utopia that has dazzled and misled very amiable and public spirited men. The upholders of capitalism are dreamers and visionaries who, instead of doing good with evil intentions like Mephistopheles, do evil with the best of intentions.

A CONSTRUCTIVE ROLE FOR MULTINATIONAL CORPORATIONS

Because of its heritage, for instance, many Americans even today fail to understand that the American market is only a subsection of the world market, and that our value system is not necessarily universal. The arrogance of the American government's desire to export its complicated antitrust concepts, for example, is viewed by the Japanese and Europeans with a mixture of amazement and hostility. These governments regard their business establishments as great national assets which furnish the revenue to support the increasing living standards of their people. It is difficult for them to understand, let alone credit, the basically adversary position taken by our government toward business. These various types of nationalism hardly create a welcome environment for world corporations.

That the world is inhospitable to multinational corporations is also reflected in the fact that many former colonies see today's world corporations as the descendants of the chartered monopolies of the imperial nations. To them, our global corporations seem to be thinly disguised government-directed instruments dedicated to the pursuit of governmental foreign policy under the guise of a commercial establishment. Their bitter experience with government-chartered monopolies did little to create a welcome environment for these new worldwide economic structures that began to grow during the great postwar international expansion. The suspicion of a modern mercantilism hangs in the air.

In spite of this, the value of world corporations is, and will continue to be, undeniable. They fuel the growth of nations and give people the wherewithal to deal with econmic misery. They can function amid diverse value systems even while they must move in a resisting medium. The principal reason the world corporations are so profoundly disturbing to so many governments, and to the citizens of so many countries, is that they represent today's visible agents of change.

Agents of change involve new ideas and values. They have never been welcome in any society. This is especially true when the carrier of new or strange values is, or is thought to be, alien to the society that is affected. The word for *foreigner,* from the Golden Age of Greece right up to the Middle Ages, was *barbarian*. It should not surprise us, therefore, that the world corporation is often unwelcome even while it is the carrier of technology that may be the best hope of closing the gap between the very rich and the very poor.

Yet the role of the world corporation as an agent of change may well be even more important than its demonstrated capacity to raise living standards. The pressure to develop the economy of the world into a real community must come, in part, from an increasing number of multinational firms which see the world as a whole. "Today's world economy . . . ," Peter Drucker has said, "owes almost nothing to political imagination. It is coming into being despite political fragmentation." The world corporation has become a new weight in an old balance and must play a constructive role in moving the world toward the freer exchange of both ideas and the means of production so that everyone may one day enjoy the fruits of a truly global society. This is a goal worthy of us all.

Walter B. Wriston, "World Corporations: Saints or Sinners?" Reprinted from *Business and Society Review/Innovation,* Winter 1973–1974.

IN DEFENSE OF THE MULTINATIONAL CORPORATION

EMILIO G. COLLADO

Emilio G. Collado, when executive vice-president of the Exxon Corporation, presented the following statement to the United Nations Economic and Social Council Group of Eminent Persons Studying the Impact of Multinational Corporations on Development and on International Relations, September 11, 1973. In it, he identifies and evaluates what he considers to be the major issues in multinational corporate relationships with host countries. He also explores areas for cooperative action by multinational corporations and governments.

In using their resources of capital and management to undertake new investment, multinational corporations are most interested in carrying on a viable business operation over time, while earning a satisfactory return on their investment. These companies are not in business, either at home or abroad, to earn quick returns, recover their capital, and then "get out" of business in a given project or country. On the contrary, decisions to make additional investments for expansion and modernization, for example, are likely to follow the initial capital commitment, so that the project is in a nearly constant state of evolution. These considerations—the long-term view of multinational corporations in making investments, and the nearly continuous renewing or enlarging of those investment commitments—are fundamental to a proper understanding of the process of international direct investment and the motives and behavior of multinational corporations.

Of course, the overwhelming majority of investments by multinational corporations lead to mutually successful long-term relationships between investor and foreign host country. In the case of Exxon, we have carried on foreign operations for more than 85 years and currently have operations in more than 100 countries. When we embark on a new venture in a foreign country we intend to remain in that country for an indefinitely long period—for as long as we can carry on successful business operations.

Why do companies invest abroad in the first place? Generally, companies respond to attractive opportunities to invest wherever they occur, at home and abroad. When market conditions indicate investment in a foreign country, multinational corporations have responded to such opportunities. In the case of extractive industries, of course, investments must be made where the raw materials are located and it is economically feasible to produce and market them. Successful discovery of foreign oil resources, for example, generally leads to a chain of investments in producing, refining,

Emilio G. Collado, "The Multinational Corporation," *Multinational Enterprise,* Exxon Corporation, undated. Reprinted by permission.

transporting, and marketing the output. Beyond the producing stage, these investments generally occur along the economically feasible transportation routes from producing areas to foreign consuming countries.

In manufacturing industries, foreign investment generally occurs in response to competitive cost conditions and other market factors, reflecting, for example, transportation costs, proximity to low-cost material inputs, availability of appropriate labor, particular aspects of foreign demand, and foreign barriers to imports. In responding to competitive cost conditions, multinational corporations do not "cause" shifts in international trade competitiveness among nations, but are largely responding to shifts which are already taking place. In doing so, they are promoting international specialization in production among nations, and are increasing the benefits of international trade to both importing and exporting nations. In the process, they are helping to raise overall living standards in both host and home countries.

No multinational corporation has unlimited resources of capital and management at its command. Consequently, a multinational corporation must choose carefully among the many investment opportunities which arise, weighing the various risks and prospective returns of new investments at home and in foreign countries. When considering long-term investments outside the home country, multinational corporations are vitally concerned that the basic "rules of the game" affecting foreign investments will remain relatively stable, or at least predictable, over time. Introduction of host country policies which result in substantial increases in taxation of foreign investment, in detailed government regulation of operating decisions, in restrictive foreign exchange controls or in substantial special privileges being granted to competing enterprises, could make an otherwise successful investment no longer viable. Moreover, investors face the additional risk in some countries of nationalization or forced sell-out of their investments. Such policies may be invoked by host governments largely to strengthen their national economies. However, if they serve to discourage foreign investors from participating, a reverse effect may well occur.

How do multinational corporations view their responsibilities to society, particularly in developing countries? I believe multinational corporations generally see their most important responsibility as conducting their particular business well—by producing a high-quality product or service efficiently, offering it at a reasonable price, and being responsive to possibilities for improving the product and the production process. In this way, the activities of multinational corporations will result in economic benefits to workers and consumers, as well as to governments in host countries. Of course, in conducting their businesses well, multinational corporations should also abide by the spirit and letter of local laws and requirements, and reflect in their general demeanor a recognition that they are guests in the countries in which they operate. I believe these responsibilities are generally accepted by multinational corporations.

The primary importance of carrying out economic functions well, however, does not suggest an ostrich-like approach of "minding one's own business" without regard to the impact of business operations on the goals of various groups. Indeed, a second level of corporate responsibilities to society lies in a sensitivity and responsiveness to the indirect impact of business operations on the society-at-large. Thus, the operations of multinational corporations must be consistent with national goals—for example, with respect to protecting the physical environment, reducing social inequities, improving labor skills, and so on. Multinational corporations generally accept these responsibilities and adapt to the host country environment. They advance the national goals of host countries not simply because it is "the right thing to do," but to a great extent because such adaptive behavior promotes a successful long-term operation in the foreign host country.

Among the most common ways in which the operations of multinational corporations have a positive indirect impact on host countries is by the introduction of more advanced technology and the training of nationals in new technical or managerial skills. In the case of Exxon, we employ the most advanced technology appropriate to the circumstances of an individual host country and the markets being served, combining our own technology with various relevant technologies developed elsewhere in the world.

In our operations, we have engaged in substantial training efforts in technical and managerial fields—locally, in other foreign areas, and also by bringing foreign nationals to the United States for training.

Beyond the areas of conducting operations well, and ensuring that these operations support national goals, multinational corporations generally accept a third level of social responsibility. This concerns efforts to enhance the broader social environment in countries in which the corporation or its subsidiary "lives and works." Increasingly, multinational corporations are viewing their proper role to include such broader areas of positive contribution to the general welfare. Thus, multinational corporations have provided financial and technical support in foreign host countries for programs in health and education, community development, and for national cultural activities, among others.

Aramco, for example, over many years in Saudi Arabia has attempted to contribute to economic and social progress by the following activities: technical and financial assistance to local businesses; construction of 45 schools and one hospital; assistance for agricultural development; construction of a 500-mile road; and more than $2 million in financial support for research to eradicate a major eye disease. In Venezuela, our affiliate has undertaken similar kinds of activities over decades. In general, when we find and produce oil in a less-developed area we carry out many projects and activities beyond those directly involved in oil production.

To mention a cooperative activity with which I am very familiar, nearly a decade ago, multinational corporations and banks from the United States, Western Europe, Canada, and Japan jointly formed the ADELA investment company. ADELA's major objective is to promote and strengthen national small business enterprises in the developing countries of Latin America, by making minority investments in such businesses. ADELA has been successful in this objective. The availability of ADELA financing has often made adequate additional financing possible for these national ventures. Today, ADELA is supported by 235 multinational corporations and banks and in eight and one-half years has disbursed over $1 billion in loans and investments. Currently, ADELA has about $350 million of outstanding loans and investments to nearly 400 enterprises in more than twenty Latin American countries. ADELA investments have been in activities ranging from agricultural processing to capital goods manufacturing. Perhaps one indication of ADELA's success is that similar cooperative efforts by multinational corporations have been initiated in the Far East and in Africa.

Such efforts by multinational corporations are undertaken because of an awareness that the future of their operations will be affected by the broader social environment in host countries and, therefore, it is in their interest to improve that environment.

MAJOR ISSUES IN RELATIONSHIPS WITH HOST COUNTRIES

Despite the infrequency of actual conflicts, the potential for conflicts in the goals of multinational corporations and governments is a cause for serious concern, particularly among host countries. This is true of industrialized countries as well as developing countries.

THE LARGE SIZE OF MULTINATIONAL CORPORATIONS

The large size of many multinational corporations, in terms of total assets or sales, particularly when compared to the economies of developing countries, is often cited as evidence of power over national economies. The vast assets and geographical scope of multinational corporations are viewed by some as indicating virtual immunity from control by national governments—in host and even in home countries. Their substantial wealth and geographical spread is believed to afford multinational corporations great flexibility in marshalling resources to virtually any task. Thus, multinational corporations have been accused of bringing about the rise and fall of currencies, weakening labor's bargaining power in individual countries, impeding the development of local industry and local research and development efforts, and of causing many other economic ills.

While there undoubtedly are some advantages to large size—for example, in carrying out effective research and development programs—multinational corporations do not have the flexibility or power to elude effective control by governments that has been suggested. Of course, multinational corporations cannot ignore market forces which render a particular activity uneconomic.

Concerning their alleged ability to escape control by governments, it should be noted that most of the wealth of multinational corporations consists of fixed assets—in the case of the oil industry, production equipment, pipelines, refineries, and service stations—which cannot be summoned to bring pressure to bear on either individual currencies or governments. On the contrary, the fixed assets of multinational corporations are potential "hostages" in foreign host countries.

To help preserve their role in managing these immovable assets over time, the subsidiaries of multinational corporations must be responsive to national laws and priorities. The many examples of unilateral government actions—imposed production and export quotas, price controls, controls on local borrowing and remittance rights, enforced sell-outs, and in some cases expropriations—and the accommodations made by multinational corporations, do not indicate that global size entails substantial power. Even the so-called "liquid" assets of multinational corporations, for example, cannot be mobilized readily in a foreign exchange crisis, since much of these consist of working capital required to carry on day-to-day operations, and there is no indication that multinational corporations have used their borrowing power to engage in currency speculation.

The success of multinational corporations in operating in many countries over long periods does not reflect an ability to escape control by governments. On the contrary, multinational corporations owe their long-term success largely to their ability to make flexible adaptations to the national requirements and goals of individual host countries, while continuing to carry on effective business operations on an international scale. As national priorities have changed in host countries, multinational corporations have recognized the need to be responsive to such changes. For example, as the desire and capability for local participation in the equity of multinational subsidiaries has grown in some countries, multinational corporations have increasingly accepted such participation. At the same time, multinational corporations have adapted to changing conditions in the world economy—in my industry, for example, by forming joint ventures with other corporations and with governments to share the burden of the huge capital requirements and risks involved in some of today's large natural resource development projects.

"DISRUPTION" BY MULTINATIONAL CORPORATIONS

Multinational corporations are also viewed, particularly in developing countries, as a potentially "disruptive" influence in the host economy. For example, a multinational subsidiary may be seen as a "disruptive" force for doing any of the following: paying wages in excess of the going rate in an area; introducing labor-saving technology when there is unemployment in the country; making some national enterprises non-competitive; increasing local incomes which results in increased imports of consumption goods; remitting substantial dividends back to the home country; and increasing the burden on limited infrastructure facilities. These "disruptions" do sometimes accompany foreign investment. However, they are not necessarily adverse to the interest of the host country.

For example, the introduction by a multinational corporation of labor-saving technology may in some cases seem inappropriate if there is unemployment in the host country. However, the economic benefits of introducing such production methods may be much greater for the host country than the use of a more labor-intensive process, even after taking into account the costs associated with alleviating the difficult social problems of unemployment. Multinational corporations generally introduce the most efficient technology appropriate to the circumstances of host countries, which may or may not be labor-saving. In most cases, of course, new foreign investments create substantial employment in host countries, directly and indirectly.

Without adopting an approach of avoiding the "disruptions" by promoting a stagnant economy, greater efforts are needed to anticipate and accommodate the inevitable disruptions accompanying the development process. Thus, where there is a potential for significant economic and social disruptions, it is important for subsidiaries of multinational corporations to keep host governments informed about their plans and to attempt to work out cooperative solutions to those social and economic problems which seem likely to arise.

DIVISION OF THE BENEFITS FROM FOREIGN INVESTMENT

Perhaps the major concern of developing countries about multinational corporations relates to the division of the benefits of foreign investment between the multinational corporation and the host country. In some cases —for example, in considering government tax revenues and balance-of-payments effects—this concern is expanded also to include the distribution of benefits between the host and home countries. Of course, some of the benefits of foreign investment to host countries, particularly in the developing world, are difficult to measure—such as the new knowledge and skills acquired by the labor force, and the impetus to the development of industries related to the foreign investment project. However, much of the host country concern seems to reflect a belief that there is a fixed amount of benefit from foreign investment to be divided largely between the investor and the host country. According to this view, one party can gain only at the expense of the welfare of the other. This belief has led some host governments to attempt to increase the benefits from foreign investment by imposing a variety of restrictions governing the participation of foreign investors in their economies.

Of course, there is no "fixed" amount of economic benefit resulting from foreign investment, and restrictive policies intended to increase the benefits to host countries are likely to have the effect of reducing such benefits by discouraging foreign investors from participating in that economy. Multinational corporations are likely to make their greatest economic contributions to host countries where government policies toward foreign subsidiaries are well established and predictable, non-discriminatory as compared to national enterprises, and not excessively restrictive.

AREAS FOR COOPERATIVE ACTION BY MULTINATIONAL CORPORATIONS AND GOVERNMENTS

Recognizing the potential for tensions and conflicts between multinational corporations and governments, there are a number of positive actions which both corporations and governments could take to reduce, if not eliminate, the potential sources of conflict.

TAX POLICY

An important objective of certain home country governments in their tax policy toward multinational corporations based in their country is that decisions to invest at home or abroad should be relatively neutral with respect to taxation. A major departure from such neutrality would occur if income earned by a foreign branch or subsidiary is subjected to double taxation—i.e., it is taxed fully by both the host and home country governments. Where substantial double taxation of foreign income occurs, the burden of two taxes would be so great that multinational corporations would simply avoid making foreign investments. Home country governments generally seek to prevent international double taxation either by exempting all foreign-source income from tax (territoriality principle), or by allowing credit for foreign income taxes paid on the foreign-source income subject to tax. However, even where the foreign tax credit is allowed, some distortions may result from differences in the tax policies of host and home country governments. Thus, further inter-governmental efforts are required to negotiate multilateral agreements to achieve greater harmonization of national tax policies, and to ensure that international double taxation is avoided. Such agreements should also seek to eliminate distortions arising from discriminatory tax treatment of foreign investment by host countries. A number of recent bilateral treaties contain a provision which precludes tax discrimination against foreign investment by host countries.

Another distortion occurs when host countries grant substantial tax incentives or offer lengthy "tax holidays" in efforts to attract foreign investment. This raises several problems. First, the availability of substantial incentives, such as "tax holidays," may distort the international allocation of investment resources, with related distorting effects on international trade patterns. While some "distortion" of investment in favor of developing countries may be considered desirable, the competition among countries in providing incentives can become so great that overly generous incentives are offered. Although host governments are willing to forego some tax revenue in the interest of attracting investment and the resulting economic benefits, this must be carefully balanced against the need to have sufficient tax revenue to meet growing demands for government services. Without careful balancing of investment incentives and future revenue needs, budgetary constraints may subsequently require host governments to deny the incentives and raise taxes substantially on all foreign subsidiaries, thus making some investments in place no longer economic. Finally, host country incentives may be rendered virtually meaningless from the start if, in the absence of tax-sparing treaties, the home country government effectively denies such incentives by applying the full home country tax rate to all income from abroad. In such cases, the home country simply picks up the tax revenue given up by host countries in their attempts to attract investment.

Such problems can only be avoided by greater international harmonization of tax incentives, including agreement on specific upper limits to the extent of incentives allowable by host countries. Also, to make the incentives effective, home countries should provide for tax-sparing in developing countries. This can be achieved most effectively by inter-governmental agreements.

VOLUNTARY "CODE OF CONDUCT" FOR MULTINATIONAL CORPORATIONS

Agreement among multinational corporations on a voluntary "code of conduct" describing broad principles of acceptable behavior in various areas would undoubtedly contribute to a better climate of understanding for the corporations generally. It would also serve to discourage some multinational corporations from the kinds of activities which can generate ill will for multinational corporations as a group. It would be impractical for such a code of conduct to set forth detailed legal rules, of course, since adherence to a set of principles does not indicate precise behavior in particular circumstances. However, an investors' code could broadly support positive adaptations to host country social and economic goals, and condemn certain undesirable forms of behavior—such as speculative foreign exchange operations, distortions in international transfer prices, or attempts to circumvent host government policies.

INTERNATIONAL COORDINATION OF GOVERNMENT POLICIES TOWARD MULTINATIONAL CORPORATIONS

Full international coordination or harmonization of national policies affecting multinational corporations is probably not feasible, and in some cases not desirable for individual countries. However, there are some policy areas in which greater coordination is possible, and would result in substantial benefits to multinational corporations and governments. Tax policy has already been suggested as a major area in which a more internationally co-ordinated approach would have mutually beneficial results. Another broad area of concern to host governments is the so-called "extra-territorial" application of home country policies to the international operations of multinational corporations. There are a number of policies in which the apparently overlapping jurisdictions of home and host countries result in a potential for conflicts. Perhaps the most common examples today are anti-trust policy and balance-of-payments policies which require remittances of foreign earnings. Among the more industrialized countries, the importance of conflicts resulting from the application of anti-trust policies is diminishing, as their anti-trust policies are becoming more similar. Concerning the general issue of extra-territoriality, however, in those areas where national policies are not likely to be harmonized, it seems clear that greater consultation among governments before the application of policy beyond national borders would have the effect of greatly reducing the potential for misunderstandings and conflicts.

National policies toward foreign investment on the part of both host and home countries is another area in which greater international coordination would be useful. By this I do not support, however, regional harmonization of host country policies for the purpose of substantially restricting the activities of foreign investors. Efforts toward a united regional policy that is largely intended to impose extensive controls over the operations of foreign multinational corporations may backfire, if the adverse business climate causes multinational corporations to undertake alternative investments outside of such regions. On the other hand, multinational corporations would be significantly encouraged to undertake new investments in developing nations if they had a greater assurance that their operations in these countries would not be subjected to substantial new forms of discrimination or controls once their facilities had been constructed. Thus, a measure of international agreement on some maximum extent of discrimination or restrictions affecting foreign investment in various policy areas—such as taxation and foreign exchange remittance policies, for example—could substantially reduce the investment risks perceived by multinational corporations. In addition, limitations on home country restrictions on foreign investment would probably have a positive effect on both investors and host countries. As the discussion continues among investors and governments, elements of a broad inter-governmental agreement could evolve and be available for individual governments to endorse voluntarily. Such action in various policy areas could have a substantial encouraging effect on potential investors in countries participating in the agreement.

While agreement may be possible initially in only a few areas, an inter-governmental agreement could include a broad commitment by host governments to submit foreign investment disputes to the international conciliation and arbitration facilities of the World Bank or International Chamber of Commerce. Irrespective of whether elements of an inter-governmental agreement in policies relating to foreign investment are eventually established, a greater commitment by developing host countries to use international conciliation and arbitration machinery in investment disputes would dramatically improve the climate for investment by multinational corporations in these countries.

ARRANGEMENTS FOR FUTURE DISCUSSIONS AMONG MULTINATIONAL CORPORATIONS AND HOST AND HOME COUNTRY GOVERNMENTS

It seems clear that a continuing exchange of views among investors and governments would contribute greatly to a better climate for understanding of their respective goals. Some useful exchanges have taken place in recent years in the various UN panels and a joint discussion of multinational corporation issues is now developing in the Organization for Economic Cooperation and Development. However, it would be desirable to provide for a continuing discussion in which the developing and industrialized countries participate equally, along with multinational corporations. It seems to me that a natural way to achieve this is to expand the UN panel on foreign investment and make it a permanent UN activity. I hope that such an effort will receive your serious consideration and active support.

DO MULTINATIONAL CORPORATIONS STAND GUILTY AS CHARGED?

RICHARD EELLS

Richard Eells, adjunct professor at the Columbia University School of Business and director of the Program for Studies of the Modern Corporation, identifies and explains four underlying criticisms of multinational companies.

Until the last three or four years, there was every reason to believe that the multinational corporation was on the brink of becoming a quasi-sovereign actor on the world stage. Every sign pointed in that direction: the enormous growth of foreign direct investment during the 1960s; the rapidly escalating demands and expectations of people around the world for the goods that large, well-managed companies could provide; the continued threat or presence of tariff barriers in the nation-states; the willingness of countries to welcome the entrance of American (and other) technology, capital, and management skills; the failure of countries in or out of the United Nations to work out procedures for regulating such companies; and much more—all this made it appear that multinational companies were about to achieve an unprecedented level of power and independence.

It was probably the enormous size of these companies and their economic—and, consequently, their social, political, and psychological—power that made their role as quasi sovereigns seem so likely. To understand this, one need look only at the enormous size of multinational corporate operations. According to Committee for Economic Development estimates, the gross world product in 1973 was valued at $3 trillion, of which some $450 billion, or 15 percent, was produced by multinational corporations. This multinational segment of the world economy is growing at an annual rate of 10 percent—a faster growth rate than that of most nations. Some economists speculate that, before the close of the century, some 300 giant multinational businesses will produce more than half of the world's goods and services.

A SUBJECT OF CONCERN

Simultaneous with this growth has been the examination and criticism of the multinational corporation. Thousands of books and articles have been published on the subject by now. And, both in this country and abroad,

Richard Eells, "Do Multinational Corporations Stand Guilty as Charged?" Reprinted from *Business and Society Review,* Autumn 1974, Number 11.

governmental interest in multinational corporations and their economic and social effects has increased enormously. In 1972 and 1973, for example, the U.S. Department of Commerce published *The Multinational Corporation: Studies on U.S. Foreign Investment,* a two-volume, comprehensive study of the subject. The United States Tariff Commission published another extensive study, *Implications of Multinational Firms for World Trade and Investment and for U.S. Trade and Labor,* at the request of the Finance Committee of the U.S. Senate. Following the revelations of ITT's involvement in Chile, the Senate Foreign Relations Committee established a subcommittee on multinational corporations. This subcommittee has held hearings on the ITT affair and the role of the oil companies in the Middle East, and plans further investigations.

Multinational corporations have been the subject of resolutions by the International Labour Conference in 1971 and by the Third Session of the United Nations Conference on Trade and Development in 1972. Also as a result of the ITT involvement in Chile, the United Nations Economic Social Council, in July 1972, adopted a motion calling for a study of "the role of multinational corporations and their impact on the process of development, especially that of developing countries, and also their implications for international relations." The Department of Economic and Social Affairs of the United Nations Secretariat has now issued a study, *Multinational Corporations in World Development,* and a U.N. Group of Eminent Persons investigating multinational corporations has recommended that a permanent division of the U.N. be established to study and monitor the performance of multinational corporations.

In addition to this interest shown by the United States and the United Nations, the governments of many other countries have sponsored studies of the multinational corporation and its effects. There has been the semiofficial Watkins report in Canada, *Foreign Ownership and the Structure of Canadian Industry,* and in Great Britain, *The Impact of Foreign Direct Investment on the United Kingdom.*

Finally, in the United States, concern about the effects of multinational corporations has expressed itself in proposed legislation. The Burke-Hartke foreign trade and investment act, first introduced in the U.S. Senate in autumn, 1971, would increase considerably the taxation of profits from foreign investment by U.S. corporations; freeze foreign trade, through the imposition of import quotas, at the average levels of 1965–69; and give the President power to prohibit the transfer abroad of whatever U.S. capital or technology he felt would create unemployment in the U.S.

From all of this evidence, it is clear that the multinational corporations had become a subject of major concern around the world. Although it has its defenders, the multinational corporation is by and large the object of criticism, a good deal of which deals with political and legal problems. Four such problems are emerging as the most important with which multinational corporations must come to grips.

THE POLITICAL AND LEGAL PROBLEMS

First, there is the problem that the large multinational corporation has become, or at least has come to be perceived as, a relatively independent center of power—a quasi-sovereign entity competing improperly, if not unethically, with the nation-state. This is very likely the most serious charge against multinational corporations. Second, the large multinational corporation is not concerned with, or, again, *appears* not to be concerned with, social justice. Third, the multinational corporation is seen as a chief culprit in the destruction of the world environment. Fourth, there is the problem of the growth of corporate intelligence networks that violate the privacy of individuals and the secrets of governments.

(1) THE QUASI SOVEREIGNTY OF MULTINATIONAL CORPORATIONS

The belief that large multinational corporations are more or less independent power centers is manifested by a quote from the 1973 U.N. report, *Multinational Corporations in World Development:*

> The manifold operations of foreign-based multinational corporations and their pervasive influence on the host country may be regarded as a challenge to national sovereignty. The challenge has, moreover, economic, social, political, and cultural dimensions which are frequently inseparable from one another. The tensions and conflicts thus generated are, likewise, the result of complex interaction between many agents in many areas.
>
> Frequently, the multinational corporation is perceived as capable of circumventing or subverting national objectives and policies.

Further, Her Majesty's Department of Trade and Industry issued a report in 1973 entitled *The Impact of Foreign Direct Investment on the United Kingdom.* In a chapter on the multinational corporation and national sovereignty, it stated:

> Both the advocates and opponents of the international corporation seem to agree that in some way inward investment restricts the national sovereignty of the recipient nation. . . . It added, Economic control/ownership by foreigners has political consequences. . . .

The relative independence of the multinational corporation is stressed in report after report. That the large multinational corporations have a standing that approaches sovereignty is seen in the fact that the Ford Motor Company and Occidental Petroleum deal directly and at considerable length with the top political leaders of a nation as large as the Soviet Union. Furthermore, these companies make arrangements with nation-states that are of greater economic (and social) consequence than many of the nations of the world are capable of. These arrangements are not called "treaties," but in terms of their significance for international affairs, they are on a par with agreements between nations.

These corporations are seen as more or less independent, depending upon which host country is involved. In the case of the developed host countries—where the largest amount of foreign direct investment is located—the problem of the independence, or the quasi sovereignty, of the multinational corporation is perhaps not so severe, and this for several reasons. First, the developed countries are experienced and knowledgeable in economic matters and do not feel as threatened as do the developing countries by the size and power of the large multinational corporations. Second, these countries are the ones that have their own multinational corporations either seeking entrance to, or already in, the country from which the entering multinational is likely to come, so there is a certain complementarity.

Not surprisingly, the multinational corporation has greater negotiating power with a developing country than it does with an economically developed country (although the largest amount of direct foreign investment is in developed countries). To be sure, developing countries have recently seen their power vis-à-vis multinational corporations increase dramatically due to the fact that they control what are feared to be increasingly scarce natural resources. But this is one of the few advantages possessed by the underdeveloped countries in dealing with large multinational firms. In general, such countries are eager, if not desperate, for economic development and feel compelled to offer the best possible conditions to companies which can help provide it.

The multinational corporation also appears to be relatively independent of its home country. It seems uncannily successful at avoiding taxation at home. It is charged with exporting jobs from its home country to countries with cheap labor. It is accused (in the United States) of almost "giving away" (through underpriced royalties) the American patrimony of scientific and technological knowledge which has resulted from the investment of American money—frequently tax money. It is accused of shuttling its enormous liquid assets between currencies in ways which have been disruptive to world monetary stability. And it is accused of pursuing its own economic goals regardless of the needs and plans of the countries which may be affected. No wonder multinational corporations seem to have the independence of sovereign political entities.

If all of these characteristics do not add up to "sovereignty" in the classical sense or even "quasi sovereignty," still there has been more independence than most political leaders now seem willing to tolerate. And so we are seeing more and more efforts to restrict the freedom of these new giants. In the United States, the Burke-Hartke bill would be a giant step in harnessing American multinational corporations. In Cuba, Chile, and the nations in the Organization of Petroleum Exporting Countries (OPEC) there have been a number of cases of nationalization and expropriation. In a number of countries, certain sectors of the economy—such as transportation, communications, banking, and insurance—have been reserved for national corporations. Bolivia, Chile, Colombia, Ecuador, Peru, and Venezuela have closed several economic sectors to direct foreign investment. The OPEC governments are moving toward complete control of the oil-producing facilities in their territories. In Canada, a foreign investment review act has been proposed. The regulation of foreign investment is being considered in Australia, and in Mexico there is now a requirement for the registration of new foreign investment. Japan long has screened foreign investment carefully, although there has been some liberalization recently.

The independence of the multinational corporation has also been challenged by the world labor movement. Worldwide striking by employees of a multinational corporation has been raised as one way of restricting the power of such a company. Professor Neil Jacoby has written in *Corporate Power and Social Responsibility:*

> Multinational business is likely also to bring the multinational labor union in its wake. Many companies in high-wage countries like the United States have built plants in low-wage nations in order to reduce costs and stay competitive in world markets. Their success in avoiding the cost-raising effects of the economic power of the national union is motivating labor unions to multinationalize. More unions are beginning to organize, to bargain, to boycott products, and to strike *across national boundary lines.* While yet incipient, labor union multinationalism may be expected to gain force in the future. If it does, it could slow the pace of multinational corporate investment.

Of course, because of divergent interests there can be competition between labor groups in different countries, but their cooperation with one another is a possibility that will restrict the power of the multinational corporation.

How successful these moves to regulate multinational corporations will be remains to be seen. Powerful social and economic forces seem to be shaping the multinational corporation for a new, powerful, and not yet clearly defined institutional role in the world. How far the quasi sovereignty of the multinational corporation will go—or be allowed to go—will be one of the major political and legal questions of the future.

(2) LACK OF CONCERN FOR SOCIAL JUSTICE

The large multinational corporations are often accused of having little concern for the lives, rights, and welfare of those with whom they deal. Of course, the argument goes, the social injustices to workers and customers are not so severe in the developed countries, where labor unions and legal safeguards are strong. But in the developing countries of the world the poor are exploited as cheap labor, and natural resources are stripped away with little return to the mass of people. That the poor of the world are exploited to supply a relatively small part of the world with an unnecessarily high level of material existence compounds the injustice.

This extreme maldistribution of material benefits is regarded by many as the largest and most serious social injustice in the world today: robbing the poor to satiate the rich. And the multinational corporation is seen as the agency through which this great injustice is perpetrated. This is a criticism with which multinational corporations will have to deal more and more in the decades ahead.

(3) THE WORLDWIDE PROBLEMS OF THE ENVIRONMENT

Then there is the fact that people in all nations, and especially in the United States, have become extremely sensitive to local and global problems of the environment. And here, too, the multinational corporation is being viewed as the culprit.

Local environmental problems—those whose main effects are felt within a limited geographical area—include noise pollution, strip mining, congestion, trash, garbage, industrial waste disposal, etc. The relative laxity of laws and restrictions in some countries may make it attractive for multinational corporations to locate polluting operations there. Indeed, some underdeveloped countries have suggested that for the sake of economic development they would be glad to import a little, or even a great deal of, pollution and become "pollution havens."

The petroleum and automobile industries provide examples of multinational business which causes *global* environmental damage. These industries are held responsible for the dramatic increase in the level of carbon dioxide in the world's atmosphere. The careless shipping of petroleum has done great damage to the life in the world's oceans. Whether out of arrogance or inability to respond, multinational corporations have been slow to answer this and other criticisms, thereby inflaming public opinion against them further.

(4) THE DEVELOPMENT OF WORLDWIDE NETWORKS OF CORPORATE INTELLIGENCE

Finally, there is the growing fear of corporate intelligence systems. Following World War II, several American organizations openly offered intelligence services to corporations. The general public is still virtually unaware of such organizations. They are staffed by men who have shifted from intelligence work in the federal government to intelligence activities in the private sector. Another little-known fact is that in recent years an increasing number of big corporations have either established private intelligence units or hired intelligence consultants from the United States intelligence community. Their prime purpose is to protect corporate secrets. However, it is likely that some corporations also use these intelligence organizations to acquire another corporation's secrets or sensitive information regarding foreign government policy which would affect their business. A whole new world of corporate intelligence has thus developed.

Tad Szulc, a noted former correspondent for the *New York Times,* recently wrote that "this emerging industrial-intelligence complex is more pernicious than the military-industrial complex about which Eisenhower warned when he left the White House in 1961."

Let us take only two examples: the oil industry and international banking. In both cases, these are companies which have highly developed professional intelligence units that may indeed rival government intelligence services. The oil companies, of course, want to know what competitors are doing or planning with regard to the search for new sources of oil, making international arrangements, arriving at marketing decisions, and so on. The oil-producing countries of the Middle East allege that the international oil companies' intelligence operations penetrate their governments as well. Also, some of the international banks in the Middle East not only study money flows and long-range economic forecasts, but also have developed highly detailed dossiers on the key people in each of the countries and carry on an intense day-to-day analysis of political power shifts.

Another aspect of this intelligence activity is its domestic use; this involves the increasing surveillance of company personnel, the detailed and often highly personal preemployment investigations, the psychological testing, the assessment of wives of potential candidates for high positions, and so forth. The question is not whether security and security clearances are necessary. It is how much surveillance—both public and private—a free society can tolerate and still be free in a meaningful sense.

The fact of the matter is that ready solutions to these problems are not at hand. Each has been studied to some degree, but there must be many more years of research and "social experimentation" before anything like a consensus on their solution is achieved. Unfortunately, there is no assurance that one of the most difficult steps of all—clearly identify[ing] the problems—has been reached.

And certainly the problems mentioned above by no means give a total picture. For example, the multinational corporation (as well as purely domestic corporations) must work out questions dealing with the structure and function of the board of directors, involving questions of inside and outside directors, the representation of noncorporate constituencies, etc.

Perhaps all of these problems could be attacked more reasonably and adequately if the university community, the business community, and the legal profession take seriously the need to develop a more adequate theory of the firm. Such a theory is needed to relate the goals of a corporation to the goals of a nation, as well as to make clear what the actual social, economic, and psychological bases of the business firm really are in the latter part of the 20th century. Such a theory must include, among other things, an examination of the issues of corporate social responsibility and business ethics. Thus far only fragments of a real theory of the firm have appeared, and they have been largely economic fragments. This will not be enough.

QUESTIONS

1. List the major criticisms levied at the multinational corporation as discussed in the preceding three articles.
2. Identify those criticisms having the most significance for: (a) host countries; (b) the future of world prosperity; (c) the prosperity and survival of the multinational companies; and (d) the U.S. socio-economic-political system.
3. In light of the facts as presented or as you know them, evaluate the validity of the major criticisms and the offsetting benefits of multinational corporate activity.
4. Do you think that Turner's condemnation of the multinational corporation is justified?
5. Do Eells and Collado answer well the major criticisms?

10

BUSINESS, ENVIRONMENT, AND ENERGY

THE ENVIRONMENTAL CRISIS

NEIL H. JACOBY

Neil H. Jacoby in this article explains the basic causes of environmental degradation, schools of thought developed to deal with the problem, and his recommendations on how to come to grips with the crisis.

Who would have predicted, even as recently as a year ago, the strong ground swell of public concern about the environment that now preoccupies Americans? The great silent majority as well as activists of the left have discovered that our country is running out of clean air and pure water. Suddenly, we all understand that smog, noise, congestion, highway carnage, oil-stained beaches, junk graveyards, ugliness, and blatant commercial advertising not only offend our senses but threaten our health and our very lives.

Now we are trying to identify the culpable parties and to demand corrective action. What are the basic forces behind environmental deterioration and why has a crisis emerged so swiftly? What are the merits of the diagnoses and prescriptions that have been advanced for the environmental problem? How can the environment be improved, and who should pay the costs? What are the respective roles and responsibilities of business and of government in restoring environmental amenities? Above all, what lessons does the environmental crisis teach about the functioning of our political and market systems, and about reforms needed to forestall other crises in the future?

We focus attention upon the urban physical environment, that is, upon the spatial and sensory qualities of the land, air, water, and physical facilities that surround the three out of four Americans who live in towns and cities. This milieu deteriorates as a result of air and water pollution, noise, industrial and household waste materials, declining quantity or quality of housing per capita, crowding, congestion, loss of privacy and recreational facilities, rising accidents and loss of time in urban transportation, and, not least of all, drabness and ugliness.

The physical environment is, of course, only one dimension of the quality of human life. In focusing upon physical factors, one excludes important social and psychological factors such as order and security, social mobility, and the social participation or alienation of the individual. All of these environmental factors, along with per capita income, wealth, health, and education, need enhancement.

Reprinted from *The Center Magazine,* a publication of the Center for the Study of Democratic Institutions, Santa Barbara, California. Volume 3 (November–December 1970), 37–48.

Spatially, the urban environment must be viewed as one subdivision of the entire global ecosystem, which also embraces rural lands, the oceans, the atmosphere surrounding the earth, and outer space. Since all parts of this system interact, ideally it should be analyzed, planned, and managed as a whole.

The urban physical environment nevertheless merits a top priority because it affects the majority of our population and, by general assent, its qualities are below the threshold of tolerability. In addition, physical factors powerfully influence the health, mental attitudes, and life-styles of urban residents, and their enhancement will elevate the social and psychological qualities of American society. One is therefore justified in focusing attention upon the physical characteristics of urban life, notwithstanding that it is a partial analysis of the global ecosystem.

Three basic forces have operated to change the urban physical environment for the worse: population concentration, rising affluence, and technological change. The overwhelming tendency of people to concentrate in cities has worsened the environment in many ways. Traffic congestion, crowding, overloading of transportation, marketing and living facilities, delays and loss of time, along with rising levels of air, water, and noise pollution, have been among the social costs of urbanization. During the half-century between 1910 and 1960 the percentage of Americans living in urban areas of 2,500 or more rose from 45.7 to 70, while the number of urbanites tripled from 42 to 125 million. Beyond doubt, the 1970 census will reveal an accelerated urbanization. Urbanization clearly brings benefits to people—wider job opportunities, richer educational and cultural fare, more individual freedom from social constraints—or else it would not have been so powerful and enduring a movement. Yet, beyond some levels of population size and density, the total costs of urbanization begin to exceed the total benefits. Discovery of the optimum size of cities and optimum density of their populations [is a] vitally important [task] confronting national planners.

A second prime mover in environmental change has been rising affluence—the expansion of annual real income and expenditure per capita. Real income per person (measured in 1958 dollars) more than doubled during the eighteen years, 1950–1968, from $1,501 to $3,409. As real incomes have mounted, each person has bought and consumed more tangible goods, thrown them away more quickly, and generated solid waste. Each person has traveled more miles per year, multiplied his contacts with other people, and rapidly expanded his usage of energy. All of this has increased air, water, and noise pollution, crowding and congestion, traffic accidents. With the number of urbanites doubling and per capita real incomes quadrupling every forty years, the problem of supplying urban amenities is exploding. One shudders to contemplate the environmental degradation that would occur if 525 million Indians, now crowded 417 per square mile, were each to spend as much as 200 million Americans living only 60 per square mile. India seeks affluence, but could she stand it?

Environmental degradation is not, of course, inherent in rising affluence. Only the particular forms and methods of production and consumption to which our society has become accustomed degrade it. Rising affluence can and should be a source of environmental enhancement.

It is often overlooked that rising per capita income results in an increased demand for environmental amenities. People naturally demand better public goods—more comfort and convenience and beauty in their communities—to match the better private goods and services their rising incomes enable them to buy. One reason for the environmental "crisis" is the frustration felt by the public with a short supply of environmental amenities available to meet a rising demand for them.

The physical environment of large American cities has not degenerated absolutely in an overall sense, but probably has been improving. People easily forget amenities taken for granted today that were lacking half a century ago. Examples are air-conditioned offices, restaurants, and homes; thermostatically controlled electric and gas heat; underground utility wires and poles; paved boulevards and auto freeways. These have widely replaced the crowded slums, the filth of unpaved streets, the drafty cold-water flats and belching chimneys of winter, and the steaming miseries of unrefrigerated summers. Even in the inner city, people today live longer, healthier, and more comfortable lives—if not happier ones—than they did before World War I. What has happened is that the overall supply of urban amenities has fallen far short of the rising effective demand for them, and the supply of certain critical goods, such as pure air and water, has virtually vanished.

The third source of the environmental problem is technological change. Advancing technology has expanded the variety of products available for consumption, made products more complex, raised rates of obsolescence and thereby added to waste disposal. It has also added immensely to the per capita consumption of physical materials and energy, with consequent increments of waste and of pollution. It has expanded the amount of information required by consumers to make rational choices in markets, thereby creating market imperfections that are the source of the contemporary "consumerism" movement. Technological change, however, is, like rising affluence, a two-edged sword; it can be used to improve as well as to degrade the environment. Technology can *reduce* material consumption and recycle harmful wastes. Examples are the replacement of bulky vacuum tubes by microminiaturized circuits in computers, or the conversion of sewage into pure water plus fertilizers. Environmental preservation calls for a redirection of our technological efforts, as well as a restructuring of patterns of consumption.

One conspicuous aspect of environmental deterioration has been the disappearance of "free goods"—amenities such as clean air, pure water, and open space—that are in such ample supply relative to the demand for them that they are not economized. Pure air is no longer free. To obtain it one must buy air-conditioning equipment and acquire a home in which to install it. Pure water must be purchased by the bottle, now that the product of many municipal water systems is barely potable. Most urban dwellers must spend large sums of money for travel in order to gain the privacy and recreation of a natural environment unavailable at home.

A second aspect of environmental change is the fast-rising importance of spatial relationships in the cities. Such factors as building heights and population densities, street layout, park location, and zoning patterns largely determine the life-styles of urban residents and the supply of amenities available to them. The atrociously bad planning of most American cities and the abject perversion of zoning and building requirements to serve short-term commercial interests are well documented. The flagrantly over-dense building on Manhattan Island has been permitted only because of popular ignorance and apathy. Now, the public is belatedly recognizing the heavy social costs that its neglect has created. Popular concern with city planning, zoning, and building development is rising. The heavy stake of the individual in the physical attributes of his community is finally being appreciated.

A third aspect of environmental change is the multiplication of interdependencies among individuals. To an increasing extent the activities of each of us impinge upon others. This is so not only because more people live in cities, but also because the scale and variety of each person's activities rise with the amount of real income he produces and consumes. Thus, no one suffered disamenity a generation ago when his neighbor played a phonograph in a suburban home; but many suffer when a neighbor's son now turns up the sound volume of his hi-fi instrument in a high-rise apartment building.

Increasing interdependency is one way of looking at what economists call the "spillover effects" or external costs of production or consumption. For example, paper mills emit chemical wastes into lakes and streams, copper smelters inject sulphur dioxide into the air, and electric generating stations throw off carbon monoxide, radioactive wastes, or hot water, depending upon their fuels. Motor vehicles cause massive air and noise pollution, traffic accidents, and vast expenditures on medical, legal, policing, and engineering services and facilities—all borne mainly by the public. These industries all generate external costs, thrust upon society in the form of loss of environmental amenities. Although reliable estimates are lacking, total external costs in the U.S. economy are of the order of tens of billions of dollars a year.

The speed with which public interest in the environment has mounted may be explained primarily by the swift decline in certain amenities below thresholds of tolerability. Although certain critical amenities, notably pure air, have been diminishing for many years, the public has suddenly become aware of critical deficiencies. Thus, the quality of air in the Los Angeles Basin deteriorated steadily after 1940. Yet only by the mid-nineteen-sixties, after school children were being advised not to exercise outdoors on smoggy days and when smog alerts were being sounded on many days each year, was decisive action taken to reduce air pollution from motor vehicles. By the sixties, people saw that the "capacity" of the atmosphere over the basin to disperse pollutants had been intolerably overloaded.

After the design capacity of any facility has been reached, amenities diminish exponentially with arithmetic increases in the load. For example, when a twenty-first person enters an elevator designed to hold twenty persons, everyone in the elevator suffers loss of comfort; and when a twenty-second person enters, the percentage loss of amenity is much greater than the 4.8 per cent increase in the number of passengers. Similarly, when the five thousand and first automobile enters a freeway designed to carry five thousand vehicles per hour, it puts pressure of inadequate space upon five thousand and one drivers, and not only upon the new entrant.

Another reason for current public concern with the environment is the gathering appreciation of inequity as some groups in society gain benefits at the cost of other groups. The automobilist whose vehicle spews out air pollution gets the benefits of rapid and convenient travel; but he imposes part of the costs of that travel upon people who are forced to breathe bad air and hear deafening noise and who must bear the costs of painting and maintaining property corroded by pollutants. Because this is manifestly inequitable, upgrading the environment by eliminating this kind of pollution will not only add to aggregate real income, but will also improve its distribution.

Before examining effective measures for enhancing the environment let us dispose of a number of partial or superficial diagnoses of, and prescriptions for, the problem. Several schools of thought have arisen.

First, there is the Doomsday School. It holds in effect that the problem of environmental degradation is insoluble. For example, Paul Ehrlich argues in his book *The Population Bomb* that it is already too late to arrest man's inexorable march to racial extinction through overpopulation, malnutrition, famine, and disease. Other criers of doom are the natural scientists who predict changes in the earth's temperature, as a result of accumulating carbon dioxide in the atmosphere, with consequent melting of the polar ice and other disasters. Although laymen are incompetent to judge such matters, they remain moot issues among natural scientists and therefore call for at least suspended judgment. Accumulating evidence suggests that population growth in the advanced nations has already slowed appreciably, and is starting to do so in many less developed lands. In any event, an apocalyptic view of the future should be rejected if only because it leads to despair and inaction. If one really believes that the future is hopeless, one will cease making an effort to improve society.

At the opposite pole is the Minimalist School. It holds that environmental deterioration is a minor problem in comparison with such contemporary issues as poverty, civil rights, and school integration. Its members argue that political leaders calling for a better environment are "eco-escapists," seeking to divert public attention from their failure to resolve these primary issues. What the Minimalists overlook is that the United States is already making progress in reducing poverty, expanding civil rights, and achieving educational integration, while it is still losing ground in arresting the decline of the urban environment. They also forget that attention to the environment does not mean neglect of poverty. On the contrary, central-city areas generally have the worst physical conditions of life and are populated mainly by low-income families. Because the poor stand to gain most from environmental enhancement, a war on pollution is one battlefront in a war on poverty. A vigorous attack on that front need not inhibit action on other fronts.

There is also a Socialist School. Its members view environmental deterioration as an inescapable consequence of capitalist "exploitation." If only private enterprise, market competition, and profit incentives were replaced by central planning and state ownership and management of enterprises, they contend, the problem would disappear. However, the socialist countries are facing more serious problems of pollution as their per capita G.N.P.'s are rising. Managers of socialist enterprises are judged by the central planners on the efficiency of their operations, and are under as much pressure to minimize internal costs and throw as much external cost as possible on the public as are the managers of private firms in market economies who seek to maximize stockholders' profits. Moreover, because a monolithic socialist society lacks a separate and independent mechanism of political control of economic processes, it is less likely to internalize the full costs of production than a market economy, with its dual systems of market-price and governmental controls. Pollution has arisen primarily from the failure of our political system, acting through government, to establish desired standards of production and consumption. If government performs its unique tasks, the competitive market system will operate within that framework to produce what the public demands without harming the environment.

The largest group of new environmentalists appears to be associated with the Zero Growth School. Its thesis is simple: since environmental degradation is caused by more people consuming more goods, the answer is to stop the growth of population and production. Nature has fixed the dimensions of the natural environment; therefore man should fix his numbers and their economic activities. We must establish a stable relationship between human society and the natural world.

Zero economic and population growth could arrest the process of environmental degradation, but could not, per se, restore a good physical environment. Were real G.N.P. constant through time, current levels of air and water pollution, noise, crowding, ugliness, and other negative elements would continue as long as present patterns of production and consumption are maintained.

Zero growth of population and production is, moreover, impossible to achieve. Because economic growth is a product of expanding population, higher investment, and advancing technology, zero growth would call for stopping changes in all three variables. This cannot be done in the proximate future, if at all. A leading population analyst has shown that even if, beginning in 1975, every family in the United States were limited to two children—an heroic assumption—population dynamics are such that this nation would not stop adding people until about 2050 A.D., when it would contain nearly 300 millions. (See Stephen Enke, "Zero Population Growth—When, How, and Why," TEMPO Publication 70TMP35, Santa Barbara, California, June 2, 1970.) While a decline in net savings and investment to zero is possible, it is extremely unlikely in view of the savings and investment rates Americans have maintained during the present century in the face of enormous increases in their real wealth and incomes. (See *Policies for Economic Growth and Progress in the Seventies,* Report of the President's Task Force on Economic Growth, U.S. Government Printing Office, Washington, D.C., 1970.) A static technology of production is inconceivable. As long as Americans remain thinking animals they will increase the productivity of work.

Finally, zero growth is undesirable. A rising G.N.P. will enable the nation more easily to bear the costs of eliminating pollution. Because zero growth of population is far in the distance, and zero growth of output is both undesirable and unattainable, it follows that the environmental problem must be solved, as President Nixon stated in his January, 1970, State of the Union Message, by redirecting the growth that will inevitably take place.

The Austerity School of environmental thought is related to the Zero Growth School. Its members assert that environmental decline is produced by excessive use of resources. They are outraged by the fact that the United States consumes about forty per cent of the world's energy and materials, although it contains only six per cent of the world's population. Believing that asceticism is the remedy, they call for less consumption in order to conserve resources and to reduce production and pollution. We should convert ourselves from a society of "waste-makers" into one of "string-savers."

The basic error here is that it is not the amount of production and consumption per capita that degrades the environment, but the fact that government has failed to control the processes of production and consumption so as to eliminate the pollution associated with them. Without such political action, consumption could be cut in half and society would still suffer half as much pollution; with appropriate political control consumption could be doubled while pollution is radically reduced. The second error of the Austerity School, which distinguishes it from the Zero Growth School, is a notion that the world confronts a severe shortage of basic natural resources. Exhaustive studies by Resources for the Future have shown the contrary: there are no foreseeable limitations upon supplies of basic natural resources, including energy, at approximately current levels of cost. Technological progress is continually opening up new supplies of materials that are substitutable for conventional materials (e.g., synthetic rubber and fibers) and lowering the costs of alternative sources of energy (e.g., production of petroleum products from oil shales, tar sands, and coal). Austerity theorists do make a valid point, however, when they observe that governmental regulation to internalize external costs can cause business enterprises to develop ways of recycling former waste materials back into useful channels.

Finally, there is the Public Priorities School. Its adherents see the problem as one of too much governmental spending on defense and space exploration, leaving too little for environmental protection. The solution, as they see it, is to reallocate public expenditures. There are two responses to this line of reasoning: public expenditures are already being strongly reordered, and in any event reallocations of private expenditures will weigh far more heavily in a solution of the environmental problem. Thus between the fiscal years 1969 and 1971 federal budget outlays on defense and space are scheduled to shrink by ten per cent, from $85.5 billions to $77 billions, whereas outlays on social security and public assistance will rise by twenty-six per cent, from $46 billions to $60 billions. The President has announced plans for further contractions of defense outlays and expansions of expenditures on the nation's human resources.

Environmental restoration does require large increases in public expenditures upon sewage disposal and water purification, parks, housing, urban development, and public transportation. Even more, however, it calls for a reallocation of private expenditures as a result of governmental actions to internalize external costs in the private sector. For example, the purchase price and operating expenses of an automobile that is pollution-free will undoubtedly be higher than for a vehicle that degrades the environment, because the auto user will be paying the full costs of his private transportation. With internalization of costs, spending on private auto transportation may be expected to decline relatively. At the same time, spending on education and housing, which produce external benefits, will increase relatively. In the aggregate, readjustments in patterns of private expenditure will far outweigh reallocation of public expenditure in a total program of environmental restoration.

Because the environmental problem is critically important and is soluble, and neither socialization of the economy, zero growth, austerity, nor new public spending priorities offer a satisfactory solution, a more basic approach must be made. A good policy for environmental improvement should improve the distribution of income among people as well as the allocation of society's resources. Governmental intervention is necessary to attain both ends.

Environmental degradation occurs, as has been shown, when there are significant external costs involved in producing or consuming commodities. A social optimum cannot be achieved when there is a divergence between private (internal) and social (external plus internal) costs. An optimal allocation of society's resources requires that the full costs of production of each good or service be taken into account. The internalization of external costs must therefore be a pivotal aim of environmental policy. (A trenchant description of the external costs of economic growth is given by E. J. Mishan, *The Costs of Economic Growth,* New York: Praeger, 1967.)

Theoretically, perfectly competitive markets in which there are no transaction costs will lead to an optimum reallocation of resources in cases of pollution via bargaining between the polluter and the person harmed by pollution, no matter which party is legally responsible to compensate the other. (See R. H. Coase, "The Problem of Social Costs," *Journal of Law and Economics,* III, October, 1960.) In practice, however, the transaction costs of education, organization, and litigation are excessively high when pollution affects large numbers of people, as it usually does. For this reason it is more efficient for government to resolve pollution problems by legislation or regulation, rather than to leave them to bilateral market bargaining. For example, government can order air polluters to reduce their emissions by x per cent. Polluters then incur (internalize) costs in order to conform to the public regulation, thereby relieving the public of even greater costs of maintaining health and property damaged by pollution.

Prior governmental action is essential because the competitive market system is incapable, by itself, of internalizing the costs of anti-pollution measures. Suppose, for example, that the automobile could be made pollution-free by installing a device costing x dollars. An automobile owner would not voluntarily install the device, because other people would reap the benefits of the cleaner air made possible by his expenditure. General Motors proved this in 1970 by a well-advertised effort to sell motorists in the Phoenix, Arizona, area a pollution-reducing kit costing only twenty-six dollars. During the first month only a few hundred kits were sold in a market with several hundred thousand potential buyers. Auto makers would not voluntarily install the device because to do so would add to their costs and put them at a disadvantage in competition with other manufacturers who did not install it. And antitrust laws prohibit any agreement among all auto manufacturers simultaneously to install, or not to install, pollution-reducing devices. Where large external costs or benefits are involved, there is a conflict between the decision that serves the self-interest of the individual and that which serves the collective welfare of the community. Community welfare can only be given the precedence it deserves by a prior governmental action regulating private behavior, followed by corporation actions to modify products, prices, and allocations of resources in order to conform to the public regulation.

Society cannot reasonably expect individual enterprises or consumers to shoulder external costs in the name of "social responsibility," because the competitive market system puts each firm and household under strong pressure to minimize its costs in order to survive. What is needed is a prior political decision that leaves all producers or consumers in the same relative position.

There are usually alternative solutions to pollution problems; each alternative should be evaluated in order to identify the least costly of them. Consider again the example of smog in the Los Angeles Basin. Among possible ways of coping with this problem are the following: controlling emissions of pollutants from motor vehicles and stationary sources by public regulation; moving people out of the basin; rezoning to reduce building density; building a rapid mass-transit system; imposing heavy taxes on private automobile operation; or subsidizing motorists to limit their auto mileage. The costs and benefits of each alternative, and combinations thereof, should be evaluated before an anti-pollution policy is adopted. The goal should always be the most efficient use of scarce resources.

All desirable things in limited supply have a cost, and there are trade-offs between desirable things. People may gain more of one thing only by sacrificing something else, and the optimum situation is reached when no additional benefits can be obtained by further substitutions. These principles apply to environmental amenities. For example, noise pollution can be reduced with benefits to health and well-being, but at the cost of larger expenditures for insulation or noise-abatement devices or a reduction in the speed or power of engines. Conceivably, utter silence could be achieved by incurring astronomical costs and by making great sacrifices of mobility, power, and time. The public decides the optimum noise level by balancing the benefits of less noise against the costs of attaining it. Government then fixes a noise standard at that point where the costs of reducing noise further would exceed the additional benefits to health and well-being. Although the calculus is necessarily rough, this is the rationale of determining standards to reduce pollution of all kinds.

Just as governmental intervention is needed to bring about the reallocations of resources needed for environmental improvement, so it is also required to levy the costs of such improvement equitably among individuals and groups in society so as to improve—or at least prevent a worsening of—the distribution of income.

There are opposite approaches to the problem of cost allocation. By one principle, polluters should pay the costs of suppressing their pollution; by another, the public should pay polluters to stop polluting. The second principle is defended on the ground that the public benefits from the reduction of pollution and should pay the costs of this benefit. Those who espouse this view hold that tax credits and public subsidies are the proper instruments of a policy for environmental betterment. Libertarians usually favor this approach because of their preference for the "carrot" versus the "stick," and their belief that public boards often come under the domination of those they are supposed to regulate.

Advocates of the first principle argue, to the contrary, that society initiates an anti-pollution policy from a current status of inequity. The problem is to restore equity as between polluters and those damaged by pollution, not to compensate polluters for a loss of equitable rights. They also observe that persons with large incomes generally generate disproportionately more pollution than those with low incomes, so that a policy of internalizing costs in the polluter will tend to shift income from richer to poorer people, with resulting gains in social well-being. The appropriate instruments for dealing with pollution are, in their view, public regulations to reduce harmful activities, or taxes and fines on polluters.

Equity requires that the costs of suppressing environmental damage be borne by those responsible for it. Public restraint of private actions harmful to the environment thus should be the dominant instrument of environmental policy. Assertion of this principle does not, however, preclude the use of taxes, fines, or lawsuits, nor does it rule out the use of public subsidies to enterprises which, through long-continued tolerance of harmful activities vital to their survival, have acquired a certain equity in them. For example, a city council might prohibit billboard advertising of off-premise goods or services, on the ground that the visual pollution costs borne by the public exceed the benefits. To enable outdoor advertising companies to finance an adjustment into other activities, a city might reasonably offer to pay them subsidies over a period of years on a descending scale.

Since the quality of the urban environment is a function of many variables, public policies to enhance the environment must utilize many instruments.

Direct governmental control of emissions of pollutants—[aural], atmospheric, olfactory, visual, or health-affecting—is now exemplified in federal and state laws governing air and water pollution, and in federal standards of noise emissions from aircraft engines. Assuming that reduction of emissions is the least costly solution, the main problems are to determine appropriate standards and enforce them. In fixing standards, the state of pollution-control technology is an important consideration. Where such technology exists and can be applied at reasonable cost, the law should simply ban emissions and enforce compliance. This appears to be true of much air and water pollution from fixed sources, such as the chimneys of manufacturing and power-generating plants. Where pollution technology is in process of development, as in the case of automobile emissions, government should fix standards that are progressively raised as time goes on.

Another way to internalize external costs is to guarantee each property owner legal rights to the amenities pertaining to his property. A California court recently awarded substantial damages to home owners near the Los Angeles International Airport to compensate them for demonstrated loss of property values because of excessive noise from airplanes. A constitutional amendment should be enacted guaranteeing every property owner a right to environmental amenities, because this would induce business enterprises to reduce or eliminate pollution in order to escape legal liabilities. However, judicial processes are so costly, time-consuming, and uneven in their results as to make other solutions to environmental problems preferable.

Governments—federal, state, and local—themselves contribute to air and water pollution, especially by discharging untreated sewage into rivers and lakes. They should internalize these costs by massive public expenditures on sewage-treatment and water-purification plants. Such outlays will, of course, ultimately be paid for by a public that presumably values a clean environment more highly than the money paid in taxes to finance such facilities.

Urban planning, zoning, and building regulations are powerful instruments for enhancing the amenities of space, privacy, recreation, housing, transportation, and beauty in our cities. If American cities are to offer ample amenities for living, much stronger governmental controls of the design, quality, height, and density of buildings, and of the layout of transportation, recreation, and cultural facilities will be necessary. Americans will have to put a much higher priority on urban amenities, if strong enough instruments of social control over property usage are to be forged. Such controls will be opposed by builders, accustomed as they are to permissive public regulation that can be bent to their purposes. Yet firm public control of land usage under a long-range metropolitan plan is one reason why such cities as London hold a strong attraction for their residents as well as for millions of foreign visitors.

Enlargement of the supply of urban amenities also calls for immense public and private expenditures on recreational and cultural facilities, housing, and public transportation systems. The many programs coming under the auspices of the federal Departments of Transportation and of Housing and Urban Development serve this end. A whole battery of incentives for the participation of private enterprise in the gargantuan tasks will need to be fabricated, including tax credits, accelerated depreciation, credit guaranties, cost-plus contracts, and direct governmental subsidies. The naive idea that private corporations can or will undertake urban rehabilitation out of a sense of "social responsibility" denies the ineluctable fact that in a competitive market economy the firm cannot devote a material part of its resources to unprofitable activities and survive. Just as government must first create a market for pollution-reducing devices before the enterprise system will produce them, so it must first create adequate incentives to induce enterprises to produce urban housing and transit systems. That the responses are swift when the incentives are strong is shown by the great strength of the housing boom after World War II, triggered by liberal F.H.A. mortgage insurance and Veterans Administration home-loan guaranties.

Above all, a high-quality urban environment requires the public to assign high values to urban amenities—to appreciate them greatly and to work hard and pay for them. So far, too few American urbanites have held such values with sufficient intensity to bring about the necessary political action. Whether recent public outcries for a better environment will be sufficiently strong, sustained, and widespread to change the historical American posture of indifference remains to be seen.

The sudden emergence of the environmental problem raises profound issues about the functioning of our social institutions. Does it betoken an institutional breakdown—a failure to respond to new demands of the public? Has the social system responded, but been seriously laggard in its responses? Does the fault lie mainly in the political or in the market subsystem of our society, wherein there are two methods by which social choices of the uses of resources are made—voting in elections and buying in markets?

Although these questions cannot be answered finally, the most defensible positions appear to be the following. First, the social system has been sluggish in responding to the higher values placed by the public on environmental amenities, but it has not broken down and the processes of resource reallocation have begun. Second, the environmental crisis was generated primarily by tardy responses of the political system, and only secondarily by faults in the market system.

If American society is to attain optimal well-being, its dual set of political and market controls must operate promptly and in the proper sequence in response to changes in social values. Political action is first needed to create a demand for environment-improving products; market competition can then assure that this demand is satisfied economically. Measures are needed to improve both political and market processes.

Our model of the dynamic relationships between changes in social values, government actions, and corporate behavior is shown in the chart below. The primary sequential flow of influence runs from changes in social values, via the political process, to changes in governmental regulation of the private sector and reallocation of public resources; thence, via the market process, to corporate reallocation of private resources. However, changes in social values are not wholly determined by shifts in levels of income and other autonomous factors. They also respond to political leadership in the legislative and executive branches of government and to the public advertising and selling efforts of corporations. Similarly, governmental actions are not responsible exclusively to shifts in the values of the public. They are also influenced in some degree by the political activities of businessmen and by corporate lobbying. These secondary flows of influence also help to determine the performance of the social system.

The model enables us to identify salient points of improvement in the system. They are to reform the political process so that government actions will more rapidly and accurately reflect significant shifts in social values, to reform the market process so that corporate behavior will more rapidly and accurately reflect changes in governmental regulation, and to reform political and business behavior so that their secondary influences will help rather than hinder. Specifically, what changes are needed in each of these three areas?

The environmental problem emphasizes once again the need for a political system capable of translating changes in social values rapidly and

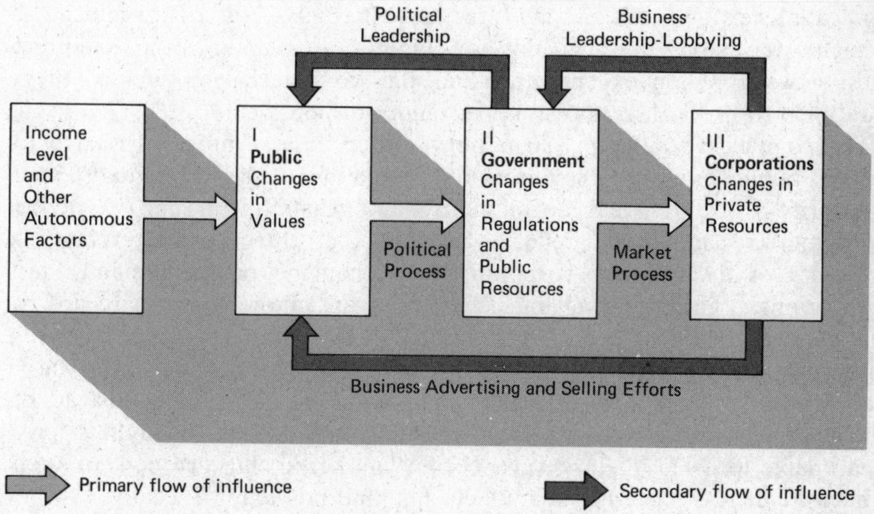

accurately into governmental actions. The political apparatus for sensing, recording, mobilizing, transmitting, and acting upon millions of changes in individual preferences must be improved. Our representative system of government must be made more representative. This raises anew the old dilemmas of participative democracy, the weaknesses of political parties, the unrepresentativeness of legislatures, and the inordinate influence of pressure groups in an age of accelerating technological, demographic, and economic change. The basic requirements for greater efficiency of the political system are better education and sustained participation in political affairs by citizens. While one may easily be pessimistic in the light of the past, there is ground for hope of improvement. Americans generally spend only a small fraction of the time and effort they devote to private goods in making choices of the public goods they purchase with their taxes. Yet purchases of public goods and services are now nearly one-third as large as purchases of private goods. During 1969 government purchases amounted to $225 billions or twenty-three per cent of a total G.N.P. of $923 billions, whereas private purchases were $698 billions or seventy-seven per cent. Rational behavior in resource allocation requires a massive increase in the time and effort devoted to public decisions. Hopefully, the present egregious under-allocation of time represents a cultural lag which will be rectified in due course.

Changes should be made in the voting process to make it function more like a market. Just as consumers record the relative intensities of their demands for different private goods by the amounts of their expenditures in markets, so voters could be enabled to record the relative intensities of their demands for public goods. Each voter could be given, say, one thousand votes, which he could cast in whatever numbers he chose for alternative aggregate levels of public expenditures and alternative patterns of allocation of each level among different objects. Finally, a maximum usage of direct links between public expenditures and the taxes levied to finance them could help to make the political system more responsive.

The competitive market system must also be made more responsive to shifts in public values and governmental regulations. Despite its undoubted superiority as a device for gauging consumers' wants, the recent rise of the "consumerism" movement reflects, among other things, a disturbing insensitivity of the business corporations to changing public demands and expectations. The foot-dragging behavior of the auto makers in regard to safety and air pollution and of the oil companies in regard to air and ocean-water pollution are symptomatic. Business corporations generally have been reluctant, if not obstructive, reactors to new social values instead of innovative leaders in satisfying them. Either their market researchers have been unable to detect them, or else correct market intelligence has not been utilized by their engineering, manufacturing, and marketing executives.

A reorientation of corporate organization is needed, from the board of directors down through corporate and divisional managers to individual plant and store executives. The board should include one or more "outside" directors chosen especially for their knowledge of corporate relationships to society, including the environment. This need should be met by the normal process of including such nominees in the slate of directors presented by management for stockholder vote, rather than by augmenting the board by special stockholder nominees, as Ralph Nader proposed to General Motors Corporation. The normal procedure is more likely to result in effective board action to improve the environment, because it avoids "bloc" politics within the board. Every single policy and action of the firm should be reviewed for its effect upon the environment. An environmental analyst, assigned to this task as a staff adviser to the chief executive, would help to assure good corporate behavior. Standard corporate policy should require all managers to include in their proposals for new operations of facilities measures for preventing adverse environmental effects. Corporations should also make more penetrating use of consumer surveys and public-opinion polls in order to keep informed of shifts in public tastes and priorities.

Reforms are also needed to ensure that the secondary influences upon social values exercised by political and business leaders are facilitative rather than obstructive. These influences are significant. For example, President Eisenhower's sponsorship of the Interstate Highway Act in 1956 and President Kennedy's proposal of a manned round trip to the moon in 1961 mobilized and activated changes in the values of the American people which led to highway and space programs each of the order of five billion dollars a year. President Nixon's leadership in 1970 in a national effort to improve the environment will probably produce even larger reallocations of resources. All three Presidents discerned deep changes in public priorities to which they gave form and implementation. Without such political leadership, readjustments would have been delayed amid mounting public tension and frustration.

American corporate leadership generally has not played a helpful role in implementing changes in social values. Whereas business lobbyists should be informing legislators of new environmental regulations desired by the public, they usually oppose such changes. Most corporate advertising is narrowly focused upon expanding public demand for existing products rather than for new products with superior environmental effects. As Henry Ford recently advised, corporate managers should "stop thinking about changing public expectations as new costs which may have to be accepted but certainly have to be minimized. Instead, we should start thinking about changes in public values as opportunities to profit by serving new needs."

This analysis of deterioration in the urban environment and of means to restore it has unveiled neither a master culprit nor a panacea. It has delineated a complex public problem requiring many instruments of policy for its solution. It has shown that the basic requirement is a citizenry that assigns higher values to urban amenities than it has in the past, and will work harder and pay more to get them. Given new social preferences, new regulations will be imposed and those long-neglected regulations on the statute books will finally be enforced. It is disturbing to reflect that a lawsuit brought by the Attorney General of the United States early in 1970 against several large corporations for polluting the southern end of Lake Michigan was to enforce a federal statute enacted in 1899. Here—as in the administration of urban zoning codes—Americans have not put high enough values upon environmental amenities to insist that private actions conform to existing public laws.

Environmental improvement will call for annual public and private expenditures of tens of billions of dollars indefinitely into the future. Profound changes will be necessary in the structure of relative costs and prices of goods, and in patterns of production and consumption. These readjustments will cause difficulties for individual companies operating on the margin of profitability and unable to pay the full costs of their products. Yet the ability of our profit-oriented enterprise system to adapt to a massive internalization of costs cannot be doubted, when one recalls its successful assimilation of the technological revolution since World War II. Over a period of time the costs and prices of products with large external costs (e.g., automobiles) would rise relatively, while those with large external benefits (e.g., homes) would decline relatively. While consumers would spend relatively less on autos and relatively more on housing, in a growing economy this would mean changes in the growth rates of different industries rather than an absolute decline in the output of any one. Also, new industries would emerge to supply the growing demand for pollution-controlling equipment and services. Profit rates and market signals would continue to guide resources in the directions desired by consumers.

The effects of environmental improvement upon the overall growth of the U.S. economy depend mainly upon how "economic growth" is defined and measured. There is a growing recognition that the true end of public policy is a steady expansion of social well-being, and that a rising G.N.P. is only a means to this end. G.N.P. is simply a measure of the aggregate output of the economy, whereas social well-being is also directly related to the composition of output, its full costs, and the uses to which it is put. If, as has been true during the past twenty years, much production included in the G.N.P. has been associated with national defense and environmental degradation, growth of the G.N.P. can be a highly misleading index of gains in social well-being. Indices of well-being should be developed to help guide long-term public policy, and G.N.P. also should be recast to provide a more meaningful measure of total output.

Assuming the existence of a strong effective demand by the public for a better urban environment, it cannot be doubted that a redirection of production to supply that demand will expand the well-being of American society. A better environment would enable people to reduce many other costs they now incur for health, property maintenance, recreation, and travel to leave uncongenial surroundings. Rising social well-being is not in conflict with an expanding G.N.P., provided that the increments of production improve the quality of life. On the contrary, growth of production is needed for that purpose. As President Nixon said in his 1970 State of the Union Message: "The answer is not to abandon growth, but to redirect it."

QUESTIONS

1. What three basic forces does Jacoby identify as causing our environmental degradation? Discuss them.
2. What schools of thought have arisen to tell us what to do or not to do? Explain their reasoning, and comment on the extent to which they promise to meet the crisis.
3. Jacoby says, "The internalization of external costs must . . . be a pivotal aim of environmental policy." What does he mean by this? Do you agree? What

problems arise in implementing this principle? What can be done to improve its implementation?

4. Explain Jacoby's model of the "Dynamic Relationships Between Public Values, Governmental Regulations, and Corporate Resource Allocations." Evaluate the significance of this model in (a) explaining the roles of business and government in dealing with the pollution problems and (b) determining how we may improve our system to deal more effectively with the pollution problems.

TRADE-OFFS IN ASSESSING ENVIRONMENTAL IMPACTS

STAHRL EDMUNDS

Stahrl Edmunds, dean of the Graduate School of Administration, University of California, Riverside, presents in the following paper some of the major trade-offs that must be considered in establishing pollution standards.

The environment is where we all live, and our business is where we work. Thus, the environment versus business represents two sides of our lives, in which we trade off health and aesthetic goals against economic goals. In this sense, environmental impacts have innumerable ramifications throughout the range of our activities, like any of the other great polarities and mysteries of living. Only a few of these interactions can be considered in a short paper, and ten topics have been selected for discussion. These are:

1. Unemployment versus the environment.
2. Inflation and the environment.
3. Capital investment costs versus pollution results.
4. Incremental costs of pollution abatement versus effects.
5. Health effects of pollution.
6. An industry example.
7. Energy effects.
8. Land use—housing densities.
9. Mineral requirements.
10. Summary and international effects.

1. UNEMPLOYMENT VERSUS THE ENVIRONMENT

The ultimate trade-off in environmental impacts has come to the fore during the current recession. President Ford commented upon it when he said, "I am for the environment, but I am also for jobs." The message is clear that jobs come first, as perhaps they should; but what is not clear is whether there is a logical connection, as implied in the statement, between environmental requirements and unemployment.

The Environmental Protection Agency commissioned a study which estimated the unemployment consequences of environmental requirements to be 0.05 to 1 percent, which is a very small part of the 9.5 percent unemployment rate in the economy (see Trade-off sheet, Item 1).

Stahrl Edmunds, "Trade-Offs in Assessing Environmental Impacts," *California Management Review,* Volume XIX, number 1, 1976. Reprinted by permission.

Unemployment and the recession are derived, at least in part, from over-pricing and price misalignments caused by inflation.

2. INFLATION AND THE ENVIRONMENT

The Council on Environmental Quality has estimated the inflationary or price effects of environmental control at ½ of 1 percent out of an annual rate that reached 14.4 percent in the first quarter (Item 2 on Trade-off sheet). Indeed about two-thirds of the price rise, or 9½ percent, is traceable to the size of government deficits during recent years, which inflated the money supply. Most of the rest of the price inflation, about 4½ percent, is attributable to specific commodity shortages, such as petroleum following the Arab oil embargo, and food shortages due to world crop failures in 1973–74.

The nonsequitur relating jobs to environment diverts attention from the government's responsibility for joblessness through failures in its monetary-fiscal policies, as well as serving as a rationalization for giving industry relief from environmental standards.

Automobile emission standards, originally set for 1975 and slipped to 1978, are to be delayed yet again to 1982 in a proposal by President Ford, which Congress may cut to 1980. The purpose of the delays are to ease automobile unemployment, which is attributable in reality to the inflation cycle and to the large gas-using cars, and also to give industry time to find solutions to the emission problem. California first imposed emission standards in 1963. The twelve years since then were not enough to move the industry to a solution; and there is little on the horizon to suggest that twenty years to 1982 will result in air quality standards being met.

Also under the rationale of saving jobs, the air quality standards on stationary sources are being relaxed to allow more sulfur oxide emissions, which will enable the use of more coal and high sulfur oils. This course of action is intended to relieve the energy shortage by enabling power companies to burn more available and cheaper fuels, thus saving jobs as a trade-off against reduced sulfur emissions in the Eastern industrial states. Atmospheric SO_2 becomes sulfuric acid in combination with moisture and particulates and is capable of health damage, including catastrophic events such as the killer smog in London during the early 1950's.

The question is, then, do we really have to step backward, or even aside, from environmental improvement because of high unemployment rates? The relationship between jobs and environmental requirements is minimal; and those who would waive environmental standards should prove their job relatedness, especially since the Environmental Protection Agency and the Council on Environmental Quality currently show that environmental impacts have contributed negligibly to inflation or unemployment.

If unemployment is the issue, it should be attacked at its cause, namely, the pre-empting of private capital flows through heavy government borrowing and inflating the money supply to finance fiscal deficits. But to make environmental improvement a scapegoat for the government's fiscal failures does nothing to cure either unemployment or environmental damage.

3. CAPITAL INVESTMENT COSTS VERSUS POLLUTION EFFECTS

The capital investment by industry in environmental abatement equipment during 1974 is estimated at $1,465 million (Item 3). Notice that 80 percent of this investment, which is principally for air and water pollution abatement, is in four industries: metal processing, chemicals, petroleum, and utilities.

The pollution abatement which has been achieved over the past eight to ten years, partially by such investments, is shown in the right column (Item 3). In water, pollution from suspended solids, chlorides, and total bacteria has been reduced, but pollutants from nitrates, phosphates, and fecal coliforms have increased.

In air, particulate pollution from combustion has decreased; but particulate pollution from industrial processing and sulfur oxide emissions from oil sources have increased.

Automobile emissions from hydrocarbons have gone down, but nitrogen oxides have increased.

That is, we still have some way to go to achieve the goals of the Clean Air Act of 1970 or the Water Quality Amendments of 1972. The clean air standards essentially call for a 90 percent reduction in emissions from the 1970 level, and the water quality amendments call for a "no discharge policy." The no discharge policy may prove to be unrealistic, or at least too costly, but it is still a legislative mandate. This leads us to consider future costs of attempting to improve air and water quality as far as seems practicable.

4. INCREMENTAL COSTS OF POLLUTION ABATEMENT VERSUS EFFECTS

Industry has traditionally made investments in pollution control for its own reasons, which may be for cost reduction, product quality, or local ordinances. The Environmental Protection Agency estimates what the "incremental costs" are to meet the federal air and water quality standards since 1970. These incremental costs, for both industry and government, are estimated at $194 billion over the ten years from 1973–1982. This amounts to an average of about $19 billion per year, or ranging from 0.7 to 1.0 percent of GNP (Item 4). Of this amount, the largest portion, or $133 billion, is for air pollution abatement, $74 billion for autos, and $59 billion for stationary sources. Industry water treatment costs are $27 billion, and governmental costs (mostly for municipal waste water treatment plants) are $24 billion. The cost of solid waste disposal and surface mining abatement is $5 billion each.

The expected improvements in air quality over a similar time period are a large (60 percent) reduction in particulate emissions, a 40 percent reduction in sulfur oxides, and some modest decreases in hydrocarbons, carbon monoxide, and nitrogen oxides.

In water quality improvement, a significant reduction in suspended solids and biochemical oxygen demand is expected, but only a small improvement in dissolved solids or nutrients.

5. HEALTH EFFECTS OF POLLUTION

Is all this cost and trouble to improve the environment worthwhile? In the end, the answer to that question depends upon our own appreciation of the environment and the amenities of nature as they enhance our life-style and satisfaction. Or, lacking that appreciation, the issue depends upon effects upon our health.

Health effects are difficult to measure because they are so interactive. The majority of cancers are believed to be induced by synthetic chemicals disposed into the environment. The body-weight of DDT and PCB in tissue has increased for all vertebrates, including man. For some species like the falcon and pelican, the disintegration of eggshell formations has endangered reproduction of young.

In water pollution, a news headline will occasionally signal grave concern, like lead poisoning in the Boston drinking water, or high chemical and coliform counts in New Orleans drinking water. About one-third of municipal water quality is rated as sub-standard. The health effects of this poor-quality water have not been isolated.

In air pollution, a concerted effort to measure health effects has produced some discernible results. For example, a study by Lave and Seskin dealing with particulates and sulfur oxides estimated that a 50 percent reduction in air pollution would be associated with a 7 percent reduction in total death rates (see Item 5).

The continuous air monitoring study in five cities (Chicago, Denver, Philadelphia, St. Louis, and Washington, D.C.) correlated daily mortality data with daily levels of carbon monoxide, nitric oxide, sulfur oxide, nitrogen dioxide, and hydrocarbons. A significant relationship was found in Chicago, where pollution levels were highest, especially between sulfur oxides (from stationary sources) and immediate death rates, and between nitric oxide (from automobiles) and mortality rates delayed or lagged several days later.

Another study of 117 standard metropolitan areas related two pollutants, particulates and sulfates, to specific diseases.

Particulate pollutions were associated with higher death rates for infants under one year of age.

Sulfate pollution was correlated with elevated fetal death rates.

For adults, sulfate pollution was significantly related to higher death rates for cancer, tuberculosis, and cardiovascular diseases.

6. AN INDUSTRY EXAMPLE

The health damage from environmental pollution is thus seen to be significant, and it warrants serious concern as well as reasonable costs to avoid adverse health effects. The question is, what are reasonable costs? And, how clean is clean enough? An impressionistic view suggests that the last 1 or 2 percent of environmental abatement is likely to entail exorbitant costs, but up to that point the trade-off between cost and damage reduction is reasonable. This impression is based upon the general observation that abatement costs increase logarithmically. Abatement costs are almost negligible for significant quality improvements in the early stages, but they become near-infinite to achieve the last 1 percent.

An industry example of such a logarithmic function is reported by Crocker in attempts to remove fluorine emissions from the stack gases of the phosphate fertilizer industry in Florida. Fluorides emitted into the air settled into grasslands surrounding wide areas around the plants where livestock grazed. The cattle acquired fluorosis from the grasses, a particularly pitiful and painful disease causing growths on the bone structure of joints until the cattle were immobilized and starved to death. Livestock owners sued the fertilizer plants, who were required by the courts to control emissions.

Emission control costs were $6.7 million to go from 90 to 95 percent efficiency in removing fluorides from stack gases, but $16 million to reach 99 percent efficiency (see Item 6). The costs for controlling the last 1 percent were steeper still, but very uncertain.

The trade-off made by the companies, rather than to control emissions beyond 95 percent, was to buy up 200,000 acres of land for $25 million. By that decision, they became such large cattle owners that it paid them to invest in pollution control equipment to protect their livestock investment.

This example tells something about the importance of internalizing costs, versus payoffs, within an industry.

7. ENERGY EFFECTS

Let us turn now to some other problems which relate to long term growth of the U.S. economy, namely, to energy, land use, and mineral requirements. The long term supply of these factors of production obviously will seriously influence the U.S. future.

The Environmental Protection Agency has experimented with two models to evaluate energy impacts in the future: one is called SEAS or the Strategic Environmental Assessment System, the other MERES or Matrix of Environmental Residuals from Energy Systems. SEAS is a base case model which related energy requirements to GNP; and MERES is a simulation data base which related energy by source and use to residual pollutants. A brief abstract of the results of a high and low growth rate projection is shown as Item 7 on the Trade-off sheet.

With a low annual growth rate of 2 percent per year, the U.S. economy will need an increase of 2 percent in natural gas, 50 percent in coal production, and 100 percent in hydro and nuclear sources. By energy conservation measures, the petroleum requirements are assumed to be controllable to around present levels.

At a high growth rate of 4 percent per year, petroleum requirements would increase 30 percent, and all other fuel sources would be at their maximum output as before in the low growth case. In other words, energy independence in this model is built upon coal and nuclear production, plus oil conservation.

The environmental effects of the high growth rate option with high abatement investment would be a 90 percent increase in particulates, a 70 percent increase in sulfur oxides, and over 100 percent increases in hydrocarbons, carbon monoxide, water pollution, and energy-related land utilization. These residual effects reflect, of course, the consequences of heavy reliance upon coal as an energy source.

Coal is our greatest energy resource, but it is a high polluting source of sulfates, particulates, and hydrocarbons, as well as water pollution and land devastation by strip mining. If coal must become a principal source of fuel for independence, can we moderate our energy requirements by other means? One such means is a different form of land use in the United States, that is, shifting from urban sprawl to higher density in housing.

8. LAND USE—HOUSING DENSITIES

A study by EPA called *The Cost of Sprawl* identified the energy requirements and pollution effects of two forms of urban development, one called high density with 0.3 acres per dwelling unit, and low density with 0.6 acres per unit. This acreage includes not only the dwelling unit but all city land allocations which go with it, such as streets, parks, schools, commercial areas, and other infrastructures.

First, the capital cost of the high density development is 44 percent less than for low, and its annual operating cost is 18 percent less (see Item 8).

The environmental benefits are even more marked, a 40 percent reduction in energy requirements, 45 percent reduction in air pollution, 50 percent in water pollution, 40 percent in auto mileage, and 30 percent in water consumption.

A change to high density urban development would greatly alter our living habits and life-styles, perhaps returning us to the urban development patterns around the turn of the century. Will the American consumer stand for such a change? That question is probably debatable. However, maybe the consumer will not have to make any choice, because the inexorable tide of events will make it for him. That is, the U.S. over-abundance of resources may run out in key materials, limit our growth, and make us live more like the rest of the world.

9. MINERAL REQUIREMENTS

In 1950, the United States consumed 2 billion tons of new minerals; by 1972 the amount had doubled to 4 billion tons. While the United States is one of the more resource-rich nations of the world, it is self-sufficient in only 2 of the 25 commodities for which world demand exceeds reserves. Indeed, the United States does not have sufficient reserves to satisfy its cumulative demands to the year 2000 for 47 out of 87 principal commodities needed to sustain its economic growth. Among the key shortages where both U.S. and world demand will exceed available reserves by the year 2000 are copper, lead, zinc, tin, natural gas, and petroleum (see Item 9). Other key resources in which the United States will become increasingly dependent upon foreign sources are aluminum, chromium, iron, and nickel—all important to industrial production.

The United States can try to increase its recycling rate of short materials. Only lead and nickel have considerable recycling at present. Raising the recycling rates in all materials is likely to be at increased costs, and certainly it will change industry usage habits.

10. SUMMARY AND INTERNATIONAL EFFECTS

The message is that life-styles are changing: in industry, as to its material usage, waste disposal, recycling, and environmental control habits; in consumer habits of housing, densities, urban development, transportation, energy consumption, pollution, and health.

Rising world prices of materials in the past few years are a precursor of the change which stems from all the world having expectations which previously were limited to the United States and Western Europe. Key materials are not sufficient to realize all those expectations; hence, prices rise. Substitute materials must be found, such as coal, nuclear, and solar energy to replace petroleum in the United States. But coal especially presents pollution problems in particulate and sulfate emissions, as does nuclear energy in radiation. These pollutants mean significant health hazards or higher pollution abatement costs.

Similarly, the automobile-petroleum problem is only partially soluble by smaller cars and energy conservation. In the longer run, energy reductions of larger magnitude by changing living habits, higher urban densities, less travel, less energy, less pollution, less materials consumption will have to occur, even to maintain something near present health environments and cost structures.

These changes, too, will have political effects, particularly in our foreign relations. As the United States becomes more resource dependent, its diplomacy will have to become more multilateral and conciliatory. With its self-sufficiency slipping into dependency upon the rest of the world for half of its commodity needs, the United States will become more of a trading nation, such as Britain or Japan, in which the trade balance on current account can send shock waves of price changes and unemployment through the economy. The price and monetary sensitivity of the U.S. economy will be greater than it has been in our more self-sufficient and isolation days. That is to say, in summary, that the trade-offs from environmental impacts will be structural and profound today and far into the future.

The idea that the troubles of the 1970's—in the form of inflation, shortages, and environmental deterioration—are a temporary aberration in the otherwise tranquil life of a bounteous nation is false, a nostalgia of yesterday's dreams. The troublous present presages the kind of future which the United States may expect; and the message is that industry and personal life-styles are just beginning profound structural changes.

Comparison and Trade-Off Data

ATTRIBUTABLE TO SOCIO-ECONOMY		ATTRIBUTABLE TO ENVIRONMENTAL REGULATION	
1. Unemployment	9.5%		0.05 to 1%
2. Inflation (1975–1st qtr.)	14.4%		
Monetary Expansion	9.5%		
Oil & Food Shortages	4.5%	Environmental Costs	0.50%
3. Capital Investment by Industry, 1974		Pollution Effects	
	$ Millions		*% Change*
Metal Mfg.	$ 482	*Water* (1963–72)	(Period)
Electrical	46	Suspended solids	−12
Machinery	42	Nitrates	+12
Auto & transp	29	Phosphates	+11
Stone & glass	58	Chlorides	−3
Other durables	73	Dissolved oxygen	0
Food	67	Total coliforms	−11
Textile	7	Fecal coliforms	+26
Paper	31	*Air* (1960–70)	
Chemical	188	Particulates:	(Per Year)
Petroleum	239	Industry	+ 1.1
Rubber	8	Combustion	−1.1
Other non-durables	5	SO_2	
Mining	28	Industrial	+3.0
Transportation	9	Combustion	+4.2
Utilities	307	Automobile (1965–73)	(Period)
Trade	80	Hydrocarbons	−30
Total	$1,699	Nitrogen oxides	+13

Comparison and Trade-Off Data—*Continued*

ATTRIBUTABLE TO SOCIO-ECONOMY		ATTRIBUTABLE TO ENVIRONMENTAL REGULATION	
4. Incremental Costs of Pollution Abatement (1973–1982)		Pollution Effects	
	$ Billions		*% Change*
Air pollution		*Air*	
Auto	74	Particulates	−60
Stationary	59	Sulfur oxides	−40
Water		Nitrogen oxides	−10
Government	24	Hydrocarbons	−20
Industry	27	Carbon monoxide	−20
Solid waste	5	*Water*	
Surface mining	5	Suspended solids	−80
Total	$194	BOD	−70
0.7% to 1.0% of GNP		Dissolved solids	−20
		Nutrients	−10
5. Health Effects of Air Pollution		Air Pollution (Particulates & SO_2)	−50%
Death rate	−7%		
Death rate reduction in:			
Fetal deaths			
Infant mortality			
Adults			
Cancer			
Tuberculosis			
Cardiovascular			
6. Fluorine Case:		Pollution Effect	
Industry Cost	*$ Millions*		*% Efficiency*
Stack gas equip.	6.7	Remove fluorine gas	90–95%
" " "	16.0	Remove fluorine gas	99%
Land cost	25.0	Purchase 200,000 acres to avoid damage	

7. Energy Budgets (1971–1978)			Pollution effects at high growth and high abatement	
	% Increase			
	Low	*High*		*% Increase*
Annual GNP growth	2%	4%	Particulates	90
Energy sources:			SO_2	70
Petroleum	0%	30%	Hydrocarbons	100
Natural gas	2%	2%	Carbon monoxide	105
Coal	50%	50%	Water pollution	120
Hydro & nuclear	100%	100%	Land utilization	110

Comparison and Trade-Off Data—*Continued*

ATTRIBUTABLE TO SOCIO-ECONOMY			ATTRIBUTABLE TO ENVIRONMENTAL REGULATION	
8. Land Use—Housing Densities Private and Public Investment			Pollution Effects	
	Density		High density as ratio to low	
	Low	*High*		*% Reduction*
Acres per unit	0.6	0.3	Air pollution	−45%
Investment (per unit)			Water pollution	−50%
Private	$40,000	$25,000	Energy	−40%
Public	8,000	5,000	Auto mileage	−40%
Total	$48,000	$30,000	Water use	−30%
% difference		−44%		
Operating cost:				
Private	$1,000	$ 800		
Public	1,200	1,000		
	$2,200	$1,800		
% difference		−18%		
9. Mineral Requirements (1971–2000) Ratio of Recoverable Resources to Demand			Recycled from Scrap % of U.S. Consumption	
	U.S.	WORLD	%	
Copper	0.9	0.9	20%	
Lead	0.5	0.4	35%	
Zinc	0.5	0.5	5%	
Tin	0.0	0.5	15%	
Natural gas	0.3	0.4	—	
Petroleum	0.1	0.6	—	
Aluminum	—	2.4	10%	
Chromium	0.0	1.4	15%	
Iron	0.7	4.9	NA	
Nickel	0.0	1.8	30%	

Data Source: Council on Environmental Quality, Fifth Annual Report, December, 1974, Superintendent of Documents, Washington, D.C.

QUESTIONS

1. How do you assess Edmunds' approach? In his trade-off analysis the correct approach to environmental controls?
2. Explain each one of Edmunds' trade-offs, considering others you wish to add.
3. How should we come to a decision about environmental controls when it appears that agreement cannot be reached by objective evaluators of the cost-benefit analysis?

4. Can you think of any changes in American life that will come about from pollution abatement that are not mentioned by Edmunds? Speculate on some styles of living that might be encouraged to prevent pollution.
5. If pollution abatement does not cost many jobs, why have American workers and labor unions not endorsed and pushed antipollution programs to a greater extent? Do recent coalitions of auto workers and manufacturers in lobbying efforts to avoid taxes on big automobiles show that the industry does not share Edmunds' assumptions?
6. In light of Edmunds' analysis of the impact of pollution abatement programs, would you favor or oppose slowing down economic growth in the near future?

DON'T CONFUSE US WITH FACTS

FORBES

Forbes magazine in the following article examines a number of arguments made by antinuclear power propagandists and finds that they ignore facts. The article also points out that reputable scientists can come to opposite positions on nuclear energy.

The Bell nuclear power plant proposed for Cayuga Lake in western New York was killed by the complaint that it would heat the nearby water by several degrees. William Brown, an industrial arts teacher in a local high school, likes to fish there. The controversy left him dead set against nuclear power.

In Wisconsin dairy country, Naomi Jacobson, a bookkeeper turned housewife, suspects that radioactive emissions from Wisconsin Electric's Point Beach plant are falling on grazing land and getting into the milk.

James Duree, a crusading Westport, Wash. lawyer, circulates cartoons of deformed children, slyly suggesting nuclear power is to blame.

In San Francisco, people worry that "crazies" (like the Symbionese Liberation Army) might use nuclear materials to terrorize society.

In the Pacific Northwest, Douglas Still, a Presbyterian minister, battles nuclear power on the grounds that it would encourage our society to continue its sinfully wasteful ways.

On such personal—and not infrequently irrational—grounds do many individual Americans fight nuclear power. For those who want to be part of an *organization,* Ralph Nader leads a loose-knit antinuclear movement. It's a strange crusade, uniting rightwingers and leftwingers, ecologists and rugged individualists in a bedfellowship as strange as existed in the heyday of the Prohibition movement just after World War I.

Despite a recent Harris poll showing that only 19% of the American people opposed the building of more nuclear power plants (63% were in favor, 18% "not sure"), the antinuclear coalition has been remarkably successful. It has certainly slowed the expansion of nuclear power.

But have the antinuclear people truly thought through the consequences of their actions? Consider the following facts:

In the next ten years, even with zero population growth, the number of U.S. households will increase 34% and the size of the labor force will rise 25%—this because of the big bulge in the birthrate during the Fifties. Whence will come the energy to power the homes and the jobs for these people? Not only will electricity have to supply the new capacity, it will also

Reprinted by permission of *Forbes* Magazine from the September 1, 1975 issue, pp. 20–34.

have to replace a part of the fast-dwindling supply of natural gas. Even adoption of the most stringent energy conservation can only delay briefly, not avert, the looming energy shortage.

It takes five to ten years to start a new generating plant and get it working. Thus there is very little time to get started on the nearly 50% expansion in the supply of electricity that the U.S. will need by 1985 (this year's rate of expansion is only 2.7%).

This kind of expansion is impossible without considerable new nuclear capacity. Additional oil-burning plants are out of the question; the U.S.' dependence on the Organization of Petroleum Exporting Countries is already frightening. Coal, while plentiful, cannot fill the whole gap. Not enough miners or transport is available to quadruple coal output in 1985—which is what it would take. (Besides, the people of Wyoming would not take kindly to reducing their state to a puddle.)

Although Nader and his allies do not like it, the fact is that organized labor leans toward the development of nuclear energy. Labor men see red when fanatical environmentalists say that a no-growth society is preferable to the risks of nuclear power. To labor, "no growth" means "no jobs." In Los Angeles, Sigmund Arywitz, an AFL-CIO County Federation of Labor head, puts labor's case bluntly: "The antinuclear people are the middle class, and if they had their way, we'd all go hungry."

But can so many people from so many walks of life be wrong about the dangers of nuclear power? FORBES' Jean Briggs has spent weeks criss-crossing the U.S., talking with both enemies and proponents of nuclear power generation. After carefully weighing the evidence and considering the motives of both sides, FORBES has concluded that the opponents are wrong. Most of their legitimate objections have been met or are on their way to resolution. Only lurid imagination can deform the children in Jim Duree's cartoons, not nuclear reactors. And as for the dangers of potential terrorists, they have far easier targets available to them than nuclear power plants.

A nuclear explosion? A big bang that would obliterate an entire city? Forget it. In a nuclear reactor, it takes the most concentrated effort to keep the reaction going. There is no way for a nuclear power plant to produce the dreaded mushroom cloud.

Why then the bitter opposition? It is sad but true that nuclear power has an aura of bad magic about it—and most people are more superstitious than they care to admit. Inside the reactor, atoms are being split and energy released and, in the process, highly radioactive and deadly materials are created. Somebody is tinkering with God's universe.

And it is all so new. As recently as 1965 there were only six nuclear power plants operating in the U.S. *vs.* 56 now. That people should fear something so new and so potentially dangerous is not at all surprising. After all, many people are still afraid to fly, 72 years after the Wright brothers made their demonstration and a full quarter-century after airplanes became the dominant mode of long-distance passenger travel. In New York City in the 1890s, the press charged "murder" when alternating current replaced direct current. Even Thomas A. Edison supported the charges. Opponents electrocuted animals in an effort to support their case.

Given its genesis in a mushroom cloud of destruction, given the hush-hush, father-knows-best attitude of its early sponsors, it is not surprising that nuclear power has become a prime target for antiestablishment movements. "We were our own worst enemies," says Dr. Norman Hilberry, former director of Argonne National Laboratory. But many of the opponents are very selective about their facts and quite cynical. Consider Ed Koupal of California, who is helping Ralph Nader organize the antinuclear fight in 16 western states. Antinuclear slogans, Koupal says, are excellent for getting otherwise uncommitted people turned on to consumerist and environmental causes.

The simple fact is that nuclear power has had a remarkable safety record, far better than that of the railroad in its early days or the airplane or even of coal generation of electricity. No member of the general public has been killed or even hurt by nuclear reactors. There have been mishaps and near-accidents, of course. But any engineer expects this from a new technology. The nuclear bugs have been carefully controlled and remarkably nonlethal.

The U.S. has never had an accidental release in significant amounts of radioactive substances into the air. It did happen in Britain in 1957, but what followed is, if anything, reassuring. Radiation levels did not become excessive. Britain's Atomic Energy Administration has closely studied the people in the area, and to date has detected not the slightest increase in cancer.

Aware that they were dealing with cosmic forces, not mere mechanics, the nuclear energy people have acted responsibly. "These machines aren't toys," says Dr. Hans Bethe, Cornell University's Nobel prize-winning physicist and a proponent of nuclear power. Adds Dr. Dixy Lee Ray, former head of the Atomic Energy Commission, "And the reactor industry people know this." The manufacturers have, however reluctantly, added safety features on top of safety features to meet the demands of critics.

Take the issue of thermal pollution. A nuclear power station creates more energy than it converts into electricity. The excess heat is dissipated into water from the stream, lake or ocean where the plant is located. This used to raise nearby water temperatures by about 20 degrees. Though some fish seemed to like the warmer water, others did not. Certainly some fish were killed, though not many.

Since 1972, however, nuclear plants (as well as other industrial plants) have had to meet federal thermal pollution standards. The standards depend on the body of water, but essentially, nearby water must be heated no more than a few degrees. The neighborhood fish seem happy.

But the issue is still being used against nuclear power. A group called

Another Mother for Peace, having lost its original cause with the end of the Vietnam war, has joined the antinuclear "crusade"; its brochure still complains about thermal pollution.

How about radiation, that deadly peril? How much of it leaks into the air and water from a nuclear plant? The answer today is a minuscule amount, a tiny fraction of the normal background radiation in which we all live. Here, too, the developers of nuclear energy have gone a long way toward defusing the arguments of their detractors. As recently as 1970, the permissible radiation was 500 millirems per year at the plant fence, five times the average background radiation but well below levels where scientists have been able to detect any effect. But since 1970 federal regulations have cut that level by 99%, requiring that the radiation released be as low as technically and economically feasible—in most cases, five millirems per year or less at the plant fence. The 56 U.S. plants now meet this tough standard.

The opponents of nuclear power blithely ignore such facts. In Wisconsin, for example, a group called LAND (League Against Nuclear Dangers) claims Wisconsin Electric is leaking radiation from its Point Beach plant, and that the radiation passes into the grass the cows eat and thence into their milk. However, the evidence LAND cites tends, in fact, to prove the opposite. The former Atomic Energy Commission reprimanded the utility for not checking out an unusually high, but still safe, reading found in one milk sample. That sample was taken in 1972; its levels have never again been found, though the milk is regularly monitored. It is quite likely that the checking equipment itself was faulty in that long-ago worrisome sample.

The days are long gone when people trusted their government implicitly. If nothing else did, Vietnam ended that. So, it is not surprising that the general public became suspicious of anything shrouded in official mystery and stamped "secret" the way nuclear matters were. There's no question but that the old Atomic Energy Commission (1946–75) hurt its own cause with its secretive, arrogant attitude. The AEC took the general attitude that laymen should leave nuclear matters to the priestly caste. People easily became convinced that the AEC was hiding something. What odd sacrifices were going on in that closely guarded temple?

The old AEC is dead, its responsibilities parceled out to the Nuclear Regulatory Commission and the Energy Research & Development Administration. Nuclear energy is no longer a private preserve of the nuclearists, but is now officially viewed in the total energy context. The damage, however, has been done.

PRODUCING A ZEALOT

Take the sad case of Dr. Henry Kendall, an articulate, learned Massachusetts Institute of Technology high-energy physicist. In 1971 Kendall became convinced there was an essential nuclear safety weakness.

As water circulates in the core of most nuclear reactors, it carries away the heat generated by the fissioning uranium. If the cooling pipes should ever break, the radioactive material decaying inside would get so hot it would melt the core. Were this to happen, the core could sink right into the earth and pollute both air and subsurface water with radioactivity.

Dr. Kendall was so convinced that the backup cooling system was inadequate that he took his case to the AEC. The AEC, in effect, told him to go jump in the lake. Largely at Kendall's insistence, however, hearings were held. They lasted two years and produced over 20,000 pages of testimony. As a result, the backup systems were greatly improved. Dr. Ian Forbes, head of nuclear engineering at Massachusett's Lowell Technological Institute, who had originally sided with Kendall, says he now is satisfied that the new system is safe.

Kendall, however, was so soured by the whole situation that he has become a propagandist against nuclear development. (It was Kendall, in fact, who got Ralph Nader interested in the subject.) Kendall still insists the cooling system backup is inadequate. Complains he, "They made some minor changes but they were basically cosmetic." No one doubts Kendall's sincerity, but his antinuclear argument now has little support among other nuclear scientists. The improved cooling system's reliability has been studied by a group of 60 scientists headed by Dr. Norman Rasmussen, head of the nuclear engineering department of MIT. The Rasmussen report concludes that the probability of all systems failing at the same time with a resulting catastrophic accident is remote indeed—perhaps like the chance of a severe earthquake occurring during a major volcanic eruption in the midst of a hurricane.

Since the Rasmussen study, the antinuclear people have been talking less about reactor safety and more about the fuel cycle. They have jumped on the question of civic safety and extended it to civil rights in connection with spent nuclear core rods. The spent fuel rods eventually have to be sent to special facilities for reprocessing in order to extract remaining usable fuel, including plutonium, one of the deadliest substances known, and to separate the wastes. What if there should be an accident in transporting the spent rods? How can the rods be guarded against terrorists?

The man who raised the terrorism issue is Dr. Theodore Taylor, the celebrated physicist who designed atomic bombs at Los Alamos. Since he raised the issue, the antinuclear propagandists have made a red herring of it: The necessary safety precautions, they charge, would mean a loss of civil liberties. (So does frisking at airports, but the civil libertarians accept that.) Dr. Taylor himself now believes the issue can be resolved economically and without mass violations of civil liberties.

Dr. Dixy Lee Ray makes a telling point in this regard: Terrorists who come in contact with fuel cores would face quick and certain death.

What about those lethal nuclear wastes? After fuel rods are reprocessed, some wastes will stay radioactive for 250,000 to 500,000 years. What can be done with such materials? Critics claim this is a moral issue: We ought not bequeath these "hot" wastes to future generations. This is a problem, certainly, but is it worse than our profligate burning of fossil fuels? Which is more harmful to posterity: leaving them with a problem capable of solution? Or leaving an earth bereft of coal and of oil?

Conventional proposals for disposing of the wastes involve solidifying it and burying it in geologically stable formations deep within the earth or perhaps in retrievable form in an underground cavern. Since the waste from a large (1,000 megawatt) reactor each year could be stored in a 4-foot cube, such proposals certainly aren't impossible.

But there are other possibilities. Ex-Argonne Director Norman Hilberry says the thing to do is find a use for them—making them profitable. Dr. Theodore Taylor suggests, as ex-AEC head James Schlesinger did before him, that if all else fails, we can always send them off in a rocket aimed at the sun. Farfetched? It may sound that way, but both Taylor and Schlesinger were speaking from knowledge.

When their safety arguments are demolished, the antinuclearists tend to retreat to an economic argument. They claim that existing nuclear plants aren't running at anything like their full capacity. David Comey, a Sovietologist turned professional environmentalist, makes much of this argument. He has tried to persuade investment bankers to avoid nuclear development as a bad risk. ("No bucks, no nukes," he chortles.) But what are the *facts?* Nuclear power plants have operated well below capacity. Because of technical and regulatory problems they have produced an average of 57% of what they were designed to produce—but even that unexpectedly low figure was somewhat better than the performance of the average large fossil-fuel plant. At current operating rates, U.S. nuclear plants in 1974 saved an estimated $800 million as compared with fossil-fuel plants of equivalent output. In the first quarter of 1975 in Philadelphia, they saved customers $17 million. In New York $24 million.

True, a nuclear plant costs more to build than either an oil- or coal-fired plant, currently $120 more per kw of capacity as opposed to coal. But the cost of nuclear fuel is so much less than either oil or coal that over the life of the plant the cost advantage is clearly nuclear's.

At Northeast Utilities, for example, the total cost—including capital cost—of a kilowatt hour produced by the company's nuclear plants is 9.63 mills; a kwh produced by its oil-fired plants costs 30.80 mills. At Wisconsin Electric, a nuclear-generated kwh costs 9.32 mills, while a coal-generated one costs 15.95. The story is much the same across the country.

COSTLY FUEL?

But what of the economic future? With the price of uranium going straight up, won't nuclear lose this advantage? Wallace Behnke, executive vice president of Commonwealth Edison in Chicago, thinks not. "Nuclear's advantage over coal is likely to increase rather than decrease," he says. Coal is just beginning to run into some of the environmental problems and licensing delays that have traditionally beset nuclear. As this happens, the cost of building and supplying coal plants is likely to escalate rapidly. At the same time, Behnke says, with greater standardization and fewer licensing delays, nuclear's costs may well stabilize.

John Hill, deputy administrator of the Federal Energy Administration, supports this view: "Taking into consideration the probable increase in uranium prices, increasing costs of uranium enrichment, the costs of reprocessing and of safeguards, it's still unlikely that nuclear power will lose its advantages."

The argument that inflation, with its huge impact on construction and capital costs, will hurt nuclear more than fossil-fuel plants does not wash. The same factors that drive up the capital costs of nuclear power plants will push up the costs of getting coal out of the ground and will impact what OPEC charges for its oil.

There remains, of course, the danger of a global uranium cartel (FORBES, *Jan. 15*). But it is questionable whether this could ever be as effective as OPEC. Uranium represents just 17% of the overall cost of nuclear power generation, as opposed to 65% for oil in oil-fired plants.

Confronted with these facts and figures, the opponents of nuclear power have one more fallback position. Nuclear power, they claim, is subsidized. It could not operate without the federal insurance provided under the Price-Anderson Act.

The argument sounds good, but is a distortion. The Federal Government had to step in because private companies are limited by their assets in the amount of insurance they can provide. So the Government wrote the insurance both to encourage the industry and to protect the public.

The truth is, however, that insurance companies *do* provide a steadily increasing percentage of the total. Maximum coverage on a single accident is $560 million. Of this, private companies now provide $125 million, up from $60 million maximum in 1957. Recently they cut their premiums 20% because of the industry's safety record. "There's no reason now," says the Lowell Institute's Ian Forbes, "that the industry can't insure itself."

DIRTY TRICKS

In California, where the art of the political dirty trick has been developed to a high degree, the antinuclear crusaders have hit upon a clever ploy. They recently qualified for the ballot an initiative that would prohibit use of California land for nuclear sites unless every individual were fully indemnified for the worst conceivable accident. If this insurance protection was not forthcoming within a year of passage of the law, no new plants could be built, and old plants would have to be derated and ultimately phased out. The initiative comes to a vote next June.

Richard Spohn, who has worked with Ralph Nader for more than five years and who was recently appointed to head the California Consumer Services Division, brags: "We did studies to determine the best way to get signatures for a petition, and then we used that technique." Politically shrewd, but it is honest?

A more recent issue is the so-called spread of nuclear weapons via nuclear reactors. The assumption underlying the argument is that the U.S. can somehow prevent other nations from having both reactors and bombs. Which, of course, is not the case. The recent sale of reactors to Brazil by West Germany is an example of that. Another example is South Africa, which has devised its own reactor, as well as its own uranium enrichment process. And, of course, India. It is difficult to see how a U.S. decision to renounce use of nuclear power would be binding on other countries, many of whom need it far more desperately than we do.

A final argument trotted out by some antinuclear people says that present nuclear plants involve an interim technology. Convinced that the breeder reactor is dying of its own technical problems, they now say we should wait for the fusion reactor. Or wind power. Or solar generation. But they know full well that large-scale use of those alternative technologies is decades away, while the electricity shortage is only a few years ahead and the oil crisis is right now.

SEEING THINGS WHOLE

Too many people have fallen into a habit of seeing issues in isolation. They oppose nuclear power, for example, because it is not a perfect answer to the energy problem. They demand, in another area, that pollution controls be carried to almost impossible lengths. They want auto safety and environmental controls with no consideration of the costs in jobs and living standards. They see life in small segments. They talk of energy conservation without, in most cases, showing any willingness to give up any of the privileges and pleasures that modern society offers. They assume, somehow, that people in other countries will willingly forego a better life so that Americans can have both a high standard of living and an ideal environment.

In a sense, this is a betrayal of the very idea of ecology, which is supposed to be concerned with the interrelationship of organisms and their environment. Hungry Indians and jobless Americans are part of this overall system, and their rights must be considered along with clean air and nuclear dangers, real and imagined. The emotional and frequently unreasonable opposition to nuclear-power generation is a prime example of one-sided environmentalism, of a failure to see things whole.

As we said at the beginning, there is also a cynical side to the antinuclear argument. It is best illustrated by the true story of a group of wealthy Bakersfield, Calif. farmers who own big ranches. Several utilities, including Southern California Edison, Pacific Gas & Electric and the Los Angeles Department of Water & Power, are proposing to build a nuclear plant in their neighborhood. It is not lost on the farmers that the plant might hurt their land values. So they are thinking of hiring a lawyer who specializes in environmental causes and fighting the plant on the grounds that "crazies" might blow it up. That is what is known as being crazy like a fox. But what does it have to do with the benefits of nuclear power to the nation as a whole?

QUESTIONS

1. Assuming that the position in this article on the safety of nuclear energy is correct, what factors account for significant and continued resistance to nuclear power in the public and in the scientific community?
2. In our contemporary, pluralistic society is it possible to be objective about the merits of radically new technologies? Is a rational-scientific approach to solving social problems and soothing the public mood likely to be effective?
3. Even if nuclear power plants are not fully safe, should society be willing to accept some risk in order to get the energy it needs for future economic growth and to maintain the quality of life in urban areas? What would be an acceptable level of risk?
4. Assume for purposes of argument that a fifteen-year moratorium is called on the construction of all nuclear power plants. What do you see as the major consequences of such a move on the quality of life, economic prosperity, poverty, inflation, unemployment, and improving the position of minorities in society?

THE ENERGY PROBLEM: WHAT SHOULD BE THE GOVERNMENT'S POLICY TOWARD BUSINESS?

JOHN C. SAWHILL

John C. Sawhill, formerly the Federal Energy Administrator and now president of New York University, briefly describes the nature of our "energy crisis" and what we should do about it.

With the Congress now out of session, those of us concerned with energy policy are now in a position to step back and review the accomplishments and disappointments of the first half of 1975 and think through some of the alternatives available. Your conference on *The Changing Business Role in Society* is a good place to begin this dialog.

Almost two years have passed since the Arab Oil Embargo began; yet the nation is no closer to a coherent effective energy policy than it was at the beginning of 1974. President Ford presented one proposal to the Congress in January, but unfortunately his proposal would have been so damaging to our already weakened economy that it was unacceptable. Congress, on the other hand, has done little more than debate the issue. Except for the strip-mining bill and the bill opening up the naval petroleum reserves to production, no major piece of energy legislation has moved through the Congress. All we have heard are charges and counter-charges and an endless parade of testimony—much of it repeating arguments that were made almost two years ago.

Some have suggested that the current situation is not wholly undesirable. The argument is that the economy is recovering more rapidly than if we had adopted the excise tax proposals of the President and that energy development is proceeding more rapidly than if some of the proposals considered by the Congress were enacted. Thus, the argument runs, we are better off without either executive or legislative action.

I reject this argument. I believe that we have a serious energy problem in the United States and that the government must take the necessary steps to solve it. In the few minutes that I have with you this morning, I would like to discuss the energy situation by first reviewing the current energy situation and outlining some perspectives on our energy problem. Then, I will discuss some areas where government involvement is essential and finally, I will

John C. Sawhill, "The Energy Problem: What Should Be the Government's Policy Toward Business?" *The Changing Business Role in Society*, George A. Steiner (ed.), Los Angeles, California: Graduate School of Management, UCLA, 1976. Reprinted by permission.

conclude by giving you some observations on my experiences in Washington and what all of us can do to make government more responsive to the will of the people.

First, let me review briefly the current energy situation. As most of you know, energy consumption has been growing at four and one-half percent per year since the middle 1960's or about fifty percent more rapidly than the growth in domestic energy supply. As a matter of fact, the supply situation has been relatively stagnant. Oil production topped out in 1970; natural gas production is now beginning to fall off; we mined more coal in 1920 than we did in 1970; and nuclear power plant schedules are being curtailed with increasing regularity.

United States Petroleum Demand and Imports

YEAR	1970	1973 (Before Embargo)	1975 (At Recession Low)	1976 (March)
Demand: Barrels Per Day (millions)	14.7	16.7	16.0	17.7
Imports: Barrels Per Day (millions)	3.4	6.4	5.0	7.7
Percent Imports to Total	23	38	31	44
Import Percentage Supplied by Arab States	6	16	25	30

Sources: *U.S. News & World Reports,* April 5, 1976, pp. 36–37; and United States Bureau of Mines, and American Petroleum Institute data.

As a result of these trends, petroleum imports have been growing rapidly. Unfortunately, in the post-embargo period, these imports are becoming more and more concentrated in the Middle East and Africa, and it is this situation which has created the "energy crisis." It is not a crisis of supply, but a crisis brought on by our increasing dependence on unstable political regimes for a vitally important natural resource.

There are a number of reasons why we must take steps to reduce our dependence. The first is economic. As we become more and more dependent on foreign sources for energy supply, we become increasingly vulnerable to price increases and thus subject our economy to manipulation by outside forces. Perhaps the best illustration of the impact of rising energy prices on the American economy is that the oil price increase which we experienced in 1973 and 1974 contributed at least one-third to our high rate of inflation during those years.

The higher prices also created a deficit in our balance of payments.

America's bill for imported oil was $8 billion in 1973, and increased to almost $25 billion in 1974. While currently the balance of payments accounts are generating surpluses, the increased usage of petroleum which will inevitably accompany economic recovery coupled with the prospect of higher OPEC prices in the fall could change the picture dramatically.

There are also national security arguments for reduced vulnerability. The United States cannot remain the economic and moral leader of the free world if we continue to become evermore dependent on insecure foreign sources for our petroleum.

Before discussing the solution to the energy problem, I would like to share with you some perspectives on energy policy. In this way, perhaps, we can agree on some of the constraints that have made it so difficult to move forward over the past eighteen months.

The first constraint is the current condition of our economy. We are still in the midst of a very serious economic recession, and while there are some signs that recovery is underway, unemployment remains high, corporate profits are depressed, housing starts and automobile sales are well below our earlier levels, and industry production has only begun to inch up. Faced with this economic situation, it is very difficult to take drastic steps to expand energy supply or curtail consumption.

At the Federal Energy Administration we conducted an in-depth study of the affect of price changes on energy supply and demand. The conclusion of our study was that an $8 per barrel price for petroleum would result in imports of about 12 million barrels per day by 1985 or about fifty percent of domestic demand. On the other hand, if the price were $12.50 per barrel, imports would fall to about 3.3 million barrels per day or less than fifteen percent of domestic demand. The problem is that the higher price—which would do much to solve our existing energy problem—would slow down the rate of economic growth. Thus, we are presented with a dilemma. We cannot move rapidly to reduce petroleum imports by raising prices unless we are willing to sacrifice economic growth, and at a time when our economy is only in the early stages of a recovery, it is very difficult to take any action which will retard this recovery. These contradictory policy objectives—reducing energy vulnerability and accelerating economic recovery—have made it extremely difficult for Congress and the Administration to resolve the question of petroleum price controls. The Congress has opted for economic recovery and the Administration for reducing energy imports.

The second perspective which is important to an understanding of the energy situation is the difficulty of expanding energy supplies in the short-run. It takes three years to develop an oil field after it is found, four or five years to open a new deep coal mine, five to build a new refinery, nine to ten years to build a nuclear plant. And these time lags are only one of the obstacles on the path toward energy self-sufficiency.

There are important environmental issues remaining to be resolved. I have recently been in touch with the governors of the Rocky Mountain States and my impression is that they remain committed to orderly development of energy resources. But, they oppose development which significantly alters the ecological balance in an area. I heard this same sentiment expressed throughout the country last summer when I conducted hearings on Project Independence. There are many Americans—and I regard myself as one of them—who regard our environmental legacy to the next generation as every bit as important as our legacy of economic growth.

A third perspective which I would like to leave with you is the difficulty of obtaining energy conservation through allocation and rationing programs. In early 1974, the Federal Energy Administration tried to fashion an equitable allocation of petroleum supplies to different segments in the economy with the help of a staff of almost four thousand people located in Washington and in ten regional offices around the country. In retrospect, I must admit we did a very poor job. It is very difficult if not impossible for bureaucrats to replace the market mechanism and make the thousands of decisions which are made daily in the marketplace. There is just no way for government officials to determine how much we should allocate to different industries and how much to reserve for consumers. I believe that a program which is predicated on an allocation or rationing scheme is doomed to failure.

The final perspective which I would like to discuss with you is a major structural change that has taken place in the oil industry in recent years. That change involves a shift in power from the giant international oil companies to the governments of producer countries. Where once the oil giants controlled oil prices and the oil distribution system, today that control is in the hands of the major producing countries. As the statements earlier this year by the Shah of Iran and other OPEC leaders indicate, the companies have lost the bargaining position they once held and are now forced to accept terms dictated by producer governments. As a result, a vacuum has been created, and the governments of the consuming countries are moving, of necessity, to fill this vacuum by entering into negotiations for oil supplies.

Much of the recent energy news coming out of Washington has focused on the question of how to get the government more involved in international oil. Earlier this year, the House of Representatives considered and rejected a proposal to create a Federal Petroleum Purchasing Agency, and Senator Frank Church of Idaho has introduced legislation calling for an Oil Import Administration. The intent of both bills is to put the U.S. government into a better position to negotiate oil prices and supplies with the producing nations. While it is unlikely that Congress will take any action on this matter in 1975, it is clear that government-industry relationships will change over time. For, as one oil man recently stated, the cost and availability of energy are too heavily affected by public interest to be left in the hands of an international cartel (OPEC) and an oil industry which no longer commands an effective position at the bargaining table.

Given these perspectives, I would now like to turn to a discussion of the areas where I think the government must become involved if the United

States is to reverse current trends and become less dependent upon foreign sources for its petroleum supply. The first important area for government involvement is in the regulation of energy prices. There has been a great deal of talk recently about the need to return to a free market. Unfortunately, this is impossible. We simply do not have a free market for petroleum. Oil prices today and in the foreseeable future will be set by the OPEC cartel, and—because oil is such an important energy source—the level of oil prices will determine the prices for other fuels as well. Thus, unless we want the managers of the OPEC cartel to set energy prices in the United States, our government must continue to regulate oil and natural gas prices. Complete deregulation would make our economy even more vulnerable to the political vicissitudes of the Middle East. Few would argue with the proposition that we need domestic oil and natural gas prices which provide adequate incentives for new production and which are high enough to curtail waste and nonessential uses. But, when OPEC establishes a price of \$11 or \$13 or even \$15, does this mean that that price is necessarily at the right level to either encourage supply or curtail demand?

We should establish one agency in Washington with the responsibility for regulating energy prices and—in an emergency—allocating supply. This agency would combine the present functions of the FEA and the FPC as well as extending its jurisdiction to other energy sources. Such an agency should be set up as an independent regulatory commission in order to remove it from the political pressures of the executive branch. It should operate under broad guidelines from Congress to gradually move toward a single price for both oil and natural gas (except natural gas currently under long term contracts), to set natural gas prices at the BTU equivalent for petroleum, and to consider both cost and market conditions in establishing prices.

The second area where government involvement is necessary is in the leasing of federal lands. Here we must resolve issues concerning both coal and oil shale leases in the west and oil and gas leases on the outer continental shelf. The coal and oil shale leasing program should contain incentives for development. I do not feel that we should permit corporations to lease lands at very low rentals without some requirement that these lands be developed within a reasonable period of time. I also feel that we should enact a realistic strip mining bill (such as the one President Ford vetoed) before opening up additional western coal lands for leasing.

On the outer continental shelf, the government has an important responsibility to balance the conflicting interest of the industry and the public. We need to begin exploring the Atlantic outer continental shelf as rapidly as possible; yet, we must do this under careful government supervision to insure that the necessary environmental precautions are taken and that the public retains a fair and reasonable interest in any energy supply which may be found. The Department of the Interior is currently reviewing a variety of leasing procedures including various forms of royalty and net profit leases. It seems to me that the net profit lease under which the federal government retains a share of the profits of any oil or gas which is found holds great promise and should be pursued. Under this concept it might be desirable for the government to share in the heavy, front-end exploration expenses and thus reduce the enormous amount of private capital now required for off-shore drilling. Such an approach would allow some of the smaller companies that do not have access to the major capital markets to compete with the major companies for oil on the outer continental shelf.

A third area for government involvement is to protect the environment. There are external diseconomies associated with pollution and for this reason government intervention is necessary to protect public health and property. Where possible, we should rely on the market mechanism rather than regulations to provide the incentives for maintaining environmental standards. For example, I would prefer a sulfur tax to the current system of regulating sulfur emission from utilities and other stationary sources. I would apply the same principle to automobile emissions and to water pollution regulations. We also need to take steps to insure that the new communities which will inevitably accompany the development of energy resources in the Rocky Mountain States do not degrade the environment or neglect human, social needs. In this regard, I would advocate a federal program which provides some kind of front-end financing for the educational, sewer and water, and transportation facilities in these communities.

One other regulatory area where government involvement will be necessary is to resolve the issues surrounding nuclear energy. The Nuclear Regulatory Commission is off to a good start but a great deal remains to be done before the country has the confidence needed so that we can proceed with the development of nuclear facilities. At the present time, there are too many unanswered questions particularly in the areas of waste management and sabotage. We must do further work on the disposal of nuclear wastes and develop more effective methods of securing nuclear facilities against the threat of sabotage before we can create the national consensus needed to move forward with nuclear reactor development. At the same time, we need to address the proliferation question and consider establishing some type of international organization to control the movement of radioactive materials.

Up to this point I have not mentioned research and development but clearly that is an area where the government will have to play an important role. In spite of significant increases over the past few years the current federal research and development budget is still barely adequate and should be increased. I would like to see increases in a number of areas with significant promise of near-term payoff such as secondary and tertiary recovery methods, more efficient conversion of fossil fuels into electricity, commercial solar heating and cooling applications, land reclamation technology, geothermal, etc.

The development of facilities to convert coal into cleaner burning fuels also needs attention. Here, I believe, the most appropriate role for the government is to eliminate some of the risks associated with this new technology. Business has the requisite technical and managerial skills and therefore should take the technical risks; the government should reduce the risks associated with severe price fluctuations. Perhaps the best way for the government to do this would be to solicit bids for new synthetic fuel facilities. Companies would indicate their requirements in terms of the price necessary to guarantee an adequate return on investment. For example, the government might guarantee a minimum price of $12 per barrel for fifty thousand barrels of oil equivalent per year over a twenty year period beginning in 1982. The companies which were successful in winning government contracts would then be in a position to obtain financing based on the government guarantee. I believe that such a system is preferable to a joint venture between government and industry because it assigns the primary responsibility to industry, which has the technical and managerial skills to build and manage these facilities.

There is another area where it may be necessary for the government to become involved in providing capital resources for energy development—the electric utility industry. Some in this industry have argued that the government should create a Utility Finance Corporation which would be in a position to purchase preferred stock of utilities and thus provide them with the equity base needed to raise capital financing. Those who favor this type of arrangement have suggested that the UFC should gain agreement from state regulatory officials at the time equity securities were purchased that rates would be increased sufficiently to pay off the investment in a reasonable period of time. At this point, I would like to know more about how the UFC would work and whether, in fact, it is needed before I would be prepared to endorse such a measure.

I have not said anything about what the government should do to encourage energy conservation. It is clear that there are a number of steps which can be taken. The most direct is to permit energy prices to increase gradually so that both business and consumers will have the incentive to use energy more efficiently. As you know I have been a strong advocate of conservation because I feel that it is our only near-term alternative and I have argued that a moderate but gradually increasing tax on gasoline would be the best way to demonstrate our resolve to use energy more efficiently in the future than we have in the past. The tax could be used to finance research and development and to improve public transportation. Other steps which could be taken to encourage the efficient use of energy include the requirement of energy labeling for appliances and autos and energy efficiency standards for new buildings. Tax credits could provide a good way to encourage the retrofitting of existing buildings to make them more energy efficient.

Let me conclude by discussing a crisis which may be potentially more debilitating than the energy crisis, and that is the crisis of confidence. These days, in the wake of Watergate and Vietnam, people appear to have lost confidence in the institutions which traditionally hold society together and provide leadership in a crisis. It is this lack of confidence which makes it so difficult to get the American people to unite behind any policy. I believe that we must restore confidence in our system before any real progress can be made toward solving our energy problem or any of our other pressing national problems. And, to do this, we must somehow change the decision-making process in our giant government and business bureaucracies so that people perceive that their leaders are, in fact, becoming more—rather than less—responsive to their constituents.

Operationally, this means that government officials and corporation executives must increasingly subject their decision-making to public scrutiny and be prepared to defend themselves against adverse criticism of special interest groups. It also means that the basis for decision-making must transcend the narrow objectives of a particular government agency or business organization and be attuned to the larger national interest. As administrator of FEA, I was forced to operate in an open decision-making environment. I had no other choice, but I would have had it no other way. Although at times it was cumbersome and frustrating, the net result was to develop more confidence in what we were doing. As a result of this experience, I believe that all of government must move toward a greater degree of openness in its decision-making. It must reach out into the community and seek ways to involve more people with different points of view in the decision-making process. It must explain to the people how and why its decisions are made. And—because honesty is inherent in openness—it must do so with the utmost of candor.

This is as necessary today as at almost any time in our past because the ultimate solving of our energy problems will require the confidence and support of the American people.

I have enjoyed the opportunity I had to participate in developing America's energy policy—first as a member of the executive branch and now as a consultant to the Congress. I hope that I will have an opportunity to serve again in the future. Of course, there were times when the job was frustrating. But, in this regard, I concur with the former Secretary of Commerce, Peter Peterson. After leaving office, he said, "The experience was costly, but it was also priceless."

QUESTIONS

1. Why does Sawhill say there is an energy crisis?
2. Do a little library research, and get data on our past and future energy production and consumption, especially with respect to oil.
3. What are Sawhill's recommendations for managing our "energy problem"? Do you agree with him? Explain.
4. Role play the different major interests in dealing with our "energy problem" from the point of view of developing a national policy that is in the public interest. Major interests in the game are OPEC, the large oil companies, the President, the Congress, the environmentalists, the energy consumer, and the small oil companies.

11

BUSINESS AND CONSUMERS

CONSUMER DISCONTENT: A SOCIAL PERSPECTIVE

ZARREL V. LAMBERT AND FRED W. KNIFFIN

Zarrel V. Lambert, associate professor of marketing and director of the Master of Business Administration Program at the University of Florida, and Fred W. Kniffin, professor of marketing and director of the Master of Business Administration Program at the University of Connecticut at Stamford, present in this article fundamental underlying causes of consumer discontent.

Consider for a moment the strategy of the firefighters in the following vignette:

> For days firemen have battled a blaze in a large industrial complex. The fire is fueled by highly combustible chemicals flowing from ruptured pipelines connected to vast liquid storage facilities. While large quantities of foam have been sprayed on the blaze, the firemen have made no attempt to shut off the pipelines that feed the fire.

When responding to consumerism proposals, allegations, and moves to extend government regulation, businessmen must direct their efforts to the springheads of these issues, or risk making a strategic error similar to the one committed by the firemen. Many past reactions to consumerism seem more indicative of uncoordinated, disjointed actions than of well-planned, coordinated, and broad substantive programs of enduring value. It is unlikely that a lasting amelioration of consumer discontent can be achieved by focusing on the fulgurant symptoms that happen to dominate attention at a given moment. Unless the basic causes that fuel consumer discontent are dealt with successfully, relief is transitory and discontent bursts forth later in the form of new symptomatic issues and complaints.

A topology that helps identify basic sources of discontent would be a valuable aid to businessmen in developing and directing affirmative actions to mitigate the problems of consumerism. In addition, it would serve to classify consumer issues, in terms of underlying causes, into groups that could be dealt with as sets rather than as separate issues, thereby enhancing the efficiency of business efforts in this area.

Such a topology exists in sociological literature under the rubric of alienation. Alienation has been a prevalent idea in sociology and related disciplines for many years. It has been the main theme in studies of political apathy, maladjustment in work, negative voting patterns, and various forms of anti-social behavior, and it is called "the central problem of our time" by some. Thus, it should not be surprising to find alienation among consumers.

The concept of alienation provides important insights into the propelling forces behind consumerism. As such it holds considerable promise for assisting businessmen in employing a strategy of positive action rather than reaction. It offers some principles for businessmen to follow in going on the offensive, in launching effective programs to deter major consumer issues from arising instead of assuming a defensive stance of reacting to issues after they have captured public and government attention, and simply trying to counter publicized accusations of vociferous consumerists.

PROS AND CONS

In discussing alienation in the consumer realm, one premise is that businessmen believe affirmative steps need to be taken to lessen consumer discontent. Needless to say, such a conviction is not universal within the business community.

Some businessmen seem to favor a negative approach, which includes such common tactics as attacks on consumerism proposals, attempts to discredit proponents, and efforts to block or water down legislative and regulatory initiatives. This approach apparently presupposes that consumer measures lack a lasting and substantial constituency among the electorate and that discontent has been incited largely by self-appointed consumer spokesmen for their own purposes. Businessmen who hold this view may feel that all they need to do is resist these pressures until the proponents tire and shift their attention to other *causes célèbres*.

Another similar notion assumes that consumerism is a faddish aspect of the more general social turmoil of the last ten years and consequently will fade from the scene. According to this notion, business has to do no more than simply bide its time. Some argue that consumerism is already waning. They point to a slowdown in the introduction of new consumer bills in Congress, the philosophies of some new appointees to federal regulatory agencies, and public preoccupation with the energy shortage and domestic economic and political woes.

On the contrary, however, there is evidence that negative approaches and inattention to consumer discontent may be shortsighted and counterproductive to business interests beyond the short run. For example, several surveys have yielded similar, alarming findings: over half of the people questioned have limited or little confidence in business, particularly large organizations. Such widespread disillusionment seems a fertile spawning ground for antibusiness sentiments and for rallying calls that are far more revolutionary than anything yet advanced by the consumer movement. Irving Kristol recently concluded that "the American corporation is in serious trouble . . ." unless the trust of the American people is regained.

Relying on a decline in consumer vociferousness as a signal of rising apathy could be dangerous. Before counting heavily on consumer apathy, perhaps one should note an observation by John Gardner of Common Cause:

> We find that the American people are not really apathetic. They just don't know how to find the targets, and if you help them find the targets, they are ready to go.

Two studies in past months show high consumer support for increasing government regulation over marketing practices. In one, 87 percent of the proposed new regulations, fourteen of sixteen, were strongly favored by a majority of those questioned.

Although fervor within government at the moment may be less than some consumerists would like, government is far from inactive in consumer-oriented matters. To cite a few of many possible examples, the FDA is requiring new information on product labels and is proposing warning labels for cosmetic products judged to have been inadequately tested. DOT is approaching the grade labeling of tires. A recently passed Senate bill extends the powers of the FTC and sets warranty standards. And who knows how aggressively the new Consumer Product Safety Commission will exercise its extensive powers in the future?

Furthermore, state and local agencies cannot be written off as dormant. For instance, the "toughest consumer protection law in the country," according to the state's attorney general, was recently enacted by Florida. The law authorizes the establishment of rules defining unfair and deceptive practices and empowers the attorney general to enter cease-and-desist orders against violators.

In a broader context, who would deny that caustic attacks on businessmen, portraying them as "villains," have receptive audiences in this day and time? Instead of simply bemoaning this situation, lashing out at attackers, or engaging in reactionaryism, businessmen have in the concept of alienation a tool for better understanding consumer discontent and, more importantly, a set of guidelines for deactivating hotbeds that nurture consumer discontent.

FORMS OF ALIENATION

Sociologist Melvin Seeman identified five forms of alienation: powerlessness, meaninglessness, normlessness, isolation, and self-estrangement. A thoughtful look at what lies behind the consumer issues that have come to the forefront in recent years suggests that they are often rooted in the first four forms of alienation.

POWERLESSNESS

Seeman defines powerlessness in broad terms as "the expectancy or probability held by the individual that his own behavior cannot determine the occurrence of the outcomes, or reinforcements, he seeks." From a consumer standpoint, powerlessness is a feeling or belief held by a person that as an individual he cannot influence business behavior to be more in accord with his needs and interests as a consumer, that he is powerless to counter detrimental actions taken by sellers and powerless to get them to respond satisfactorily to complaints.

The consumer movement is so replete with a sense of consumer powerlessness that definitions of consumerism come close to that of powerlessness. Note, for example, how evident powerlessness is in this following statement: "Consumerism is a social movement seeking to augment the rights and power of buyers in relation to sellers." More pointedly, Mary Gardiner Jones, when a member of the FTC, stated: "There is abroad in our country . . . a pervading sense of public powerlessness." A sense of powerlessness is often reinforced by spokesmen of national stature, not the least of whom is Justice William O. Douglas, who in speaking at a large university recently claimed that large corporations are running the country through their extensive influence in Washington.

The hotly contested legislation to establish a federal Consumer Protection Agency is symptomatic of the perceived imbalance in power between consumers and business. Proponents of the bill see it as a means of increasing the power of consumer representation and interests, vis-a-vis those of business, in proceedings of regulatory agencies. One illustration is Senator Muskie's call to put buyers of products "on a better footing" with the sellers.

Empirical studies as well as letters to government agencies reflect the extreme degree of powerlessness felt by some consumers. One survey revealed that 40 percent of those questioned who had been victimized by outright fraudulent practices failed to report the incidents to enforcement agencies because they believed authorities would be unable or unwilling to take any action. Another study found that over 56 percent of the households that experienced dissatisfaction with products did not seek corrective action from the seller. One reason, according to the researchers, may be that buyers do not expect any results and consequently do not go to the trouble of seeking remedies.

The popularity of "action line" features in newspapers and on radio and television also attests to consumer feelings of powerlessness. People see these as a cudgel for getting companies to respond satisfactorily to the grievances of individual consumers.

Consumer feelings of powerlessness can take various guises. One is the belief of some persons that they cannot exert any influence on business decisions concerning what products will or will not be placed on the market, their quality level, warranty coverage and duration, price, satisfactoriness of services, and so forth. Consequently, they harbor feelings like those of alienated voters who see themselves as being able only to exercise a negative choice between candidates offered to them by political bosses. Regardless of business opinions to the contrary, many consumers think their wishes carry virtually no weight in determining the market alternatives offered to them. This perceived powerlessness leads to discontent because, "Buyers want the right to influence products and marketing practices. . . ."

Another guise of powerlessness is the consumer frustration that results when a firm is inert, indifferent, or otherwise unresponsive to requests for corrective action. Illustrations abound. One of the most common is the inability to get a seemingly simple correction made in one's credit account, which is computerized. An additional example is the failure to obtain a remedy, or perhaps even a concerned hearing, when the product or service fails to meet what the buyer thinks are reasonable expectations. Although the firm's intentions may be admirable, the consumer's attitude is determined by what happens to him—he feels wronged and powerless to obtain satisfaction. It might be noted in passing that both of the problems cited have led to proposed legislation, the Federal Fair Credit Billing Act in the first instance and a statute to establish minimum performance standards and warranty service in the second.

Proposals to allow consumers greater use of class-action suits, thereby increasing their legal power in coping with perceived wrongs and unresponsiveness by business, reflect a third guise of powerlessness. Still another is a feeling of being manipulated by business. It is expressed most commonly in the form of an accusation that buying preferences and wants are manipulated. Rosenthal portrays it this way:

> The consumer is in serious need of help. . . . [In] the drugstore aisle, on the auto showroom floor, across the cash register everywhere, the consumer must face Madison Avenue, the whirling computer and the motivational research psychologist. . . . Standing alone, the American consumer cannot deal with this power in the marketplace.

Galbraith describes this kind of perceived consumer powerlessness as "the management of those who buy goods."

Illustrations like these are mentioned to help executives recognize manifestations of consumer powerlessness, not to point an accusing finger at businessmen or to trot out perennial allegations. Businessmen should recognize that a sense of powerlessness, along with other forms of alienation, can be based on imagined or superficial conditions as well as fact. It is a subjective feeling, attitude, or state of mind. But regardless of whether or not the perceived conditions are real, the consumer is alienated until the conditions are alleviated. Since powerlessness is a function of perception, the degree of alienation experienced can vary widely among consumers facing similar conditions.

In coping with real or imagined powerlessness consumers frequently follow a strategy of calling on a strong third party, often government, to intervene in their behalf to protect and promote their interests. Similarly, some will join or otherwise support consumer organizations and activists, such as Ralph Nader, who seem capable of exerting influence.

Alleviation of consumer powerlessness is thus a major challenge facing businessmen. Public relations campaigns that paper over problems or propagandize and fail to deal with basic causes of powerlessness are not likely to achieve significant and lasting results.

What, then, can the business community do? The purpose here is primarily to illuminate major sources of discontent and point the way for businessmen to devise and implement resourceful new initiatives. While some possible affirmative actions are mentioned in the following paragraphs, any allusions to a comprehensive list would be premature and presumptuous at this time, since efforts to devise remedial measures are still in their infancy.

WHAT CAN BE DONE ABOUT POWERLESSNESS?

Five areas are presented briefly below to sketch some types of affirmative actions open to a firm. They are (1) a corporate mechanism and willingness to implement consumer proposals, (2) an information system that monitors consumer concerns and irritants, (3) corporate conditioning and mechanisms for rapidly alleviating consumer dissatisfactions, (4) a control system to prevent practices that inadvertently produce consumer dissatisfaction, and (5) employee training, evaluation, and compensation methods that are incentives for satisfying consumers.

First, a corporate willingness to conscientiously listen to consumer proposals and to seriously consider and implement them where possible forestalls powerlessness by giving consumers a sense of having some voice or influence. In a day of credibility gaps and cynicism, the listening and implementation effort must be more than window dressing. Unless consumers see it as being sincere, the effort is wasted. Convincing explanations for not adopting measures that are touted as serving consumer interests must be widely communicated to consumers. There also must be a communication channel to top power centers in the firm. Part of the success of the Giant Food supermarket chain, which has been noted for its consumer-oriented actions, is attributed to the power of its consumer adviser in working with senior vice-presidents. Being customer oriented as espoused by the marketing literature of the 1960s is simply not enough.

Second, powerlessness can be combated by a marketing-consumer information capability that informs top executives when consumers see ill effects on their quality of life and well-being coming from the firm's practices and products. This goes far beyond conventional marketing research that is concerned with product preference tests, advertising research, and the like. It entails actively researching irritations, apprehensions, and dissatisfactions felt by consumers so that remedial steps can be taken. In contemporary jargon it means learning what's bugging consumers.

Third, corporate conditioning and mechanisms for responding quickly and satisfactorily to consumer complaints are an obvious yet woefully neglected means of preventing powerlessness and resentment. In addition to conditioning personnel to handle consumer problems rapidly, organizational structures and devices must exist to quickly resolve consumer grievances into feelings of being treated sympathetically and acceptably. Examples of what has been done include:

So-called "cool" lines, which enable frustrated consumers to get a concerned response.

"Buyer Protection Plans" which provide reasonable warranty coverage and minimize customer difficulty and inconvenience in obtaining warranty service. In this vein, AMC's plan appears to be a notable success.

Too often glaring and prolific sources of frustration are allowed to exist unnecessarily, leaving consumers with feelings of having no recourse.

Fourth, install a system of controls that identifies and corrects practices that needlessly produce dissatisfaction. Harmonizing product performance and buyer expectations is one of several possible focal points of such a system. For instance, advertising and salesmen's enthusiasm, if not tempered with concern for post-purchase satisfaction, can lead prospective customers to expect performance that won't be delivered. Buyer dissatisfaction occurs if performance is below expectations regardless of how well the product might function based on design specifications. One study observed that the number of consumers who were dissatisfied because the product failed to live up to the producer's claims or the buyer's expectations was nearly twice the number dissatisfied because the product was defective. As with any control system, the purpose is to bridle a type of cost—dissatisfaction and its consequences—although in this instance there is no time-honored and refined scheme of measurement.

Fifth, employees, including management personnel, should be trained and compensated for achieving customer satisfaction. Typically, personnel are promoted and rewarded for short-run sales, profits, production levels, or other achievements that ignore, if not run counter to, customer satisfaction. A district manager, for example, whose promotion and bonuses over the next two to three years depend solely on district profits, is apt to give consumer satisfaction a low priority relative to profits. To be fully consumer-conscious, a firm must appreciate such realities.

MEANINGLESSNESS

Seeman describes meaninglessness in general terms as "a low expectancy that satisfactory predictions about future outcomes of behavior can be made." In the case of consumers, meaninglessness occurs when they feel shackled and incapable of judging and choosing intelligently from among alternative products, brands, or dealers because of inadequate information. That is to say, they feel unable to predict reliably the outcomes of alternative purchase behaviors.

A sense of meaninglessness is very evident among consumers, as is illustrated pointedly in the conclusion of a book on consumer problems:

> The American consumer is in a perpetual state of bewilderment and doubt because no matter how he may try, he often doesn't know what he is buying. He doesn't know because he isn't told.

Meaninglessness also is evident in an FTC report, which concluded that consumers waste a sizable portion of their expenditures because they have insufficient knowledge about the products being purchased.

It is particularly antagonizing when consumers believe that firms could provide more information but are withholding it instead. Even more alienating, if believed, is the intentional exploitation of consumer ignorance, which according to an FTC report, some firms practice. Many consumers have come to believe that they have a right to more adequate information in the marketplace. And two past American presidents have told them exactly this. Thus, for business not to furnish the information can be interpreted as a violation of their rights as consumers.

Nondescript, unintelligible product claims also contribute to meaninglessness. Consumerists have spoken out repeatedly against such practices as making incomplete comparisons and senseless claims that provide no information that is useful as a basis for purchase decisions. Probably more disconcerting are promotional statements that actually mean something other than the obvious interpretation. When the practices of whole industries are questioned, the consumer who is already suspicious is likely to form attitudes that have long-run detrimental effects for all business.

"Now, more than ever, [the consumer] wants information and guidance he can rely on," according to Herbert D. Eagle, president of Sales and Marketing Executives International. Consequently, meaninglessness looms as a large source of discontent.

Perceived insufficiency of information is the central theme in a host of consumerism measures, such as several FDA moves to get more data as well as common product names on food, cosmetic, and drug labels, efforts by FTC staffers and others to find a means for grading the performance of competing products, unit pricing, proposed legislation mandating easily understood warranties, open dating, and publication of government test data on products. Activism across a broad front will probably continue as long as the lack of adequate information is seen as a major deficiency in the marketplace.

WHAT CAN BE DONE ABOUT MEANINGLESSNESS?

Businessmen can lessen consumer meaninglessness by providing what buyers consider an appropriate amount of easily understood, objective information about product characteristics, dangers and limitations, and comparative value. The information should conform to what consumers consider useful from their perspective. That is, the informational desires of consumers must be determined, and then the communication programs developed to satisfy these consumer needs.

Some laudable efforts have been made by business and government-business groups to improve the flow of meaningful information to consumers. One illustrative and noteworthy action is the "Guiding Principles for Responsible Packaging and Labeling" by the National Business Council for Consumer Affairs. Another is the new industry-developed plan for labeling meats, which indicates where the cuts come from on the animal and uses standardized names for different cuts. Many other examples could be cited, including publication of objective buying guides and establishment of energetic offices of consumer information by some firms. If these efforts are to attain optimal effectiveness, however, firms may have to become more aggressive in disseminating this type of information to consumers.

If businessmen fail to devise means for ensuring that consumer desires for information are satisfied, expanded government intrusion is almost a certainty. Mary Gardiner Jones has stated that if business does not furnish enough information to consumers, the government will. Some steps by business may even pay off in short-run, traditional terms, as open dating of foods seems to be doing.

NORMLESSNESS

Normlessness can be described as a belief that businessmen engage in socially undesirable, unethical, and unjust marketing practices to achieve their corporate goals. In fact, some businessmen hold feelings of normlessness themselves in the form of an attitude that payoffs, various deceptive practices, or other types of unethical behavior are necessary to compete effectively. It is evident, for instance, in the publicized case of an owner of an appliance store chain, who based his marketing strategy on a "bait and switch" philosophy. When this business philosophy was questioned, he argued defiantly that "bait and switch is the American way." On the consumer side, normlessness is reflected in suspicion, cynicism, and in some instances a nearly complete distrust of business.

The undercurrent of normlessness among consumers can be seen in several recent events. Witness the quick, almost instinctive allegations of misconduct and conspiracy against major oil companies when the prospect of a fuel shortage caught public attention. Earlier, when meat prices rose rapidly, first reactions of many were to suspect meat processors and food chains of profiteering. Then there is the mother who wrote to the author of a column on shoplifting, saying that as a parent she completely approved of shoplifting by teenagers because "each business is just as greedy and dirty and underhanded as the next. . . ." And one could hardly overstate the normlessness felt by the consumer who expressed in a letter to a government consumer affairs office, "All we need to understand is that we are dealing with organized dishonesty on a huge scale." In one study, over 20 percent of the people believed they had been cheated or deceived in a recent purchase.

Manifestations of less extreme feelings of normlessness include beliefs that firms put their own interest ahead of consumers, that producers deliberately design products to wear out so replacements can be sold, that improvements and safety features are withheld from the market when this is to the advantage of the producer. Skepticism of advertising is another manifestation.

Undoubtedly consumer normlessness has been amplified by the many publicized allegations and exposés in recent years. These run the gamut to the unconscionable, including the knowing sale of hazardous toys and contaminated foods, alleged cover-ups of critical safety defects in products, promotion of ineffective and useless drugs, and intentional misrepresentation of combustible materials as nonburning. Normlessness seems to exist in almost every facet of the consumer marketplace. Even some pet lovers have charged that advertising claims of dog food producers are grossly overstated. In the face of so many accusations, it would almost be surprising if numerous consumers were not distrustful of business.

Recognizing that normlessness exists in the minds of consumers, the responsible businessman faces the task of undertaking affirmative actions to regain consumer confidence. Little good is accomplished by lamenting that business has been unjustly maligned, that only a few firms are guilty, or that business is being used as a whipping boy. Many consumers simply believe otherwise, and businessmen must demonstrate anew that they merit the consumer's respect and trust. A senior automobile executive was cognizant of this when he stated:

> People have said we in the industry will cheat you and steal from you. A lot of what's been said is erroneous but this is how many people feel and we must do something to change this.

WHAT CAN BE DONE ABOUT NORMLESSNESS?

To overcome consumer normlessness, businessmen will have to demonstrate through their practices and dealings that customers are treated fairly, that business will do more than merely meet minimum technicalities of the law in dealing with customers. In the words of Herbert D. Eagle, "Today people are demanding the truth. They want honesty and fairness." Thus, the atmosphere created by business must be one of justice and fair play.

To achieve effective and full implementation of honesty and fairness doctrines, it may be necessary for the firm to promulgate specific "do's and don't's" for various organizational subunits and supporting companies such as advertising agencies and dealers. Personnel at all levels must be convinced that the firm is sincere and scrupulous.

Pious proclamations [made] by top management that conflict with demands made on subordinates and are not supported by the firm's reward and advancement system will be largely ignored. Middle-level and junior executives, if pressured by sales and profit objectives without any weight given to consumer welfare, can be expected to act accordingly. The same is true for companies having a supporting role. Despite righteous calls by management for truthful advertising, for instance, the firm's ad agency may be tempted to follow the approach described in S. S. Baker's confessional if the agency's performance is evaluated solely on the basis of sales volume:

> The usual thinking in forming a campaign is first, what can we say, true or not, that will sell the product best? The second consideration is, how can we say it effectively and get away with it. . . .

Personnel may have to be trained and then given periodic retraining on evolving consumer norms and ethical expectations of business. Otherwise, personnel may continue practices that once were ethically acceptable to consumers but now are potent contributors to consumer normlessness. What was just plain good business sense in the past may be currently regarded, as the result of changing consumer concepts of fairness, as grossly unjust. What is ethically acceptable and what is not must be judged against consumer norms rather than those of industry executives, since the two sets of ethical norms may not necessarily be in agreement at all times. Periodic audits may be conducted to ensure that training is in line with current consumer norms and that personnel are following their training and not an outmoded business sense.

A complete audit of the firm's activities that affect consumers is a means of pinpointing those that foster normlessness. Like marketing audits that are used to evaluate a firm's marketing programs and indicate ways to improve, audits can be made of a firm's practices to assess their contribution to consumer normlessness and to determine ways to lessen the problem.

ISOLATION OR CULTURAL ESTRANGEMENT

Persons who experience cultural isolation or estrangement perceive the things, beliefs, and goals that are very important to most members of society as lacking value and validity, as providing little or no meaningful satisfaction, as being purposeless or bankrupt. Individuals with these attitudes have a feeling of dissociation, disenchantment, and lack of identification with society.

In describing this form of alienation, sociologist Gwynn Nettler indicates that there is usually an outspoken dislike for American mass culture, including automobiles, television, radio, and the press, popular magazines, advertising, conventional religion, and national spectator sports. The familiar objects, art forms, products, and values of society are criticized and repudiated as being mass-produced, standardized, and vulgar. Much of what makes up our so-called consumer culture is seen as exploitative *kitsch* which provides little intrinsic satisfaction. In the words of Charles A. Reich:

> Our culture has been reduced to the grossly commercial; all cultural values are for sale, and those that fail to make a profit are not preserved. Our life activities have become plastic, vicarious, and false to our genuine needs, activities fabricated by others and forced upon us.

Business, as seen by some culturally estranged people, epitomizes and perpetuates the culture they find offensive. Thus the marketplace becomes a high-profile target for venting their resentment and frustration. Specific consumer issues serve as rallying causes and vehicles for expressing negative sentiments about the culture. In a sense business becomes something of a scapegoat.

WHAT CAN BE DONE ABOUT ESTRANGEMENT?

Cultural estrangement is probably the most difficult form of alienation for business to overcome, since it stems principally from a repudiation of society's primary values and beliefs, in contrast to being solely attributable to business practices in the marketplace.

In the process of setting policies and making decisions, attention can be given to maintaining a low-profile target for cultural dissatisfaction. Based on an understanding of the factors that inflame the culturally alienated, business actions can be formulated so that they do not inadvertently flaunt these irritants. In addition, resources might be devoted to promoting an uplifting of public values such as environmental conservation and others leading to an improved quality of life.

MULTIPLE FORMS OF ALIENATION

Numerous consumers experience simultaneously two or more forms of alienation, which intensifies their discontent. Some prevalent combinations are (a) meaninglessness and powerlessness, and (b) normlessness and powerlessness. Criticism levied against business frequently reflects multiple forms of alienation. Thus, concerted actions directed at all forms of alienation are needed to effectively mitigate consumer disaffection.

SUMMARY

The concept of alienation, long a theme in sociology, offers businessmen a basis for understanding major sources of consumer issues and a means of collating the countless issues into groups, based on similarities, so that mitigating actions can be undertaken more efficiently and effectively. Principal components of alienation—powerlessness, meaninglessness, normlessness, and cultural estrangement—serve to explain general types of discontent among consumers that give rise to specific points of contention. With these components of alienation in mind, businessmen can devise strategies for forestalling consumer issues before they fester to the point of capturing public and government attention.

QUESTIONS

1. John Dewey once wrote that "conceptions . . . are general answers supposed to have a universal meaning that covers and dominates all particulars. Hence they do not assist inquiry. They close it" (in *Reconstruction and Philosophy*, 1948). Does the conceptual framework in this article illuminate new aspects of the consumer movement or mask diversity that does not fit into the categories?
2. Does a conceptual framework that focuses on alienation adequately explain factors underlying consumerism such as rising expectations and changing cultural values? What about the coincidence of the rise of a great leader for consumerists like Ralph Nader?
3. Do the authors underestimate the importance of real abuses of the public trust by business as a motivating force behind consumer indignation?
4. Could this conceptual framework of alienation be instructively applied to other contemporary movements in the business community such as the environmental movement and the civil rights movement? If not, is the problem in the shortcomings of the analytical framework or in a real disparity in the nature and fundamental causes of the latter movements?

CONSUMERISM AND MARKETING

MAX E. BRUNK

Max E. Brunk, professor of marketing, Cornell University, rejects the idea of the helpless consumer and in the following address examines some of the non-consumer forces behind consumerism and their implications to business in what he calls the "meddlesome Seventies."

Consumerism is a movement of activists who champion issues which appear to be beneficial to consumers. This definition is blunt and to the point. It will not make the consumerist happy, for it exposes the spurious inference that there is, outside the marketplace, a bona fide movement of consumers who join in common cause on their own behalf. Nevertheless, in order to understand the growth, strength and power of consumerism one must realize that it is not a movement of consumers themselves. The term implies protection of the consumer but the flood of proposals for ways and means of protecting the consumer are not generally traceable to those seeking protection for themselves. To the contrary the specific issues of consumerism are initiated by those who, for assorted reasons, seek to protect others from harm. It is this third party involvement in a buyer-seller relationship that gives consumerism its uniqueness. The consumer activist, regardless of motive, is indeed a crusader.

Time will not permit an exploration of all the motives of the consumerist. They obviously range from selfish to unselfish, from dishonest to honest, from ignorant to the well-informed. Regardless of motive the consumer activist contends that consumers should be protected from physical and economic harm, that consumers should be informed and educated in product knowledge, that consumers should have a choice in the marketplace and finally that consumers should have proper legal redress for wrongs. These aims are similar to the four consumer rights identified by President Kennedy in his 1962 address on consumer interests . . . the right to safety, the right to be informed, the right to choose and the right to be heard. On the surface one can scarcely argue with such virtuous aims until one realizes that under consumerism they are subjected to third party interpretation and in this sense may or may not be in the consumer interest.

In a normal market relationship the buyer's right to accept or reject in the marketplace imparts a very forceful economic meaning to these aims consistent with each individual's particular set of values. But competitive enterprise is rejected by the consumerist who identifies protection in terms of third party values. And because such values can always be made to appear rational they are condoned and often vigorously supported by the general pub-

Talk Before the National Broiler Council in Atlanta, Georgia, October 7, 1970. Reprinted by permission of the author.

lic. As a result an endless myriad of laws, regulations and coercions is rapidly displacing the free decision of the individual in the marketplace and the right of the consumer to choose increasingly becomes a mockery.

Without much doubt I reveal my personal convictions on consumerism. I think most of all I resent the hypocrisy of the politics behind consumerism . . . the illusion that someone is doing something for me when in fact they are only doing something, at my expense, to serve their own selfish political interests. I hear business leaders today claiming that consumerism is anti-business. They have fallen victims to the hypocrisy of consumerism. They are mistaken. Consumerism is aimed at the consumer. Business can adjust and endure under consumerism much better than consumers. To business, consumerism merely closes the doors to certain opportunities, redirects business effort or alters the competitive advantage one business might have over another. But look what it does to the consumer who pays the cost and loses the benefits that a prohibited product or service could have provided.

I reject the contention that the consumer is ignorant, stupid or uninformed merely because her actions are not consistent with either my beliefs or the beliefs of any professional consumerist. In my opinion consumers with dollars in their pockets are not by any stretch of the imagination weak. To the contrary they are the most merciless, meanest, toughest market disciplinarians I know. I reject the thesis that there is any one universal value in marketing that can be made applicable and acceptable to all 200 million American consumers. Any businessman trying to capture the favor of the consumer knows this. They know that the value and needs of different consumers change with almost every purchasing decision. Surely we need to distinguish between the proper role of government in protecting consumers from deceptive practices and the inappropriate role of serving as intermediary between buyers and sellers in making value judgments.

In our zeal to protect the "innocent" consumer we need recognize that each protective step puts an added limit on our productive capacity as a nation. It may be argued that a wealthy nation can afford such luxury and, while this is true, we need also to take into account the price we are paying for consumerism.

Risk is inherent in every consumer purchase . . . in every consumer act. The efforts of man to eliminate risk in the marketplace contain much political appeal but are nonetheless futile because the reduction of one kind of risk must always be accompanied by a compensating increase in another kind of risk. The cost of protection is deprivation. The restricted use of D.D.T. not only keeps people from being harmed but also increases their exposure to malaria. The proper balance between these two risks is a value judgment for society to determine. We can, if we desire, achieve a high degree of auto safety by reducing speed but society rejects the sacrifice and instead with the safety belt accepts a lower safety level requiring less sacrifice. Some of the most protected members of our society are the inmates of our prisons. The distinguishing characteristic of these unfortunates is that they know the personal cost of their protection by having an acute awareness of their deprivations. But the cost of consumer protection is not so apparent. We have no way of putting a value on the sacrifice in foregone products and services that a free market could provide. We would not have the violence on our campuses or streets today if the disruptors bore greater risks of being penalized. The increased violence we tolerate is the price we pay for reducing the risk of penalizing the innocent. The jurist who said that it is better to let a hundred guilty persons go free than convict an innocent man either did not understand the nature of risk or had little respect for social order. In 1747 Voltaire wrote "It is better to risk saving a guilty person than to condemn an innocent one." Later Blackstone wrote "It is better that ten guilty persons escape than one innocent suffer." Now, once again, our odds are up and I'm beginning to wonder what par really is for the innocent man.

So far I have identified the consumerist only as a kind of self-appointed, omnipotent guardian of the consumer. Who is the consumerist? Where do his ideas come from? What gives him motive? To some degree I think we are all consumerists at some time or another. We all have ideas about how other people should behave or be made to behave. When we get worked up about some issue we may even become activists and try to force our opinions on others. However, the most potent and dangerous consumerists are found in the ranks of elected public officials, career public workers, authors and writers, college professors, school teachers and preachers . . . people who have time on their hands to worry about others . . . people whose status depends on publicity and popularity. It is interesting to observe that the consumerist sometimes has as much difficulty convincing the consumer of her need for protection as in convincing a regulatory body to do something about it. But in final analysis the consumerist with the real punch is the elected official who champions laws, the appointed official who establishes regulations, or the self-appointed crusader who needs only to release a report or make a speech to hit the headlines. I doubt that my Congressman is responsible for the eight sets of seat belts that came in my last car but I got them and I paid for them. While some Congressmen deem it expedient to play on the political opportunities of consumerism we can be thankful that most of our public representatives, perhaps much better than the general public, understand the shams of consumerism. In a very real sense these responsible representatives often protect the consumer from the consumerist.

So far I have talked in broad generalities. Perhaps a specific illustration can do more to expose consumerism in its true light. This is dangerous because there are supporters to be found behind almost any consumer issue. I know I could get some support for banning alcoholic drinks from the market and if I tried hard enough I might even find some support for banning milk. I have heard it said that if strawberries were a manufactured product they would be restricted from the market today because so many people are allergic to them!

Anyway my little story has to do with unit pricing. Some consumerist got the bright idea a few years ago that if all products in the retail store were marked as to price in equivalent units of pounds, quarts, square feet and the like then the consumer could better identify the best buy. There was an implied assumption that the variety of package sizes on the market [was] a calculated attempt to deceive the consumer.

Gradually the idea began to catch on and more and more people began to accept and champion it. I know of no strong bona fide consumer support for the idea but I do know of a lot of passionate pleas by consumerists who thought the idea had merit especially for people on a tight budget. Finally the proposal gathered enough steam to be ordered in effect by the Department of Consumer Affairs in New York City. But before it could be invoked the courts ruled that the Department had no authority to require conformance. The matter currently rests there while steps are being taken to establish the needed authority. [Ed.: New York City now has unit pricing in grocery stores.]

But as in any fight charges and countercharges flew around rather wildly. The merchants claimed that the costs of so marking products would be prohibitively expensive . . . that the net increase in cost would have to be borne by the consumer. The consumerists claimed that such marking would enable some consumers, and particularly those who needed it most, to save up to 10 percent on their grocery bill. But no one really had any facts though the idea sounded plausible and workable. This is the typical way consumerist issues arise and generate support, not among consumers, but rather among those who would like to do something for the consumer. It also reveals the typical negative reaction of the business community which serves only to add the fire of certainty to the consumerist's eyes.

Fortunately this is one idea that could be tested with a reasonable degree of preciseness and one of my colleagues at Cornell, Professor Daniel Padberg, undertook to do just that with a midwestern chain. The most interesting of his conclusions is that both the costs and benefits were grossly overstated. The costs in the smallest stores ran to over 4 percent of the sales value but in large supermarkets they amounted to less than a tenth of one percent of sales. But a check of product movement indicated no significant shift in purchases by the consumer. In two broad food categories the consumer actually traded up to the higher cost per unit item, in the cereal category she traded down and there was no change in the others. Surveys of consumers shopping these particular stores revealed that awareness of the availability of the information was greatest among the high income, well-educated consumers. Despite these findings, the only real facts on the issue available, it is my prediction that the consumerist will continue to champion unit pricing, will continue to talk about how it will benefit the poor and eventually succeed in getting widespread regulations making unit pricing mandatory.

The issue of unit pricing did not originate from any factual base and accordingly facts are not likely to alter the decisions of those who champion its cause. It makes no difference that the theory of unit pricing is based on a false and strictly materialistic premise. It makes no difference that it gives the large merchant a competitive advantage over the small. It makes no difference that the wealthy take greater advantage of the information than the poor. Even if the benefits are not very great it may be argued that the costs are insignificant. At least the consumer doesn't need a computer when she shops and she gained a notch in her right to be informed. But is the cost really insignificant if we add this to the hundreds of other laws and regulations that have been so forced on the consumer within the last several years? I believe this case illustrates practically all the generalities I described in the first part of my talk. Now it is time to turn to the subject of how the business community—how the marketer—can live in the era of consumerism . . . the era of the meddlesome Seventies.

It is clear that the marketer now needs to keep an eye on both the consumer and the consumerist. The activities of the consumerist [are] causing the consumer to increasingly rationalize her actions in the marketplace and this verbal justification is in turn affecting her behavior. Shrewd marketers in the past have always responded more to the actions of the consumer than to her talk. The literature of market research is full of examples in which the consumer said one thing but did another. This is nothing more than the inability of one to always sound rational in explaining actions. In fact none of us likes the thought of being unable to explain our actions in some logical way to a second party. All I am saying is that consumerism is stirring up a self-consciousness in consumers and that marketers in the future will need to give greater heed to materialistic values that can be easily rationalized by the consumer.

On the other side of this coin is the risk that marketers will overreact to what they hear from consumerists. To some degree I think we are going through this stage today. I know of at least one major chain which attempts to appeal to the consumer by quickly adopting almost every consumerist idea that comes along. Sometimes it pays. Sometimes it doesn't. The point to keep in mind in trying to separate the good from the bad is that most of the talk comes from consumerists while the real action comes from consumers.

In considering the impact of consumerism on marketing, any industry should recognize that consumerism breeds on suspicion of the motives of business. Something has to be wrong, someone has to be unhappy for consumerism to exist. The consumerist sees different sized packages on the market not as an attempt to meet the differing requirements of people but rather as a deliberate effort to confuse the consumer. In the consumerist's mind fractional ounce contents have nothing to do with efficiency or cost savings but [are] used to make comparative pricing difficult. Codes are put on packages to hide vital information from the consumer. Colors and printing are used to deceive. Packaging is used to cover faulty merchandise and advertising is designed to make people act impulsively against their better judgment. The list is endless, and it always will be, for this is the nature of consumerism. However, I believe this observation tells us that the more business conducts its affairs in the open—lives in a goldfish bowl so to speak —the less it will be subject to the whims of the consumerist.

Permit me to give a simple example. As you know the red meat industry code dates many of its prepared meats with a four digit number. The first and last digit added are the month, the two center digits the day of the month. The packer uses this information for the identification of a given lot if for some unforeseen reason he must make a withdrawal from the market. But that is not the point. The cryptic code causes the consumerist to think that something is being hidden from them. Writers take delight in letting people in on how to read the "secret" code. Once the code is translated the fact that it has little meaning to the consumer is inconsequential. Why does the business community bait the consumerist like this? Wouldn't it be much better to use a simple lot number or perhaps even better to print an open date on the package? There has been so much publicity on this in recent months that the consumer is beginning to wonder about all those funny numbers stamped on all canned goods. After all the consumer is buying and eating the stuff. Isn't she entitled to know?

This little example may sound trivial to you but I assure you it is not so considered by the industries involved. It's not at all unlike the truth-in-lending law. How many consumers do you think wanted this law for their own protection. How many thought it might be a good idea for someone else? How much more do you now know about interest rates and carrying charges than before the law was passed? How many dollars has it saved the consumer? Regardless of how you choose to answer, the truth-in-lending law is now safely tucked away on the books where it can be forgotten. The few mills of marketing margin that it will permanently cost may even be worth the silencing of the consumerist on this issue. I only regret that it has freed the consumerist to dream up some other issue that might hurt me more.

Consumerism is made up of little issues each affecting . . . relatively few consumers or businesses. It thrives on the importance of being unimportant. It enlists the passive support of the majority against the vigorous opposition of the few and in this way it grows on our economy like a cancer. You people in the broiler industry are not particularly concerned about truth-in-lending, code dating, auto or mine safety. In fact not being involved they may sound like pretty good ideas to you. But I rather expect you may see some problems and exorbitant costs in such things as Federal inspection that are not apparent to the auto dealer down the street.

On the surface one might expect the specific issues of consumerism to serve as a congealing force uniting an industry in defense behind a common cause. But we forget that industries such as yours are made up of competitors and that most consumer issues do something to alter competitive advantage. Any new law or regulation that costs your competitors more than it costs you or that weakens your competitors product franchise more than yours might not on the surface look so bad to you. Recognizing the way the market works you know that it is not so much your absolute costs as your relative costs that determine your profit position and being in a relatively favorable position you may even feel tempted to oppose the majority point of view of your fellow industry members. Of course the fallacy of this thinking which tends to destroy the cohesiveness of an industry is that competitive advantage created from such issues is very short lived. If your competitive advantage lies in some distribution network, package design, freezing process or the like you only succeed in forcing your competition into following your pattern of doing business. And you are right back where you started unless in the meantime your competitors have found a better way of doing it.

Viable members of any trade organization never lose sight of the fact that competitive position within an industry must always be subservient to the competitive position among different industries. In fact the strength of any trade organization largely depends on its members' willingness to compromise on issues affecting the industry. No good member of a trade association always gets his way. I have digressed into this little sermon because consumerism can and often does threaten the cohesiveness of an industry.

There is one other timely concern of the marketer and that has to do with current efforts to center the issues of consumerism in one governmental agency, office, bureau or department. Provision for such an office came out of Senate Committee hearings this past week and the House has already acted on a somewhat different version of the same measure. Mr. Nader in particular has been outspoken for the creation of a Department of Consumer Affairs, calling this the most important consumer legislation ever.

At the present time the organization of government permits consumer interests to be served in a wide variety of ways. One study several years ago revealed that no less than 33 Federal departments are engaged in various phases of consumer protection. These agencies were involved in 118 different consumer protective activities requiring the services of 65,000 full-time employees. In addition there were 178 other programs indirectly related to the consumer interest. And this is but a small part of the activity that goes on in Washington and at the state and local levels where we also have extensive policing of a wide variety of marketing processes from weights and measures to sanitation and trade practices. This all adds up to a highly protected consuming public and it raises a number of questions. Would the consumer interest better be served by concentrating these activities in a singular agency? Can such an agency serve as an effective spokesman for the consumer in the promulgation of new laws and regulations? What interest groups would be most influential with such an agency? To what degree should such an agency act as intermediary between buyers and sellers?

In the past government has established consumer protection laws and regulations in response to needs as they arise. The administration of these activities has been delegated to agencies and departments accustomed to working with the special businesses involved, be it agriculture, finance, commerce, drugs, labor, housing or what not. The proposal for a central consumer agency shifts the audience center from supplier to buyer and by this process cuts across our total economy. Because almost every issue of consumer protection is related to the operational idiosyncrasies of the supplier involved, such an agency would encounter both conflict and duplication of effort with every other department of government. It may be that this is typical of government but I don't think it is good government.

How effective a spokesman for the consumer such an agency might be is demonstrated by the past activities of the President's Special Assistant for Consumer Affairs. During its eight-year gestation period much effort has been made to gain consumer, business, and labor support for the program. Many talks have been given, press conferences held, and consumer meetings scheduled. Although the office of Special Assistant has carried White House identity and has been served by three different, highly respected and competent ladies, the general public has never really taken the office very seriously. It should be apparent to the most ardent supporter of the program that bona fide consumer interest has failed to develop.

Apparently the consumer already knows that any remedial action he deems necessary is most directly accomplished as a result of his actions in the marketplace. He also knows that the marketplace respects his actions either when he is in the minority or with the majority. He does not expect to impose his consumption values on his neighbor anymore than he expects his neighbor's values to be imposed on him.

Regardless of any new agency that might be created to represent the consumer and regardless of the growth of consumerism, the only true reading of the consumer is to be obtained by observing her actions in the marketplace. There can be no true spokesman for the consumer other than the actions of the consumer herself. Try as she might she will rationalize her actions but she cannot explain them in full. That is why she cannot tell you what new or modified goods and services would better serve her needs. In marketing research I have spent the better part of my life ringing consumer doorbells in a futile effort to get [consumers] to tell me how some product or market service can be improved or what new products or services they want, only to find that in response they failed either to visualize their alternatives or identify the true values to which they in final analysis respond. The consumer, in her mute but effective way, can only bring all her value considerations to bear in response to what is offered her. She has her own built-in protective device. If you displease her . . . if you do not offer her the best alternative . . . if indeed you deceive her in terms of her own values, she simply and quickly votes "no" in the marketplace. That is the miracle of the free market . . . the miracle the consumerist refuses to recognize.

QUESTIONS

1. Who and what is behind "consumerism"?
2. Do you accept Brunk's assertion that consumerism is more likely to affect the consumer adversely than it will the marketer? Why does he say this?
3. Brunk rejects the idea of one federal agency to handle consumer affairs. Are his reasons acceptable to you?
4. What are your feelings about the general tenor of this article?

12

BUSINESS AND MINORITIES

WHAT DOES "EQUAL EMPLOYMENT OPPORTUNITY" REALLY MEAN?

WILLIAM H. BROWN III

William H. Brown III, formerly chairman of the Equal Employment Opportunity Commission, Washington, D.C., outlines in detail in the following speech what types of discrimination may take place and what the courts and the government can and will do about them.

As you know, recent amendments to federal law make discrimination in employment illegal, and assign responsibility for its identification and elimination to the federal agency of which I am Chairman. I want to discuss with you implications of this legislation for your operations.

THE ISSUE

First, I want to tell you about a magazine article I read recently about a County Executive of one of our larger counties.

The article told of the executive's warning to his department heads to "alert all staff" against the possibility of "some ultraliberal organization" prodding job applicants into taking advantage of the new federal law. The warning came in a memorandum which said that the county might have problems if a departmental head *said the wrong thing* and the applicant subsequently filed a charge of discrimination.

"Frankly," the memorandum stated, "I expect the county will have a charge filed against it, in any event, by some ultraliberal organization attempting to create an issue." Well, we at EEOC have news for that County Executive: No one has to "create" an issue of discrimination. Discrimination exists today in both public and private employment, in all types of jobs, at all levels, against every minority, and both sexes.

What I want to discuss with you today is the dimension of that discrimination, the way in which it has been defined by the courts, and the amendments to Title VII which give EEOC increased powers to eliminate it.

MEANING OF "MERIT" EMPLOYMENT

I am particularly glad to have an opportunity to discuss the legal requirements to eliminate discrimination with a group such as yours. You represent

From *Proceedings, 1972 International Conference on Public Personnel Administration.* Reprinted by permission of the International Personnel Management Association, 1313 East 60th Street, Chicago, Illinois 60637.

official state and local government agencies charged with the responsibility for the administration of state and local government merit systems. These systems have been designed to establish the principle of merit employment—the principle that the selection and promotion of employees must be based, not upon some extraneous factor, but upon their ability to do the job.

Title VII of the 1964 Civil Rights Act, the law which we enforce, requires basically the same thing. It requires that the particular extraneous factors of race, sex, or ethnic origin must not be a factor in any employment system; it establishes instead a "merit" employment principle of ability to perform the job for which the individual is being considered, recruited, selected, or promoted.

As you may know, the jurisdiction and coverage of EEOC to enforce Title VII has recently been expanded by amendments which became effective on March 24th of this year. Whenever a new law is passed there is some delay in understanding its full impact until cases work their way through the courts. While the applicability of Title VII prohibiting discrimination in employment is new to your agencies, the basic principles of Title VII are not. A body of precedent has been established by the courts which will, I believe, offer sufficient guidance to you in considering the implications of the new law.

The new law reinforces the principle of merit employment—employment based upon the ability to do the job. However, to be completely frank, I also think that a careful examination of the way in which the state and city personnel systems of this country have been run in recent years will suggest that full compliance with the law will require some new thinking on your part. It will require a new and careful look at the way in which you do business; it will require careful understanding of just what discrimination is and how it exists in your operations, and it may require new types of employment action to eliminate discrimination. It may, in short, require a whole new understanding of the full dimensions and scope of the term "merit" employment.

Let me explain. I view the term "merit" employment the same as the term "job relatedness." This is the standard imposed by the United States Supreme Court for determining whether employment practices comply with Title VII. Just because some state and local agencies say they are operating on the basis of the merit system doesn't mean they are in compliance with Title VII. Indeed, there is a substantial possibility that many of them are in violation, or at a minimum, in serious need of re-examination, because the mechanisms that they use to evaluate "merit," albeit in good faith, are not in fact, job related. They are not, in fact, adequate predictors of job performance.

DEFINITION OF DISCRIMINATION

This standard of "job relatedness" has developed over the last several years as we have become more sophisticated in our understanding of what discrimination in employment really is. I find that there is much misunderstanding about this term, both in terms of the law, our history, and our society. Over the last seven years, we and the courts have gone through several stages in our understanding of how discrimination works.

STAGE I: EVIL INTENT

The first stage is fairly simple to understand. It assumed that discrimination was essentially a human problem—an evil state of mind on the part of some individual. It was evidenced by signs such as "No Irish Need Apply"; or the advertisements in many newspapers dividing job opportunities into those for "white" and those for "colored." The investigation of this kind of discrimination focused on proving the intent of the employer and whether he "meant" to exclude someone for an unlawful reason. The remedy focused on educating the person and establishing brotherhood activities designed to eliminate this type of evil state of mind.

STAGE II: UNEQUAL TREATMENT

The second stage focused not on the intent or the state of mind, but on the actions of the person accused of discrimination. The standard applied was one of "unequal treatment." Was a black person treated differently than a white person; an Anglo treated differently than a Chicano; or a man treated differently than a woman? The investigation focused primarily on what happened to a specific identifiable individual or limited group of individuals, and attempted to determine whether they had been treated differently than someone of another racial, ethnic, or sexual group. If illegal or unequal treatment was identified, the remedy was fairly simple: Find the people who had been treated unequally and treat them in an equal fashion.

STAGE III: UNEQUAL EFFECT

Recently, a third stage of the definition of discrimination has been developed in legal decisions. The most important decision was the case of *Griggs* v. *Duke Power,* in which the Supreme Court considered two hiring standards applied equally and uniformly by the Duke Power Company—a requirement that a job applicant pass a written test and a requirement that a job applicant have a high-school diploma. Requirements similar to those exist in most merit systems.

The Supreme Court determined that these requirements were applied equally to all applicants regardless of race. Therefore, there would have been no violation of the law if the definition of discrimination were limited to "unequal treatment." Further there was no "evil intent" involved, as the Supreme Court found that the company was even engaging in various community activities to improve job opportunities for minorities.

With such a record, how could the Duke Power Company possibly be in violation of the law? It can be and it was, because the Supreme Court has made it perfectly clear that employment practices, even those which are neutral on their face and equally applied to people of all races, might still be illegal if their impact is to exclude people of one group more than those of another. Specifically, speaking for an unanimous court, Chief Justice Warren Berger said:

> If an employment practice which operates to exclude Negroes cannot be shown to be related to job performance, the practice is prohibited.

What does this mean? It means that in examining employment practices we must go through a two-part analysis. Part one: Does the employment practice operate to exclude Negroes or women or Chicanos or another protected group? This can usually be discovered by a simple examination of the statistical make-up of your work force. The second step in the analysis is to determine what particular practices have operated in such a fashion as to exclude minorities and women, and to determine whether those practices are job related. In this examination, the court made it clear that the burden of proof is not upon the minority group individual who believes that the practice which has excluded him is not job related, but the burden is on the employer utilizing the practice to prove its job relatedness.

While the Supreme Court decision focused on two specific employment practices—the use of certain tests and requiring a high-school diploma—the language used by Chief Justice Berger has much broader application than these two practices. Clearly his language requires a complete re-evaluation of all our employment practices. I should like to outline for you some of the court cases interpreting Title VII in the private sector and those dealing with public employment under the provisions of earlier federal laws, so that you may anticipate the types of practices that may be illegal and begin to eliminate them with nondiscriminatory remedial practices.

The most important thing to remember is that discrimination need not be a matter of malicious intent. Not only the courts but the Congress [has] made it clear that general business rules and procedures may in themselves constitute systemic barriers to minorities and women.

The same indictment must be made of the operation of many aspects of the civil service system. Indeed, the report of the Senate Labor Committee on the recent amendments clearly observed that:

> Civil service selection and promotion techniques and requirements are replete with artificial requirements that place a premium on "paper" credentials.

This report also points out that similar requirements in the private sector had been held illegal in cases such as *Griggs,* and called upon the United States Civil Service Commission to:

> Undertake a thorough reexamination of its entire testing and qualification program to ensure that the standards enunciated in the Griggs case are fully met.

I think you should undertake a similar "reexamination."

DISCRIMINATION IN STATE AND LOCAL GOVERNMENT

Measured against the standards established by *Griggs* what, then, are some of the particular troublesome areas of state and local government to which such examination should be devoted?

1. RECRUITMENT

The courts have recognized that recruitment systems are often discriminatory. Specifically, if you have an all-white or male work force, and there is a heavy element of word-of-mouth recruitment in which job applicants learn about vacancies from existing employees, this may perpetuate the all-white or male character of the work force. This is clearly illegal under Title VII. A recent survey showed that your major recruitment sources are your job-announcement, local employment services, and a heavy dose of referrals from present employees. If any or all of these systems produce a segregated recruitment pool, they must be changed or improved. The remedy is to institute new recruitment systems which will have the result of obtaining an integrated recruitment pool.

2. HIRING STANDARDS AND CRITERIA

Any hiring standard such as educational level, amount of experience, requirement that an applicant not have an arrest record, or requirement that an applicant not have a garnishment against him, which may operate statistically to exclude more blacks than whites, or such as a height requirement which may exclude more women or Chicanos than Anglos, are illegal unless you can establish, by a clear-cut validation study, that the requirements you are utilizing are specifically related to the job performance for the specific jobs for which the individuals are being selected.

Incidentally, the survey showed that 28 percent of you use residence as a requirement for unskilled jobs. Unless you can prove people with a certain residence do the job better, this may be illegal in a geographic area that is predominantly of one race. The survey showed 66 percent of you disqualify applicants if they have arrest or conviction records. The courts have already said that to use arrest records this way is probably illegal unless you can prove specific job relatedness. It is probably also illegal, at least, for certain types of convictions. The survey also showed 22 percent require a high-school diploma for unskilled jobs, and 94 percent require it for the entry-level office worker.

3. WRITTEN TESTS

It is the position of our agency that if you are utilizing a written test as a preemployment selection device, which 88 percent of your agencies are, and the failure rate for blacks, Chicanos, or women is higher than the failure rate for whites, Anglos, or men then you must sustain the burden of proof of establishing a clear preponderance of statistical evidence that the test can actually predict adequate performance of the actual job for which the individual is being tested. If it is not accomplishing this, then its use must cease.

The demand for validated employment tests does not mean an end to *merit* employment principles but, rather, the opposite. It means return to true merit. It means that you must be able to prove that you are in fact measuring "merit" in terms of the ability to perform the job. That is the only merit which we should be measuring anyway.

4. RULE OF THREE SELECTION SYSTEM

Another method commonly used in personnel systems to help appointing officials select qualified candidates for vacant positions is the Rule-of-Three or the Rule-of-Five, which requires officials to select from the top three or the top five in the list of candidates. Some methods require the selection of the highest ranking candidate. Of 300 state and local government personnel systems in one sample, only 43 percent permitted an appointing official to select any qualified applicant.

I think the courts will deal very critically with these selection systems requiring selection from a list of the top three or top five, for the same reason that mandating a high-school diploma is unlawful. If you find that a system utilizing the "Rule of Three" operates in such a way that Negroes are, in fact, qualified for the jobs but not appearing on the final selection lists, then the system is operating to exclude Negroes. I think you will be required by the courts to prove the job necessity of this selection system. This will be very difficult. Remember that the others on the list of those qualified are, by definition, qualified even if they are not included in the top three. I think you will find the courts looking with some substantial lack of sympathy upon any system which permits exclusion of qualified blacks.

5. PROMOTION SYSTEMS

There are significant deficiencies between seniority systems utilized in private industry and promotion systems used in public employment. There are sufficient basic similarities, however, that the principles developed with respect to the former are applicable to the latter. For example, courts have required the elimination of seniority systems in private industry in which departmental or job seniority had operated to freeze blacks into jobs to which they were discriminatorily assigned at the time of their initial hire. These were replaced with plantwide or other broader-based seniority systems, which avoid continuing to penalize blacks because of prior discrimination.

Similarly, rigid civil-service job classification systems which freeze categories of employees into certain lines or job series may be discriminatory since they limit rights to move from one series to another. Where the failure to be assigned to that series in the first place was discriminatory, the failure to permit their promotion out of that series or their transfer into another series will simply perpetuate the discrimination and is therefore illegal.

REMEDIES

If discrimination is found to exist, what will you be required to do? The answer is to eliminate it, all of it, to make certain it won't return, and develop a remedy for those who have been victims. Prior to the passage of Title VII, the courts had already begun to do a thorough reexamination of state and local government standards and required remedial action. For example, in a case involving the Mississippi Highway Patrol, the court enjoined the use of a test "not proved to be significantly related to successful job performance."

The patrol was ordered not to introduce new standards more stringent than those applicable prior to the case; it was ordered to affirmatively recruit blacks by advertising in black media, visiting black schools, and other actions; and it was, of course, required to maintain records on applicants by race in order to determine compliance with the court order.

In another case involving the Alabama Highway Patrol, a court ordered that 50 percent of those hired be black until such time as 25 percent of the patrol were black; and that no training be implemented unless 25 percent of those in the training course were black. The court required aggregating existing registers and waiting lists, if necessary, to reach this remedial goal, and further ordered affirmative recruitment efforts including "regular recruitment visits to predominantly Negro schools." Similar decisions requiring numerical remedies have been required by the courts in dealing with the Minneapolis Fire Department and a number of other government employers.

Recent newspaper stories regarding reactions to statements by the President have led some public commentators to ask whether there has been or will be a change in the policy of the federal government or the EEOC in requiring this type of remedy for employment discrimination. I should like to reassure this group that regardless of what interpretation may have been placed upon certain developments by the press, there is no change in the policy of the federal government or the Equal Employment Opportunity Commission concerning appropriate remedies for the elimination of discrimination in employment. These remedies are based upon the statutory duty of the Equal Employment Opportunity Commission to identify and eliminate discrimination in employment. We are not concerned with "quotas" or "preferential treatment" in the abstract where there is no discrimination. What does concern us at EEOC and throughout the federal government is the legal obligation to eliminate all discrimination. Sometimes the action taken to eliminate discrimination may be voluntary if an employer—such as the merit systems for which you work—conducts a comprehensive self-audit and determines that certain action is necessary to bring its operations into compliance with the law.

For example, the state of Pennsylvania recently conducted an extensive survey and examination of its employment practices. It concluded that certain substantial remedial steps were necessary and subsequently developed an excellent remedial program. More often, such action is necessary in the context of an enforcement or compliance procedure before an administrative agency such as EEOC. In either case the standard of remedy must be consistent with those required by the courts.

The Supreme Court has given us a great deal of guidance regarding a standard of remedy, and has made clear the distinction between preferential treatment, as some might call it, and remedial treatment which is necessary to eliminate discrimination. In the case of *Swann* v. *Charlotte-Mecklenberg Board of Education, 402* U.S. 1, the court spoke directly to the issue in pointing out that if all things were equal, certain remedial practices might not be necessary or appropriate. All things, however, are not equal where segregation or discrimination have existed. The remedy for such discrimination may be:

> . . . awkward, inconvenient, and even bizarre in some situations and may impose burdens on some; but all awkwardness and inconvenience cannot be avoided in the interim period when remedial adjustments are being made to eliminate the . . . (discrimination or segregation).

Among the cases which the Supreme Court discussed was the case of *United States* v. *The Montgomery Board of Education,* 395 U.S. 225, in which the District Court had set a remedy requiring a specific racial ratio in faculty assignments and the Court of Appeals had changed this part of the remedy. The Supreme Court reversed the Court of Appeals decision and reinstituted the numerical remedy. It specifically permitted the use of a mathematical ratio as a starting point in the process of shaping a remedy. The Supreme Court pointed out "awareness of the racial composition of the whole school system is likely to be a useful starting point in shaping a remedy to correct past" discriminatory practices. Careful reading of the Supreme Court decision makes it clear that where discrimination exists it must be entirely eliminated and the remedy adopted must be appropriate to such elimination.

The use of what, I believe, may appropriately be called "numerical remedies" was clearly endorsed by the Supreme Court in this case. Such terms as "quotas" and "preferential treatment" and "discrimination in reverse" have had many meanings to many different people and have unfortunate connotations. The important thing to this agency and the federal courts is that, where discrimination exists, it must be eliminated, and where such elimination requires a numerical remedy, it is part of the policy of our agency to obtain the remedy that has been approved by the Supreme Court. Much public controversy has developed in this area because newspaper reporters and others may not be aware of current legal definitions of discrimination established by the courts and followed by the EEOC in its case-processing activity. Thus, much of the action including the requirement of a "numerical remedy" necessary to eliminate discrimination in employment appears harsh to those who do not understand the law, and the fact that discrimination is defined as more than just plain evil intent or unequal treatment. But even if they do not understand the legal definition of discrimination, they certainly can understand the words of the Supreme Court that "all things are not equal" where discrimination exists.

PROCEDURE UNDER NEW LAW

In closing I should like to outline very briefly the procedural context in which we will be applying the principles I have outlined above:

1. *Charge Filed with EEOC.* The case begins when an aggrieved party files a charge with us or the initiation of a charge by one of our Commissioners where the possible existence of discrimination has been brought to (his/her) attention.
2. *Investigation.* Extensive investigation of the facts is conducted in order to determine exactly what happened and how your employment systems operate.
3. *Deferral.* In a situation where there is a state agency administering an enforceable fair employment practices law, our investigation is delayed for at least 60 days to permit deferral of the case to a state or local anti-discrimination agency administering legislation comparable in scope to Title VII.

Our records indicate that there are presently 33 state fair employment practices commissions to which deferral is appropriate.

A number of the agencies represented here have asked us whether we will be deferring to agencies administering state grievance procedures or other employee appeal procedures which include a nondiscrimination component. The statute does not permit such deferral. It makes it clear that a state law or city ordinance must prohibit the practices prohibited by Title VII and establish an agency specifically for the purpose of providing remedies for such practices and it clearly does not contemplate deferring for investigation to those agencies, which, in fact are the agencies against which the charge might be filed. This does not prohibit your agency from taking vigorous action to assure that its practices and those of other state agencies are in compliance with the law, but it does prohibit us from deferring to you for investigation charges against yourself or against other agencies.

4. *Finding and Conciliation*. If discrimination is found you will be notified of that fact and provided with an opportunity to eliminate the discrimination through informal methods of conciliation.
5. *Enforcement*. If conciliation fails, the statute provides two enforcement mechanisms—one governmental and one private. The EEOC can refer the case to the United States Attorney General who may bring a suit in Federal District Court. If the U.S. Attorney General does not bring such a suit, the individual who filed the charge with us in the first place may bring one on his own, and if the experience in the private sector is any guide, will do so in many cases.

In concluding, let me urge you to start immediately on the work of extending the principle of merit employment to individuals of all races, ethnic origins, and sex. Let me urge you to conduct the first step in the examination of your practices proposed by the *Griggs* case, that is, determining whether there is a statistical disparity in your work force. Let me suggest that if our experience with state and local governments today is a guide, you will not need an elaborate computer but simply a glance around the room to determine that violations exist. Let me suggest finally that as you reexamine the operation of your employment systems in order to eliminate this statistical disparity, you do so with an imaginative and creative hand to extend the principle of merit employment to its fullest possible extent, which was not limited to rigid rules and tests but was instead designed to assure that the taxpayer gets his money's worth every time a government employee is recruited, hired, or promoted.

Merit principles were not implemented to assure the rigid following of procedures which no longer serve their purpose. They were not implemented to require the utilization of "phony credentials" nor were they implemented to protect the jobs of those of us who design, administer, and interpret written tests. Every time a black, Chicano, or a woman is excluded from recruitment, hiring, or promotion by the rigid operation of the system that does not in fact measure merit or job relatedness, the taxpayer is gypped and the principles of merit employment sabotaged.

I look forward to joining with you in a great common effort to extend the concept of merit employment and to assure that all government jobs are filled with people who really can do their job regardless of race, religion, sex, color, or national origin. Gentlemen and ladies, you have my best wishes for success in this great common endeavor and my promise that, if you do not succeed voluntarily, we will use the full powers of the law recently passed by Congress to encourage your compliance with whatever steps are necessary to obtain it.

QUESTIONS

1. Do the benefits of providing "equal employment opportunity" to society exceed the economic, governmental, and individual costs of strict enforcement? Explain.
2. Do you foresee a day when it will not be necessary for government machinery to compel adherence to Title VII? What changes in society would have to take place? What problems would stand in the way?
3. Do you feel that the definition of discrimination given here is too broad? Is it a mandate for federal government aggrandizement of power over private enterprise and state and local governments?

EXPLODING SOME MYTHS ABOUT WOMEN MANAGERS

WILLIAM E. REIF, JOHN W. NEWSTROM, AND ROBERT M. MONCZKA

William E. Reif, associate professor of management, Arizona State University; John W. Newstrom, associate professor of management and assistant director of the Bureau of Business and Economic Research, Arizona State University; and Robert M. Monczka, visiting associate professor of management, Michigan State University, report in the following article the results of a survey among 164 organizations that explodes major myths about managerial differences between men and women and the ability of women managers to contribute to the achievement of organizational objectives.

Are women managers different from their male counterparts in ways that affect job performance and, therefore, their ability to contribute to the achievement of organizational objectives? Are there substantial reasons for excluding them from managerial positions to the extent that they are excluded today?

The organization's answer to both questions generally has been "yes" largely because of a wide variety of assumptions, or myths, about women managers. Some representative assumptions are:

Women are more emotional and sensitive to the feelings of others, while men are rational and cooly objective in their relationships with others.
Women are uncomfortable in a man's world.
Women work as a hobby or for luxuries and, as a result, lack the ambition, aggressiveness, and dedication necessary to excel in business.
Women have higher rates of sickness and absenteeism.
Women do not understand statistics.

On the assumption that women are significantly different from men in important ways, many organizations have taken the position that special training and development programs are required to prepare women for management positions. In an article entitled "Management Development for Women," Brenner presents a set of recommendations for setting up effective programs to prepare women for management. One of his four underlying assumptions is that women require special programs, because "in general, they have different skills and different attitudes toward the managerial role than men do."

Companies are not alone in establishing separate management training programs for women. Educational institutions, such as the University of Michigan's Division of Management Education, conduct programs that are directed to women, apparently on the assumption that women's needs are different. The brochure for one program, "Management Briefing for Women," states that the three-day seminar has been designed to "meet the needs of women who wish to develop their managerial skills." Great care was taken, however, not to offend any prospective participants by stressing that women are invited and encouraged to participate in all management seminars.

While special treatment appears to be the dominant approach, there are writers and practitioners who believe that women should participate in the same management and supervisory training programs as men, both in and outside the organization. A recent survey of twenty prominent business firms found that although some interest was expressed in special programs for women (on the assumption that inferiorities are commonly found in women), only one firm had what could be classified as a special development program. Interestingly enough, one other company excludes women entirely from its management-development programs. The overall survey report cautions against the use of special programs unless they are open to all persons who need added exposure in a particular discipline. Otherwise, such programs may take on negative connotations and continue to promote the myth that women, along with other minority groups, are innately less capable of performing effectively as managers.

REVIEW OF RELEVANT RESEARCH

Is there evidence that women managers are different—psychologically and socially—from men? If women are different in ways that account for variances in managerial performance, special considerations are probably warranted. If, on the other hand, they are not different in these ways, it is time to engage in more meaningful discussions of the role of women in business. This review of research findings is not intended to be exhaustive but is meant to be representative of what is known about the capabilities of women to manage.

In testing for differences in level of measured ability and knowledge in twenty-two dimensions related to business, the Johnson O'Connor Research Foundation's Human Engineering Laboratory found that there are no differences between men and women in fourteen categories, women excel in six, and men excel in two areas. Women are superior in finger dexterity, graphoria, ideaphoria, observation, silograms, and abstract visualization, while men excel in grip and structural visualization. These results, and others, led to the following observation:

> The aptitudes which seem to underlie successful management are: Objective Personality, Abstract Visualization, and high English Vocabulary. Equal numbers of men and women possess objective personality and high vocabulary. More women have abstract visualization than men. The

ratios are three women in four, one man in two. Theoretically at least, there ought to be more women in management than men.

An exhaustive review by Knowles and Moore of the research contributions concerned with female biology and socialization factors by Bennis, McClelland, Maccoby, Gizberg, Hoffman, Rossi, Masters and Johnson, and others, led them to conclude that the one difference that biologists, psychologists, social psychologists, and sociologists all seem to agree on is women's greater concern for relationships among people.

> About the only testable difference between men and women seems to be women's greater ability in interpersonal relationships . . . the manager of the future will need to be more people-centered, more able to work with people than to exercise position power.

In his book *Managing Women in Business,* Ellman raised the question, "How different are women?" His research led to the general conclusion that, "From an analysis of the data . . . it may be seen that the differences between men and women are far less important than the similarities between them." He suggested that there is some evidence to support the contention that women are more concerned with associates and friends, the quality of supervision, and the surroundings of a job, while men are more interested in the benefits of a job, opportunities for education and advancement, and pay.

The noted Harvard psychologist David McClelland, in trying to synthesize the thousands of psychological studies indicating sex differences, remarked that "the problem is not lack of information, but making sense out of a surfeit of facts." He went on to identify women as more interdependent, more interested in people than things, less analytical, and less manipulative of things than men.

A recent article by Crowley, Levitin, and Quinn attempted to dispel some ill-founded stereotypes of the "average woman." The study found that a significant sex difference does exist in the importance women place on having co-workers who are friendly and helpful. However, women and men attach the same importance to having a competent supervisor rather than having a nice supervisor who is concerned with the welfare of subordinates. The study also provided some support for the proposition that women are more concerned than men with the hygiene aspects of their jobs (such as good hours, pleasant physical surroundings, and convenient travel to and from work).

This study also revealed that women and men are equally concerned that their work is self-actualizing, equally discontented with intellectually undemanding jobs, and equally concerned with opportunities for getting ahead on the job. Overall, these research findings show that there are "more on-the-job similarities between men and women than differences."

Another recent study by Lirtzman and Wahba investigated the capability of women to assume managerial roles, especially aspects related to the decision-making process. The results clearly do not support the contention that women will adopt a sex-role-related strategy in a competitive situation under conditions of uncertainty. In discussing the practical implications of their findings, the authors concluded:

> From a practical point of view these findings raise questions about the traditions of business which bar the accession of women to high organizational positions precisely because it is expected that women will "naturally" act according to sex related roles; that is, noncompetitively.

All of these research findings, although not conclusive, strongly suggest that many of the assumptions that women managers are basically different from men ("different" usually meant as inferior) are not well supported by facts.

A SOCIAL-PSYCHOLOGICAL VIEW OF WOMEN MANAGERS

Most of the research on women managers takes a predominantly psychological approach and is concerned with understanding the attitudes, values, and beliefs women hold about themselves and their work-related roles. Once this psychological make-up is established, strong inferences are made about how women will behave in a business situation. Less attention has been given to understanding how women relate to the environment within which they operate, their attitudes about it, and the extent to which the socialization process has affected their view of the managerial role and the congruence between their self-concept and role expectations.

The psychology of women managers cannot be understood outside the social context and social pressures that direct and support their behavior. The purpose of this study is to provide information about women managers' perceptions of their work environment and to see if their views of the formal and informal aspects of organization are significantly different from those of men. If their social perceptions are different, there would be some basis for predicting sex differences in personality and social conduct. This, in turn, would lead one to conclude that women should be treated differently and that certain modifications in organizational climate would be in order. It would also lend credence to the need for special training programs for women so that they could be conditioned to more nearly fit the role expected of them as managers.

One of the most significant features of this study is its concern for how women managers themselves perceive their work environment. Other studies have found it more convenient to ask men, such as a group of personnel directors, what they think women's attitudes are, or to use a sample of women from the general population, most of whom are not managers and have no aspirations to become managers. There is reason to believe that, psychologically and sociologically, there is just as much difference between female managers and nonmanagers as there is between male managers and nonmanagers. One could also expect there to be more commonality among managers, male and female, than between managers and nonmanagers.

METHODOLOGY

The semantic differential technique was used to measure men and women managers' perceptions of their formal and informal organizations. The semantic differential was chosen because of its ability to measure perceptions along two independent dimensions, evaluative and potency. The evaluative dimension measures perceptions of the "goodness" or "badness" of organizational concepts. In other words, are they believed to be valuable and beneficial to the individual in satisfying his needs? The potency dimension measures perceptions of the "strength" or "weakness" of particular concepts, or the extent to which they are pervasive in the work environment and influential in affecting individual behavior.

The research instrument was developed by selecting eight concepts to represent the formal organization and eight to represent the informal organization. The concepts are:

Formal Organization Concepts

Authority
Job description
Performance appraisal
Chain of command
Policies
Controls
Organizational objectives
Supervisor

Informal Organization Concepts

Voluntary teamwork
Clique
Personal influence
Co-worker evaluation
Social interaction
Group cohesion
Social group membership
Grapevine

Bipolar adjective pairs were chosen through a judgmental selection process that took into consideration their appropriateness for the concepts being studied and their high factor-loading scores. The bipolar adjective pairs selected to record perceptions of the evaluative dimension were: fair-unfair, good-bad, valuable-worthless, pleasant-unpleasant, and clear-hazy. The potency pairs were: strong-weak, hard-soft, and large-small.

The sixteen-page questionnaire was administered to 286 men and 55 women who were participants in management-development programs. They represented 164 organizations, the majority of which were business and government organizations. The organizations varied in size from less than 50 to more than 20,000 employees and had annual sales or revenues from under $250,000 to over $500 million.

Statistical analyses of the data included (1) calculation of the evaluative and potency means for each of the sixteen concepts and for the formal and the informal organizations overall; and (2) application of the standard "t" test to determine if significant differences exist between male and female perceptions of the formal and the informal organizations.

RESEARCH RESULTS

The individual and overall means of the eight formal and eight informal concepts for the evaluative and potency dimensions are shown in Tables 1 and 2. The relatively high mean scores along the evaluative dimension for both men and women indicate that the concepts representing the formal and

Table 1 Formal and Informal Organizational Concepts, Evaluative Means

	EVALUATIVE MEANS*	
CONCEPT	WOMEN	MEN
Formal		
Supervisor	6.22	5.84
Organizational objectives	6.12	5.99
Authority	6.00	5.71
Performance appraisal	5.93	5.48
Job description	5.84	5.44
Policies	5.79	5.69
Chain of command	5.77	5.74
Controls	5.77	5.60
Overall means	5.93	5.69
Informal		
Voluntary teamwork	6.01	5.79
Group cohesion	5.67	5.41
Personal influence	5.56	5.09
Social group membership	5.49	5.12
Social interaction	5.47	5.21
Co-worker evaluation	5.12	4.67
Clique	3.29	3.12
Grapevine	3.06	3.31
Overall means	4.96	4.72

* Minimum score = 1.00; maximum score = 7.00.

informal organizations, with the exception of clique and grapevine, were perceived to be quite good, that is, valuable to the respondents in satisfying their needs (Table 1). The mean scores along the potency dimension, although lower than the evaluative scores, reveal that the organizational variables were generally perceived to be quite strong and influential in affecting behavior (Table 2).

Table 2 Formal and Informal Organizational Concepts, Potency Means

CONCEPT	POTENCY MEANS* WOMEN	MEN
Formal		
Organizational objectives	5.72	5.35
Authority	5.24	5.33
Policies	5.13	5.05
Performance appraisal	5.12	4.77
Supervisor	5.05	5.15
Controls	5.00	5.12
Chain of command	4.98	5.03
Job description	4.87	4.72
Overall means	5.14	5.07
Informal		
Personal influence	4.86	4.86
Voluntary teamwork	4.85	4.74
Group cohesion	4.82	4.74
Social group membership	4.61	4.38
Grapevine	4.55	4.18
Co-worker evaluation	4.52	4.39
Social interaction	4.45	4.50
Clique	3.85	3.89
Overall Means	4.56	4.46

* Minimum score = 1.00; maximum score = 7.00.

FORMAL VERSUS INFORMAL CONCEPTS

The data show that the formal organizational concepts were perceived by men and women to be better (more valuable) and stronger (more influential) than the informal ones. Voluntary teamwork and group cohesion were the only informal concepts that compared favorably with the set of formal organization variables. For men and women the evaluative means of all other informal concepts were lower than the lowest of the formal concepts. Along the potency dimension women respondents viewed *all* formal concepts as more influential in affecting behavior than any of the informal concepts. For men all formal concepts except job description and performance appraisal were perceived as stronger and more influential than any informal organization variables.

Clique and grapevine had the lowest composite evaluative and potency means of all sixteen variables, indicating that they were viewed as relatively bad and weak. The fact that they were perceived as weak and having little influence on individual behavior is fortunate. Although the difference is not statistically significant, it is interesting to note that women managers perceive the grapevine to be more influential in affecting behavior than men.

WOMEN'S AND MEN'S PERCEPTIONS

In order to get a clearer picture of how men and women view the formal and informal aspects of organization the standard "t" test was employed. For men it revealed that along the evaluative dimension there is a statistically significant difference between all formal concepts and six of the eight informal concepts, the exceptions being voluntary teamwork and group cohesion. Along the potency dimension there is a significant difference between six formal concepts (an except performance appraisal and job description) and all informal concepts. Men clearly view the two sets of organizational variables differently. They perceive the formal organizational concepts as being more valuable in satisfying needs (evaluative dimension) and more influential in affecting behavior (potency dimension) than the informal ones.

For women, along the evaluative dimension there is a significant difference between four formal concepts (supervisor, organizational objectives, authority, and performance appraisal) and five informal concepts (social group membership, social interaction, co-worker evaluation, clique, and grapevine). And along the potency dimension there is a significant difference between six formal concepts (all except chain of command and job description) and three informal concepts (co-worker evaluation, social interaction, and clique). Women apparently do not make such a sharp distinction between the formal and informal organizations, and do not have as great a tendency as men to look to the formal organization for the satisfaction of needs and cues for appropriate behavior. The data show, however, that although men perceive concepts relating to the formal organization as significantly more valuable and influential than those of the informal organization, women view the formal organizational aspects even more positively than men.

The standard "t" test also was used to determine if statistically significant differences exist between men and women in the ways they perceive the various components of the formal and informal organizations along the evaluative and potency dimensions. Table 3 lists the differences at the 0.05 significance level for seven of the sixteen organization concepts along the evaluative dimension and two concepts along the potency dimension.

Table 3 Significant Differences in Perception of Organizational Concepts Between Men and Women

CONCEPT	EVALUATIVE DIMENSION SIGNIFICANT DIFFERENCE AT 0.05 LEVEL	POTENCY DIMENSION SIGNIFICANT DIFFERENCE AT 0.05 LEVEL
Organizational objectives		x
Supervisor	x	
Authority	x	
Performance appraisal	x	x
Job description	x	
Personal influence	x	
Social group membership	x	
Co-worker evaluation	x	
Overall		
Formal organization	x	
Informal organization	x	

Of the eight formal concepts, women consider four (supervisor, authority, performance appraisal, and job description) to be more valuable in satisfying their needs, and two (organizational objectives and performance appraisal) to be more influential in affecting behavior than men. The way women responded to performance appraisal is of particular interest. Other research implies that women managers are discriminated against when it comes to promotion. If they really feel this way one would expect them to view performance appraisal negatively. On the contrary, this study found that women view performance appraisal as significantly more valuable and influential than men.

Women perceive three of the eight informal concepts significantly differently from men along the evaluative dimension. They view personal influence, social group membership, and co-worker evaluation as more valuable in satisfying needs. This result is consistent with other research and lends support to the proposition that women place higher value on interpersonal relationships, especially those with peers. It is somewhat surprising that although these three informal concepts are perceived as more valuable by women, they are not perceived as being significantly more influential in affecting behavior.

In all cases the significant differences in perception of the work environment between men and women are a product of the more positive feelings women have about the formal and informal organizations. Along the evaluative dimension women regard the total organization to be significantly more supportive of need satisfaction.

This finding does not support the many opinions expressed in the literature that the world of business is foreign to most women and that they do not fit comfortably in managerial roles.

CONCLUSIONS

The results of this research, along with the other reported findings, lead to several conclusions about women managers.

First, men and women managers are more similar than dissimilar in their feelings about the organizational climate within which they work. This conclusion is based upon their perceptions of the sixteen concepts that were chosen to represent the formal and informal organizations. Primary differences were found to exist in the more positive views that women have of the formal organization and its ability to satisfy needs, and the extent to which they value interpersonal relationships as evidenced by higher evaluative mean scores for personal influence, social group membership, and co-worker evaluation. No significant differences exist between men and women that would limit the capacity of women to perform effectively in managerial roles.

Second, women managers tend to view the organization as an integrated whole. Men, on the other hand, differentiate between formal and informal organizational concepts and clearly prefer the formal organization, both in terms of its value in satisfying needs and its influence on individual behavior. One implication of this finding is that women managers may find it more satisfying to work in an organization in which the technical (formal) and social (informal) aspects are compatible and supportive of their needs for affiliation and other socially derived forms of gratification. This kind of work environment would be very consistent with the organization-development (OD) approaches of organizational behaviorists, who contend that the most effective systems are those that are capable of maintaining a climate that allows individuals to experience need satisfaction and at the same time supports the organization's efforts to achieve its objectives.

Third, this study proposes that decisions made about women on the basis of their sex, without considering such individual factors as background, education, experience, personality, and potential, are likely to be wrong. It appears that many of the stereotypes of women are not representative of women who hold or aspire to responsible positions in business. Moreover, the supposed sex differences in personality, abilities, and attitudes about work for the most part have not been based upon empirical observations of women managers but have resulted from judgments about traits that have been rightly or wrongly attributed to women in general.

This conclusion does not imply that women on the average are equal or superior to men in all capacities that are important for managers. It simply argues that women should be considered on the basis of their personal qualifications in the same way that men are. On that basis it is realistic to assume that there are many women who are well qualified for management positions.

Fourth, the need to establish special management-development programs for women is questioned. This is especially true of programs whose purpose it is to "condition" women so that they will feel more at home in business. The results of this study indicate that women managers do not perceive their environment as threatening or dissatisfying but as highly supportive. It is recommended that a more effective change strategy would be to modify the beliefs of those persons who do not think that women are capable of managing, rather than to change the attitudes of women about their roles at work. Special training programs may be in order, but not for the group for which they were originally intended.

In conclusion, there is considerable research evidence to support the fact that women managers psychologically are not significantly different from their male counterparts and that they may possess even superior attributes and skills in some areas related to managerial effectiveness. From a social psychological standpoint—that is, how they view themselves as a part of the environment within which they operate—this study has shown that women managers have much in common with men. Differences do exist, but mostly in ways that would serve to *increase* the probability of women

The Peter Principle bluntly reveals how people advance in institutional bureaucracies. "In a hierarchy every employee tends to rise to his level of incompetence." That is, people who do their work well tend to get promoted until they finally land a job too difficult for them. At that point they stop getting promotions, which leads to Peter's Corollary: "In time, every post tends to be occupied by an employee who is incompetent to carry out his duties." Thus, according to Peter, real work in an organization is performed only by those who have not yet reached their "final placement" of incompetence.

Commenting on the Peter Principle in the *Harvard Business Review,* one professor of management suggested that organizations are still able to function—despite the incompetents—because women and other suppressed minorities, such as blacks and immigrants, are not permitted to rise to positions they cannot handle; they remain instead in jobs they can perform efficiently. But the real flaw in the Peter Principle is probably simpler: Most employees are not promoted high enough to test their mettle. If six equally competent individuals are working in a department, and one of them is promoted over the others to his final level of incompetence, five competent people remain to do the job. And there they probably stay, for their new incompetent boss is not likely to get any further promotions to make room for them.

From HUMAN BEHAVIOR/*Man and the Organization* by Rafael Steinberg and the Editors of TIME-LIFE Books © 1975, Time, Inc., pp. 78–79.

functioning well as managers. It is recommended, therefore, that organizations begin treating women as equals, not because of moral obligations or pressures from outside interest groups to improve female-male ratios, but because they would more effectively utilize valuable human resources.

QUESTIONS

1. In what major ways are women managers alleged to be different from men managers?
2. To what extent has the available research, exclusive of that of this article, confirmed or disproved these allegations?
3. Describe the research design of this article. Would you recommend any major changes in the methodology? Explain.
4. What major conclusions did the authors of this article draw from their research?
5. Are the results of this research convincing to you? Do the results agree with your general observations?
6. What further research on this subject would you recommend?

NO EASY VICTORIES ON THE VOYAGE TO EQUALITY

JACQUELINE PINCKNEY

Jacqueline Pinckney, manager of the Equal Employment Opportunity Program Development, General Electric Company, discusses in the following paper equal opportunity policies of General Electric, problems that have been encountered in fulfilling the policies, and actions that the company has taken to achieve its objectives.

Writing some 2000 years ago, a philosopher observed: Affairs go according to the conditions of their time, and plans must be made in accordance with the way affairs are going now. My assignment is to share with you one corporation's approach to providing equal employment opportunities—to summarize our policy, describe some of the creative programs that have been implemented, and to comment on their results. Before doing so, however, we need to assess the environment as a way of understanding the broader view and perhaps adjust our expectations based upon the way affairs are going now.

First, to state the obvious: The economic downturn of 1974–75 has had an adverse impact on employment levels in general, and on minority employment levels in particular. Economists predict that America still faces a long and painful period of high unemployment for the rest of the decade. In time, a larger and larger proportion of the unemployed will be those with little or no job experience, notes one observer, most of them young and a disproportionate number of them black. Severe social stresses are predicted as high rates of unemployment tend to impede movement toward social or economic equality. The already grim conditions suffered by minority youth will become grimmer still, and the overall position of minority persons in the society may not improve. Concomitantly, it is felt that progress toward equality for women may slow down.

As the economy slowed down, minorities and women were adversely affected—largely because employers followed the seniority provisions of their bargaining unit contracts, and the LIFO principle—last in, first out—applied, although some attempts were made by employers to implement shortened work weeks and similar approaches to sharing the work. Predictably, there have been clashes over the seniority question and a number of cases are now in the courts. In one instance, civil rights advocates have proposed the concept of "retroactive seniority" for employees who initially

Jacqueline Pinckney, "No Easy Victories on the Voyage to Equality," *The Changing Business Role in Society,* George A. Steiner (ed.), Los Angeles, California: Graduate School of Management, UCLA, 1975, pp. 1–14. Reprinted by permission.

were denied jobs because of their race and/or sex, and they suggest that such constructive seniority is a way to help minority and women workers keep jobs won for them through litigation of discrimination cases or through conciliation agreements.

The "rightness" or "wrongness" of layoffs based on seniority caused traditional allies in the civil rights movement to clash at the NAACP convention in June. On the one hand, Herbert Hill, National Labor Director of the NAACP stated: "There are some who argue that seniority is a vested right. This, of course, is sheer nonsense. The argument that white men have a prior right to a job and that blacks must wait until there is full employment before they too can work is the essence of the racist mentality." However, William Pollard, Director of Civil Rights for the AFL-CIO and a member of the NAACP Board of Directors, took sharp issue, saying: "A lot of people are falling victim to cliches and shibboleths, rather than listening to the issues. Seniority did not create the recession, and the abolition of it won't cure it."

Second, at the end of ten years since passage of the Civil Rights Act, twenty years since the Supreme Court ruling on school integration, and 199 years since the declaration, "All men are created equal," millions of our citizens do not believe the promise of America will be fulfilled. One would expect a different state of affairs following the Sixties—a decade when shouts of "black power" and "black is beautiful" moved masses and changed history. But the expectation is too great and the reality unchanged.

In the private sector, despite the excellent efforts exerted by the corporate world to fulfill its obligations to legal and social responsibility, to ensure the right of all persons to work, and to advance on the basis of merit and ability, there are people who state that, unfortunately, not all the artificial, arbitrary, and unnecessary barriers to equal employment opportunity have been removed. This viewpoint is confirmed in some quarters by the status of blacks today, notably as summarized in the April 1975 issue of *Fortune*. In the article, "Black America: Still Waiting for Full Membership," the authors note that great shortcomings persist amid what most white Americans see as immense accomplishment in moving the U.S. toward racial equality. They cite the ever-increasing number of blacks who hold political office, or who are enrolled in higher education as examples of progress; however, they suggest that these gains are tempered by economic disparities.

16% of black families have less than $3,000 annual income, compared to 5% of white families.

In the middle income brackets, $7,000–$12,000 annual income, the percentage for both black and white families is 26%; however, in the majority of black families, both husband and wife must work to attain this income level.

At the top of the scale, family incomes above $15,000, blacks number 16% compared to 38% of white families. Money may not buy everything, but income is a major determinant of well-being.

The primary source of earned income is employment, and blacks have made employment gains—gains which are particularly noticeable where federal contracts and subsidies have provided leverage, forcing employers to take affirmative action in hiring and upgrading. But, the authors note, while more and more companies have increased their numbers of minority managers and professionals, blacks argue that few of these positions have real authority; most are "window dressing" jobs, or are involved with minority employees or sales to minority markets rather than mainstream operating jobs. These and other developments cited in *Fortune* point up the fact that, while minority progress over the years is demonstrable, "it has been below the level of minority expectations and is offset to some degree by comparable and sometimes greater gains for whites."

Third, women have joined the equal rights battle and their expectations were also high in the early days of the movement. However, in 1975 the gap has widened between women's expectations and performance of our societal institutions—business, government, academia, and the religious community. Among the modest gains: In politics, the first woman governor was elected in her own right; a woman was appointed secretary of Housing and Urban Development. Women comprised 20% of law school enrollments in 1974, and 25% of incoming medical students were women. More modest gains were registered in the arts, science, show business, education, publishing, and sports. But, the progress of women has been hampered by tokenism, chauvinism, and women's own reluctance to abandon their traditional roles.

Fourth, corporations continue to feel heavy pressure from government, minority and women activists, and youth—with at least tacit support from the general public—to serve as the main catalyst for change.

How does the corporation respond to these pressures while dealing with other weighty problems? Where does corporate social responsibility begin and end? Is it realistic to expect immediate solutions to deep-seated, centuries' old problems? Is it realistic to expect the corporation to redress all the wrongs of society—of poor health, bad housing, faulty family structure, drug abuse, educational and cultural deprivation—all those factors which impact on the worker long before he or she arrives at the plant gate? Where do we draw the line?

Although some view the corporation as monolithic, it is, in fact, a multifaceted institution whose managers must balance the claims of many constituencies—employees, shareowners, public interest groups, government, customers, suppliers, bankers, and the competition. It's been said the complex and clashing claims of constituents are harder to assess and resolve than ever. For example, managers intent on serving the corporation's long-term future may feel the need to bend to the desires of public interest groups concerned about pollution. The stockholders, on the other hand, might worry more about the impact of pollution control on current earnings. To take another case, if a supplier raises prices sharply, the corporation's managers may choose to absorb some of the costs rather than drive customers to competing products. But the managers will probably have to defend that action to their bankers when it comes time to negotiate a new loan. It's like walking a tightrope daily—without a net.

Perhaps it was this concept of the managerial balancing act which inspired this comment by GE Board Chairman, Reg Jones, in a recent *Forbes* article:

> Jones sees his biggest challenge as keeping GE in tune with the times. 'I am concerned,' he says, 'not so much with developing enough business managers per se as I am with developing business managers who have the sensitivity and concern for external factors to permit them to operate successfully in what I see in the years ahead as a much more hostile environment than we know today.'
>
> Every businessman will know what Jones is talking about: The increasing way in which politics, ecology and consumerism and the like are intruding into the business decision-making process. It is no longer enough for a manager to be profit-minded and efficiency-minded; he must factor in a good many influences which will never appear on a balance sheet. Rather than merely complaining about these 'outside' influences, GE has already begun to work them into its decision-making process; witness the way such matters as minority hiring are given weight in the Company's strategic business planning.

This same article provides some insight about GE's organizational structure which may be a useful preface to our discussion of equal opportunity policies and practices at GE:

> From the outside, at least, GE is a managerial nightmare, more conglomerate than most conglomerates. Just consider the variety of complex management problems GE poses down through its nine groups and 48 divisions. Its growing chemical and plastics businesses eat up great gobs of capital, while its toaster, flatiron and other small appliance lines are mainly labor-intensive. Its utility equipment business juggles order backlogs stretching to the next decade, while its lamp and consumer products businesses live week to week. General Electric's aircraft engine and aerospace managers depend on just a handful of giant customers, while its refrigerator, air conditioner and other major appliance managers must deal with perhaps 100 million notoriously fickle American consumers.
>
> Some GE businesses, such as batteries and heat pumps, call for growth strategies, while others, such as vacuum tubes, are best harvested for cash flow. Some rely on international markets; others are strictly domestic. Some involve the most sophisticated new technologies; others can be worked out on the back of an envelope. Nearly all have a high labor content, but some require platoons of Ph.D.s while others need only warm bodies to operate.

Few will debate that managing a company as complex as GE requires sophisticated management methods and systems. Our equal employment measuring system is one of the most comprehensive in industry. It's built into our official written policy, which begins:

> General Electric is committed to equality of opportunity, a basic goal of a free society. Profitable, responsive growth and the business success of the General Electric Company, as well as the personal growth of individuals, result from enhancing and utilizing the abilities of individuals to the fullest extent practical within the framework of the business environment. By hiring, compensating, training, promoting and in all ways providing fair treatment to employees on the basis of merit, the effectiveness of the Company's operations can be maintained while enhancing both the nation's economic progress and that of individuals.

This principle was first enunciated in 1935 by President Gerard Swope and has been emphasized by four succeeding Chief Executive Officers. Today's policy centers on this paragraph:

> It is the policy of the General Electric Company to provide employment, training, compensation, promotion and other conditions of employment without regard to race, color, religion, national origin, sex or age, except where age or sex are essential, bona fide occupational requirements.

The Company's policy goes on to recognize that while such a written statement of purpose provides an essential base on which to build, a declaration alone is insufficient in realizing equality of opportunity. The policy calls for affirmative action on several key fronts:

> Action programs designed to bring more minority people and women into the GE work force and to identify those who have the capability and initiative to move up through the ranks.
>
> "Outreach" programs to "seek out individuals whose potential has not been developed" and assist them in meeting employment standards and qualifications necessary to sustain the Company's performance in a highly competitive economy.
>
> Leadership not only at the local but also at the national level.
>
> Performance relating to equal opportunity goals as one primary measurement of management. Annual Equal Opportunity reviews are conducted at both the operational and corporate levels of the Company, with the Corporate EEO staff assigned responsibility for monitoring Company-wide progress toward equal opportunity goals.

As business men and women, we must place the question of equity or equality on the basis that any realistic business organization in today's social environment has to learn to integrate the newer social expectations and responsibilities of equal opportunity with the rigorous disciplines of a competitive business arena.

Based on these considerations, we are interested in results that not only meet the government's explicit requirements, but also open up opportunities for us to utilize the talents of women and minorities more fully and at progressively higher levels of responsibility. Further, we recognize that results won't flow automatically, and that managers need exposure to new procedures and decisions in an area which many of them may find difficult and unfamiliar.

The result is that General Electric has an action-oriented philosophy as well as a Company-wide system to accelerate the upward mobility of minorities and women. Chairman Jones has noted that "this sense of commitment starts with the Board of Directors." During 1973, the Public Issues Committee of the Board made its first order of business an in-depth review of the Company's equal employment policies and practices. In 1974, a black man was elected to the Board, which as a whole has consistently supported proposals to upgrade opportunities for minorities and women. As for top management's view, Chairman Jones has commented: "There is no aspect of General Electric to which management assigns greater importance than to fulfill our commitments as an equal opportunity employer . . . the men and women joining us can be assured that they will be measured not on the basis of color or sex, not by race or religion or country of origin, but by the single criterion of performance."

Conscientious implementation of this equal opportunity policy over the years has turned words into actions and statements of intent into measurable progress. Here are some examples:

The obvious first step in improving opportunities for minorities at General Electric is to put more people from minority groups on the payroll. GE has done that. At the end of the second quarter of 1974, the number of minority employees at General Electric was at an all-time high, totaling 35,719, and representing 11.3% of the Company's U.S. work force. At the end of 1968, the comparable figures were 21,583 or 6.9%. Thus minority employment had increased by 65.5%, while total company employment rose only 1%. These statistics were made available in a special section of the *GE Investor,* a quarterly publication for shareowners, in the fall of 1974. We also reported gains in key job categories—managers, professionals, and skilled crafts.

From year-end 1973 to year-end 1974, minority managers increased by 25.5%, while total managers grew by only 3.5%. In the professionals category, the total climbed by 1.1%, while minority professionals increased by 14.3% in that period.

Since 1968, minority professionals have more than doubled, while minority managers experienced nearly a four-fold increase. These gains are indeed significant because of the technical orientation of many of GE's businesses. Similar increases have been achieved in other categories. For example, in December 1974, minorities held 6.9% of the skilled crafts jobs, an increase since 1968 of 66.6%, from 2,340 to 3,898.

On an individual basis, minority men and women are serving the Company in a wide variety of high-level assignments, including positions as manager of research, corporate medical director, union relations negotiator, traveling auditor, plant manager, strategic planning manager, sales engineer, quality control supervisor, general manager, manager of technical resources operations, and legal counsel.

Minority employees have a special voice in shaping the Company's equal opportunity programs and performances via a panel of minority employees from across the Company who come together to assess what is being done and to recommend future courses of action and improvement to management.

Business considerations have also given the issue of equality for women a high priority among the concerns of General Electric management, ever mindful of women's consumer clout as the principal and regular buyers in most families. Since many of our consumer products and major appliances are purchased by women, there is added incentive to exert a leadership role in the area of employment opportunities for women.

The Company has defined four objectives in a program to provide equal employment opportunities for women: to be responsive to the government's requirements; to use womanpower effectively; to establish goals, priorities and measurements for management; and to gain men's and women's understanding and awareness of the problems both face in enabling women to move into more challenging career paths.

Total women's employment at the end of 1974 was 27% or 79,722. At the upper end of the spectrum, the number of women in managerial positions has more than quintupled since 1968, while women in professional jobs nearly doubled. In August of 1974, the Company elected its first woman Vice President, heading GE's Corporate Consulting Services. Her election, capping 30 years of service, illustrates the up-from-the-ranks aspect of the Company's human resource system; most of the gains registered by women in the managerial, professional, and skilled crafts areas are the result of promotions from within the Company.

Some GE women have broken new ground, venturing into careers which have not been traditionally sought by women—as welder, fork truck operator, plant protection policewoman, factory forewoman, and aircraft test pilot. Women are employed on the Company's traveling auditor staff, and they hold staff positions in business planning, employee and public relations, legal operations, and investment securities analysis. As with minorities, a women's panel of key professionals has been organized to survey programs for women and bring suggestions for improvement to the attention of top management. The panel has brought to the fore, for example, the need for new efforts to change traditional perceptions of women in responsible jobs. Carefully structured "awareness seminars" and other programs have helped both men and women rethink their attitudes regarding women's roles in the world of work.

But sheer statistics of hiring and upgrading minority persons and women don't tell the entire story of equal opportunity as practiced at General Electric. The Company goes beyond these activities to conduct vigorous recruitment programs designed to reach minorities and women and attract them to GE careers. These recruitment programs take a number of forms. On a Company-wide basis, a high priority is given to recruiting minorities and women among college students. In the recruitment of minorities, for example, GE recruiters yearly visit more than 25 predominantly black campuses in the U.S., with especially intensive efforts directed at six predominantly black four-year engineering schools. And in its general recruiting at hundreds of campuses nationwide, 700 recruiters make special efforts to interview and refer minority and women candidates among college seniors. Through these efforts, employment of minority college graduates represented 15.3% and women 12.4% of the total college graduates hired in 1974.

These Company-wide efforts are strengthened by programs initiated by specific operations. As an example, black students with technical degrees are recruited for Corporate Research and Development's Industrial Research Graduate Study Program. An Industrial Intern Program for Women has been established in Philadelphia by the Switchgear Equipment Division in cooperation with the University of Pennsylvania's Wharton School of Finance and Commerce. The program provides professional assignments for women students before they begin MBA studies and offers them permanent positions on completion of their advanced degree work. In Erie, Pennsylvania, an unusual program initiated by the Transportation Systems Division enables women liberal arts graduates to work toward positions in manufacturing methods and planning.

Cooperative work programs and summer jobs provide important channels through which minorities and women gain a first exposure to GE careers. Example: Co-op assignments in accounting and finance for minority candidates resulting from a program established by Schenectady's Steam Turbine-Generator Financial Operation in conjunction with New York City Community College. Our recruitment extends beyond programs for college-level candidates, however. The Company's Chicago Hotpoint Relations Operation, for instance, seeks local minority people for the training programs it conducts under U.S. government sponsorship. In the latest of these programs, the operation achieved a high retention rate of 75% of those recruited.

General Electric has a long tradition of conducting training and development programs that help employees develop to their maximum potential and provide future leadership. Today, each of these programs seeks to increase the participation by minorities and women.

For college graduates, we conduct a number of Company-wide programs, including:

Financial Management Program—a one- to two-year program for graduates with special aptitude and interest in financial careers.

Manufacturing Management Program—offered primarily to those with engineering degrees who wish to work toward positions in manufacturing.

Technical Marketing Program—for engineering and other technical graduates seeking responsible positions in technical sales and application engineering.

Field Engineering Program—intensive training and field assignments for engineering graduates interested in installation, maintenance, and troubleshooting at customer locations worldwide.

Engineering Management Program—for specially qualified engineering graduates interested in innovative product design and development.

Employee Relations Management Program—one to two years of intensive and varied assignments leading to positions in managing human resources effectively.

Sales Financing Program—conducted by the GE Credit Corporation principally for finance and business graduates.

In addition, many components sponsor their own rotational programs for college graduates in such areas as major appliance sales management and technical disciplines. Minorities and women have steadily increased their participation in these developmental programs.

In addition to conducting its own professional development programs, General Electric makes it possible for employees to study at nearby educational institutions, offering reimbursement of tuition for acceptable academic performance in approved college-level job-related courses.

GE's self-development opportunities are by no means limited to individuals with college degrees. On a Company-wide basis, the Individual Development Plan reimburses tuition to any hourly or non-exempt salaried employee with at least six months' service who takes college or non-college courses which will contribute to his or her general career development.

At Crotonville, New York, the Company operates its own Management Development Institute, with professional and managerial studies tailored to various stages of employee development, from entry-level positions to advanced executive workshops. Indicative of the increased participation in these courses by minorities and women, a recent offering of the Institute's Managerial Skills Development Course, designed for people who want to work toward managerial positions, included 32% minority and 17% women in its enrollment.

Complementing these Company-wide activities are literally hundreds of development and training programs conducted by individual components at plant locations throughout the country. Probably the best known of these activities is "Hotpoint High" in Chicago. Enrolling nearly 1,100 in the past year, this program offers basic high school courses, taught within GE facilities. Supplementing "Hotpoint High" are courses in quality control and middle management, as well as apprenticeships for electricians, pipefitters, millwrights, machinists, and tool and die makers. Most of the participants are members of minority groups.

General Electric is delivering on the promise of its written policy to provide leadership in advancing equal opportunity at both national and local levels. One area for attention has been the problem of attracting more minorities into technical career paths. National figures point up the problem: In engineering, for example, in 1968, only 314 black Americans earned bachelor's degrees in engineering—less than 1%. By 1974, the number of black engineering grads was reported at 743, a 137% increase, but only 1.79% of total engineering degrees awarded. There were 1.033 Spanish surnamed engineering graduates in 1974 (including 397 degrees awarded by the University of Puerto Rico); and 32 American Indians in the class of 1974, or 0.07%. In total, 1,808 members of these three minority groups received engineering degrees, or 4.35% of the 41,407 degrees conferred. If none of these grads decided to go on to graduate school or into non-industrial careers, each of the "Fortune 500" companies could theoretically hire just 3.6 minority engineering graduates from the class of '74. That's the dimension of the supply problem. (Similarly, women comprise less than 2% of engineering graduates.)

This problem is compounded by the fact that upward mobility for minorities and women into the executive ranks depends in large part on increasing the numbers of minorities and women with technical degrees. As an indicator, a number of our top managers have four-year technical degrees. Our thesis, consequently, is that increasing the number of minority people who are qualified engineering graduates will prove of significant help in accelerating their entry into the top managerial ranks and mainstream positions.

On a national scale, we are joining with government agencies, other companies, educators, and minority leaders to encourage greater numbers of minority students to select technical careers. To spearhead efforts aimed at minority youth, Reg Jones is serving as Chairman of the National Advisory Council on Minorities in Engineering, formed by the National Academy of Engineering to lead a national drive to increase the number of minority engineering graduates from the present 1,500 per year to some 4,000 to 6,000 per year within a decade. As one phase of this national effort, the Minority Engineering Education Effort Task Force, under GE leadership, has identified more than 8,000 minority high school graduates who have expressed an interest in engineering careers. This Task Force has also contacted some 10,000 students to make them aware of an engineering career's potential and its attainability.

General Electric has also initiated its own Program to Increase Minority Engineering Graduates. Examples of its far-ranging activities include the following:

More than 10,000 young people have toured Expo-Tech, a mobile exhibit designed to motivate minority junior high school students to investigate engineering careers. Traveling to such cities as Philadelphia, Washington, Erie, Cleveland, Cincinnati, Lynchburg, Virginia, and Bridgeport, Connecticut, the show is housed in a 40-foot expandable van in which 17 "operate-it-yourself" exhibits make engineering more understandable and approachable.

In Syracuse, New York, GE participates with Cornell University in a Mini-Co-Op program in which sophomore students spend a week assigned to minority engineers to learn their job responsibilities.

In Philadelphia, the Switchgear Equipment Division contacts Lincoln University sophomores who have good records in physics, mathematics, chemistry, and science, to inform them about engineering.

In California, the Vallecitos Nuclear Center fields a team of managers who conduct workshops for high school counselors of Spanish surnamed students.

Concern for augmenting the numbers of qualified minorities in engineering and business is also evident in many of the educational grants made by the General Electric Foundation, an independent trust. In 1974, $1,070,152 out of a total educational support budget of $3,408,778 was allocated by the Foundation for programs aimed at strengthening engineering and business academic offerings in predominantly black schools, strengthening dual-degree programs linking predominantly black liberal arts schools with major engineering schools, and stimulating other innovative programs in engineering.

The Foundation has also established a series of grants to support Tech-Vocational Education programs, encouraging the development of secondary school courses and curricula designed to point young minority people toward technical careers.

The long-range objective of General Electric's equal opportunity policy and practices is to contribute toward development of a truly open society—one in which race and sex have no part in limiting the self-fulfillment of the individual. Short-range programs to get us on that long-range trajectory as summarized herein reflect a conscious and conscientious effort to meet the Company's commitment to a program of well conceived and workable, doable corporate social responsibility. But to expect that one segment of society—business—can and should provide a full spectrum of development and opportunity is to overlook the myriad of factors that may aid or hinder—factors such as home environment, parental guidance, education, self-concept, peer perception, and role models. In the broadest sense we need a better integration of the home/school and work environments to assure maximum opportunity for individuals to reach their full potential. Moreover, because the corporation is a creation of society, a mirror of contemporary mores, the corporation responds to societal needs whether couched as strident demands or pathetic pleas for help. Thus national priorities and goals are needed to shore up the weaknesses in the delivery system. The sad state of education in the inner city ghetto, the barrio, the small town in the South, or in rural areas is illustrative. It is here that learning is discouraged and future careers so often blighted. For many minority youths to achieve a professional career, family patterns of non-achievement must be overcome, and basic skills acquired without assistance at home and/or in a school which defies learning. Corporations have spent millions of dollars aiding school dropouts, helping programs such as the Opportunities Industrialization Centers, and providing basic education programs to functionally illiterate prospective employees. Inevitably, however, the schools and the basic learning institutions must do a more effective job if discrimination and unequal opportunity are not to be perpetuated.

Overcoming the barriers to women's full utilization requires making a fundamental change in attitudes and behavior, to dispel the unrealistic image of what is proper "women's work" versus "men's work." It may mean a massive communications and guidance effort starting at the grammar school level to overcome the lack of true information about the scope of careers and widened options, and the lack of realization that these choices are available to women. More fundamentally, it means unravelling a tangled snarl of myths, half truths, and misconceptions about sex role differentiations that have hampered men and women for centuries.

Driving, creative, innovative efforts to solve problems is the essence of life—for a civilization, or an individual, or a corporation. Measuring the social effects of business decisions is the newest and most difficult of the many challenges faced by business men and women these days, and it does indeed require a driving, creative effort. And GE will continue the policy and practices that ensure equal employment opportunity and upward mobility for minorities and women. True, it's a legal requirement, involving regular governmental "compliance reviews" that measure the Company's progress. More than that, however, as Chairman Jones has stated: "Above that, it's a moral requirement—it's expected of us as a socially responsible corporate citizen and it's essential to the self-respect of those of us employed by the Company. At the same time, fortunately, it makes good economic sense for the country . . . and good business sense in keeping our operations profitable."

Finally, scattered but symptomatic events of recent years and the further development of societal trends confirm that there is clearly a competitive edge to be won by those corporations who take imaginative, farsighted, innovative steps to capitalize on minority gains in education and income to develop manpower and marketing opportunities, and to capitalize on the large number of women who are already well educated, well motivated, and well adjusted to the world of work. To do so means corporate social responsibility—and corporate survival.

In closing, I should like to add one further thought: Life is not a series of easy victories, of winning every round or arriving at neat solutions to every problem. Winning the battle of equality won't be an easy victory. But then, difficulty is an excuse which history never accepts. And finding neat solutions to societal problems has to be a shared venture. "The hard reality," as John D. Rockefeller 3rd observed, "is that no one sector of our society is competent to deal with these problems—not business, not government, not labor, not the non-profit organizations. The only answer is that all sectors must become involved, each in its own distinctive way, but in full and collaborative relationship with the others." Let us resolve, then, to become involved—each of us bringing our expertise, our creativity, and our own individual brand of excellence to the task. Each of us can make a difference—and all of us should try.

QUESTIONS

1. The author gives a look inside the complex equal opportunity program of an industrial giant. Are you impressed with the efforts and results revealed here? Why or why not?
2. Is there anything that General Electric is not doing to further equal opportunity that you think might be done? If so, what?
3. Do you agree with Pinckney that there is "clearly a competitive edge to be won" by companies that aggressively pursue affirmative action goals? Why or why not? If so, do you think General Electric could have embarked on some of the programs mentioned in this article at an earlier date?
4. Would you describe the General Electric program as a creative and farsighted one or as a simple compliance effort to satisfy the government and pressure group demands?

13

RENOVATING GOVERNMENTAL REGULATORY MACHINERY

THE CONSENSUS ON THE MAJOR ISSUES ABOUT THE BUSINESS-GOVERNMENT RELATIONSHIP

NEIL H. JACOBY

Neil H. Jacoby, editor of the proceedings of a seminar held at the Graduate School of Management, University of California at Los Angeles, to reassess the business-government relationship, summarizes the results of the seminar in the following wide-ranging overview.

Readers who have studied the papers submitted by participants in the UCLA Seminar on the Business-Government Relationship, and who have read the ensuing dialogue, probably are now considering how this far-ranging colloquy can be recapitulated. Summing it up is a delicate and difficult task, to be undertaken with caution. The summarizer must try to avoid errors in interpreting the views of the participants; and he must avoid interjecting his own biases. However, it is necessary to attempt a recapitulation, if the product of the seminar is to take on a distinct and recognizable character, and is not to remain a mere jumble of unconnected ideas and proposals.

We propose to recall, in turn, the major issues on the agenda of the seminar . . . Then, we shall endeavor briefly to present the propositions pertaining to each issue upon which there appeared to be a substantial consensus among the participants.

THE CHARACTER OF THE PRESENT RELATIONSHIP

The initial question posed for discussion was: How should the present U.S. business-government relationship be characterized? A bewildering variety of descriptions were given. Government and business in the United States were variously described as enemies, antagonists, opponents, and adversaries. The participants used colorful analogies to describe the relationship, varying from guerrilla warfare, to the medieval church and state, to the tension between labor unions and business managements, to porcupines making love (very, very carefully!).

There was general agreement, however, that the current business-government relationship could well be described as "adversary" in nature. Officials of government characteristically look upon themselves as probers, inspectors, taxers, regulators, and punishers of business transgressions. Businessmen typically view government agencies as obstacles, constraints, delayers, and impediments to economic progress, having much power to stop and little to start. A considerable measure of mutual suspicion prevails. Each adversary lacks knowledge and understanding of the role, motivation, problems, and modes of action of the other. It was universally agreed that the current relationship is seriously defective and that it must be improved if our society is to make satisfactory progress toward its goals.

THE TREND IN THE RELATIONSHIP

A second question is whether the American business-government relationship has been worsening or improving through time. Again, there was agreement among the participants that the relationship has been deteriorating. The goals and values of our burgeoning, affluent, urbanizing, and technologizing society have become more numerous, more complex, more interrelated, and harder to reconcile. As a consequence, conflicts among various interest groups in society have multiplied, trade-off relationships have become harder to measure, social priorities have become more difficult to establish, and social consensus has become harder to achieve.

Our governmental institutions, inherited from the small, relatively poor agrarian society of our past, are not coping rapidly enough with the social problems of today. Unresolved issues about energy, the environment, urban transit, housing, poverty, drug use, and crime have piled up. Government has been tardy in weighing social values, in establishing trade-off relationships, and in making the rules needed to guide the private sector. Business has often been insensitive to changing social values, and obstructive rather than facilitative in adjusting to them. A better educated and hypercritical public holds a low level of confidence in both institutions.

WELLSPRINGS OF MALFUNCTIONING

A third basic issue is how changes in the social and technological environment have affected the U.S. business-government relationship. Four major changes in the structure and values of American society since World War II have had a profound impact: *First,* a truly national society has emerged out of local and regional societies. *Second,* what Daniel Bell has called the "communal society" has arisen, marked by relatively greater emphasis upon public goods and the internalization of external costs. *Third,* the American public holds rising expectations and now considers itself "entitled" to good jobs, excellent housing, and other amenities. *Fourth,* there has emerged a deep concern for the quality of life.

These value changes have multiplied the number of *political* decisions that have to be made relative to the number of decisions made in *markets.*

More of the political decisions are unpopular because they involve clashes of conflicting interests in which *everyone* has to give up something. As a result, the political system has become clogged. Whereas the market disperses responsibility for unpopular decisions, the political process focuses responsibility—and politicians try to evade it. Hence, we have the current crisis in the political system.

Technological changes have also played an important role. Designing new modes of urban mass transit, creating new cities, reducing environmental pollution, developing new energy supplies and controlling the new information technology—all these tasks call for innovations in governmental structures and some need public-private joint ventures. Technological changes are also forcing the need for new institutions of *international* decision making and management, especially in respect to the new satellites in the sky used for communication, navigation, weather prediction and control, and the assessment of natural resources.

Many differences between U.S. business and government can also be traced to the divergence of their underlying ethical systems. Business espouses and practices individualism, whereas government operates on a collectivist ethic. The business ethic emphasizes and rewards or punishes individual *in*equalities, whereas collectivists emphasize the equality of individuals.

Finally, the malfunctioning of the business-government relationship is due in considerable degree to public ignorance of the respective responsibilities of these two institutions in our pluralistic society. This being so, better economic and political education for citizenship must be part of the remedy.

FLAWS IN BUSINESS BEHAVIOR

What features of business performance are responsible for the flawed relationship with government? Although it was clear that members of the seminar found more fault with government than with business, they were critical of many aspects of business performance. Many censured business leaders for insensitivity to changing social values, such as the public demand for less polluting and safer automobiles that emerged during the late 1960s; and for opposing instead of cooperating with government in designing regulations to express these values. Businessmen were faulted for preoccupation with short-term results—next quarter's profit-and-loss statement—rather than with their long-term performance.

The ethical behavior of businessmen in dealing with governments also received sharp criticism, particularly efforts to "buy" political favors with campaign contributions, or with promises of lucrative jobs to civil servants in regulatory agencies. Although the officials of government and of labor unions are equally culpable, it was thought that business leaders set the standards of behavior in American society and therefore bear a special responsibility. One participant argued that it was the political *weakness* of business, which lacks a constituency, that leads to excessive lobbying in order to protect its legitimate interests.

Businessmen also received adverse comment for their ignorance of government and their lack of understanding of the problems and constraints under which government officials labor. Business was also taken to task—along with government—for raising the expectations of the public to unrealistic heights through its sales promotional efforts. With respect to one widely held belief—that big business wields inordinate political power—the participants emphatically disagreed. At least since World War II, the stream of federal government legislation and regulation has contradicted the notion that big business wields the dominant influence in American society. On the contrary, many held that its political weakness should be a source of concern.

FAULTS OF GOVERNMENT

Although business was assigned a share of the blame for a relatively unproductive relationship with government, the consensus of the seminar was that the archaic structure and processes of American government bear the major responsibility. Nearly all of the participants commented upon the much heavier load of decision making that falls upon government today, and the halting, inaccurate way in which the political system translates public preferences into operational programs. The U.S. political system was variously described as a "Tudor polity," "chaotic," "overloaded," and unresponsive to the "fields of force" of contemporary life. A "horse-and-buggy" structure of state and local governments has led to a fiasco in environmental control; and it threatens to fragment the national markets that undergird the productivity of the U.S. economy. Likewise, in the rest of the world the proliferation of national governments and a strident nationalism threaten the integrity of world markets. Everywhere, *governmental structure is contradictory to the imperatives of business efficiency.*

There was unanimity in the view that government has expanded too rapidly relative to the private sector, and that its low productivity forms an increasingly heavy drag on social progress. This low productivity may be attributed, in part, to the central motive of government, which is to provide services and jobs, whatever the cost. In part, it is due to the lack of a market test of the value of government services to the public. Several participants emphasized the need to provide *incentives* for efficient administration of public programs, as well as for innovative thinking. And steps should be taken to make the tenure of civil servants less secure, so that they will be more responsive to the citizens.

The choicest terms of excoriation of government, however, were reserved for its regulation of business. There were no dissenters from the proposition that governmental regulation of business at the present time is widely inept, wasteful, and in need of radical therapy. The joint public-private management agency type of regulation—such as the ICC, the CAB, or the FPC—generally has failed to serve either the interests of the consumers they were intended to protect or the interests of the enterprises they were supposed to control. "Functional" regulation of particular business activities, such as product safety or labor relations, is a more recent development; but many government forays into this field are still on trial. A law of entropy appears to govern regulatory agencies; when new, they perform vigorously in the public interest; as they age, they degenerate into custodians and spokesmen for their respective industries. This suggests that regulatory agencies be given a limited life, extensible only after a periodic congressional appraisal demonstrates their net value to society. The regulatory process itself suffers from endemic diseases, which were described as *Penncentralization, Lockheedization, Legalization,* and *Consultantization.* It exhibits biases in favor of represented interests and against innovations.

The recent tendency of governments to compel business firms to shoulder the costs of carrying out such social programs as environmental improvement and worker safety, in order to "economize" government expenditures, is burdening American business in international competition. It is attenuating the private enterprise system. There was also a consensus among the participants that the governmental attack on big firms in concentrated industries, exemplified by the Industrial Reorganization Bill of Senator Hart and by much antitrust litigation, was counterproductive and should be abandoned. A redirection of antitrust resources to root out restrictive practices in the economy would raise productivity, reduce inflation, and enhance business-government relationships.

REPRIVATIZING GOVERNMENTAL PROGRAMS

A fundamental issue is whether the boundary line between the public and the private sectors of the U.S. economy is properly drawn. Is government attempting to produce commodities and to perform services that could more efficiently be produced by profit-seeking enterprises? The consensus of the seminar was that U.S. governments on all levels have grown too rapidly during the last decade for the efficient management of their myriad activities. During this hectic expansion, they have intruded unwisely into some fields better cultivated by the private sector.

A "reprivatization" of such functions as the design, evaluation, and administration of health and welfare services would be desirable. Other candidates for transfer to the private sector are the insurance operations of the Veterans Administration, the uranium enrichment operations of the Federal Energy Agency, and the fire protection and waste disposal services of municipal governments. It is not even clear that the U.S. Postal Service

Corporation should monopolize the mails. Participants in the seminar repeatedly stressed the unique function of government to set social priorities and to establish programs; and its inherent weakness as the manager of ongoing production operations that emanate from those programs. Here, it appears, is a fruitful field for reform.

LESSONS FROM OTHER INDUSTRIALIZED NATIONS

The question was repeatedly raised whether the American business-government relationship is as productive as those in other large nations with democratic political systems and market economies. Are there features of the relationship in such countries as Britain, France, Germany, and Japan that the United States should emulate? In particular, when American-based corporations go abroad and multinationalize their operations, are they handicapped by the fact that the U.S. government adopts an attitude of neutrality toward them, whereas the governments of most foreign countries treat their companies, in effect, as instruments of their national policy?

The consensus of the seminar was quite clear that there is little of practical value that the United States can import from the business-government relationships in other countries. The reason is that the relationship between these two institutions is imbedded in the matrix of the entire social system, of which they are only a minor part. The interactions of the public and the private sectors of the U.S. economy are much more heavily determined by what goes on in the entire social system than by the actions of either business or government per se. Nations whose social systems differ from our own will develop different business-government relationships, inappropriate for transplantation to the United States. Notwithstanding this negative response to the issue, members of the seminar were quick to recognize that the United States lacks an adequate theory or model of its social system. There is an urgent need to develop such a model in order to legitimize social institutions and processes presently lacking a theoretical foundation. This is an undertaking as difficult as it is important, however, because valid social theories are rare works of personal inspiration; they cannot be bought with money.

WHAT SHOULD THE RELATIONSHIP BE?

Just as a wide variety of adjectives were employed to describe the *present* business-government relationship, so was a broad spectrum of terms advanced to characterize the *ideal* relationship. It was said that business and government should "collaborate," "cooperate," or "act in concert." The simile of a symbiote was invoked as a model, implying a mutually beneficial coexistence of these two social institutions. "Peaceful coexistence," a phrase borrowed from the literature on Soviet-American relations, was also suggested as the proper delineation of the relationship.

Participants in the seminar were quite emphatic, however, in rejecting any idea of unity, or even of confederation or partnership. These words evoked the image of an excessively close relationship between big business and big government, which would pose a threat of dominance of other social institutions and would be inconsistent with the social pluralism that has always been an American ideal. It was generally believed that a certain amount of tension and arm's-length dealing *should* characterize the government's relationship with business, just as this should be present in its relationship to such other institutions as the labor union, the church, or the university.

Some participants held that the ideal relationship is, indeed, one of "adversaries," but that it should not be obstructive or abrasive in character. While we may reasonably expect the relationship to move from guerrilla warfare to peaceful coexistence, we would not wish it to proceed to a status of outright community. Confrontation should be replaced by cooperation; not by concert or combination.

A recurrent theme of the dialogue was the unfortunate ignorance of most businessmen about the motivations, powers, and constraints of governmental officials; and of governmental officials about the competitive imperatives and the market discipline to which the businessman is subject. The general conclusion was that the leaders of both institutions require a fuller education in the differences, as well as the similarities, of leadership roles in business and in government.

TOPICAL PRIORITIES

The seminar devoted much time to the task of identifying specific topics, within the vast range of business-government interrelationships that deserved top priority for research or education. By using the iterative type of Delphi technique, it was found that seven topics were rated highest by the group. They were, in order:

1. Reform of governmental regulation of business
2. Conditions of business-government collaboration in resolving social problems
3. Public finance of election campaigns
4. Adoption of growth-oriented taxation policies
5. Design of new types of public-private enterprise
6. Implementation of the planning function in government and business
7. Education for leadership in government and business

These seven subjects were selected from a list of twenty subjects reviewed by all participants in the seminar, plus additional subjects that various participants proposed. In view of the wide range of subjects from which the selection was made, and because there was a sharp drop in the number of votes given any topic after the first seven, it is clear that there was a pronounced consensus on the importance of these seven topics. The ratings, it should be added, reflect the consensus of the participants not only on the intrinsic importance of the topics, but also on the probable productivity of research and educational efforts by the Norton Simon Commission. They were chosen, in short, because they have the potential of producing the highest social payoffs.

It is not surprising that reform of governmental regulation of business was assigned top priority. We have seen that four participants in the seminar chose to devote their papers to this subject; and a recurrent topic of the dialogue was flaws in regulation. A rising tide of public and professional economic criticism of business regulation has appeared, and a growing literature has analyzed its effects upon the economy and the society. The Brookings Institution has published numerous reports in its Studies of the Regulation of Economic Activity; and the American Enterprise Institute for Public Policy Research has published numerous Evaluative Studies. Groups of economists at several U.S. universities, notably Massachusetts Institute of Technology, the University of Chicago, and the University of California, Los Angeles, have participated in the examination.

The great preponderance of this literature is adverse in its assessment of the effects of governmental regulation upon the vigor and growth of U.S. business enterprise and its capacity to serve the demands of the public. We need not here review the many critical studies that have been published . . . The point is that a substantial scholarly literature now exists, assessing the goals, processes, and results of efforts by the federal government to control the behavior of business enterprises in different industries, or business's performance of different functions. This provides the foundation on which to build new regulatory principles and procedures or, in some instances, to curtail or abandon regulation altogether. The consensus of the seminar was that all of the regulatory agencies need a periodic "shaking up," that some should be reoriented, and others terminated.

We shall not pause to comment on the other six high-priority topics identified by the members of the seminar. All are well-known to observers of the contemporary national scene. Like reforming the regulation of business, all have been the subject of study by many governmental or private bodies. Few will dispute the need for further investigative work to fill gaps in our knowledge about these subjects, for the development of public policies with respect to them, and for education of the public in the nature of these policies.

A STRATEGY FOR CHANGE

We come, finally, to consider how a program, or series of programs, intended to improve the U.S. business-government relationship, can be implemented. What relative emphasis should be put on research to discover new knowledge, synthesis of existing knowledge, and education to communicate knowledge to those who need it? What are the desirable time dimensions and financial requirements of an effective program? What individual and institutional expertise should be called upon to make inputs? How can the influence of a program be maximized?

Although there were one or two dissentient voices, most of the conferees advised that emphasis in any program mounted by the Norton Simon Commission should be placed upon efforts to *synthesize* existing knowledge and to *communicate* it to the political and economic leaders of our society as well as to the public. American society is like the farmer who declined to take advice on better farming techniques from the county agricultural agent on the grounds that he was "not farming as well as he already knew how to!" Our universities and other institutions for public policy analysis have already developed many of the concepts needed to improve the performance of both government and business and the relationship between them.

The central need is not research to produce more knowledge, but integration of what is known and communication of the product to those able to act. As one participant said: "The important thing is to pick issues that are central, develop consensus on needed reforms, and then dramatize the matter." It was felt that the Commission should be a catalyst for action, organizing existing knowledge and giving it visibility. The Commission was advised to review the records of past commissions on public policy, in order to identify factors that led to their success or failure. Ineffective *communication* of reports to the public seems to have been a prolific cause of failure. One successful prototype was the Committee for Economic Development, which took leadership in the enactment of the Employment Act of 1946 and the Marshall Plan of 1948.

With respect to the magnitude of an effective program to improve the U.S. business-government relationship, it was believed that anything less than a five-year effort would be less than optimal, and that a minimum budget of $400,000 to $500,000 per year would be necessary.

The participants suggested that the Commission sponsor a variety of specific programs. Among some of the more striking proposals was a conference on "corporate crime," a conference on corruption in public office, and an essay contest among college students on ways to improve public-private sector cooperation. The Commission was counselled to place on its agenda only issues of immediate practical interest to large numbers of people, and to offer specific proposals to cope with these issues.

POETIC MEDITATIONS

An altogether delightful development was the submission of some poetic meditations by Professor Kenneth E. Boulding, inspired by his attendance at the seminar. As his readers well know, Professor Boulding is a master of the rhymed couplet and serves as the unofficial poet laureate of the American Economic Association. His lyrics affirm, in a poetic vein, points previously made in ponderous prose!

The public fist is thinly gloved:
Business, feeling much unloved,
Thinks Government is out to get it
And if it does we may regret it.

Business, more than in the past,
Feels itself to be harassed.
For power to stop becomes an art
More powerful than the power to start.

When things become a little sour
We call on countervailing power.
And, as the tension slowly mounts,
The countervailing is what counts.

Business meets a messy fate
If it tries to be a State;
Business leaves us in the lurch
When it tries to be a Church;
Business makes itself a fool
When it tries to be a School;
Business drowns in love of pelf
When it tries to be itself;
Business might as well enjoy
Living as a whipping boy.

The imminent approach of death
Will clear the mind and sweeten breath.
So agencies are most effective
That die on reaching their objective.

Creating crises may be how
We all could learn from Chairman Mao.
So troubles should not much dismay us
Who seek the best amount of chaos!

QUESTIONS

1. How, according to the seminar participants, may the present business-government relationship be best characterized? Would you add any others?
2. In what ways are business performance and government actions responsible for the faults in the relationship?
3. What is involved in "reprivatizing" government programs? Is this a good or bad idea?

4. Outline what you think would be the proper relationships between business and government in the United States for today. How about the year 2000?
5. If you were to list the major priorities in the business-government relationship that should be the subject of research and action for change, would you agree with the seminar participants? Where would your list differ and why?
6. Do you agree with the recommendations of the seminar to the Norton Simon Commission for improving the business-government relationship in this country? What other measures would you recommend?

THE LIMITS OF LEGAL COMPULSION

JOHN T. DUNLOP

John T. Dunlop, in his capacity as Secretary of Labor, prepared remarks for the White House staff on problems of government regulation and methods to improve them. The following is an article drawn from those remarks.

In recent years a rapid expansion of government controls has been associated at the same time with a growing dissatisfaction with the effects of regulation. Scholarly books and journals have offered detailed criticisms of specific regulatory policies, but these analyses have neither slowed the growth of formal regulation nor encouraged the development of alternative approaches to problems.

The issue confronts those involved in public policy generally. The Department of Labor, however, is an unusual vantage point from which to survey different types of regulatory programs and the arguments about their usefulness. In recent years the Department has been assigned one of the most extensive sets of regulatory programs in the Federal government. In 1940 the Department administered 18 regulatory programs; by 1960 the number had expanded to 40; in 1975 the number stands at 134. At present the Department has responsibility for promulgating and administering complex regulations under the Occupational Safety and Health Act, the Urban Mass Transportation Act, the Consumer Credit Protection Act, the Davis-Bacon Act, the Civil Rights Act of 1964, the Equal Pay Act, the Employee Retirement Income Security Act, and many others. All of these regulatory programs establish substantive—and in many cases quantitative—definitions of acceptable conduct for employers, employees, and third parties.

The Department thus provides examples for a broader comparison between essentially private methods for rule-making within a broad and general governmental context—exemplified by collective bargaining—and the more intensive approach of governmental promulgation of mandatory regulations.

A distinction also needs to be drawn between economic regulation of prices, rates or fees and related conditions of entry to a market, on the one hand, and social regulation, on the other, affecting conditions of work such as discrimination, health and safety and the like. In the case of economic regulation it may often be appropriate to raise the question of whether the interests of a sector and the public may not better be served by deregulation. In the field of social regulation, while some deregulation may be appropriate, the major areas of review are likely practically to be concerned with methods

John T. Dunlop, "The Limits of Legal Compulsion," New York: *The Conference Board Record,* March 1976, pp. 23–27. Reprinted by permission.

of regulation, involvement of those affected, enforcement, compliance approaches and communication to those affected. Regulation to achieve a public purpose continues, but the central concern is the methods, approaches and mutual attitudes of the regulators and the regulatees.

Over the years regulation has proved to be a practical and effective approach to some social and economic problems. The inspection of meat and poultry is an obvious example and suggests the sort of concerns that prompted the development of regulation in the late 18th century. In the words of a foremost student of administrative law, Kenneth Culp Davis, "Practical men were seeking practical answers to immediate problems. . . . What was needed was a governmental authority having power not merely to adjudicate, but to initiate proceedings, to investigate, to prosecute, to issue regulation having force of law, to supervise." From these perceived needs developed the structure of modern regulation, an approach which is now used, without significant modification, as our principal policy tool for dealing with occupational disease, discrimination, dangerous toys and pollution.

THE REGULATORY PROBLEM

A major reason for the attraction of regulation over the years has been the belief that it is a speedy, simple and cheap procedure. It should be apparent that the administrative procedure is by no means fast or inexpensive, but the prevailing belief is that it is. This misconception, in large part, is due to the fact that the constraints on the rule-making and adjudicating activities of regulatory agencies are not widely perceived or appreciated. Perhaps, too, because the majority of Congressmen are lawyers, and not business executives, labor leaders, economists or labor mediators, they are apt to think of social and economic problems in legal terms. For these and other reasons, when a problem acquires national attention—as pollution, inflation and occupational disease have in recent years—the natural reaction has been to create a new regulatory agency to deal with it. There are a variety of problems with this approach.

1. The first problem with regulation is that it encourages simplistic thinking about complicated issues. To get regulatory legislation passed in a pluralistic society often requires the evocation of horror stories and the mobilization of broad political support. To quote Professor Wilson: "Political inertia is not easily overcome, and when it is overcome, it is often at the price of exaggerating the virtue of those who are to benefit (a defrauded debtor, a sick industry) or the wickedness of those who are to bear the burden (a smog-belching car, a polluting factory, a grasping creditor)."

2. Second, designing and administering a regulatory program is an incredibly complicated task. How successfully and efficiently occupational disease or discrimination in hiring practices will be reduced depends not just on the kind of goals set by Congress or a few key decisions by civil servants

in Washington but upon tens of thousands of individual actions taken by business firms and private citizens across the country. Ensuring compliance with a regulation is far more difficult than promulgating it, though that too can be a complicated and lengthy process. There are, for example, 5 million workplaces and 1,200 OSHA inspectors. All affected parties can never be notified of a new rule's existence, and thus reasonably be expected to comply —and the means of informing regulatees of new rules (mainly through publication in the *Federal Register*) are severely inadequate.

3. Third, oftentimes policies that appear straightforward will have unintended consequences which can create problems as severe as those with which the regulations were intended to deal. For example, the Wagner Act meant to encourage the development of unions and collective bargaining, but its concept of "exclusive representation"—where the employees in a unit decide which union, if any, they want to represent them in bargaining with management—contradicted the traditional union principle of "exclusive jurisdiction"—in which all workers in a particular craft or industry are legitimately represented by one union. The Wagner Act had the effect of encouraging competition between unions for members, hence disputes between unions and changing the internal governance of organized labor—an entirely unintended effect. Article XX of the AFL-CIO Constitution was later adopted to provide a method for mitigating these disputes through limited arbitration; competitive elections, rational bargaining structures and union jurisdiction are not entirely compatible. It is very hard for affected groups to perceive the longer-term and often unintended consequences of regulation.

4. Fourth, the rule-making and adjudicatory procedures of regulatory agencies tend to be very slow, creating conflicts between the different groups involved, and leading to weak and ineffective remedies for the people the programs aim to help. Early experience demonstrated the need for the regulatory agencies' procedures to include the same sort of safeguards to ensure fairness that were present in the judicial and legislative processes. The result eventually was the Administrative Procedure Act of 1946, which established formal procedures for the promulgation of rules and the adjudication of cases. The purpose was to ensure that each party affected by a proposed rule would have an opportunity to present its views, thereby limiting the possibility that regulations or decisions would be arbitrary, unworkable, or unfair.

Common sense recognizes the importance of these procedures, but while they are designed to make regulation fair, they can also make it rigid. When a regulatory program is imposed immediately upon passage and the administrative agency lacks authority to adjust the law to fit the realities of business practices—as is the case with some requirements of the new pension law (ERISA)—the result is often rules based on abstractions which are fair and effective in some settings and pointless and burdensome in others. In the case of one ERISA provision, for example, the Department of Labor received over 220,000 individual requests for exemption, some taking more than 12 months to process. The procedure is lengthy and complicated: if an exemption is proposed, it is then published in the *Federal Register* and comments are solicited; a public hearing can be requested and if, as a result, the exemption is modified, then the procedure may be repeated. The process is often prolonged by different groups taking advantage of procedure to advance their interests; thus, a legitimate exemption may take months to obtain.

5. Fifth, the rule-making and adjudicatory procedures do not include a mechanism for the development of mutual accommodation among the conflicting interests. Opposing interests argue their case to the government, and not at each other. Direct discussions and negotiations among opposing points of view, where mutual accommodation is mutually desirable—as in collective bargaining—forces the parties to set priorities among their demands, trading off one for another—creating an incentive for them to find common ground. The values, perceptions, and needs of each become apparent. And some measure of mutual understanding is a by-product. As compulsory arbitration undermines the willingness of the parties to bargain conscientiously over the differences, so regulation lessens incentives for private accommodations of conflicting viewpoints. Public hearings encourage dramatic presentations and exorbitant demands and the government's disclosure rules and the Advisory Committee Act inhibit private meetings between the affected parties and the agency.

The regulatory agency is thus ignorant of the parties' true positions, and is forced to guess each interest's priorities and needs from the formal and often extreme public statements the parties have presented at public hearings. The regulatory process encourages conflict, rather than acting to reconcile opposing interests. Moreover, there is a sense that it is wrong for the regulatory agency to try to bring parties together and develop consensus. Relying on public and highly formal proceedings makes the development of consensus extremely difficult, if not impossible. And unless this consensus can be developed, neither party has any stake in the promulgated rule, thus is free to complain that it is biased, stupid or misguided. Moreover, each side is free to continue the controversy in the form of endless petitions for review, clarification and litigation before the agency and the courts. Nothing is ever settled because true settlement can come only through agreement, consent or acquiescence.

6. A sixth problem is that regulatory efforts are rarely abandoned even after their purpose has been served. As James Q. Wilson has pointed out: "Both business firms and regulatory agencies operate on the basis of a common principle: Maintain the organization . . . for the public agency that means creating and managing services (or a public image of services) that please key Congressmen, organized clients, and the news media."

A parallel problem affects the agency's body of regulations: repealing or modifying those rules is a lengthy and complicated process and is rarely done. Thus the code becomes bloated with anachronistic and rarely enforced regulations that nonetheless have the force of law and could be applied at the convenience of a compliance officer. Trivial and important regulations are mixed; to the regulatee the program appears irrational and arbitrary. Also, as the body of rules expands, it becomes increasingly more difficult and expensive for the regulatees to figure out what is required of them. In this way, the agency and its rules remain in place long after their usefulness has been served.

7. A seventh problem involves the legal gameplaying between the regulatees and the regulators; the tax law is the classic example, but it is typical of regulatory programs in general. The regulatory agency promulgates a regulation; the regulatees challenge it in court; if they lose, their lawyers may seek or find another ground for administrative or judicial challenge. Congressional amendments may be developed. Between a challenge to the regulation's basic legality, pressure on the agency for an amended regulation, and administrative and judicial enforcement proceedings, there is ample opportunity for tactical strategies, allegations of ambiguity, pleas of special circumstances and the like.

It should be a first principle that no set of men is smart enough to write words around which others cannot find holes when the stakes are high.

8. An eighth problem with regulation concerns the difficulty encountered by small and medium size firms in complying with the regulations of the various agencies, and the problems the government has in trying to enforce compliance. Many regulations do not well fit the circumstances of small enterprises. It is often difficult if not impossible for small to medium size firms to keep track of the large number of regulations issued by various agencies. And there is little reason to do so; the chances of a small or medium size firm being inspected are minute, and if it is inspected and found to be in violation fines for a first offense are usually small. Thus, it may make practical business sense for a firm to put off the expenses required to achieve compliance until after an inspection has specified those changes which have to be made. Compliance cannot be compelled through a police effort in every workplace, given any practicable levels of funds and personnel.

To a degree "public examples"—where a company found in violation is given harsh and visible treatment—encourages other companies to come into compliance. But this tactic is generally unsuccessful for several reasons: nearly every company—particularly small ones—has a good or plausible excuse for not being in compliance (e.g., they were not aware of the regulations), thus, a large fine tends to get whittled down to a small one through the successive stages of administrative review; also, such tactics are perceived to be unfair and generate strong resentment in public opinion and the press and create hostility to the program and attempts to change it in the political arena.

9. Ninth, over time as the rule-making and compliance activities of regula-

tory agencies become routine, it grows increasingly difficult for the President and the agency to attract highly qualified and effective administrators into leadership positions. As the quality of leadership declines, problems often receive increasingly less imaginative treatment or no attention at all.

10. Tenth, uniform national regulations are inherently unworkable in many situations because the society is not uniform. There are significant differences among industries and sectors and regions of the country. Consequently, a regulation may be unrealistically harsh in one industry or sector or part of the country and too lenient in another.

11. An eleventh problem is what is called "regulatory overlap," where a number of different regulatory agencies share some of the same responsibilities. Although the creation of a new specialized agency probably heightens effectiveness in one field, the danger is that a series of uncoordinated steps, each quite sensible in [itself], can set up a feedback of unanticipated consequences that is overwhelmingly negative. No one regulatory program is ever able to see the problems through the eyes of those subject to regulation, and the total consequences of regulatory programs on the firm or industry are never perceived. There is no mechanism in government to add up these consequences. Moreover, jurisdictional conflict among agencies, even with the best of good will, consumes vast amounts of time and energy and stimulates general disrespect for governmental agencies.

TOWARD IMPROVEMENT

It is not realistic to expect any significant reduction in the number of Federal regulatory programs in the immediate future; in fact, it is likely that the political processes and the Congress will seek to add new ones. Regardless of the theoretical merits of regulation, it is important, as a practical matter, that more attention be given towards improving the quality of regulation. In a sense, accommodation with practical reality has always occurred. While some inspectors in the field enforce the letter of the law, others develop an array of informal operating rules of thumb which drafters of the regulations never thought of, or indeed rejected. Sometimes these rules of thumb call for nonenforcement in trivial cases or where application of a rigid rule would be unreasonable. "Policy-makers" would do well to address explicitly that which lower level implementers will do anyway—though unevenly—through the application of common sense or prejudice. The following suggestions are designed to make the regulatory process more responsive to the problems cited above.

First, *the parties who will be affected by a set of regulations should be involved to a greater extent in developing those regulations.*

The way regulations are currently developed is inherently contentious and acts to maximize antagonism between the parties. The result is poorly framed rules, law suits, evasion and dissatisfaction with the program by all parties. In our society, a rule that is developed with the involvement of the parties who are affected is more likely to be accepted and to be effective in accomplishing its intended purposes.

There is no single way by which the parties can be involved in the rule-making process, but a method is suggested by the Department of Labor's recent experience with section 13(c) of the Urban Mass Transportation Act. UMTA gives grants to cities to take over failing private transit systems. Section 13(c) requires that funds not be granted until the Secretary of Labor has certified that employees would not be adversely affected by the Federally funded activities. This requirement has caused substantial delays and confusion as unions and private managers or city officials haggled over what constituted equitable compensation. Rather than prepare regulations, the Department brought together union and transit representatives and got them to prepare a three-year agreement as to what protection employees should receive as a consequence of the Federally funded activities. The Department mediated and provided technical assistance helping to create the standards to apply to individual cases presented to it. Processing time will be very noticeably reduced.

This approach is not necessarily applicable without modification to, say, OSHA or ERISA, but it represents a useful spirit of reliance on private mechanisms which sometimes can achieve a program objective most efficiently.

Second, *anachronistic and unnecessary regulations should be repealed and, in the future, rules should be promulgated with greater reluctance.* It is an open question as to how many regulations a business, particularly one of small or medium size, can absorb. Not only is it difficult for the regulatee to figure out what is required but it is equally hard for compliance officers to determine violations. Often they rely on a small percentage of the rules with which they are familiar; thus the trivial rules are enforced as often as the important ones. This causes annoyance with the program without producing substantial benefits.

Third, *greater emphasis should be placed on helping regulatees achieve compliance, especially through consultation.* Trying to force compliance primarily through threats of inspections and stiff fines has not proved successful. It has worked against acceptance of the programs by isolating the regulators (and their expertise) from the regulatees and creating antagonism and distrust between the two. As pointed out earlier, the chances of a small or medium size business ever being inspected are minute and the cost of coming into compliance is often high. If the business executive asks the agency for technical assistance, in effect the person is asking to be inspected; at least this is the common perception. The regulatory agencies have the expertise to deal with complicated, technical problems such as pollution and occupational disease. But because the programs appear punitive, there is little constructive interplay between the regulators and the regulatees.

Fourth, *the activities of the various regulatory agencies need to be co-*

ordinated better. As it is now, a single firm may be under the purview of OFCC, OSHA, the Wage and Hour Administration and a variety of other programs. Simply the number of forms required poses a substantial burden, again, encouraging antagonism for the programs. More significantly, the jurisdictions may overlap. As a long-range goal, perhaps some consolidation and more coordination and sensitivity can occur.

Fifth, *regulations must be made to reflect differences between industries, sectors, and geographic regions.* A rule that is fair and workable in New York may be excessively severe or unnecessary in Utah. Similar problems exist between industries and types of enterprises and labor organizations. Uniform, national rules may assure equity but they do not reflect the reality of the workplace.

And six, *the actions of the various regulatory agencies need to be brought into greater harmony with collective bargaining.* Many of these programs undermine relations between organized labor and management, as when issues of safety and health, apprenticeship and training, and pensions are placed under government regulation. Without limiting its responsibility to administer the law, and recognizing that some laws are designed explicitly to change the results produced by private collective bargaining, there are ways to involve the parties better to achieve practical and acceptable solutions.

THE CENTRAL ISSUE

The country needs to acquire a more realistic understanding of the limits to the degree to which social change can be brought about through legal compulsion. A great deal of government needs to be devoted to improving understanding, persuasion, accommodation, mutual problem-solving and informal mediation. Legislation, litigation and regulations are useful means for some social and economic problems, but today government has more regulation on its plate than it can handle. In many areas the growth of regulations and law has far outstripped our capacity to develop consensus and mutual accommodation to our common detriment.

It has well been said that the recreation and development of trust is the central problem of government in our times. The development of new attitudes on the part of public employees and new relationships and procedures with those who are required to live under regulations is a central challenge of democratic society. Trust cannot grow in an atmosphere dominated by bureaucratic fiat and litigious controversy; it emerges through persuasion, mutual accommodation and problem-solving.

ECONOMIC VERSUS POLITICAL RATIONALITY

A major threat to our socio-economic-political system today and tomorrow arises from the clash between economic and political rationality. What is rational in one area may not be rational in the other, and vice versa. Political decision making is concerned with social justice, the public welfare, governance by consent of the governed, equalitarianism, and majority rule. Decision making in the economic world is based upon return on capital commensurate with risk, ownership power, efficiency, self-interest, and comparative authoritarian decision making. This is oversimplified but sets the contrast.

As government controls over economic life expand, and the thrust inevitably is toward more rather than less, the introduction into the economic system of political decisions also expands. One result, of course, is to make the economic system operate more in conformance with the will of the community. Another result may be to hobble the ability of the economic system to fulfill its responsibilities in producing goods and services efficiently.

The Editors

QUESTIONS

1. Would Dunlop's suggestion that "the parties affected by a set of regulations should be involved to a greater extent in developing those regulations," lead to a greater and perhaps unhealthy domination of government by business interests? How would someone like Ralph Nader respond to this idea?
2. Would Dunlop's suggestions for improvement serve to mitigate all the difficulties he describes? If not, what problems would remain, and what suggestions do you have for their alleviation?
3. What are some additional problems of regulation that you can think of that were not covered by Dunlop?

THE CASE FOR ECONOMIZING ON GOVERNMENT CONTROLS

MURRAY L. WEIDENBAUM

Murray L. Weidenbaum, Edward Mallinckrodt Distinguished University Professor, Washington University, presents some of the abuses of federal regulatory power over business and pleads for a fundamental rethinking of federal controls.

It is always tempting to compare the ugly reality of what we oppose with the enchanting ideal of what we propose. This surely seems to be the case with the current wave of expanding government controls over the private sector.

Are some consumer products unsafe? Are some working conditions unhealthy? Are some physical environments deteriorating? Are some employers discriminating in their personnel practices? The standard answer seems to be clear: Just establish another corps of federal officialdom with power to right these wrongs.

Of course, one must possess the personality of a Scrooge to quarrel with the desirability of safer working conditions, better products for the consumer, combating discrimination in employment, or reducing environmental pollution. And, to be sure, the programs established to deal with these issues have at times yielded substantial benefits to the public.

But, unfortunately, any realistic evaluation of the actual practice of government regulation does not comfortably fit the notion of benign, beneficent, and wise men and women making altogether sensible decisions in the society's greater interests. I must report that, in my study of the subject, I find instead waste, bias, stupidity, arrogance, concentration on trivia, conflicts among the regulators, and, worst of all, arbitrary and often uncontrolled power. Let me cite chapter and verse.

THE COST OF REGULATION

Purchasers of new cars produced in the United States in 1974 paid approximately $3 billion extra for the equipment and modifications needed to meet federal requirements. Mandatory auto buzzers and harnesses (the widely detested "interlock" system) will rapidly fade into history as examples of the highhandedness and wastefulness of government regulation. Over 40 per-

Murray L. Weidenbaum, "The Case for Economizing on Government Controls," *Journal of Economic Issues,* Vol. 9, No. 2, June 1975, pp. 205–218. Reprinted by permission.

cent of the owners of those expensive contraptions disconnected them or otherwise found ways of avoiding their use prior to their elimination by the Congress. Nevertheless, the phenomenon of government adding to the costs of private production of goods and services as a convenient way of achieving public objectives without spending much, if any, government money on them seems likely to continue.

Less dramatic but often equally expensive types of federal regulation remain with us. The agencies carrying them out are surely proliferating. In the past decade alone, we have seen the formation of the Consumer Product Safety Commission, the Occupational Safety and Health Commission, the Environmental Protection Agency, the Federal Energy Administration, the Cost Accounting Standards Board, the National Bureau of Fire Prevention, the Mining Enforcement and Safety Administration, the National Highway Traffic Safety Administration, the National Transportation Safety Board, the Federal Metal and Nonmetallic Mine Safety Board of Review, and the Occupational Safety and Health Administration, to cite some of the better known.

The administrative cost of this galaxy of enforcers (approximately $2 billion a year to support a regulatory workforce in excess of 63,000) represents merely the tip of the iceberg. It is the costs imposed on the private sector that are quantitatively important, and the major costs show up in the added expenses of business firms which must comply with various directives. A substantial "inflationary multiplier" thus must be applied to the direct outlays for federal controls.

The process of federal regulation gives rise to a variety of added business costs. U.S. Steel estimates that its superintendents and foremen spent 4,000 man-hours in 1972 guiding inspectors through its coal mines. The need for government inspectors also has siphoned off experienced supervisory personnel. Consolidation Coal is said to have lost 600 foremen to the ranks of federal inspectors.

A direct private cost resulting from the expansion of government controls is the growing paperwork burden imposed on business firms: the expensive and time-consuming process of submitting reports, making applications, filling out questionnaires, replying to orders and directives, and appealing in the courts from other rulings and regulatory opinions. As of 30 June 1974 there were 5,146 different types of approved public use forms, in addition to tax and banking forms. Individuals and business firms spend over 130 million man-hours a year filling out all the necessary federal reports.

The lack of understanding between regulators and those they regulate is vividly conveyed in the interchange reported by a small manufacturer who attended a federal meeting on the paperwork burden. When he was advised not to worry about the matter personally but have his staff complete the forms, he replied: "When I attend this meeting the staff is right here with me. It's me."

A small, 5,000 watt radio station in New Hampshire reported that it spent

$26.23 just to mail to the Federal Communications Commission its application for renewing its license. An Oregon company, operating three small television stations, reported that its license renewal application weighed 45 pounds. At the other end of the spectrum, one large corporation, with about 40,000 employees, uses 125 file drawers of back-up material just to meet the federal reporting requirements in the personnel area. The personnel manager contends that one-third of his staff could be eliminated if there were no federal, state, or local reporting requirements.

The U.S. Office of Management and Budget estimates that the reporting burden imposed on U.S. business by the federal government increased by 50 percent between December 1967 and June 1974. Major new programs were the principal source of the increase—occupational safety and health activities, Medicare and Medicaid, environmental protection regulations, and equal employment compliance.

There are many other hidden costs that arise as a result of federal regulatory legislation. The Jones Act, requiring cargo shipments from one U.S. port to another to be made by U.S. vessels, adds 8 to 10 cents per million cubic feet to the cost of transporting liquified natural gas between Alaska and the West Coast. Attempts to avoid this "tax" result in the roundabout and more expensive process whereby Alaska exports the gas to other countries, and the mainland United States imports it from the South Pacific and Russia.

Another hidden cost is the reduced rate of innovation that may occur as the result of government controls. The longer it takes for some change to be approved by a federal regulatory agency—a new or improved product, a more efficient production process, and so forth—the less likely the change will be made. Professor William Wardell of the University of Rochester School of Medicine and Dentistry has concluded that as a result of more liberal policy in the United Kingdom toward the introduction of new drugs, Britain experienced clearly discernible gains by introducing useful new drugs, either sooner than the United States or exclusively. Professor Sam Peltzman of the University of Chicago estimates that the 1962 amendments to the Food and Drug Act delayed the introduction of effective drugs by about four years and added $200–$300 million a year to consumer costs.

The private costs of government regulation arise in good measure from the attitudes of the regulators. To quote a member of the Consumer Product Safety Commission: "When it involves a product that is unsafe, I don't care how much it costs the company to correct the problem," and no one can fault the commission for not putting its money (and yours and mine) where its big mouth is. In one recent case where an offending company had not posted a label on its product bearing the correct officialese ("cannot be made non poisonous"), it was forced to destroy the contents. If you do not care about costs, apparently you do not think about such economical solutions as pasting a new label on the can.

In contrast to the great attention given to the benefits that are expected to flow from each and every new regulation, the costs usually are ignored. Let "them" pay for it; "they" can afford it; that seems to be the public attitude. The economic model underlying this approach is quite unusual. Government mandated costs of private production are assumed neither to be shifted forward to consumers nor backward to the factors of production. The costs presumably simply come out of profits, but without interfering with the needed flows of saving and investment—the proverbial "free lunch."

TRIVIA AND NONSENSE

An expected result of the lack of attention to the costs of regulation is the opportunity for bureaucrats to engage in all sorts of exercises in trivia and, on occasion, sheer nonsense. What size to establish for toilet partitions? How big is a hole? (It depends upon where it is.) When is a roof a floor? What colors should various parts of a building be painted? How frequently are spittoons to be cleaned? There actually are people willing to take our tax dollars to establish and administer regulations dealing with just these burning issues. And these are not historic relics, but directives promulgated during the 1970s.

Picture the plight of the small businessman who tries to deal with the Occupational Safety and Health Administration (OSHA) rules without paying for expensive outside assistance. I have tried to by requesting copies of the introductory materials provided by the agency. Some examples stagger the mind. Let us begin with a supposedly simple matter, the definition of an *exit*. My dictionary says that *exit* is "a passage or way out." For OSHA enforcers, defining *exit* is a challenge to their bureaucratic instincts, and they are not found wanting. To OSHA, an *exit* is "that portion of a means of egress which is separated from all other spaces of the building or structure by construction or equipment as required in this subpart to provide a protected way of travel to the exit discharge." Obviously, I had to define "a means of egress" as well as an "exit discharge." Leaving seems to be easier than entering, at least the Kingdom of OSHA. *Exit discharge* is defined merely as "that portion of a means of egress between the termination of an exit and a public way." But now let us tackle "means of egress." Brace yourself. OSHA defines this as "a continuous and unobstructed way of exit travel from any point in a building or structure to a public way and consists of three separate and distinct parts: the way of exit access, the exit, and the way of exit discharge. A means of egress comprises the verticle and horizontal ways of travel and shall include intervening room spaces, doorways, hallways, corridors, passageways, balconies, ramps, stairs, enclosures, exits, escalators, horizontal exits, courts, and yards." The careful reader will note that, unlike the dictionary, OSHA is unable to provide a definition of *exit* which does not contain the word *exit*. And exit is a comparatively easy one. Try ladder, where the reader literally has to cope with three renditions of the same tedious set of definitions plus one trigonometric function.

The puzzlement over OSHA regulations extends to the chairman of the Occupational Safety and Health Review Commission, the independent agency created to hear appeals from rulings by OSHA inspectors. In response to a question about one vague standard: "What do you think it tells us to do?" he lamented: "I have no idea—and I don't think OSHA could tell you either, before an inspection, citation, complaint, hearing and post-hearing brief. I submit that there isn't a person on earth who can be certain he is in full compliance with the requirements of this standard at any particular point of time."

The operation of the Occupational Safety and Health Act provides a pertinent example of how government regulation can lose sight of the basic objective. A company, particularly a smaller one without its own specialized safety personnel, which invites OSHA to come to the plant to tell the management which practices need to be revised to meet the agency's standards, instantly lays itself open to citations for infractions of the OSHA rules and regulations. The law makes no provision for so-called courtesy inspections.

In order to circumvent the problem, one regional office of OSHA suggests that companies take photographs of their premises and send them to OSHA for off-site review. After all, if the inspectors do not actually "see" the violations, they cannot issue citations for them. The more naïve among us may believe that the basic purpose of the law is not to punish businessmen or to seek out the most costly and cumbersome method of meeting the statutory requirements, but to achieve a higher level of job safety. One can also hope that OSHA is undergoing a form of "on-the-job training" for new regulating agencies and that future rules and their interpretations will be less onerous. It is unfortunate, however, that business and consumers must serve as involuntary guinea pigs in the process.

OSHA, to be sure, does not have a monopoly on regulatory foolishness. An examination of the proposed Uniform Guidelines on Employee Selection Procedures is revealing. The guidelines were drafted by the U.S. Equal Employment Opportunity Coordinating Council in order to assure that selection procedures, in both the public and the private sectors, do not discriminate against any group on the basis of race, color, religion, sex, or national origin. The objective surely is a worthy one. Yet the proposed guidelines have been challenged by such professional organizations as the American Society for Personnel Administration and Division 14 of the American Psychological Association.

A mere reading of the proposed regulations reveals the basis for concern. Smaller employers would have great difficulty in understanding the regulations, while large and small companies alike would find compliance difficult and expensive. The Coordinating Council does try to ease the burden on employers, but the result surely challenges the understanding of the typical executive:

> If a criterion-related or construct validation study is technically feasible in all other respects, but it is not technically feasible to conduct a differential prediction study when required by subparagraph 14a(5) below and the test user has conducted a validation study for the job in question which otherwise meets the requirements of paragraph 14a below, the test user may continue to use the procedure operationally until such time as a differential prediction study is feasible and has been conducted within a reasonable time after it has become feasible.
>
> A selection procedure has criterion-related validity, for the purpose of these guidelines, when the relationship between performance on the procedure and performance on at least one relevant criterion measure is statistically significant at the .05 level of significance. . . . If the relationship between a selection procedure and a criterion measure is significant but nonlinear, the score distribution should be studied to determine if there are sections of the regression curve with zero or near zero slope where scores do not reliably predict different levels of job performance.

Should these guidelines be enforced, the result is likely to be not fairer testing, but a shift from what would become more costly and cumbersome procedures to the simpler but far more bias-prone subjective interview.

BIAS AND DOUBLE STANDARDS

The image of the all-wise and judicious government administration of controls is severely tested when we see how bias can be introduced into the process in the most innocent manner. The responsibility for doing the basic research underlying new job safety and health regulations has been assigned to the National Institute of Occupational Safety and Health (NIOSH) in the Department of Health, Education, and Welfare. In early 1974, NIOSH signed an agreement with the Amalgamated Clothing Workers union under which an official federal study of safety and health hazards in the clothing industry is to be conducted by a union employee and paid for by the union. In reporting this strange arrangement, OSHA noted that the union will help obtain the cooperation of plant managers. It is interesting to contemplate the reaction of management to an investigation of its premises by its union in behalf of the government!

The double standard at times followed by federal regulators can be another cause for concern over the extent of the power entrusted to them. The Environmental Protection Agency (EPA) is now studying the possible pollution which may result from the catalytic converters it has mandated for 1975 automobiles. Both private and government researchers have shown that the new "antipollution" equipment may produce harmful amounts of sulphuric acid mists, which can irritate the lungs. The catalytic converters also emit platinum, which, in the words of the director of EPA's fuel and additive research program, is "really adding a new thing to our environment." Apparently, there is no significant amount of platinum in our air or water at the present time.

Just think of the government and public outrage which would have resulted if a private business firm had taken such action without submitting a detailed environmental impact statement.

WHICH GOOD IS BETTER?

Perhaps it is inevitable, but the proliferation of government controls has led to conflicts among controls and controllers. In some cases, the rules of a given agency work at cross purposes with each other. For example, OSHA mandates back-up alarms on vehicles at construction sites. Simultaneously, the agency requires employees to wear earplugs to protect them against noise, which can make it extremely difficult to hear the alarms. More serious and more frequent are the contradictions between the rulings of two or more government agencies where the regulated have little recourse.

The simple task of washing children's pajamas in New York State exemplifies how two sets of laws can pit one worthy objective against another, in this case ecology versus safety. Because of a ban on phosphates in detergents, the mother who launders her child's sleepwear in an ecologically sound way may risk washing away its required fire-resistant properties. In 1973, in an effort to halt water pollution, New York State banned the sale of detergents containing phosphates. Less than two months later, a federal regulation took effect requiring all children's sleepwear in sizes 0 to 6X to be flame-retardant. New York housewives now face a dilemma, because phosphates are the strongest protector of fire-retardancy. Phosphates hold soil and minerals in solution, preventing the formation of a mask on the fabric that would inactivate flame-resistancy. Soap and, to a lesser degree, many nonphosphate detergents redeposit those harmful items during the wash cycle. What does a conscientious mother do in a phosphate-banned area to avoid dressing her children in nightclothes that could burn up. Smuggle in the forbidden detergent? Commit an illegal act of laundry?

The controversy over restrooms furnishes another example of the conflict among different regulations and also demonstrates that common sense at times may be in short supply. The Labor Department, in administering its weighty responsibilities under the Occupational Safety and Health Act, has provided private industry with detailed instructions concerning the size, shape, dimensions, and number of toilet seats. On the basis of a long accepted biological argument, some type of lounge area is required to be adjacent to women's restrooms. However, the Equal Employment Opportunity Commission has entered this vital area of government-business relations. The commission requires that male toilet and lounge facilities, although separate, must be equal to those provided for women. Hence, either equivalent lounges must be built adjacent to the men's toilets, or the women's lounges must be dismantled, OSHA and state laws to the contrary notwithstanding. To those who may insist that nature did not create men and women with identical physical characteristics and needs, we can only reply that regulation, like justice, must be blind.

ARBITRARY POWER

The instances of waste and foolishness on the part of government regulators may pale into insignificance when compared to the raw arbitrary power that can be, and at times is, exerted by federal regulators. To cite a member of the Consumer Product Safety Commission: "Any time that consumer safety is threatened, we're going to go for the company's throat."

That this statement is not merely an overblown metaphor can be seen by examining the case of Marlin Toy Products, Inc., of Horicon, Wisconsin. The firm's two main products, Flutter Ball and Birdie Ball, were plastic toys for children, identical except that one contained a butterfly and the other a bird. The toys originally held plastic pellets that rattled. This led the Food and Drug Administration in 1972 to place the products on its ban list; if the toys cracked, the pellets could be swallowed by a child. The company recalled the toys and redesigned its product line to eliminate the pellets and thus be removed from the ban list. Now enter the newly formed Consumer Product Safety Commission (CPSC) in 1973, which had assumed responsibility in this area. Because of an "editorial error," it puts Marlin products on its new ban list, although there is no longer any reason to ban them. Apparently, the commission incorporated an out-of-date FDA list. The error was called to the commission's attention, but it replied that it was not about to recall 250,000 lists "just to take one or two toys off." Marlin Toy Products reports that it was forced out of the toy business and had to lay off 75 percent of its employees due to the federal error. It is ironic to note that the commission, which specializes in ordering companies to recall their products if some defective ones may have been produced, refuses to recall its own product when there is a defect in every single one.

A more humorous instance of the CPSC's failure to abide by its own standards involves the toy safety buttons which the commission intended to distribute in fall 1974 in an effort to make consumers more safety conscious. Only after producing 80,000 buttons did the commission learn that its product was dangerous to children because of the lead paint and the possibility of breaking off and swallowing pieces of the button. Unlike the procedures that it expects of the companies its regulates, the commission presumably ran its tests after, rather than before, production. Fortunately, the commission realized its error prior to making public distribution of the buttons. Hence, only a waste of resources and tax dollars was involved.

It would be easier to excuse the commission for its blunders were it not for the arbitrary nature with which it exercises its power. Literally, a producer can be guilty unless he or she proves his or her innocence. The CPSC has ruled that "articles not meeting the requirements of the regulation are to be considered as banned even though they have not yet been reviewed," that is, even if CPSC has not seen them or is unaware of their existence.

There are limits to the extent to which the commission uses its vast powers, but one recent call was almost too close for comfort. The Consumer Product Safety Commission actually considered, but ruled against, banning a book as a hazardous product. The concern was over scientific textbooks that allegedly fail to warn young readers of the inherent dangers in some experiments. In its ruling, the commission did warn publishers to be aware of this potential problem.

It also appears that federal regulators literally do not have to obey the law. One such case involves the Kennecott Copper Corporation and the Environmental Protection Agency. The source of the company's complaint is the lack of an EPA approved plan for the state of Nevada to meet federal clean air standards. A tentative plan was submitted in January 1972, but more than two years later the federal agency had neither approved it nor offered an alternative, as required by the Clean Air Act. The act stipulates EPA must act within six months. Kennecott is going ahead on its own with a $24 million project to clean up emission from its Nevada smelter, hoping that ultimately it will receive the agency's approval. Kennecott has notified EPA that it plans to sue the agency for failure to obey the Clean Air Act of 1970. Such notification is required before the suit can be instituted.

The literature does not give much attention to the role of the government official as inspector. Yet this uninvited visitor tends to make his or her appearance with considerable frequency, and often without prior notice. The Supreme Court recently ruled that air pollution inspectors do not need search warrants to enter the property of suspected polluters as long as they do not enter areas closed to the public. The unannounced and warrantless inspections were held not to be in violation of constitutional protection against unreasonable search and seizure.

The OSHA inspectors can go further. They have so-called no-knock power to enter the premises of virtually any business in the United States without a warrant or even prior announcement. Jail terms are provided in the law for anyone tipping off an OSHA "raid."

Nor are such arbitrary actions limited to the legislative and executive branches. One recent judicial decision on environmental regulation surely must leave the business community shaking its head in wonderment. A federal district judge in Texas ordered the private developer of a community project near San Antonio to pay the attorney's fees for four citizens groups, even though the private developer was not even a party to the suit (it was filed against the federal government, which had accepted the developer's environmental impact statement) and the citizens groups had lost the case. The court proclaimed the interesting doctrine that, since private citizens carry much of the burden of seeing that federal environmental policy is carried out, awarding them their costs—even if they lose—will help ensure that information concerning projects and their impact on the environment will become public (*Sierra Club* v. *Lynn,* West. Dist. Tex.).

THE POSSIBLE SHAPE OF THINGS TO COME

We can obtain some understanding of the future consequences of the path on which the nation has embarked by examining that sector of U.S. industry which already has gone down the road of government control to the greatest degree. Over a period of three decades, the major defense contractors have grown accustomed to the federal government making the basic decisions about which products are to be produced, how the firm is to go about producing them, and how capital is to be provided. In the process, the federal government has assumed a major portion of the risk and the role of the entrepreneur.

One senior Pentagon official described with considerable enthusiasm his visit to a large defense contractor and its role with the military service regulating its operations: "I was impressed with the complete interrelationship of the Service/contractor organizations. They are virtually co-located. . . . The Service is aware of and, in fact, participates in practically every major contractor decision." It may not be altogether coincidental that the two largest and most government-dependent of the defense contractors—Lockheed and General Dynamics—are precisely the firms whose products have come under greatest attack for cost overruns and other basic shortcomings. More C5As and TFXs (to cite two of their better-known products) would seem to be rather poor precedents for future public policy.

This article is not intended to be a simpleminded attack on all forms of government control over industry. A society, acting through government, can and should act to protect consumers against rapacious sellers, individual workers against unscrupulous employers, and future generations against those who would waste the nation's resources. But, as in most areas of life, the sensible questions are not matters of either/or, but rather of more or less. Thus, we enthusiastically can advocate stringent controls to avoid infant crib deaths without simultaneously supporting a plethora of detailed federal rules and regulations dealing with the color of exit lights and the maintenance of cuspidors.

A NEW DEPARTURE

We need a fundamental rethinking of the attitude that government increasingly should involve itself in what traditionally has been internal business decision making. Viewing the process of determining national priorities as a two-step affair is one possibility. The first step should continue, as at present, to focus on determining how much of our resources should be devoted to defense, welfare, education, and so forth, at least to the extent that these basic issues are now decided by design at all.

This determination should be accompanied by a tentative allocation of responsibilities among the major sectors of the economy. Such indicative planning would recognize that the constant and increasing nibbling away at business prerogatives and entrepreneurial capacity has a very substantial cost: reduced effectiveness in achieving basic national objectives, notably (to use the language of the Employment Act) "maximum employment, production, and purchasing power."

At a time when cost-benefit analysis has become fashionable, we should not be oblivious to the very real effects of converting ostensibly private organizations into voluntary agents of the federal establishment. Rather, the nation should determine which of its objectives can be achieved more effectively in the private sector and attempt to create an environment which is more conducive to the attainment of those objectives.

It is reasonable to anticipate that primarily social objectives, such as improved police services, would continue to be the primary province of government. But primarily economic objectives, notably training, motivating, and usefully employing the bulk of the nation's work force, would be viewed as mainly the responsibility of the private sector, and especially of business firms.

The new model of national decision making hardly calls for an abdication of government concern with the various problems discussed here. Rather, it would require a redirection of the methods selected to achieve those ends. In the environmental area, for example, the current dependence on direct controls would be reduced in favor of the more indirect but powerful incentives available through the price system. Specifically, imaginative use of "sumptuary" excise taxation, such as we have grown accustomed to in the cases of tobacco products and alcoholic beverages, can be used to alter basic production and consumption patterns. The desired results would not be accomplished by fiat, but by making the high-pollutant product or service more expensive relative to the low-pollutant product or service. The basic guiding principle would be that people and organizations do not pollute because they enjoy messing up the environment; they pollute because it is easier or cheaper to do so. In lieu of a corps of regulators, we would use the price system to make polluting harder and more expensive. A similar opportunity for sumptuary taxation in lieu of government controls is now presenting itself with reference to energy.

In the job safety area, the law seems to have lost sight of the basic objective: a healthier working environment. As we have seen, the current emphasis is on punishing violators. In the more positive spirit suggested here, the basic thrust of occupational safety and health legislation would be changed from prescribing and proscribing specific practices to focusing on desired reductions in the accident and health hazard rates in a given factory or industry. It is doubtful that there is an invariant way of achieving that desirable result. Changes in equipment, variations in working practices, training of employees, and leadership on the part of management all may be practical alternatives. Presumably we should opt for the mix of methods which entails the least cost, and those combinations probably would vary from plant to plant and over time.

Perhaps one of the least understood forms of government control is over the direction of the flow of saving and investment. This is accomplished through the use of the government's credit power, involving "off-budget" agencies such as the Export-Import Bank, loan guarantees such as those given the Lockheed Aircraft Corporation, and establishment of a galaxy of government-sponsored borrowers and lenders (usually referred to by their nicknames, "Fanny Mae," "Ginny Mae," "Sally Mae," "Fanny Rae," and "Freddy Mac"). None of these federal instrumentalities do much to add to the available pool of investment funds. Rather, they bid funds away from unprotected and truly private borrowers. In every period of tight credit, there is a predictable clamor to set up still more federal credit agencies to "protect" borrowers not now under the federal umbrella. Clearly, a more positive and fruitful approach would be to create an economic environment which provides more incentive to save and thus results in a larger pool of investment funds becoming available to the society as a whole.

The moral of the tale should be clear by now: Because of the very substantial costs and other adverse side effects to which they give rise, the existing array of government controls over business should be given a new and hard look by society. Substantial attention should be paid to the possibility of cutting back or eliminating those controls that generate excessive costs and other disadvantages. Rather than blithely continuing to proliferate the usage of government controls over business, alternative means of achieving important rational objectives should be explored and developed.

QUESTIONS

1. Do you agree with the underlying indictments of government regulations presented by Weidenbaum?
2. Do you think the evidence presented by the author for regulatory reform is a sufficient basis for a major overhauling of government regulations? Specifically, what do you recommend?
3. Can you think of any areas where there should be more rather than less government regulation of business? Be specific.
4. Do you agree with the author's prescription for reforming the regulatory machinery? Explain why or why not?

CHANGING MODES OF GOVERNMENT REGULATION OF BUSINESS

JOHN R. MEYER

John R. Meyer, the 1907 Professor of Transportation, Logistics, and Distribution, Graduate School of Business Administration, Harvard University, and president of the National Bureau of Economic Research, Inc., examines the changing fashions in government regulation and recommends a few new approaches.

THE JOINT PUBLIC-PRIVATE MANAGEMENT AGENCY

Early government regulation of industry in the United States was characteristically of the type in which a special agency, usually a creature of Congress, helped manage a particular industry's affairs, often in considerable depth and detail. The Interstate Commerce Commission (ICC), the Federal Communications Commission (FCC), the Federal Power Commission (FPC), the Securities and Exchange Commission (SEC), the Civil Aeronautics Board (CAB), the Nuclear Regulatory Commission (NRC), state public service and public utility commissions—all fitted this basic pattern.

Diverse motives stimulated these early regulatory efforts. Consumer protection was nearly always prominent in the publicly professed motives, and it may even have been dominant in some cases, e.g., the SEC. Development and promotion of a "struggling" infant industry was the major consideration in other instances, e.g., the FCC, AEC, and CAB. Cartelization or stabilization of an industry's markets was still another major incentive. Many scholars believe that this cartelization motive largely explains the ICC's relationship to the railroad industry in the late nineteenth century, and the ready acquiescence of the trucking and inland waterway common carriers to ICC regulation during the 1930s.

The performance of these regulatory agencies in meeting their real or professed objectives has been at least as diverse as their origins and motivations. The general scholarly consensus today is that consumer protection has *not* been a major accomplishment of regulation. Even if an agency starts with emphasis on consumer interests—so the argument goes—the highly individualistic, even personalized, relationship between the agency and the regulated industry is such that, as the industry matures, the temptation to indulge in cartelization becomes overwhelming. Thus, many observers see the CAB as going through a cycle in which it began with promotion and development as its major objective, slid into a more consumer-oriented stance toward the end of the second decade of its existence, and now is drifting into a cartelization-stabilization mode. Similarly, many less skeptical scholars would characterize the ICC as starting with consumer interests paramount, but then accommodating or even promoting cartelization in order to achieve real power in industry affairs.

Neither have the agencies done exceedingly well in protecting *producer* interests, if, indeed, that was their goal. Regulated industries have produced relatively low rates of return on net worth, although common carrier trucking and banking appear to be partial exceptions to the rule. In 1972, three regulated industries ranked near or at the bottom in rate of return: Air Transport at 6.6 percent, Class I Railroads at 3 percent, and Investment Funds at 2.5 percent. These percentages contrast with a 12.1 percent average return for all manufacturing, 12.4 percent for the service industries, and 11.3 percent for trade. Financial difficulties and bankruptcies are rather commonplace in the railroad, airline, and securities industries.

Earnings deficiencies are also suggested by the apparent insufficiency of capital in some regulated industries, notably the electric power industry. In particular, insufficient incentive to invest is alleged in some regulated industries, despite rapidly growing demands for their products. The natural gas industry is cited as the worst recent example of this phenomenon; and many would also claim that electric utilities and telephones constitute apt illustrations of the same problem.

FUNCTIONAL REGULATION

Given this failure to meet either producer or consumer objectives, it is not surprising that alternatives to the joint public-private management format of regulation have arisen. By far the most important alternative has been "functional regulation." Functional regulation started as early as the turn of the century in the form of the antitrust laws. The Federal Trade Commission (FTC), the Robinson-Patman Act, and similar efforts to eliminate "predatory pricing" and other forms of "anticompetitive" behavior also go back many decades. Government's objectives in enacting such legislation are not always clear or consistent. For example, the so-called "fair-trade" laws that permit the fixing of minimum prices represent, in the view of many observers, an attempt to extend the principle of cartelization and thus are anticompetitive in effect.

In general, functional regulation applies to business performance in carrying out a narrow, well-defined business function, in contrast to the application of joint-management regulation to practically all aspects of an enterprise's performance. And functional regulation usually embraces business firms in several industries or throughout the economy.

Examples of functional regulation abound, and the number of instances has grown rapidly within the last decade or so. The most important example, from an economic standpoint, has been the effort to establish an "incomes policy," regulating increases in wages, prices, rents, interest, and dividends. The methods range widely, of course, from "jawboning" to "guideposts" to "freezes" and mandatory controls. The real and psychological impacts can hardly be overestimated. Indeed, economists, public officials, businessmen, and labor leaders are only beginning to sort out their thoughts on the difficult issues involved.

Regulations aimed at environmental improvement are a second economically important category of functional regulation. Environmental controls are not restricted to air and water depollution, but extend to billboards, junkyards, plant location, and so forth. On the whole, the environmental regulations of the last half decade or so constitute an eloquent example of public policy outracing the underlying information or knowledge base. Because complex system interactions or interdependencies are often involved in environmental problems, and the secondary and tertiary effects of a given policy are often not obvious, functional regulations not uncommonly have produced results contradictory to their primary or intended effects.

A third relatively new category of functional regulation has to do with safety both of products and of working conditions. There have been intensified efforts in fields of traditional concern, such as drug certification and coal mining. And regulations have extended into completely new areas, such as automobile design. The development of new technologies, particularly nuclear power, has also led to an increase in government involvement in the safety of employees and of the public.

Attempts to achieve better flows of information to consumers constitute another relatively recent development in functional regulation. Truth-in-lending and unit prices are two important examples. Again, historical roots are relatively deep and long-standing; but only within the last decade has governmental activity become significant. Continued price inflation and the greater involvement of women in politics and business may promote this type of regulation, which could be the "growth sector" of government regulation in the future.

THE PUBLIC-PRIVATE ENTERPRISE

Other important alternatives to either conventional joint-management or functional regulation have emerged in recent years, motivated to some extent by disappointment with previous forms of business regulation. The most important example is certainly the joint public-private enterprise. The Federal National Mortgage Association (Fannie Mae or FNMA), the Communications Satellite Corporation (COMSAT), the U.S. Postal Service, and the proposed Federal National Railway Association (Fannie Rae) exemplify the new species.

The new public-private enterprises have an interesting diversity of origins and motives. Fannie Mae represents a spinoff of a successful government activity that apparently no longer needed the special protection and aid of government to survive, and could benefit from exposure to the competitive pressures of private enterprise. COMSAT embodies a government effort to aid the private sector in developing a new and expensive technology. It contrasts with the joint public-private management agency used to promote new technologies until the late 1940s; indeed, the former AEC may be the last of the "old species." Fannie Rae (assuming it comes into being) would be motivated by failure rather than success: The objective would be to "bail out" the Northeast railroads, a notoriously unsuccessful but economically important sector of the private economy. Fannie Rae would also represent a recognition of an important failure in conventional regulation. Similarly, the Postal Service emerged from failure, though in the public rather than the private sector.

The current fascination with public-private enterprises has led to suggestions to create analogies to the American Telephone and Telegraph Company in other sectors of the economy. For example, a great deal has been said about the adaptability of the "AT&T approach" to the railroad industry; and the question has been debated whether COMSAT should be made more in the image of AT&T. The key questions about the adaptability of the AT&T approach to other industries would appear to be the prevalence of scale economies in these industries and the degree to which they are natural monopolies.

Interest in the public-private enterprise also appears to have been stoked by observation of Japan's postwar economic success. Many would attribute it largely to the unusual degree of cooperation between the government and large private enterprises in Japan. Of course, there were other explanatory factors, such as large pools of underutilized agricultural labor, a considerable initial gap between world industrial technology and Japan's technology, and very favorable (but unsustainable) terms of trade for manufactured goods as against unprocessed commodities. Also, the adaptability of Japanese methods to other societies remains to be established.

THE PROPENSITY TO DEGRADATION IN REGULATORY AGENCIES

The obvious question is whether the new approaches, functional regulation, and the joint public-private enterprise, will succeed to any greater extent in achieving their professed objectives than the old-style joint-management agencies. The answer is probably *yes* in the short run, and *no* in the long run. A major regularity in previous government efforts to regulate business is the propensity for degradation to occur over time. Late nineteenth-century reports suggest, for example, that the ICC was then a very exciting innovating institution. It represented an important new departure in public policy and attracted some of the best talent of the time. Similarly, there is considerable objective evidence to support an opinion that the SEC has never again been quite as vital as it was in its first few years, when it was under strong and knowledgeable leadership and attracted fine young talent to its staff.

Not all regulatory agencies, of course, follow from the day of their inception an undeviating downward trend in quality and responsiveness. New appointments to many of the regulatory commissions, particularly to the chairman's seat, have often resulted in at least a temporary revival. Nevertheless, most such revivals have been only cyclical fluctuations around a basic downward trend.

If aging is the problem, how does one incorporate change into the regulatory system? One simple legalistic way would be to establish for any new agency an arbitrary cutoff of its life, at say ten years. However, the realities of bureaucratic self-survival, plus the considerable potentiality for a growing community of interests between the agency and the industries being regulated, suggest that any such cutoff date would never be realized. Political inertia would be too large to overcome.

The potentialities for unbiased appraisal of performance that are implicit in the joint public-private enterprise give this approach its special attractiveness. A public-private enterprise, usually being somewhat dependent upon private external financing, would be more exposed to the "corrective audit" that constitutes a fundamental contribution of organized financial markets to a market economy. The extent to which this correction would work in practice, though, is uncertain. Many observers contend that "the audit" really is inoperative, even for completely private enterprises, given the increasingly professional character of managements and the alleged divorce of ownership from control. Moreover, the ultimate corrective in the private sector, the formal takeover by another enterprise, would ordinarily not be available to the joint public-private enterprise. Finally, access to *public* funds could obviously moderate much of the normal financial discipline of capital markets. The experience of other countries with joint enterprises, such as many international "flag" airlines, lends strong confirmatory evidence to these fears. Even with all these limitations, however, the joint public-private enterprise should be somewhat more susceptible to pressures for change than an established government bureaucracy.

The public-private enterprise is mainly a substitute for the joint-management agency. Some forms of regulation, especially those that are functional in character, seem unadaptable to the joint public-private enterprise approach. The usually preferred alternative to formal governmental action to achieve safety, or consumer protection, or any other functional objective, is "self-regulation" by the firms or industries involved. Occasionally, too, spontaneous associations of affected parties such as the Consumers Union and similar organizations may come into being to achieve functional regulatory objectives. On the whole, though, these efforts have probably been less than fully successful. In fact, their failures often induce formal government entry into the field. Nevertheless, in the interests of maintaining options, public policy might consider making grants to support or elicit more private efforts at regulation. A similar line of argument could also justify the tax preferences now given to various forms of cooperative associations.

A central theme in designing future business-government relationships might be the development of even more experimentation and diversity—perhaps to the point of deliberately inducing overlapping jurisdictions between public and private agencies. For example, government agencies, joint public-private corporations, and private enterprises might all compete with each other in providing mail services to the public. Also, change should be institutionalized for government regulatory agencies. A formal cutoff date or a periodic reappraisal of an agency may not work; but it is at least worth a try. The very act of reappraisal should create an opportunity to insert alternative points of view into the record. In a world of limited options, this may be the best that can be done.

QUESTIONS

1. Do you believe that the functional regulation proposed by Meyer can overcome the deficiencies of much of the current regulation of industry? Explain.
2. Does the establishment of public-private enterprises promise a useful method to avoid inappropriate federal regulation?
3. Study the available literature on the U.S. Postal Service, and make a presentation of the pluses and minuses of the public-private enterprise.
4. Do you believe that Meyer's proposal to establish an arbitrary limit to the life of a new agency will prevent regulatory degradation?

HISTORICAL ACCIDENT

JOHN P. CARTER

John P. Carter, professor of business administration, University of California at Berkeley, hypothesizes how a slightly different sequence of technological developments in the transportation industry might have produced a very different social structure in the United States and, of course, different social values.

A slightly different sequence of invention might have produced a very different social structure of the present transportation industry. We had railways before highways because we learned how to lay smooth-running lines—the rails, before we learned how to lay smooth-running surfaces—the roads. As long as only animal power was available, that sequence may not have been important. But we learned how to apply steam power to locomotion before we learned how to develop the road. Moreover, working iron was known before vulcanization of rubber was discovered. Thus, railways were in local use, in mines and the like, by the end of the eighteenth century. Steam locomotion was invented at the beginning of the nineteenth century, but it was nearly the middle of that century before portland cement and vulcanized rubber were developed. Steam carriages were tried before then, but they were heavy and fragile and soon broke up under the shocks of iron wheels on cobblestones. The rail gave the steam engine a smooth place to run, and the railways were so obviously superior to any previous form of transport that all energies were devoted to railway construction for the following century. The big impact of portland cement and vulcanized rubber on transport had to wait until the invention of the internal combustion engine.

But suppose portland cement and vulcanized rubber had been invented prior to, or concurrently with, the application of the steam engine to locomotion. Isn't it possible that a form of the highway era would have evolved immediately, and that the railway era would never have occurred? Smooth-surfaced lanes would have permitted steam carriages and trucks to operate, and quite possibly steam truck and trailer combinations. Roads were already a well-known technology, and their business form was the turnpike.

Road vehicles are maneuverable and can turn out almost anywhere for crossing or overtaking. When railways were first developed for public use, that is, not merely for industrial use, it was supposed that they would be public highways just like any road or turnpike. But rail technology lacks flexibility. Its virtue, that it is guided by two smooth thin lines, is also its major handicap, because some form of central planning is required for meeting or overtaking trains. That led to the requirement that all trains be under a single control and to the assumed corollary that single control meant single ownership. That was the original source of the railway bureaucracy.

And this was the basis of the first large-scale organization. The railway industry, as is well known, offers such substantial indivisibilities that there are important economies of scale, and hence strong monopolistic tendencies. But suppose we had gone directly to a steam-powered highway era: would there have been the same economies of scale and monopolistic tendencies? I think not. The cement highway would probably have adopted the organization of the turnpike, whether ownership turned out to be public or private. The turnpike was open to all who paid the tolls. While there might have been few manufacturers of steam carriages, there is no reason to suppose that there would be few buyers. Even the mature automobile industry today, while marked by few manufacturers, has very large numbers of buyers. It might be that if the highway era had evolved in the early nineteenth century instead of the early twentieth, the land transportation industry might have developed with a large number of independent producers, in the manner of the international shipping industry or the segment of the trucking industry now carrying exempt commodities. This means that a competitive market would have evolved along the standard definition of competition: so many buyers and so many sellers that no one buyer or seller can affect the price.

Instead, we had the emergence of the largest industrial organizations known in society up to then, the technology of which dictated a monopoly position. But did the requirement that all trains be subject to a single central traffic controller also require single ownership? The primitive quality of communications techniques in the early nineteenth century may well have triggered the single-ownership requirement. By trial and error (mostly the latter), it soon became clear that trains could not operate on a "see and be seen" formula of traffic control. A train has very limited braking ability and zero capability for other evasive action. Fairly early on, trains were controlled by timetable, varied by written train order. The trainmaster could not communicate with train crews once they had left the terminal; until the invention of the telegraph he could not even communicate with the other terminal. Train crews had to meet trains at the crossing points. To avoid indefinite delays, there were sometimes provisions that if the opposing train did not arrive, the train could proceed cautiously to the next siding. Since the opposing train would be running late, and in a hurry, curves could become quite exciting.

Safe operation, without a communication system, thus could involve very long delays. Those would hardly be compatible with a system of a large number of competitive users of the railway lines. Delays would strike at random, but their economic impact might be so great that a couple of them could wipe out a small businessman. Steam locomotives were like airplanes: they required fuel and water and they could not be shut down en route. Thus, their ability to tolerate delay was quite limited. A train might have to be abandoned while the locomotive sought more water, or the crew might have to gather fuel. And it would have been easy for one competitor, in these conditions, to sabotage his rival. Although managers may not have analyzed it at the time, it was probably lack of communications ability between the traffic controller (trainmaster) and the train crews that required the single ownership of the rail line and the train operation. Only by that could the risks of serious delay be borne equitably by all train movements.

It was the actual sequence of inventions that produced the railway monopolies. The popular reaction to those monopolies produced the state regulatory agencies and the Interstate Commerce Commission. The latter often has served as the example for later legislation controlling transport. The enormous indivisibilities of railways led to the concept of ruinous competition when multiple lines served the same markets so that in 1920 the certificate made its appearance: new railways could not be built without a certificate of public convenience and necessity from the ICC. In fact, by 1920 railways were being abandoned rather than constructed. Never mind, a certificate was required for abandonment also.

Why were railways being abandoned by 1920? Obviously, because the highway era had arrived. The highway era resulted from the invention of the internal combustion engine, which, in the following half century, entirely displaced steam as the source of transportation power. Highway transportation is essentially competitive and ubiquitous. The man-machine ratio is 1:1; very little capital is required to enter the industry. Limited skill is required to operate the machine. Since the vehicle moves freely on the smooth surface of the road, no elaborate administration is required to provide separation of the movements. A few simple rules suffice to let the system operate on a "see and be seen" basis.

So what model did Congress apply when the trucking industry was placed under ICC control? The railway model. Certificates were required for entry and rates had to be published. The certificates provided fixed routes. Carriers were not to use the ubiquitous highway network. The individual independent truck driver suddenly needed a large administrative office like a railway. Formerly, when he was ready to carry a cargo, he had gone to a broker just as a shipowner does today.

And in 1938, when air transportation was brought under control of the Civil Aeronautics Authority, the railway model was again applied. Air transport is the most flexible of all forms of transport. Airports must be close enough together to meet the range of the aircraft, and navigational systems must be provided so that the aircraft knows its location and the location of conflicting traffic. "See and be seen" is not effective in overcast even at DC-3 speeds. Yet air traffic control was not provided by the airlines but by another federal agency, the Civil Aviation Administration, now the FAA. Nevertheless, Congress arranged that airlines obtain certificates for fixed routes, just as if they were railways. Even skipping a stop, overflying a major traffic center such as Elko, Nevada required federal permission. Air transportation is technologically the most innovative of all forms of transport, yet the CAB has never voluntarily permitted a new company to enter the industry on a permanent basis. The dominant companies in the industry are the same companies that were there in 1938. They have become fewer through merger. Congress has required the CAB to issue certificates to others, but there is hostility to new managements, which might have new ideas for organizing air transport.

So we have a situation in which the historical accident of a few decades in the sequencing of inventions generated the large-scale organization that the railway technology seemed to require. The railway pattern, once evolved, was accepted by Congress, and apparently by the nation at large, as the organizational model for all subsequently invented transport technologies. And that included the relationship between industry and government.

"What if" games are never easy, but it ought to be interesting to hypothesize how the transport industry and organization would have developed had adequate road surfaces and vehicle springing been known when steam power was applied to locomotion. Steam carriages with solid rubber tires might have run on concrete roads. Adhesive abilities would have been much greater than those for the steel wheel on steel rail. Hence, concrete roads could have been built with much less engineering and earth moving than required for railway construction. (The engineering skills necessary for the construction of low-gradient railway lines had already been developed during the canal construction era.)

Some railway construction no doubt would have taken place, but essentially as an extension of the early use of railways in mines. Railways might have been built as essentially industrial carriers to handle heavy coal and ore movement. Even now, well through the twentieth century, some railways are still being built to handle coal and ore traffic. Under some conditions, no better technology has yet been invented for the long-distance repetitive movement of bulk commodities. The industrial railways built in the nineteenth century might not have been common carriers, or common carriers only of a few minerals. The basic common-carriage transportation might have been provided by rubber-tired steam carriages operating along concrete roads.

Such steam-carriage operation might well have been to a small organizational scale. The steam carriage of the early nineteenth century would surely have been relatively more expensive and relatively less convenient than the internal combustion engine truck of the early twentieth century. Like the steam locomotive, it would have required two men to operate it, one man to tend the fire and boiler, the other to drive the vehicle. It would have been relatively heavy because of the water and its range would have been limited by the availability of additional water supplies. The corner filling station that would have evolved a century earlier would have sold coal and water.

But organizationally, there would have been room for many entrepreneurs.

Nothing in the technology dictated a large organization. There might have been some scale economies in marketing for those who chose to operate regular lines. That was the experience of nineteenth-century steamship companies. Maintenance and repairs could be contracted, as shipping companies do. A maintenance base would have had to stand on its own feet, as do airline bases, by contracting for the maintenance of equipment belonging to others to maintain capacity operations.

With many entrepreneurs monopoly would have been less easy to organize and maintain. With entry available to those with little capital, the shipping field provides an analogy. Shipping conferences have led uneasy existences. But domestic steam-carriage operation would have taken much less capital and a much smaller organization than the ownership of even a single vessel. Presumably, a two-man steam carriage could have tramped cargo a century ago just as a two-man tractor and refrigerated trailer tramps cargo now. But monopoly pressures in transportation, with free entry into the steam-carriage business, would not seem to be different from monopoly pressures elsewhere in the economy. That is, the established would like to prevent the entry of newcomers. Transportation by steam carriage would not have required the invention of a whole special set of organizations to deal with transportation. The ICC and the CAB need never have emerged. All of that business and governmental organization development because of the accident of a few decades in the timing of inventions!

But now we have the communications ability to control the movements of many transport units by a single traffic controller no matter who may be the owner of these units. The FAA does that quite successfully. FAA control techniques could be applied to rail transport; anyone could then lease a locomotive and cars, hire a crew from the union, pay the tolls to the railway company, and run his train for his own account under FAA-type control. Why do we still need the large transport organizations and their accompanying government bureaucracies?

QUESTIONS

1. How credible, in your opinion, is speculation of the kind found in this article? What makes such historical perspectives useful in the contemporary world?
2. Can you speculate where society may be at the crossroads today in terms of the development by business executives of applied technology? What, for example, are the likely consequences of developing nuclear energy before solar energy?
3. Were technological factors of primary importance in blueprinting government regulation of transportation or were other factors of equal or greater importance? Are there other factors of significance that Carter does not mention? If so, what are they?

14

SHOULD WE SLOW DOWN ECONOMIC GROWTH?

GROWTH VS. NO GROWTH: AN EVALUATION

ROLAND N. MCKEAN

Roland N. McKean, Commonwealth Professor of Economics, University of Virginia, examines and evaluates in the following article the case for no growth.

"Growth" is a harmless neutral concept meaning merely "a growing" or "an increase." If growth meant an increase in well-being in terms of an agreed-upon criterion of well-being, it could hardly be opposed. Objections to growth must refer to the increase of particular magnitudes—in population, GNP, or power consumption—that cause negative growth of well-being according to some criterion. What is really objected to, then, is *negative or uneconomic growth* according to certain concepts of social welfare.

Disagreement about these matters is bound to occur, because *any* kind of growth will injure some individuals, and in the real world all injured persons will not be compensated. Moreover, even if they could be compensated, some might not like the outcome: in any group decision, there is a basic value or criterion judgment about which members of the group may disagree. To discuss costs or gains from any kind of growth or from anything else, however, one must keep in mind a criterion that determines how costs and gains are to be measured. In this paper I will use the concept of "economic efficiency," according to which gains (or costs) are priced at whatever individuals would voluntarily pay, at the margin, to have (or avoid) them. This means accepting (or stimulating) the values that would emerge from a voluntary exchange system. One could substitute a different criterion and, although similar phenomena would occur, the values attached to them could differ.

Throughout the paper I will use the term "economic growth," as I believe most other persons use it, to mean increases in GNP or some such indicator of aggregate final output. In a sense this is a misuse of the word "economic," for growth would hardly be economic—hardly an economical use of resources—if it entailed certain costs that were not being counted (as is the case with GNP). It is convenient, however, to use the term "economic growth" in this fashion, since this usage is widely accepted. Moreover, except where I specifically mention population growth my discussion will pertain to economic growth.

POSSIBLE INTERPRETATIONS OF THE CASE FOR NO GROWTH

Let us examine alternative ways of interpreting the arguments in favor of retarded or zero growth. Critics of economic growth may mean that it

Reprinted by permission of *Daedalus,* Journal of the American Academy of Arts and Sciences, Boston, Massachusetts. Fall 1973, pp. 207–227, *The No-Growth Society.*

constitutes two steps forward and one step back—that it has bad side effects which partly offset the good effects. In that event, it makes sense to see if reducing the bad effects can yield net gains. It would not make sense, however, simply to eliminate growth, for in these circumstances, one would sacrifice the two steps forward in order to avoid one step backward. (The use of penicillin is perhaps analogous. It makes sense to prescribe it with care and regulate its use so as to reduce the undesirable side effects, but not to eliminate it altogether.) In this situation, most indexes of growth are misleading, of course, if they are mistaken for indexes of growth in welfare, for in terms of well-being they may reflect the two steps forward but little or none of the backsliding. Also, it might be noted that the distribution of benefits and injuries is not uniform. To recipients of benefits (perhaps the young and upwardly mobile), growth may seem lovely; while to the injured (among them the elderly or long-time residents who preferred their city when it was half its present size), economic growth may appear to be an undiluted evil.

Alternatively, critics of "economic growth" may mean that expansion of the economy has so many bad side effects that it really constitutes two steps forward and three steps back. As before, it would be sensible to try to reduce the steps backward as long as the effort yielded net gain. If reducing the bad side effects were too costly to be economical, however, it would be appropriate to stop the growth—in other words, to prevent the two steps forward in order to eliminate the three steps backward. Such a policy employs a meat axe instead of a scalpel, yet it is the best one can do when using the scalpel results in too many disadvantages. An analogous situation may exist with respect to many pollution policies. In terms of economic efficiency one might think initially that households should be charged for throwing away bottles according to the costs imposed on other people. Their actions, not the production of such bottles, should be made more expensive. Because of heavy monitoring costs, however, it may be more economical to retreat to a "second-best" measure, a tax on disposable bottles, or even the prohibition of such bottles. Or, to take an extreme example, it is *conceivable,* though not likely, that prohibiting the internal combustion engine would be preferable to the alternatives, given the transaction-and-intervention costs associated with voluntary contracting, government charges for spillovers, or government regulation.

It is possible, finally, that some opponents of growth believe its effects to be solely bad ones. In that case, stopping such growth would be an unambiguous improvement. I do not believe the consequences are so simple, however, and doubt that many other persons do.

EVALUATING THE COSTS OF GROWTH

Personally I do not think that the most highly publicized costs of growth are by themselves so ruinous and unmanageable. With the possible exception of the carbon dioxide layer around our atmosphere, which is probably no more imminently destructive than another ice age, deterioration of the physical environment is unlikely to cause cataclysmic disaster. Mainly it will bring about a declining level of material well-being. The world will turn out to be less rich and sweet smelling than a few people for a few decades thought it was. To have 90 percent instead of 60 percent of individuals poor again, or to have life expectancies shorter again, would be deplorable but not unspeakably disastrous (especially since high levels of material wealth and lower death rates may not have relieved man's anguish enormously anyway).

Realistic scenarios for the future would allow for the adjustments that even stubborn, stupid *Homo sapiens* can hardly avoid. To be sure, as far as forms of pollution are concerned, they result from the kinds of interdependencies in which individual action gets one almost nowhere. As Schelling has pointed out even more vividly than most, individual decisions where negotiation costs are high (as they would be if we tried to hire each other to be less noisy) can trap societies in myriad and extremely persistent "nonoptimal" situations. Nonetheless, if the costs of inaction become high enough, some private agreements (to use soundproofing, for example) will seem worth the transaction costs, and government measures will appear to be worth the intervention costs. As an example of the latter, people will even adopt decimal systems if the costs of doing nothing grow large enough. Similarly, as environmental quality deteriorates, people will, through voluntary contracts and the political process, divert their resources from material goods to environmental types of material well-being. People will have to sacrifice some of both, of course, but they can still end up with a bit of fun as well as filth—as in the lifestyle, say, of Elizabethan England, which may have been pretty awful in certain ways yet left some room for pleasure and creativity.

Admittedly, the political process, either within or among nations, does not respond in a timely or precise fashion—and I have little faith, incidentally, that governments will avoid thermonuclear wars, though I put them aside here—but at least it provides gross responses to gross increases in the demand for public goods. These responses will be *truly* gross, though, if debate and adjustments are postponed until crises prompt government action. In such circumstances, it seems especially likely that people will turn to bare-hands controls and large government-operated anti-externality programs instead of making relatively wide use of price mechanisms. In other words, while economic growth will inevitably bring government adjustments to avoid disasters resulting from growth as such, these inevitable responses are likely to be clumsy and to cause unnecessarily large government.

In the private sector there will be many automatic adjustments. Prices, while they will not follow appropriate paths where resources are not owned privately, or markets do not exist, or prices are regulated, will eventually respond in a gross fashion even under these adverse conditions. (Watch the prices of fish and gas over the next decade.) These price changes will also help strike a balance between environmental quality and other forms of material wealth. Thus, I assert, along with numerous others, that a sensible scenario for the future portrays declines of wealth and a series of painful adjustments, including a leveling off or decline of population, but not a sudden collapse of any kind.

The exhaustion of nonrenewable resources would bring about similar adjustments as we became poorer. It would be an unlikely coincidence for technological advances to maintain per capita income indefinitely; economic growth will probably become negative someday. (This is not much of a forecast; as Singer says about the basic logic of *The Limits to Growth,* it's like a meteorologist predicting rain—sometime!) But all resources will not simultaneously and suddenly vanish without advance warning. There will be signals that this ore or that material is rapidly becoming more difficult to obtain. Prices will rise, inducing people to shift to substitutes—perhaps even buggies for automobiles or card games for television. Anticipating further price increases, speculators (that is, all of us) will find it profitable to store scarce materials, not for distant posterity but to apportion them out over a thirty- or forty-year period, and some would subsequently be kept for high-value uses over subsequent thirty- or forty-year periods. These apportionments will help make the process of getting poorer a matter of painful but not catastrophic adjustment.

These prospects raise in starkest form the question, "How much are we willing to sacrifice for posterity?" Clearly people will make enormous sacrifices for their children and grandchildren. They *may* also wish to put aside extra resources for the well-being of distant generations yet be unwilling to do so unless they are assured that others will also do so. This free-rider difficulty raises the issue, "Can public policy promote economic efficiency (in terms of the wishes of the existing population) by extra conservation efforts?" Individual values on this point are difficult to discern. I don't honestly know whether I would voluntarily give up one quarter of my disposable income even if this would, with 100 percent certainty, prevent extinction of the human race 1000 years hence. I rather doubt if people do care much about what happens thousands of years from now, and doubt therefore if the free-rider problem is very significant. For most people the preferred compromise may be to profess, but not really demonstrate, concern about the distant future. Such a pretense lets us eat our cake yet also satisfy our need, for the sake of sanity or a greater sense of purpose, to believe that mankind has a future. If we explicitly disavowed any concern about the distant future, of course, the consumption of our minerals and durable capital stock would be nothing to worry about, but I shall not entertain this extreme possibility.

Population growth will, whenever extra persons add more to total social cost than they contribute, reduce material well-being and accelerate environmental deterioration and the use of exhaustible resources. Here too, however, it is impossible for me to visualize a situation in which people, even acting individually, would fail completely to make adjustments as the negative marginal social product of people became larger and larger. Their adjustments would hardly be those which would be optimal in a hypothetical world of zero transaction costs and therefore zero free-rider difficulties, but there would be reductions in birth rates and increases in death rates as extra bodies produced less useful output and more undesirable consequences. Minor disasters might be involved in this process but not sudden unprecedented madness or famine or plague. Nonetheless, the disadvantages of deliberately limiting population growth seem relatively small and hence the case for it is comparatively strong.

Other possible side effects of growth, however, worry me as much as conventional forms of pollution and poverty. These other consequences produce or aggravate what might be called poverty of the spirit. They can be regarded as unconventional forms of pollution, since, analytically viewed, all side effects are similar to pollution: they stem from overuse or suspected overuse of some resource (with economic efficiency as the criterion) because the consent of the damaged parties is not bought. Thus, if our individual actions spread disease or despair, they use up people's health without purchase of their consent. The following external effects of growth, although we know little about them yet, may be as ominous as its threat to material well-being as such.

I believe that, from now on, many types of growth—in, for example, population, urban density, and material affluence—increase the probability of pervasive controls and ownership by government. So far data do not show any marked correlation between growth of GNP and proliferation of government. Indeed up to this time statistics suggest that the size of government or the pervasiveness of oppressive controls and the scale of output are inversely related, because freedom from restrictions has surely promoted economic growth. Recent "exponential" increases, however, are unprecedented, and bring into play another set of causal relationships.

For one thing it is obvious that Robinson Crusoe needed neither markets, government, nor behavioral rules to cope with interdependencies. As soon as Friday arrived, however, there arose both production and consumption interdependencies. Some of these—Crusoe's use of Friday's labor and Friday's use of Crusoe's hut—could be taken into account by voluntary exchanges. As specialization and population densities increase, however, many interdependencies arise—my use of others' air or your use of others' peace and quiet—that cannot be taken into account by bargaining because of high transaction costs. The resulting (potentially relevant) side effects multiply in number and significance as growth, which involves ever greater specialization, continues. The two extreme choices confronting people may be to accept an increasing degree of interference with each other, which is frustrating, or to vote for various majority-rule government restrictions, which are also frustrating. In certain cultures part of the behavioral discipline that continued growth will demand might be accomplished by custom instead of coercive regulation, but generating instant or appropriate traditions is difficult. In any event, to be viable, behavioral rules have to be voluntarily accepted as a result of enlightened self-interest, and free-rider and other difficulties make it unlikely that such "social contracts" will evolve. I conclude that people will move in both of these directions but with much emphasis on the use of government, on coercive restrictions imposed by majority coalitions who object to particular spillovers. But majority rule, like any other political process, is a meat cleaver method of resolving conflicts. It leaves more people dissatisfied than would smoothly working markets (which are largely unavailable for resolving the conflicts under discussion because of transaction costs). Unresolved conflicts will become deeper and more numerous. The bargaining process in government will cost more and achieve less. In short, government, as we allocate more and more burdens to its decision-making process, will become a more costly and embittering process.

Affluence itself, even apart from production interdependencies, causes potentially relevant externalities. Interdependencies arise because A wishes to help B or, more likely, wishes to take something away from B. In this instance, growth increases the likelihood of pervasive government intervention to impose complex schemes and counterschemes for wealth redistribution. Economic growth may bring some conflicts over wealth distribution closer to home. Maybe the poor feel envy more keenly when many slightly wealthier persons are in their immediate vicinity than they do when a few filthily rich persons live in some remote village on Long Island. Moreover, regardless of whether attempts to resolve such conflicts produce government expansion, affluence and the resulting expansion of opportunities multiply certain types of overt conflicts to be resolved by government (though as I note later, growth eases the resolution of other conflicts). The simple increase in the number of alternatives confronting people puts them in conflict with each other more often. If transaction costs are low, conflict resolution by bargaining is comparatively easy. If such costs are high, however, the market offers little help. Thus the proliferation of conflicts *where transaction costs are high,* ulcer generating in itself, increases the probability of an expanding and increasingly unpleasant role for government.

Rising incomes will be devoted partly to government anyway—to defense, new services, and various public goods. Despite their desirable features, these all yield bigger, more discordant government and feelings of helplessness on the part of individual citizens. Voters, in deciding whether or not to vote, to inform themselves, to write their Congressmen, face a formidable free-rider situation. Why should I inform myself when the chances of my deciding an election or influencing anything, even of affecting the decisions of others to vote or inform themselves, are infinitesimal? As a consequence, government seems, from the standpoint of each voter, to have enormous arbitrary power. The disgruntled citizen cannot turn to a competitor, and, as government grows, he feels a growing sense of impotence, especially when, as inevitably happens from time to time, a particularly petulant and power-hungry person climbs to the top. Moreover, at best, the purchase and distribution of goods and services by government yield frustration, because almost no one, except the famous median voter on each issue, gets the amount or kind of defense or Medicare that he prefers for his tax dollar. Also, it should be remembered, the public goods themselves (defense or highways for example) inflict distressing external impacts without purchasing the consent of the damaged persons. In general, then, while growth may be neither a necessary nor a sufficient condition for big government, I am convinced that from now on extra growth increases the probability of bigger and more conflict-ridden government.

Other more speculative impacts of population and economic growth may rob life in the future of much flavor and quality. With growth there is pervasive change and perhaps a reduction in the probability of durable nonsuperficial relationships. In a large and mobile population, for example, the chances of encountering or dealing with a person a second time and the chances of frequent or persistent dealings are comparatively small. The village pub tends to become an urban cocktail bar; the department store is not conducive to regular sessions around a pot-bellied stove. New social organizations arise, of course, but *if,* on balance, the process of growth reduces the chances of having durable nonsuperficial relationships, this in itself is a considerable loss, for much of life is an almost pathetic search for such relationships.

More importantly, however, change and the impersonality of relationships may contribute to the decline of customs and behavioral rules which have, in the past, helped to reduce many external costs that people would otherwise have inflicted on each other. At best there is a serious free-rider problem involved in people's decisions as to whether to be friendly or courteous, to take garbage cans to the rear of the house, to serve as witnesses, to refrain from making noise, and even to be honest. Why should I do my bit, which is just a drop in the bucket, when other people may not reciprocate? Through the centuries man developed ethical rules, and often enforced them by threats of retaliation, ostracism, and eternity in hell, to cope with various free-rider difficulties. Along with the decline of religion which threatened personal punishment and allowed no free riders, larger and more mobile societies suffer a decline in the possibilities of personal retaliation or ostracism, a decline which undermines behavioral codes and aggravates free-rider problems. In large cities, accordingly, while there are forces pushing in different directions, there appears on balance to be less warmth, courtesy, trust, and adherence to behavioral codes than in small towns. Suburban neighbors hesitate less than village neighbors to ignore nearby screams, to use chainsaws on Sunday mornings or head-lighted power mowers at night. In crowded, impersonal, yet affluent societies, it costs more and is worth less to by-standers to interfere with muggings. Witnesses step forward less often. Even a high degree of honesty, which, for the entire group, is extremely economical in social and business intercourse, may now cost more than it is worth to many individuals. One person's future dealings with any other person will be few, he feels no obligation because of personal ties, and he cannot count on others to provide reciprocal favors according to the old rules. In my judgment, increasing material wealth, specialization, and population may exacerbate all these factors. They do not change our taste for morality or a behavioral code; they simply make it more costly and less rewarding to each individual to be considerate of others and to adhere to customs or ethical rules. In other words, growth tends to undermine the "social contracts" that are so important to the enforcement of amenity rights and the functioning of capitalism.

These observations are highly speculative, for many variables and uncertain relationships are involved. Furthermore, and this deserves emphasis, I am not suggesting that things were better under Peter the Great. On balance, life was probably dreadful for most people in most earlier eras, and at present it may be getting better every day, but this is irrelevant. The relevant question is this: if growth is not, or will not in the future be, a free lunch, are there policies that could make us better off in the decades ahead than we would otherwise be?

Another force helping to generate some of the above side effects as well as others is the rising value of time, in terms of real income that can be earned per hour, which results from economic growth. Increases in personal income influence a person's choice between work and leisure and his choice among leisure activities. The extra income makes him able to afford more leisure and time-consuming activities, but the higher earnings per hour make such pursuits more expensive to him. That is, he has to sacrifice more to take an hour off. This causes him to substitute relatively more productive uses of leisure time for those that yield constant results per hour (such as walking in the woods). In many cases this "substitution effect" dominates the "income effect." Hence, as Linder has pointed out, one often finds capital and other inputs being used to save time or make each hour more productive, and less time devoted to uses of time that cannot be made more productive. One observes more leisure activities involving television sets, cameras, automobiles, boats, and TV dinners, and fewer leisure activities using mainly a person's time.

What concerns us here are the possible repercussions on others of these new choices by each individual. Thinking and decision making are among the uses of time that are becoming relatively expensive, so unless citizens gradually come to value these activities more, they may spend less time on them. Each of us has a stake, however, in getting other citizens to be well informed, to think about issues, and to make decisions carefully. Perhaps the impact of rising real incomes is offset by other developments, but this may be another way in which growth is aggravating the free-rider difficulties that plague the democratic process. Is growth pushing us more and more toward quick decisions, the acquisition of superficial information about numerous subjects, and centralization of effective power? If so, it may further increase the difficulty—the cost, that is—of governing ourselves.

Moreover, the costliness of time further exacerbates the problem of establishing nonsuperficial friendships. Giving genuinely concerned attention to each other is relatively expensive. It is more efficient to go to cocktail parties than to spend time with one friend at a time. Such results of individual decisions make it more costly for each of us to obtain the approval and attention we crave. Along this line too, paying attention to old people becomes prohibitively expensive so that we simultaneously struggle to prolong their lives and manage to make their lives almost unbearable.

All of these effects seem as serious to me as the prospective decline in material well-being. People can apparently endure considerable poverty or physical hardship if struggling still yields slight improvements, and if they feel as though they can influence events somewhat. If struggle results in virtually no response, however, if events seem increasingly to be beyond the individual's control, then a deeper sort of poverty sets in than just the material sacrifices of having more pollution and fewer goods. Trying to deal with bureaucracy, even in a comparatively small organization like a university, or to do anything about spillovers that result from the erosion of rules and respect for individuals can make life frustrating and tasteless. Whatever happens to GNP, a sufficient decline in control over their lives can render many people hopelessly depressed or violently angry.

Also, to the extent that growth beyond some point does aggravate these spillovers, taking steps to check economic and population growth itself might be a more economical way of reducing the external costs than trying to alleviate the spillovers while reaping the desirable consequences of growth. In other words, it is conceivable that growth yields net disadvantages yet that direct attacks on the disadvantages cost more than they gain. For instance, how, at low cost, can public policy directly promote economical behavioral codes or a more thoughtful citizenry? It is also conceivable, though, that by implementing a low-growth policy, government could alleviate the erosion of behavioral rules and the other spillovers described above.

It should be stressed that the relevant magnitudes are the marginal advantages and disadvantages of growth. Clearly, up to some point population and economic growth contributed more than it cost. No man is an island; there are economies of agglomeration—a wide range of choice in shopping, for example—for which people make great sacrifices and tolerate certain diseconomies. Beyond some point, however, these forms of growth yield decreasing marginal returns, increasing marginal costs, and ultimately net marginal disadvantages. These net marginal disadvantages may climb rapidly as growth rates soar even if past growth has brought rich rewards.

To keep things in proportion, however, I must admit that attributing the above costs to economic growth is highly speculative. Other variables obviously contribute to the expanding role of government, the slump in respect for the individual, and the crumbling of useful traditions. Perhaps growth has nothing to do with these phenomena.

Past evidence is far from illuminating. Clearly, growth is neither a necessary nor a sufficient condition for the existence of such side effects. Some societies have had high population densities or high rates of economic growth without marked difficulties. Other societies have exhibited these effects without startling population or economic growth. Conflicts, externalities, powerful and pervasive government, and changing behavioral codes go back to the beginnings of man. Finally, regardless of the magnitudes of such phenomena, and even if growth would henceforth *help* produce them, everyone is free to make different value judgments about their significance. None of us gets up each morning and asks, "What can I do today for economic efficiency?" For example, some, especially those who are on top, or think they will be on top, do not feel that the average individual's frustration matters much unless it threatens revolution.

My personal feeling, however, is that something is going wrong in terms of satisfying individual demands, and that congestion, interferences, and government expansion are contributing to the malaise. In recent years, writers and artists attract unusually large audiences by portraying the frustrations and emptiness of life, and there is pervasive resentment of the constraints imposed by families, fellow citizens, firms, governments, and other organizations. Whether or not growth has played a significant role in the past, I cannot help believing that continued growth will make it harder and harder for us to avoid interfering with each other, harder and harder for us to govern ourselves.

EVALUATING THE COSTS OF NO GROWTH

We should now examine the principal costs of stopping growth and try to make some comparisons with alternative policies. Maybe growth will appear to be like democracy: the worst possible situation one can imagine—except for the alternatives. In the case of retarding population growth, apart from the difficulties of implementation, I cannot believe that the costs could be great. The consequences of settling for no more than four billion human beings on this planet, or 250 million in the United States, could hardly be catastrophic. If additional people still yield a positive net return at all, it is a modest one, and, at worst, limiting population would sacrifice a modest amount of material well-being. In saying this, I am assuming that one or two children per couple would yield most of the value of offspring as a consumption good. If most people have an intense desire to spawn and rear large families, then growth might yield a high return to the existing population even if the adverse effects on living conditions were serious. The basic dilemma would then be more difficult. Even so, at some population level, externalities would make it economical to ask people to give up demands for large families in order to meet other intense demands.

The case is not quite so clear when one considers implementation, though here too I am comparatively optimistic regarding the retardation of population growth. One can visualize controls that would be ominous and horrible, like selective sterilization, or the selective elimination of children, perhaps along lines adopted by the Spartans. Another ancient Greek practice, forcing everyone over sixty years of age to drink poison hemlock, might not actually be so bad, except for the fact that exceptions, discretionary authority, and corruption would arise. In connection with population control, however, at least in comparison with many other kinds of government controls, I am somewhat sanguine about the prospects for nonhorrible actions.

On the whole I believe working toward low or zero population growth, if it does not come about naturally, would probably be worth the cost. Maybe I am naive to trust that advocating and debating such a policy will not lead to some tyrannical form of genocide. However, while I realize that mankind reverts to bestiality at the drop of a hat, I do not believe that a proposal or precedent for population control would greatly *increase* the probability of bestial actions. A nation could try exhortation, education regarding birth control, and moderate taxes per child, though I doubt their effectiveness. When these methods fail, a certificate system could be introduced unilaterally, with immigration controls applying to those countries that fail to adopt similar systems. I don't see that this in itself would give underdeveloped nations great cause for complaint.

How would one set about stopping economic growth? Putting a legislative ceiling on the GNP would hardly affect anyone's behavior, since the GNP is merely the result of adding together various components that are determined by a host of variables. The only way to do anything would be to work on the variables that affect investment and consumption behavior. Government would have to do things to influence particular output decisions rather than just say grandly, "Let there be no growth."

Establishing ceilings and controls on each industry's output would convert a private enterprise economy into a centrally planned one, thereby losing the coordination provided by markets. The result, I assert, would be clumsily inefficient, at least in terms of conventional criteria. If detailed central planning was the only way to achieve no growth, I would chalk this up as an awesome cost of a no-growth policy. Let us look, however, at other ways of reducing economic growth in a mixed economy.

Outputs could be reduced, though in a rather haphazard fashion, by measures short of detailed planning, such as limiting the work week to say thirty hours. Such a step would still require a lot of repugnant enforcement and loop-hole-plugging activities, perhaps even the monitoring of consumption and the use of leisure time. Furthermore, measures like limiting hours of work are extremely imprecise tools, which would cut back on many services that contribute little to pollution or depletion yet entail many of the disadvantages of central planning.

In my view the least unappealing type of mechanism would be to tax all output of goods for both consumption and investment, and devote the proceeds to environmental repair. With the objective of no growth, the taxes and outlays would be adjusted to hold constant some such output indicator as GNP, and one would simply hope that outcome yielded an appropriate amount of pollution and exhaustible resource use. I am using the word "pollution" to represent all the external costs discussed earlier, since most of them, if they are functions of growth, would be held down to varying extents by the cessation of growth. For present purposes the kind of tax—sales, value added, turnover, or income—does not matter much; the pattern of output curtailment would differ under different kinds of taxes, but this whole technique of curtailing aggregate output—or, as I noted above, any known technique—is a rather clumsy way to reduce pollution and consumption of depletable resources. (I will also neglect repercussions on and from interest rates in order to concentrate on directly pertinent impacts.)

Note how imprecise the linkage is between no growth and these undesired effects. One could have no growth of the GNP and still be polluting or using up energy sources at various rates. One's conclusion depends partly on how one measures growth, but practically any index will have only a loose connection with the increase in pollution or the consumption of exhaustible resources. For example, as costs of production rise due either to pollution or to the inaccessibility of selected resources, the prices of goods might rise while the quantities produced fell, and the indicator of final output might not increase. The actual level of pollution will depend upon the composition of the output and the way it is produced—upon the extent to which pollution is cleaned up after being generated, or is prevented by shifting to new "cleaner" outputs or by producing the old outputs in more expensive ways. Also, the combination of outputs and methods of production may either increase or decrease the consumption of energy and other nonrenewable resources. Thus, simply holding GNP or any other practicable index of output constant to reduce pollution or the consumption of stored-up energy is like holding a consumer's total budget constant in order to reduce his disposal of trash along the highway or his consumption of fats. The linkage is indirect and different for different kinds of trash or fats. As for the linkage between GNP and its undesired impacts, some forms of output are associated with high rates of pollution and depletion of nonrenewable resources; others are not.

If, however, we start regulating particular outputs, we're back in the business of detailed planning in order to do something other than just stop growth. If we start taxing particular outputs, we're trying to curtail the side effects rather than growth per se (which may turn out to look very sensible but which is not the topic at hand). Keeping in mind the imprecision of these linkages, let us consider the costs or disadvantages of tax expenditure programs that would prevent any increase in, say, the cumulative measure of consumption plus investment plus government expenditures for *goods* (as opposed to goods plus services).

There are several significant disadvantages of zero economic growth, some inherently associated with a static as opposed to a dynamic economy, and some connected with the particular measures required to implement a ZEG policy. First and most obvious, the sacrificed consumption and investment would obviously have been desirable from the standpoint of existing persons. Also, some of the investment in durable facilities would have created returns for near future generations. Hence, if we stop economic growth to promote one set of objectives, we must give up the at least partially offsetting material benefits. In a free economy this would mean giving up not exactly what you and I personally visualize as frills but whatever consumers in general regarded as their least important purchases, presumably including quality and quantity in most categories of goods—food, housing, books, music, art, medical care, and so on. In a planned economy, it would mean giving up, again not what you and I think of as frills, but whatever the planning establishment regarded as marginal—education, research, or welfare programs. In other words, whether you think pollution and resource depletion constitute one or three steps backward, you have to sacrifice the two steps forward if your remedy is stopping the growth of total output. Below, I will argue that this sacrifice would be larger under a no-growth policy than under an alternative approach.

In the short run there would be transitional difficulties. The shock of taxes to prevent growth, though it would depend upon factors about which we know little, might be considerably greater than defense mobilization or demobilization, for the policy would throw most industries into readjustments. Unlike mobilization, which changes the composition of output, the no-growth policy would, in addition, stop investment and growth of total output. Accompanying this resource re-allocation would be a traumatic adjustment of attitudes as people were confronted, even gradually, with a drop in real income in comparison with their previous expectations, with the prospect of no future wage increases except perhaps for superior individual performance, and with the prospect of a relatively static society. Such a shock often has a sharp impact on one family; when it occurs simultaneously to everyone, the difficulties might be smaller, or they might be greater.

A more serious problem is that a no-growth policy would heighten distribution conflicts within the nation and among nations. (Note, however, that if my earlier arguments are correct, no growth would reduce certain other conflicts attributed to growth—interferences with each other as a result of noisy equipment, other manifestations of affluence, and crowding, whereever there were high transaction costs.) Consider distribution conflicts within a nation. People resent it less when someone else gets a promotion or a higher income if they suffer only a comparative rather than an absolute loss. It is easier to dispense rewards if one can give *A* a promotion or higher income without taking anything away from *B*, harder if one can award something to *A* only if it is taken from *B*. When industries are expanding, when the pie is growing, it is possible for Negroes or young people to move into unions or better jobs or new occupations without anyone else suffering in an absolute sense.

No growth, however, might sharpen these conflicts and make it more difficult for politicians to encourage free entry into occupations and industries or to allow freely moving prices and rates of hire, more difficult for collective bargaining and government processes to work satisfactorily. British experience suggests that lack of growth may "produce as many and as unpleasant stresses on the social and political economy as industrial growth can impose on the ecological and natural resources of the globe." No growth may imply sharper distribution conflicts and the costs associated with them in terms of resources devoted to bargaining and conflict resolution and, perhaps more important, resources of the spirit squandered in anger, bitterness, and violence.

Conflicts among nations would be exacerbated for these as well as other reasons. If all nations did agree to retard economic growth, the underdeveloped nations would find it more difficult, whatever the agreed-upon formulae, to get ahead. Such countries would probably find the door forever closed to anything approaching the incomes enjoyed by the advanced countries. They would find it more difficult to bring about changes in resource allocation (and, as Beckerman points out, they may object to endless prospects of dressing up in archaic costumes and studying folkdancing to amuse the tourists).

But the conflict in interests is so sharp that it is hard to imagine worldwide agreement to limit growth. The United States, for instance, has about 6 percent of the world's population and consumes about 40 percent of the world's fossil fuel and other outputs. Suppose the United States pushes for an agreement to stop economic growth in order to reduce pollution and the use of exhaustible resources. It is difficult to imagine the underdeveloped nations agreeing to large sacrifices for the sake of the rest of the world, and, in view of the sensitivity of advanced nations about national security, one can hardly foresee their making large concessions. Without a world-wide agreement, however, the free-rider problem makes it hard to imagine unilateral or small-group action.

What do these conflicting interests among nations signify for the costs of a no-growth policy? They imply that it would require tremendous negotiation costs and sacrifices of "national security" and "fairness among nations" to implement a no-growth policy. An alternative way to put the point is simply to say that the chances of any nation's adopting no-growth policies are slight. Some people might even argue that no-growth postures would produce extra temptations and less deterrence and hence increase the chances of thermonuclear war. In view of the complexities, however, about all one can say, it seems to me, is that the potential provocations and probabilities for thermonuclear war are large in any case, and probably not significantly different whether there is continued growth or not.

Another speculative, yet perhaps important, consideration is the set of sacrifices entailed by having a more nearly static society. Under a no-growth policy, it would necessarily be less rewarding than before, in comparison with other activities, to search for changes in technology, to seek to identify changes in taste, or to shift resources. In short, changes, which may seem too attractive currently, would become less rewarding, relative to "housekeeping" and status-quo production, than at present. Initially there would be considerable re-allocation of resources in response to the new taxes and government programs. Investment in growth-promoting innovations would become relatively unattractive, however, since growth promotion would no longer be permitted. This might have some desirable consequences, such as reducing the adverse impacts of "future shock," but it would also have some deleterious ones. For one thing man craves variety, a degree of uncertainty, and the hope that he may find some satisfying purpose in life. One can vividly appreciate these desires by asking himself the old but illuminating question: "Would life be satisfying if it consisted merely of pushing buttons to stimulate the pleasure centers of the brain?" A static society is, to some extent, less conducive to the pursuit of varied objectives than is a growing society. With fewer possibilities of change, people might feel they had less "adventure," less hope of discovering some larger purpose in life, less hope of something better ahead.

A closely related yet less speculative cost of the reduced rewards for change would be the weakening of incentives for producing knowledge and cultural diversity. It would be possible, naturally, for some discovery and cultural innovations to occur, but study, research, new knowledge, and innovation would almost certainly be less rewarding than in a growing society, and fewer resources would be devoted to them. Although wages and rewards in general would be lower than in a growing economy, those available for growth-promoting activities would be especially affected. If government officials found it rewarding to sponsor research and selected innovations, resources devoted to them could be maintained or even expanded, but it is doubtful whether, in such a context, voters and politicians would give strong support to these activities or that in any case an atmosphere conducive to exploration could be maintained. Successful research depends greatly on serendipity and unforeseeable interdependencies with other types of research. All in all, I am fairly confident that no-growth policies would reduce aggregate success in research and development and diminish the chances of solving particular technological problems. This sacrifice of knowledge might be terribly important, not merely because man craves exploration and knowledge for its own sake, but also because technological developments, especially those pertaining to energy and biology, might reduce problems of pollution and exhaustible resources and contribute enormously to the well-being of posterity.

My biggest objection to a no-growth policy, however, is closely related to my principal apprehension concerning unbridled growth. I believe that measures to induce no growth would likewise produce a government role that would intensify our "spiritual poverty." The taxes imposed to stop growth of consumption and investment would yield large revenues. The spending of these revenues in ways consistent with no growth would, I have suggested, be better than detailed planning, but would nonetheless bring relatively large and discretionary government.

We cannot know for sure whether the revenues collected would exceed those involved in a more finely tuned attack on pollution and resource exhaustion. For the reasons stated below, however, I believe that direct attacks on many of the side effects (*a*) would yield more than they cost (in which case the blunt-instrument approach of checking growth is not the appropriate one, at least initially), and (*b*) would result in smaller government spending programs and less discretionary authority than a growth-reduction approach aimed at yielding the same abatements in pollution and resource depletion.

Given the variability of the input-output connections between growth and different forms of pollution, no growth would leave the economy with too much of some forms and too little of others for its efficient operation. It is a ham-handed strategy somewhat like, to take an extreme analogy, reducing a city's power supply by 10 percent in order to reduce fires, accidental electrocutions, and atrocious movies; cutting down on power usage would eliminate some unknown quantities of these phenomena, but only by chance the appropriate ones.

AN ALTERNATIVE POLICY

In my view the more economical approach to spillover abatement is probably to launch frontal attacks on the conventional externalities with the aim of reducing each form as long as the gains promise to exceed the costs. Moreover, it would often be economical to minimize the government's role, particularly its discretionary role, by using price mechanisms: effluent charges, liability reassignments (to fasten external costs on those activities that generate them), congestion fees, external-cost taxes on commonpool resources like fish, and other spillover charges. These devices would be "fine tuning" compared to regulations or government-operated abatement programs. The levying of externality-charges and the fixing of liabilities on someone in the causal chain would probably use fewer resources and less government than would achieving the same amount of pollution abatement via growth reduction. In many instances, of course, transaction costs, such as those of collection and enforcement, would make it uneconomical to use such price mechanisms in the neat and complete manner in which they could be employed in a hypothetical zero-transaction-cost world.

Similarly the logical straightforward thing to do about nonrenewable resources, if voters do want to preserve more for posterity, would be to tax the use of those particular resources, to tax outputs of petroleum (instead of giving depletion allowances to stimulate exploration), coal, uranium, ores, and so on. The size of such taxes could be adjusted by trial and error to yield the desired degree of deterrence, and the revenues could be used to reduce other taxes. (What degree of deterrence to strive for would have to be determined by the political process; we have no other criterion concerning interference to leave more for posterity.) To be realistic, however, a more effective means of doing something for posterity is probably to attempt to develop the fusion reactor and ways of tapping geothermal energy. After all, to the extent that one is concerned about distant generations, he presumably has the average person of the future in mind. One surely cares no more about unknown people of the twenty-fifth century than about those of the thirty-fifth. The relevant "posterity" is therefore an exceedingly large number of persons. Parceling out x tons of copper or y billions of GNP among an almost infinite number of people does little for the average person. The cost of our doing *much* for the average member of posterity would be fantastic, especially if we tried to do it through simple conservation. The cost of developing technologies to keep future energy costs down promises to be somewhat less fantastic; furthermore, success would bestow benefits on our immediate descendants for whom we have special concern.

Economic growth as conventionally measured would be retarded by a combination of finely tuned attacks on orthodox forms of pollution, plus conservation or research on energy sources, plus population control. While the benefits of growth would naturally be diminished, so would the "subtle" external costs because resulting reductions in affluence, the value of time, and crowding would remove some of the pressures which may contribute to superficial relationships, the erosion of behavioral rules and ethical codes, government expansion, and other spillovers. These subtle spillovers may be important, and I don't like simply to accept whatever this policy would do to them. But the no-growth policy would also let them lie wherever no growth dropped them. All I can say is that if further reductions in these effects appeared to be worth the cost, and if no growth appeared to be the economical way to curtail them, then further reductions of growth might be considered.

CONCLUSIONS

Thus, I would expect highly undesirable effects either from untrammeled economic and population growth or from government interventions to stop economic growth. As for population growth, I can visualize steps to retard or stop it that in my judgment promise more gains than costs. I do not see any disastrous costs from having a constant population, nor do I see a high probability of ruin from the implementation of such a policy.

It is conceivable that the most economical means of conserving exhaustible resources and of relieving various forms of pollution is the meat-axe approach represented by a no-growth policy, but this seems improbable when one considers alternatives even in a crude and cursory fashion. The preferable course, it seems to me, would be to attack directly conventional forms of pollution (making use of effluent charges and price mechanisms wherever they appear to be economical), and to tax the use of nonrenewable resources. This direct and more finely tuned approach would, of course, reduce growth and final output, as conventionally measured, thereby generating some of the costs and benefits attributed to no growth. Whether it reduced the growth of the GNP to 1 percent, to zero, or to a negative 2 percent would not be highly relevant as long as its impact on pollution and the exhaustion of resources was one in which gains exceeded sacrifices. The parts of the GNP that this policy would reduce are those that produce more social cost than gain, and the parts it would preserve are those that yield more social gain than cost. The by-product reduction of economic growth, in combination with zero population growth, would also diminish most of the subtle side effects discussed above, assuming that they are related to crowding, affluence, and material outputs. (Unfortunately, just as with a no-growth policy, these side effects might not be alleviated in the appropriate amounts.) Perhaps most importantly, this policy would keep government from being quite as large, pervasive, discretionary, quarrelsome, and costly as it would be under a no-growth policy. In comparison with such a direct attack on the difficulties, a zero economic growth goal seems a little like trying to eliminate the clouds in order to get better-lighted offices. It is not always an error to manipulate proxies (the best way to a man's heart and all that), but I judge that it would be inefficient to do so in this instance.

Our conclusions are:

1. If the present growth trends in world population, industrialization, pollution, food production, and resource depletion continue unchanged, the limits to growth on this planet will be reached sometime within the next one hundred years. The most probable result will be a rather sudden and uncontrollable decline in both population and industrial capacity.

2. It is possible to alter these growth trends and to establish a condition of ecological and economic stability that is sustainable far into the future. The state of global equilibrium could be designed so that the basic material needs of each person on earth are satisfied and each person has an equal opportunity to realize his individual human potential.

3. If the world's people decide to strive for this second outcome rather than the first, the sooner they begin working to attain it, the greater will be their chances of success.

From Dennis Meadows, et al. *The Limits to Growth.* New York: Universe Books, 1972, pp. 23–24.

QUESTIONS

1. What is McKean's definition of "growth"?
2. Enumerate and explain the major costs and problems of growth. Do you agree with McKean's evaluation of them?
3. Does the author respond convincingly to advocates of slowing down growth such as Meadows in his *The Limits to Growth?* (See box.)
4. How do you appraise McKean's conclusion that growth will bring bigger and more conflict-ridden government?
5. How can one measure the "costs" of bigger government against the "benefits" of economic growth in such a way as to determine when and at what point economic growth should be restrained? Is this a good question to ask? If not, what might be a better question to deal with this issue?
6. How may growth reduce the amenities of life? Is it inevitable that growth will reduce such amenities?
7. Is economic growth the primary cause of our socio-economic-political problems?
8. What, according to McKean, are the major costs and problems of slowing down or stopping economic growth? Do you agree with him? Explain your position.
9. What are McKean's solutions to the problems of growth and their control? Do you agree with him? Are there other alternative solutions that you recommend? Explain.

THE FUTURE OF MANKIND

HERMAN KAHN

Herman Kahn, founder and director of the Hudson Institute, long-time leader in the futurist movement, and author of a number of highly respected books, such as (with Anthony J. Wiener) *The Year 2000: A Framework for Speculation on the Next Thirty-Three Years* and (with B. Bruce-Briggs) *Things to Come,* presents in the following excerpt from his Franklin Lecture an imaginative and provocative rebuttal to those who foresee catastrophe in the future if we do not slow down growth.

There are two basic views of the future of mankind. One is the so-called neo-Malthusian point of perspective, which emphasizes the population explosion, the exhaustion of energy sources, the disappearance of pollution space, the growing income gaps, and the increasing difficulty of decision making. In every way we face disaster. The Club of Rome studies by Professor Meadows and Professor Forrester attempted to show that no matter what you did in the next ten to twenty to fifty years, mankind would run out. Typically in these computer printouts, half the world will die.

The other view of the future, the post-industrial (or super-industrial), is almost the exact opposite. It argues mankind is going through a really interesting transition. Sometimes when people talk about a point in history, all they really mean is a period of time between two transitions. Nothing very exciting. But I want to use "transition" in a different sense today. I am told that when Adam and Eve were thrown out of the Garden of Eden, Adam turned to Eve and said, "We are living in an age of transition." That's what I mean by "transition." A transition is marked by a radical difference.

Now I sometimes try to make this terribly dramatic. If you ever want to make yourself look like a profound speaker in front of an audience, one trick is to use very big numbers; refer to the fact that there are a billion stars in the galaxy, or a billion galaxies in the universe. How many people think about that many numbers at one time? Very few. Or we can say that mankind has been on earth for two million years. How many studies go back that far? Very few.

Our study starts two million years ago. I have examined every year for the last two million years quite carefully. I did that to get a perspective on the issue. There is a lot of trivia, but basically there are only two issues of any importance. Actually, if you are a religious individual, you will have a

Herman Kahn, "The Future of Mankind," in *Man and the Future of Organizations, 1973–1974 Franklin Foundation Lecture Series,* Volume 4, Carl A. Bramlette, Jr., and Michael H. Mescon (eds.), Atlanta, Georgia: School of Business Administration, Georgia State University, 1975, pp. 17–26. Reprinted by permission.

third incident, but we may not agree to what that incident is. I won't bother discussing it. (I am referring here, of course, to the Covenant of God with Abraham.)

What were the two incidents? The first was the agricultural revolution, about ten thousand years ago. Mankind went from a nomadic, food-gathering, almost animal type of existence to civilization. Civilization means civic culture, living in cities. And you don't have cities without agriculture. Rather interestingly, the standard of living probably didn't change. If you want to get a sense of how people lived in this period in terms of their yearly income, you can argue that no culture in world history went far below $50 or above $300 per capita. A country like Colombia, which now has $350 per capita, is in this sense richer than the richest culture of history until the last two hundred years. After the agricultural revolution, there was a long time when absolutely nothing happened; it took about eight thousand years for the revolution to spread around the world.

The second important incident in history occurred about two hundred years ago: the so-called Industrial Revolution. For the first time in world history there was sustained economic growth. For the first time, people got richer every year. In some years the rich got poorer and in other years the poor got poorer, but by and large the rich got richer and the poor got richer. England is considered the home of the Industrial Revolution. If you look at the English growth rate for the last two hundred years, you can argue fairly persuasively that they grew on an average of about 2.3 percent a year. That is not very good by current standards, but it is terribly exciting in that it was the first time in world history anything like that had ever happened. A 2.3 percent yearly growth rate is equivalent to a tenfold increase every hundred years or a hundredfold every two centuries. Thus the total English Gross Product today is about one hundred times what it was two hundred years ago.

Some of us now believe that we are going through a third interesting incident or transition. We call it the transition to "the post-industrial culture." We think this transition will probably be seen as largely having occurred during the next ten to twenty years. If we are correct, it will be one of the unique points of world history.

Look at the world population. It stayed very low, perhaps ten million, for thousands and thousands of years, then gradually started to grow. It grew very fast in the sixteenth and seventeenth centuries and now has reached about 2.1 percent a year. It seems very clear the curve of world population is going to turn over and flatten out at about 15 billion people—give or take a factor of 2.

There are no respectable long-range population predictions in the twentieth century. As you know, someone making a prediction usually gives a high, medium and low figure. This is the first time you will have one that is going to be right. Let's predict 15 billion, give or take a factor of 3! I will be a little surprised if the world population is much less than 7 billion or much more than 30 billion. That prediction is different from 100 billion and is substantially more than the two or three billion that Forrester's computer gives you after the starvation.

How well will these people live? As always, lousy; but they will be well off in some ways. The growth rate of the Gross World Product for the last twenty years reached 5 percent. That is very rapid. It doubles every fourteen years, and increases by a factor of about 10 every fifty years, or a factor of 100 every hundred years. That's quite rapid. I think the Gross World Product will reach about $300 trillion, plus or minus a factor of 5. These figures will give you a sense of orientation. We are at $4 trillion right now, so even if it turns out to be $60 trillion, that is 15 times more than today. It is pretty big. If it turns out to be $1,000 trillion, that is very big. That implies a per capita income of something like $5,000 (give or take a factor of 3).

Now you have a nice precise picture of the world of the future. There are a lot of people, but they are not coming out of your ears, and a fantastic amount of goods and services is being produced. That is the picture. How sure are we of this picture as opposed to the opposing picture of starvation and disaster? They obviously are as different as night and day. Let me give you a little of the evidence for the two pictures. Obviously I am not going to discuss it in detail because it would take me at least five or six hours. We have a seminar at the Institute in which we take two days to discuss it.

Now let's go back to the neo-Malthusian point of view. I said that the Gross World Product doubled every fourteen years. Let's start this discussion in 1973. If you assume that the gross use of resources is proportionate to the Gross World Product, which is a little pessimistic, you will ask yourself how long it will take to use up resources. That depends on how many resources there are. The Forrester and Meadows studies assume there are about 250 years of resources left. That seems like a very optimistic assumption. About the only thing that will last more than 250 years at the current rate of consumption is coal. According to the Bureau of Mines, everything else will run out. So you can't accuse us of cheating at that point. By 1986, you will have doubled the use rate but used more than fourteen years because you are using more in the end than in the beginning. In fact, you use up twenty years. So if you start off with 250 years, by 1986 you use up twenty years; that gives you 230. But in 1986, your use rate is twice as fast, so that gives you 115. Do the same calculation to the year 2000; you use up twenty years; that's 95, half of that is 47. If you keep doing this, in the year 2020, you are finished. Resources are out. According to the calculation, if you are off by a factor of 2, you can add another fourteen years. What if you are off by a factor of 10? Add another fifty years. So somewhere between fifty and one hundred years in the future, this entire wonderful mechanism we have been building for the last two hundred years—

since the Industrial Revolution—turns out to be a fraud. We've all been living in one huge delusion; so goes the calculation.

And the calculation doesn't stop there. It says if you aren't out of resources, pollution will get you. How does that work? Well, we know that right now in many parts of the world pollution is beginning to press upon health, life, and safety. Pollution is proportionate to the Gross World Product. That is optimistic if anything. It is probably worse than that. If you increase the pollution every fifty years by a factor of 10, it is going to be intolerable. In a hundred years, that is a factor of 100. Even if you save 90 percent of the pollution—that is a factor of 10 increase—in another hundred years you are still going to be dead. And, so this calculation goes, you can't save 90 percent. So pollution gets you.

If pollution doesn't get you, the "gaps" will get you. Sometimes people say the rich get richer and the poor get poorer. That is clearly wrong if you mean absolute income. But the gaps do increase. Every year somebody in the aid business, often the President of the World Bank, will make the following speech: "The developed world gets $3,000 per capita, the underdeveloped world gets $200 per capita; the gap is $2,800. In ten or fifteen years, both of these numbers will double to become $6,000 and $400 respectively. The gap becomes $5,600 and you are twice as bad off as you were before." Is that a reasonable remark? Somebody must think it is reasonable or that speech wouldn't be made every year.

If the gaps don't get you, decision making gets you. It becomes more and more difficult to make decisions that are appropriate—too many rapid changes, too many governments, too fractionated—is the picture fairly clear? We face total disaster.

Now if you believe that, there is a moral implication. What is the moral implication? Drop out! Don't be part of this corrupt system. Don't contribute to the death of mankind. If you can't stop it, the least you can do is watch it.

When a friend of mine was applying for his first aid project, I asked him a whole series of questions, and he finally got mad and said, "You remind me of a joke I heard. There was this man who was a station guard and they asked him what would he do if he saw two trains on the same track.

He said, 'I would throw the signal.'

'What happens if the signal is broken?'

'I would flag him: STOP!'

'What if there is no flag?'

'I would wave my hands.'

'What if they couldn't see you?'

'Well, then I would call my sister.'

'What would you call your sister for?'

'She would like to watch, too!' "

That is the basic and the only moral thing someone could do. According to this view, anybody trying to increase productivity, trying to train people to do a productive job or increase achievement orientation, is guilty of a war crime. His efforts are speeding up this death and making it larger. This kind of belief has important consequences. It can change your entire culture.

You might want to ask what kind of person would hold this viewpoint. Well, we had a poll this afternoon on the two views of the future, and I was really shocked. I've taken this poll about a hundred times, but I suddenly realized that it's always been in the northeastern United States and California, and in England, Japan, and Holland, and prestigious universities in Europe. This morning when I took the poll, people voted 1 to 4: 80 percent voted for the post-industrial perspective and 20 percent for the neo-Malthusian beliefs. At a place like Harvard or Yale or Columbia, the vote will be 10 to 1 the other way. There has been no exception to this. I haven't done scientific sampling, but you don't have to when you take a poll dozens of times.

The neo-Malthusian belief is being taught throughout the world today at prestigious universities. They have a right to believe it. Let me give you the history of the neo-Malthusian belief in terms of The Club of Rome studies, although there is more to it than that. The Club of Rome is a group of about 75 of the most prestigious industrialists, scholars, publicists, and writers in the world. They asked Professor Forrester of the Massachusetts Institute of Technology to do a study on the current predicament of mankind. Professor Forrester is a very distinguished individual. He's reported to have earned about $20 million on the magnetic core memory and to have given one or two million dollars to the school. Not many professors have those credentials. He's not a fly-by-night. He did this study and came out with the neo-Malthusian results I just gave you. The Club of Rome reviewed the study and asked Professor Meadows, also of MIT, to check the results. He came out with more dramatic and more catastrophic results. The studies were released at the Smithsonian Institute—not a fly-by-night organization. About two hundred of the best minds in the world are there. According to the press, nobody really objected to the results except people from the third world. We know why they objected: they can't afford to go back and tell their people they are going to be poor. It gives them a terrible moral dilemma. The only way to solve their problem was to reject the study.

What is wrong with Forrester's and Meadows' work? It is terribly difficult to prove a study like this is wrong. These are both very competent people, but their studies are not competent—I will make that as a flat assertion. I've debated this with Professor Forrester in a three-hour debate and I've discussed it with Meadows. They made lots of mistakes; I'll mention a few of them. But that in itself isn't sufficient to negate their work. People always make mistakes in studies, yet often their studies will still be right because the basic idea is right. The Forrester-Meadows position is a terribly persuasive one—the conception of a "finite bowl" (whatever I use, you can't have; whatever you use, I can't have; whatever we both use, our grandchildren can't have). But resources are not like a homogeneous substance in a finite bowl. Resources are processes and skills; the more I use, the more I have, within limits. Resources are like muscles you exercise. I can have my skill and I can teach it to you; we can both use it and our grandchildren will do even better. This is particularly true with technological skills, which are cumulative.

Now let's assume I am trying to show that something survives. When we started the study, we thought that you wouldn't be able to make any *a fortiori* arguments—that you would have to depend on new technologies, new inventions, rising to the occasion. It turns out to be quite different. To give you an example of what I mean, consider agriculture. Let me assume I have fifteen billion people in the world. I want to feed them well. That will require roughly a ton of grain per person. A very poor society can feed five people with a ton of grain. But this is going to be a rich society—meat, eggs, vegetables. So it's one person per ton (roughly U.S. standards today). That is fifteen billion tons. If I am using current technology, I can get about three tons per hectare. So I need about five billion hectares, which is roughly fifty million square kilometers. Do we have fifty million square kilometers of agricultural land? The answer is no. That is approximately the total amount of level land in the entire world. I just proved that just to live well we will run out of the main resource—land. I could stop the calculation at that point. To be fair to the Forrester-Meadows people, they did not. They said, well, actually you can do better than three tons per hectare. You can raise the price of grain, use more fertilizer, employ better agricultural practices and more irrigation; you can double crop, triple crop, and do all kinds of things. With such changes you might get an increase of a factor of 10. Let's say now you need only five to ten million square kilometers to feed the world. Is the problem solved? No! If you use this much fertilizer and insecticide, it will drain into the rivers, lakes, and oceans of the world, and pollute the place beyond description. Even if you eliminate 90 percent of the pollution, it's not enough. It doesn't work. That's where Forrester and Meadows stop.

But actually, pollution is not inevitable. There are about five ways to have basically pollution-free agriculture. Let me give you the most obvious. How many people here have heard of hydroponics? Very interesting. My educated audiences have never heard of it. Hydroponics is growing something in a nutrient pool. Hydroponics will cut pollution down to zero and save enormously in inputs. It uses much less water, much less insecticide, much less fertilizer. It can be done. We did it in World War II. Even today, you find some people growing young wheat by this method. Rapid transportation by airplane killed hydroponics because it would have been used in the small islands of the Pacific, or for off-season crops. You can use greenhouses with hydroponics; you can stack them and get as much as you want out of them. What I have just shown is that we really do have resources and that pollution need not contribute to the problem.

What about the income gaps? I will make just one comment. Rapid economic growth is always associated with the creation of income gaps—for some people get rich much faster than others, and the gaps themselves stimulate enough economic growth by pulling them out. The hydroponic method will be developed in the rich countries of the world first. Then this technology will be used in the rest of the world. The gaps are what make this possible. You couldn't give the hydroponic method to everybody at the same time.

What about decision making? Farmers are very stubborn people. How can you get them to shift to hydroponics? How many will you have to shoot, Stalin would ask. Can we handle their problem? Yes, very easily. Tell the farmer that until 1950 we were able to treat air and water in the United States as free commodities. Now we can't. What we would like to do now is put effluent charges on polluting activities so that people treat air and water as costly goods. In principle, if you are an economist and want to find the most efficient charge for polluting a river, you would decide upon a level of purity. Next you would determine the cost of removing a pound of pollutant from a river that was pure or of subsidizing somebody for not putting pollutants in. Then you would charge everybody who does the polluting exactly that price. When someone puts in a pound, you take out a pound some place else. We are suggesting that it is better to charge twice the removal cost. For every pound someone pollutes, you take out two pounds. The more he pollutes, the cleaner the river becomes. Therefore we put on these effluent charges. Then we raise the price of grain and tell the farmer if he shifts to hydroponics he can make money, but if he continues to farm in the classical fashion, he can go bankrupt.

The Club of Rome studies all make three big mistakes. First, investigators didn't ask themselves how to solve the pollution problem. They made an assumption that you couldn't do better than 90 or 95 percent, which simply is not true. Every pollution program I know of in the United States, northwest Europe and Japan is going to do more than 90 to 95 percent for the next ten years. Secondly, they underestimated enormously the power of a price system in forcing decisions, in making them easy to take. It is terribly easy to take the decision I just mentioned—the charge for polluting—the farmer raises his prices so that he makes money.

It is terribly difficult to order people to give up their way of life and to go to hydroponics, which is a factory way of life. One of the things about the future which many people (including myself) don't like is that it is likely to involve the elimination of this kind of traditional activity. If you go to Europe, you will find there is no wilderness there except in Scandinavia. My guess is that this will be true world-wide in ten years. Now many people here like the wilderness. They think it's great. Some people think the wilderness is essential to survival. That's not true. Go to Europe. France isn't dying because it has no wilderness. Still, if you are an American, you've been raised near a wilderness. You generally think it is very important. Look at the wilderness very hard, because it will not be there very long.

I am saying that you can't solve all problems. You can't fix the world so that everybody has what he wants. But what you can do is to give everybody in the world a very high income. The income is real. What do we mean by real? I would guess that Americans 50 to 100 years from now may have a typical income of say, $50,000 per capita. That means a median family income of $100,000 a year. What do you do with that $100,000 a year? You can have two or three houses, four cars, two helicopters, and three submarines, but you will diaper the baby yourself. There are no maids. You wash your own dishes. The comment has been made that one good maid is worth a house full of appliances. That is still true. One thing you are going to find out here is that the richer Atlanta gets, the lower the quality of life of the upper middle class will become. Maids get tough, traffic jams increase, and so on.

I have a theorem that if you are a member of the upper middle class, the best country to live in is one where the per capita income is about $1,000. Define the upper middle class as those who have three to ten times the average per capita income. Consider three cases. Take Colombia, or Korea, which has roughly $300 per capita. The upper middle class would have about $1,000 to $3,000. Or consider the case of countries with $1,000-per-capita income, such as Central Mexico, Southern Brazil, Portugal, or Spain. The upper middle class would have $3,000 to $10,000. Third, look at the United States, with a $6,000-per-capita income. Here the upper middle class will have $20,000 to $60,000. In which country do you think the upper middle class lives best—the $300-, the $1,000-, or the $6,000-per-capita country? It would be the $1,000. In Colombia with only $3,000 you might have three or four live-in maids, but you don't have an automobile, and you don't have access to travel or to modern medicine. You know there are a lot of things lacking. In a $1,000-per-capita country, your income would increase to $10,000. Now you have the automobile, you have the appliances, you have the travel, you have the good university, and you also have three maids. You have a car, but no traffic jams. You have status. You have immunity from the petty cares of life. Here in the United States, you have three-car families, but also traffic jams. The rich don't like it. One feels sorry for them, but not terribly so. Now, the rich don't do badly. They may live two hours from work as in New York and Los Angeles, but many of them take seaplanes to work. A seaplane is very expensive, but if the trip takes just ten minutes and you earn $50 an hour, it is very inexpensive. One reason that almost worldwide hostility has grown is recognition by the upper middle class that their standard of life will go down as everyone else's goes up. The rich will do well in all circumstances, which is characteristic of the rich. Does everybody notice that the rich tend to live well? The middle class will live fairly well. Even the poor will live relatively well. But the upper middle class will find its standards going down. Well, that's the picture of the future, which in many ways is very grim and in many ways very pleasant.

QUESTIONS

1. Kahn makes light of the warnings of contemporary Cassandras who feel mankind is falling behind in the struggle for survival. What basic differences exist between his assumptions and those of scholars like Meadows? Who do you think is likely to be more accurate in this area—the optimist or the pessimist?
2. Is the "post-industrial culture" described by Kahn really "one of the unique points of world history"? Or is Kahn flattering his own generation without real cause?
3. Do you think Kahn really examined every year for the last 2 million years carefully, or did he have student assistants do it for him?

. . .

15

SHOULD WE HAVE NATIONAL AGGREGATE ECONOMIC PLANNING?

THE HUMPHREY-JAVITS BILL TO ESTABLISH A SYSTEM TO PRODUCE A BALANCED ECONOMIC GROWTH PLAN FOR THE UNITED STATES

HUBERT H. HUMPHREY AND JACOB K. JAVITS

United States Senators Hubert H. Humphrey and Jacob K. Javits presented in both houses of the Congress in 1975 a bill to amend the Employment Act of 1946 so as to provide machinery for the federal government to develop a national aggregate economic plan. This proposal has raised sharp controversy. In this paper, the Humphrey-Javits bill is described, and in the following papers, arguments pro and con are presented.

The Humphrey-Javits bill was simultaneously introduced in the Fall of 1975 in the U.S. Senate and House of Representatives, 94th Congress, 1st Session, as an amendment to the Employment Act of 1946. It provides for the development in the United States of a Balanced Economic Growth Plan.

The preamble of the bill points out that at the time of introduction the United States was suffering from severe economic problems. These problems, such as double digit inflation and very high unemployment, were due largely to a previous "failure to develop a long-term national economic policy" which in turn created "fundamental imbalances in the economy." The authors of the bill assert, therefore, that there is a major national need for a National Plan.

The accompanying chart shows the major agencies involved in the development of the plan and the flow of action. Central in the process is the Economic Planning Board. This board, composed of three members appointed by the President, by and with the advice and consent of the Senate, is responsible for: (1) preparing and submitting to the Council on Economic Planning a proposed Balanced Economic Growth Plan, (2) seeking active participation of people throughout the United States, (3) evaluating and measuring the achievement of the goals and objectives of approved Balanced Economic Growth Plans, (4) reviewing major programs and activities of the federal government to see whether they are consistent with any approved Plan, and (5) coordinating long-range planning activities of the federal government to assure consistency with any approved Plan.

The Act provides for the establishment of a Division of Economic Information within the Board to secure and disseminate information for and resulting from the development of a Plan. The Board is also required to

Prepared by George A. Steiner from the original Humphrey-Javits bill.

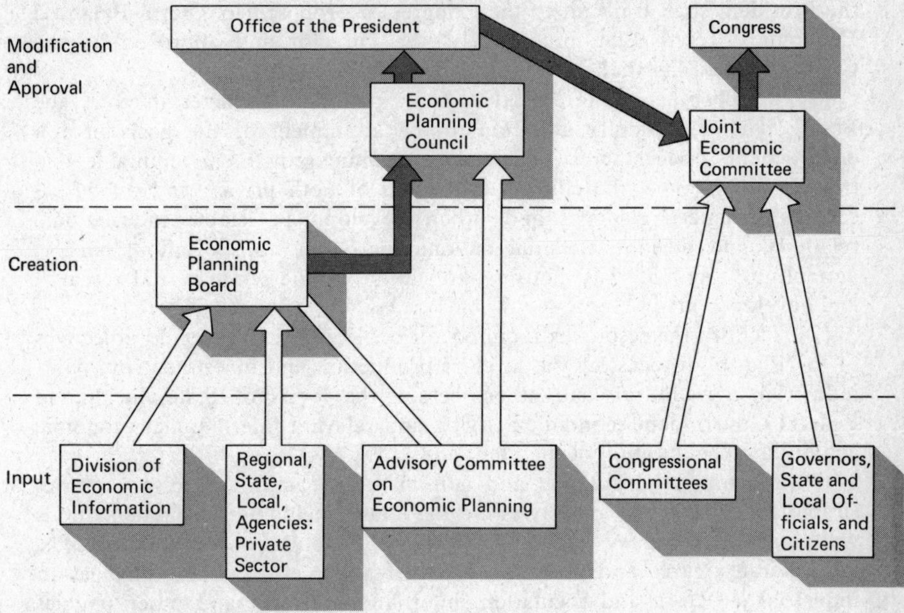

From "Notes From the Joint Economic Committee," Congress of the United States, Volume 1, Number 19, July 1, 1975, p. 7.

establish procedures to insure widespread consultation with regional, state, and local planning agencies in the preparation of the Plan. When the President submits a Plan to the Congress, the Board, within sixty days, must transmit it also to the Governor of each State and other appropriate local agencies. The Governors then may submit a report about the Plan to the Joint Economic Committee of the U.S. Congress. Regional, State, and local agencies may request the Economic Planning Board to review their plans to see whether they are consistent with the National Plan.

The Act also provides for the creation of an Advisory Committee on Economic Planning. This Committee will consist of four members appointed by the President, four members appointed by the Speaker of the House of Representatives, and four members appointed by the President of the Senate. The Committee elects its own Chairman and is supposed to meet not less than twice a year. Members shall be appointed from among representatives of business, labor, and the public at large. This Committee also is authorized to establish regional or industry subcommittees to furnish advice and assistance to it in the formulation and implementation of the Plan. The fundamental purpose of the Committee is to furnish advice and assistance to the Board in the preparation and review of the Plan.

Section 208 (a) of the Humphrey-Javits bill describes the substance and transmission of the Balanced Economic Growth Plan, as follows:

Sec. 208 (a) *Not later than April 1, 1977,* and biannually thereafter, the President shall transmit to the Congress a proposed long-term Balanced Economic Growth Plan prepared by the Director and approved by the Council. The Plan shall—

(1) establish economic objectives for a period to be determined by the Board, paying particular attention to the attainment of the goals of full employment, price stability, balanced economic growth, an equitable distribution of income, the efficient utilization of both private and public resources, balanced regional and urban development, stable international relations, and meeting essential national needs in transportation, energy, agriculture, raw materials, housing, education, public services, and research and development;

(2) identify the resources required for achieving the economic objectives of the Plan by forecasting the level of production and investment by major industrial, agricultural, and other sectors, the levels of State, local, and Federal Government economic activity, and relevant international economic activity, for the duration of the Plan; and

(3) recommend legislative and administrative actions necessary or desirable to achieve the objectives of the Plan, including recommendations with respect to money supply growth, the Federal budget, credit needs, interest rates, taxes and subsidies, antitrust and merger policy, changes in industrial structure and regulation, international trade, and other policies and programs of economic significance.

(b) The President shall submit to the Congress with the proposed Plan a *Report* prepared by the Board and approved by the Council. *The report shall*—

(1) provide whatever data and analysis are necessary to support the objectives, resource needs, and policy recommendations contained in the Plan;

(2) provide an examination of longer-term economic trends beyond the period of the Plan and recommend objectives with respect to the goals outlined in subsection (a) (1);

(3) compare the actual results with respect to matters referred to in subsection (a) since the submission of the previous Plan with the projected results of the Plan when submitted and indicate (A) the reason for any failure to achieve the objectives of that Plan, (B) the steps being taken to achieve the objectives of the previous Plan, and (C) any necessary revisions in the Plan.

This section of the Act is presented in full because it is clear that the Act calls for a national aggregate comprehensive type of long-range plan but does not specify precisely what it shall be. The Board obviously has great flexibility in developing the details of the Plan.

When the Board completes a plan it is presented to the Council on Economic Planning, another agency created by the Act. The Council shall consist of the Chairman of the Economic Planning Board, who shall be the Chairman of the Council; the Secretaries of State; Treasury; Defense; Interior; Housing and Urban Development; Transportation; Agriculture;

Commerce; Labor; Health, Education, and Welfare; the Attorney General; the Chairman of the Federal Reserve Board; the Chairman of the Council of Economic Advisers; the Director of the Office of Management and Budget; the Administrator of the Federal Energy Administration; and the Chairman of the Advisory Committee on Economic Planning.

The function of the Council is to review and make revisions, as deemed necessary, in the Balanced Economic Growth Plan and, upon approval, to transmit the Plan to the President. Also, the Council is supposed to review on a regular basis progress in the implementation of the Plan.

The President then transmits the Plan to the Joint Economic Committee of the United States Congress. The Plan is also transmitted to each standing committee of the House of Representatives and Senate, and each joint committee of the Congress. Within 60 days after receipt each of these committees is supposed to send to the Joint Economic Committee a report giving their views of the Plan and recommendations on all matters within their jurisdictions. The Committee on the Budget of the Senate and of the House of Representatives shall report on the recommendations of various committees concerning budget policy for the Plan.

The Joint Economic Committee then will hold hearings and not later than 105 days after the submission of the proposed National Economic Plan to the Congress, it will report to the House of Representatives and to the Senate a concurrent resolution stating what the Congress approves or disapproves in the proposed Plan. It will report on findings of the Congress and make recommendations as to actions needed.

Not less than 135 days after submission of the proposed Plan the Congress shall act on the concurrent resolution submitted by the Joint Economic Committee. Upon adoption of the resolution the Plan is submitted to the President.

When the President receives the Plan he may make such modifications as he sees fit. If there are revisions the President must resubmit the Plan to the Congress not later than 30 days after receipt of the concurrent resolution. Not later than 30 days following receipt of the revised Plan the Congress shall, by concurrent resolution, approve or disapprove the Plan in whole or in part.

It is not entirely clear in the Act what happens if the Congress and the President do not agree. The Act does say, however, that the President and the Board may not take action under section 212 with respect to any part of the Plan which has not been approved or which has been disapproved by the Congress.

Section 212 of the Act contains features with enormous implications. This section specifies that:

> (a) The President, with the assistance of the Board, shall take appropriate actions to insure that the departments and agencies of the executive branch will carry out their programs and activities in such a manner as to

further the objectives of the Plan, and to *encourage* State and local governments and the *private sector* to carry out their programs and activities in such a manner as to further the objectives of the Plan.

(b) Whenever the Board determines that any department or agency of the Federal Government has submitted any budget request to the President or the Congress, or proposed any legislation, rule or regulation, or undertaken any other activity which may have a significant effect on the achievement of the goals and objectives contained in an approved Balanced Economic Growth Plan, the *Board may require the head* of such department or agency to submit a *detailed* statement to the Board assessing the consistency of the proposed budget, legislation, rule, regulation, or other action, with the Plan, together with the reasons for any significant departure from such goals and objectives.

Both Senators Humphrey and Javits and proponents of the bill say that it is "indicative" and not mandatory. This section of the bill clearly makes it mandatory for the President to use the powers of the executive branch, which are enormous, to implement the Plan. It is difficult to get any other meaning from this provision.

Finally, it should be noted that the bill provides for the establishment within the Congressional Budget Office of a Division of Balanced Growth and Economic Planning. This Division, headed by a Deputy Director of the Budget Office, will serve as staff to the Joint Economic Committee with respect to its review and development of the National Economic Plan.

QUESTIONS

1. Explain the machinery that the Humphrey-Javits bill proposes to establish in order to develop a national economic plan.
2. Assuming that you agree with the basic idea of our developing a national aggregate economic plan, do you think this is the preferred mechanism?
3. The Advisory Committee on Economic Planning is authorized to get regional and local advice and assistance in the formulation and implementation of plans. How might this be done? Is this a good idea?
4. Do you think it is likely that Congress will agree on a plan prepared by the executive branch?
5. Section 212 says that the President, once the plan is approved, "shall take appropriate actions" to ensure that the executive branch acts to further the objectives of the plan. Does not this provision make the plans more mandatory than indicative?
6. Is it a good idea to establish the type of machinery envisioned in this proposed legislation without specifying in some detail the nature of the plans that should be forthcoming?
7. Do you think the proposed legislation would be good or bad for this society? Explain your position carefully.

LAISSEZ FAIRE, PLANNING, AND REALITY

ARTHUR SCHLESINGER, JR.

Arthur Schlesinger, Jr., Albert Schweitzer Professor of the Humanities at the City University of New York and winner of Pulitzer prizes in history and biography, endorses the Humphrey-Javits bill in the following article.

In recent weeks the main lines of President Ford's thinking about the economy have emerged with commendable clarity. In the name of "maximum freedom for private enterprise," he is proclaiming a crusade against the awful state of "regulatory bondage" in which, as he sees it, the American government is holding the oppressed and helpless American businessman. "I hear your cries of anguish and desperation," he told one audience of capitalists, as if they were inmates of a Soviet forced labor camp. "I will not let you suffocate." If only he had shown comparable sympathy for Solzhenitsyn!

Inveighing against "the mistaken, stupid idea that regulation protects people," the President argues that the public interest can be served best "through the market place" and proposes de-regulation as a primary goal of national policy. As for inflation, his solution for that, he recently acknowledged, is mass unemployment. "As you bring down the inflation," he has said, "*We* [an interesting pronoun] may have to suffer for a short period of time higher unemployment than we like." He has called for the partial denationalization of atomic energy, with the future production of enriched uranium turned over to private ownership (apparently under terms that guarantee profits to the private owners). The "critical choice" in the months ahead, he tells us, is between a "free" economy and "an economy whose vital decisions are made by politicians while the private sector dries up and shrivels away."

A certain amount of this may be discounted as the pre-campaign oratory of a man who has a natural concern about heading off Ronald Reagan. But enough of it corresponds to what we know about Gerald Ford as a Congressman to suggest that he probably is, on this range of questions, personally the most conservative President since Herbert Hoover. One doubts whether Eisenhower or even Nixon had Mr. Ford's gallant confidence that the unregulated market place is a sure guarantee of full employment, stable prices, decent wages and working conditions, protection for the consumer and truth in the securities markets. One must call this confidence gallant because it runs squarely against the evidence of history. It was, of course, the sad but indisputable fact that the unregulated market place achieved none of these

From *The Wall Street Journal,* July 30, 1975. Reprinted by permission of the author.

things which got the national government into the business of regulation in the first place.

MARKET PLACE FAILURES

And it is also the fact that the unregulated market place is patently unable to deal with urgent problems in our day. It has manifestly failed, for example, to control inflation while avoiding mass unemployment. Friedrich von Hayek, the high priest of laissez faire, admitted the other day that, under his creed, "We cannot avoid substantial long-term unemployment." Ford's own economists expect high unemployment till the end of the decade. Nor can the unregulated market place contain the administrative power over prices exerted by concentrated industries. Nor can the unregulated market place cope with problems like oil that are essentially political rather than economic in character. Nor can the unregulated market place bring about the reconstruction and expansion of our mass transit system which would be both helpful in re-employment and essential in the conservation of energy. Nor can the unregulated market place meet the nation's needs for health care, education, housing, welfare, solvent cities and environmental protection.

It is the obvious impotence of the unregulated market place in face of the hard problems of our time which has led some members of Congress—notably Senators Hubert Humphrey and Jacob Javits—to introduce the Balanced Growth and Economic Planning Act of 1975. This bill springs in part from a group called the Initiative Committee for National Economic Planning; and I must declare my own interest, for I was among those who signed that committee's statement. More formidable signers include economists like J. K. Galbraith, Wassily Leontief and Robert R. Nathan, labor leaders like Leonard Woodcock of the UAW, Arnold Miller of the Mine Workers and Jerry Wurf of the Federation of State, County and Municipal Employes and, it should be noted, business leaders like Robert McNamara, Stanley Marcus, Philip Klutznick, Robert Roosa of Brown Brothers Harriman, William F. May of American Can, W. Michael Blumenthal of Bendix, J. Irwin Miller of Cummins Engine, Arjay Miller of the Stanford Business School and Alfred C. Neal of the Committee for Economic Development.

The Humphrey-Javits bill would be regarded as innocuous in any other highly industrialized country. It would create an Economic Planning Board in the Executive Branch, establish procedures for industry and labor participation in the setting of economic targets and provide for congressional approval or disapproval of all plans developed by the board. The essence of the planning would be the gathering of information, the estimation of national resources and requirements and the coordination of national policies. There would be no enforcement authority, no interference with the making of private decisions, no revision of the pattern of ownership, no action except on the basis of legislation. The bill, in short, would give the nation the analytical, though not the enforcement, machinery to do for itself what every large corporation does every day in the way of advance planning.

Our radicals are naturally suspicious of all this. They recall that the idea of national planning received its first powerful endorsement in this country before World War I from George W. Perkins of J. P. Morgan and Company. They recall the summons to national planning during the Depression by men like Gerard Swope of General Electric and Henry I. Harriman of New England Power. They recall Joseph P. Kennedy writing in 1936, "An organized functioning society requires a planned economy. . . . Planned action is imperative, or else capitalism and the American scheme of life will be in serious jeopardy." They remember how business took over the NRA in the early New Deal, as it has taken over nearly all the regulatory agencies that cause President Ford such distress.

In view of all this, it is astonishing to note the hysteria the Humphrey-Javits bill has provoked in fundamentalist business circles. Walter B. Wriston of Citicorp has called it "a program designed to destroy the free-market system and with it our personal liberty." Wriston even challenges the proposition that "government regulation of goods and services is a legitimate function of government." Thomas A. Murphy of General Motors predicts that "inevitably someone—maybe all of us—would lose some freedom." This overkill is, I say, astonishing, except for those venerable enough to remember the same hysteria with which business leaders in other days fought Social Security, unemployment compensation, stock exchange regulation, the guarantee of bank deposits, food stamps, the Employment Act of 1946—fought, indeed, all the forms of government intervention which, by saving business in 1975 from a ghastly collapse in the style of 1929–32, permit savants like Wriston and Murphy to run on so about the beauties of the market place. If those earlier attacks on government regulation had succeeded, one shudders to think what real trouble the nation would be in today.

HISTORY'S SPECIAL RELISH

I do not believe that national planning is a panacea. The left wing fear that business will capture the planning mechanisms is not without substance. The European and Japanese experience in national planning reveals problems as well as achievements. In addition, the failure of economic (and all other types of) foresight is a salient fact of life. History outwits us all, and does so all the time, and seems to take special relish in outwitting businessmen and economists.

Still, when laissez-faire zealots object that planning will infallibly get us into a mess, one can only comment that it is hard to imagine a greater mess than the refusal to plan has got us into already: the worst inflation in a generation, the highest unemployment in 35 years, the worst decline in real output in nearly 40 years, the worst deficit in the balance of payments ever, the worst peacetime budgetary deficits ever, the worst energy shortages ever, the worst crises in municipal finance ever. Is more of this the glorious future that Ford, Wriston, Murphy and the rest are holding out to the American people?

And it is sheer irresponsibility to denounce the mild Humphrey-Javits measure as contemplating, in Wriston's phrase, an "economic police state." It was the same sort of irresponsibility that led most Americans to stop paying any attention to the self-righteous and self-serving wails of business leaders in the 1930s. If the American businessmen want W. H. Whyte to write a sequel to his sterling book of 1952 "Is Anybody Listening?," Wriston and Murphy are pointing out the direction in which they should go. It is almost as irresponsible for an American President to pretend that the country can get along without government regulation. For the reality is that we will continue to have government regulation—and that we will not lose our freedom.

Joseph P. Kennedy's question of 40 years ago is still to the point: "Should we try to have a balance between regulation and individualism, or should we revert to an uncontrolled individualistic scheme?" The answer is self-evident: We must strive for a better balance—a balance that will enable us to meet some of the problems the unregulated market place can never meet—and stop confusing our minds and dissipating our energies by trying to transform manageable differences over degree into a religious war.

IN OPPOSITION TO THE HUMPHREY-JAVITS BILL

T. A. MURPHY

T. A. Murphy, chairman of the board of General Motors Corp., explains in the following article why he is opposed to national comprehensive planning.

I have read the July 30 article "Laissez Faire, Planning and Reality" by Arthur Schlesinger Jr. Since I am among those whose remarks on the subject he has characterized as expressions of "hysteria" and "overkill," I would like to take this opportunity to respond. Mr. Schlesinger states that we are concerned only with "manageable differences over degree." I wish this were true, but I am rather inclined to agree with Senator Javits' statement (Journal, July 8) that we are engaged in "a great national debate on the American economy and its future," and our differences are not of degree but of principle.

At the outset, we should be clear on what this debate is *not* about. No one questions the need for government intervention in situations where one person's unrestricted freedom can seriously inhibit the rights of others. Some standards in areas like safety and environmental protection, for example, are necessary. The issues in these areas involve the levels of particular standards—the question of whether their cost to society exceeds their benefit. While admitting the necessity of some types of regulation, it should be remembered that the areas in which one individual's free choice unduly impairs the rights of others are far more limited than government planners commonly assume. (If, for example, I were to prefer a car with lighter and consequently less expensive bumpers, it is hard to see how my free choice would materially impinge on the welfare of anyone else. Nevertheless, my choice has been restricted by government regulation.)

I cannot imagine that Mr. Schlesinger is so naive as to believe that the current proposals for national planning are merely designed to enable the government "to do for itself what every large corporation does every day in the way of advance planning." If all we were talking about were government plans that are comparable to business plans, there would indeed be nothing to debate. Government units, of course, should try to anticipate future demands on their resources and plan to meet them, just like any private business. We wish them well at it and would like to see them do an even better job. But that isn't the issue.

Unlike a business, a government may not only plan—it may also com-

From *The Wall Street Journal,* August 18, 1975. Reprinted by permission of The Wall Street Journal, © Dow Jones & Company, Inc. 1975. All Rights Reserved. Also reprinted by author's permission.

mand. A business can set goals only for itself; a government body can set goals for other people as well. General Motors, for example, can and must plan the future production of cars but, contrary to popular myth, cannot compel anyone to buy them. Moreover, we try to plan production on the basis of what we anticipate people will want, not according to our idea of what they ought to buy. Every rational businessman knows that responding to consumer demand is more profitable than trying to change it.

The inherent limitations of business planning have been vividly illustrated in our industry during the last two years. Despite our best efforts to forecast demand, precipitous switches in consumer tastes left the industry with too many large cars last year and too many small ones today. The consumer, as always and as it should be, has had the final word. A government plan or "national goal" can, however, be imposed on consumers whether they like it or not, and this is the kind of planning that the great debate is all about.

The national planning that Mr. Schlesinger advocates involves much more than improved economic forecasting and coordination of current regulatory activities. Despite his statement that "there would be no enforcement authority, no interference with the making of private decisions," the Humphrey-Javits bill expressly contemplates additional "legislative and administrative action" to "achieve the objectives" of *a proposed* "growth plan."

There really are only two ways to allocate resources in a society: by consumer choice or by government edict. The decisions are either decentralized and flowing from the bottom up or they are centralized and flowing from the top down. It really comes down to the question of who is to decide: the individual consumer speaking through the marketplace or the economic planner speaking through the legislative and administrative process. In the interests of individual freedom as well as efficiency, I come down on the side of the customer deciding for himself.

The history of attempts to control the allocation of resources through the political process is dismal, whatever the period or wherever in the world you care to observe. The current economic "mess" which Mr. Schlesinger attributes to a "refusal to plan," has in fact been seriously aggravated by the hangover from an unfortunate experiment in political planning—peacetime wage and price controls. Selective political price controls, such as those on natural gas, continue to cause untold harm. It is hardly a coincidence that the railroads, the airlines and the public utilities, which have been subjected to the most lasting and the most detailed governmental controls, are among our most troubled industries. It is similarly hardly a coincidence that the economic progress of entire nations seems to be inversely related to the degree of political interference in the market process.

Mr. Schlesinger, in citing some of the shortcomings of today's economy, tried to set up a straw man of an "unregulated marketplace (which) is patently unable to deal with the urgent problems in our day," and he gives unemployment and inflation as examples of problems the marketplace has failed to control. Surely Mr. Schlesinger cannot believe that the marketplace caused inflation or that it alone could control it; it is Mr. Schlesinger's government planners who caused inflation through excessive spending and expanded money supply. Few businessmen, straining as we all are to meet government standards, edicts, guidelines, and codes, would agree that the marketplace is unregulated. Ours is a mixed economy, but the government planners do not acknowledge the part that their remedies of regulation have played in worsening our economic ills. Instead, free enterprise, the victim, is termed the villain of the piece, and the prescription is to increase the dosage of regulation which has helped to lay him low.

An adverse effect on our material prosperity, however, is not the only, or even the most important, reason for rejecting national planning. We are concerned ultimately with the threat to individual freedom. It is very well to talk, as the sponsors of planning do, about "the regional and local participation by citizens in every part of the nation," but no one can really believe that "national planning" will be undertaken in myriads of town meetings. Comprehensive national planning must ultimately involve the coercive powers of vast federal agencies which we must expect will be as remote from the influence of ordinary citizens as those which exist today. And that remoteness, although our friends on the other side will never admit it, actually is the whole point of a planning scheme. If national planners merely ratified those allocations of resources which citizens themselves would choose there would be no excuse for the planners' existence.

We already live in a wonderfully planned society, one in which each citizen in effect participates directly in a continuing referendum on every single item in a finely detailed platform. The marvelous difference from state planning is that ours is planned to be free—and we all ought to work to keep it that way.

QUESTIONS

1. Compare the fundamental issues about national economic planning advanced by Mr. Schlesinger and Mr. Murphy.
2. Mr. Murphy rejects national economic planning because he feels it will eventually trigger the coercive powers of federal agencies and thus reduce individual freedom. How does Mr. Schlesinger reply? Which side are you on?
3. Can government national economic planning be justified on the grounds that corporations do it every day, as argued by Mr. Schlesinger? Explain your position.
4. Is our choice, as explained by Mr. Murphy, government control or individual initiative?
5. Mr. Schlesinger says we need national economic planning because the unregulated market has messed things up. Mr. Murphy says we have a messed-up economic situation because of inept government planning and regulation. Where do you stand in this debate?

PROPOSAL FOR A NATIONAL POLICY ASSESSMENT AND ACTION PROGRAM

GEORGE A. STEINER

George A. Steiner explains in the following article why he is opposed to the Humphrey-Javits bill and other proposals for national aggregate planning but makes suggestions for federal government long-range planning.

In the Spring of 1975 Senators Humphrey and Javits introduced a bill in the Senate (S. 1795) which proposed the establishment of machinery in the federal government for developing a comprehensive national economic plan for the United States. A major purpose of the bill is to "provide for the development of a Balanced Economic Growth Plan, embodying coherent and realizable long-term economic goals, consistent with the Nation's economic resources and identifying the policies and actions that would be required to attain such goals." While the bill is specific about the establishment of various boards and agencies it does not prescribe the type of economic plan which will be prepared. That would evolve over time and within the broad policies laid down in the legislation.

The Humphrey-Javits bill is not likely to be passed this year but there seems little doubt that the forces which gave rise to it will continue. On the basis of past and current discussions of this subject I expect the demand will be patterned after the French system. While details of the Humphrey-Javits bill differ from the French system there are remarkable similarities.

In defending his bill Senator Javits observed that it "has opened a great national debate on the American economy and its future." Indeed it has, and rightly so, for there is strong disagreement about the need for and consequences of national economic planning in this country. On the one hand are those who take the position that the free market is a myth and national planning is needed to assure balanced economic growth. Many others see in the acceptance of this position an eventual replacement of the free market by government intervention either by design or an inevitable irreversible march of events. At the other extreme are those who reject outright national economic planning. T. A. Murphy, Chairman of the Board of General Motors Corp., for example, says: "We already live in a wonderfully planned society, one in which each citizen in effect participates directly in a continuing referendum on every single item in a finely detailed platform. The marvelous difference from state planning is that ours is planned to be free—and we all ought to work to keep it that way."

Adapted from George A. Steiner, "Proposal For A National Policy Assessment and Action Program," *Planning Review,* September 1975 (the journal of the NASCP).

In between these positions is another, namely, that there is great dissatisfaction with the way the economic system has been operating and "We therefore urge that provision be made for planning at the highest level of the United States government and through regional, state and local units of administration." This is a position taken by The Initiative Committee for National Economic Planning in its "The Case for Planning," and endorsed by a surprising number of prominent leaders in business, government, and the professions.

It is not the purpose of this paper to debate the validity of these positions. I accept the premise that the real issue is not a centralized dictatorial planning system versus no national planning at all. The real issue is: how can national integrated planning be designed to strengthen rather than weaken or supplant the current free enterprise system?

If we are to be spared the potential disasters from inappropriately designed national planning it is imperative that businessmen, as well as other groups, become deeply involved in the debate about what kind of a planning system we should have. This debate should cover a wide range of issues, many of which cannot be examined in this paper.

In this paper I wish to point out to businessmen, and government planning designers, that there are lessons of experience from corporate planning which have high applicability to national planning. They explain why French-type national planning is inapplicable to the United States. They also suggest a type of national integrated planning which is more appropriate to this country today. Finally, I explain why the word "planning" should be avoided in discussions of national planning.

SOME CHARACTERISTICS OF FRENCH-TYPE AGGREGATE PLANNING

The first French plan was launched in 1946 and was called the Plan of Modernization to indicate that its major aim was to repair the ravages of war. It was stimulated by the Marshall Plan for Europe, which was developed by the United States government. Since then there have been seven five-year plans, the last of which will begin in 1976 and end in 1980.

In the successive plans there have been four different conceptions of purpose which have been mixed in varying combinations: (1) to provide an understanding of alternatives open in using national income; (2) to specify the structure of production, growth changes in industries, and supply characteristics of the economy; (3) to lay out programs to correct problems, such as transportation and energy; and (4) to describe conditions needed for full employment with stable prices and a favorable balance of payments.

Planning begins with a Gross National Product (GNP) target objective. The GNP is then broken down into public consumption, housing, gross capital formation, and so on. Production levels and estimates of required investments in different sectors are then calculated by an input-output analysis. These estimates are then given to commissions whose members are drawn from industry, labor, and government. Horizontal commissions are formed to deal with economy-wide matters such as finance, productivity, and manpower. Vertical commissions deal with industrial segments of the economy such as transportation, steel, chemicals, and so on. Plans are integrated and when a workable synthesis is achieved the results are presented to Parliament for debate, following which the government approves the plans.

A number of features of this system are of interest to us here. First, the plans are prepared for branches of economic activity and not for companies or products. General objectives are set but individual companies are free to act as they choose. Second, the planning involves the effort of thousands of experts from business, professions, government, and industrial associations. Third, the plans are implemented by a mixture of psychological, structural, institutional, legislative, and administrative methods. Pierre Massé, a long-time President of the French Planning Commission, used to say the plan was "less than imperative but more than indicative." The French begin with indicative directions, then use persuasion, and then, if required, incentives for direct action. The government intervenes directly only when important imbalances appear to be imminent. By far, however, most of the implementation of plans rests on voluntary actions by decision makers in both the private and the public sectors.

Managers of larger firms are influenced by the plans, especially in making their investment and financial decisions. Executives of smaller firms say their decisions are little influenced by the government's plans.

French planning has by no means been considered an unqualified success by observers. Overly ambitious targets induced excessive investment and price inflation in 1957–58 and again in 1962–63, for instance. The targets of the sixth plan (1971–75) are so far from reality that the entire process is being seriously questioned. On the positive side, however, the system has produced very useful information, an acceptance of the importance of planning, better communications among major groups about national problems, and improved economic and planning education for decision makers. So, the French experience has been a "mixed bag."

APPLICABILITY OF FRENCH NATIONAL PLANNING TO THE UNITED STATES

The United States does not have a national aggregate integrated long-range plan, but it does have many long-range plans which are national in scope. For instance, the Park Service in the Department of [the] Interior has detailed long-range plans for our national parks. The Federal Aviation Agency has long-range plans for airport and traffic safety improvement. The Bureau of the Census has long-range plans for collecting statistics. Only during World War II did we have in this country anything approaching a national aggregate plan and it was far from complete in coverage.

We need aggregate integrated planning in the United States but at this time it should not be of the French type. My reasons are as follows:

First, there is a high probability that the type of communications among businessmen typified in the French planning system would be considered illegal in the United States. Our antitrust laws are quite explicit about competitor's discussing and planning to act cooperatively in their economic relationships. The Humphrey-Javits bill does not call for collaboration of businessmen but rather charges an Economic Planning Board to "seek the active participation by regional, State, and local agencies and instrumentalities and the private sector through public hearings and other appropriate means to insure that the views and proposals of all segments of the economy are taken into account in the formulation of the Plan."

This sounds agreeable and democratic but it is difficult to understand how an integrated long-range economic plan which has any depth and creditability to it can be prepared without major and detailed contributions by businessmen who deal operationally, rather than theoretically, with the kind of numbers needed in preparing a national plan. This fact became quite obvious in the only preceding experiences of the United States with national aggregate planning. During World War II and the Korean War the majority of employees in the federal government's production-control agencies were businessmen because they knew better than anyone else how specific economic forces affected the business sector with which they were familiar. To assure this needed realistic injection into planning requires, as the French found out, extensive consultation among businessmen and that is contrary to our antitrust laws.

Second, the sheer size and complexity of the economy of the United States cautions against any attempt to encompass it all in an overall, integrated long-range plan which presumes to provide guidance for decision making in both the private and public sectors. It may be useful to try to capture the entire economy in one grand model for statistical purposes. But, to use such models for operational decisions is quite another matter. Proponents of national planning speak of the Plan as being primarily a source of information to be used by everyone without coercion. Yet, the Humphrey-Javits bill requires that the President make policy recommendations to the Congress to achieve the objectives of the Plan and also requires him to ". . . take appropriate actions to insure that the departments and agencies of the executive branch will carry out their programs and activities in such a manner as to further the objectives of the Plan, and to encourage State and local governments and the private sector to carry out their programs and activities in such a manner as to further the objectives of the Plan." To do so the Chief Executive obviously must use "informational" planning data for operational purposes.

Our experts have not recently received high grades in forecasting general economic activity even one year ahead, let alone for longer distances. They have much less accuracy in forecasting particular sectors of the economy. For instance, who predicted the 1975 low level of automobile production?

Our economic system is much too complex and dynamic to encompass in a single comprehensive plan which may be used for operational purposes. Goals which are established when plans are made may very quickly become quite unrealistic and government actions taken to assure them may make matters worse. The wide gap between target projection and reality is a major failure of the fifth French plan.

Third, there are strong psychological aversions by many people to this type of planning that will not easily be overcome. Many people, for instance, see in such planning the first step to some type of central government planning and strongly resist it.

Fourth, there are political and administrative issues which would inevitably create problems. For instance, such planning would strengthen the hand of the executive branch as compared with the legislative branch. It would also tend to shift power from executive administrators to staff experts. Such shifts in power are not likely to be accepted easily in today's Congress, which has become increasingly jealous of its powers.

If French-type national planning is inappropriate for the United States, and if we need national long-range planning, the questions is: What should be done?

MAJOR LESSONS OF BUSINESS LONG-RANGE PLANNING EXPERIENCE APPLICABLE TO NATIONAL PLANNING

Before addressing that question, I want to comment on five major lessons of experience with corporate planning that should influence its answer. In presenting these lessons I recognize, on the basis of a number of years of my personal planning experience in both government and business, that there are great dissimilarities between planning in the federal government and that in even the largest companies in the private sector. There are, however, enough similarities to justify careful consideration of over twenty years of experience with corporate planning.

It is also quite important to observe that whatever is done must clearly reflect understanding of these similarities and dissimilarities. The way the planning process is organized must be tailored to the unique characteristics of the federal government's structure, operation, and traditions as well as the value systems and decision-making styles of dominant personalities in the government. This is the first lesson of business experience.

Second, there must be a strong commitment by the President, his Cabinet, and Congressional leaders to the idea that long-range planning is necessary and that it should become an integral part of decision making in government. As we learned in corporate planning, it is not enough for top management to be dedicated to long-range planning. Top administrators must somehow also convey and make understood their depth and strength of commitment to all others in the organization.

Commitment means many things. To illustrate, it means becoming involved in the planning process, assuring that the planning process is appropriate to the unique circumstances of the organization, allocating sufficient resources to do the job, and making current decisions on the basis of the plans.

Third, experience has taught us that organizations that create a comprehensive planning system for the first time should "make haste slowly." Eating dinner in one gulp is likely to produce indigestion. We know that the introduction of a planning system into an organization is an event which brings many changes, not the least of which is an alteration of power relationships. Unless the introduction is done carefully, cautiously, and circumspectly, it can easily create more problems than it solves and the planning system will, at best, be ineffective. Attempting to do too much too soon is a major pitfall to be avoided.

Fourth, before a long-range planning system is introduced into an organization top management must have a very clear understanding of the purposes the system is supposed to achieve and who is to do what and when. A plan to plan should be prepared. In government, the tendency is to lay down a broad policy and then to evolve details in a sort of "muddling through process." This is not the best way to proceed in launching a long-range planning system.

Fifth, great care should be taken to assure that concern over techniques does not divert planners and managers from the fundamental substantive purposes of planning. If this is not done, manipulation of numbers becomes more important than the meaning of numbers. The process becomes encrusted with formal procedures and rituals. In this event the exercise becomes pedestrian and, as a result, the creativity, innovation, and imagination which is needed for effective planning erodes and disappears.

Finally, the planning process must be continuous. When modern formal corporate planning first began in the United States there was a tendency to make five year plans and not change them until it became clear that they needed revision. That policy did not work very well. Now, virtually all companies that have a comprehensive formal planning system go through the process on a fixed cycle, usually once a year. This should also be the policy for any aggregate planning system introduced in the federal government.

It is pertinent to note here that, with the exception of the last consideration, the collapse of the Program Planning Budgeting System in the federal government was due in very large part to the fact that each one of these criteria for effective planning was ignored. Some time ago, through an extensive mail survey, I sought to determine (with Professor Schollhammer) the major pitfalls which ought to be avoided if corporate planning was to be effective. The above pitfalls were among the more significant ones identified by practitioners to be avoided. I also asked respondents how happy they were with their planning systems. My study showed an almost perfect correlation between dissatisfaction with planning and entrapment in these pitfalls.

WHAT SHOULD BE DONE?

If we should not create an aggregate integrated long-range planning system, what should we do? I suggest that we should limit our initial efforts to five areas of action, namely, (1) hammering out national goals, (2) undertaking a situation audit, (3) laying out action programs in selected areas, (4) developing better information for planning, and (5) developing a public planning consciousness.

NATIONAL GOALS

A primary and obvious task is to develop a set of national goals which have some consensus. President Eisenhower appointed a Commission on National Goals which made its report in 1960. There never was before nor has there since been any comparable effort. The time has arrived to define major national goals and to redefine them on a continuous basis.

The first set of goals might be prepared by a Presidential Commission but the function should be lodged in a permanent organization preferably located in the Executive Office of the President. The goals should cover more than economic targets because our system has a multiplicity of goals which are interrelated. Such a set of aims, together with some estimates of priorities, would serve as a fundamental foundation for planning throughout government and in the private sector.

Major goals should, of course, be divided into subgoals. Care should be taken, however, not to define too many subgoals nor to attempt to secure a perfect coordination among all goals. As goals are defined more concretely at lower levels of abstraction, conflicts will increasingly appear.

The goals should be set only after public debate. In the process of goal formulation all major groups in society should be heard, including business. I believe that the process of setting goals will stimulate useful national debate and the goals themselves will be used as valuable guidelines by those doing planning both in the public and private sectors.

THE SITUATION AUDIT

In business planning, making the so-called situation audit involves the collection and analysis of all relevant data useful in planning and in the process of identifying major opportunities and threats. It is essential that the areas for which data are to be accumulated, the type of data to be collected, and the depth of analysis to be devoted to specified data, should be very carefully circumscribed. This is so because not even the largest and most wealthy company can afford to examine in detail all information which might have a bearing on planning.

So it should be with government. The potential scope of data relevant in a comprehensive national long-range plan staggers the imagination. Hence, the boundaries must be very carefully defined. In conformance with the considerations mentioned earlier the first effort to prepare a situation audit should be narrow and modest.

SELECTED ACTION PROGRAMS

The next step in business planning, following the situation audit, is to choose those opportunities and threats which the company wishes to address. Strategies, policies, and detailed plans of action are then prepared to exploit opportunities, avoid threats, and solve problems. Similarly, following the situation audit, public long-range planning should proceed to identify those major programs for which detailed plans should be prepared. Again, the scope should be selective rather than comprehensive. I have in mind selecting for detailed planning such areas as energy, transportation, housing, productivity, or future raw material shortages. The areas for which detailed plans are made will change from year to year, but periodically, as noted previously, all program plans should be reviewed and modified in light of changing environment. In other words we should not develop plans at one point in time to last for many years. As in business the plans should be revised periodically. A one-year cycle may be too rapid for government; perhaps a two-year cycle would be better. There should also be, of course, a reasonable amount of integration among the program plans.

Making program plans is a critical step. In the past we have identified many major problems which subsequently arose. A number of past studies, including the Paley Commission Report of 1952, identified the current energy problem. Our problem in this country is not so much identification of problems that lay ahead as determining what should be done about them when they are identified.

In the future we must agree on specific actions which should be taken to deal with selected opportunities and threats. Again, first efforts should be modest in number and scope.

DEVELOPMENT OF BETTER INFORMATION FOR PLANNING

There is no other nation of the world that collects more comprehensive, detailed, and illuminating data about its activities than the United States. Yet, there are gaping holes both in the availability of needed data and techniques to improve their usage in planning. For instance, during the energy crisis last year the federal government was embarrassed with the paucity of information it had about the industry. In dealing with the recession in early

1975 the government found it had insufficient information about business inventories. Our GNP measure, as well as our Cost of Living Index, are not as reliable as they should be.

There should be an assessment of data needs for better planning and a gradual strengthening of our data base. Here again, we should proceed with caution, for data accumulation is expensive and when poorly conceived can create all sorts of problems in and out of government.

PLANNING CONSCIOUSNESS AND PARTICIPATION

Even the comparatively modest effort I have outlined above, not to mention a comprehensive national long-range planning program, will not succeed without the development of a new planning consciousness throughout society. We shall be unable to deal with the complex problems of this society without a much better understanding of the meaning and need for long-range planning in the public sector.

A planning consciousness is needed to inject widespread participation in any national planning effort. Not only, of course, must there be participation in the process by leaders and staff in the Congress and executive branch, but there must be citizen participation at this level as well.

Furthermore, planning of an appropriate nature must be pushed down through lower levels in the federal government as well as in state and local governments. Large corporations with diverse and decentralized operations learned long ago that best results in planning were achieved when planning was decentralized and done on the basis of broad guidelines from central headquarters. Here again, government can and should learn from experience in the private sector.

Space does not permit elaboration of these suggestions. But I feel compelled to add that in the public sector, as in the private sector, it is crucial that new mechanisms be invented to follow these prescriptions in such a fashion as to improve rather than restrain progress in planning. With unimaginative and routine planning processes it is easy to hobble the planning effort.

Among other reasons for the development of a planning consciousness and participation is that we must not allow national planning to be done exclusively by an elitist group. Only by the leavening influence of many participants, in and out of government, will dangers inherit in comprehensive government planning be avoided.

PLANNING VERSUS NATIONAL POLICY ASSESSMENT AND ACTION PROGRAM

Throughout I have used the word planning. Unfortunately, planning is a pejorative word when applied to federal socio-economic activities. There are many reasons for this, not the least of which is the fact that thirty to forty years ago we witnessed the rise of national economic planning systems around the world to strengthen the hands of dictators. Planning became associated with dictatorial governments which functioned in ways quite contrary to our views of the role of government and the operation of the economic system. Because of such deep-seated antipathy to the word planning when applied to government I suggest that it be discarded and other words be found to describe the process we are talking about here.

I suggest the phrase National Policy Assessment and Action Program to describe what we are talking about here. This phrase highlights the fact that it is national policy with which we are concerned. It says, also, that we are not alone concerned with assessment but also with action programs.

THE ROLE OF BUSINESSMEN

Whatever is done to improve national long-range planning in the public sector will be significantly improved if the lessons painfully learned about long-range planning in the private sector are understood and applied. For this reason I propose that a series of dialogues begin between business men and women and those in the federal government concerned with developing, doing, and using a national integrated long-range planning system. I do not have in mind conferences where each group lectures to the other. Rather, I propose working sessions to deal with the many problems and issues associated with getting on with the job of long-range planning in government.

I do not have in mind a continuous dialogue among the same people. This might be acceptable but I think there are enough different problems and issues to tax the minds of many people in and out of government. So, I suggest a somewhat loosely coordinated series of dialogues involving many people in the public and private sectors.

I do not have in mind that in these conferences the discussion will include substantive matters. Rather the discussion should be concerned with techniques, procedures, lessons of experience in organizing the process and in doing it, and matters related to systems operations.

CONCLUDING COMMENT

To summarize, I know of no more pressing problem in the United States than that of developing a capability to identify major problems that lay ahead and to implement plans to deal with them. There is no reason why we cannot do this. A comprehensive aggregate integrated long-range national plan is not at this time the preferred approach, in my judgment. But we should begin to develop a more selective aggregative approach. In doing this I think that the lessons of corporate planning in business can have valuable applicability to government in what I call a National Policy Assessment and Action Program. In this endeavor I believe that business men and women personally can make a significant contribution in engaging in continuous dialogue with government officials about preferred procedures until the process becomes perfected.

QUESTIONS

1. The author of this article takes the position that the debate about national economic planning should not be whether or not to have it but precisely what kind of planning we should have. Do you agree or disagree? Explain your position.
2. Why does the author say that French-type national integrated planning is not what we should adopt in the United States? Do you agree with his assessment?
3. Steiner identifies some major lessons of business comprehensive integrated planning that are applicable to national planning. To what extent does the Humphrey-Javits bill apply these lessons?
4. Appraise the appropriateness of the recommendations made for national integrated planning as an appropriate method to improve national economic performance while at the same time preserving the major strengths of our socio-economic-political system.

16

DIVERSE VIEWS ON THE FUTURE OF THE CORPORATION AND CAPITALISM

THE EMERGING PUBLIC CORPORATION

JOHN KENNETH GALBRAITH

John Kenneth Galbraith, professor emeritus of economics, Harvard University, and long-standing severe critic of corporations, in the following article argues for what he calls the "evolutionary view of the corporation," which, in essence, is the tendency for large corporations to become assimilated to the state. He says this tendency is essentially irreversible.

There are two disparate views of the modern, large corporation—two very different views of General Electric and General Motors and General Dynamics and General Mills and General Foods. These and the other generals—something less than a battalion, about a thousand in all—contribute close to half the production of goods and services in the United States. The distinction is between what may be called the "traditional" and what may be called the "evolutionary" view of the large corporation.

THE TRADITIONAL APPROACH

In the traditional view, a deep and, indeed, unbridgeable chasm divides the state from the firm. The differentiation between the government on one side and private enterprise on the other is fully accepted. Regulation of private enterprise by the state may be necessary, but such control as there may be is subject to a heavy burden of proof. The general right that the corporation be free from interference is deeply imbedded in our history and tradition. The right is further protected by what might be called corporate privacy. You can't regulate what you don't know about. The government can ask for information only after establishing a specific need to know. It is almost as though there is a broad presumption that what one does not know about corporate behavior does not hurt anyone.

The corollary of this view is that the corporation is kept honest and its operations are kept aligned with the public interest by the fact of competition. It is the market, not the state, that serves as the ultimate regulatory force. The market is an expression of public will, manifested in everyday purchases of goods and services; and since the public cannot be in conflict with itself, the corporation must respond to public needs. This is what puts the burden of proof on state intervention and makes such intervention neces-

John Kenneth Galbraith, "The Emerging Public Corporation." Reprinted from *Business and Society Review,* Spring 1972, Number 1, pp. 54–56.

sary only if, somehow or other, the orders and signals of the marketplace have failed.

Admittedly, many who hold this view concede that the market can, indeed, fail. Firms can become too large, monopoly and oligopoly can replace competition, the state can be influenced or even suborned by the great corporations. It's quite possible, to paraphrase Marx, that the state becomes, in fact, the executive committee of the corporate bureaucracy. But in this view, the solution lies not in controlling corporate power, but in dissolving it—in reviving the market and in restoring competition. The conditions under which private business can truly be private must thus be reestablished. At this point, there is always an appeal for the rigorous enforcement of the antitrust laws and the breaking up of the giants.

PRIVATE ENTERPRISE BECOMES PUBLIC

The evolutionary view of the corporation is sharply at odds with the traditional one. It says that the development of General Motors, Jersey Standard, and General Dynamics invokes, at some stage in growth and in power, a clear, clean break with the economics of the private firm in the classical market. At some point, these overwhelming large firms become, and I emphasize this term, *public institutions*. The clichés of private enterprise serve primarily, at this point, to disguise the essentially public character of the great corporation, including its private exercise of what is in fact a public power. Such a corporation fixes its prices, controls its costs, integrates backwards so as to control the supply of its raw materials, and influences, persuades, and, on occasion, bamboozles its customers. The giant corporation has powerful enough leverage in the community that getting what it needs from the government becomes pro tanto sound public policy. It has, on frequent occasions, a hammerlock on the Pentagon.

The most striking example of such a corporation, or the one on which one can take the strongest position, is the highly developed and fully specialized weapons firm—Lockheed, for example. Lockheed's physical plant is extensively owned by the government and leased to Lockheed. The company's working capital comes from the government in the form of progress payments. Its business comes all but exclusively from the government. Its cost overruns are socialized. Its capital needs—even those resulting from the mismanagement of its civilian business—are guaranteed by the government. Only its earnings and the salaries of its executives are in the private sector. Is such a firm private? Well, under the Constitution I am reminded that a man is entitled to believe anything!

The line between private and public enterprise in cases such as Lockheed is so exotic as to be ludicrous. This demarcation is, in fact, a device for diverting the attention of the public, the congressional committees, and the Comptroller General from what is in fact managerial error, executive perquisites, lobbying for new expenditures (including new weapons systems), profits, and political activity by executives and employees—all of which in a de jure public bureaucracy (or a full-fledged public corporation like the Tennessee Valley Authority) would be subjects of the greatest concern. Thus is public business hidden behind the cloak of corporate privacy.

But the specialized weapons firms, in this view of the corporation, are only the obvious case. General Motors, a different example, both sets the prices for its cars, and, in conjunction with the other automobile companies, foreign and domestic, does so for all cars. This has great effect on the public. General Motors negotiates wage contracts, and this likewise has great public effect—such public effect as has persuaded the President of the United States, in one of the more radical of his several recent radical moves, to place the price system in abeyance—a plank not part of the 1968 Republican platform. (I'm not criticizing the act, mind you.) General Motors also designs cars and incorporates or rejects safety features, also with public consequence. Its emphasis on engine design has public effect, as does the level of emissions therefrom. And General Motors powerfully influences highway construction. Few, if any, of our state legislatures make decisions that have greater impact on the public than are made annually by this one corporation. And its decisions as to what it will make, where it will produce, and what and from whom it will import have considerably more international impact than those of the very important men—my one-time colleagues in the State Department—who preside with no slight rancor over the affairs of, let us say, Chad or Mali.

The evolutionary view of the corporation therefore accepts its tendency to become assimilated to the state and regards this tendency as essentially irreversible. This view no longer presumes that the corporation has private affairs that should be protected from public scrutiny. It follows that while autonomy in the corporation's operations may have practical merit, there is no longer a presumption against public regulation. While there remains the danger that the firms will regulate their regulators, it is precisely such regulation—not the rehabilitation of market constraints nor, parenthetically, voluntary virtue—to which one must look for the protection and advancement of the public interest.

LIFTING THE VEILS

While I have presented two opposing views of the corporation with strict impartiality, it should not come as a surprise that I believe the evolutionary view has far more going for it than the traditional view.

The antitrust laws—basic to the traditional view—are eighty years old, approaching their centenary. The last really important dissolution occurred sixty years ago. This is not prima facie an encouraging record. Each new generation of reformers has held that only the feckless ineptitude and cowardice of its predecessors has kept the market from being restored. And then each new generation, its bravery notwithstanding, has also failed. I believe we can safely and however sadly conclude that if these laws were ever going to work wonders for anyone but lawyers, they would have worked them by now. And I argue that confidence in the efficacy of these laws has provided considerable support for irresponsible corporate power, in that the laws sustain the hope and perpetuate the myth of the all-powerful marketplace. These laws keep alive the illusion that public business is private, and they keep the burden of proof on those who propose regulations or even call for disclosure. And these laws totally suppress the possibility—many would say the specter—of the ultimate development of public ownership. I suggest that no one could do more for General Motors than this.

I do not object to according autonomy to the corporation. It is necessary for effective administration and effective production. There is no doubt that the independent entity, the autonomous corporate organization, is a highly useful device for undertaking and conducting complex industrial tasks. The fact that such an organization has emerged where steel must be manufactured in megatons, automobiles made in the millions, and chemicals processed on a vast scale, added to the fact that something very like the corporate entity has appeared in societies as diverse as those of the United States and the Soviet Union, indicates the utility of the autonomous corporate device. But in the evolutionary view of the corporation, autonomy is not a right by matter of principle; it is merely a pragmatic decision.

Accordingly, where there is a clash between corporate goals and the public interest—as with the safety of products, industrial effects on the environment, the effect of price and wage settlements on the economy, the equity of profits, or the appropriateness of executive compensation—there is no natural right of the corporation to be left alone. And I come here to a very important point: There is no barrier—in the developed case of specialized weapons firms like Lockheed or the incompetent ones like Penn Central, for example—to stripping away the purely artificial facade of private enterprise and converting such corporations into fully publicly owned enterprises. The one thing worse than a General Motors whose public character is recognized is a General Motors whose public character is denied. And the one thing worse than a General Dynamics that is publicly owned and publicly controlled is a General Dynamics that is publicly owned but privately controlled.

There is no magic in stripping away the myth that the market controls the modern corporation, and no magic in stripping away the hope that it sometime could be made to do so. I am quite convinced that divesting the corporation of these cloaks is the very first step toward any useful program for reform.

WHAT IS THE FUTURE OF THE CORPORATION?

REGINALD H. JONES

Reginald H. Jones, chairman and chief executive officer, General Electric Company, says that there are powerful forces pushing for the demise of private corporations but that if the larger corporations take appropriate action in their own and in the public interest the large private corporation will continue to play a major role in society.

I am deeply honored by this opportunity to address the Detroit Economic Club. Your reputation is so imposing, and your roster of speakers is so distinguished, that one feels obliged to stretch a bit for a subject worthy of the audience.

Like most businessmen, I have been addressing most of my public comments to the immediate problems of our economy—inflation, recession, and capital formation. But today, with your indulgence, I would like to step back a bit and take a longer, more philosophical look at a deeper question: the future of the corporation itself.

It would be hard to imagine a more directly concerned audience than this. Last August, *Fortune* magazine listed, for the first time, the top fifty industrial corporations of the world. Twenty-four of them are based in the United States. Ten of the top twelve are American. In fact, three of the top five are headquartered right here in Detroit—General Motors, Ford, and Chrysler. General Electric was number six, so I feel a rather direct interest myself.

THE ISSUE IS SURVIVAL

It seems to me that we have reason to be concerned whether the corporation as we know it—the characteristic institution of our American enterprise system—will survive into the next century. Great social and institutional changes are taking place that will necessarily affect the corporation, and especially the larger firms that are the core of our nation's industrial system.

We in management are no strangers to change. The corporation has survived and prospered precisely because it *is* highly adaptable to changing circumstances. In fact, corporations are perhaps the principal agents of change in the United States, with a highly successful record as engines of human progress. It is not by coincidence that the United States created the first and only trillion-dollar economy in the world. That is the result of our traditions of political and economic democracy, in which the profit-and-loss

From an address to the Detroit Economic Club, Detroit, Michigan, November 25, 1974. Reprinted by permission of General Electric.

disciplined private corporation, rather than the government, is the primary economic instrument.

One would think that an institution which has been so spectacularly successful would have an assured future—at least for another century or so. But curiously, it is almost impossible to find any prophet who sees much of a future for the investor-owned corporation.

WHAT THE PROPHETS SAY

Even the most friendly futurists, such as Daniel Bell, Herman Kahn, and Peter Drucker, forecast trouble. As the economy shifts from goods to services, in terms of occupation and output, we become a "post-industrial society." And the question they ask—and we in management must answer—is whether the post-industrial society will also be a *post-business* society.

Other prophets are less generous. More than a century ago Karl Marx predicted that capitalism would collapse of its own inner contradictions, to be superseded by socialism or communism. Many people around the world still accept this as a historical necessity, and are working to move history along by one means or another.

The gloomy historical philosopher Oswald Spengler, writing of the "Decline of the West" at the beginning of this century, prophesied that our civilization is doomed to end with a great final struggle between Money and Power—business and government. And the inevitable outcome, he said, will be the triumph of Caesarism, raw power triumphant over economic and political democracy.

More recently, the prophets have taken a different tack. John Kenneth Galbraith and Richard Goodwin believe that the bureaucratic necessities of operating an industrial system—the disciplines it imposes on all concerned—will inevitably cause the major corporations to be absorbed by the state, the central planning and controlling bureaucracy.

Then there is the consummate pessimism of Robert Heilbroner. He predicts that the pressures of human population on the earth's resources will inevitably bring us into a system of worldwide rationing and control, wherein such bizarre oddities as private enterprise and private decision-making—at least with respect to industrial resources—simply could not be allowed. Thus the challenge extends to *all* industrial democracies, to their economic *and* political structures.

Now these are the observations of intelligent and serious men, and they are not to be ignored. It's my impression that they tend to overstate the weaknesses of the private enterprise system, and underestimate its creative power and adaptability. Nevertheless there *are* bureaucratic tendencies; there *are* worldwide trends to planned economies; there *are* crises that make the public yearn for strong, authoritarian controls.

EXAMINING THE VULNERABILITIES

My purpose today is not to predict the end of the corporation—far from it—but to surface some of its vulnerabilities, a subject that I think is especially important for those of us with managerial responsibilities. Absorbed as we are with the day-to-day tasks of running successful businesses, we cannot ignore the dangers to the survival of the system itself. Preserving and strengthening the best economic system ever developed is one of our basic responsibilities to future generations.

With this responsibility in mind, let's examine some of the vulnerabilities.

A SHIFT IN VALUES

The deepest challenge comes from a basic shift in the values and beliefs that undergird our society. The counterculture is not a passing phenomenon. The values that have supported and vitalized our business system—the belief in rationality, objectivity, efficiency, self-discipline, thrift, hard work—these values seem to be losing their power. Science and technology, once universally admired, are becoming objects of suspicion.

The shift in values is not confined to the young. As C. Jackson Grayson pointed out in the *Harvard Business Review,* both labor and business nowadays often seek to reduce competition, not encourage it. Increasingly, Americans distrust the market system and demand that government step in to assure them of economic benefits. Much of the public has come to feel that controls—in other words, central planning—are not only desirable, but superior. Grayson concludes, "We are very near the point where further centralization will change our present system into one that can no longer perform its function efficiently."

And at that point, the sustaining rationale for the private corporation disappears.

FINANCIAL STARVATION

Another serious vulnerability is the possibility of financial starvation. Corporations cannot survive without a steady infusion of capital investment in new plants and equipment and new technology. Without this, the system runs down, loses its competitive capability in the world, and fails to satisfy the economic needs of society.

American business today is suffering from several decades of underinvestment. Ever since the depression, public policy has systematically favored the stimulation of demand, the redistribution of wealth, and the growth of government services—and given the needs of producers much lower priority. Now we pay the piper.

Between now and 1985, it is estimated that the capital investment needs of the private sector will be on the order of $4.5 trillion. That compares with $1.5 trillion invested in the past dozen years. Where will that enormous amount of private capital come from?

With real profits declining, investors leaving the stock market, and business going deeper and deeper into debt, the possibility of a capital shortage is not academic.

Major corporations with serious financial problems—Pan Am, Penn Central, Lockheed, Con Edison, Grumman, and others—have been reluctantly turning to the government as financier of last resort. Perhaps that seems a long step from regarding government as the financier of first resort. But if consumption-oriented tax policies continue over time to dry up the sources of voluntary savings and investment, then the United States will turn increasingly to government financing, and the power to tax could ultimately become our primary source of capital. And that, of course, would be the end of capitalism and private enterprise.

UNCONTROLLED INFLATION

Another and related vulnerability that must be faced is the possibility that today's double-digit inflation, if it is not brought under control, could lead to political and economic chaos. Dr. Kissinger has solemnly reminded us of the disruptive social and political effects of inflation, and the vulnerability of the Western democracies.

On the other hand, excessively stringent measures to stop inflation lead to a down-spiralling recession. Thus we walk an economic tightrope between inflation and recession.

Either of these problems, getting out of hand, could conceivably lead to demands for major changes in our economic system, with some form of socialism brought into being under the guise of emergency reform measures. The top 100 corporations—the most visible targets of control—would be the most vulnerable in such a situation. That's one reason why we cannot regard a harsh recession as an acceptable solution for our problem of inflation.

PLANNED ECONOMIES

Yet another area of vulnerability is the fact that American corporations are increasingly obliged to compete on the international scene with state enterprises and state-controlled economies. How can individual companies hope to compete effectively against the power of national treasuries, and their power to tax people to cover their inefficiencies or advance political objectives?

As more and more of the world turns toward planned economies—using the whole resource base of a nation like one single economic enterprise—we in the United States might, in self-defense, find ourselves drifting in the same direction. The temptation to join the march toward government planning and control may be stronger than we think. Well-meaning proposals for federal planning commissions to prevent shortages and anticipate problems have in them the seeds of a planned economy.

Another variation of this theme is the trend toward socialism in Europe.

Unlike the United States, the labor movement in Europe has a Marxist tradition and is trying in several countries to gain control of private industry through the use of political power. This would be a very remote possibility in the United States, with the present leadership of our labor unions, but it is a live issue in West Germany, for example, where private industry is threatened by two major propositions.

One is a bill for what is called increased "co-determination." That is, the managing Board of Directors would be made up of 50% representatives of the employees and 50% representatives of the shareholders, with provisos that make it easy for the employee bloc to exert substantial control.

The other is a so-called profit-sharing proposal under which a certain percentage of industry's profits are distributed annually to employee trusts in the form of stock. Because of co-determination in the banks which manage the trusts, employees and their unions could gain effective control over these shares, which in a few years would amount to a controlling interest in the whole economy. The step from there to a labor government and full socialism could be very short indeed.

In an excellent book entitled *British Nationalization 1945–73,* R. Kelf-Cohen points out that the nationalization of Britain's basic industries was not brought about by a great national desire for socialism, but by pressure from the trade unions—the dominant elements of the Labour Party—in order to attain better control over the management of these industries.

Now the labor movement in the United States, unlike its European counterpart, has not formed a political party. It has been content to work—very successfully—within the traditional two-party system. Furthermore, American unions are for the most part strong supporters of the private enterprise system. Nevertheless, if the European trade unions, with their strong Marxist orientation, were to push Europe still further into socialism, this could not fail to affect the United States in the long run.

REGULATION TO EXTINCTION

But the most insidious vulnerability, and the one most likely to change the major corporations into mere arms of the government, is the slow, ever-more entangling web of regulations by which the power of decision is being transferred from the Board Room to federal agencies in Washington. I need not recite here the long litany of statutes and regulations by which the federal government tells business what it may and may not do. The threat of federal charters and the licensing of corporations would be the last straw. Every one of these regulations is introduced as a protection for the public, and every one is said to be adopted for our own good. The cumulative effect is what we must be concerned about.

Public policy has for decades favored growth of the public sector over the private sector. Expenditures by all governments in the U.S.—federal, state, and local—amounted to 10% of the gross national product in 1929. They have increased every decade and now stand at 32% of the economy. (Including off-budget items, Milton Friedman says it's now 40%!) If the long trend continues, they will be about 50% by the end of the century. The question is—when government is such a pervasive element, at what point do we cease to have a market-oriented, private enterprise economy?

We have, of course, a highly mixed economy at the present time, and the distinction between public and private enterprise is being blurred. As Professor Galbraith put it in *Atlantic* magazine in 1967, "It requires no great exercise of the imagination to suppose that the mature corporation, as it develops, will eventually become a part of the larger administrative complex associated with the state. In time the line between the two will largely disappear. Men will marvel at the thin line that once caused people to refer to General Electric, Westinghouse, and Boeing as *private* business."

IS IT WORTH SAVING?

What are we to make of all this? If it is all so inevitable, should we plan accordingly? If the major corporations—the core of our private enterprise economy—are ultimately to be controlled or absorbed by the federal government, should we cynically start positioning our companies for power roles in the bureaucracy to come? Or do we have, in our private enterprise system, some freedoms and values that must be preserved for future generations?

I'm sure I know your answer. Historians tell us that situations of freedom are rare and not very long-lasting in the five-thousand-year history of civilization. What we have developed here in the United States, political and economic democracy, has never been developed elsewhere on such a scale. It would be to our eternal dishonor if we were to let it be destroyed.

There's more at stake than the private enterprise system. If too many of our economic liberties are lost, our political and civil liberties will follow. A government that controls our economic life will soon control the rest of life. Freedom is indivisible.

This is, of course, an old-fashioned message. But then, so is socialism. The struggle between liberty and tyranny, people and governments, is a very ancient struggle, and every generation must work out its own accommodation.

BEWARE THE ELEPHANT

None of us, I'm sure, expects a return to the *laissez-faire* doctrine in which government plays no significant role in the economy. That day is gone.

Nor can we afford the kind of divisive adversary relationship between government and business that so frequently has us working at cross-purposes.

Rather, we need a relationship built on mutual respect and mutual support for common objectives. On some technical projects where the risks and costs are too large for individual corporations, business and government will have to work together if the job is to be done. We will need more government support for economic objectives overseas—a really effective foreign *economic* policy. But as one of my associates says, "Beware of getting into bed with an elephant. If he ever rolls over, you've had it."

We'll need to have a proper understanding about who does what, with government determining national objectives and policies, and private enterprise getting the economic work done. Though both business and government serve the public, we must insist on maintaining the essentially private, market-oriented character of the corporation, and try to reverse the long, uninterrupted trend of expanding the government sector at the expense of the private sector of the economy.

How can this be done? My purpose today has been to examine the vulnerabilities, not to present a Grand Plan for Salvation. But certain principles would seem to be basic.

DEVELOP A CONSTITUENCY

First, business must develop a constituency of hard-core supporters. As Irving Kristol has pointed out, "No institution in our society can endure without a constituency—a substantial number of people who are loyal to the institution and who will quickly rally to its defense when it is in trouble. Yet the modern corporation is just about the only major institution of our society which does not have such a constituency."

As Kristol explains, "Constituencies are not born but created—and once created, they need constant cultivation. Politicians understand this, but corporate managers do not."

Kristol stresses the share owner constituency, but I think it's larger than that. Our natural constituency is the middle class that not only invests in, but works in, and buys from the corporation. These are the people with a direct economic and political stake in the corporation's success. We in management need to cultivate their loyalty; engage in serious two-way communications; and specifically ask for their help when we need it.

All of us are aware that this is more easily said than done, or we would have done it long ago. So-called economic education programs for the public have failed miserably, and programs to sell the free enterprise system like you'd sell soap are an insult to the people. In my view, we'll have to win our constituency issue-by-issue, like any successful politician, demonstrating how specific proposals will affect the lives and pocketbooks of the people whose support we need. People don't want lectures. They want answers to problems, and assurance that we really care about the things that concern them.

VOLUNTARY ACTION TO PREVENT REGULATION

Another basic principle is to resist unnecessary governmental interference with business decision-making. This is one principle that every businessman seems instinctively to understand, but unfortunately we have too often been purely reactive, forever in a defensive posture. The best defense is a good offense. We must anticipate public criticism and take the necessary action to make regulation unnecessary.

In retrospect, it appears that industry did not anticipate the strength of public feeling that could be aroused on the subjects of safety and environmental pollution. The auto industry particularly has been hurt by the legislative over-reaction.

Energy conservation and consumer information are areas where the danger of excessive regulation runs high today. An ounce of prevention here will be worth a *ton* of cure. Industry must take the initiative in developing *voluntary* standards such as the energy-efficiency ratings of the air-conditioning industry, and move out front with effective programs of consumer education.

Or if legislation is needed or inevitable, as in the case of pension reform, then industry can help to assure a sensible outcome by coming up—on its own—with legislative proposals that are responsive to the real problems.

It's the excesses, the needless and heedless use of governmental power, that must be avoided—primarily through voluntary action that anticipates public concern.

CONSCIOUS EVOLUTION

But more important than resistance to excessive regulation is the positive performance that wins and holds the support of our constituencies. As Irving Shapiro said here a few weeks ago, the American public, the sum total of all our constituencies, is highly pragmatic. It supports institutions that deliver the goods.

Thus the basic strategy for corporate survival is to anticipate the changing expectations of society, and serve them more effectively than competing institutions.

This means that the corporation itself must change, consciously evolving into an institution adapted to the new environment.

PLURALISTIC SOCIETY

Consider the changes. It's quite clear that the United States can no longer be called simply "a business society," as we were from about the Civil War to the end of World War II. Today, we are a pluralistic society, in which many competing groups and institutions strive for power and influence. Thus more decisions will be made, and more resources will be allocated, by political processes rather than the market economy. We must adapt to that.

Moreover, as I mentioned before, the U.S. economy is primarily engaged in the production of services, not goods. Though the production of food, materials, and manufactured products is still this country's basic strength on the world scene, six out of ten of our people are engaged in the services sector, and that will increase to seven out of ten in the 1980's. Higher priority is being given to such things as health care, education, municipal services, travel, and recreation. Does this mean that the post-industrial society will also be the post-business society? Not at all. For one thing, industry has a big challenge to provide the equipment that will make the inflationary services sector more productive. And with some imagination, corporations can provide—as businesses—many of the services now provided by governments and other institutions. This too means adapting to a more political climate.

THE WORLDWIDE OPPORTUNITY

Looking further ahead, we see that the easily available sources of energy, food, and materials on this planet are being used up. Unless the world wants to settle for a regimen of shared poverty, we will have to tackle the economic and technological task of developing the more difficult secondary sources. Nuclear power, for example, as well as oil; intensive farming of submarginal land; farming and mining of the sea; and development of substitutes for scarce metals. These are tasks of economic development for which the private corporation has shown itself to be eminently suited, though it will require adaptation to a new relationship with governments in all nations.

And while the United States may be entering its "post-industrial" phase, most of the nations of the world are striving to reach the industrial level. Who is best qualified to provide the know-how, the technology, and the organizational skill required in the developing nations? The initiative has already been taken by the corporations, many of which are now operating on a world scale.

There are many critics of the so-called multinational corporations, but as Peter Drucker points out, "Business is the only institution capable of being multinational . . . The nation is too small a unit to make rational economic decisions." If the gap between the rich and the poor nations is to be narrowed, the business corporation has the best chance of succeeding because it is the only effective international institution we've got.

NEW DIRECTIONS

These, then, are some of the directions in which the corporation should be evolving:

. . . toward a new and more productive relationship with government;
. . . toward competing more effectively for influence and resources in a pluralistic society;
. . . toward business ventures in the fast-growing services sector;
. . . toward the development of new technologies, new sources of food, fuel, and raw materials;
. . . and toward economic development on a world scale, to help narrow the gap between the rich and the poor nations.

These are noble and self-justifying purposes, but they do not assure the successful future of the corporation. For we have many points of vulnerability, as I have tried to show today.

The sportswriter Damon Runyon once wrote, "As regards the human race, it's 9-to-5 against." At this juncture most of the prophets seem to give the same odds against the long-term survival of the corporation.

But we have all seen the underdog emerge as the winner because he had the will and the energy to prevail.

That's the challenge: in the words of William Faulkner, "not merely to endure, *but to prevail.*"

> . . . if American capitalism is to maintain and increase its vitality, it must do a better job of integrating its economic and social functions. Toward this end I would offer three suggestions. First, corporations must develop more effective tools for measuring the social, as well as economic, costs and benefits of their actions.
>
> . . .
>
> Second, businessmen must take the initiative to spell out more clearly and positively the longer-range economic and technical implications of current proposals for social problem-solving.
>
> . . .
>
> Finally, we must press forward on the national level to create broader and more viable long-range goals, to assess what business can and cannot do to meet those goals, and to set more comprehensive strategies to combine the strengths of public and private resources.
>
> David Rockefeller, "The Essential Quest for the Middle Way," in Leonard Silk, ed., *Capitalism: The Moving Target,* New York: Quadrangle/The New York Times Book Co., 1974, pp. 97–98.

THE CRISIS OF CAPITALISM: A MARXIST VIEW

JOHN G. GURLEY

John G. Gurley, professor of economics at Stanford University, picks up from where he left off in the third reading in this book to explain in the following article the Marxist view about the viability and future of capitalism, a view, of course, not shared by the defenders of capitalism.

Marxists today consider capitalism to be an imperialist system that exploits much of the world, in the sense that it uses power—economic, political, and military—to control other people and their resources for the purpose of unduly benefiting itself. This international and hierarchical system, many Marxists believe, reached its peak in the early decades of this century, although, within the system, some countries have subsequently gained while others have lost. Since that time, global capitalism has been confronted by another expanding ideology and movement—Marxian socialism—and by other potent adversaries, the total impact of which has been to reduce its ability to expand in the world economy and thus to prosper from this activity. Contemporary capitalism, Marxists contend, must expand to remain viable, but it is increasingly difficult for it to do so. That is essentially the crisis of capitalism today. Its future depends on how this contradiction is resolved.

. . .

International capital is both more active and more confined than it was several decades ago. Large areas of the world have been removed from its control and it is threatened by enemy forces, at its borders and within its smaller circle. But within these tighter confines, international capital has made the most of its opportunities—its energy has risen with the compression of its domain. It has strengthened and expanded its position in the advanced capitalist nations; temporarily gained dominance in such countries as Brazil and Iran, which are likely to become major powers in the world; intensified its influence elsewhere, as in Egypt; to a small degree, drawn the Soviet Union and Eastern Europe back into global capitalism's dominion; and in general has taken maximum advantage of the Sino-Soviet split. Nevertheless, when one surveys the sweep of the 20th century, it is almost impossible to avoid the conclusion that capitalism has declined as a world force, in that it has lost much control over the world's resources and markets.

While the structure of international capitalism has been impaired during this century, U.S. capitalism as an integral part of it grew in stature throughout the period until, at the close of the Second World War, it found itself supreme. However, since about 1965 the going has become much rougher. The world is now considerably less receptive to the expanision of U.S. capitalism.

Marxists do not have a uniform position about the viability and future of U.S. capitalism. However, the following propositions would probably elicit much of their support: (1) Capitalism must expand to survive. (2) For the United States and other major capitalist nations, expansion must take global form. (3) Expansion has become more difficult, more costly, riskier, and more controversial. (4) These and other factors have weakened the ability of the U.S. capitalist class to extract surplus value from the system. (5) U.S. capitalists, with government help, will attempt to regain their previous position of strength by promoting measures to weaken their adversaries. (6) The responses of "the adversaries" to these counterattacks will do much to determine the shape of U.S. society in the future.

. . .

If U.S. monopoly capital is to regain its former position, there will need to be stepped-up foreign programs of economic and military aid, counterinsurgency, military force when required, and so forth. Toward the same end, the U.S. government could continue its attempts to bring Marxist nations (*e.g.,* the U.S.S.R. and Eastern Europe) back into the fold of global capitalism by granting more and more concessions to them. It could also raise its efforts to gain more secure footholds in the dictatorial countries now emerging as future economic giants (*e.g.,* Brazil, South Africa, Iran, Nigeria, and Indonesia). Moreover, the U.S. government could press for even greater superiority in the world trade of weapons of destruction.

[T]he nature of the responses of people here and abroad to monopoly capital's counterattack will determine, to some significant extent, whether this mode of production will survive much as it is or be greatly transformed. The responses of labor, consumer-interest groups, anti-capitalist movements abroad, and others may be mild and conciliatory. If so, the U.S. capitalist class and its national security managers will be able to revitalize American capitalism and achieve high growth rates by capturing even a larger share of the nation's income and wealth. While this outcome is possible, it will not be likely if capitalism's problems are as serious as argued above. For, if the roots of the difficulties are deep, capitalists' solutions to their problems would have to be so damaging to the working classes and others as to elicit from them something closer to fury than to conciliation. In this event, either of two outcomes would most likely result: (1) the conversion of monopoly capitalism into a neo-fascist society, or (2) its transformation into a socialist one.

The first outcome would occur if a weakening capitalist class, in the face of stiff opposition, is unable by democratic means to solve its problems, and so is forced to subordinate itself to a strong, repressive state that seeks solutions to the problems by dictatorial decrees. The neo-fascist regime would serve both itself and monopoly capital by oppressive control over the working class, by racist measures aimed at gaining "white support" and dividing workers, by the active employment of military force at home and overseas, and by a law-and-order regimen making illegal many social, economic, and political activities that are now within the law. Such a political system might have the support not only of a desperate capitalist class but also of a frightened section of the middle class, threatened by workers and haunted by racist fears.

The second path would be traversed only if large numbers of people, victimized by monopoly capital's drives, came to see the welfare of the capitalist class as basically destructive of the welfare of most other people; and if, in the process of struggling against each demand as it arose, they developed new goals, different values to live by, and a new conception of the world around them—all in opposition to existing capitalist forms. Socialism would then be accepted by the majority of people who, having learned from discussion and practical activity by confronting monopoly capital's proposed solutions to its problems, had themselves changed—into socialists.

The transformation of the capitalist mode of production into the socialist mode would probably take place gradually, with collective ownership of industries (at the national, local, and enterprise levels) proceeding by degrees as one group of privately-owned corporations after another demanded "outrageous" sacrifices by others in order to save themselves; with national and regional planning being developed in stages to meet problems incapable of being solved by private markets; with workers gradually gaining control of their modes of work and the structures of rewards for work; with consumers, in cooperation with workers, transforming products to fit their needs rather than a profit-making compulsion; and with people reassessing and changing the aims and methods of monopoly capital in foreign policy to favor democracy over repressive capitalist modes of production.

Only when people, confronted by the repeated summons to bail out the capitalist class at great public expense, gain an understanding that their interests are sharply opposed to those of monopoly capital—only then will they, having changed themselves in the process, be in a position to change their world.

However, if U.S. capitalism does survive this century, the chances are that many of its democratic accompaniments will not. In the long run, democracy seems less compatible with a monopoly capitalism in deep trouble than it does with a socialism that comes out of American traditions. Competitive capitalism—free enterprise—was consistent with many personal freedoms, but monopoly capitalism has been eroding those freedoms with its drive to preserve itself. Monopoly capitalists and their national security managers have proven over and over again, by their actions on the world scene, that, when the chips are down, they prefer capitalism to democracy.

Freedoms for capital clearly have taken precedence over freedoms for people.

In conclusion, it is possible, but unlikely, that U.S. monopoly capitalism will go largely unchallenged in its destructive endeavors to restore its own health. If, as seems more likely, it *is* seriously challenged, the outcome would probably be a neo-fascist state—the retention of monopoly capitalism by repressive means. One should also allow, however, for the outside chance that capitalism will survive by reforming itself to the satisfaction of most people. One might recall that, after the Reformation had crowded Catholicism into a narrow corner of Western Europe, the Catholic Church, with its new Society of Jesus, carried out reforms in a Counter-Reformation that before long enabled it to recapture much of what had been lost to Protestant movements. It should also be remembered, though, that the Jesuits were reinforced by Spain's military forces and by the Inquisition. Does monopoly capital have its own group of Jesuits—its Society of Adam Smith—in the wings?

There is *also* an outside chance for the transformation of monopoly capitalism into a socialism that would restore, revitalize, and extend the best democratic practices to be found in America's traditions. This could be the outcome only if monopoly capital repeatedly failed to extricate itself from its deepening difficulties and in the process thoroughly educated large numbers of people to its own necessities. At that point, the issue of capitalism or socialism would turn on whether monopoly capital still had sufficient support to impose repression. If not, a socialist America would be born.

"I would be prepared to make a bet, though I shan't be there to collect, that by the year 2000, the essential framework [of America] will be remarkably similar to what it is today."

Lord C. P. Snow, "Hope For America," *Look,* December 1, 1970, p. 33.

. . .

"Thus, *whether we are unable to sustain growth or unable to tolerate it,* there can be no doubt that a radically different future beckons. In either eventuality it seems beyond dispute that the present orientation of society must change. In place of the long-established encouragement of industrial production must come its careful restriction and long-term diminution within society. In place of prodigalities of consumption must come new frugal attitudes. In these and other ways, the 'post-industrial' society of the future is apt to be as different from present-day industrial society as the latter was from its pre-industrial precursor."

Robert L. Heilbroner, *An Inquiry into the Human Prospect,* New York: W. W. Norton & Company, Inc., 1974, p. 94 (italics in original).

THE CORPORATION AND LIBERAL DEMOCRACY

IRVING KRISTOL

Irving Kristol, Henry R. Luce Professor of Urban Values, New York University, argues in the following statement that there is danger for private corporations in becoming integrated into the public sector, and that if this integration does happen, it will adversely affect our liberal democracy.

. . .

Whether for good or evil—and one can leave this for future historians to debate—the large corporation has gone "quasi-public," i.e., it now straddles, uncomfortably and uncertainly, both the private and public sectors of our "mixed economy." In a sense one can say that the modern large corporation stands to the bourgeois-individualist capitalism of yesteryear as the "imperial" American polity stands to the isolated republic from which it emerged: Such a development may or may not represent "progress," but there is no turning back.

The danger which this situation poses for the American democracy is not the tantalizing ambiguities inherent in such a condition—it is the genius of a pluralist democracy to convert such ambiguities into possible sources of institutional creativity and to avoid "solving" them, as a Jacobin democracy would, with one swift stroke of the sword. The danger is rather that the large corporation will be thoroughly integrated into the public sector, and lose its private character altogether. The transformation of American capitalism that *this* would represent—a radical departure from the quasi-bourgeois "mixed economy" to a system that could be fairly described as [a] kind of "state capitalism"—does constitute a huge potential threat to the individual liberties Americans have traditionally enjoyed.

One need not, therefore, be an admirer of the large corporation to be concerned about its future. One might even regard its "bureaucratic-acquisitive" ethos, in contrast to the older "bourgeois-moralistic" ethos, as a sign of cultural decadence—and still be concerned about its future. In our pluralistic society we frequently find ourselves defending specific concentrations of power, about which we might otherwise have the most mixed feelings, on the grounds that they contribute to a general diffusion of power, a diffusion which creates the "space" in which individual liberty can survive and prosper. This is certainly our experience vis-à-vis certain religious organizations—e.g., the Catholic Church, the Mormons—whose structure and values are, in some respects at least, at variance with our common democratic beliefs, and yet whose existence serves to preserve our democracy as a

Reprinted with permission of Irving Kristol from *The Public Interest,* No. 41, Fall 1975, pp. 139–141.

free and liberal society. The general principle of checks and balances, and of decentralized authority too, is as crucial to the social and economic structures of a liberal democracy as to its political structure.

Nevertheless, it seems clear that the large corporation is not going to be able to withstand those forces pulling and pushing it into the political sector unless it confronts the reality of its predicament and adapts itself to this reality in a self-preserving way. There is bound to be disagreement as to the forms such adaptation should take, some favoring institutional changes that emphasize and clarify the corporation's "public" nature, others insisting that its "private" character must be stressed anew. Probably a mixture of both strategies would be most effective. If large corporations are to avoid having government-appointed directors on their boards, they will have to take the initiative and try to preempt that possibility by themselves appointing distinguished "outside" directors—directors from outside the business community. At the same time, if corporations are going to be able to resist the total usurpation of their decision-making powers by government, they must create a constituency—of their stockholders, above all—which will candidly intervene in the "political game" of interest-group politics, an intervention fully in accord with the principles of our democratic system.

In both cases, the first step will have to be to persuade corporate management that some such change is necessary. This will be difficult: Corporate managers are (and enjoy being) essentially economic-decision-making animals, and they are profoundly resentful of the "distractions" which "outside interference" of any kind will impose on them. After all, most chief executives have a tenure of about six years, and they all wish to establish the best possible track record, in terms of "bottom line" results, during that period. Very few are in a position to, and even fewer have an inclination to, take a long and larger view of the corporation and its institutional problems.

At the same time, the crusade against the corporations continues, with the "new class" successfully appealing to populist anxieties, seeking to run the country in the "right" way, and to reshape our civilization along lines superior to those established by the marketplace. Like all crusades, it engenders an enthusiastic paranoia about the nature of the Enemy and the deviousness of His operations. Thus, the *New Yorker,* which has become the liberal-chic organ of the "new class," has discovered the maleficent potential of the multi-national corporation at exactly the time when the multi-national corporation is in full retreat before the forces of nationalism everywhere. And the fact that American corporations sometimes have to bribe foreign politicians—for whom bribery is a way of life—is inflated into a rabid indictment of the personal morals of corporate executives. (That such bribery is also inherent in government-aid programs to the underdeveloped countries is, on the other hand, *never* taken to reflect on those—e.g., the World Bank—who institute and run such programs, and is thought to be irrelevant to the desirability or success of the programs themselves.) So far, this crusade has been immensely effective. It will continue to be effective until the corporation has decided what kind of institution it is in today's world, and what kinds of reforms are a necessary precondition to a vigorous defense—not of its every action but of its very survival as a quasi-public institution as distinct from a completely politicized institution.

It is no exaggeration to say that the future of liberal democracy in America is intimately involved with these prospects for survival—the survival of an institution which liberal democracy never envisaged, whose birth and existence have been exceedingly troublesome to it, and whose legitimacy it has always found dubious. One can, if one wishes, call this a paradox. Or one can simply say that everything, including liberal democracy, is what it naturally becomes—is what it naturally evolves into—and our problem derives from a reluctance to revise yesteryear's beliefs in the light of today's realities.

WILL U.S. CAPITALISM SURVIVE?

OTTO ECKSTEIN

Otto Eckstein, professor of economics, Harvard University, and president of Data Resources, Inc., discusses a few major defects of capitalism but responds affirmatively to the question: "Is the capitalist system worth saving?"

The future order of society can never be foreseen, for it is the product of social inventions not yet made. The United States has been a capitalist country since her founding. But capitalism may have performed its mission, accumulated the physical and human capital, institutionalized the process of technological progress, and achieved sufficient living standards. Will capitalism die of boredom? Will it be succeeded by a better social order designed for new and different goals? Or will our society be superseded by more vigorous peoples, ideas, cultures? Could Maoism really be the wave of the future?

One hundred years from now, the economic system will be very different. Technology will be unrecognizable; education and consumption levels will be far greater; new information technologies and techniques for modifying human behavior will surely alter the economic system. But will the economic system still be "capitalist"?

Today's capitalism is already characterized by the large corporation, which is hard to distinguish from a socialist state enterprise. The corporation is an institution for managing the productive activities of tens of thousands of workers, for introducing technological changes, for developing markets, and for accumulating the nation's capital. How then does our modern capitalism differ from other systems? And what is worth preserving for a hundred years?

Today's capitalism is still based on private property, and the individual corporation is still free to make the larger part of its business decisions freely and without government approval or control. Within the enterprise, the manager is free to manage the productive activities as he sees fit—though "he" may be a corporate committee. Outside the corporate sector, today's capitalism is still a part of a democratic system of individual freedom, free choice as to job or shopping, and family property rights that allow wealth to be fractionally passed on from generation to generation.

Otto Eckstein, "Will U.S. Capitalism Survive?" Reprinted from *Business and Society Review/Innovation,* Summer 1974,

EXPANDING GOVERNMENT POWER

The last ten years have seen some significant changes in the character of our capitalist system. Following the New Deal, the relation between business and the state was stable, with business reasserting its independence to a degree. But beginning in the mid-1960s, government broadened its regulatory scope in a variety of ways. The economy's overloading of the natural ecological system produced a detailed set of pollution control regulations. The consumer was given various forms of protection against marketing practices employed by business. The right to hire new workers was modified to require equal opportunities for blacks, women, and other groups. The conditions for the work place were regulated more precisely. Price and wage controls, at least briefly, affected this critical aspect of market behavior: And most recently, the energy problems have created a new set of public interventions.

The present government's philosophy runs counter to these expansions of public power. But the excesses of this administration—in which business shares the blame—have now backfired, and will probably bring into office a Congress and a president more keen on social change. As a result, the period of consolidation will be cut short and the country will more quickly embark on another round of social reform.

The shape of the coming agenda is not yet clear, and little creative thinking is being done. But a major attempt to change the distributions of income and of wealth seems in the offing. The unfortunate McGovern initiatives of 1972, so strongly rejected in that election, did not really disappear from the agenda, and the drive for tax reform and a negative income tax is now more likely to reach a successful conclusion.

INCOME AND WEALTH REFORM?

Can the American capitalist system stand a major new attempt at equalizing the distribution of income and wealth before it has digested the newly defined scope of regulation by government? This depends on the skill with which it is done and on what else is happening in the economy. For one thing, the present imbalance between a scarce supply of capital and an abundant supply of labor is producing a substantial shift of income growth from wages to profits. Thus, the division of income between profits and wages can stand some redress through distributive reform. While such tax changes will reduce the rate of capital formation and prolong the period of capital shortage, some increase in corporate taxation would not be decisive for the economy's successful development. In any event, the modern corporation has shown considerable ability to shift taxes forward through higher prices, backward through lower wages, or no place at all by finding new loopholes to replace the old.

On the personal side, a massive attempt to change distribution of income seems less in the cards since the futility of an excessively progressive income tax was amply demonstrated in the 1940s and fifties. Personal tax reform is more likely to eliminate some of the horizontal inequities through tougher provisions for minimum income taxes, lesser differentials for capital gains, and other such measures.

The taxation of wealth is probably the strongest candidate for massive changes in policy. The estate and gift taxes have eroded since World War II. Their ability to raise revenue remains very small and the means of avoidance are general. The taxes lead to distortion in the disposition of wealth, including the encouragement of charity, but the ability of wealthy families to stay that way is clearly retained. The actual reform proposals in the areas of taxation of estates, gifts, and trusts are very moderate, and even the broad wealth taxes that have been advanced are usually proposed at low rates.

IS THE CAPITALIST SYSTEM WORTH SAVING?

This is, perhaps, the toughest question of all. Now that the principles of managing the modern corporation can be taught to young men and women in business schools and the institutional structure of the well-functioning productive enterprise is thoroughly understood, it may be that the need for the inequities of capitalism is past.

My judgment remains that we cannot do without capitalism in the foreseeable future. We still need the organizing principle of the profit motive for the productive enterprises. The socialist countries are in earlier stages of economic development; while they can achieve high rates of growth in old, heavy, capital-intensive industries where the state's ability to force capital accumulation has a high reward, they have shown themselves to be very weak in those industries more directly aimed to satisfy the needs of the population through consumer goods. In the technology-intensive areas the socialist countries have shown strong results only in the military segment. Perhaps future techniques of behavior modification will make it possible to achieve alternative motivations to replace the economic motive, and will make the subordination of the individual to some collective will a more practical system than it has shown itself to be so far. But I see no reason to seek to hasten the day when the individual foundation of the society is gone and we entrust civilization's fate to a particular leadership class that retains power through psychological technologies or brute police power.

The defense of the capitalist system is that it works. If it is to survive, it must show the ability to successfully solve the new problems of environmental preservation and of consumer protection. It must also manage the next round of reform, particularly in the income and wealth distribution fields, in ways that preserve sufficient incentive to have the system function, improve the efficiency of the system, and preserve its ability to accumulate sufficient capital. The system will be best served by those who face these matters squarely and seek not only to move the system to assimilate these new impulses, but also to reform the quality of government so it will handle its growing responsibilities honestly and effectively.

A SYSTEM WORTH IMPROVING

LEON H. KEYSERLING

Leon H. Keyserling, president of the Conference on Economic Progress and former chairman of the President's Council of Economic Advisors, explains in the following article why capitalism is worth improving and saving.

What is capitalism? In the United States, *capitalism* essentially means that the predominant portion of production and distribution is in private hands, operating under the rewards and incentives of what we usually call the profit system, even where government directly creates large demand for goods and services.

This "private enterprise" is complemented or supplemented by many public or government activities, some relatively independent of private enterprise but affecting it greatly, others affecting it directly. Essential to the whole process is a system of political democracy and personal freedom which contains many purely economic aspects. We have a system of responsible free government and responsible free enterprise, which we constantly attempt to steer between the Scylla of excessive aimlessness or *laissez-faire,* and the Charybdis of excessive centralization and government fiat.

The system has evolved and will continue to do so. Most well-informed people in 1900, or even in 1928, would have called what we welcome today "socialism" rather than "capitalism." But looking backward, I would say instead that we have been progressing, and still are, toward a more socially minded society rather than toward socialism, that being a system where the major instruments of production and distribution are in public hands, not guided by the profit motive as we employ it.

Our system has many blemishes, and our virtue consists in recognizing them. But I am convinced that during the past four decades we have made an unparalleled record of progress—economic, social, and what might be called civil. And we have done this under our free institutions with remarkably little turmoil and upheaval by historic tests. We should aim to improve the system, not abandon it.

Looking toward the future, one may forecast in what directions we think our system is moving, or define purposefully in what directions we want it to move and how much we can impel the system in these directions. Of course, some forecasts are necessary, but the record of mankind's progress has involved an increasing degree of control or command over existing circumstances, rather than mere resignation to them.

Leon H. Keyserling, "A System Worth Improving." Reprinted from *Business and Society Review/Innovation,* Summer 1974 Copyright 1974, Warren, Gorham, and Lamont, Inc. 210 South Street, Boston, Massachusetts.

Further, stress upon forecasts instead of purposefulness has made our actions, at least on the national policy, belated, *ad hoc,* inadequate, and quite inconsistent. We have also tended to adhere to the maxim that if we take care of today, tomorrow will take care of itself. We would do much better to follow the rule that if we take care of tomorrow, today will take care of itself. We sorely need a longer-range perspective.

I believe that our towering central problem domestically, both short-range and long-range, both in terms of cause and consequence, is the unsatisfactory distribution of income among our people and the inadequate allocation of available resources to needed public goods and services. Much of the neglect is due to the prevailing position among economists that there is a sharp dichotomy between what is good for the economy in narrow "economic" terms, and what is good in terms of enlarged distributive justice and our priority domestic needs. If this dichotomy existed, it would confront the capitalist system with an insoluble dilemma. For it would mean that capitalism can achieve optimum progress in narrow economic terms only if we tolerate human and social conditions and civil and political consequences sure to undermine capitalism in the long run.

Fortunately, the accepted dichotomy is imaginary. After forty years of study, I am sure that a listing of what is best for the capitalist system in purely economic terms would be practically identical with a listing of what is best for the nation and the people in terms of distributive justice and domestic priorities. Not only is sustained and optimum economic growth by far the most certain and creative road toward fulfillment of priorities and distributive justice, but correspondingly, fulfillment of priorities and the ends of justice is a veritable *sine qua non* for sustained optimum economic growth.

Our country's repeated and costly departures from optimum growth have been due, in the main, to distributive imbalances which have prevented increases in ultimate demand (private consumption and public outlays) from keeping pace with our burgeoning power to produce—to the detriment of all. If this were promptly recognized, those focusing upon optimum growth and those focusing upon distributive justice would perceive the essential mutuality of their interests. And this would enlarge the voluntary consents and reduce the divisive elements in our democracy.

ROLLER-COASTER PROSPERITY

From early 1953 until now, we have gone through four cycles comprised of periods of inadequate upturn (with each upturn at its peak tending to leave us with more idle resources than the previous upturn), stagnation, and absolute recession. We are now in the second or even third stage of a fifth such cycle. Comparing our actual performance with optimum growth at reasonably full use of our resources, this "roller-coaster prosperity" has, since 1953, caused us to forfeit more than $1.8 *trillion* of national production, measured in 1970 dollars, and about 48 million man-years of employment opportunity (translating all types of unemployment, including part-time and concealed, into the full-time equivalent). Meanwhile, assuming tax systems not too different from those actually in effect, roller-coaster prosperity has deprived us of an *additional* 430 billion dollars of public outlays for goods and services, which would have been applied to satisfying our domestic priorities and distributive justice.

If national policies are not altered drastically, I estimate that the real average annual growth rate in the future will be about the same as that since 1953. This would mean another $1.7 *trillion* forfeiture in national production through 1980, and corresponding forfeitures of other types. This is what our system really cannot afford.

As for a policy of optimum economic growth, the first widespread objection arises from the belief that our economy is already so productive that we should concentrate instead upon distributive justice and domestic priorities. I have already indicated the false nature of this dichotomy. Moreover, this course would be divisive and exacerbating beyond description. Deficient economic growth means high-level unemployment, the ultimate economic and social evil. And any mature measure of our domestic needs and aspirations reveals incontestably that we need and can use the manifold benefits of economic growth as far ahead as we can see.

Despite recurrent agitation, the evidence that the natural resource outlook will not permit optimum economic growth is not compelling nor even persuasive. The preponderance of evidence points to science, technology, and human ingenuity obtaining the natural resources required to restore and sustain optimum economic growth. A temporary and even exaggerated "energy crisis"—which we could largely have avoided by the policies I recommend here—should not now throw us off the track. And if the prospect of specific resource exhaustion were to threaten our capabilities, the new approaches to policy-making I am advocating would be even more urgent.

Many of the ecological objections to growth would throw out the baby with the bath water. Pollution control requires programs which will consume vast resources. To obtain these resources, without prolonging the present travesty of setting one priority in competition with another, will require optimum economic growth.

MEANS WITHOUT ENDS

The basic reason that national and other economic policies have done so poorly by the standards of economic growth, priorities, and justice can be stated simply. Whenever fiscal policies, monetary "guideline" or "control" policies, and others have been used either to restrain or to stimulate the economy, they have not been tied to quantified and integrated goals for growth, priorities, and justice. As a result, the increased or decreased purchasing power resulting from these efforts has allocated income and resources in directions which have ignored equilibrium and aggravated imbalances, in addition to being regressive in important cases.

This has been essentially true of "anti-inflationary" policies proper. For prices and wages are not ends in themselves; they are merely means toward ultimate objectives. Ironically, these "anti-inflationary" policies have greatly aggravated inflation, for they stem from the erroneous theory that deliberate departure from reasonably full resource use restrains price inflation. All empirical observation in the past two decades or longer reveals that the *reverse* is true, and that sustained optimum economic growth would average far less net price inflation than roller-coaster prosperity. Besides, price increases may be bad, neutral, or good, depending upon their distributive effects.

As a result of the foregoing errors, our national economic policies and related social policies are all in disarray; they are improvised, piecemeal, and inconsistent, instead of having unity and consistency. They attempt to cure evils after they occur, instead of looking and working ahead. They are more preoccupied with means than with ends, and therefore they do not properly adjust the former to the latter.

To take two vivid examples: National policy has driven millions of farm people into urban areas, where they have swelled the unemployment ranks and welfare roles; also, the acute food shortages of today and tomorrow have been in the making for many years. And rather than a successful war against poverty employing a few strategic measures based upon experience, we have conducted an errant experimentalism, which spawned an endless medley of unsuccessful, disillusioning policies and programs, eventually turning us away from what we most need to do.

To remedy all this, I have proposed legislation which I call a *National Purposes Act*. Under this Act, the Council of Economic Advisors would help the President develop long-range quantified goals (to be included in his *Economic Reports* to the Congress), so balanced as to resource and income allocations as to promote optimum growth, priorities, and distributive justice. The abolition of poverty in America in less than a decade should be a major goal.

Long-range and integrated goals should also be set in such areas as energy, food, transportation, resource development, antipollution, education, health, housing and urban renewal, and the restoration of our rural population to reasonable parity of income and public service with others. The adjustment of policies to ends, now so inadequate, would thus be facilitated. The entire perspective would be revised from year to year, in light of evolving experience. We would learn by doing, and be stimulated by achievements.

My proposal does not predetermine the range or scope of government programs, but merely insists that government programs stop flying blind. Indeed, the process would greatly reduce the proliferation and duplication of programs and policies and provide a new test of their effectiveness. The goals for income and resource allocation would not be mandates for private enterprise, but instead guides for government undertakings. This new perspective would, however, reduce the degree to which government and private enterprise work at cross-purposes and shed light upon the best divisions of responsibility. In an economy performing well, private enterprise might even carry a larger share of the load. Under this approach it would also become much easier for a watchful public to assess and influence government action.

Such an approach is imperatively needed and well within our capabilities. Rarely has our economic performance and social harmony been in greater danger than now. This is not because the *absolute* situation is worse than in some earlier times, but rather because the legitimate expectations of the American people have, happily, been enlarged. Never was the promise of the future greater, if we act rightly and in time.

CHAPTER SIXTEEN QUESTIONS

1. Arrange the "futures" seen for capitalism by the authors on a spectrum from optimistic to pessimistic, and briefly describe each.
2. What major problems are perceived in present-day capitalism that must be corrected if the system is to survive?
3. Explain whether or not you think those actions suggested by the authors to strengthen the corporation and the capitalistic system will likely be taken in the next few decades?
4. Evaluate Galbraith's solution of nationalizing the corporation.
5. Examine in detail the Marxist position presented by Gurley, and with the information given in the other articles of this chapter, plus your own reasoning, explain whether or not you agree with his position.
6. Kristol takes the position that if the corporation were made a public institution it would mean the loss of individual liberty. Gurley takes just the opposite position, namely, that individuals will benefit with socialism. Which do you think is correct?
7. Is Eckstein correct in thinking that since we can teach people to manage the modern corporation, we can teach them to undertake the reforms needed to reduce past inequities of capitalism?
8. Evaluate Keyserling's proposal for a National Purpose Act. Is such a move likely? Is it practical?
9. What is your scenario for the corporation and capitalism over the next quarter century? Explain and defend your position.